Causes
Time (459)
Class (88x)
Comp. of Sex. + Place (454).

Critical Issues
In Canadian Society

edited by

Craig L. Boydell

Carl F. Grindstaff

Paul C. Whitehead

Holt, Rinehart and Winston of Canada, Limited
Toronto, Montreal

Craig L. Boydell
Assistant Professor
Department of Sociology
The University of Western Ontario

Carl F. Grindstaff
Assistant Professor
Department of Sociology
The University of Western Ontario

Paul C. Whitehead
Assistant Professor
Department of Sociology
The University of Western Ontario

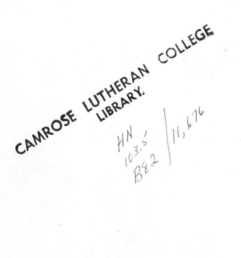

Copyright © 1971 by
Holt, Rinehart and Winston of Canada, Limited
Toronto, Montreal

ISBN: 0-03-928084-5

Printed in Canada

1 2 3 4 5   75 74 73 72 71

Preface

One of the principal problems that students and teachers of sociology in Canada have faced has been the paucity of relevant materials dealing with the Canadian situation. While it may be argued that in areas of theoretical development or methodological technique, the country of origin is of little importance, the fact of the matter is that it is easier to understand and relate such things when the supporting materials are taken from our own experiences.

The purpose of this book is to bring together a broad range of materials that bear directly on the Canadian scene in relation to a variety of critical issues.

The major headings we have used to catalogue these issues are Population, Physical and Social Environment, Minority Groups, Canadian Identity, and Deviant Behaviour and the Administration of Justice. Most of the articles in each of these sections are descriptive and arranged to complement the variety of available texts in both introductory and upper level social science courses.

We feel that this book has three principal advantages. First, all materials deal with topics that are not only specifically relevant to, but also about, Canadian society. Second, all papers are contemporary and thus reflect both the "state of the art" and the latest thinking and research on each of the issues discussed. Over eighty percent of the items included appeared between 1968 and 1971; of these, more than half appeared in 1970 and 1971. Third, this book of readings brings together articles from a wide variety of sources and presents some of the best scholarship available on each of the critical issues. Many articles are taken from scholarly journals such as *The Canadian Review of Sociology and Anthropology*, from reports of the Royal and Senate Commissions (for example, the Task Force on Housing and the Royal Commission on the Status of Women), from books such as Harold Cardinal's *The Unjust Society* and F. G. Vallee's *Kabloona and Eskimo* and a number of papers have been prepared especially for this volume. One article that originally appeared in French is translated while some others have been considerably edited. This collection of materials allows most instructors to assign readings that previously have been too expensive or somewhat inaccessible, especially for large classes of students who might have to share the few copies of books and journals available at the library.

We have labelled the major issues developed in this reader as "critical" not only because they are matters that the media bring to our attention daily, but also because they are issues that the current generation of students and researchers find most relevant to their lives and their society. They are also issues that, for the most part, were not long ago defined as strictly personal problems, or legal problems, or engineering problems, or medical problems. Now they are increasingly thought of as issues upon which social science research and ultimately societal action can have a positive effect. Indeed, some of them are now being defined exclusively as *social science problems*. While social science research and recommendations are surely no panacea for social ills, the perspectives they offer must in many cases be taken into consideration when policy decisions are made. Further, policy decisions with respect to these major areas are being made daily in Canada.

Not all of the critical issues discussed in this volume are treated in the same way, or with the same approach. Each has had its own genesis and development and each calls for a different level of description and analysis. We have selected for inclusion, those materials that best describe the current status of the issues and the direction in which Canadian society is moving relative to them. The section on population, for example, deals not only with the problems of fertility increase or fertility control, but also with the current debates over contraception and abortion.

Pessimists claim that man has already lost the environmental battle while optimists claim that man is only on the verge of losing it. It is a war that has to be waged on two fronts: one physical (air, water) and the other social (poverty and housing). The economic roots of air and water pollution are well documented. The solutions to these problems, however, are often reduced to mere political footballs. Thus, we must examine such issues not only in the technical sense, but also in the context of the total social framework within which they occur. Poverty, poor housing and unemployment are certainly problems for individuals who endure them, but they are not individual problems. They are structural problems that have their origins in the social organization of our society. The alleviation of poverty, poor housing and unemployment will necessitate changes in the economic, political and social structures which give rise to the differential access to the rewards that our society has to offer.

Descriptions of several minority groups in Canada were chosen because as a collective entity they illustrate the relative powerlessness of minorities to control their own lives, regardless of how much any single group attempts to change its situation. There are certainly degrees of powerlessness, but all minority groups suffer exclusion from full participation in the society to some extent, whether they be Indians, Eskimos, blacks, or immigrant groups.

Every large group of people at one time or another wrestles with the development or maintenance of its identity. Canadian society is no exception, but the social and historical context within which it faces this problem is a unique one. Canadian identity is inexorably linked to conflicts of dependence and independence in important areas of social life: history, economics, politics, education, communication, and even sports. The section on Canadian identity examines these areas and illustrates the difficulty of trying to gain and maintain a viable identity in the face of pressures to assimilate to a larger and more powerful force.

The last unit of this book deals with Deviant Behaviour and selected problems in the Administration of Justice. Selected types of deviant behaviour are chosen for analysis: crime, delinquency, and problems related to the use of alcohol and other drugs. Crime and delinquency are major issues that not only affect official agencies such as the courts and the police, but also are related to our neighbourhoods, schools, and even our personal freedoms.

Individuals are involved in crime and delinquency, but again the roots of the problem can often be traced to the social organization of our society and the processes through which individuals become socialized into the social and legal values of Canadian culture.

Alcohol and drug use have become increasingly important issues in Canada. Many Canadians use alcohol for a variety of purposes: ceremonial, ritual and convivial – it presents no problems for them. For other Canadians the use of alcohol is problematical and they become defined as deviant. There has been concern over the use of drugs other than alcohol for some time, but that concern has become most pointed in the past few years due to extensive drug use among young people of all social classes. Several parallels between the use of alcohol and the use of drugs are drawn and these have to do with the issues of legal control and the statistical distributions of the rates of use of these substances. Societal responses to deviant behaviour can sometimes be the source for further problems. Hence, selected issues in the administration of justice are examined relative to the types of deviance considered in this Chapter.

While as co-editors we are equally responsible for the organization and integration of these materials, this book would have not been possible, of course, were it not for the fact that authors and publishers were gracious enough to allow their work to be reprinted. We are most appreciative.

C.L.B.
C.F.G.
P.C.W.

Table of Contents

B. Social Environment

3   Minority Groups   *233*

4   Canadian Identity   *357*

5   Deviant Behaviour and the Administration of Justice *439*

A.   Crime and Delinquency

B.   Alcohol Use and Alcoholism

C.   Drug Use and Abuse

D.   Selected Problems in the Administration of Justice

Contributors

Craig L. Boydell, Department of Sociology, University of Western Ontario, London, Ontario.

R. M. Boyce, Department of Psychiatry, Victoria Hospital, London, Ontario.

David Brown, Student, Department of Political Science, University of Toronto, Toronto, Ontario.

Harold Cardinal, President, Indian Association of Alberta, Member of the Board of National Indian Brotherhood.

Donald H. Clairmont, Department of Sociology and Anthropology, Dalhousie University, Halifax, Nova Scotia.

Robert Cliche, Lawyer and Leader of the New Democratic Party of Quebec.

Barry Commoner, Department of Botany, Washington University, St. Louis, Missouri.

David A. Croll, Chairman, Special Senate Committee on Poverty.

Jan de Lint, Alcoholism and Drug Addiction Research Foundation of Ontario, Toronto, Ontario.

G. Edward Ebanks, Department of Sociology, University of Western Ontario, London, Ontario.

Dianne Fejer, Alcoholism and Drug Addiction Research Foundation of Ontario, Toronto, Ontario.

John E. K. Foreman, Faculty of Engineering Science, University of Western Ontario, London, Ontario.

P. J. Giffin, Department of Sociology, University of Toronto, Toronto, Ontario.

Alastair Gillespie, Liberal Member of Parliament, House of Commons, Ottawa, Ontario.

Carl F. Grindstaff, Department of Sociology, University of Western Ontario, London, Ontario.

Jacques Henripin, Department of Demography, University of Montreal, Montreal, Quebec.

Lewis Hertzman, Department of History, York University, Toronto, Ontario.

John Hogarth, Osgoode Hall Law School, York University, Toronto, Ontario.

Margaret E. Hughes, Faculty of Law, University of Windsor, Windsor, Ontario.

Warren E. Kalbach, Department of Sociology, University of Toronto, Toronto, Ontario.

Merrijoy Kelner, Department of Sociology, University of Toronto, Toronto, Ontario.

Bruce Kidd, Freelance writer, member of the National Advisory Council on Fitness and Amateur Sport.

Lucien Laforest, Department of Behavioural Science, Department of Social Medicine, University of Sherbrooke, Sherbrooke, Quebec.

R. D. Lawrence, Author, Expert on Conservation.

James MacKinnon, Student, Department of Political Science, York University, Toronto, Ontario.

Hugh MacLennan, Department of English, McGill University, Montreal, Quebec.

Denis W. Magill, Department of Sociology, University of Toronto, Toronto, Ontario.

Robin Mathews, Department of English, Carleton University, Ottawa, Ontario.

Lynn McDonald, Department of Sociology and Anthropology, McMaster University, Hamilton, Ontario.

Patricia Musson, United Community Services, London, Ontario.

Martin O'Malley, Toronto Globe and Mail, Toronto, Ontario.

R. W. Osborn, Department of Population Dynamics, The Johns Hopkins University, Baltimore, Maryland. Currently on leave of absence acting as Advisor to the Training Research and Evaluation Center, Pakistan Family Planning Council, Lahore, Pakistan.

Sylvia Ostry, Special Manpower Studies and Consultation, Dominion Bureau of Statistics, Ottawa, Ontario.

K. V. Pankhurst, Canadian International Development Agency, Ottawa, Ontario.

Philip Resnick, Student, Department of Political Science, McGill University, Montreal, Quebec.

Albert Rose, Department of Social Work, University of Toronto, Toronto, Ontario.

T. J. Samuel, Research Branch, Department of Manpower and Immigration, Ottawa, Ontario.

Mildred A. Schwartz, Department of Sociology, University of Illinois, Chicago, Chicago, Illinois.

Wolfgang Schmidt, Alcoholism and Drug Addiction Research Foundation of Ontario, Toronto, Ontario.

Benjamin D. Singer, Department of Sociology, University of Western Ontario, London, Ontario.

Reginald G. Smart, Alcoholism and Drug Addiction Research Foundation of Ontario, Toronto, Ontario.

James Steele, Department of English, Carleton University, Ottawa, Ontario.

Leroy Stone, Consultant on Demographic Research, Dominion Bureau of Statistics, Ottawa, Ontario.

W. D. S. Thomas, Department of Obstetrics and Gynecology, Vancouver General Hospital, Vancouver, British Columbia.

Ben Tierney, Ottawa Correspondent for Southam News Services.

Courtney Tower, Hopkins, Hedlin Limited, Economics Communications, Toronto, Ontario.

F. G. Vallee, Department of Sociology and Anthroplogy, Carleton University, Ottawa, Ontario.

Edmund W. Vaz, Department of Sociology, University of Waterloo, Waterloo, Ontario.

J. E. Veevers, Department of Sociology, University of Western Ontario, London, Ontario.

Mel Watkins, Department of Economics, University of Toronto, Toronto, Ontario.

Paul C. Whitehead, Department of Sociology, University of Western Ontario, London, Ontario.

1 Population

The population of the world is growing at a rate of two percent per year, adding two more human beings to the world total every second of the day. By the year 2000, this *population explosion* will have increased the number of people on the earth to nearly seven billion. Such growth cannot continue unchecked and population increase must be brought under control. Most Canadians realize that such a problem does exist and that steps are needed to remedy the situation, but they do not feel that such population problems apply to Canada. This is probably true; the population explosion and its effects around the world apply only indirectly to Canadians, even though as consumers we tend to use far more than our share of natural resources. In North America as a whole, we account for approximately six percent of the world's population but we consume about 50 percent of the goods and services produced from resources. Thus, although we do not add large numbers of people to the world total, we, more than anyone, upset the population-resource balance.

At the same time, when we focus only on Canada, we find that our population growth due to natural increase (births minus deaths) is not extreme, about one percent per year, and this growth does not place pressure upon our ability to survive or to live under relatively affluent conditions. The estimated population of Canada in June, 1970 was 21,377,000, an increase of approximately 17 percent since 1961 (this increase includes net immigration). During this period of time, the crude birth rate, the number of births per 1,000 population, has declined from 26 to 18. This drop in the birth rate is reflected in Table 1 which shows the number of children 0-4 years of age decreasing by over 17 percent from 1961 to 1970. Although the pressures from population are not serious in terms of survival, this does not mean that the variables involved in population change (births, deaths, and migration) are not important to our society. There are many situations which significant numbers of people in our country see as undesirable, and which are brought about by changes, or lack thereof, in population variables.

The first article in this section, "The Fertility Crisis in Quebec," which is adapted from a pamphlet written by the Council of French Life in America, reverses the modern population problem – the Council says that Quebec needs *more* people through increased fertility. This article indicates that the crude birth rate in Quebec has been falling at a steady rate since 1921 (except for

TABLE 1

The Population of Canada, 1961-1970

Age	1970	1961	Percentage Increase 1961-1970
Total	21,377,000	18,238,200	17.2
0–4	1,868,300	2,256,400	−17.2
5–9	2,301,400	2,079,500	10.7
10–14	2,297,100	1,856,000	23.8
15–19	2,068,200	1,432,600	44.4
20–24	1,851,800	1,183,600	56.5
25–44	5,369,800	4,871,000	10.2
45–64	3,944,300	3,168,000	24.5
65+	1,676,100	1,391,100	20.5

Source: *D.B.S. Daily*, January 12, 1971, p. 2.

1951) and by 1966 there was a lower birth rate in Quebec than in the rest of Canada.[1] This is contrary to the popular image many Canadians have regarding fertility patterns in Quebec. The Council goes on to point out that this fertility decline in the province may be detrimental to Quebec's obtaining financial considerations from the federal government and in maintaining provincial political and social power. They foresee the need for the Quebec government to have inducements for higher fertility, so that Quebec can maintain its political, cultural and social influence in Canada. Quebec officials feel that the smaller proportion of the total Canadian population in Quebec resulting from lower fertility will bring about a reduction of its *equal partnership role* in Canada.

Whereas some organizations in Quebec may desire higher rates of fertility, the principal issue in Canada relating to fertility is birth control. Only in the last decade have laws prohibiting the dissemination of birth control information been repealed throughout Canada. The item included here, "Important Things to Consider and Do About Family Planning," is a typical information pamphlet describing the types of birth control methods most widely used in Canada, showing the advantages and disadvantages of the various procedures. However, although not illegal, most of the family planning techniques under consideration in this pamphlet are not acceptable to large segments of the Canadian population, specifically Roman Catholics. A section of Pope Paul's Encyclical Letter on the regulation of birth, *Humanae Vitae,* is reprinted here. It clearly condemns *artificial* methods of birth control and states that the only licit practice of birth limitation is the rhythm method.

The statement of the Canadian Bishops on this Encyclical indicates agreement, but also recognizes "that a certain number of Catholics, although admittedly subject to the teaching of the encyclical, find it either extremely difficult or even impossible to make their own all elements of this doctrine" (page 22). Ultimately, according to the Bishops, it is a matter of faith and conscience. "Counsellors may meet others who, accepting the teaching of the Holy Father, find that because of particular circumstances they are involved in what seems to them a clear conflict of duties, e.g. the reconciling of conjugal love and responsible parenthood with the education of children already born or with the health of the mother. In accord with the accepted principles of moral theology, if these persons have tried sincerely but without success to pursue a line of conduct in keeping with the given directives, they may be safely assured that whoever honestly chooses that course which seems right to him does so in good conscience." The entire statement of the Bishops is given in this section.

The debate concerning acceptable methods of birth control will undoubtedly continue for some time to come. However, there are many sectors of the Canadian population that want to control fertility. This is particularly true at the individual level. Although there have been no definitive studies carried out in Canada, it has been estimated that from forty to fifty percent of all births in Canada are accidental, that is, unplanned by the mothers at the time of conception.[2] The next article, "Vasectomy as a Birth Control Method," examines one method not already described by which couples who have the number of children they desire protect against further pregnancies – male sterilization, the vasectomy. Grindstaff and Ebanks briefly describe the types of families who undergo the operation and then proceed to analyze previous fertility and contraceptive usage histories of these people to determine why the vasectomy was deemed necessary.

The men having the operation were rather typical of the general population, perhaps slightly above average in terms of income, occupational, and educational attainments. These men and their wives had more children than they desired to have when they were first married and the vasectomy was chosen as a sure and safe method of birth prevention. Approximately forty percent of all of the children born to these couples were accidental and unplanned. All other forms of birth control had been employed by the people with varying degrees of success (the pill was most successful but even here there were some failures) and the couples were not willing to take future chances. Perhaps the major reason for the operation was that no more children were desired, but the median age of the wife, just over 30, made pregnancy a possibility for a long time to come. Therefore, for most couples, a method that was very effective for at least ten years was needed. The vasectomy was such a method. There were no recorded cases of pregnancies after the vasectomy had been performed.

The next four items in the section on population deal with the most controversial method of individual population control, the abortion. First, "The 'Liberalization' of the Canadian Abortion Laws" by Jean Veevers compares the old and new legislative policies of the government. The major change in the law is that it recognizes not only physical health as a legitimate reason for having an abortion, but also that the mental health of the woman is an important consideration. However, Veevers argues that the amendments have failed to make abortion legally available to all women whose physical or mental health would be endangered by carrying a pregnancy full term. The principal reasons cited for this failure are: lack of clarity in the concept of mental health, lack of representation of qualified personnel other than medical doctors on therapeutic abortion committees, lack of procedures for a woman to present her own case before a committee, lack of appeal channels, and lack of hospital space. Veevers concludes that the amendments to the criminal code have not significantly liberalized the abortion laws and in some instances, additional *roadblocks* have been erected.

The second article on abortion, "Therapeutic Abortion in a Canadian City" by Boyce and Osborn, documents the increase in the number of abortions being performed in one Canadian city: from 119 between 1962 and 1968 to 166 in 1969 alone.[3] The authors describe some specific case histories and provide the rationale for the granting of abortions. The third and fourth selections on the topic of abortion are taken from the Royal Commission Report on *The Status of Women in Canada*. The first of these selections indicates that there may be as many as 100,000 illegal abortions performed in Canada each year. If this is so, then twenty percent of all pregnancies in Canada end in abortion (there are approximately 400,000 births each year). Most of these abortions are thought to be performed on married women who already have children. The commission concludes that women must have the right to control their own bodies and they "recommend that the Criminal Code be amended to permit abortion by a qualified medical practitioner on the sole request of any woman who has been pregnant for twelve weeks or less."

The second selection from *The Status of Women in Canada* is a minority statement from one of the commissioners, Jacques Henripin, that opposes the report's recommendations on abortion. Henripin writes that the respect for life, at any age, is the key issue. He says that the problems relating to abortion, that is, the sanctity of life, "cannot be answered by attitudes and laws which, in the final analysis, are based only on convenience . . . the problem of abortion cannot be resolved by considering solely the psychological and physiological benefits or the advantages for the family which may derive from the destruction of the foetus."

Fertility and its control is not, however, the only population component that is a problem in our society. There are mortality differentials between provinces, regions, and various groups of people. Two of the most critical indicators of social progress are the levels of maternal and infant mortality. Maternal mortality is usually defined as the number of deaths to women in childbirth per year per 10,000 maternities. In Canada, the rate is approximately four per 10,000, which is about average in the Western World. However, the article by Thomas titled "Maternal Mortality in Native British Columbia Indians, a High-Risk Group" shows that there are large variations between sub-groups of people, even when these groups live in the same general geographic location. Thomas found that Indians made up about 2.4 percent of the population of British Columbia but accounted for 5.7 percent of all live births and 16.1 percent of the maternal mortality between 1955 and 1965. This disproportionate number of maternal deaths of Indian mothers is attributed to geographic, socio-economic, and medical factors.

Infant mortality is defined as the number of deaths to children under one year of age in any given year per 1,000 live births in that year. Canada ranks 13th among major industrial countries with an infant mortality rate of 22. Again, the variations among groups within Canada are large. Musson in her article "Infant Mortality in Canada" shows the declining incidence of infant mortality over time, but she also illustrates the continuing discrepancies between groups. For example, the rate for the white population is approximately one-fourth that of the rate for the Eskimo population. Again, geographic, socio-economic, and medical factors are cited as causes of the observed differences.

Migration can also be an important population characteristic relating to societal organization and resulting in social and economic problems. "Migration Between Canada and the United States" by Pankhurst shows that migration between the two countries up to 1964 was larger than had been thought previously and that the interchange was growing, especially among professionals and skilled workers. Also, the *brain drain* loss of Canadians to the United States in the 1950's and early 60's was not as large as many scholars had suggested. Pankhurst says that the major reason for the interchange between the two countries was the growing interdependence of the two national economies resulting in a scarcity of high-level manpower.

The short excerpt from Samuel's publication "The Migration of Canadian-Born Between Canada and the United States of America 1955 to 1968" updates the Pankhurst article and indicates that Canada has probably had a *brain gain* rather than a *brain drain* in relation to migration with the United States. Such a gain is, however, not without its problems. The final article in this section, "The Universities: Takeover of the Mind" examines the controversial issues of large numbers of non-Canadians (particularly Americans) teaching in Canadian universities and having major influence on the total process of university training. According to the authors, Steele and Mathews, the migration of university teachers to Canada from the United States has a negative effect upon the quantity and quality of Canadian content in course work. To quote directly from the article: "Americanization exists at a number of levels: in numbers and attitudes of faculty, in course offerings, in ideological orientation of studies, in hiring procedures and preferences, in the failure of concern about the limited opportunities for Canadian students. A change of heart is necessary in Canadian higher education."

In addition, we are attracting more and more people from the United States. In the first nine months of 1969, some 15,500 people had migrated to Canada from the United States, making the Americans second to the British (18,600) as the largest number of any single nationality coming to Canada.[4] Indications are that at least thirty percent of these migrants are in professional occupations. Thus, even the seemingly indirect effects of migration can become a critical issue for Canadian society.

Footnotes

1. Actually, more recent data from 1968 show that Quebec had the lowest birth rate of all provinces, just over 16.3 births per 1,000 population. This low rate is attributed to later ages of marriage in Quebec and to birth control methods even among Catholics. Source: *Canadian Magazine*, February 14, 1970, p. 4.

2. "In the Fall of 1956, the Alfred Polity Research Bureau found the relationship of planned to accidental birth was 1.5 to 1. Forty-nine percent of parents reported the child planned, 36 percent said the birth was accidental, and 15 percent said they could not remember." Jean Veevers, "Maternal Attitudes Towards Pregnancy," *VARIAbles*, the Journal of the Sociology Club, University of Alberta, 4, February, 1965, p. 29.

3. A recent survey in this city has shown that in 1970, 675 therapeutic abortions were performed.

4. *Canadian Magazine*, February 14, 1970, p. 3.

The Fertility Crisis in Quebec[*]

The Council on French Life in America
(translated by Katya von Knorring)

Introduction

The Council of French Life published the following statement in a 1967 edition of *Vie Française,*

> The most crucial problem that confronts Quebec is not political, economic or educational, but one concerning family size. If births continue to decline in Quebec, neither independence, nor wealth, nor immigration can assure the survival of the French Canadian people. The Quebec government must be asked without delay for a birth-rate policy, and more broadly a family policy.[1]

Ever since this problem was made public, it has preoccupied the leaders of the Council on French Life. During their plenary session in Moncton, New Brunswick in September of 1967, they developed the framework for a paper concerning this question, after consulting the enlightened views of an eminent French sociologist, R. P. S. de Lestapis, Professor of Family Sociology at the Paris Catholic Institute.

In reply to the Council's request for documentation, the French sociologist prepared a paper of 21 single-spaced typewritten pages. With the permission of author and Council this text appeared in the July-August, 1967 edition of *Relations.* Just before the session began, de Lestapis sent the Council a recent copy of the Codes for social security, public health, family and social welfare, published by the *Librarie Dalloz* in Paris.

The Fertility Crisis

The Decline

Broadly speaking, the fall of the birth rate in Quebec came about in the following manner: a high of 65 births per 1,000 people at the beginning of the English regime in 1770; a high of 37.6 births per 1,000 (in 1921) since Confederation and a drop to 16.5 per 1,000 in 1967. In this part of the report, the description of the birth rate crisis is limited to Quebec (which is the major contributor to the French Canadian population), since it is impossible to obtain figures for the whole of the French population in Canada. The present situation in Quebec and in Canada depends above all on the fertility of Quebec mothers. Even here we may suppose, and legitimately so, that the rate of fertility of the French Canadian mother in Quebec is roughly equivalent to that of any mother in Quebec, whatever her origin.

More serious still, the decline in number of births in Quebec, which began in

[*]Adapted from a study by the Council on French Life in America.

1960, continues to accelerate. According to Dr. Parrot it has varied between 0.5 percent and 3.2 percent each year, from 1960 to 1965. It reached 7.8 percent as early as 1965, and nearly 10 percent in 1966.[2] In absolute figures, Quebec reached a peak in 1959 with 142,400 births. This total fell in 1965 to 120,000, and to less than 100,000 in 1967, despite the increase in population. Between 1959 and 1965 the decrease of births in Quebec was 16 percent. In order to grasp this declining trend more fully, let us remember that Quebec recorded 95,000 births in 1942 in a population of 3,400,000, and the same number (95,000) in 1967 in a population of nearly 6,000,000.

What sort of future can Quebec anticipate from the demographic viewpoint? If this decline were to continue at its present rate, natural growth would reach a stalemate by 1975 and the population would quickly go down as a result. One would have to foresee a catastrophic decrease in the French-speaking community in Quebec by the year 2000, assimilation combining with the demographic decline. Statisticians have calculated that if birth control continues to be practised in Japan at the present rate, after four centuries there would not be a single Japanese. Obviously, life does not flow in such a precise mathematical rhythm, but nevertheless a certain number of these statistical projections must be taken very seriously.

Quebec and Canada

If the problem is viewed from a Canadian perspective the future of the French group is hardly any less disquieting. The French group has maintained a proportion of 30 percent since Confederation simply because of its high birth rate. However, at the present time Quebec ranks eighth among the provinces with regard to births.[3] In comparing Quebec with the other major province in Canada, Ontario, we note that: for Quebec the birth rate has decreased from 28.5 in 1959 to 19.0 in 1966, a decrease of 33 percent; while for Ontario, the rate has decreased from 26.4 in 1959 to 19.0 in 1966 – a decrease of 20 percent.

TABLE 1

Birth Rates for 1965

	Total	Rate for Every 1,000 People	Proportionate Distribution
Canada	418,595	21.3	100.0
Newfoundland	14,740	30.3	3.5
Prince Edward Island	2,517	23.4	0.6
Nova Scotia	16,524	22.0	3.9
New Brunswick	14,175	23.1	3.5
Quebec	120,607	21.2	28.8
Ontario	141,610	20.8	33.8
Manitoba	19,976	20.9	4.8
Saskatchewan	20,494	21.6	4.9
Alberta	32,664	22.7	7.8
British Columbia	33,669	18.5	8.0

TABLE 2

Birth Rates for 1966

	Total	Rate for Every 1,000 People	Proportionate Distribution
Canada	387,710	19.4	100.0
Newfoundland	14,084	28.5	3.6
Prince Edward Island	2,199	20.3	0.6
Nova Scotia	15,220	20.1	3.9
New Brunswick	12,722	20.6	3.3
Quebec	109,878	19.0	28.3
Ontario	131,942	19.0	34.0
Manitoba	18,007	18.7	4.6
Saskatchewan	19,037	19.9	4.9
Alberta	30,593	20.9	7.9
British Columbia	32,502	17.3	8.4[4]

A comparison of Tables 1 and 2 clearly reveals that a fall in the birth rate is the general trend in Canada. However, the tendency is stronger in Quebec (2.2 percent) than in Canada as a whole (1.9 percent). In 1965, Quebec accounted for 28.8 percent of the births in Canada, while in 1966, the figure decreased slightly to 28.3 percent. Ontario had 21,000 more births than Quebec in 1965, and 22,000 more in 1966. Finally, Quebec's birth rate ranks seventh among the provinces. Quebec falls far behind its rival for Labrador, Newfoundland.

In order to pinpoint the problem, let us compare Quebec with the country's largest and most prosperous province, Ontario. A document prepared by the States General in November, 1967, bearing the title *La Famille et la Politique Familiale*, provides the following points of comparison:

TABLE 3

Birth Rates for 1921–1966

Year	Quebec	Ontario	Canada
1921	37.6	25.3	29.3
1931	29.1	20.2	23.2
1941	26.8	19.1	22.4
1951	29.8	25.0	27.2
1961	26.1	25.3	26.1
1962	25.2	24.6	25.3
1963	24.4	24.1	24.6
1964	23.5	23.2	23.5
1965	21.2	20.8	21.3
1966	19.0	19.0	19.4

These figures indicate that Quebec's birth rate, which in 1921 was twelve points above that of Ontario and eight points above the Canadian average, has dropped below the latter, and is equal of that of Ontario in 1966. But the population of Ontario is nearly one million greater than that of Quebec, and Ontario registered 22,000 more births than Quebec in 1966.

The Increase in Quebec

Let us now consider the increase in population in Quebec itself. It was 21.6 percent in 1901-1911, 21.8 percent in 1921-1931, 15.9 percent in 1931-1941, 21.7 percent in 1941-1951, and finally 13.6 percent in 1961.[5] A population which has almost doubled between 1931 and 1961 only produces a twenty percent increase in births. We shall see that the situation is still more serious than these figures reveal, for one additional growth factor must be considered — that of immigration.

Migration

Dr. Paul Parrot indicates (in the unpublished works which he has so obligingly passed on to us), that the increase in population in the province of Quebec up to 1951 had been caused only by births. This does not mean that no immigrants have settled in Quebec, but that, for several reasons, the total immigrant population has changed nothing with regard to the total statistics. This is not the case after 1951. The increase in population surpasses that of births by 94,035 from 1951 to 1956; by 111,374 from 1956 to 1961; and by 67,720 from 1961 to 1966. Note that the periods studied here are quinquennial. The mortality rate should also be taken into consideration, a rate which will necessarily increase with the aging of the population, and which will have the greatest effect on the French Canadian segment, as the immigrants are generally quite young.

Another factor worthy of examination, but about which nearly no information is available, is the emigration of Quebeckers to other provinces and other countries, especially the United States. We only know that this movement exists, and that it will persist unless the prosperity of Quebec grossly surpasses that of Ontario, British Columbia and the United States in particular.

The 1961 census revealed that 268,445 citizens born in Quebec were resident in another Canadian province. This exodus may be explained in several ways, notably, the fact that the standard of living is 27 percent higher in Ontario than in Quebec. *Le Soleil*, of January 4, 1968, reports that 38,000 Canadian citizens moved to the United States in 1966 and that this number nearly doubled the following year, as 50,000 Canadians had crossed the border by October 1, 1967. Finally, a work document produced by the States General entitled *Le Peuplement et L'Immigration* confirms that in 1963, 77,000 citizens had left Canada, of whom thirty percent lived in Quebec. Unfortunately these documents give no references.

French-Speakers in Quebec

We have discussed the increase in population in Quebec. We should now direct attention to the increase in French-speakers in Quebec. We know that 68,000 Quebeckers of French origin have succeeded in anglicizing themselves in their native province. According to the 1961 census figures there were still 130,345 New Canadians who become English-speaking, and finally, that the English in Quebec very rarely learn to speak French. In 1961 there were 567,057 Quebeckers of British origin, and approximately 700,000 English-speaking residents.

The problem of the anglicization of these two hundred thousand Quebec

9

citizens should be further scrutinized. To begin with, we should establish that the geographical centre of this phenomenon is Montreal, where three-quarters of British manpower is concentrated in Quebec, and where British influences over finance, commerce, and international enterprises are most accutely felt.

Montreal and Quebec

Dr. Lomer Pilote has maintained in *Le Devoir* (August 30, 1966) that French Canadians could become a minority on *L'Ile de Montréal* by 1986. This hypothesis could become tragically true if the following factors continue to work against us: the lowering of the birth rate, an increase in British immigration, and the growing anglicization of French Canadians and of new settlers in Montreal. According to Dr. Pilote, Metropolitan Montreal (L'Ile de Montréal, L'Ile de Jésus and the Comté de Chambly) had a population of 2,253,000 in 1961. The English Canadians numbered 390,000 (out of half a million in the whole province) and the New Canadians 483,000 (out of about half a million also in Quebec). Thus the French Canadians numbered 1,380,000, that is 61.7 percent of the total Montreal population.

The States General in turn sounded the alarm in the paper *Le Peuplement et L'Immigration*; the author writes:

> In 1961 greater Montreal constitutes 35 percent of the population of Quebec. It receives 82.6 percent of the immigrants in the province. Nine out of ten immigrants join the English-speaking element: 167,182 New Montrealers speak only English, and 38,370 speak only French.

Before establishing a vast and costly immigration programme in Quebec, would it not be prudent to ask if these new arrivals are not contributing to submerging us? And would it not be more practical to spend the millions which the operation will cost us, in encouraging our own births? History has taught us that to maintain oneself with foreign support is a grave indication of decadence in a people. It is no more expensive to produce more citizens than to adopt them, and from the national point of view, it is a safer method.

What does Montreal represent as far as the rest of the province is concerned? During November 1967 the States General in Montreal examined the question. In their document, *Le Peuplement et L'Immigration*, they confirm that 70 percent of the population of the province of Quebec is concentrated in the areas surrounding the cities of Quebec and Montreal. One out of two Quebeckers lives in greater Montreal. The urban population of Montreal city itself represents 35 percent of the total Quebec population.

This concentration and imbalance continues to grow. From the beginning of the century, the concentration has moved from one out of four Quebeckers living in Montreal, to one out of three. Another suspected phenomenon is that of depopulation of other regions in the province. Between 1951 and 1956 all the counties in Quebec underwent an increase in population. Between 1956 and 1961 the population had dropped in eleven counties, and in sixteen between 1961 and 1966.

The Montreal region has become an active centre of anglicization for New Canadians and even French Canadians. It is in the process of absorbing the rest of the province. If this fact is not recognized, by the year 2000 the province of Quebec will be called Montreal, and will have become the nucleus of Anglo-American language and civilization.

The Aging of the Population

Finally, the most direct consequence of the decrease in births is the aging of the population. According to a projection by Dr. Parrot the proportion of Quebeckers under 19 years of age will have decreased by one half, from 1960 to 1980.[6] On the other hand, the proportion of Quebeckers above 60 years of age will have doubled, in this same time span. A man such as François Hertel would be well justified in reiterating his famous apostrophe, uttered as he left Quebec for the first time: "I'm leaving the old France for the new."

Perhaps we shall become an aged population. The review *La Famille et la Politique Familiale* points out one of the consequences of this aging process: "A birth rate which is too low gradually transforms the socio-economic dynamism of a nation, minimising investments in the future, for centralisation of current spending." This sociological jargon means that generations of pleasure-seekers produce generations of impotent people, that an egotistical craving for pleasure and a refusal to sacrifice anything in life bring the worst calamity possible upon any community: that of precocious senility.

Conclusion

It is time to bring these questions to a close and to form a conclusion. The conclusion is cruelly obvious: French Canada is on its way to losing the demographic battle which it had so successfully fought for three centuries, and this even in Quebec. We have the choice of three remedies: to make French culture the dominant culture in Quebec as it was between 1760 and 1850; to favour immigration which would be of benefit to our group; above all to adopt energetic measures so that the birth rate of French Canadian women will increase to the level of the 1950's. We must point out immediately that the first two remedies would have no effect and would be well nigh impossible unless the third were put into successful operation. The example of France shows us that this third possibility is feasible and all that remains is to imitate here, what has already been done in our former mother country.

Footnotes

1. *Vie Francaise*, March-April, 1967, p. 230.
2. *Le Devoir*, January 20, 1967.
3. Jacques Henripin in *Le Devoir*, March 1, 1967.
4. Figures from the demographic service, in Quebec.
5. Unpublished works of Dr. Paul Parrot, on the decline of births in Quebec. (Editor's note: It should be noted that the census figures for the increase from 1951-1961 is 29.7 percent. The increase from 1961 to 1968 would be approximately 13 to 14 percent.)
6. Paul Parrot, unpublished notes.

Important Things to Consider and Do About Family Planning*

G. D. Searle and Company of Canada Limited

The Different Ways to Control Birth

There are several ways to protect a woman from becoming pregnant. Some of the newer methods are easier and more acceptable to use, and more reliable than the methods available before 1960. *The pill* is an excellent example.

There is no *one* method, however, that suits every couple. Therefore, couples who want to plan their families are wise to consider *all* methods – and to discuss them with a physician and perhaps their religious adviser – before making a decision. Often a couple may try several methods before finding the one that's best for them. All the methods of birth control described in this leaflet have been used by thousands of couples.

How Pregnancy Occurs

In order to better understand how birth control methods work – and why they must be used correctly and consistently to be effective – it is helpful to understand what takes place in a woman's body to allow a baby to develop.

CHART 1

The Female Reproductive System	and What Happens Before a Baby Starts to Grow
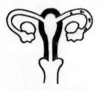	1. In most women, an egg cell is released from one or the other of the two ovaries about once every 28 days. It travels through the Fallopian tube to the uterus (womb).
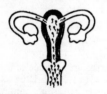	2. During sex relations, the husband deposits special cells (sperm) in the vagina. These sperm travel from the vagina, into the uterus, then into the tubes. If one of the sperm cells unites with the egg cell which has been released, the egg is fertilized—and a baby begins to develop.
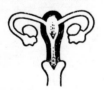	3. If the egg cell is *not* fertilized, it disintegrates in about 24 hours. Then during the menstrual period, the disintegrated egg, along with the lining of the uterus, is carried away when bleeding occurs. This is the beginning of a new menstrual cycle.

*Used by permission of G. D. Searle and Company of Canada Limited.

How to Protect Against Pregnancy

To protect against pregnancy it is necessary to prevent the sperm cell from meeting an egg cell. When you intentionally do something to prevent such a meeting, you are practicing birth control. Some of the different ways of preventing the sperm and egg from meeting are described in Chart 2. You will notice that in order to use some of these methods you will need to see a doctor.

Select the Birth Control Method You Prefer

Selecting a method of birth control should be a decision of both husband and wife. If a particular preparation or device is distasteful to either partner, another method should be considered. In reaching a decision, you should be able to answer "yes" to the following questions:

1. Is the method easy enough so you'll use it all the time? No matter how reliable the method, pregnancy may result if it is not practiced consistently and correctly.

2. Is the method one which will not interfere with the enjoyment of the sex act? Sex relations are a very important part of a satisfying marriage, and the birth control method selected should not interfere with its enjoyment by either partner.

3. If complete privacy is needed to use a particular method, does your home situation permit such privacy? This is particularly important where there are young children, or if other adults share the home. Bathroom facilities may be a factor.

4. Does it allow you to maintain the intimacy of love-making? Most married couples prefer spontaneous love-making. They want a method of birth control which does not make it necessary to interrupt love-play in order to use a device or preparation to prevent pregnancy.

5. Can you be reasonably sure an unwanted pregnancy will be prevented? If there is undue worry as to the reliability of a birth control method, marital tension may result.

Consult a Physician or a Family Planning Clinic

After you and your partner have thought about and talked about birth control and the method you think you would like to use, you would be wise to discuss it further with a doctor – even if you do not need a prescription. There are private physicians and family planning clinics you can ask for advice and assistance – and for the answers to any question you may have. In this way you can be sure you thoroughly understand – and know how to use – the method of birth control you have chosen.

A physical examination is important. In fact, such an examination is *essential* if you are planning to use the pill, the intrauterine device or a diaphragm. It is also recommended that every woman have a vaginal and breast examination at least once a year. The doctor may discover minor medical problems which can be corrected before they become big ones. The examination may be slightly

CHART 2

Questions and Answers About Birth Control Methods Most Widely Used in Canada

	The Pill	Intrauterine Devices
What is it?	A combination of synthetic hormones very much like those a woman produces in her own body. There are many varieties of the pill available on prescription. The most commonly used type employs a balanced combination of progestin and estrogen in each pill. The hormone action of this type of pill is similar to that of the hormones secreted by a healthy woman at times when ovulation is normally inhibited. Dosages of this type of pill have been reduced to the point where one of the newest contains only 1 mg. of the active progestin. Another type, used in the sequential method, consists of two kinds of pill. One kind is taken for 15, or 16, days and the other for five days. The combination pill, however, is considered to be the more certain one of preventing unwanted pregnancy.	A small object (loop, spiral, ring) made of plastic or stainless steel.
How does it work?	Prevents the ovary from releasing an egg cell. With no egg cell present, a woman cannot become pregnant.	It is inserted into womb by a doctor and left there indefinitely. Exactly how it works to prevent pregnancy is not completely known but it does not prevent the ovary from releasing eggs.
How reliable is it?	Virtually completely sure if you follow directions. Rates higher in effectiveness than any other method.	Not as effective as the pill, but will prevent pregnancy in a majority of instances. However, it may be expelled unknowingly. Ordinarily not recommended for women who have not had children as it Is difficult to insert in such cases.
How do I use it?	Ask your doctor. The most usual schedule is one pill a day for 21 consecutive days each month, beginning five days after the menstrual period starts. Essentially this 21-day cycle is repeated each month until you wish to try to have a baby.	Inserted by a doctor. It is important to return at least once a year for a thorough examination. Must also be checked frequently, by feeling to make sure it has not been expelled.
What about side effects and other occurrences?	The majority of women experience few, if any, side effects. In studies, less than 5 percent discontinued use of the newer low dose combination pills for this reason. However, occasional side effects, some of them serious, may occur. If they do, you should discuss them with your doctor. The more common ones usually occur in early cycles of use, then ordinarily diminish rapidly or disappear.	Many women have no problem. Others have cramps and bleeding between menstrual periods. In a relatively few cases, the device has perforated the womb and entered the abdomen. If there is excessive discomfort the doctor will remove the device.
Does it affect sex relations?	Many couples say they enjoy sex relations more because they do not worry about pregnancy.	There is little or no feeling of its being in the womb. If properly inserted, neither partner should be aware of it.
Where can I get it or where can I find out more about it?	Consult your doctor, or family planning clinic. Your doctor or the clinic doctor will talk with you and examine you before prescribing the pill. The clinic, or a local pharmacy, will fill the doctor's prescription. Your doctor, or the clinic, can answer your questions, and will probably give you informative material to accompany your prescription.	Obtained from a private doctor or family planning clinic. The doctor will examine you and decide if the device is suitable.

Diaphragm	Condom	Chemical Methods	Rhythm
A flexible, cup-shaped device made of rubber, inserted before intercourse. It is used with vaginal cream or jelly.	A thin sheath or cover made of rubber or similar material. It is worn over the penis during sexual intercourse.	A vaginal foam, jelly, cream, suppository or tablet. A special powder or fluid, applied with a sponge, is also available.	A plan of avoiding sexual intercourse during the wife's fertile period —that is, just before and just after an egg has been produced in her body.
It is placed in the vagina to cover the entrance to the womb. If properly inserted, it prevents sperm from passing into the womb.	It catches and holds the husband's sperm, so they cannot enter the vagina and fertilize an egg cell.	Acts in the vagina by coating the surfaces and the entrance to the womb. Destroys sperm cells and may act as a mechanical barrier as well.	Most women release an egg cell about once a month—usually about 14 days before menstruation. This may vary from month to month and it is necessary to determine as accurately as possible when an egg will be produced.
If used correctly, many women have a high degree of success. Among consistent users, about 2 or 3 women out of 100 become pregnant each year. If diaphragm is improperly placed or becomes displaced during intercourse, pregnancy can result.	It offers good protection if the husband uses it correctly and consistently. Failures are due primarily to tearing of the condom or to its slipping off during the sex act.	Not rated as effective as the first four methods described, although some women have used them successfully. Vaginal foams rate somewhat higher in effectiveness than the other chemical methods.	Uncertain unless the menstrual cycle is regular and you can accurately figure out your fertile period. Correct use means having no sex relations for the specified time—often as long as half of each month.
The doctor will fit you and show you how to insert it. You should return to the doctor at least every two years, and after each pregnancy, to have the diaphragm checked for size.	The husband puts it on his penis after erection, and well before climax. For extra protection the wife should use a contraceptive jelly, cream or foam.	Read and follow the instructions. Must be used before each sex act. Provides protection for about an hour.	Consult a doctor or a rhythm clinic for help in determining when your fertile period is likely to be each month. You will need to keep records of previous menstrual periods for a number of months.
None, if properly inserted. Some women do not like to insert a diaphragm. Others find it distasteful to remove and clean.	No physical side effects.	No physical side effects.	No physical side effects.
If properly inserted, neither husband nor wife should feel it.	Some couples object to the condom because they must interrupt activity to use it. Some men dislike it because it interferes with their full sexual enjoyment.	Drainage of the preparation from the vagina is objectionable to some couples. Foaming tablets may cause a temporary burning sensation.	Most couples are unwilling—or unable—to refrain from sex relations for the length of time required to be "safe".
A private doctor or family planning clinic can supply you.	At any drug counter. No prescription is required.	At any drug counter. No prescription required.	Consult a doctor or family planning clinic.

uncomfortable for the few minutes it takes, but it is certainly not painful and you have no reason to fear it. A nurse is on hand to assist you.

If you don't like one method of birth control, don't hesitate to ask your doctor about changing to another. People differ, and what suits a relative or friend may not necessarily suit you. The doctor is the best one to advise you.

When you are ready to have a baby, stop using whatever method of birth control you have chosen. After the birth of your child, start practicing birth control again. Spacing your children in this way will enable you to give *each* one the attention and care he deserves.

Remember, a planned for and wanted family is much more likely to be a secure and happy family.

On the Regulation of Birth: *Humanae Vitae**
(abridged)

Pope Paul VI

Hence conjugal love requires in husband and wife an awareness of their mission of *responsible parenthood*, which today is rightly much insisted upon, and which also must be exactly understood. Consequently it is to be considered under different aspects which are legitimate and connected with one another.

In relation to the biological processes, responsible parenthood means the knowledge and respect of their functions; human intellect discovers in the power of giving life biological laws which are part of the human person.

In relation to the tendencies of instinct or passion, responsible parenthood means that necessary dominion which reason and will must exercise over them.

In relation to physical, economic, psychological and social conditions, responsible parenthood is exercised, either by the deliberate and generous decision to raise a numerous family, or by the decision, made for grave motives and with due respect for the moral law, to avoid for the time being, or even for an indeterminate period, a new birth.

Responsible parenthood also and above all implies a more profound relationship to the objective moral order established by God, of which a right conscience is the faithful interpreter. The responsible exercise of parenthood implies, therefore, that husband and wife recognize fully their own duties towards God, towards themselves, towards the family and towards society, in a correct hierarchy of values.

In the task of transmitting life, therefore, they are not free to proceed completely at will, as if they could determine in a wholly autonomous way the honest path to follow; but they must conform their activity to the creative

*Used by permission of the United States Catholic Conference. Taken from "On the Regulation of Birth, *Humanae Vitae*, Encyclical Letter," Section 10 through Section 17, pp. 6-11.

intention of God, expressed in the very nature of marriage and of its acts, and manifested by the constant teaching of the Church.

These acts, by which husband and wife are united in chaste intimacy, and by means of which human life is transmitted, are, as the Council recalled, "noble and worthy," and they do not cease to be lawful if, for causes independent of the will of husband and wife, they are foreseen to be infecund, since they always remain ordained towards expressing and consolidating their union. In fact, as experience bears witness, not every conjugal act is followed by a new life. God has wisely disposed natural laws and rhythms of fecundity which, of themselves, cause a separation in the succession of births. Nonetheless the Church, calling men back to the observance of the norms of the natural law, as interpreted by their constant doctrine, teaches that each and every marriage act (*quilibet matrimonii usus*) must remain open to the transmission of life.

That teaching, often set forth by the magisterium, is founded upon the inseparable connection, willed by God and unable to be broken by man on his own initiative, between the two meanings of the conjugal act: the unitive meaning and the procreative meaning. Indeed, by its intimate structure, the conjugal act, while most closely uniting husband and wife, capacitates them for the generation of new lives, according to laws inscribed in the very being of man and of woman. By safeguarding both these essential aspects, the unitive and the procreative, the conjugal act preserves in its fullness the sense of true mutual love and its ordination towards man's high calling to parenthood. We believe that the men of our day are particularly capable of seizing the deeply reasonable and human character of this fundamental principle.

It is in fact justly observed that a conjugal act imposed upon one's partner without regard for his or her condition and lawful desires is not a true act of love, and therefore denies an exigency of right moral order in the relationships between husband and wife. Likewise, if they consider the matter, they must admit that an act of mutual love, which is detrimental to the faculty of propagating life, which God the Creator of all, has implanted in it according to special laws, is in contradiction to both the divine plan, according to whose norm matrimony has been instituted, and the will of the Author of human life. To use this divine gift destroying, even if only partially, its meaning and its purpose is to contradict the nature both of man and of woman and of their most intimate relationship, and therefore it is to contradict also the plan of God and His will. On the other hand, to make use of the gift of conjugal love while respecting the laws of the generative process means to acknowledge oneself not to be the arbiter of the sources of human life, but rather the minister of the design established by the Creator. In fact, just as man does not have unlimited dominion over his body in general, so also, with particular reason, he has no such dominion over his generative faculties as such, because of their intrinsic ordination towards raising up life, of which God is the principle. "Human life is sacred," Pope John XXIII recalled; "from its very inception it reveals the creating hand of God."

In conformity with these landmarks in the human and Christian vision of marriage, we must once again declare that the direct interruption of the generative process already begun, and, above all, directly willed and procured abortion, even if for therapeutic reasons, are to be absolutely excluded as licit means of regulating birth.

Equally to be excluded, as the teaching authority of the Church has frequently declared, is direct sterilization, whether perpetual or temporary, whether of the man or of the woman. Similarly excluded is every action which, either in anticipation of the conjugal act, or in its accomplishment, or in the development of its natural consequences, proposes, whether as an end or as a means, to render procreation impossible.

To justify conjugal acts made intentionally infecund, one cannot invoke as valid reasons the lesser evil, or the fact that such acts would constitute a whole together with the fecund acts already performed or to follow later, and hence would share in one and the same moral goodness. In truth, if it is sometimes licit to tolerate a lesser evil in order to avoid a greater evil or to promote a greater good, it is not licit, even for the gravest reasons, to do evil so that good may follow therefrom; that is, to make into the object of a positive act of the will something which is intrinsically disorder, and hence unworthy of the human person, even when the intention is to safeguard or promote individual, family or social well-being. Consequently it is an error to think that a conjugal act which is deliberately made infecund and so is intrinsically dishonest could be made honest and right by the ensemble of a fecund conjugal life.

The Church, on the contrary, does not at all consider illicit the use of those therapeutic means truly necessary to cure diseases of the organism, even if an impediment to procreation, which may be foreseen, should result therefrom, provided such impediment is not, for whatever motive, directly willed.

To this teaching of the Church on conjugal morals, the objection is made today ... that it is the prerogative of the human intellect to dominate the energies offered by irrational nature and to orientate them towards an end conformable to the good of man. Now, some may ask: in the present case, is it not reasonable in many circumstances to have recourse to artificial birth control if, thereby, we secure the harmony and peace of the family, and better conditions for the education of the children already born? To this question it is necessary to reply with clarity: the Church is the first to praise and recommend the intervention of intelligence in a function which so closely associates the rational creature with his Creator; but she affirms that this must be done with respect for the order established by God.

If, then, there are serious motives to space out births, which derive from the physical or psychological conditions of husband and wife, or from external conditions, the Church teaches that it is then licit to take into account the natural rhythms immanent in the generative functions, for the use of marriage in the infecund periods only, and in this way to regulate birth without offending the moral principles which have been recalled earlier.

The Church is coherent with herself when she considers recourse to the infecund periods to be licit, while at the same time condemning, as being always illicit, the use of means directly contrary to fecundation, even if such use is inspired by reasons which may appear honest and serious. In reality, there are essential differences between the two cases; in the former, the married couple make legitimate use of a natural disposition; in the latter, they impede the development of natural processes. It is true that, in the one and the other case, the married couple are concordant in the positive will of avoiding children for plausible reasons, seeking the certainty that offspring will not arrive; but it is also true that only in the former case are they able to renounce the use of marriage in the fecund periods when, for just motives, procreation is not desirable, while making use of it during infecund periods to manifest their affection and to safeguard their mutual fidelity. By doing so, they give proof of a truly and integrally honest love.

Upright men can even better convince themselves of the solid grounds on which the teaching of the Church in this field is based, if they care to reflect upon the consquences of methods of artificial birth control. Let them consider, first of all, how wide and easy a road would thus be opened up towards conjugal infidelity and the general lowering of morality. Not much experience is needed in order to know human weakness, and to understand that men – especially the young, who are so vulnerable on this point – have need of encouragement to be faithful to the moral law, so that they must not be offered some easy means of eluding its observance. It is also to be feared that the man, growing used to the employment of anti-conceptive practices, may finally lose respect for the woman and, no longer caring for her physical and psychological equilibrium, may come to the point of considering her as a mere instrument of selfish enjoyment, and no longer as his respected and beloved companion.

Let it be considered also that a dangerous weapon would thus be placed in the hands of those public authorities who take no heed of moral exigencies. Who could blame a government for applying to the solution of the problems of the community those means acknowledged to be licit for married couples in the solution of a family problem? Who will stop rulers from favouring, from even imposing upon their peoples, if they were to consider it necessary, the method of contraception which they judge to be most efficacious? In such a way men, wishing to avoid individual, family, or social difficulties encountered in the observance of the divine law, would reach the point of placing at the mercy of the intervention of public authorities the most personal and most reserved sector of conjugal intimacy.

Consequently, if the mission of generating life is not to be exposed to the arbitrary will of men, one must necessarily recognize insurmountable limits to the possibility of man's domination over his own body and its functions; limits which no man, whether a private individual or one invested with authority, may licitly surpass. And such limits cannot be determined otherwise than by the respect due to the integrity of the human organism and its functions, according to the principles recalled earlier, and also according to the correct understanding of the "principle of totality" illustrated by our predecessor Pope Pius XII.

Statement of Canadian Bishops on the Encyclical *Humanae Vitae**

Pope Paul VI in his recent encyclical *On Human Life* has spoken on a profound human problem as is clearly evidenced by the immediate and universal

*The English and French versions of the Statement of the Canadian Bishops on the Encyclical Humanae Vitae: © 1968 Canadian Catholic Conference, Ottawa. All rights reserved.

reaction to his message. It is evident that he has written out of concern and love, and in a spirit of service to all mankind. Conscious of the current controversy and deep differences of opinion as to how to harmonize married love and the responsible transmission of life, we, the Canadian bishops, offer our help to the priests and Catholic people believing it to be our pastoral duty.

1. Solidarity with the Pope

We are in accord with the teaching of the Holy Father concerning the dignity of married life, and the necessity of a truly Christian relationship between conjugal love and responsible parenthood. We share the pastoral concern which has led him to offer counsel and direction in an area which, while controverted, could hardly be more important to human happiness.

By divine commission, clarification of these difficult problems of morality is required from the teaching authority of the Church.[1] The Canadian bishops will endeavor to discharge their obligation to the best of their ability. In this pursuit we are acting consistently with our recent submissions to the federal government on contraception, divorce and abortion, nor is there anything in those submissions which does not harmonize with the encyclical.

2. Solidarity with the Faithful

In the same spirit of solidarity we declare ourselves one with the People of God in the difficulties they experience in understanding, making their own, and living this teaching.

In accord with the teaching of the Second Vatican Council, the recent encyclical[2] recognizes the nobility of conjugal love which is "uniquely expressed and perfected through the marital act."[3] Many married people experience a truly agonizing difficulty in reconciling the need to express conjugal love with the responsible transmission of human life.[4]

This difficulty is recognized in deep sympathy and is shared by bishops and priests as counsellors and confessors in their service of the faithful. We know that we are unable to provide easy answers to this difficult problem, a problem made more acute by the great variety of solutions proposed in an open society.

A clearer understanding of these problems and progress toward their solution will result from a common effort in dialogue, research and study on the part of all, laity, priests and bishops, guided by faith and sustained by grace. To this undertaking the Canadian bishops pledge themselves.

3. Christian Conscience and Divine Law

Of recent years many have entertained doubts about the validity of arguments proposed to forbid any positive intervention which would prevent the transmission of human life. As a result there have arisen opinions and practices contrary to traditional moral theology. Because of this many had been expecting official confirmation of their views. This helps to explain the negative reaction the encyclical received in many quarters. Many Catholics face a grave problem of conscience.

Christian theology regarding conscience has its roots in the teaching of St. Paul.[5] This has been echoed in our day by Vatican II: "Conscience is the most secret core and sanctuary of a man. There he is alone with God, whose voice echoes in his depths."[6] "On his part, man perceives and acknowledges the imperatives of the divine law through the mediation of conscience. In all his activity a man is bound to follow his conscience faithfully, in order that he may come to God, for whom he was created."[7] The dignity of man consists precisely in his ability to achieve his fulfillment in God through the exercise of a knowing and free choice.

However this does not exempt a man from the responsibility of forming his conscience according to truly Christian values and principles. This implies a spirit of openness to the teaching of the Church which is an essential aspect of the Christian's baptismal vocation. It likewise implies sound personal motivation free from selfishness and undue external pressure which are incompatible with the spirit of Christ. Nor will he succeed in this difficult task without the help of God. Man is prone to sin and evil and unless he humbly asks and gratefully receives the grace of God this basic freedom will inevitably lead to abuse.

4. Teaching Office of the Church

Belief in the Church which is the prolongation of Christ in the world, belief in the Incarnation, demands a cheerful readiness to hear that Church to whose first apostles Christ said: "He who hears you hears me."[8]

True freedom of conscience does not consist, then, in the freedom to do as one likes, but rather to do so as a responsible conscience directs. Vatican Council II applies this concept forcefully. Christians therefore "must always be governed according to a conscience dutifully conformed to the divine law itself, and should be submissive towards the Church's teaching office, which authentically interprets that law in the light of the gospel. That divine law reveals and protects the integral meaning of conjugal love, and impels it towards truly human fulfillment."[9]

Today, the Holy Father has spoken on the question of morally acceptable means to harmonize conjugal love and responsible parenthood. Christians must examine in all honesty their reaction to what he has said.

The Church is competent to hand on the truth contained in the revealed word of God and to interpret its meaning. But its role is not limited to this function. In his pilgrimage to salvation, man achieves final happiness by all his human conduct and his whole moral life. Since the Church is man's guide in this pilgrimage, she is called upon to exercise her role as teacher, even in those matters which do not demand the absolute assent of faith.

Of this sort of teaching Vatican II wrote: "This religious submission of will and of mind must be shown in a special way to the authentic teaching authority of the Roman Pontiff, even when he is not speaking *ex cathedra*. That is, it must be shown in such a way that his supreme teaching service is acknowledged with reverence, the judgments made by him are sincerely adhered to, according to his manifest mind and will."[10]

It follows that those who have been commissioned by the Church to teach in her name will recognize their responsibility to refrain from public opposition to the encyclical; to do otherwise would compound confusion and be a source of scandal to God's people. However, this must not be interpreted as a restriction on the legitimate and recognized freedom of theologians to pursue loyally and conscientiously their research with a view to greater depth and clarity in the teaching of the Church.

It is a fact that a certain number of Catholics, although admittedly subject to the teaching of the encyclical, find it either extremely difficult or even impossible to make their own all elements of this doctrine. In particular, the argumentation and rational foundation of the encyclical, which are only briefly indicated, have failed in some cases to win the assent of men of science, or indeed of some men of culture and education who share in the contemporary empirical and scientific mode of thought. We must appreciate the difficulty experienced by contemporary man in understanding and appropriating some of the points of this encyclical, and we must make every effort to learn from the insights of Catholic scientists and intellectuals, who are of undoubted loyalty to Christian truth, to the Church and to the authority of the Holy See. Since they are not denying any point of divine and Catholic faith nor rejecting the teaching authority of the Church, these Catholics should not be considered, or consider themselves, shut off from the body of the faithful. But they should remember that their good faith will be dependent on a sincere self-examination to determine the true motives and grounds for such suspension of assent and on continued effort to understand and deepen their knowledge of the teaching of the Church.

The difficulties of this situation have been felt by the priests of the Church, and by many others. We have been requested to provide guidelines to assist them. This we will endeavor to accomplish in a subsequent document. We are conscious that continuing dialogue, study and reflection will be required by all members of the Church in order to meet as best we can the complexities and exigencies of the problem.

We point out that the particular norms which we may offer will prove of little value unless they are placed in the context of man's human and Christian vocation and all of the values of Christian marriage. This formation of conscience and this education in true love will be achieved only by a well balanced pastoral insistence upon the primary importance of a love which is human, total, faithful and exclusive as well as generously fruitful.[11]

5. Preliminary Pastoral Guidance

For the moment, in conformity with traditional Christian morality, we request priests and all who may be called to guide or counsel the conscience of others to give their attention to the following considerations.

The pastoral directives given by Pope Paul VI in the encyclical are inspired by a positive sacramental approach. The Eucharist is always the great expression of Christian love and union. Married couples will always find in this celebration a meeting place with the Lord which will never fail to strengthen their own mutual love. With regard to the sacrament of penance the spirit is one of encouragement both for penitents and confessors and avoids both extremes of laxity and rigorism.

The encyclical suggests an attitude towards the sacrament of penance which is at once less juridical, more pastoral and more respectful of persons. There is real concern for their growth, however slow at times, and for the hope of the future.

Confession should never be envisaged under the cloud of agonizing fear or severity. It should be an exercise in confidence and respect of consciences. Paul VI invited married couples to ". . . have recourse with humble perseverance to the mercy of God, which is poured forth in the Sacrament of Penance."[12] Confession is a meeting between a sincere conscience and Christ Our Lord who was "indeed intransigent with evil, but merciful towards individuals."[13]

Such is the general atmosphere in which the confessor and counsellor must work. We complete the concept with a few more particular applications.

In the situation we described earlier in this statement (par. 17) the confessor or counsellor must show sympathetic understanding and reverence for the sincere good faith of those who fail in their effort to accept some point of the encyclical.

Counsellors may meet others who, accepting the teaching of the Holy Father, find that because of particular circumstances they are involved in what seems to them a clear conflict of duties, e.g. the reconciling of conjugal love and responsible parenthood with the education of children already born or with the health of the mother. In accord with the accepted principles of moral theology, if these persons have tried sincerely but without success to pursue a line of conduct in keeping with the given directives, they may be safely assured that whoever honestly chooses that course which seems right to him does so in good conscience.

Good pastoral practice for other and perhaps more difficult cases will be developed in continuing communication among bishops, priests and laity, and in particular in the document we have promised to prepare. In the meantime we earnestly solicit the help of medical scientists and biologists in their research into human fertility. While it would be an illusion to hope for the solution of all human problems through scientific technology, such research can bring effective help to the alleviation and solution of problems of conscience in this area.

6. Invitation to Social Pastoral Action

The whole world is conscious of the growing preoccupation with the social impact of all men's thoughts, words and actions. Sexuality in all its aspects is obviously an area of the greatest human and social impact. The norms and values which govern this so vital human concern merit the attention and cooperation of all. Our world evolves at a frightening rate, creating at once a vivid sense of unity and a set of conflicting forces which could destroy us.

This concern will be fruitful only if it leads all of us to recognize our true human worth in the possession of our inner powers by which we are distinctively ourselves with the full recognition of our complementary sexual differences on the physical, the psychological and the spiritual plane. Only in this manner will we achieve marriages that are truly unions of love in the service of life.

To this end there must be brought into play all the positive forces of the family, the school, the state, the Church. No one may stand aloof, nor are there really national boundaries in a matter of such universal application. With this in mind we call on all members of the Church to realize the importance of the process of education for marriage on every level from the very youngest to the various possibilities of adult education.

Without wishing to specify in detail we single out for special mention a few aspects which may have richer possibilities. We place first the dialogue and cooperation, which have been so encouraging, among all members of the Church and, through the ecumenical movement, with other Churches.

We note with deep satisfaction the spread and strength of so many activities calculated to prepare for marriage or to deepen the appreciation of married persons of this sublime state. For example, marriage preparation courses, family apostolates, discussion groups, etc.

Educators, too, are to be commended for their growing attention to the question. Everywhere the problem of sex education and family life is being studied. And this education is happily being deepened by scientific research and diffused through the creative use of mass media. Nothing less than this mobilization of all human forces will suffice to meet the challenge of divisive and destructive forces which begin deep in the willful selfishness of man and inhibit the true expression of his love. We pledge ourselves to the pastoral priority of encouraging and promoting these programs whenever and wherever possible.

We conclude by asking all to pray fervently that the Holy Spirit will continue to guide his Church through all darkness and suffering. We, the People of God, cannot escape this hour of crisis but there is no reason to believe that it will create division and despair. The unity of the Church does not consist in a bland conformity in all ideas, but rather in a union of faith and heart, in submission of God's will and a humble but honest and ongoing search for the truth. That unity of love and faith is founded in Christ and as long as we are true to Him nothing can separate us. We stand in union with the Bishop of Rome, the successor of Peter, the sign and contributing cause of our unity with Christ and with one another. But this very union postulates such a love of the Church that we can do no less than to place all of our love and all of our intelligence at its service. If this sometimes means that in our desire to make the Church more intelligible and more beautiful we must, as pilgrims do, falter in the way or differ as to the way, no one should conclude that our common faith is lost or our loving purpose blunted. The great Cardinal Newman once wrote: "Lead kindly light amidst the encircling gloom". We believe that the Kindly Light will lead us to a greater understanding of the ways of God and the love of man.

Footnotes

1. *On Human Life*, n. 4 and 18.
2. *On Human Life*, n. 8.
3. "The Church Today," n. 49.
4. "The Church Today, n. 51.
5. Rom. 14:23 and I Cor. 10.
6. "The Church Today," n. 16.
7. *On Religious Freedom*, n. 3; "The Church Today," nn. 16, 17.
8. Luke 10:16.
9. "The Church Today," n. 50.
10. *Constitution on the Church*, n. 25.
11. *On Human Life*, n. 9.
12. *On Human Life*, n. 25.
13. *On Human Life*, n. 29.

Vasectomy as a Birth Control Method[*]

Carl F. Grindstaff and G. Edward Ebanks

Rationale for the Study

In 1851-61, the crude birth rate in Canada (number of live births per 1,000 people in the population) was 45. In 1970, this rate is approximately 18. Not only have the birth rates decreased but the average family size has declined from a normal five or six children per family at the turn of the century to one of two or three children in the 1970's. In addition, women are completing their childbearing at an earlier age. Fifty years ago, it was not uncommon for a woman to have a child in her late thirties or early forties. Today, this is a relatively rare event. In fact, it is estimated that approximately 75 percent of all families are now complete in terms of the number of children desired before the woman is thirty years of age. This new demographic pattern creates an important and serious situation. At age 30, with all the desired children and with fifteen more years of potential childbearing ahead of them, what can the couple do to prevent the occurrence of additional pregnancies?

Standard birth control techniques range in sophistication and reliability from *coitus interruptus* to the *pill*. However, all known and available contraceptive techniques have certain drawbacks. Traditional methods such as *coitus interruptus* and the rhythm method are uncertain and take a great deal of planning, self control, and restraint to be even partially effective. All previous studies have shown that failure rates related to these methods are high. The chemical methods such as jellies and creams are relatively unreliable and distasteful to perhaps a majority of the couples that have used them.

The condom and diaphragm are fairly effective if used properly, but there is always the danger of accidental pregnancies resulting from defects and/or damages as well as the slipping of the devices. Also, some people indicate that these contraceptives interfere with sexual enjoyment and spontaneity. The intrauterine devices are excellent in terms of protection if used properly, and so long as they are correctly placed. However, many women cannot use these devices since they either involuntarily expel them, or must remove them because of a variety of side effects, such as cramps, pain, bleeding and infection. The idea of a foreign body in the uterus does not appeal to many women and to this is added the fear of uterine cancer. Finally, the oral contraceptive is the most sophisticated birth control measure of its kind available. If used according to directions, it is virtually foolproof. There are some uncomfortable side effects in many women such as headaches, weight gain and cramps, but recently there have been more serious questions raised relating the pill to cancer and blood clotting. The evidence on this point has been inconclusive, but many women have discontinued the use of the pill, and many do not take the pill for more than a few years consecutively. Thus, for every method currently in use as a nonpermanent birth limitation technique, there are some problems related to health or to failure. There is at present no perfect chemical or mechanical contraceptive method.

Given these deficiencies, more and more married couples who have completed

[*] Not published previously; written specifically for this volume.

their family size are turning to sterilization as a means of birth control. Traditionally, it was the female who underwent an operation such as salpingectomy or tubal ligation in order to prevent future pregnancies. Just a decade ago, 75 percent of all sterilization operations were performed on females. Such operations are, however, painful, expensive, and require rather intensive hospital care for at least a week. Recently, the male sterilization operation known as vasectomy has become more popular due to publicity, ease of the operation, the relative painlessness, the low cost, and perhaps other factors. Today, 75 percent of all sterilization operations are performed on men and estimates indicate that such operations have quadrupled in the past four years.

The vasectomy is a surgical procedure which makes the male sterile. It involves the cutting and tying of the *vas deferens*, the tubes which carry the sperm from the testicles to the penis and hence prevents the transmission of the sperm to the female. Physiologically, this operation does not interfere with sexual intercourse and erection and ejaculation still take place during the sex act, but the sperms are reabsorbed by the body. Therefore, in the successful vasectomy, there is no sperm deposited into the uterus during intercourse to fertilize the female ovum.

The purpose of this paper is to describe the types of men who undergo the operation in terms of their socio-economic characteristics, to determine the reasons for having the vasectomy, and to examine previous birth control techniques that were used to see the effectiveness of such techniques.

Methodology

This study was conducted in a large Canadian city during 1970 with the co-operation of two local urologists who performed approximately 85 to 90 percent of the operations in the city. Questionnaires were mailed to 800 men who had undergone a vasectomy from 1966 to 1969 in this city. Over 500 of the questionnaires were returned, approximately 63 percent of the total mailed. This is considered an excellent rate of return for a mailed questionnaire even in spite of the condition that it is a special population, since consideration should be given to the fact that some of these people had the operation for as much as three years prior to the survey and have consequently changed addresses. We have reason to believe that the respondents are representative of the population of 800 since before sending out the questionnaire we had obtained the age and occupational distributions of the total 800 men and these distributions did not vary significantly from our returned questionnaire on these two variables.

The Findings

Background Characteristics

There are no current data available on the socio-economic characteristics of the general Canadian population with which our respondents could be compared. The latest information published concerning the city where most of the respondents live was the 1961 census. Unfortunately, income, educational, and occupational positions have changed markedly since that time making com-

TABLE 1

Socio-economic Characteristics of Families Undergoing Vasectomy

HUSBAND'S OCCUPATION	Number	Percent
Professional and Manager	158	31.3
Clerical and Sales	67	13.2
Skilled	106	20.9
Semi-skilled and Unskilled	140	27.7
Other	35	6.9
Total	506	100.0

HUSBAND'S EDUCATION	Number	Percent
Less than High School	98	19.4
Some High School	213	42.1
Completed High School	125	24.7
Some University	23	3.8
Completed University	47	9.2
No Response	4	.8
Total	506	100.0

Median School Year Completed: 10.5 years

WIFE'S EDUCATION	Number	Percent
Less than High School	46	9.1
Some High School	242	47.8
Completed High School	166	32.8
Some University	34	6.7
Completed University	13	2.6
No Response	5	1.0
Total	506	100.0

Median School Year Completed: 10.8 years

FAMILY INCOME	Number	Percent
Under $5,000	34	6.7
$5,000–$9,000	243	48.1
$9,000 plus	209	41.3
No response	20	3.9
Total	506	100.0

Median Family Income. $8,600

HUSBAND'S RELIGION	Number	Percent
Protestant	372	73.5
Catholic	55	10.9
Jewish	0	0.0
Other	13	2.6
None	60	11.8
No response	6	1.2
Total	506	100.0

WIFE'S RELIGION	Number	Percent
Protestant	382	75.5
Catholic	61	12.0
Jewish	2	.4
Other	10	2.0
None	46	9.1
No Response	5	1.0
Total	506	100.0

Note: Fifty-five of the 506 couples show a different religious affiliation between wife and husband.

HUSBAND'S AGE AT OPERATION	Number	Percent
Under 30	82	16.2
30–34	132	26.1
35–39	141	27.8
40–44	97	19.2
45 plus	54	10.7
Total	506	100.0

Median Age: 36.4 years

WIFE'S AGE AT OPERATION	Number	Percent
Under 30	156	30.8
30–34	144	28.5
35–39	122	24.1
40–44	71	14.0
45 plus	13	2.6
Total	506	100.0

Median Age: 33.4 years

parisons on such characteristics with our respondents meaningless. It would appear, however, that the respondents are rather typical of the larger population, perhaps a bit above average in terms of occupational, educational, and income attainments. Table 1 shows these and other background characteristics. There are more professionals and managers among the respondents than semi-skilled and unskilled people. Both the husband and the wife have slightly higher median school grade completed than the general population. The husband had completed 10.5 years of schooling on the average and some 13 percent had attended university. The wife's educational attainment is similar, 9.3 percent had been to university and the average amount of schooling completed for the wife was 10.8 years. The median family income is approximately $8,500, which is probably a bit higher than the median family income found in the city as a whole.

Religious affiliation indicates that the respondents are 75 percent Protestant, 10 percent Catholic, 10 percent no religion, and 5 percent other. The city's population is about 75 percent Protestant, but it is also about 20 percent Catholic. Thus, there is an underrepresentation of the latter religious group among the men who had undergone the vasectomy. This is to be expected given the official Catholic opposition to such a procedure.

The median age of the husband is 36.4 years, with 16 percent under the age of 30. The wife is younger with a median age of 33.4 and 31 percent under the age of 30. Without some permanent form of birth control, a large proportion of these women would have had 10 to 15 years of potential childbearing to face, when it is obvious that they desired no more children. This point is illustrated in Table 2.

TABLE 2

Number of Living Children at the Time of the Vasectomy and Number of Children Desired by Husband and Wife at the Time of Their Marriage

Number of Children	Couples With Living Children		Desired By Husband at Marriage		Desired by Wife at Marriage	
	Number	Percent	Number	Percent	Number	Percent
0	5	1.0	31	6.1	32	6.3
1	19	3.8	20	3.9	16	3.2
2	124	24.5	219	43.3	191	37.7
3	145	28.7	80	15.8	86	17.0
4	109	21.5	63	12.5	92	18.2
5	67	13.2	9	1.8	8	1.6
6 or more	31	6.1	14	2.8	16	3.2
No response	6	1.2	70	13.8	65	12.8
Total	506	100.0	506	100.0	506	100.0
Total Number of Children	1,690		1,090		1,169	
Children Per Family:	3.38		2.50		2.65	

Table 2 shows the number of living children belonging to the couples at the time of the survey and hence at the time of the operation and also the number of children the husbands and wives desired at the time of their marriage. Generally speaking, the couples had over 30 percent more children than they had wanted when they were first married. The respondents average 3.38 children per family while the husbands and wives had originally desired 2.50 and 2.65 children per family respectively. The modal category for the number of children living is three while the modal category for the number desired by both husband and wife is two. It is clear that more children were conceived than were wanted.

Why the Vasectomy

Table 3 shows the major reasons the respondents gave for choosing the vasectomy as a method of birth control.

TABLE 3

Reasons for the Vasectomy Operation*

Reasons	Number	Percent
We Had All of the Children We Wanted	369	72.9
We Had All of the Children We Could Afford	263	52.0
Wife Was Dissatisfied With Other Contraceptive Methods	203	40.1
Other Contraceptive Methods Had Failed	138	25.7

*The totals add to more than 506 couples and 100.0% because the respondents could choose more than one reason.

Nearly three-fourths of the respondents indicated that they underwent the operation because they as a family had all of the children that they wanted. In addition, over 50 percent indicated that they had all of the children they could afford. In a sense then, the vasectomy can be viewed as a *desperation act*. The respondents do not want any more children and the vasectomy guarantees them that no *accidents* will occur. Over 99 percent of the men said they knew that once the operation was performed that they could never again make their wives pregnant. There were no reported cases of pregnancies from the respondents after the operation had been performed. Other major reasons for having the operation were dissatisfaction and failure with other contraceptive methods. In addition, many couples found that the use of some contraceptives reduced their sexual pleasure.

TABLE 4

Most Influential Person in Arriving at the Decision to Have the Operation

Person	Number	Percent
Husband	141	27.9
Wife	22	4.4
Husband and Wife Equally	321	63.4
Another person	22	4.3

Table 4 provides information as to who was the most influential person in arriving at the decision to have the vasectomy operation – the husband, the wife, or someone else. As might be expected, most couples (63 percent) said that it was a joint decision, with both the husband and wife equally taking part in the decision. Over 25 percent replied that the husband was most influential. This reinforces the statement made by the men that they had all the children they could afford. Rarely was the wife or another person mainly responsible for the decision to have the vasectomy.

Effectiveness of Contraceptives Used Prior to the Vasectomy

Table 5 shows that approximately 97 percent of the respondents had used some form of birth control technique prior to sterilization. The table also provides information as to the number of failures (accidental pregnancies) using various methods. It should be kept in mind that these are very general figures and do not take into consideration length of time used nor the order of the method.

TABLE 5

Previous Contraceptive Use and Accidental Pregnancies Occurring While Employing the Various Contraceptive Methods

Used a Contraceptive Method Prior to the Vasectomy Operation	Number	Percent	
Yes	489	96.6	
No	15	3.0	
No Response	2	.4	
Total	506	100.0	

Accidental Pregnancies	Couples	Pregnancies	Index*
Method			
Rhythm	140	138	.99
Coitus Interruptus	176	144	.82
Douche	51	29	.57
Diaphraghm	187	105	.56
Vaginal Foams and Jellies	126	55	.44
Condom	279	110	.39
Intrauterine Device	83	31	.38
Oral Contraceptive	323	27	.08

Total Accidental Pregnancies: 639
Total Couples Using Birth Control: 489
Average Number of Accidental Pregnancies Per Couple: 1.31

*Index: $\dfrac{\text{Pregnancies}}{\text{Couples}}$

There were 639 accidental pregnancies reported by the 489 couples who were using some birth limitation technique at the time that the pregnancy occurred. This averages to 1.3 accidental children per couple, or about 39 percent of the total number of living children that the couples have. The term *accidental pregnancies* as used here means that the children were unwanted and unplanned at the time of conception, and not necessarily unwanted over the duration of the marriage. Again, this high failure rate was a strong motivating force to have the operation.

Table 5 also shows the failure index for the various contraceptives employed. The rhythm method was the least reliable with 138 pregnancies for the 140 couples who had used this method, an index of .99. The most successful technique employed was the pill, with a failure index of only .08, and most of these failures were undoubtedly caused by improper use. However, many couples found the oral contraceptive unsatisfactory because of health reasons.

The IUD and diaphragm show relatively high failure indices, .38 and .56 respectively. Once more, the major reasons for the lack of success with these techniques would be improper use, but it illustrates the pregnancy dangers these couples faced even with relatively sophisticated devices.

When all the contraceptive methods that were employed are taken as a group, and their failure index calculated by the order in which they were used regardless of what particular methods they were, the results were as reported in Table 6.

TABLE 6

Accidental Pregnancies by Time Order of Method Used

Method	Couples	Pregnancies	Index*
First Method	461	313	.68
Most Common Techniques as First Method			
Condom: 159 couples			
Coitus Interruptus: 114 couples			
Second Method	400	185	.46
Most Common Techniques as Second Method			
Diaphragm: 91 couples			
Oral: 91 couples			
Condom: 90 couples			
Third Method	276	86	.31
Most Common Techniques as Third Method			
Oral: 103 couples			
Diaphragm: 41 couples			
Fourth Method	148	48	.32
Most Common Techniques as Fourth Method			
Oral: 67 couples			
IUD: 22 couples			
Fifth Method	60	11	.18
Most Common Techniques as Fifth Method			
Oral: 28 couples			
Foams: 11 couples			

*Index: $\dfrac{\text{Pregnancies}}{\text{Couples}}$

The general decreasing trend of this index is most likely a result of three factors: (1) the length of time the methods were used decreases with the order of the method; (2) the increasing reliability of the more recent methods, the use of which increases with the order of the method; and (3) the more care taken with the later methods to avoid pregnancy. After the second method, by far the most popular technique used was the pill. The condom and then *coitus interruptus* (withdrawal) were used most often as a first method. However, even with the relative success of later methods, the respondents turned to vasectomy as a *sure* means of birth prevention. When asked if they had it to do over again would they still choose the vasectomy, 99 percent of the respondents indicated that they would still undergo the operation and that they were satisfied with the results.

Conclusions

The men undergoing vasectomy were found to be rather typical of the general population, perhaps a bit above average in income, occupational, and educational attainments. As families, they had more children than they desired to have when they were first married, and nearly 40 percent of all births were accidental. That is, they were unplanned and unwanted at the time of conception. All other forms of birth control had been used with varying degrees of success and satisfaction, but there were certain problems with every technique employed.

The median age of the wife was approximately 33 with more than 30 percent under 30. With from 10 to 15 years of potential childbearing still to come, these respondents decided that the vasectomy was one sure, safe, and reliable method of birth prevention. After the operation, satisfaction was found to be nearly universal.

Vasectomy as a birth control technique is being rapidly diffused across Canada. This will continue despite the liberalization of the abortion laws. Female sterilization is almost certain to become more widespread with the recent developments in techniques for performing them. There are indications that with the unsatisfactory nature of most of the chemical and mechanical methods of contraception male and female sterilization will increase as too will abortion. It may be true that Canada does not have a population problem in the sense it is used with regards to the developing countries, but the individual couples have their family planning problems. These couples are ever in search of a sure, safe and easy way of ensuring that they have only the desired number of children. Couples spacing pregnancies will find vasectomy unsuitable but couples permanently terminating their childbearing will increasingly find the answer in sterilization.

References

Cobb, David, "The Operation—Then No More Children," *The Canadian Magazine*, September 20, 1969.

Gallup, George, Gallup Poll, "Voluntary Male Sterilization Favoured by 53% of Adults," *Press*, Binghampton, New York, September 3, 1970.

Kantner, Jack, Allingham, Jack and Balakrishnan, T. R., "Oral Contraception and the Fertility Decline in Canada 1958-1968," paper presented at the annual meeting of the Population Association of America, Boston, Massachusetts, April, 1968.

London Free Press, London, Ontario, March 24, 1970.

McGill University, *Birth Control Handbook*, August, 1970.

Poffenberger, Thomas, "Two Thousand Voluntary Vasectomies Performed in California: Background Factors and Comments," *Marriage and Family Living*, 25, November, 1963.

Porter, John, *Canadian Social Structure*. Toronto: McClelland and Stewart Ltd., 1967.

Simon Population Trust, *Vasectomy: Follow-up of a Thousand Cases*, December, 1969, Cambridge, England.

Toronto *Globe and Mail*, March 28, 1970.

The Liberalization of the Canadian Abortion Laws[*]

J. E. Veevers

In June of 1969, the Canadian Parliament passed a controversial series of amendments to the Criminal Code which included, among other reforms, the specification of certain limited circumstances under which therapeutic abortions could be lawfully performed. The purpose of the present article is to outline the legal changes, and to comment briefly on the consequences and implications of the amendments.

The Original Abortion Legislation

The Criminal Code of Canada, passed in the 1953-1954 session of Parliament, appears at first reading to contain two sections which clearly prohibit all abortions.

Section 237. (1) Everyone who, with intent to procure the miscarriage of a female person, whether or not she is pregnant uses any means for the purpose of carrying out this intention is guilty of an indictable offence and is liable to imprisonment for life. (2) Every female person who, being pregnant, with intent to procure her own miscarriage, uses any means or permits any means to be used for the purpose of carrying out her intention is guilty of an indictable offence and is liable to imprisonment for two years. (3) In this section, *means* includes: (a) the administration of a drug or other noxious thing, (b) the use of an instrument, (c) manipulation of any kind.

Section 238. Everyone who unlawfully supplies or procures a drug or other noxious thing, or an instrument or thing, knowing it is intended to be used or employed to procure the miscarriage of a female person, whether or not she is pregnant, is guilty of an indictable offence and is liable to imprisonment for two years.

In practice, however, doctors and hospital abortion committees were able to perform therapeutic abortions with no record of prosecutions[1] because of the existence of an additional section:

Section 209. (1) Everyone who causes the death of a child that has not become a human being, in such a manner that, if the child were a human being, he would be guilty of murder, is guilty of an indictable offence and is liable to imprisonment for life. (2) This section does not apply to a person who, by means that, in good faith, he considers necessary to preserve the life of the mother of a child that has not become a human being, causes the death of the child. Theoretically, Section 209 might apply to any person. In practice, it was interpreted to refer to any qualified medical doctor, who could legally perform a therapeutic abortion if he could establish that it was necessary to preserve the life of the mother, and if, as with all surgery, it was performed with due care and skill. Unfortunately, although the code did define when a

---

[*] Not published previously; written specifically for this volume.

child became a human being,[2] it was unclear whether or not section 209 dealt with miscarriage, as well as with the death of a child at parturition.

The Abortion Amendments

In 1969, the ambiguity concerning Section 209 was resolved by the simple addition of the words "in the act of birth", making it irrelevant to abortions. Section 237 was retained, but was amended by the addition of four subsections.

(4) Subsections (1) and (2) do not apply to

(a) a qualified medical practitioner, other than a member of a therapeutic abortion committee for any hospital, who in good faith uses in an accredited or approved hospital any means for the purpose of carrying out his intention to procure the miscarriage of a female person, or

(b) a female person who, being pregnant, permits a qualified medical practitioner to use in an accredited or approved hospital any means described in paragraph (a) for the purpose of carrying out her intention to procure her own miscarriage, if before the use of those means, the therapeutic abortion committee for that accredited or approved hospital, by a majority of the members of the committee and at a meeting of the committee at which the case of such female person has been reviewed,

(c) has by certificate in writing stated that in its opinion the continuation of the pregnancy of such female person would or would be likely to endanger her life or health, and

(d) has caused a copy of such certificate to be given to the qualified medical practitioner.

(5) The Minister of Health of a province may by order

(a) require a therapeutic abortion committee for any hospital in that province, or any member thereof, to furnish to him a copy of any certificate described in paragraph (c) of subsection (4) issued by that committee, together with such other information relating to the circumstances surrounding the issue of that certificate as he may require, or

(b) require a medical practitioner who, in that province, has procured the miscarriage of any female person named in a certificate described in paragraph (c) of subsection (4), to furnish to him a copy of that certificate, together with such other information relating to the procuring of the miscarriage as he may require.

(6) For the purposes of subsections (4) and (5) and this subsection,

(a) *accredited hospital* means a hospital accredited by the Canadian Council on Hospital Accreditation in which diagnostic services and medical, surgical and obstetrical treatment are provided;

(b) *approved hospital* means a hospital in a province approved for the purposes of this section by the Minister of Health of that province;

(c) *board* means the board of governors, management or directors, or the trustees, commission or other person or group of persons having the control and management of an accredited or approved hospital:

(d) *Minister of Health* means

(i) in the Province of Ontario, Quebec, New Brunswick, Manitoba, Alberta, Newfoundland and Prince Edward Island, the Minister of Health,

(ii) in the Province of British Columbia, the Minister of Health Services and Hospital Insurance,

(iii) in the Provinces of Nova Scotia and Saskatchewan, the Minister of Public Health, and

(iv) in the Yukon Territory and the Northwest Territories, the Minister of National Health and Welfare;

(e) *qualified medical practitioner* means a person entitled to engage in the practice of medicine under the laws of the province in which the hospital referred to in subsection (4) is situated; and

(f) *Therapeutic abortion committee* for any hospital means a committee comprised of not less than three members *each of whom is a qualified medical practitioner*, appointed by the board of that hospital for the purpose of considering and determining questions relating to *terminations* of pregnancy *within that hospital.*

(7) Nothing in subsection (4) shall be construed as making unnecessary the obtaining of any authorization or consent that is or may be required, otherwise than under this Act, before any means are used for the purpose of carrying out an intention to procure the miscarriage of a female person.

The amendments state that *no* abortion can be considered lawful unless it has first been approved by a formal therapeutic abortion committee at an approved or accredited hospital.[3] The law is inconsistent with respect to the conditions under which violation is deemed to have taken place. When a woman who believes herself to be pregnant attempts to obtain an illegal abortion, the law is concerned only with the preservation of fetal life, and she cannot be found guilty unless she is actually pregnant. When other individuals are involved in attempts to procure an illegal abortion, the law is concerned both with the criminal destruction of fetal life, and with the intention to commit the crime, and participants may be found guilty whether or not the woman is in fact pregnant.

Consequences of the Abortion Amendments

If the intent of the abortion amendments was to make abortion legally available to all women whose physical or mental health would be endangered by the completion of a particular pregnancy, then the legislation has been, and will continue to be unsuccessful. The problems inherent in its initial specifications are complicated and magnified by the unwieldly machinery created for its implementation. Some of the more obvious problems are outlined below.

1. The Concept of Mental Health

A very important addition in the abortion amendments is the provision that abortion is justified not only when the mother's life is threatened, but also when her health would be endangered by carrying the pregnancy to term. The critical word *health* is not defined by the legislation. If, as Morgentaler suggests, we adopt the World Health Organization's definition of health as not merely an absence of disease, but "a state of complete physical, mental and social well-being," then any unwanted pregnancy could be construed as a threat to health.[4] Although the revised abortion laws have been in effect for only a short time, at least one study has already attempted to assess the actual workings of therapeutic abortion committees. Smith and Wineberg interviewed doctors serving on committees in six public non-Catholic hospitals in Toronto and Winnipeg. After reviewing the various interpretations which are given to the idea of mental health, they conclude that there are such wide discrepancies in usage that the term is "meaningless" as a legal or medical standard.[5] It is twisted and reinterpreted as necessary to cover a wide range of other reasons for abortion that the committee recognizes as valid, but which are not directly supported by the law. For example, abortions granted on socio-economic grounds may be viewed in terms of the psychological trauma of financial stress. All of the committees studied reported that they would consider a substantial risk of fetal deformity to be in itself a valid reason for abortion. Although the law does not recognize this reason directly, the decision can be rationalized in terms of the psychological trauma assumed always to accompany the bearing of a deformed child.

The absence of a clear or consistent working definition of mental health has led to radical fluctuations in the probabilities that a particular request for an abortion will be granted. These discrepancies appear to be related to such diverse factors as the woman's occupation, her sophistication and skill in interpersonal manipulation, or the committee's perception and evaluation of her as a *responsible* or *moral* person.

2. Membership of Committees

If the definition of health is expanded to include the psychological as well as the physiological, there seems little justification for limiting membership on therapeutic abortion committees only to qualified medical doctors. Although doctors may be especially well versed in matters of physical health, there is no reason to assume that they are also equally proficient in their judgments of social and psychological attributes, and membership on the committee might usefully be extended to other qualified professionals such as psychologists, social workers, and sociologists, or even, as Parker suggests, to clergymen and lay men and women.[6]

Abortion committees composed partly of nonmedical personnel might not only consider a wider range of reasons as legitimate grounds for abortion, but might be considerably more liberal in the granting of official consent. As the editor of a Nova Scotia medical journal has noted: "As doctors are notoriously conservative, they will be slow to use even the little leniency that the law now allows."[7] Only a few doctors would agree with Morgentaler's strong pro-abortion statement to the Canadian Medical Association, in which he concludes that: There is no way the medical profession can evade this responsibility (to the individual woman and to the community) now that it has received such wide powers to shield women from the consequences of unplanned, undesired, unintended, and unwanted pregnancies.[8] The personal philosophies of many doctors would lead them to continue to oppose abortions on moralistic grounds. For example, the letters in reply to Morgentaler's position compared it to the Nazi's solution to the Jewish problem[9] and deplored the philosophy of modern humanism which ". . . intent upon saving humanity from misery, plunges it into death."[10]

The legal stipulation that a committee member must be a doctor "other than a member of a therapeutic abortion committee for *any* hospital" has been the cause of much confusion. Some hospitals take it to mean that a doctor cannot be a judge of one of his own cases; others infer that no gynecologist who *ever* performs abortions is eligible, and recent consultations of Toronto hospitals with the Deputy Attorney General have failed to resolve the issue. As a result, one committee has no gynecologist at all, and others are considering replacing gynecologist members.[11]

3. Consideration of Cases

The practical working of abortion committees has created additional restricttions not required by the law. All of the committees surveyed by Smith and Wineberg require that every case they consider be brought before them and be supported by at least two doctors, and many prefer that one doctor also be a psychiatrist if the abortion is to be requested on mental health grounds.[12] There is nothing in the law itself to suggest that a woman could not be represented to the committee by some other person, not necessarily a medical doctor, or even that if desired, she could not go directly to the committee and plead her own case. The referral system which has been commonly adopted requires the professional attention of at least five doctors, rather than the three specified by the law. Although the duplication of resources may be expensive and time consuming, a more important consequence is the fact that the procedure creates an additional barrier for the pregnant woman in that before she can place her case before a committee she must first find a doctor to recommend her. The predisposition of the doctor whom she consults may be a critical factor in obtaining or not obtaining an abortion. Such a doctor is, of course, not bound by any factors other than his personal morality and professional judgment, and is not required to justify a negative decision to an abortion board or anyone else. The optimum time for performing an abortion is within the first twelve weeks of pregnancy. Since a woman may sit six weeks before confirming the fact that she is pregnant, she has only about six weeks to solicit a referral from a doctor, obtain a positive decision from the committee, and arrange for the abortion itself to be performed. Any delay in these steps may seriously complicate the abortion procedure.

4. Appeals

In virtually all legal decisions, provision is made for some kind of appeal for re-consideration to a higher authority. The Abortion Amendment is unique in that it does not incorporate any such formal appeal mechanisms. Half of the committees studied had no procedures for appeal and re-application, and the remainder had divergent policies. Since one abortion committee had no authority over any others, presumably a woman could take her case to another hospital committee, assuming that she could find a sympathetic doctor, and that the arrangements and delays did not postpone the decision until such time as an abortion could no longer be safely recommended.

5. Accredited and Approved Hospitals

Although the medical procedure involved in an abortion may, in most cases, be safely performed in a doctor's office the Abortion Amendment specifies that the abortion must be performed not only in a hospital, but in an accredited or approved hospital. While one cannot fault legislators for wanting the best medical facilities available for all citizens, the stipulations that abortion may be performed only in certain hospitals makes obtaining an abortion unnecessarily difficult and expensive. One of the common arguments against permissive abortion policies is that, if abortions were to be readily available, the demand for them would be so great that hospitals would be swamped with patients and thus would be unable to provide the necessary beds and doctors without seriously interfering with medical attention available for other health problems. This argument is specious on two grounds. First, in our society once a woman is pregnant she is going to demand some kind of medical attention within the next nine months. The choice is not between an abortion or no medical help, but between a short stay in hospital to have an abortion or a longer stay in hospital to have a baby. Second, for many abortions there are no clear indications for hospitalization, and the procedure might be performed safely in a doctor's office, or on an out-patient basis.

Conclusions

The Abortion Amendments do not fulfill the intention of the law to make a legal therapeutic abortion available to everyone whose health would be endangered by carrying a pregnancy to term. The Amendments as presently written are vulnerable to three major criticisms.

1. The Amendment Does Not Liberalize

Prior to the 1969 amendments, an abortion might be performed by any doctor who was convinced, and if necessary able to prove, that the termination of a pregnancy was necessary to save a woman's life. Now such an operation can be performed only in certain hospitals after the doctor has the consent of at least three colleagues. The law allows no exceptions for emergency conditions. The specification that all abortions must be performed in certain specified hospitals adds complications and difficulties which may be unnecessary from a strictly medical standpoint. Most abortions might be safely performed in a doctor's office or on an out-patient basis. Finally, although the recent legal changes have lead to an increase in the numbers of requests for abortions: ". . . the Amendments reported to liberalize the law on therapeutic abortion have not affected the hospital's rates of approval."[13]

2. The Abortion Committees Add Extra Nonlegal Requirements for Obtaining an Abortion

Although there is nothing in the law specifying how a woman's request for an abortion is to be presented, committees routinely do not accept for consideration cases presented by the woman herself, or by some one acting in her behalf, unless her representative is a medical doctor. This procedure makes obtaining an abortion more difficult on two counts. First, it necessitates that, on her own initiative, a woman find at least one doctor who is sympathetic with her plight. Second, it requires the professional consideration of five doctors, rather than the legally required three. Although almost all other legal decisions are subject to appeal, many committees routinely deny requests for reconsideration.

3. The Abortion Committees are Inconsistent in Their Interpretations of the Amendments

The concept of mental health is so open to idiosyncratic and expedient definitions that it has been interpreted largely in terms of the personal biases and preferences of individual committee members. Some of the judgments involved clearly involve moral rather than medical or legal pronouncements. In practice, most but not all of the committees surveyed incorporated rape, incest and extreme youth as legitimate reasons for abortions without further evidence of danger to mental health. The composition of committees varies both in size (from three to eight) and in professional qualifications. Of the six committees surveyed, only one out of twenty-six doctors was female. Given such discrepancies, it is not surprising that hospitals vary in their predisposition to accept nonmedical reasons for abortion, and that the rates of acceptance of cases brought before the committees range from 75 percent to 95 percent.[14]

Footnotes

1. G. B. Parker, "Bill C-150: Abortion Reform," *The Criminal Law Quarterly*, 11, 1968, p. 268.
2. Sec. 195. (1) A child becomes a human being within the meaning of this Act when it has completely proceeded in a living state from the body of its mother, whether or not (a) it has breathed (b) it has independent circulation (c) the navel string is severed. a) A person commits homicide when he causes injuries to a child before or during its birth as a result of which the child dies.
3. K. D. Smith and H. S. Wineberg, "A Survey of Therapeutic Abortion Committees," *The Criminal Law Quarterly*, 12, 1970, p. 283.
4. H. Morgentaler, "Abortion," *Canadian Medical Association Journal*, 102, 1970, p. 876.
5. Smith and Wineberg, p. 306.
6. Parker, p. 274.
7. Anonymous, "Abortion," *Nova Scotia Medical Bulletin*, 49, 1970, p. 34.
8. Morgentaler, p. 876.
9. C. P. Harrison, "Therapeutic Abortion," *Canadian Medical Association Journal*, 102, 1970, p. 1209.
10. C. Heine, "Abortion," *Canadian Medical Association Journal*, 102, 1970, p. 1211.
11. Smith and Wineberg, p. 285.
12. *Ibid.*, p. 287.
13. *Ibid.*, p. 293.
14. *Ibid.*, pp. 288-292.

Therapeutic Abortion in a Canadian City *

R. M. Boyce and R. W. Osborn

In spite of widespread public, political and medical interest, relatively little has appeared to the present time in the way of clinical studies on the subject of therapeutic abortion in Canada. Prior to the introduction on June 27, 1969,

*"Therapeutic Abortion in a Canadian City" by Dr. R. M. Boyce and R. W. Osborn, originally published in *The Canadian Medical Association Journal*, 103: 461, 1970.

of new federal legislation respecting therapeutic abortion, the senior author became concerned with changes in conditions under which therapeutic abortions were being performed in the study city and their number. A review of these changes was begun in 1968.

The study city, London, Ontario, is an ideal city for such a review. The population of about 200,000 and the dominance of the city over a large number of smaller urban and rural areas provide some of the aspects of a large metropolitan centre. It is also representative of much of Ontario in that it is relatively old and densely settled with a predominantly Protestant population of English extraction. The fact of its being a *typical* Canadian city is attested by the frequent use of the area by market research companies. The dominance of the city over a large land area of Southwestern Ontario includes the responsibility of providing much of the specialized health care for this region. There is one large general hospital of 1000 beds at which all of the therapeutic abortions in the study were performed (the second general hospital in the city is smaller, has Roman Catholic affiliations and no abortions were performed there). Thus the opportunity was provided for observing changes in the number of therapeutic abortions and in the increasing use of psychiatric grounds for the operation. During the study period, only five psychiatrists were concerned in the large number of cases in which psychiatric consultation was sought.

Procedure

It was decided to study the years 1962 to 1968, inclusive. This span includes the years in which therapeutic abortion was not often done and extends up to the year preceding the change in law. Complete data for the period after 1968 are not available, but it was believed that a detailed study of the changes occurring over the earlier period would provide insights into present developments.

The hospital records of all the patients undergoing therapeutic abortion in this period were reviewed. The historical material, records of examination, and all consultation reports in the case records were perused to discover the grounds for abortion. In many instances more than one reason was given. As it was not always possible to establish the primary reason in a given case, all reasons given were recorded. An attempt was made to discover possible clustering of reasons occurring in the period studied. This involved an ordering of the data so that the patients with identical grounds, or patterns of grounds, could be enumerated. The total number of cases seen in psychiatric consultation and the number of cases seen by each of the psychiatrists were also determined.[1]

Cases were grouped according to diagnosis, age, marital status, religion, number of previous pregnancies and duration of pregnancy at the time of interruption; these features, where pertinent, were also viewed over the total time period. The number in which hysterectomy or sterilization was performed was ascertained. The number of therapeutic abortions performed during the year that legislation was enacted (1969) was obtained and grouped according to month, bearing in mind that the new legislation became effective June 27, 1969.

Brief questionnaires were sent to major hospitals in Canada to determine the number of abortions done during 1969. Private hospitals in Toronto and Montreal were also contacted.

TABLE 1

Basic Medical and Demographic Characteristics

Characteristic	Number	Percent*
Number of therapeutic abortions per year		
1962	4	3.3
1963	9	7.5
1964	10	8.4
1965	12	10.1
1966	14	11.8
1967	28	23.5
1968	42	35.3
Marital status		
Married	77	64.7
Single	30	25.2
Separated, widowed, divorced	12	10.0
Age (years)		
13–15	4	3.3
16–19	7	5.9
20–24	24	20.2
25–29	20	16.8
30–34	20	16.8
35–39	27	22.7
40–44	17	14.3
Religion		
Roman Catholic	18	15.1
Anglican	23	19.3
United	37	31.1
Other Protestant	32	26.9
Other	9	7.5
Previous pregnancies		
None	26	25.0
1	16	15.4
2	14	13.5
3	22	21.2
4	8	7.7
5	7	6.7
6 or more	11	10.6
No data	15	—
Duration of interrupted pregnancy (weeks)		
3–6	7	6.1
7–8	28	24.3
9–10	14	12.2
11–12	20	17.4
13–14	22	19.1
15–16	13	11.3
17+	11	9.6
No data	4	—
Additional medical action after abortion		
Hysterectomy	16	13.4
Tubal ligation	39	32.8
Contraceptives	4	3.4
Psychotherapy	6	5.0
Tubal ligation recommended (not done)	1	0.8
No additional action indicated	53	44.5

*No data cases excluded from percentage distributions.

41

Results

The number of operations performed increased slowly until 1967 when the number was double that for the preceding year (Table 1). From 1967 to 1968 the number of therapeutic abortions increased by 50 percent. The total number performed during the years 1962 to 1968 was 119. Throughout the period the majority of the respondents were married and were over 30 years of age. In keeping with the religious characteristics of the area over three-quarters of the patients were Protestant.

One-quarter of the patients had had no previous pregnancies, and low-parity women (three or fewer pregnancies) accounted for over 70 percent of the cases. Sixty percent of the terminations were at 12 weeks or under and 9.6 percent were of 17 or more weeks' duration.

Operations producing sterilization (hysterectomy or tubal ligation) were carried out on 46.2 percent of the patients, but in an almost identical number of cases no additional medical action was taken.

The relatively rapid increase in the number of therapeutic abortions performed in London has continued throughout 1969. The number increased by 295 percent between 1968 and 1969 (Table 2). Indications are that the number during 1970 will be even higher, as the operations performed during the first months of 1970 have continued at the November-December 1969 level, i.e., about 30 per month.

TABLE 2

Number of Therapeutic Abortions per Month, 1968-1969

Month	Number 1968	Number 1969	Month	Number 1968	Number 1969
January	4	10	August	5	9
February	1	4	September	5	5
March	2	9	October	5	15
April	6	13	November	1	29
May	4	12	December	6	37
June	1	10			
July	2	13	Total	42	166

The number of abortions performed in London is not typical of the rest of Canada in 1969. Thirty-one of 43 hospitals contacted provided information on their experience. Of those who did not reply five were general and seven were private hospitals. Of the 31 hospitals providing information one hospital in Eastern Canada reported 291 abortions and one in Western Canada reported 109. One Ontario hospital reported 179; another, 63. In the remaining 27 hospitals an estimated total of 186 therapeutic abortions were carried out.

The sharp increase in abortions performed in London after 1966 suggests the possibility that the nature of the recipients may have also changed. In order to pursue this possibility, the period was subdivided: 1962-1966 and 1967-1968. As can be seen in Table 3, in the later period there was a higher proportion whose marital status was single. Further, the patients in the 1967-1968 group were younger and more likely not to have had a previous pregnancy. The data suggest that it is becoming less difficult for a single, young, nulliparous woman to receive a therapeutic abortion.

TABLE 3

Changing Characteristics of Therapeutic Abortion Recipients, London, 1962-1966, 1967-1968, in Percentages

Characteristic	1962-1967	1967-1968
Marital status		
Married	75.5	57.1
Single	16.3	31.4
Other	8.2	11.4
Age		
13–15	2.0	4.3
16–24	20.4	30.0
25–34	38.8	30.0
35–44	38.8	35.7
Previous pregnancies		
0	18.6	29.5
1	20.9	11.5
2	9.3	16.4
3	27.9	16.4
4–5	14.0	14.8
6 and over	9.3	11.5
Duration of interrupted pregnancy (weeks)		
3–9	47.9	23.9
10–13	29.2	37.3
14–16	18.8	25.4
17+	4.2	13.4
Additional medical action after abortion		
Hysterectomy	16.3	11.4
Tubal ligation	18.4	42.9
Psychotherapy	6.1	4.3
Other	8.1	1.4
None indicated	51.0	40.0

New techniques appear to have made possible abortion at relatively late stages of pregnancy. Nearly 39 percent of the 1967-1968 recipients were aborted of a pregnancy of 14 or more weeks' duration. Perhaps the most dramatic finding in this table is the marked increase in tubal ligations in the later period, particularly in older married women.

Bearing in mind that multiple grounds for the interruption of pregnancy are often given in a single case, in Table 4 the number of cases in which each of the reasons was given has been totalled. For example, in 58 cases depression was given as the reason (or at least one of the grounds) for abortion. The percentage distribution for the entire 1962-1968 period and for each of its subdivisions is presented.

As can be seen in Table 4, only 19.2 percent (45 cases) of the grounds given were based on medical reasons, rubella, gross exposure to radiation or genetic defects. With the exception of the relatively infrequent mention of rape or mental retardation, the overwhelming remainder of the reasons given were psychiatric considerations; depression, lack of external support and potential suicide risk account for a majority of these.

TABLE 4

Grounds or Reason for Abortion—1962-66 and 1967-1968, in Percentages

Grounds for Abortion	Total 1962–1968 Number	Total 1962–1968 Percent	1962–66	1967–68
1. Depression	58	24.8	20.6	27.5
2. Lack of external supports, i.e. lack of any helpful or supporting relatives or friends or any sort of emotional help immediately available	35	15.0	12.0	16.9
3. Considered to be a potential suicide risk	35	15.0	14.1	15.5
4. Medical reasons (exclusive of rubella)	27	11.5	16.3	8.5
5. Rubella (exposure to or actual evidence of infection in the patient)	15	6.4	12.0	2.8
6. Displaying evidence for disorganization (disorganizing potential or psychotic potential)	15	6.4	7.6	5.6
7. Previous postpartum serious (usually psychotic) psychiatric illness	11	4.7	3.3	5.6
8. Rape	5	2.1	1.1	2.8
9. Onset of psychosis or more severe illness, i.e. evidence of more serious symptomatology of beginning disorganization	5	2.1	3.3	1.4
10. Patently psychotic	6	2.6	1.1	3.5
11. Immaturity	8	3.4	1.1	4.9
12. History of a definite previous psychotic illness other than during the postpartum period	4	1.7	2.2	1.4
13. Severe identity diffusion	5	2.1	3.3	1.4
14. Mental retardation	1	0.4	—	0.7
15. Gross exposure to radiation	2	0.9	2.2	—
16. Attempted suicide	1	0.5	—	0.7
17. Genetic reasons (two children mentally retarded)	1	0.4	—	0.7
Total	234	100.0	100.0 (92)	100.0 (142)

During the seven-year period changes occurred in the grounds on which abortion was recommended. The major changes observed between the 1962-1966 and 1967-1968 periods were the relative increase in the instances of depression (27.5 percent from 20.6 percent) and lack of external support (16.9 percent from 12.0 percent) and a decrease in the submission of medical reasons (8.5 percent from 16.3 percent) and rubella (2.8 percent from 12.0 percent) as grounds for abortion. Because of the small number in many of the categories, other changes are difficult to discern.

Not all cases fit into the classification of grounds given in Table 4. On a limited number of occasions in 1968 there was presented a constellation of circumstances or a *general socio-economic climate* surrounding the individual which, in its total thrust, made continuance of pregnancy hazardous to the patient's health or general functioning. Illustrative cases may be cited:

Case 1. – Extreme economic strictures. This patient has five children, and an additional child would only pose added financial burdens. There was severe *hyperemesis gravidarum* with all five previous pregnancies; during one pregnancy the patient was pre-eclamptic. There were persisting varicose vein problems despite vein stripping in 1953.

Case 2. – A 44-year-old woman who wished to have no more children. Rh incompatibility existed but there were no problems with any of her previous three pregnancies.

Case 3. – A person presenting some degree of depressive reaction occurring in a *pathological personality*. All five children of this patient are in the care of the Children's Aid Society for economic reasons and because of the incompetence of the mother. The patient was bent on abortion by illegal means if therapeutic abortion was refused. Alcoholism of a severe degree existed in both the patient and her husband. (General socio-economic climate.)

Case 4. – During five other pregnancies the patient presented anxiety and depression nearing panic. She had strong uterine contractions throughout each pregnancy as well as repeated urinary tract infections. These combined to cause long periods at home in bed or in hospital, and the patient's current fear was of going through the same process again. There was also a history of losing a pregnancy at 7½ months gestation owing to placental separation (*abruptio*) after which she developed a transitory compulsive desire to kidnap a neighbour's child.

TABLE 5

Reason or Reasons for Therapeutic Abortion

Reasons	Number of Cases	Percent
Rubella	14	11.8
Medical reasons (excluding rubella)	19	16.0
Depression plus medical reasons	6	5.0
Depression plus potential suicide risk	12	10.1
Depression plus lack of external supports	11	9.2
Depression, lack of external supports and potential suicide risk	15	12.6
Lack of external supports plus other grounds	9	7.6
Other multiple grounds	33	27.7
Total	119	100.0

The frequency and percentage distribution of the most commonly noted grounds or clusters of grounds is presented in Table 5. In 14 cases rubella was the sole reason given in support of the recommendation for abortion. Medical reasons only (exclusive of rubella) were the only grounds to support the recommendation in 19 cases. The combination of depression and medical reasons was given in six cases. Where several grounds were presented, a frequent pattern was the combination of depression with other medical or psychiatric grounds. In a large number of cases the lack of external supports was a factor in the decision to recommend the abortion.

Psychiatric consultations were obtained in 83 of the total of 119 cases. One psychiatrist was involved in nearly one-half (40 cases) of all consultations (Table 6). The data indicate that as psychiatrist A increased his activity, the other psychiatrists also became involved with an increasing number of cases.

TABLE 6

Number of Cases Seen in Psychiatric Consultation by Each Psychiatrist (per year)

Year	Psychiatrists A	B	C	D	E	Total
1962	—	—	—	—	—	—
1963	2	—	—	—	—	2
1964	2	1	—	—	—	3
1965	5	—	3	1	—	9*
1966	7	1	1	1	—	10
1967	7	2	4	3	—	16
1968	17	4	11	7	3	42
Total	40	8	19	12	3	83*

*One other psychiatrist was involved in a single case in 1965, making the total for the year 1962-1968 period 83.

Discussion

The major rise in the number of therapeutic abortions in this centre was in 1967. While the undertone of change in attitudes in society (reflected in the proposal of change in the law and the final enactment of new law) is undoubtedly a factor, the increase has not been due solely to greater pressure from the community. The attitude of physicians has played a large part. This can develop when only one or two physicians feel quite strongly on the subject, feel reasonably confident that they are acting within the law and proceed to recommend abortion in a relatively liberalized fashion. This seems to have occurred here as one of the psychiatrists, more or less dramatically, began to support more requests for abortion for patients referred to him. By virtue of his role within the group of psychiatrists, through presentation of cases at conferences, through lectures and other means, his feelings and attitudes have been made fairly widely known, with subsequent channelling of patients to this psychiatrist by obstetricians and other community physicians. Some of the other psychiatrists have also, in varying degree, adopted freer attitudes.

At the present time, when consultation is indicated, the opinion of one psychiatrist together with the written opinion of the referring physician is accepted as sufficient by the hospital abortion committee. During the years studied, attempts were made to establish the policy of obtaining more than one psychiatrist's recommendation, but this was not always easily arranged. In some instances the patient (and her physician) may consult different psychiatrists until a supporting recommendation is gained, i.e. she may *shop around*, putting the psychiatrist in the role of judge and rendering a waste of time all psychiatric opinions given prior to the one containing a positive recommendation for abortion. It would seem more realistic for the family physician to use the psychiatrist's opinion for what it is worth in formulating his own course of action and recommendations.

We must acknowledge that abortion is performed in a large number of cases not because of psychiatric but because of social factors, often because of the distress that continuing the pregnancy will cause others. Most noticeably this is seen in the parents of young unmarried girls, in the anguish they experience in contemplating social reaction to themselves as well as their daughter. The doctor is asked to end a pregnancy because it is not socially condoned. It is especially in the frequently encountered absence of effective *external supports* – parents, friends or others – that we find ourselves confronted by what is actually a social problem, only potentially a psychiatric one. Decisions and action in these situations should probably not be solely in the hands of the psychiatrist. This is the opinion expressed in the recent report of the Group for the Advancement of Psychiatry,[2] an organization usually productive of soundly reasoned recommendations, "that psychiatrists . . . begin to recognize their own limitations and back away from the invitation to accept responsibility for making decisions that more appropriately rest in the broader community".

The family physician is often the most informed person regarding the patient, her circumstances, her social and community setting, and possibly he should have the major role in forming decisions, together with the patient.

The Board of Trustees of the American Psychiatric Association have recently approved the position that "a decision to perform an abortion should be regarded as strictly a medical decision and a medical responsibility. It should be removed entirely from the jurisdiction of criminal law. Criminal penalties should be reserved for persons who perform abortions without medical license or qualifications to do so. A medical decision to perform an abortion is based on the careful and informed judgments of the physician and the patient."[3] The Committee on Therapeutic Abortion of the Canadian Psychiatric Association is presently considering recommending to the association that it put forward a similar position statement and that appropriate discussions with other medical bodies and government be requested.[4]

Present-day agitation and concern raise the issue of abortion on demand or on request, not a new concept by any means; within two to three years after being made available the situation was reached in Hungary, in 1959, where the number of legal abortions exceeded the number of births.[5] There are many lines of approach or argument with respect to this concept, the foremost being that a woman should have the right to control what happens to her own body. In a pregnancy, however, there exist in the woman biologically active parts of two people. The male may take no interest or responsibility and then the woman is left with the problem herself; but this is not always the case and sometimes others (e.g. families) may realistically be a part of it. So far as the physician is concerned in this circumstance he should always have the prerogative and the responsibility to decide with his patient whether his actions or prescriptions are advisable and justified. Rarely should a patient be alone in reaching major decisions of a fundamental nature which have many ramifications and when many issues are involved. We rarely do anything completely independently and when we do it can be a devastating and destructive experience. This is especially true of actions in which one is seemingly totally isolated from the opinions, attitudes and behaviour of the rest of the immediate world or where strong polar attitudes coexist in that world. We nearly always have to grab at least someone in deciding on major actions; such actions can in fact be meaningless if we don't, and our intentions can easily become blurred both to others and to ourselves. And the other person is expected to invest something of himself or herself into the situation. If no one is there, some part of us easily becomes hardened, scarred or destroyed as a result. This is especially so in a younger person. Solutions other than abortion may emerge from this confrontation or exchange.

In the overview, society must still work out its attitudes with more humanity. The lack of self-respect and the fear of being devalued are repeatedly expressed in the origin and crises of many problem pregnancies. This low self-esteem can be seen in families producing an unhappy girl who craves at least something she can feel belongs with her (a child), or a poorly differentiated, disturbed boy who rapes a girl. The great number of pregnancies that are undesired in fear of possible or actual social rejection really reflect man's lack of tolerance for his fellow man. These situations converge in a need to make each other's lives and families more secure and confirmed as valuable.

Footnotes

1. One of the authors has been the consultant involved in assessment of some of these cases, has worked closely with all of the other consultants who have been involved and is aware of their psychiatric orientation and attitudes. Many of the patients have been seen by two or more of these consultants; some have been seen, or their situation reviewed, in a departmental conference within the hospital Department of Psychiatry.
2. Group for the Advancement of Psychiatry, Committee on Psychiatry and Law, *Group Advance, Psychiat.* (*Rep.*), 7, 1969, p. 1.
3. H. Rosen, *Amer. J. Psychiat.*, 126, 1970, p. 1299.
4. A. J. Preston, personal communication to Canadian Psychiatric Associations Committee on Therapeutic Abortion, April, 1970.
5. C. Tietze and H. Lehfeldt, *J.A.M.A.*, 175, 1961, p. 1149.

The Status of Women in Canada: Abortion*

Report of the Royal Commission, September 28, 1970

We can expect that birth control will be practised by Canadian women through increasingly reliable and readily available methods. This may in time lead to a reduction in the incidence of abortion. We doubt that abortion can be eliminated entirely. We must therefore consider abortion and the laws that apply to it. At one time abortion was a serious threat to the life of a woman. Today, due to improved surgical techniques it is safer during the first 12 weeks of pregnancy to undergo an abortion than to continue the pregnancy. It is possible that new methods of abortion may be even safer. Abortion is permissible in some states and countries for pregnancies ranging from 12 weeks to 26 weeks – by which time the foetus is generally considered to be viable. A few countries set no time limit on abortion at the woman's request.

To put this question in perspective let us consider the evolution of society's attitude towards unwanted pregnancies. Abortion is one of the oldest forms of birth control: techniques for abortion are mentioned in some of the earliest medical texts. Abortion was considered morally wrong in the Jewish and Chris-

*Report of the Royal Commission on *The Status of Women in Canada*, Sections 226 to 243, pp. 281-287, 1970. Reproduced with the permission of Information Canada.

tian traditions, though it was not until 1869 that the Roman Catholic Church equated early abortion with murder and imposed excommunication of anyone, including the mother, procuring it at any time. English common law did not consider abortion a serious crime if procured before quickening, when the movements of the foetus in the womb are first felt. It did not become a statutory crime in England until 1803.

Demands for liberalization of the law followed. The Women's Co-Operative Guilds supported reform and the British Medical Association called for clarification of the law. It was not until 1938, however, that the first decisive move for reform was made when a London surgeon challenged the law. In this case abortion was ruled to be justified "if the doctor is of the opinion that the probable consequence of the birth will be to make the woman a physical or mental wreck."[1] This ruling applied in England until 1967 when the British Parliament enacted a more liberal law permitting abortion when two physicians are of the opinion that: "(1) . . . The continuance of the pregnancy would involve risk to the life of the pregnant woman, or of injury to the physical or mental health of the pregnant woman or any existing children of her family, greater than if the pregnancy were terminated; or (2) there is substantial risk that if the child were born it would suffer from such physical or mental abnormalities as to be seriously handicapped."[2]

The evolution of the law on abortion was much slower in Britain than in some other countries. Sweden, for example, passed a law in 1939 authorizing abortion on specific medical, humanitarian and eugenic grounds. Japan and some countries in Eastern Europe have also adopted more liberal attitudes towards termination of pregnancy. Legal grounds for abortion in those countries can be classified in the categories of socio-medical, eugenic, therapeutic or socio-economic, and the practice, if not the letter, of the law is equivalent sometimes to abortion on request. The long practice of legal termination of pregnancy in those countries is reflected in their very low female death rate due to abortion. For example, Czechoslovakia reported a death rate of about 2.5 per 100,000 abortions in 1961-64; Japan had about the same rate between 1959-63.[3]

Countries with more liberal abortion laws have sharply reduced the number of illegal abortions, though these have not been completely eradicated even in countries such as Hungary, where abortion is granted on request. Illegal abortions survive for several reasons such as the lack of privacy offered by the official procedure, the cost of the operation and hospitalization, the shortage of adequate medical staff and hospital space and the lack of information among some segments of the population.

In the United States, efforts have for some years been made to persuade state legislatures to adopt statutory exceptions to the general prohibition of abortion, particularly in cases of rape, incest and deformed foetus. About 10 states had taken action along these lines by 1967. More recently the reform movement has pressed for complete repeal of the prohibition of abortion, on the grounds that a woman has the right to decide whether or not to bear a child. Dramatic developments towards reform are now taking place in legislatures and courts. Two recent State Supreme Court decisions[4] have extended the "right to privacy" to cover termination of pregnancy. In September 1969 Mr. Justice R. A. Peters of the Supreme Court of the State of California, in one of these cases, stated: "The rights involved in the instant case are woman's rights to life and to choose whether to have children. . . . The fundamental rights of the woman

49

to choose whether to bear children follow from the Supreme Court's and this court's repeated acknowledgement of a 'right to privacy' or 'liberty' in matters related to marriage, family and sex." At the same time four state legislatures (Hawaii, New York, Alaska and Maryland) were considering bills granting abortion on the request of the woman under different conditions which have to do with residency requirements, performance of the operation by a qualified physician in a licensed hospital, and the period of time after the beginning of the pregnancy. The New York bill has been passed and came into effect on July 1, 1970. However judicial interpretation of the law may settle the issue in the United States when the United States Supreme Court renders judgment in appeal on the abortion cases mentioned above.

The amendment of the Canadian Criminal Code in 1969 adapted the law to current medical practice by allowing, under section 237 (4) of the Criminal Code,[5] a qualified medical practitioner in an accredited or approved hospital to procure a miscarriage if the hospital's therapeutic abortion committee, by a majority of its members, has certified in writing that the continuation of the pregnancy would endanger the life or health of the woman. This formal procedure may make it even more difficult for some women to obtain a therapeutic abortion than it was in the past. The principal benefactor of this law is the medical profession which will know exactly under what conditions a therapeutic abortion can be performed and criminal responsibility avoided. It can even be argued, and illustrated by the experience of other countries, that a therapeutic abortion committee has the effect of reducing the number of therapeutic abortions performed by a hospital.[6] The current law cannot be relied upon to reduce the number of illegal abortions or the maternal deaths and injuries that follow the improper medical practices used in many illegal abortions. The first report issued by the Dominion Bureau of Statistics since the Code was amended shows that only 235 illegal abortions were performed over a three-month period in six provinces: Prince Edward Island, Nova Scotia, New Brunswick, Saskatchewan, Alberta and British Columbia.

Requiring the approval of a hospital therapeutic abortion committee has the effect of limiting the possibility of obtaining legal abortion.[7] Approval is not easily obtained and involves delay. For many women in remote areas there is no nearby hospital, accredited, approved or otherwise. Under the present law, they cannot get legal abortions even though qualified medical practitioners may be at hand, unless the life of the mother is endangered.

Is there a case, then, to broaden the grounds for abortion in Canada? It is common knowledge that illegal abortions are taking place. The number cannot be accurately known; estimates range from 30,000 to 300,000 a year. Dr. Serge Mongeau[8] gives an estimate for Quebec of from 10,000 to 25,000 annually, for Canada the figure would be 40,000 to 100,000. If the estimate of 100,000 were accurate, it would mean that one pregnancy in five is being aborted by illegal means. Prosecution is not an indication of the number of illegal abortions, since an average of only 30 persons are convicted each year. Law enforcement is non-existent except in a few cases where the woman's life has been seriously endangered.

Who are the women who seek abortions? Most national statistics indicate that the majority are married and already have two or three children.[9] For example, a study made in Sweden of women who had abortions showed that 66 percent were married. In Czechoslovakia, the proportion of married women among those seeking legal abortions was 82 percent in 1962. In the United States, the Kinsey Report, in 1953, indicated that of 5,293 women interviewed, 1,044 admitted having had abortions; of these, 11 out of 20 were married; the great majority had been aborted by a doctor.

Fifteen years ago there was no public demand for legalized abortion. However, in a national opinion survey released on March 7, 1970, a Gallup Poll of Canada showed that 43 percent of the adult population favoured legislation that would permit a woman to terminate pregnancy at any time during the first three months. Another type of survey carried by the French and English editions of *Chatelaine* in January 1968 indicated that the respondents were certainly in favour of liberalizing the the abortion laws. Fifty-six percent and 54 percent of the respondents of the English and French versions, respectively, felt that the law on legal abortions should copy Britain's new law, while (respectively) 32 percent and 25 percent believed that it should be granted at the request of the women. Combining these two groups would show that more than three-quarters of *Chatelaine*'s respondents, both English and French, favoured abortion on request or close to it.

During the public hearings of this Commission many organizations and individuals urged the liberalization or the repeal of all abortion laws. We also heard eloquent appeals to retain them. Some people consider the foetus as being a human life and for them abortion amounts to murder. Others believe that the foetus, though having the potentiality of human life, is not yet a human being, and consequently these people do not regard abortion as harming any existing person. The conviction that women have the right to make their own decisions about abortion was often expressed in the formula: "A woman should have control of her own body." Three excerpts from briefs illustrate this point of view: "This is a problem for which only the woman involved can answer. She knows her circumstances and her emotional limitations. She alone should be allowed to make the decision. We cannot and dare not stand in judgment. This one additional pregnancy may be the 'final straw' to break one otherwise reasonably stable home . . . who then cares for any other children? . . . who then cares and pays for her broken health, physical and mental?"[10] "The law should be amended to permit abortion at the mother's request after she has received the best medical advice available. Such legislative reform would then allow the Canadian woman complete dignity as a person with full rights, no longer subject to a discrimination imposed in a different century by an altogether different society."[11] "We do not feel that the proposed changes in abortion legislation go far enough in giving women control over their own bodies."[12]

Public opinion seems to have moved very quickly in the same direction. There is now in New York and a dozen other American cities a National Clergy Consultation Service on Abortion, begun three years ago, which refers about 25,000 women a year to physicians in the United States and abroad. Many American Roman Catholics favour the repeal of laws against abortion rather than in their liberalization, preferring to leave the matter to the conscience of the individual rather than see it delineated in a statute. Most Protestant churches take a similar view. During our public hearings, women of all faiths pleaded for a repeal of abortion laws.

It is not the function of this Commission to give preference to one trend of religious opinion over another. Moral judgments change with time or when seen in other and wider perspectives.

A law that has more bad effects than good ones is a bad law. We believe the present abortion law should be amended. As long as it exists in its present form thousands of women will break it. Breaking the law forces them to resort to methods that seriously endanger their physical and emotional health. The present law also discriminates against the poor, who do not have the means to get an abortion, for example, by going outside the country.

We have come to the conclusion that each woman should have the right to decide if she will terminate pregnancy. We believe that a woman who has been the victim of rape or incest should not be forced to bear a child. We propose that the approval of a hospital abortion committee be no longer required and that the decision be made by the woman after consultation with her physician. Anytime during the first 12 weeks of pregnancy is considered to be a relatively safe period in which to perform an abortion.

Therefore, *we recommend that the Criminal Code be amended to permit abortion by a qualified medical practitioner on the sole request of any woman who has been pregnant for 12 weeks or less.*

Further, *we recommend that the Criminal Code by [sic] amended to permit abortion by a qualified practitioner at the request of a woman pregnant for more that 12 weeks if the doctor is convinced that the continuation of the pregnancy would endanger the physical or mental health of the woman, or if there is a substantial risk that if the child were born, it would be greatly handicapped, either mentally or physically.*

Footnotes

1. Rex *v*. Bourne, 1938, 3 All England Reports, p. 615.
2. Abortion Act 1967, Elizabeth II 1967, Chapter 87.
3. Figures are subject to various methods of reporting in different countries, and comparisons should be made with caution.
4. People *v*. Belous in California, September, 1969, and United States *v*. Vuitch in Washington, D.C., November, 1969.
5. Criminal Law Amendment Act, 1968-69, *Statutes of Canada*, 1968-69, Chapter 38.
6. In New York where formely [sic] therapeutic abortions had to be reported to the Health Service, there was a decrease of 65 percent of such abortions from 1943 to 1962, following the appointment of hospital abortion committees. Another factor could be the reduction of clinical indications calling for such an operation, as a result of medical development in this field.
7. Abortions may be performed only in accredited or approved hospitals. A hospital is accredited by the Canadian Council on Hospital Accreditation if it provides certain facilities: in January 1970 of the 948 general hospitals in Canada only 450 were accredited. Hospitals may be approved by the provincial ministers of health: it is not known how many fall within this category.
8. Dr. Serge Mongeau and Renée Cloutier, *L'Avortement*, Montreal, *Les Editions du Jour*, 1968.
9. Malcolm Potts, "Legal Abortion in Eastern Europe," *The Eugenics Review*, 59, 1967, p. 232, and Dr. Serge Mongeau and Renée Cloutier, *L'Avortement*, Montreal, *Les Editions du Jour*, 1968, p. 76.
10. Brief No. 250.
11. Brief No. 29.
12. Brief No. 437.

The Status of Women in Canada: Abortion*

Jacques Henripin, Member of the Royal Commission, A Separate Report, September 28, 1970

Abortion

I cannot subscribe to the position taken by the majority of Commissioners on abortion (Chapter 4, paragraphs 226 to 243 inclusive), and more particularly to recommendations Nos. 126 and 127, paragraphs 242 and 243.

It is not easy to run counter to the trend of a large section of public opinion which is calling with increasing insistence for almost total liberalization of our abortion laws. But not every man or woman shares such views and it should perhaps be pointed out that our Commission heard eloquent, even moving, appeals in favour of the retention of our present law and some even asked for a return to stricter measures. To me, these appeals do not reflect the views of doctrinaires; they are based on respect for human life, which is a fundamental principle in the code of Western ethics, exceptions having been made for legitimate defence, war and the punishment of certain crimes.

I am well aware that this is not a simple problem amenable to hard and fast principles. There is some doubt as to when human life really begins and as to whether a foetus becomes a *human being* when it is a day, a week, a month or three months old. It is possible that the concept of human life – convenient in its obvious simplicity – does not in fact correspond to a reality so lucid that what is human and what is not can be clearly defined. The reality interpreted by this concept probably embraces a whole range of intermediary degrees of what we call *human*. In other words, human life is not – strictly speaking – an absolute. Nor can we close our eyes to the fact that this relative value attached to human life is reflected in the mores of our society: all is not done that could be done to save human lives.

But, such uncertainty, such an elusive reality, cannot be answered by attitudes and laws which, in the final analysis, are based only on convenience. In my view, the problem of abortion cannot be resolved by considering solely the psychological and physiological benefits or the advantages for the family which may derive from the destruction of the foetus.

Unless we admit the scarcely tenable view that there is no such thing as a human being before birth, we are forced to compare the advantages of such a brutal solution as abortion with the *value* of the being to be destroyed. In each individual case, we must weigh – and it may be a delicate operation – the gravity of destroying a more or less human life against the advantages which the mother, in particular, may gain. I do not wish to minimize these benefits nor the hardships suffered in some cases where an abortion may prove to be the only solution. But I cannot bring myself to deny the respect we owe to living beings in the process of becoming men and women. Unhappily, these are not matters which can be solved by a formula and there is no simple solution

*Report of the Royal Commission on *The Status of Women in Canada*, Sections 6 to 12, pp. 422-423, 1970. Reproduced with the permission of Information Canada.

which will satisfy everyone. Personally, I must admit that I do not know how serious a situation should be to warrant an abortion.

I feel this is no reason for doing away with legislation. We cannot resolve our uncertainties by sweeping away inconvenient restraints. I am therefore of the opinion that our present Canadian law provides an acceptable instrument for regulating the behaviour of Canadians in the matter of abortion, and I am not convinced that there should be further liberalization of the law. What is important now is that an honest effort be made, in hospitals and by doctors, to set up the machinery which the law provides for its application and which is still sadly lacking.

This machinery could probably be improved. Hospital committees responsible for making decisions could include not only doctors but also specialists who would perhaps be better able to assess the non-physiological aspects of the cases considered. A woman asking for an abortion should be entitled to a hearing before the committee. I also feel that the present law could be changed in two respects: first, abortion could be allowed in the case of rape or when it is clear that the child will be born seriously deformed; secondly, certain penalties could be reduced.

Maternal Mortality in Native British Columbia Indians, a High-Risk Group *

W. D. S. Thomas

In their review of 145 maternal deaths which occurred in the Province of British Columbia during the years 1955 to 1962, Carpenter and Bryans[1] noted that there was an alarming discrepancy between the mortality rate for the native Indian women of the province and that of the non-Indian population. They also noted that 50 percent of the deaths due to postpartum hemorrhage occurred in native Indian women. This paper presents a detailed study of the 26 maternal deaths which occurred among native British Columbia Indians during the years 1955 to 1965.

Methods

The case records of the Maternal Welfare Committee of the British Columbia Medical Association from 1955 to 1965 were reviewed and all patients of North American Indian origin were selected for study. No distinction was made between registered and non-registered Indians. Only direct and indirect obstetrical deaths were studied, and all definitions and classifications used were

*"Maternal Mortality in Native British Columbia Indians, a High-Risk Group" by Dr. W. D. S. Thomas, originally published in *The Canadian Medical Association Journal*, 99: 64, 1968.

those recommended by The Canadian Medical Association Committee on Maternal Welfare.[2]

Results

One hundred and sixty direct and indirect obstetrical deaths were recorded during the 11-year review period. Twenty-six of these women were native Indians. Indian deaths therefore accounted for 16.1 percent of the maternal deaths during that period. During the same period 23,830 Indian and 388,720 non-Indian live births were recorded, making a total of 412,550 live births in the Province of British Columbia.[3] The obstetrical death rate for the Indian population was 1.09 deaths per 1000 live births and that for the non-Indian population was 0.346 deaths per 1000 live births. The overall obstetrical death rate for the Province of British Columbia was 0.392. Based on the 1965 population figures, the Indians made up 2.4 percent of the population of British Columbia. This small segment of the population was responsible, therefore, for 5.7 percent of the live births and for 16.1 percent of the maternal mortality during the years 1955 to 1965.

Causes of Death

The causes of death in the 26 Indian mortalities are summarized in Table 1.

TABLE 1

Causes of Indian Maternal Deaths in British Columbia, 1955-1965

A. Hemorrhage—Total	16
Atonic uterus or retained placenta	12
Abortion	2
Ectopic pregnancy	1
Inversion of uterus	1
B. Infection—Total	6
Puerperal	1
Prolonged rupture of membranes	2
Abortion	1
Hepatitis	1
Pneumonia	1
C. Cardiac—Total	3
D. Thromboembolic—Total	1

Hemorrhage was by far the most common cause of death, accounting for 61.5 percent of the total number of fatalities. It is of interest that during the same period only 21.6 percent of the 134 recorded non-Indian deaths were due to hemorrhage. Infection was the second commonest cause of death among the Indians, although it ranks third behind vascular accidents in the causes of maternal death in the general population. Toxemia was not recorded as the cause of death in any of the Indian mortalities. The low incidence of death from toxemia, despite the general lack of prenatal care in the Indian population, was noted by Carpenter and Bryans,[4] and it was suggested that there may be some genetic or dietary protection against toxemia in the Indian race. Deaths from the sequelae of criminal abortion are quite uncommon among the Indian population. Only three such deaths were recorded among the Indian deaths studied. This is in marked contrast to the non-Indian population, in which 37 of 134 deaths studied were due to complications of abortion. Although the incidence of illegitimate pregnancy is high among the Indian race, such pregnancies tend to be accepted and are allowed to continue to term. Criminal abortion is therefore much less of a problem than it is among the non-Indian population.

Preventability

Twenty-five of the 26 Indian deaths were classified as preventable when judged against the ideal academic standard used by the Maternal Welfare Committee. In 19 cases the patient herself was deemed responsible, in four cases the physician was judged responsible, and in two cases both patient and physician were implicated. The high incidence of patient responsibility reflects the frequent refusal of the Indian woman to seek medical aid even when she is in serious trouble.

Factors Influencing Indian Maternal Mortality in British Columbia

1. Age and Parity

Advanced age and high parity are common factors contributing to high mortality rates among Indian women. In the 26 patients under review the average age was 31.8 years with a range of 20 to 44 years. Average parity was 6.8, with a range of 0 to 19. There were 10 patients who were in the dangerous position of being over 35 years of age and of a parity greater than 5. Most of the deaths in these patients were from postpartum hemorrhage due to uterine atony.

2. Lack of Prenatal Care

Only 3 of 26 Indians who died had received any prenatal care. The reasons for lack of prenatal care are multiple. Firstly, many Indian women are poorly motivated and even when medical services are available they will not make use of them. Repeated deliveries at home attended only by the husband or a native midwife have made them complacent. Secondly, the vast area of the province and the nomadic nature of some Indian groups make it impossible to reach all pregnant women even with field nursing personnel. For example, pregnant women have been known to accompany their husbands to isolated fishing villages accessible only by sea. They may be gone for several months, during which time no prenatal care is possible.

3. Geography

The land area of the Province of British Columbia is roughly 366,000 square miles.[5] Much of its mountainous and climatic conditions are extreme. Many areas are accessible only by air, and during the winter months flying is often restricted owing to weather conditions. For administrative purposes the Federal Indian Health Services have divided the Pacific region, which encompasses all of British Columbia, into three zones or areas as indicated on the

Figure 1
Indian and Northern Health Services Facilities (Pacific Region)

map (Figure 1). These are the Miller Bay zone, centred at Prince Rupert (Miller Bay), the Coqualeetza zone, centred at Sardis, and the Vancouver area, centred at Nanaimo. There are roughly 9000 registered Indians in the Miller Bay zone and 8000 in the Vancouver area; the rest of the 45,000 registered Indians reside in the Coqualeetza zone. At the present time maternal health services and education are carried on by field nurses under the supervision of regional medical health officers. Approximately one-third of the public health nursing services for Indians is provided by the Provincial Health Department nurses in order to avoid duplication of nursing services and to minimize the amount of travel required. At the present time there are eight public health nurses serving the Miller Bay zone and one full-time medical health officer located at Prince George. In the Coqualeetza zone there are seven nurses and one medical supervisor. In the Vancouver area, which includes Vancouver Island and the coast up to Bella Bella, there are six public health nurses and two medical officers who do a great deal of travelling. Nearly all travelling is by automobile, and an attempt is made to visit all major Indian settlements at least once a month.

4. Medical Economics

At the present time local medical practitioners are paid for the services rendered to those Indians whose care is paid for by the Indian Health Services on a fee-for-service basis, at 75 percent of the present provincial medical fee schedule. Unfortunately, the Indian population tends to be located in areas of the province where there are fewer doctors. As these doctors are frequently overworked, they sometimes cannot provide the necessary time and effort to bring ideal medical care to the Indian. The factor of lower payment doubtless plays a contributory role. This lack of uniformity in government-financed medical care

57

which works to the disadvantage of the Indians is expected to be corrected with the institution of jointly sponsored Federal-Provincial medical care.

A Case History of a Typical Indian Maternal Death

The following case history is typical of many Indian maternal deaths and illustrates many of the factors already mentioned.

> A 44-year-old Indian woman, para 13, gravida 16, was living in a remote settlement which was three-and-a-half hours by boat from the nearest hospital. She had made one prenatal visit at about 30 weeks' gestation, when her hemoglobin was found to be 10.0 g. She was given an intramuscular injection of iron and a supply of an oral iron supplement, but she did not return for further visits. She went into spontaneous labour at 41 weeks and was delivered at home with only a native midwife present. No drugs or anesthetic agents were available. She had a retained placenta and suffered a profuse postpartum hemorrhage. She died en route to hospital. This death was classified as a direct obstetrical and preventable death.

Methods Which Might Help to Reduce Indian Maternal Deaths

1. Medical Referral Centres

Greater efforts should be made to select those Indian women with poor obstetrical histories, such as previous cesarean section or previous postpartum hemorrhage, from remote communities and to send them to referral centres where obstetrical complications can be adequately handled. This will require a concerted program of education because most Indian women are loath to leave the family unit even under the most serious circumstances.

2. Education

Every effort must be made to educate the Indian population with regard to the importance of antenatal care, family planning and other matters pertaining to maternal welfare. Significant advances in this area have already been made with the development of Native Community Health Workers. Intelligent, interested and respected members of the native community are being trained by the Indian Health Services in all aspects of public health, with the hope that they will return to their home environment and help to raise the standard of public health in their own area. Attempts have also been made to bring together the chiefs and leaders of the Indian community to meet with medical health officers at workshops where the problems of the Indian community are discussed.

3. Birth Control

Every effort must be made to provide methods to control the fertility of the Indian female, particularly those in the higher childbearing age group. At present, oral contraceptive agents are being provided by the field nurses on

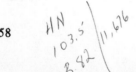

prescription of local medical doctors. The intrauterine device is also being utilized in many instances where oral contraceptives have proved impractical. The provision of contraceptive information and materials has succeeded in reducing the Indian birth rate to 34.6 per 1000 in 1966, which is approximately half of that which existed five years ago. However, this rate is still very high when compared with the figure of 17.3 per 1000 which was the birth rate for the overall population of British Columbia in 1966.

4. Sterilization

The wider use of sterilization is strongly advocated, particularly where age and parity are high and contraceptive measures have obviously failed. Such a policy can be supported by the convincing evidence already quoted that establishes the high maternal risks of advancing age and parity. If sterilization had been performed after a parity of five and an age of 35 years, 10 of 16 deaths due to postpartum hemorrhage would have been avoided.

Conclusion

In an 11-year period from 1955 to 1965, 16.1 percent of the maternal deaths in the Province of British Columbia occurred in Indian women who comprise 2.4 percent of the population and account for 5.7 percent of the total births. Sixty-one percent of these deaths were due to postpartum hemorrhage. High parity, advancing age, lack of prenatal care and geographic isolation were major factors contributing to most of these deaths. In order to reduce the number of preventable obstetrical deaths among Indian women we must teach them the importance of prenatal care and ensure that these services reach all of them. We must remove high-risk patients from remote areas and bring these women to referral centres for confinement. We must make medical care available to all Indians on an equal basis with the white population. Finally, we must be more liberal in providing birth control measures and offering sterilization for those who are a particular risk owing to greater parity and age.

Summary

Maternal deaths among native Indians of British Columbia account for a disproportionate amount of the total provincial maternal mortality. The case histories of the 160 maternal deaths studied by the Provincial Maternal Mortality Committee from 1955 to 1965 were reviewed. The maternal mortality rate for the non-Indian population during that period was 0.346 per 1000 live births, while the rate for the native Indian population was 1.09. Twenty-six Indian deaths were recorded. The major causes of death were hemorrhage and infection. It is concluded that because of geography, socioeconomic factors and lack of medical care, the native Indian population of British Columbia represents an unusually high-risk group with regard to maternal mortality. The greater use of contraception and a more liberal sterilization policy in this high-risk group are strongly advocated. Further efforts to extend the benefits of antenatal and intrapartum care to the Indian population are necessary, particularly to reduce the high incidence of death due to unattended hemorrhage.

Footnotes

1. C. W. Carpenter and F. E. Bryans, *Canadian Medical Association Journal*, 92, 1965, p. 160.
2. Canadian Medical Association, Committee on Maternal Welfare, *C.M.A.J.*, 85, 1961, p. 550.
3. (a) British Columbia, Department of Health and Welfare, Vital Statistics Division, Vital statistics of the Province of British Columbia, Report, 86th, 1957, Victoria, B.C.: Queen's Printer, 1959.
   (b) British Columbia, Department of Health Services and Hospital Insurance, Vital Statistics Division, Vital statistics of the Province of British Columbia, Report, 93rd, 1964, Victoria: Queen's Printer, 1966.
   (c) British Columbia, Department of Health Services and Hospital Insurance, Vital Statistics of the Province of British Columbia, Report, 94th, 1965, Victoria: Queen's Printer, 1967.
4. C. W. Carpenter and F. E. Bryans, *op. cit.*, p. 160.
5. Canada, Bureau of Statistics, Information Services Division, Canada Year Book Section, *Canada Year Book*, 1961, official statistical annual of the resources, history, institutions and social and economic conditions of Canada, Ottawa: Queen's Printer, 1961.

Infant Mortality in Canada[*][†]

Patricia Musson

Introduction

The purpose of this paper is: to examine patterns of infant mortality for the Eskimos of the Northwest Territories, to reflect these patterns against those experienced by the entire Canadian population, and finally to offer some tentative reasons for the differentials.

The limited period 1958 to 1968 has been chosen for two reasons: firstly, the author believes that data on Eskimos prior to this period is sufficiently inaccurate to obscure rather than clarify the analysis,[1] and, secondly, prior to 1958 infant mortality by cause was not tabulated. An examination of the factors that may affect the quality of the data used will be presented to reveal their strengths and weaknesses.

The first year of life remains the most vulnerable to mortality, excluding years of old age (60+). The infant mortality rate is one of the most sensitive single indices of conditions existing in a country. It reflects trends in general mortality, public health, sanitation, housing, and of economic development, as well as practices of infant feeding and care because infants more than any other group depend so completely on environmental conditions and the attention of others for their survival.

The level of infant mortality has an effect on future growth of the population. Reductions in infant mortality have contributed to the Eskimos' staggering

* Not published previously; written specifically for this volume.
† The author wishes to express her thanks to Dr. D. I. Poole for his assistance in the formulation of this article.

annual growth rate of 5.93 for the period 1961 to 1966. No country with a developed economy can support such growth in its total population for very long.

Measures of Infant Mortality

For convenience, the conventional infant mortality rate[2] is defined as the number of deaths under one year of age that occur during a calendar year per 1000 births during the same period.

The life table infant mortality rates and the life expectancies at age zero have been calculated by the Public Health Section of the Health and Welfare Division of the Dominion Bureau of Statistics, and are used here by permission of the Division.

No attempt has been made to calculate the cause of specific infant mortality rates due to the small number of deaths in each category. Rather, each cause or category of causes has been taken as a percentage of all deaths.

The Data

Two types of errors can exist in vital data: errors of coverage (the failure to contact entire households to register all vital events) and errors of characteristics (the failure to accurately record social and demographic variables). For the Eskimo, many factors exist that increase the likelihood of the occurrence of the above types of errors. The first, and most obvious, factor is geography. There is limited access to the Arctic in that transportation and communication systems are limited and there is considerable difficulty in locating a small population (approximately 12,000) in a land mass of 1,304,903 square miles. Secondly, it is difficult to obtain full public support and cooperation when Eskimos may not fully comprehend the significance of registering vital events because of low levels of literacy, high levels of poverty, the language barrier between registrar and registrant, and the lack of communication facilities. Thirdly, vital statistics should relate the population or the event to a specific area. This involves being able to identify the dwelling or location where each person is being counted. The seminomadic life style of the Eskimo and his use of temporary housing of snow or skin frustrates this attempt and results in both omissions and duplications. Also, enumeration and registration have largely been carried out by the Royal Canadian Mounted Police supplemented by doctors, nurses, other paramedical personnel, priests, ministers and the like. For all these persons these tasks were of low priority. The two types of errors mentioned occur in Canadian data generally but because of the factors mentioned above, there is a greater probability that they occur more frequently in the Eskimo data.

Although these problems do exist they do not totally invalidate any analysis of either population or any comparison between populations. Knowing that such limitations exist demands only that a cautious approach be taken to the analysis of trends or the explanation of differentials.

This discussion will cover the period 1958 to 1968, for both populations. For the first time, in 1958, Eskimo infant mortality data were available by cause (Internation List A). The Vital Statistics for Eskimos were unpublished material obtained directly by the author from the Analysis Unit of the Vital Statistics

Division of the Dominion Bureau of Statistics, and it should be noted that this material is only for the Northwest Territories. Vital statistics for all of Canada were drawn from the *Canadian Vital Statistics*, a DBS publication.

Levels of Infant Mortality

Eskimo infant mortality has fallen from 252 infant deaths per 1000 live births in 1958 to 91 in 1967 while the infant mortality rate for Canada during the same period has gone from 30.2 in 1958 to 22.0 in 1967 (Table 1). Eskimo infant mortality, while declining at an extremely rapid rate, is still four times the rate experienced by the country as a whole.

TABLE 1

Infant Mortality Rates for Eskimos (Northwest Territories) in Canada, 1958-1968

Year	Eskimos (N.W.T.)	Canada
1958	252	30
1959	209	28
1960	221	27
1961	198	27
1962	189	28
1963	159	26
1964	97	25
1965	100	24
1966	112	23
1967	91	22
1968	births not known	21

Source: Analysis Unit, *Vital Statistics*, Dominion Bureau of Statistics.

The remarkable decline experienced in Eskimo infant mortality is further demonstrated in a partial life table (Table 2). Q_0 is the risk or probability of dying during the first year of life. The probability of dying in that first year has been halved during the five-year interval and contributes to the addition of eleven years on the life expectancy at age zero (e_0). Life expectancy at age zero

TABLE 2

Life Table Comparisons of Eskimos of the Northwest Territories and All Canadians

Eskimos		Q_0	e_0
1960-1963		.195	45.3
1965-1968		.099	56.5
		Eskimos (1960-63)	Canada (1960-62)
Q_0	M	.214	.031
	F	.174	.024
e_0	M	43.4	68.4
	F	47.4	74.2

Source: Public Health Section of the Health and Welfare Division of the Dominion Bureau of Statistics.

refers to the number of years, on an average, newborn infants may expect to live. Note that in the second part of Table 2, the probability of an Eskimo infant dying is approximately seven times that for any (the average) Canadian during the period. (Note: The periods are not exactly comparable, but the bias would be in favour of a decreased probability of dying for Eskimos and if anything this produces a smaller differential than actually the case.)

TABLE 3

Neonatal Mortality Rates, Eskimos (Canada) and Canada, 1962-67

Year	Eskimos (Canada)	Canada
1962	53	21
1963	59	21
1964	26	20
1965	41	18
1966	34	18
1967	31	17

Source: Analysis Unit, *Vital Statistics*, Dominion Bureau of Statistics.

Deaths to babies under 28 days old are often referred to as neonatal deaths. Although included in overall infant mortality, they are often treated separately, because the neonatal mortality rate serves as an approximate index of indigenous mortality factors[3] such as birth injuries and congenital malformation predating birth, factors which are difficult for public health measures to conquer or even to influence. A pattern of decline can be noted for both populations with more rapid declines being characteristic of the Eskimos.

Interpretation

It is established that although both populations are experiencing declines, and the Eskimo rate is declining more rapidly, Eskimo infant mortality is still significantly higher than Canadian mortality. In order to explore the reason for this we must examine the causes of death among Eskimo infants.

Ill-Defined and Unknown Causes

Ill-defined and unknown causes account for a large proportion of the infant deaths recorded for both the Eskimo and Canadian populations (Table 4). It would be reasonable to say that the greater the percentage of deaths appearing in this category, the more suspect the rank order of all other causes of death become. There is no evidence that the distribution of these deaths, if known, would be the same as the distribution of all known causes; in fact, we have reason to believe the contrary. Such deaths would most likely be a part of a single category. Deaths due to unknown causes will continue to decrease as the number of trained medical personnel and facilities increase. In 1958, there were nine nursing stations, two clinics and one hospital in the Northwest Territories.[4] In 1967 there were 21 nursing stations, two clinics, six health centres and eight hospitals.[5] This increase parallels the decrease in the proportion of deaths in this category for the Eskimos.

TABLE 4

Selected Causes of Infant Death as a Percentage of All Infant Deaths

A. Eskimos (Northwest Territories), 1958-68.
B. Canada, 1958-68.

Causes		1958	1959	1960	1961	1962	1963	1964	1965	1966	1967	1968
Infectious and Parasitic (1-43)	A.	2.8	—	4.3	2.1	10.3	2.4	1.8	3.6	3.2	11.3	—
	B.	1.5	—	1.9	—	1.3	—	.9	—	1.1	—	.8
Neoplasms	A.	—	—	—	—	—	—	—	—	—	—	—
	B.	.3	—	.3	—	.3	—	.4	—	.3	—	.4
Diseases of Nervous Systems	A.	—	2.2	3.5	4.1	6.2	4.8	12.3	8.9	3.2	13.2	7.7
	B.	2.0	—	1.9	—	1.7	—	1.8	—	2.0	—	1.5
Respiratory System	A.	21.3	24.7	30.4	26.8	28.9	23.8	31.6	19.6	45.2	24.5	40.4
	B.	14.5	—	13.7	—	11.9	—	10.4	—	9.8	—	9.7
Digestive System	A.	8.3	8.6	7.0	6.2	7.2	4.8	3.5	3.6	8.1	9.4	1.9
	B.	5.6	—	5.2	—	4.4	—	3.4	—	3.4	—	2.7
Congenital Malformations	A.	10.8	—	1.7	1.7	7.8	10.0	—	13.8	3.1	—	8.3
	B.	15.8	—	15.9	—	17.2	—	17.6	—	19.3	—	19.0
Ill-Defined and Unknown	A.	44.4	39.8	35.6	33.0	24.7	32.1	24.6	35.7	11.2	13.2	26.9
	B.	23.8	—	24.7	—	26.6	—	29.2	—	29.5	—	30.1

Diseases of the Respiratory System

Respiratory diseases are the major identified causes of mortality to Eskimo infants in the Northwest Territories. There are several reasons for this, the first and most important of which is the condition of housing. A survey conducted in 1963 and 1964 indicated that of 817 one-room dwellings in the Eastern Arctic, only 81 had fewer than three persons living in them.[6] Culturally, climatically, and economically the Eskimo has always tended to live in a single-room dwelling making crowding and spread of disease major problems. Culturally, the tradition of having one's family close by is still important in that cold and lonely land's climate. Heating is easier in a small crowded single-room dwelling because body heat is sufficient to heat the home and finally, most Eskimos do not have the means to afford a larger dwelling let alone heat it.

Respiratory diseases occur among infants because there is such a high incidence of these diseases in the adults, and this is further aggravated by the habit of spitting on the floor. Public health programmes are presently attempting to alert the people to the danger of this habit in the transmission of communicable diseases.

As discussed above in the section on unidentified causes of death, access to hospitals and nursing stations is inadequate although there have been attempts in recent years to solve these problems. Lay dispensers are appointed in small settlements to treat minor diseases or injury, and to arrange for a doctor, a nurse, or evacuation. In 1967 there were attempts to involve native persons as lay dispensers. Eskimo families are issued a medical pack containing penicillin tablets, antibiotics, ointments and pediatric tetracycline as well as dressings. These could be used effectively by seminomadic or isolated families as the contents were explained in an accompanying pamphlet with illustrated instructions in Eskimo syllables. Of all respiratory diseases, pneumonia accounted for a majority of the deaths in this section for Eskimo infants. The proportion of children dying because of respiratory diseases remains high in the Eskimo community. The varying proportion from year to year is a function of the small actual numbers of Eskimo and infant deaths.

Infections of the Newborn

Infections of the newborn account for a large proportion of deaths for Eskimos in infancy, particularly if one considers only the proportion of deaths due to diseases of known causes. Such infections are aggravated by the sanitation problems experienced in the North. Lack of standards for basic needs result in water supplies becoming polluted and *gastro-enteritis* as well as infections of the newborn ensue, especially in the summer months. The permafrost prohibits the construction of efficient and inexpensive sewers. The native habit of leaving excreta in the living area, which is already crowded, is an obvious health hazard.

In 1967, three posts were provided in the Northwest Territories for sanitation experts and one for a health educator program in an attempt to improve the environment and to educate the Eskimos in the principles of personal and community hygiene. This, however, is an extraordinary task for four men on a land mass of 1.3 million square miles.

Congenital Malformations

Congenital malformations do not account for a steady proportion of infants deaths for Eskimos, but they are responsible for a substantial and seemingly growing proportion of infant deaths. The author is inclined to speculate that as fewer deaths are recorded under ill-defined and unknown causes, the proportions of infants dying from congenital malformations will increase.

Remaining Causes and Factors

Nearly all causes of infant deaths are aggravated by nutritional deficiencies. The reduction of the principal food source, the Caribou, has taken place at the same time as the Eskimo population is expanding at a staggering rate. As a result, most food needs to be imported, and this creates transportation and distribution problems. While there is a wide variety of food, the prohibitive costs force the native peoples to purchase less expensive foods which are high in carbohydrates and low in protein, fat and vitamin content. The high costs are again due to transportation, prices, the difficulty of storage, the small volume, and the lack of competitive pressures. As a result, diets have deteriorated to "bannock" and tea which leads to deficiencies in vitamins A and B. This, in time, may explain the relatively low resistance to infection. Recently, attempts to rectify this have been implemented in a program to supply pregnant and lactating mothers and all children with greater quantities of vitamins and iron.

Another problem is food loss through spoilage. Molds, food spoilage bacteria, and other similar pressures appear to be as common in the Arctic as elsewhere.[7] Formula feeding is becoming more and more common and it is not as nutritious or safe (germ free) as breast feeding. In Alaska, for example, 60 percent of native children under two years were formula fed according to a 1962 survey.[8]

Many infant deaths in the Arctic might be avoided by having trained medical personnel in attendance at the birth since that pattern can be inversely related to mortality of infants (Table 5).

TABLE 5

Attendance of Medical Personnel, 1964

	Eskimos Percent	Canada Percent
Doctor present	37	62
Nurse only	27	20
Lay person only	36	18

Source: *Report on Health Conditions*, 1965, Sessional Papers, Northwest Territories.

Conclusions

The infant mortality rate for Eskimos was nearly ten times that of other Canadians in the late 1950's and early 1960's. During the past decade this differential has been narrowed considerably, but the Eskimo infant mortality rate is still some four times greater. Improvements have been made in reducing the causes of Eskimo infant mortality; that is, lack of medicines and medical facilities, poor sanitation, poor housing, and insufficient diet, but it is obvious that greater efforts must be made in the future.

Canada has the means, the technology, and the resources to remove the remaining differential between Eskimos and the rest of the Canadian population. Problems in housing, heating, sanitation, and nutrition indirectly relate to the loss of life among infants. These problems can be solved if the will to solve them is sufficient to provide the necessary human and monetary resources.

Footnotes

1. This is discussed in detail and statistically analyzed in an unpublished Master's Thesis by the author.
2. S. Chandrasekar, *Infant Mortality in India*, 1901-55. London: George Allen and Unwin Ltd., 1959, p. 69.
3. United Nations, Bulletin No. 6, 1962, New York, United Nations, 1963, p. 62.
4. "A Symposium on Northern Medical History," *Canadian Medical Association Journal*, 100, March, 1969, pp. 521-524.
5. Sessional Paper No. 5, *Report on Health Conditions in the Northwest Territories*, 1966.
6. "Home Economics Education in the Northwest Territories," *Canadian Nutrition Notes*, 23, No. 8, October, 1968, p. 93.
7. E. Scott, et al., "Nutrition in the Arctic," *Arch Environ Health,* 17, October, 1968, p. 605.
8. E. Scott and D. Helter, "Nutrition of a Northern Population," W.H.O. Geneva Conference, 1962.

Migration Between Canada and the United States*

K. V. Pankhurst

Heavy investment in the industrial countries of the world in producing information is not, regrettably, matched by adequate critical review and analysis. Despite the commonplace recognition that inferences from crude statistics are subject to the risk of being false, or at best misleading, those inferences continue to be drawn from material that is incomplete and inadequate, and this proposition unfortunately holds for the current view of movements of people between Canada and the United States.

The Extent of Migration

The view that is currently accepted about the population movements affecting Canada since the war can briefly be described as follows. In the broad context of a movement of people from the underdeveloped countries of the world to Europe, and from Europe to Canada, and from Canada to the United States, Canada received population from Europe, mainly Britain, at the rate of about

* "Migration Between Canada and the United States" by K. V. Pankhurst originally published in *The Annals of the American Academy of Political and Social Science*, 367, September, 1966, pp. 53-62. Pankhurst is Director of Economics, Canadian International Development Agency.

125,000 a year, and lost roughly 40,000 a year to the United States. The movement of people into Canada has included about 23,000 professional and skilled workers a year, constituting about 18 percent of the total number of immigrants. Migration from Canada to the United States has been at the rate of about 40,000 a year, and has included a relatively larger proportion of high-level manpower: about a half of those emigrating to join the labor force (21,000) has consisted of professional and skilled workers (10,000). Canada is thought to have provided recently about a quarter of the scientists and engineers moving to the United States, and has contributed nearly as many workers in these two categories as Britain, western Germany, Holland, and France put together.[1]

The current view continues further to make two main inferences from these observations. The first is that there is a loss of professional and skilled manpower to the United States, but that this *brain drain* is more than compensated by the number entering from Europe, so that Canada has a net *brain gain*.[2] The loss to the United States is explained variously by references to such factors as the generally higher levels of wages and salaries in the United States, income differences in particular occupations, greater employment opportunities, greater support of research and development, propinquity, and a warmer climate. Secondly, the difference between the numbers entering Canada from other countries and those leaving for the United States has led, first, to the proposition that Canada is near to its optimum population and above its capacity to absorb immigrants, and also to variations of that proposition – such as, that some immigrants or Canadians are displaced from employment or that their movement to the United States creates opportunities for more immigration into Canada than would otherwise have been possible.

The evidence on the subject of movements of people between Canada and the United States is fragmentary and generally unsatisfactory. It falls into three main types. The first is data about the main *flows* of migrants. The second is information about *stocks* at the time of national censuses of population. The third is from detailed empirical studies of movements among particular occupational groups.

Between Canada and the United States, there are six main flows of people that can usefully be identified: (1) Canadian residents emigrating to the United States, (2) Canadian residents returning to Canada to resume residence after a period of residence in the United States, (3) Canadians entering and leaving the United States as tourists, (4) American residents emigrating to Canada, (5) American residents returning to the United States to resume residence after a period of residence in Canada, and (6) American residents entering and leaving Canada as tourists. Since most free countries control immigration for residence but do not maintain a control of tourists entering, or of residents and tourists leaving, administrative sources do not provide complete information about these movements. Tourist movements are, however, very large compared with recorded migration, and may well conceal some migrants. Data about immigration into the United States and Canada from the immigration services of the two countries deal with the gross movements of people intending to take up residence, and they exclude returning residents. Some data on returning residents exist, but the Canadian data about this category appear to include only some of the Canadian or other British citizens resuming residence in Canada.[3] The series on returning residents from Canada to the United States exists only before 1956.[4]

The view presented by the recorded flows in the six-year period ending in 1955 is of a net movement of population from Canada to the United States (Table 1). During these years, estimated immigration into Canada averaged about 144,000 a year. By comparison, the gross movement to the United States may seem large (32,000 a year). After allowing for gross migration from the United States to Canada, the apparent net difference between movements across the United States-Canadian border was equivalent to roughly one-sixth of the numbers entering Canada. The differences between the two recorded flows of returning residents do little to alter this view of the net loss from Canada, and suggest that only about one person in eight leaving Canada for the United States returned to Canada.

TABLE 1

Migration To and From Canada, 1950-1955 (thousands)

Migrations		Total 1950-1955		Annual Average
Immigration into Canada from All Countries		865.8		144.3
Gross Recorded Emigration to United States		194.4		32.4
Gross Recorded Immigration from United States		54.7		9.1
Difference between Gross Movements to and from United States		139.7		23.3
Returning Residents Recorded				
United States to Canada	24.9		4.2	
Canada to United States	19.4		3.2	
Net Difference		5.5		0.9
Net Recorded Movements from Canada to United States		134.2		22.4

Sources: L. Parai, *Immigration and Emigration of Professional and Skilled Manpower during the Post-war Period*, and estimates by Department of Citizenship and Immigration.

That view rests largely upon a calculation which accepts the recorded numbers of returning residents, but the possibility of quite a different view, and of an alternative estimate of the numbers returning to Canada from the United States, emerges from an examination of changes in the stock data. A comparison of changes in the enumerated population of Canada between the Censuses of 1951 and 1961 (Table 2) indicates net migration of Canadian-born to the United States of not more than about 5,200 a year, compared with a recorded gross emigration to the United States of about 28,000 a year, and suggests a return flow to Canada of up to 24,000 a year from the United States. An examination of the United States Censuses (Table 3) yields an estimate of the net loss of Canadian-born of the same order of magnitude, 4,500 a year. Estimates of the other components of migration indicate a return flow of United States residents from Canada in the range of 5,000 to 8,000 a year (Table 2).

The estimates derived from the stock data have their deficiencies, which arise from several sources. They are residuals which are subject to differences in the degree of underenumeration and to errors in the immigration estimates used and the death rates assumed. Nevertheless, while both sets of calculations are primitive and inconclusive, they serve to indicate that the naïve view of a substantial loss of population from Canada to the United States, which has been

TABLE 2

Estimated Emigration from Canada to the United States, 1951-1961 (thousands)

	Canadian born (1)	Foreign born (2)	U.S. Citizens (3)	Total (1+2)
1. Residents in 1951	11,950	2,060	69	14,009
2. Intercensal Recorded Immigration from all Countries	7	1,536	82–103[a]	1,543
3. Intercensal Births	4,463	5[b]	—	4,468
4. Intercensal Deaths	971[c]	349[c]	6–11[c]	1,320
5. Gross Survivors	15,449	3,252	140–166	18,700
6. Residents in 1961	15,394	2,844	88	18,238
7. Estimated Emigration and Net Outflow of Returning Residents to all Countries, 1951-1961	55	408	52–78	462
8. Recorded Emigration to U.S., 1951–1961	282	117		400
9. Estimated U.S. Citizens Returning to U.S. from Canada			52–78	52–78
10. Estimated Gross Outflow to U.S.	282	117	52–78	452–478
11. Estimate of Residents Returning from U.S. to Canada	230–245[d]	n.a.		230–245
12. Estimate of U.S. Residents Returning from Canada			52–78	52–78
13. Estimated Inflows (+) and Outflows (−) Not Recorded in Official Canada-U.S. Migration Statistics	+(230–245)	n.a.	−(52–78)	+(152–193)
14. Unrecorded Inflows from the U.S. as Percent of Recorded Emigration to the U.S.	82–87			38–48

[a] The recorded immigration of all U.S. *residents* is 103. It is assumed here that the component of non-U.S. nationals immigrating from the U.S. was no more than 20 percent.
[b] Births occurring in the U.S. to mothers normally resident in Canada.
[c] Deaths of foreign-born persons were estimated by Camu et al. on the basis of Canadian 1956 survival rates. Estimated deaths of Canadian-born is the difference between total recorded and estimated foreign-born deaths. The range of deaths of U.S. citizens has been obtained by applying the over-all death rate of the Canadian-born and the foreign-born and using the respective results as the limits of the range.
[d] Since 94 percent of the Canadian-born persons residing outside Canada lived in the U.S. in 1956 (U.N., *Demographic Yearbook*, 1956) it has been assumed that the recorded emigration of Canadian-born persons to the U.S. represented 94 percent of the emigration of Canadian-born persons to all countries, which must then have been 300. Subtracting the difference between gross survivors and residents in 1961 (row 7), yields an estimate of 245 for the unrecorded inflow from all countries. Assuming that at least 94 percent of this inflow was from the U.S., indicates a range of 230–245.

Sources:
1. P. Camu, E. P. Weeks, and Z. W. Sametz, *Economic Geography of Canada*, Toronto, 1964, p. 69.
2. *1961 Census of Canada*, Bulletin 1.2–7. Ottawa: Queen's Printer, 1963.
3. *1951 Census of Canada*, Vol. 1. Ottawa: Queen's Printer, 1953.

formed from observations solely about the recorded flows from Canada, requires modification.

Thus, we have two very different pictures of the extent of migration from Canada to the United States. One view, based upon a single calculation suggests that Canada loses population to the United States equivalent to about a quarter of gross immigration from there, and that only about one Canadian emigrant in eight to the United States returns to Canada. The alternative estimate, based upon two independent calculations, indicates that seven out of eight Canadians return from the United States. These two estimates may not mark the full range

TABLE 3

Estimated Number of Canadian-Born Returning to Canada from the United States, 1940-1960 (thousands)

Population and Migration	1940-50[a]	1950-60[b]
Canadian-born Residents in the United States at Beginning of Decade	1,040	1,005
Recorded Intercensal Migration of Canadian-born from Canada to United States	140	290
Estimated Intercensal Deaths of Canadian-born in United States	90	100
Gross Canadian-born Survivors in United States	1,090	1,195
Canadian-born Residents in the United States at End of Decade	990	950
Estimated Number of Canadian-born Returning to Canada	100	245
Estimated Net Movement of Canadian-born to United States	40	45

[a] Excluding Alaska and Hawaii.

[b] Including Alaska and Hawaii.

Sources: P. Camu, E. P. Weeks, and Z. W. Sametz, *op. cit.*, Table 3:2, p. 60; Department of Citizenship and Immigration, Ottawa.

of possibilities within which the truth lies, but it seems likely that the loss of Canadians to the United States is much smaller than has been thought. Considering all migrants between the two countries, it now appears that the ratio of emigration from Canada to immigration is about two to one rather than four to one. What may be more important, however, is that there appears to have been substantially more movement between the two countries than has been thought.

The Structure of Migration

While the size of the new movement from Canada still requires further careful study, the view of the structure of the movement has to be based upon fragmentary information and is consequently more obscure. Of the *gross* emigration to the United States from Canada roughly one-quarter is professional and one-quarter skilled,[5] but, because the occupational structure of the people recovered from the United States is not known, there is at present an insufficient basis upon which to make any judgment about the character of the net movement southwards. If the distribution of the occupational characteristics of the people moving northwards is the same as those of the southward migration, the net loss to Canada of professional and skilled manpower would be of the order of three thousand a year. The extent to which there is a larger or smaller *brain drain* than this figure therefore depends upon whether the return flow and the American immigrants to Canada contain a larger or smaller proportion of highly qualified people, and upon the relative levels of experience and education in the flows northward and southward. Evidence about the movement of a few occupational groups indicates a variety of trends, and it must be expected that, even if comprehensive data were available, they would display wide variation.

A forthcoming study by D. Dyck[6] indicates a tendency among scientists and engineers for the more able graduates to move to the United States for both higher-degree study and employment. The study analyzes the geographical mobility of the 1955 class of graduates of Canadian universities in science and engineering. Of the male graduates (199 scientists and 1,236 engineers), 35 scientists and 81 engineers took postgraduate degrees in the United States. Of each of these two occupational groups obtaining higher degrees, a larger proportion received training to the doctoral level in the United States (Table 4).

TABLE 4

1955 Class of Scientists and Engineers from Canadian Universities: Distribution of Higher Degrees by Country of Study

Graduates	Percent of Total Obtaining Higher Degrees	
	Master's Degree	Doctoral Degree
Scientists		
In Canada	37	63
In United States	6	94
Engineers		
In Canada	84	16
In United States	69	31

Source: D. Dyck, "The Geographic Mobility of the 1955 University Graduates from Science and Engineering Courses in Canada," to be published.

Of these two groups, the majority (65 percent of the scientists and 57 percent of the engineers) returned to Canada on graduation, but a larger proportion of the more highly qualified people remained in employment in the United States (Table 5).

This was more evident among the scientists than among the engineers. Those who entered employment in the United States after graduating from an American university tended to remain in the United States: in fact, it is estimated that none of those taking employment in the United States after graduation returned to Canada within the ten-year period observed. On the other hand, the members of the class moving to the United States for study or employment and remaining there are few. Moreover, those who worked in the United States and subsequently returned to Canada spent a relatively short time in the United States: in the case of both the scientific and the engineering groups, the mean length of employment abroad in any country (mainly the United States) was 1.6 years, which was long enough for the respondents to obtain valuable experience, but is unlikely to have been long enough to develop full potential value for the employers.

Generally, it appears that there is a net migration of engineers to the United States, which could be increasing. There is no adequate information about movements of scientists, but those scientists who are university teachers may be part of a net movement into Canada. According to a study made by the Association of Universities and Colleges of Canada,[7] the numbers of university teachers returning to or entering Canada from the United States were estimated to have exceeded those leaving Canada for the United States, the ratio rising from 1.6 to 1 in 1957, to 2.3 to 1 in 1958, and 2.8 to 1 in 1962. Moreover, in 1962 there were twice as many returning Canadian university teachers as Canadian emigrants in the group. Another fragment of information emerges from a study by H. G. Grubel and A. D. Scott, who have

TABLE 5

1955 Class of Scientists and Engineers Graduating from Canadian Universities: Distribution by Country of Employment and by Degree Level, 1964

Graduates	Number	Percent of Distribution by Degree Level		
		Bachelor	Master	Doctor
Scientists				
Working in United States, 1964	22	5	23	72
Total working abroad, 1964	27	7	19	74
Working in Canada in 1964:				
Employed in U.S. during 1955-1964	17	—	12	88
Total employed abroad during 1955-1964	23	9	17	74
Never employed abroad	144	28	23	49
Total working in Canada in 1964	167	26	22	52
Engineers				
Working in United States, 1964	81	52	31	17
Total working abroad, 1964	107	54	31	15
Working in Canada in 1964:				
Employed in U.S. during 1955-1964	40	65	30	5
Total employed abroad during 1955-1964	88	76	18	6
Never employed abroad	1,031	84	12	4
Total working in Canada in 1964	1,119	84	12	4

Source: D. Dyck, *op. cit.*

found "that there are approximately as many U.S.-born and -trained economists teaching in Canada as there are Canadian-born and -trained economists in teaching positions in the United States."[8] In view of the fact that there were probably very few American economists in Canadian universities shortly after the war, this is a striking indication of change.

University teachers entering and leaving Canada had very similar distributions of higher degrees: in 1957 and 1958, 49 percent entering and 46 percent of those leaving held a doctoral degree, and in both groups 83 percent had a Master's degree. In 1962, 46 percent of both groups had a doctoral degree, while 86 percent of the immigrants and 79 percent of the emigrants held a Master's degree. Since the inflow of university teachers is roughly three times as great as the outflow, the rapid expansion of Canadian universities appears to be encouraging a large *brain gain* from the United States which will be of critical importance in the domestic production of *brains*.

Although there is some loss of high-level manpower from Canada to the United States, it may be that the size of this *brain drain* is smaller than has been supposed, and that instances can be found of a gain in other occupations. Since examples have been found of a net loss, a net balance, and a net gain, it seems important that further attempts should be made to identify the occupational groups in each of these categories, both for practical reasons and also in order to help begin to understand the processes of migration.

Reasons for Migration between Canada and the United States

Since the war, migration between Canada and the United States has increased in both directions. Canadian residents moving to the United States nearly doubled from 1946 to 1964, and estimates of the return flow of Canadian residents suggest that it was more than twice as high from 1950 to 1960 as in the previous decade (Table 3). United States residents migrating to Canada also increased, but less rapidly, rising by 23 percent from 1946-1948 to 1961-1963 The professional and skilled-worker components of these movements have risen, those moving from the United States to Canada increasing by a factor of 2½ from 1950 to 1963, while those leaving Canada for the United States rose by 65 percent from 1946 to 1963. The rate of increase in the movement of professional workers alone was faster still, and the influx of university teachers into Canada has been shown to have become extremely rapid.

In view of these observations it follows that the explanation and evaluation of the movements have to be conceived in wider terms than hitherto. Simplistic explanations of the attractiveness of the United States in terms of such factors as higher income and a warmer climate is no longer adequate (if they ever were) because they can apply only to the movement southwards across the border. It is not sufficient simply to assess the factors behind the movement from Canada. It has become increasingly important to understand why the movement takes place in both directions.

Two explanations of the southward drift – propinquity and climatic differences – also apply to the northward movement. In a history of migration between the two countries, propinquity has led to the establishment of social, cultural, and demographic links which are hard to assess in relation to the other factors. It is also time to question the idea that the movement to the United States is induced by a warmer climate. The American climate in some parts is more rigorous in summer and in winter than even the adjacent regions of Canada. While tourists may move south towards the sun in winter and north to escape it in summer, it has yet to be established that this kind of consideration is a major factor in migration movements for employment.

What may be a more important reason for the existence, growth, and structure of the movements between Canada and the United States is the character of the growth of the two countries. While Canada remains small in relation to the United States, it has become large enough for a secondary manufacturing sector to emerge and for the distributive and service sectors to expand. Before this development Canada imported a relatively large amount of knowledge, skill, and technology in the form of commodities and services. While the commodity trade between the two countries continues to increase and promote specialized production on either side of the border, Canada has developed an increasing need for knowledge, skill, and technology embodied in people rather than in products.

The growth of demand and of production in the two economies since the war provided the conditions for an increasing integration of ownership and of production, both within each of the two countries and between them, and for an intensification of specialization. Specialization, like love and science, knows few international obstacles. The increase in specialization that is made possible by larger scale has also emerged in higher education.

The possibility of higher earnings in the United States than in Canada may perhaps be part of the mechanism by which people are attracted to move to the United States. It is not, however, sufficient that there should be some difference in earnings. Earnings have been higher in the United States, but neither

TABLE 6

Per Capita Earnings[a] in Canada and the United States, by Selected Occupations, 1959

Occupations	Canada[b] $'000	United States[c] $'000	Ratio of U.S. to Canadian Earnings
All Occupations	4.52	5.61	1.24
Professional and scientific	7.09	8.40	1.19
Engineers	7.79	8.63	1.11
Natural scientists	7.19	7.95	1.11
Physicians, surgeons, dentists	14.91	17.78	1.19
Academic teachers and principals	8.84	7.91[d]	0.90[d]
Managerial	6.96	9.00	1.29
Craftsmen, foremen, operatives, related workers (including miners)	3.91	4.95	1.26
Clerical	3.96	5.20	1.30
Sales	4.83	6.70	1.39
Service	3.61	3.81	1.06
Laborers (including loggers and fishermen, including farm laborers and miners)	2.53	3.43	1.35

[a] Mean annual earnings of males 25–64 years of age.
[b] Canadian nonfarm labor force. Estimates, assuming that the relative change of average per capita earnings of each group between 1959 and the 1960-61 census year was equal to the change in average per capita labor income during the same period, which was 1.87%.
[c] U.S. experienced labor force.
[d] The U.S. data include junior colleges and institutions in the southern states.
Sources: D.B.S., *Census of Canada 1961*, "Population Sample: Incomes of Individuals," Bulletin 4.1–2, Table B6; U.S., Department of Commerce, *United States Census of Population, 1960*, "Occupation by Earnings and Education," PC(2)-7B, Table 1. The exchange rate in 1959 averaged at U.S. $1 = Can. $0.959, Bank of Canada, *Statistical Summary*.

sufficiently higher to attract a larger southward migration nor to check the northward flow. The extent of the difference may be important. A crude comparison of average earnings – unadjusted for differences in price levels[9] or for the different patterns of expenditure which a migrant incurs in adapting to a society with its own pattern of goods available for consumption, customary patterns of expenditure, and climate – shows a pattern of differences which are relatively smaller for the scientific and professional groups which have shown the fastest increases in migration between the two countries (Table 6).

The gap in incomes has become narrower since the war, for most workers, but whether it is a cause or an effect of increased mobility between the two countries is not clear. The narrowing of the gap is also associated with a more rapid increase in the capital-labor ratio in Canada.[10] Scientific and professional earnings, however, appear, on the basis of a few scraps of evidence, to have risen at about the same rate in Canada and the United States, except for university teachers, whose earnings widen the gap.[11] At present the size of the migration movements is still small compared with the two labor forces, especially in the United States, and are thus unlikely to have much effect upon relative earnings.

The extent of opportunities for employment, especially of a specialized nature, may be a more important factor in the development of increased migration between Canada and the United States in view of the growth of the labor forces on both sides of the border. For example, the movement of engineers to the United States, which is large compared with other occupations, appears to be associated with a relatively small difference in earnings, and with a much larger field of employment: engineers in the United States constitute 1.3 percent of a much larger labor force, compared with 0.7 percent in Canada. Conversely, the net movement of university teachers into Canada appears to be induced by the growth of employment opportunities in Canadian universities, which is about two and a half times as fast as in the United States and also large in relation to the domestic supply of university teachers, whereas university salaries are lower in Canada and rising less rapidly.

The suggestion that the extent and character of employment possibilities are a key factor in migration, especially of scientific and professional workers, must remain in the status of a tentative hypothesis. Limitations of space prevent the subject from receiving the attention that it appears to deserve as one of the more important developments in the social and economic life of Canada and the United States.

Footnotes

1. C. Freeman and A. Young, *The Research and Development Effort in Western Europe, North America, and the Soviet Union*. Paris: Organization for European Co-operation and Development, 1965, Table 9, p. 76.

2. For example, L. Parai, *Immigration and Emigration of Professional and Skilled Manpower during the Postwar Period*, Special Study No. 1, Economic Council of Canada. Ottawa: Queen's Printer, n.d., p. 34, sgg.

3. Canadian data on returning residents do not include returning residents who are citizens of other countries than Canada or Britain, and they are re-enumerated as immigrants.

4. *Canada Year Books*, quoted in L. Parai, *op. cit.*, p. 219.

5. Since the occupations of the emigrants are those which they declare an intention to pursue, there is probably an unknown amount of upward subjective bias.

6. D. Dyck, "The Geographic Mobility of the 1955 University Graduates from Science and Engineering Courses in Canada," to be published. I thank my colleague for making some of the data available for this paper.

7. Edward F. Sheffield, "The Migration of High-Level Manpower to and from Canada," unpublished. The study dealt with members of the teaching staffs of Canadian universities and colleges who left Canada and with those who entered Canada to accept university teaching appointments. The effective samples were 70 percent, 71 percent, and 93 percent of university teachers in Canada in the three years, respectively.

8. Herbert B. Grubel and Anthony Scott, "The International Flow of Human Capital," *American Economic Review*, 56, No. 2, May, 1966, pp. 268-274.

9. A study in progress by the Dominion Bureau of Statistics indicates that the average price levels in Canada and the United States (expressed in domestic dollars) are fairly close together, that is, the difference between the two levels is indicated by the exchange rate, *vide* Economic Council of Canada, *Second Annual Review*, Ottawa, 1965, p. 54.

10. Economic Council of Canada, *op. cit.*, Tables 3-7, p. 66.

11. Canadian Association of University Teachers, *Bulletin*, 14, No. 3, February, 1964, p. 38.

The Migration of Canadian-Born Between Canada and the United States of America 1955 to 1968[*]

T. J. Samuel

Brain Drain

Finally, the *brain drain* issue may be considered briefly since this usually the context that provokes a discussion on the population movements between Canada and the U.S. Brains have always shown a tendency to go where they feel they are appreciated. Canadians are no exception.

In modern terminology, however, discussions often center around the words *brain drain* or *brain gain*. These terms imply that the large scale emigration/immigration of certain groups of people in the labour force will have an unfavourable/favourable effect on the economic and social development of the country. This assumption is neither universally valid for all countries nor uniformly applicable to the same country at different points of time. Its validity rests on the economic and social development attained by the country concerned, the degree and level of utilization of the "brains," the destination of these migrants, the type of contact they maintain with the former country and their accomplishments in their country of adoption.

Countries worried about the *brain drain*, often ignore the *brain gain* that sometimes more than compensates, as in the case of Canada, for the loss. Commenting on the emigration from Canada to the U.S. of scientists and engineers equivalent to 29.8 percent of first-degree earners in science and engineering during 1957-61, Grubel and Scott observed: "These statistics are misleading in the case of Canada since they take account neither of the reflux from the United States nor of the inflow from other countries into Canada, both of which are known to be substantial."[1] Louis Parai[2] and K. V. Pankhurst[3] also have pointed this out.

Even the assumption that a net loss of brains through migration is inimical to the welfare of the losing country is being questioned.[4] An immigrant's remittances to his former country, the possibility of influence being yielded by him in the country of adoption to the advantage of his former country, the chance that the emigrant's departure might highlight the handicaps he faced in the home country, and the overall increase in productivity such moves may cause, are some of the advantages attributed to the country supplying these professional emigrants. This point of view has not gone unchallenged, however.[5]

The above discussion is based mostly on the assumption of permanent migration. As was found in our study, however, part of the migration is only temporary, in the sense that a certain number return *home* after a period. On the debit side of such temporary migration is the loss to the Canadian economy from the failure

* "The Migration of Canadian-Born Between Canada and the United States of America, 1955 to 1968," by T. J. Samuel, Research Branch, Department of Manpower and Immigration, Chapter IX, "Brain Drain" and Chapter X, "Summary of Findings," pp. 41-43.

of these emigrants to contribute to the gross national product of Canada – both directly and indirectly. On the other hand, it is quite likely that the temporary migrant will return better equipped intellectually, socially and economically and that the education, training, experience, social outlook and attitude he obtains in the U.S. will enable him to better contribute to the future growth of the Canadian economy. "If such population movements are discouraged," warned Tom Kent, former deputy minister of Manpower and Immigration, "the interplay of knowledge and experience and resources between the two countries would inevitably be reduced in a great many ways."[6] Migration should not be conceptualized only as a response to economic opportunity. It can also be instrumental in creating economic opportunities.

It is an indisputable fact that human capital, like physical capital, is becoming increasingly mobile. In the absence of any physical controls, the circulation of human capital might, in the future, become quite significant. Such movement will be aided by the increasing trend towards professionalism in many occupations. Just as international trade enhances the efficient utilization of resources, international circulation of human capital is likely to do so in the realm of human resources. As suggested by Harry Johnson, "In the production and utilization of human talents, as in the production and utilization of commodities, self-sufficiency is likely to be far less efficient than international specialization and exchange."[7]

A certain amount of emigration of Canadian-born professionals to the U.S.A., therefore, even if it is not affected by the recent introduction of controls, need not be viewed with undue alarm. Perhaps such movement may be more aptly described as *brain trade* or *brain exchange* rather than as *brain drain* or *brain gain*. In this process of *brain trade*, the U.S.A. had a surplus in 1961-65 to the extent of about 2,000 a year. This dwindled to less than 500 in 1966. In 1967 Canada had, perhaps for the first time in the history of migration between this country and the U.S., a surplus of over 500, and in 1968 over 1,000.[8] It appears that a net gain for Canada in this process of exchange of professionals may be considered a mixed blessing. The recent discussion on the implications of the increasing proportion of American teachers in Canadian universities is a case in point.[9]

Summary of Findings

To sum up the main findings of the study, it has been found that the emigration of Canadian-born to the U.S. has lost much of its significance as a drain on Canada's human resources. Fewer people are emigrating to the U.S., and of those who do, more are returning to Canada. The return migration has been around 35 percent of Canadian-born emigrants during the period 1955-60 and 40 percent in the period 1960-68. The net migration of Canadian-born to the U.S. was about 19,000 a year in 1955-59, and according to estimates the rate rose slightly to 20,000 in the period 1960-65 and fell to 16,000 in 1966-68.

An increasing proportion of professionals among the emigrants, greater cultural uniformity of recent emigrants, failure of many of them to raise their earnings to U.S. levels, and the social and political conditions in the U.S.A. may have induced higher rates of return migration. An increasing rate of return migration is also suggested by the declining proportion of Canadian-born opting for U.S.

citizenship. On the other hand, the imposition of legal barriers to entry into the U.S. and the increasing importance of climatic considerations might reduce the rate of return migration.

The principal characteristics of Canadian-born emigrants to the U.S. during the period 1955-59 were the following: the number of females exceeded the number of males; and they were better educated than the Canadian and U.S. population in general. Their earnings in the U.S., however, did not reflect the level of education they had attained. They did improve their earnings when compared with the earnings of the same age groups in Canada, but not as compared to the earnings of corresponding age groups among U.S. whites. Non-professionals, who formed the majority, were older and had a lower rate of return migration than professionals. Nearly half of the professionals who emigrated in the period 1955-59 had returned to Canada by 1960.

The push and pull factors causing migration are found to be applicable to both emigration and return migration. It is suggested that the non-economic factors are more important for professionals than for non-professionals.

The *brain drain* could be better understood if considered as a process of exchange of brains, or *brain trade* mutually beneficial to both Canada and the U.S.A. rather than a *drain* or *gain*. Even if looked at from the viewpoint of *drain* or *gain*, Canada is currently having a net *gain* of brains from the U.S.A.

Footnotes

1. H. G. Grubel and A. D. Scott, "The Immigration of Scientists and Engineers to the United States, 1949-61," *Journal of Political Economy*, LXXIV: 4, August, 1966, p. 373.
2. Louis Parai, *Immigration and Emigration of Professional and Skilled Manpower during the Postwar Period*, Special Study No. 1, Economic Council of Canada. Ottawa: Queen's Printer, p. 34.
3. K. V. Pankhurst, "Migration Between Canada and the United States," *The Annals of the American Academy of Political and Social Science*, 367, September, 1966, p. 57.
4. Herbert Grubel and Anthony D. Scott, "The International Flow of Human Capital," *Proceedings of the American Economic Association*, 1966, p. 273.
5. Thomas Brinley, *The International Circulation of Human Capital*, pp. 490-493.
6. Speech delivered by Tom Kent in Alberta on the Second Centenary Week of University of Alberta, *The Globe and Mail*, March 8, 1967, p. 29.
7. Harry Johnson, "The Economics of the Brain Drain: The Canadian Case," *Minerva*, III, No. 3, Spring, 1965.
8. Department of Justice, *Annual Reports of the Immigration and Naturalization Service*, 1964-68; Department of Manpower and Immigration, *Immigration Statistics*, 1964-68 and Louis Parai, *loc. cit.*, p. 204.
9. It has been alleged that American professors are *taking over* Canadian universities and in particular social sciences and humanities faculties thereby threatening the development of Canadian culture. Patricia Welbourn, "Made in U.S.A.," *The Ottawa Journal Weekend Magazine*, March 22, 1969, pp. 2-6.

The Universities: Takeover of the Mind[*]

James Steele and Robin Mathews

Foreign scholars are always welcome in Canadian universities. Nevertheless, it is a matter of concern that in recent years the proportion of Canadians on academic faculties has been diminishing rapidly. In 1963 approximately 539 university teachers immigrated to Canada; in 1965, 1,048 entered the country; by 1967 the annual number rose to 1,986, a figure which represented some 12 percent of the total number of university teachers in Canada that year.[1] Of these, some 857 came from the United States, 457 from Great Britain, 100 from India, and the remainder from other countries. In 1968 Canadian universities employed about 2,642 additional faculty.[2] Of that number the vast majority were non-Canadians; 1,013 entered from the United States, 545 from Great Britain, and 722 from other countries. Thus it appears that only about 362 Canadians have been hired. Statistics describing precisely the cumulative effect of this influx on the citizenship composition of each and every Canadian university faculty do not exist. Nevertheless, certain related information may be considered roughly indicative of what has happened.

An analysis of 1961 census data has shown that of Canada's 8,779 male university professors, 2,238, or 25.5 percent, were foreign born, and 6,541 or at least 74.5 percent were Canadian born and therefore probably Canadian citizens.[3] Mr Max Von Zur Meuhlen of the Economic Council of Canada discovered through a survey of the 1967 arts and science calendars of fifteen Canadian universities[4] that, of the two-thirds of those faculty members in non-professional disciplines for whom a first degree was listed, 51 percent obtained their first degree outside of Canada. This percentage is a rough indication of the citizenship composition of those faculties.[5] Thus there is evidence for believing that the proportion of Canadians in Canadian universities has diminished by about 25 percent between 1961 and 1968, a change which has probably occurred for the most part since 1965 when the number of scholars immigrating to Canada began to rise sharply.

Information from particular campuses has not been gathered yet in a complete or consistent way. But first studies bear out the gravity of the situation. A survey conducted at Simon Fraser University in 1967-8 shows that 68 percent of faculty in professorial ranks were not Canadian citizens. A similar survey conducted by the University of Alberta[6] reveals that 60.8 percent of full-time faculty in 1961-2 were Canadian. By 1968-9, the proportion had dropped to 47.2 percent. In a study made by the University of Waterloo information services,[7] it is estimated that in 1964 about 68 percent of faculty were Canadian. By 1968 the proportion had declined to about 57 percent. The figures for the Faculty of Arts at Waterloo, however, are more alarming. In 1964-5, about 60 percent of Arts faculty members were Canadian. By 1969 the proportion had dropped to about 49 percent.

Intensive study of disciplines and departments throughout Canada must be undertaken if we are to gain a full understanding of the relations that exist

*Reprinted from *Close the 49th Parallel, etc.: The Americanization of Canada*, edited by Ian Lumsden, by permission of University of Toronto Press, © University of Toronto Press 1970.

between citizenship of faculty, citizenship of graduate students, course offerings in general, and attitudes towards Canadian information. But early studies here also give some indication of a relation between the paucity of Canadian material available and the heavy participation of non-Canadian scholars. A survey done by Michael Kennedy[8] reveals that in 1968-9 at the University of Alberta, the Sociology Department, made up of nineteen non-Canadians and four Canadians by calendar count, offered seventy-nine undergraduate and graduate courses, only one of which is described in the calendar as pertaining to Canada. In the Political Science Department, with six of thirteen staff members Canadian, sixty-six courses were offered, seven concerned with Canadian matters. Only two of these courses dealing with Canadian particularities were offered to undergraduates.

At the University of Waterloo a similar situation was found.[9] An examination by calendar of the citizenship composition of the Departments of Economics, English, Fine Arts, History, Philosophy, Political Science, Psychology, and Sociology/Anthropology revealed that every chairman was a US citizen, that a minority of full professors were Canadian, while about half were US citizens. In the Sociology Department, with about six Canadians among the twenty members, sixty-two undergraduate and graduate courses are offered. None is described in the calendar as dealing with Canadian problems. In the Department of English only two courses in Canadian literature are listed among the ninety or so undergraduate and graduate courses offered.

In the Political Science Department of Laurentian University, Sudbury,[10] with one Canadian in five members, only a half course is offered on Canadian government. The English Department, with three Canadians of ten members, offers no Canadian literature. The Geography Department, with two Canadians of five members, offered no Canadian geography in the last two years but will begin to do so in 1969-70. The evidence indicates that the proportion of non-Canadians on faculty affects the offerings involving Canadian material.[11]

Departments of History, English, Political Science, and Sociology give some indication of departmental interest in matters pertaining to Canada, because they are able to offer courses with an ostensibly Canadian content. One can only speculate, however, about departments less observable. What, for example, is the interest in Canadian particularities of the Psychology Department at Simon Fraser University, which on January 1, 1969 had fifteen members, thirteen of whom were non-Canadian, ten of whom were US citizens?

Clearly the statistics of the issue are of critical importance. At the simplest level they suggest that too few Canadians are being urged to excellence, are being helped to continue study, or are being hired when qualified personnel are sought for positions in the universities. Wherever the failure lies, the decline in the proportion of Canadians reveals discrimination against Canadians, a failure to make opportunities available to them, and so a breach of public trust. But Canadians do not suffer discrimination in employment alone. The figures which suggest that Canadians are presently in a minority and that Canadians are being employed in a decreasing ratio indicate root and branch discrimination against able Canadian students and against the community which makes possible Canada's higher educational institutions.

That is another way of saying that there has been, in the last decade, a dramatic failure of planning, co-ordination, and administration on the part of departments of education, senior administrators in education, and national organizations concerned with the welfare and operation of the universities. Moreover, the statistics reveal a demoralized concept of Canada held by those groups; for no self-respecting country in the world would permit itself, willingly, to fall into the condition that Canada presently suffers in its institutions of higher learning. The situations described at Alberta, Waterloo, and Laurentian, for example, result in large measure from the diminishment of the number of Canadians on staff and the increase of non-Canadians who are often seriously ignorant of the Canadian fact.

The condition must be seen in the broader context of Americanization of the country on a number of levels. We know that Canadians suffer more invasion by US media than almost any other country in the world. We know that Canada is smothering from US economic takeover. We know that some US *international* unions have for decades been eating at the heart and spirit of Canadian unionism.[12] We know that Canadian students at all levels are strongly influenced by US educational texts and materials.[13] And we know that studies of critical importance to the understanding of Canada – of critical importance, moreover, to the maintenance of academically self-respecting university communities – often are totally lacking or shabbily and superficially treated outside the mainstream of *important* material. We are presently conferring degrees upon Canadian students who are often so ignorant of their own country that they are a disgrace to it, and an indictment of the degree granting institutions from which they come.

More than in any other country, because of the proximity of the United States and its often oppressive influence on many aspects of Canadian life, studies in the Canadian experience should be available to every Canadian student in the fullest range and at the highest academic level possible.

It is sometimes argued that US citizens are present in the Canadian universities in a proportion of about 15 to 20 percent, and so are not a significant part of the Americanization of Canada. Without for a moment underestimating the serious threat of concentration by any non-Canadian group in Canadian educational life, the unique quality of US participation must be seen clearly for what it is, in relation to the conditioning of the US academic himself and to the general deluge of Americanization in Canada.

As the examples from Laurentian, Waterloo, and Alberta show, the concentration of US citizens in certain disciplines affects course offerings. Moreover, it affects the disposition and direction of what superficially seem to be studies not necessarily related to national consciousness. One of the few examinations of work produced by students in an area of US faculty concentration is that of Professor J. Laurence Black. His information is frightening:

> . . . let me cite a case referred to me by a marker for a first year course at my university, Laurentian (and I am using Laurentian University here simply as a typical example; I assume it is no better or worse than other Canadian universities in this regard). Some 260 students in this course were required to prepare a term essay on one of several topics. Of 50 students who attempted an essay on *race relations*, almost half treated the problems faced by the American negro. Only 5 dealt with distinctly Canadian racial difficulties: three with the Indian in Canada, two with the negro in Halifax. Some, but not many, mentioned the French-English dialogue but only one felt this was important enough to treat it separately. . . . Most of those who wrote on ethnic minorities and

immigration limited themselves to studies on large American cities. Of more than 100 essays on the family, nearly all parrotted their American texts on the suburban family in the United States – only four spoke of the Canadian family. A large number described bureaucracy in the United States and gave the impression that we cannot even develop our own ideology – in many there were comparisons made with the bureaucracy in the Soviet Union, often quite irrelevantly and inevitably to show that their system was worse than the American one. The most devastating blow to my Canadianism, however, was the fact that several Canadian students used the terms *my*, *ours*, *us*, when they were actually referring to the United States. There are no Canadian faculty members in that particular Department.[14]

The attitude that invites Canadians to consider US information as *universal, non-nationalistic, cosmopolitan*, is a product of US nationalism and *manifest destiny*, linked intricately to the so-called *objective* ideology of the behavioural sciences. Intensively preconditioned to believe that US information is un-coloured by *petty nationalism*, some US citizens and intellectually colonialized Canadians come to the point of being able to say, as a US writer did recently in *Canadian Dimension*: "The United States has a long past in training university personnel, but American scholars are not bringing American culture with them but the accumulation of world knowledge. If Canadians want home-grown propagandists, that is their affair, but the ensuing result should not be called universities."[15] This naïvely universalist attitude is characteristic of many, though not all, US citizens exerting power or forming groups in the Canadian university. The outcome is clearly observable.

The general flood of Americanization in Canada has resulted in colonial-mindedness among many Canadians. They appear to believe US citizens are superior administrators. How else, for instance, could one explain the fact that in 1968-9, the dean of arts, the two associate deans of arts, and the deputy dean of arts at Waterloo University were all US citizens? Colonial-minded Canadians, unfortunately, assist US citizens to Americanize Canadian universities. American hiring centres are visited; Canadian applicants lose out. American graduate qualifications are applied; Canadian graduate students lose out. US ideas of *significant* information are applied; Canadian studies lose out. Even worse, through the failure to advertise openings consistently and demonstrably in Canada Canadians have been automatically excluded. The failure is not simply one of carelessness or disorganization. It is to some extent an effect of psychological Americanization. To go to the US hiring centres and procure US citizens, without regard for Canada and Canadian needs, guarantees *excellence, the highest standards, the latest information* – which many US citizens and colonial-minded Canadians believe to be unavailable in Canada.

By far the largest proportion of foreign scholars recently entering the Canadian universities have come from the United States. Canadian universities are becoming Americanized in direct relation to the number of US citizens present, *the number of Canadians absent*, and the increasing influence of Americanization in other sectors of Canadian life.

Professor Allan Smith of the History Department at the University of British Columbia, unequivocally describes the situation:

> For Canada cosmopolitanism and internationalism mean, in fact, conti-nentalism. Opening our frontiers to the world means in practise opening

them to the United States. A policy of cultural laissez-faire means, *not* that we subject ourselves to a wide variety of ideas emanating from a host of different sources bearing in upon us with equal intensity. Inevitably, owing to the sheer size and weight and proximity of the American cultural establishment, it means that we are subjected to one set of ideas emanating from one source. The open door is acceptable, and even desirable, but to leave it wide open would make Canada's cultural and intellectual life a mirror image of the American, instead of the proximate reflection it is now. Canadians, like Holmes' man in the crowded theatre, are compelled to apply their principles with circumspection, owing to the situation in which they find themselves.[16]

Finally, a very clear indication of the kind of nationalism felt by US scholars in Canada is revealed in the study by David Brown and James MacKinnon. Their examination of political scientists in Canada led them to make the following observations:

> Presumably, non-Canadians who have come to Canada with the intention of becoming Canadians will gradually come to look at politics in ways that are relevant to Canadian students. But our results show that most immigrant professors do not intend to become Canadians. Fewer than one-third are engaged in research on Canadian problems; two-thirds of Canadians are. Fewer than 30 percent of the Americans who replied believe they will be teaching here in 10 years' time. Ninety percent do not intend to become Canadian citizens. By contrast nearly half of those of other nationalities plan to become citizens.[17]

Americanization exists at a number of levels: in numbers and attitudes of faculty, in course offerings, in ideological orientation of studies, in hiring procedures and preferences, in the failure of concern about the limited opportunities for Canadian students. A change of heart is necessary in Canadian higher education. But it needs to be prepared for. Governments should take some first steps to set the Canadian university on the road to recovery, and Canadianization. They must pass legislation to ensure reasonable and consistent advertising in Canada of all new positions in Canadian universities. They must also insist, by legislation, that Canadian citizens administer the Canadian universities. To that end they should legislate that Canadian citizenship be made a necessary qualification for all new appointments to administrative positions from chairman to chancellor inclusive. They must strive more effectively than in the past to bring Canadians back to Canada. Complaints are continually made that Canadians of excellence are helped in no serious way to repatriate when they leave Canada to study or work. Moreover, in order to give greater incentive to Canadian scholars, governments must re-examine their policies of awards. And they must pass legislation of a hortatory nature, calling upon universities to strive as a general policy to employ Canadians of excellence in order to ensure that Canadians remain or eventually become a clear two-thirds majority of full-time faculty members in each department.

Such legislation would form the basis for the development of universities sensitive to the aspirations of the Canadian community. And with respect for non-Canadian scholars, Canadian universities would soon begin to demonstrate a full and proper regard for the Canadian student and a concerned awareness of the particular problems and needs of the Canadian community. Without such a change in direction, no one can hazard a guess as to what will happen as the university in Canada becomes increasingly irrelevant to Canadian life, and as the Canadian people become increasingly aware of its irrelevance.

Footnotes

1. Not every immigrant intending to be a university teacher would have found employment as such, but the Department of Manpower and Immigration affirms that the correlation is very high. Any discrepancy here would tend to be counterbalanced by other factors. For example, those who entered Canada to teach as "non-immigrant visitors" are not represented at all in these immigration figures. For an authoritative discussion of the reliability of this correlation see Louis Parai, *Immigration and Emigration*, pp. 95-97.

2. This is our estimate. It includes the net increase of 2,287 reported by the Dominion Bureau of Statistics and an allowance for *turnover* owing to deaths, retirements from the profession, and emigration, at the rate of 2.1 percent of the previous year's total faculty population of 16,378.

3. L. Parai, *Immigration and Emigration of Professional and Skilled Manpower During the Post-War Period*, Special Study No. 1, Economic Council of Canada, Ottawa, 1965, p. 224.

4. Acadia, Dalhousie, St. Francis Xavier, Memorial, Sir George Williams, Trent, Mc-Master, Waterloo, Western Ontario, Laurentian, York, Victoria, Calgary, Manitoba, British Columbia.

5. There are several biases in the figure which would tend to cancel each other out. Foreign faculty members who took their first degree in Canada were counted as Canadians; Canadian faculty who took their first degree abroad were counted as foreign. The proportion of foreign faculty among the one-third of faculty members for whom no first degree was listed was probably larger than among those whose first degree was known, because the first degree or its equivalent is not as common in Europe as in Canada.

6. "Analysis of Full-time Faculty at the University of Alberta − By Country of Birth," in Robin Mathews, Cyril Byrne, and Kenneth McKinnon, "The University of Waterloo: A Special Study," presented to the Minister of University Affairs *et al.*, August, 1969, Appendix, Item One.

7. "Waterloo's Faculty and the 'Non-Canadian Controversy'," Waterloo *Gazette*, June 4, 1969.

8. "Number of Canadian Courses and Canadian Teachers in the Department of Political Science, Sociology, History, and Psychology at the University of Alberta (1968-9)," in Mathews, Byrne, and McKinnon, "The University of Waterloo," Appendix, Items 2a and 2b.

9. Mathews, Byrne and McKinnon, "The University of Waterloo."

10. J. Laurence Black, "Americans in Canadian Universities, II," *Laurentian University Review*, 2, No. 4, June, 1969, p. 111.

11. At Winnipeg University, for example, the only Canadian on the Political Science Department there resolved to use two U.S. and three Canadian texts instead of four out of five U.S. texts for an introductory Political Science course in 1969-70. Professor Rodgers gave his department chairman written notice of the new list. In the fall some one hundred and twenty students unanimously approved of the change for their course. Professor Rodgers received a letter from the chairman of his department on September 15, "insisting I use the four out of five American texts or else face 'disciplinary steps'." R. S. Rodgers, Letter to the Editor, *Uniter*, Winnipeg University, September 29, 1959, p. 13.

12. Charles Lipton, *The Trade Union Movement of Canada: 1827-1959*, Montreal, 1966.

13. Kenn Johnson, "This Courier Investigation Indicates the Extent of U.S. Influence on Canada's Schools," *Educational Courier*, May, 1969, pp. 69-75.

14. "Americans in Canadian Universities, II," pp. 110-111.

15. David Rodnick, "Academic Chauvinism," *Canadian Dimension*, 6, No. 2, July, 1969, p. 2.

16. "An Open Letter on Nationalism and the Universities in Canada," no date, distributed personally.

17. "Teaching Canadians the American Way," *Globe and Mail*, Toronto, June 18, 1969.

2 Environment

A. Physical Environment

As we wrote in the preface to this volume, pessimists claim that man has already lost the battle to save the environment while optimists claim that man is on the verge of losing that battle. In Part A of this section, we examine pollution problems relating to the physical environment; specifically air, water, and noise. We also attempt to show that the roots of such problems are not only economic, but also political and social in nature. While we have attempted to focus on problems that are particularly Canadian, it is clear from our selections that pollution knows no political boundaries and that it is impossible to entirely disassociate Canada's environmental problems from those of border areas in the United States.

In the first article of this section, "The Ecological Facts of Life," Commoner provides a succinct summary of the interrelated biological processes that constitute the earth's ecosystem. He goes on to argue that modern technology has undermined the stability of the ecosystem, which is essential to the survival of all living things. "Modern technologies act on the ecosystem which supports us in ways that threaten its stability; with tragic perversity, we have linked much of our productive economy to precisely those features of technology which are ecologically destructive."

"The Poison Makers" relates the political situation to the pollution problem. Should we expect the federal government to take a leadership position in the solution of the environmental crisis? Governments have in fact passed laws but they are often slow to enforce them. The "right" of people or agencies to pollute has not been denied. According to this article, no piecemeal activity can hope to be successful. A systems approach must be employed that recognizes all elements of the ecological world as interdependent and that international cooperation is essential if pollution is to be controlled. The important factor in bringing this type of total political involvement to fruition is education in its broadest sense. With many people informed as to the dangers of pollution, pressures can be brought to bear on the political institution. Ultimately, according to Lawrence, each individual must make a commitment that he will be responsible for solving the pollution crisis.

The third article, "Who Will Save the Great Lakes?" is a specific example of a pollution problem that affects large numbers of Canadian residents. Again, a basic question is formulated. Is it possible to clean up the Great Lakes?

If possible, who will undertake the job? The article describes the polluted condition of all the lakes, even Lake Superior to some extent. There is no question that the lakes and the society that depends on them are in trouble. The original question posed in the article is left unanswered. The time to act is now, but who will be the initiator of that action?

An International Joint Commission composed of the United States and Canada has attempted to deal with some of these questions about pollution. In 1965, the report on "Pollution of Rainy River and Lake of the Woods" was issued by this Commission. The area is one of the most beautiful in North America, used by both industry and recreation. It was found that "the waters of Rainy River are being polluted on each side of the international boundary to an extent that is injurious to property and a hazard to health." The pollution comes from pulp and paper mills together with municipality wastes, and thus the Commission recommended that these industries and towns be required to install pollution control facilities. Whether such specific types of cooperative programmes will be successful in the long run remains to be seen.

Water pollution is a major problem, but it is not the only resource that requires pollution control. In "Air Pollution," the Conservation Council of Ontario discusses some of the problems that relate to man's contamination of the air. Air pollution has been associated with many kinds of respiratory diseases, and also to degenerative processes such as cancer of the lungs. Almost all air pollution results from the burning of fuels in one form or another, and the conventional solution to the problem has been to develop a process that would permit a more complete combustion of fuels (that is, the electric car or perhaps "lead-free" gasolines). We know that automobiles account for over 50 percent of the air pollution in our major cities and it is here that the most urgent action is needed. We are putting too much contamination into the air for natural wind currents to dissipate, thus we must begin to take remedial steps to eliminate pollution at its source. This requires improved technology, continuing research, and most of all, public concern. If an awareness of the problem is present and there is pressure exerted by large numbers of people, then the first step to a solution has been taken.

Although most of us recognise water and air pollution as issues that must one day be resolved, we seldom think about a less tangible form of pollution, excessive noise. The article "Talk Louder I Can't Hear You," describes the health problems associated with the amount of noise that is present in our daily environments: "Damage to ear . . . begins at 85 decibels. . . . The average decibel count in urban areas is about 75. It is increasing at the rate of one decibel per year. This means that everyone will be completely deaf by the year 2,000." While the logic is not inexorable, the point is made clearly.

According to Foreman, "Noise Pollution in Modern Day Society," noise may be defined as "unwanted sound." Essentially, it is an energy waste product much like the other forms of pollution. Noise contributes not only to possible loss of hearing, but also to a whole range of other physical as well as psychological conditions. Hence the personal and societal ramifications of such disturbances can be extremely serious. After elaborating on the major aspects of noise pollution, Foreman outlines some possible directions that solutions might take, and in the process cites current legislative attempts to deal with excessive noise.

Given this information about pollutants of the physical environment, what can be done? In "The People vs. Pollution," Courtney Tower documents what some people are doing both with and without official support. For example, Pollution Probe obtained a national 90 percent ban on DDT. A Toronto organization is preparing strategies for all Canadian governments to use against pollution. SPEC (Society for Pollution and Environmental Control) is active in British Columbia in bringing information to the public. TV stars, the mass media, housewives, workers – many segments in the society – are voicing their opposition to the continuing pollution trend.

B. Social Environment

We have chosen to focus primarily on social environment issues as they relate to urban areas in Canada. This is not to say that problems such as poverty, housing, and unemployment do not apply to rural areas (we do have some data concerning rural Canada), only that the magnitude of the problems and the numbers of people affected are far greater on the urban scene. Contrary to many popular conceptions of the Canadian settlement pattern, we are one of the world's most urban nations. The 1971 census will show that some 75 percent of Canada's people live in urban areas. This is, for example, a higher proportion of urban residents than can be found in a majority of industrialized countries, including the United States. In addition, approximately 50 percent of all Canadians live in major metropolitan areas and nearly 25 percent in the two major urban centres of Montreal and Toronto.

The first article in this section, "The Urbanization of Canada" by Leroy Stone, does not amplify any particular problem, but it does provide a thorough description of the historical trend toward urbanization in Canada. The degree of urbanization has doubled since 1900 and every region was at least 50 percent urbanized by 1961. The largest growth rates in the past two decades have been in *suburbia*. The metropolitan areas have spread out, resulting in transportation complexities and taxation losses to the central cities. Migration rates into the metropolitan areas remain high and the effects of population redistribution will be important causal factors as to the kind of society Canada will be in the future.

One of the major social issues that Canada will have to face in the 1970's is the prevalence of poverty, particularly in the urban cores. The first of two Senate Committee Reports on poverty discusses the situation as it affects the country as a whole. According to the chairman of the session, Mr. Croll, four and one-half million people are considered poverty stricken. Half of this group is made up of the disadvantaged: the aged, the sick, the disabled; while the other half consists of the working poor. They are employed, but they do not earn enough income to rise above the objective conditions of poverty. According to Croll, welfare programmes are not adequate, and he recommends that the total system be scrapped and a new start made. The most equitable solution is adequate employment, but if certain types of employment are not sufficient to provide the necessary incomes needed to avoid poverty, then there needs to be a national minimum level of income.

The Privy Council provides personal insights by discussing particular individuals who must face poverty and its effects every day. Perhaps the major contribution of this short article is that it reiterates the notion that poverty is a cycle, a culture, a treadmill that goes on and on. "If we draw a profile of a Canadian living in poverty, he looks like this: He lives in a substandard, crowded home; he has a poor education; his health is bad; his income is low; and as for the stream of Canadian life – socially, economically, politically, culturally, he's not with it. His living conditions are bad because his income is low. His education is poor, probably because he came from a poor home. His health is bad because his living conditions are bad and always have been bad. His income is low because he has poor health and a poor education."

The final selection examining poverty is another Special Senate Committee Report which is a brief submitted by the Government of Manitoba on the "Social Development Approach to Poverty." Poverty can be understood more fully when examined not as an individual phenomenon, but as a deficiency in the total social order. Poverty is "a function of the dispersion range in the distribution of both wealth and power in today's society." An attack on poverty not only involves providing a sufficient income, but also changing the process by which the income is provided. Poverty is not the *fault* of the people who are poor, but rather the system is a function to which their lives are oriented. A guaranteed annual income is seen as only one aspect of the fight against poverty, and it is not an instrument that initiates wealth redistributions. The major factor in the struggle to eliminate poverty is a reconstitution of the social order (through taxes perhaps) so that income disparities are not so widespread, regardless of what level they assume.

A number of times in the preceding papers about poverty, the importance of housing in relation to the poor, especially in the cities, was highlighted. The next three articles in this volume describe the housing problem in Canada. Albert Rose's article "Their Own Fault" carries a rather facetious title that indicates that the inadequacy of housing is the *fault* of the people themselves. Actually, he sees the primary *fault* in the community that perpetuates poverty by not providing sufficient incomes, even for the people who do work. Although this piece was written in the late 1950's, the insights into inadequate housing issues are still relevant today.

The final two selections on housing are taken from the Federal Task Force on Housing and Urban Development, headed by Paul Hellyer. The first selection, "Impressions," describes the overall setting of housing patterns throughout Canada. Particularly in the urban areas they find that much of what is going on, even in housing development, is haphazard and does not follow any adequate overall plan. "No Task Force impression is more vivid of mind or depressing of spirit than those formed amid the blight and slum of Canada's larger cities." A sense of urgency in facing up to the urban housing problem is what is most needed. The necessity to act while action is still possible is the overall *impression*. While members of the Task Force found that action is being taken, they feel that it is not as well planned or comprehensive as it needs to be.

The second section from the Hellyer Task Force Report provides recommendations for "Social Housing and Special Programs" and "Urban Development." First of all, the government should finance extensive research into the social and psychological ramifications of public housing. The Task Force implies that there is a lack of community development or involvement in such projects; that they form the basis of an antiseptic and sterile existence. As an alternative, the

Task Force recommends that consideration be given to income supplements that would enable low income families to purchase their own homes. Finally, they recommend that special attention should be given to the housing problems of Canada's native peoples.

On programmes of urban development, the Task Force takes the position that only through regional programmes can urban planning be accomplished effectively. The report also takes a strong stand on property ownership. "Where necessary, municipalities revise property assessment practices to encourage, rather than penalize, the maintenance and improvement of residential properties by the private owners." If minimum standards are not complied with, then the owners should be required to destroy the premises at their own expense. It becomes the responsibility of the Canadian governments to show initiative in planning housing facilities that meet the needs of the Canadian people.

The final article in the Social Environment section is "Unemployment in Canada" by Sylvia Ostry. Throughout, she is concerned with the characteristics of the unemployed, regardless of the total level of unemployment. In Canada, females tend to have lower rates of unemployment than males, primarily because females are generally in sectors of the economy "less susceptible to unemployment," but also because Canadian women are less likely to remain in the market looking for work after they lose a job.

In general, the older the person, the less likely he is to be unemployed. Single people have higher unemployment rates than any other marital status group. This is partially a reflection of the age composition of this group but not entirely so (see Table 6). In fact, when age is controlled for, unemployment rates of single females are generally lower than for other groups.

Unemployment rates by occupational status indicate that white collar people are less likely to be out of a job than any other group, while labourers have the highest rates of unemployment. Unemployment duration also varies by age, sex, and occupation, and long duration periods are especially severe for unskilled workers. Regional variations are also discussed, with the Maritimes in general and Newfoundland specifically showing the highest rates of unemployment.

In conclusion, the physical and social environmental issues that confront Canada in the 1970's are many, and they will require both hard work and patience to solve. By and large, the recognition of the issues is accomplished. The solutions may be much more difficult to realize.

The Ecological Facts of Life*

Barry Commoner

The ecological facts of life are grim. The survival of all living things – including man – depends on the integrity of the complex web of biological processes

*Reprinted from *No Deposit – No Return*, edited by Huey D. Johnson, published by Addison-Wesley Publishing Company, 1970, pp. 2-16. Used by permission of the author. Originally, a background paper prepared for the 13th National Conference of the U.S. National Commission for UNESCO, 1969. Reprinted in *No Deposit – No Return* with the permission of the U.S. National Commission for UNESCO.

which comprise the earth's ecosystem. However, what man is now doing on the earth violates this fundamental requisite of human existence. For modern technologies act on the ecosystem which supports us in ways that threaten its stability; with tragic perversity we have linked much of our productive economy to precisely those features of technology which are ecologically destructive.

These powerful, deeply entrenched relationships have locked us into a self-destructive course. If we are to break out of this suicidal track we must begin by learning the ecological facts of life. If we are to find the road to survival we must discover how to mold the technology to the necessities of nature, and learn how these constraints must temper the economic and social demands on technology. This, I believe, is the momentous task which now confronts mankind. . . .

It is the purpose of this contribution to provide some factual background to the foregoing assertions.

The Origin of the Ecosystem

The global ecosystem in which we now live is the product of several billion years of evolutionary change in the composition of the planet's skin. Following a series of remarkable geochemical events, about two billion years ago there appeared a form of matter, composed of elements common on the earth's surface, but organized in a manner which set it sharply apart from its antecedents – life. Themselves the products of several billion years of slow geochemical processes, the first living things became, in turn, powerful agents of geochemical change.

To begin with, they depleted the earth's previously accumulated store of the organic products of geochemical evolution, for this was their food. Converting much of this food into carbon dioxide, the earth's early life forms sufficiently increased the carbon dioxide content of the planet's atmosphere to raise the average temperature – through the "greenhouse" effect – to tropical levels. Later there appeared the first photosynthetic organisms, which reconverted carbon dioxide into the organic substances that are essential to all living metabolism. The rapid proliferation of green plants in the tropical temperature of the early earth soon reduced the carbon dioxide concentration of the atmosphere, thereby lowering the earth's temperature and depositing a huge mass of organic carbon which became in time the store of fossil fuels. And with the photosynthetic cleavage of water, the earth for the first time acquired free oxygen in its atmosphere. By shielding the earth's surface from solar ultraviolet radiation (through the concurrent appearance of ozone), this event enabled life to emerge from the protection of an original underwater habitat. With free oxygen available new, more efficient forms of living metabolism became possible and the great evolutionary outburst of proliferating species of plants and animals began to populate the planet. Meanwhile terrestrial plants and microorganisms converted the earth's early rocks into soil and developed within it a remarkably complex ecosystem; a similar system developed in surface waters. Taken together, these ecosystems control the composition of the soil, of surface waters and the air, and consequently regulate the weather.

There is an important lesson here. In the form in which it first appeared, the earth's life system had an inherently fatal fault: The energy it required was derived from the destruction of a nonrenewable resource, the geochemical store of organic matter. The primeval life-system became capable of continued existence only when, in the course of evolution, organisms appeared that converted carbon dioxide and inorganic salts to new organic matter – thus closing the loop and transforming what was a fatally linear process into a circular, self-perpetuating one. Here in its primitive form we see the grand scheme which has since been the basis of the remakable continuity of life: the reciprocal interdependence of one life process on another.

In the course of further evolution the variety of living things proliferated; new interactions became possible, greatly enriching the network of events. Cycles were built on cycles, forming at last a vast and intricate web, replete with branches, interconnections and alternate pathways; these are the bonds that link together the fate of all the numerous animals, plants, and microorganisms that inhabit the earth. This is the global ecosystem. It is a closed web of physical, chemical and biological processes created by living things, maintained by living things, and through the marvelous reciprocities of biological and geochemical evolution, uniquely essential to the support of living things.

The Basic Properties of the Ecosystem

We know enough about some parts of this vast system to delineate the fundamental properties of the whole. These properties define the requirements of any activity – including human society – which is to function successfully within the ecosystem of the earth.

Because they are fundamentally circular processes and subject to numerous feedback effects ecosystems exhibit nonlinear responses to changes in the intensity of any single factor. Consider, for example, the ecological processes which occur in surface waters, such as lakes and rivers. This is the cycle which links aquatic animals to their organic wastes; these wastes to the oxygen-requiring microorganisms that convert them into inorganic nitrate, phosphate and carbon dioxide; the inorganic nutrients to the algae which photosynthetically reconvert them into organic substances (thereby also adding to the oxygen content of the water and so providing support for the animals and the organisms of decay); and algal organic matter to the chain of animals which feed on it, thus completing the cycle.

Since it is a cyclical system with closed feedback loops, the kinetic properties of this ecosystem are strikingly nonlinear. If the load of organic waste imposed on the system becomes too great, the demand of the bacteria of decay for oxygen may exceed the limited oxygen content of the water. When the oxygen content falls to zero, the bacteria die, the biological cycle breaks down, and organic debris accumulates. A similar nonlinearity is observed in the growth of algae. If the nutrient level of the water becomes so great as to stimulate the rapid growth of algae, the dense algal population cannot be long sustained because of the intrinsic limitations of photosynthetic efficiency. As the thickness of the algal layer in the water increases, the light required for photosynthesis that can reach the lower parts of the algal layer becomes sharply diminished, so that any strong overgrowth of algae very quickly dies back, again releasing organic debris. These are relatively simple examples of the ubiquitous propensity of ecosystems for strongly nonlinear responses, for dramatic overgrowths and equally dramatic collapse.

Because the chemical events that occur in an ecosystem are driven by the meta-bolism of living things they are subject to the special constraints of biological chemistry. One important characteristic is that the rate of chemical reactions in living cells, being determined by the catalytic action of enzymes, is subject to the considerable specificity of enzymes for their substrates. Another feature is a consequence of the long course of evolutionary selection which has been at work in living things. Living cells are capable of carrying out an enormous variety of particular chemical reactions. What is remarkable, however, is that the number of different biochemical substances which are actually synthesized in living cells is *very much smaller* than the number of substances which could, in theory, be formed – given the types of reactions which can occur. Thus conditions suitable for the separate chemical reactions which give rise to both *dextro* and *levo* amino acids are present in cells – but because of the stereo-specificity of the relevant enzyme system only the synthesis of the *levo* forms occurs at an appreciable rate. Because of similar constraints, cells produce many fatty acids with even-numbered carbon chain lengths, but no fatty acids with odd numbers of carbons. Similarly, organic compounds which contain *no* groups are singularly lacking in living things.

Thus, living systems have had a long opportunity to, so to speak, try out the enormous variety of biochemical reactions that *could* take place in the cell. In effect, the biochemical constituents now found in living cells represent the survivors of this evolutionary trial, presumably selected for their compatibility with the essential features of the overall system of cellular metabolism. This situation is analogous to the tendency of genes found in current organisms to be maximally advantageous – i.e., that nearly all mutations to alternative genes are lethal. Therefore in the same sense, we can expect that the entry into an ecosystem of an organic reagent not normally found in living systems is likely to have deleterious effects on some living organisms.

The feedback characteristics of ecosystems result in amplification and inten-sification processes of considerable magnitude. The fact that in food chains small organisms are eaten by bigger ones and the latter by still bigger ones inevitably results in the concentration of certain environmental constituents in the bodies of the largest organisms at the top of the food chain. Smaller organ-isms always exhibit much higher metabolic rates than larger ones, so that the amount of their food which is oxidized relative to the amount incorporated into the body of the organism is thereby greater. Consequently, an animal at the top of the food chain depends on the consumption of an enormously greater mass of the bodies of organisms lower down in the food chain. Therefore, any *non*-metabolized material present in the lower organisms of this chain will be-come concentrated in the body of the top one.

Because of the circularity of ecosystems and their complex branching patterns, the behavior of any given living member of the system is dependent on the behavior of many others. The specific relationships are varied: one organism may provide food for another; one organism may parasitize and kill another; two organisms may cooperate so closely in their livelihood as to become totally dependent on each other. As a result of such relationships, a change in the population of any one organism is likely to have powerful effects on other populations. Because of these numerous interconnections, a singular cause and effect relationship is rare. Instead a given intrusion on an ecosystem is likely to have effects which spread out in an ever-widening circle from its original source, affecting organisms and parts of the environment often very remote from the initial point of intrusion.

The stability of an ecosystem is achieved by a complex network of dynamic equilibria which permits alternative relationships to develop when any particular link in the network becomes inoperative. In a very simple form, this relationship is illustrated by a common farmyard practice. The farmer who wishes to maintain cats in order to control mice will provide for the cats an alternative source of food, in the form of a doorstep dish of milk. Otherwise, the cats might kill so many mice as to run out of food; they would then leave the farm in search of richer fields, if it were not for the milk on the doorstep. There is an increasing body of more sophisticated evidence to support the generalization that the stability of an ecosystem depends closely on its degree of complexity, on the fineness of the ecological web.

The cyclical processes of an ecosystem operate at an overall rate which is determined by the intricate coupling of the numerous separate events that constitute the whole. One result is that the ecosystem web has a kind of natural resonance frequency which may become evident in periodic fluctuation in a particular population of organisms – for example, seven-year locusts. Similarly, an ecosystem seems to be characterized by a specific "relaxation time" – that is, a rate at which it can successfully respond to an external intrusion by means of internal readjustment. Hence, we can expect the system to maintain its integrity only so long as external intrusions impinge on it at a rate which is compatible with the natural time-constant of the cycle as a whole. Thus, an environmental change – for example, in temperature – which develops slowly may permit organisms to adapt or to evolve adaptive forms, and the system as a whole can persist. In contrast, a rapid, cataclysmic environmental change, such as that which trapped the arctic mastodons in fields of ice, can override the system's natural rate of adaptation and destroy it.

Human Intrusions on the Ecosystem

This brief summary gives us a working knowledge of the system that constitutes the environment – a system generated by the evolution of the vast variety of living things on the earth. But among these living things is man, an organism which has learned how to manipulate natural forces with intensities that go far beyond those attainable by any other living thing. For example, human beings expend in bodily energy roughly 1,000 kilowatt hours per year. However, in highly developed countries such as the United States and Canada the actual expenditure of energy per capita is between 10,000 and 15,000 kilowatt hours per year. This extension of the impact of human beings on the ecosphere is, of course, a consequence of technology. Prehistoric man withdrew from the atmosphere only the oxygen required for respiration but technological man consumes a far greater amount of oxygen to support fires, power plants and chemical processes. The carbon dioxide produced by technological processes has measurably altered the carbon dioxide concentration of the atmosphere. Technology has had effects on the ecosystem which approach the magnitude of the natural processes themselves. Technology has also introduced into the environment substances wholly new to it such as synthetic pesticides, plastics and man-made radioisotopes.

What we mean by environmental deterioration is the untoward effect of human activities, especially technology, on the quality of the environment and on the stability of the ecological processes which maintain it. Given the previous list of ecosystem properties it is illuminating to determine the degree to which our major technological activities are consistent with them. Such an inquiry reveals that much of our technology is, in its very success as a productive enterprise, a grave threat to the stability of the ecosystem. Some examples follow.

Sewage Treatment Technology

One of our best developed technologies is sewage treatment, a technique intended to convert the noxious organic materials of human wastes into innocuous materials that could be assimilated into the aquatic ecosystem. This technology reflects an excellent understanding of *part* of the aquatic cycle: that given sufficient oxygen, aquatic microorganisms can convert organic matter to innocuous inorganic products which are readily carried off in surface waters. By domesticating such microorganisms in artificially aerated sewage plants we can indeed convert nearly all of the organic matter of sewage into inorganic products and discharge them to rivers and lakes.

So far, so good; the fatal stress of an overburden of organic matter on the stability of the aquatic cycle is avoided. But given the circularity of the process, it is evident that now a new stress must appear, this time the impact of excessive inorganic nutrients on the growth of algae. And given the nonlinearity involved in the growth of dense algal populations we ought to expect trouble at this point. And indeed the trouble has come – but it has been largely unexpected. Only in the last decade, when the effects of algal overgrowths had already largely destroyed the self-purifying capability of an ecosystem as massive as Lake Erie was the phenomenon recognized as a serious limitation on the technology of sewage treatment. In effect, the modern system of sewage technology has failed in its stated aim of reducing the organic oxygen demand on surface waters because it did not take into account the circularity of the ecological system on which it intruded. Because of this circularity the inorganic products of sewage treatment were themselves reconverted to organic nutrients by the algae, which on their death simply reimposed the oxygen demand that the treatment was supposed to remove on the lakes and rivers. This failure can be attributed, therefore, to a simple violation of a fundamental principle of ecology. The price that we pay for this defect is the nearly catastrophic pollution of our surface waters.

The Nitrogen Cycle

One of the great fundamental cycles in the ecosystem is that traversed by the element nitrogen. In this cycle the vast store of the element in the nitrogen gas of the air is converted to the organic materials of the soil and water; the latter is in turn transformed ultimately to nitrate, which is in turn the source of organic forms of nitrogen in plants and in the animals that feed on them. Finally, such organic matter is returned to the soil as waste, completing the cycle. The nitrogen cycle of the soil is of enormous importance in agricultural technology, being the basis for the yields of protein and other nitrogenous foods which it produces.

95

In natural soils nitrates are produced slowly in the soil by the action of microorganisms on humus. Once free in the soil, nitrate is quickly taken up by plant roots and converted to proteins. Most plants ordinarily contain little free nitrate and in an efficient natural soil system nitrate production and removal are so dynamically balanced as to keep the nitrate level of the soil relatively low as well. As a result little of it leaches into surface waters, so that the concentration of nitrate in surface waters is ordinarily only of the order of a few parts per million.

In Canada and the United States, as in most advanced countries, the nitrogen cycle has been subjected to major changes arising from new agricultural technology. One important change has been the development of a break in the physical continuity of the nitrogen cycle, especially in the Midwest. Originally, in the Midwest cattle were raised and fattened largely by grazing in pastures, from which they acquired their nutrition and to which they contributed organic wastes which maintained the natural fertility of the soil. As indicated earlier, in such a natural system the nitrogen cycle in the soil operates with low levels of soil nitrate, so that relatively little of the latter leaches into surface waters.

However, in recent years, a major change has taken place: most cattle are removed from the pasture for a considerable period of fattening in confined feedlots. Here, feed is brought to the animals and their wastes become heavily deposited in a local area. The natural rate of conversion of organic waste to humus is limited, so that in a feedlot most of the nitrogenous waste is converted to soluble forms (ammonia and nitrate). This material is rapidly evaporated or leached into ground water beneath the soil, or may run directly into surface waters during rainstorms. This is responsible, in part, for the appearance of high nitrate levels in some rural wells supplied by ground water, and for serious pollution problems due to eutrophication in a number of streams in the Midwest. Where feedlot manure is allowed to reach surface water untreated it imposes a heavy oxygen demand on streams already overloaded by municipal wastes.

A livestock animal produces much more waste than a human being, and the total waste produced by domestic animals in the United States is about ten times that produced by the human population. Much of this waste production is confined to feedlots. For example, in 1966 more than ten million cattle were maintained in feedlots before slaughter, an increase of 66 percent over the preceding eight years. This represents about one-half of the total United States cattle population. Because of the development of feedlot techniques, the United States is confronted with a huge waste disposal problem – which is considerably greater than the human sewage which we are attempting to handle with grossly inadequate treatment.

The physical separation of livestock from the soil is related to an even more complex chain of events, which again leads to severe ecological problems. When, as it has in much of the Midwest, the soil is used for intensive grain production rather than pasturage, the humus content is depleted; generally such soils now contain about one-half the humus present before intensive agriculture was introduced (e.g., ca. 1880). In order to maintain and increase crop productivity, farmers have resorted to increasingly heavy applications of inorganic fertilizer, especially of nitrogen. Since 1945 the annual use of inorganic nitrogen fertilizer in the United States has increased about 14-fold. This has yielded an appreciable increase in crop productivity. However, in a humus-depleted soil, porosity is reduced; as a result plant roots are not adequately aerated and their efficiency in withdrawing nutrient salts from the soil is diminished. In these conditions, the crop may be well nourished by using inorganic fertilizer to maintain a high nitrate level around the roots. However, since efficiency of nutrient uptake is low, a good deal of the nitrate is not taken up by the crop, but leaches into ground water or drains from the fields into lakes and streams. Where streams traverse heavily fertilized farmlands, for example in Illinois, nitrate concentrations in excess of the levels which lead to algal overgrowths have been observed consistently in recent years. Nearly all the streams in Illinois are now polluted by algal overgrowths. When such streams are the source of municipal water supplies – as they are in some Illinois towns – there is a risk of infant methemoglobinemia, due to the conversion of excess nitrate to nitrite in the infant's digestive tract.

We see in the impact of modern agricultural technology on the nitrogen cycle gross violations of a number of basic ecological principles. Feedlot practice breaks the physical continuity of the cycle, transferring organic wastes from large soil areas, where they can be accommodated into the natural cycle, to confined places, or surface waters. Here the heavy, rapid influx of organic matter or of its inorganic degradation products stresses the natural system beyond its capacity to accommodate, and the cycle breaks down, destroying the self-purifying capacity of surface waters and intruding nitrates in toxic amounts into livestock and man. Reflected in this situation is the propensity for the multiplication and spread of ecological perturbations, and the inability of an ecosystem to accommodate a stress which is imposed at a rate which exceeds the system's natural rate of response.

The most serious long-term effect of modern agricultural technology on the nitrogen cycle may be due to its effects on the natural complexity – and therefore stability – of the soil ecosystem. For example, modern agricultural systems have increasingly reduced the use of legumes which, with their associated bacteria, are capable of restoring the organic nitrogen content of the soil through fixation of nitrogen taken from the air. Recent studies, especially of tropical areas, suggest strongly that microbial nitrogen fixation is far more important in maintaining the nitrogen cycle than believed previously. There appear to be numerous bacteria, not only in legumes, but widely associated with many different species of plants that are capable of rapid conversion of air nitrogen into useful soil materials. When this subject has been more fully investigated, it is likely to be found, I believe, that such widespread bacterial nitrogen fixation has been a major factor in maintaining the natural fertility of soil not only in the tropics but in temperate regions as well.

What is particularly alarming is that this natural process of nitrogen fixation is seriously disrupted by inorganic nitrogen fertilizers. It has been known for some time from laboratory experiments that when nitrogen-fixing bacteria are exposed to excessive amounts of nitrate, the process of nitrogen fixation stops. Under these conditions nitrogen-fixing bacteria may not survive, or if they do, may mutate to nonfixing forms. It is probable, therefore, that the widespread use of inorganic nitrogen fertilizer is depleting the natural population of microbial nitrogen-fixers, upon which we would have to rely considerably in any program to restore the natural efficiency of the soil. Here then is an instance in which a new technology – intensive use of inorganic nitrogen fertilizer – cuts important strands in the web of ecosystem processes, thereby impoverishing the structure of the system, laying it open to collapse under the continued stress of the technology, and diminishing the opportunities for recovery.

Synthetic Detergents

The story of the nondegradable detergents introduced into the environment during the period 1945-65 is now well known, but the lessons are worth recording here. This technological failure was again the result of a lack of concern with one of the distinctive features of natural biological systems – that their chemical events are governed by the extreme catalytic specificity of enzymes. The nondegradability of these detergents was due to the failure of the enzymes in the bacteria of decay to break down the carbon-carbon bonds in the organic backbone of the detergents, a process which these bacteria readily carry out on natural hydrocarbon chains such as those of fatty acid soaps. The failure can be traced to the fact that the nondegradable detergents possessed a branched carbon skeleton, for it is quite characteristic of degradative enzymes to prefer unbranched chains over branched ones. For fifty years this specificity has been known to biologists and has, in fact, for a long time been employed in starch technology to produce highly branched residual dextrins from partial enzymatic degradation branched starches. Here again is the technological failure of a massive intrusion into the environment which resulted from a lack of concern with one of the fundamental principles of ecology – the extreme specificity of chemical events in natural biological systems.

The nondegradable detergents have now been largely replaced by straight-chain substances which are, therefore, accessible to the action of bacterial enzymes. But this change still fails to make modern detergent technology compatible with the demands of ecology, for the new detergents, like the old ones, contain considerable amounts of polyphosphate. The massive introduction of this material into the surface waters through municipal sewage (the phosphate released to surface waters from this source has increased about 27-fold since 1900) has sharply increased the nutrient available to algae and has, therefore, exacerbated the effect of sewage treatment technology on algal overgrowths. A good deal of the pollution due to algal overgrowths can be traced to phosphate imposed on surface waters by detergents in municipal wastes – again a failure to observe the ecological facts of life.

Insecticides

One important aspect of the biological capital on which agricultural productivity depends is the network of ecological relationships that relate insect pests to the plants on which they feed, and to the other insects and birds that, in turn, prey on the pests. These natural relations serve to keep pest populations in check. Pests which require a particular plant as food are kept in check by their ability to spread onto other plants; the other insects which parasitize and prey upon them exert important biological control over the pest population.

What has happened in attempts to control cotton pests – where the great bulk of synthetic insecticide is used in the United States – shows how we have broken down these natural relations and allowed the normal pest-regulating machinery to get out of hand. Here the massive use of the new insecticides has killed off some of the pests that once attacked cotton. But now the cotton plants are being attacked instead by new insects that were never previously known as pests of cotton. Moreover, the new pests are becoming increasingly resistant to insecticide, through the natural biological process of selection, in the course of inheritance, of resistant types. In the Texas cotton fields, for example, in 1963 it took fifty times as much DDT to control insect pests as it did in 1961. The tobacco budworm, which now attacks cotton, has been found to be nearly immune to methylparathion, the most powerful of the widely used modern insecticides.

In certain important cotton-growing areas the insecticides kill off insect predators and parasites, which are often more sensitive to the insecticide than the pest itself. The result: insecticide-induced outbreaks of pests. Finally, DDT affects liver enzymes which inactivate sex hormones; one result is that DDT causes abnormal shell formations in birds, which is the apparent cause of the sharp decline in the population of certain raptorial species.

If we continue to rely on such broad-spectrum insecticides recovery of the natural forms of control will become increasingly difficult. Where restoration of natural biological control has been successful, it has depended on a natural reservoir of insects which are predatory or parasitic toward the pests; if, through widespread dissemination of insecticides species that make up this natural reservoir are lost, biological control may be difficult to reestablish.

The ecological failures involved in the use of DDT and related insecticides are only too evident: The failure to anticipate that an unnatural substance such as DDT is likely to be incompatible with the evolution-tested system of cellular biochemistry; the failure to take into account the effect of food chains on the accumulation of DDT in the bodies of top carnivores, including man; the failure to appreciate the multiple relationships which regulate the population of a given insect; the failure to anticipate the nonlinear responses which cause massive insect outbreaks.

And again, this is an instance in which a new technology is destructive of the natural biological capital – the biological systems of control – upon which we must depend for stable agricultural productivity.

Some Other Examples

In further support of the generalization that we consistently fail to take into account basic ecosystem properties in our recent technological developments, certain other examples are worthy of brief note.

A long list of examples can be provided which show that the effects of amplification and biological interactions on substances newly introduced into the ecosphere have been ignored. Apart from the earlier example of DDT these include: the accumulation of iodine 131 in the thyroids of animals and human beings following dissemination of this radioisotope from nuclear explosions and, more recently, from peaceful operation of nuclear reactors; the appearance of toxic levels of mercury, applied to seeds in the form of mercurial fungicides, ultimately in the eggs of hens fed on the grain produced on the plants grown from such seeds. A particularly striking example of such a failure to take into account ecological amplification effects in technological considerations was reported recently by Tamplin, relative to radioactive wastes from nuclear reactors.[1] Starting from the radioactive materials, which according to AEC standards would be allowed to enter a typical ecosystem during reactor operation, Tamplin has calculated the effects of amplification in the food chain. He shows that, following passage through the food chain, certain radioisotopes released into a river at allowable concentrations can become concentrated in fish at levels which exceed the maximum permissible concentrations if used as human food.

The multiple consequences of environmental intrusions have also been un-anticipated by technological planners. Consider a proud example of modern technology, the Aswan High Dam on the Upper Nile River. The dam has already cut down the flow of nutrients to the Mediterranean, reducing the algal popula-tion and the productivity of the local fishing industry. At the same time the dam, and its attendant irrigation system, is likely to cause catastrophic in-crease of snail-borne schistosomiasis in the Egyptian population. Another example of such "ecological backlash" is the unexpected effect of a campaign to control malaria in remote mountain villages in Sarawak, Malaysia. The insecticides not only killed mosquitoes, but also poisoned cockroaches as well; these were eaten by the village cats, which died. As a result, disease-bearing rodents – primarily controlled by the cats – invaded the villages and serious epidemics resulted. The natural balance was finally restored when the Royal Air Force organized a parachute drop of a force of fresh cats for the villages.

The Economic Benefits and Ecological Hazards of Technology

The technologies which are responsible for the environmental problems cited above were designed for, and have in fact achieved, important benefits to human welfare: increased food production through the intensive use of in-organic nitrogen fertilizer, and through improved cattle-feeding techniques; improved control of harmful insects through the use of insecticide sprays; im-proved crop yields due to the use of mercurial fungicides. Most of our major new pollutants are similarly connected to technological benefits. Photochemical smog is a consequence of the development of the efficient and widely used, modern high-compression gasoline engine. Due to their elevated operating temperatures high-compression engines bring about the combination of nitrogen and oxygen in the air. And smog is the result of a complex chain of chemical events triggered by the release of nitrogen oxides. Similarly, nuclear reactors improve our power resources, but at the same time pollute the environment with man-made radioisotopes and with excessive heat.

These pollution problems arise, not out of some minor inadequacies in the new technologies, but because of the very success of these technologies in accom-plishing their designed aims. A modern sewage treatment plant causes algal overgrowths and resultant pollution *because* it produces, as it is designed to do, so much plant nutrient in its effluent. Modern, highly concentrated, nitrogen fertilizers result in the drainage of nitrate pollutants into streams and lakes just *because* they succeed in the aim of raising the nutrient level of the soil. The modern high-compression gasoline engine contributes to smog and nitrate pollution *because* it successfully meets its design criterion – the development of a high level of power. Modern synthetic insecticides kill birds, fish, and useful insects just *because* they are successful in being absorbed by insects, and killing them, as they are intended to do.

Moreover, there are usually sound economic reasons for the specific technological design which leads to environmental deterioration. This is particularly evident in the case of the intensive use of inorganic nitrogen fertilizer. Since 1945 the cost of farm labor, land and machinery in the United States has risen about 50-60 percent; but in that time the cost of fertilizer has *declined* about 25 percent. Moreover, intensive use of fertilizer, especially of nitrogen, provides a quick return on the farmer's investment; a fertilizer investment made in the spring is quickly reflected in the return obtained from the crop in the fall. As a result intensive fertilizer use has become crucial to the farmer's economic success. Certain government policies have intensified this effect. For example, the establishment of the Land Bank system has encouraged farmers to grow more crop on less land. This can be accomplished by very intensive use of nitrogen fertilizer, which permits a marked increase in the number of crop plants grown per acre. Similarly, feedlot operations represent a more economically efficient use of agricultural investment than do purely grazing operations.

We can expect, therefore, that efforts to reduce such environmental hazards will compete with the benefits available from the technological process, at least in economic terms. Thus, a nuclear power plant *can* be built in such a way as to reduce the resultant radioactive or thermal pollution. But this increases the cost of plant construction, raises the price of power and reduces the plant's competitive position with respect to other types of power production. Similarly, it would be possible to reduce nitrate pollution from feedlots by requiring the installation of complete (i.e., including tertiary treatment) disposal systems for the resultant wastes, but this would reduce the economy of the feedlot operation, perhaps below that of old-fashioned pasture operation. Organic fertilizers could be reintroduced in place of inorganic nitrogen fertilizer, but since the latter are cheaper to obtain and to spread, crop production costs would rise.

Equally complex relationships encumber most of our major pollution problems. It is now apparent that urban pollution due to photochemical smog cannot be achieved without supplanting present individual use of gasoline-engine transport with electric-powered mass transit systems, or possibly by replacing them with steam-driven vehicles. The first of these actions would require a massive new economic burden on cities which are already unable to meet their social obligations; the second course would mean a serious disruption of one of the mainstays of our economy, the automobile industry. The construction of nuclear power plants is now governed by certain federal standards regarding allowable emission of radioactive wastes. These represent a distinct – if poorly evaluated – health hazard resulting, for example, from the accumulation of iodine 131 in the thyroid. If emission standards are made more rigorous, the added expense might render the nuclear power industry incapable of competing with fossil fuel power plants. This would severely curtail a major federally-financed technological program, and would clearly require a serious political decision.

There is an important generalization to be derived from these observations: Part of the social value of new technological processes – their productivity and economic efficiency – depends on the *avoidance* of a reckoning with the important social costs represented by the ecological hazards which they cause. In effect, the social utility of such new technology is delicately balanced on a scale which can be readily tipped by actions designed to prevent their hazards to the environment. Such a corrective action becomes, thereby, a trigger which can readily set off major economic, social and political sequelae.

In sum, environmental pollution is not to be regarded as an unfortunate, but incidental, by-product of the growth of population, the intensification of production, or of technological progress. It is, rather, an intrinsic feature of the very technology which we have developed to enhance productivity. Our technology is enormously successful in producing material goods, but too often is disastrously incompatible with the natural environmental systems that support not only human life, but technology itself. Moreover, these technologies are now so massively embedded in our system of industrial and agricultural production that any effort to make them conform to the demands of the environment will involve serious economic dislocations. If, as I believe, environmental pollution is a sign of major incompatibilities between our system of productivity and the environmental system that supports it, then, if we are to survive we must successfully confront these economic obligations, however severe and challenging to our social concepts they may be.

Footnote

1. Arthur R. Tamplin, et al., *Prediction of the Maximum Dosage to Man From the Fall-out of Nuclear Devices.* V, "Estimation of the Maximum Dose from Internal Emitters in Aquatic Food Supply," UCRL-50163, Livermore: Lawrence Radiation Laboratory, 1968.

The Poison Makers*

R. D. Lawrence

You read about it. You taste it and you see it; and yet you do not fully believe that pollution is a dirty word. Perhaps you feel uneasy about it at times, particularly when the attention of the press, radio and television is focussed on it. But you really do not believe that pollution has the power to reach out and touch you, and you are wrong. As you read this, the wastes that you have helped to make have already put their contaminated mark upon you and upon your family. You and yours are soiled by pollution; you may never become clean again.

Yesterday you may have felt slightly out of sorts. Last month you were sure you had been invaded by one of those vague "viruses" that have become so fashionable these days. If you put your mind to it, you will surely recall that for some time now you have been off colour. Nothing serious, you have probably said to yourself as you carried on with the task of living; but the vague feelings of being unwell have worried you now and then.

*Taken from *The Poison Makers* by R. D. Lawrence, Thomas Nelson and Sons Limited (Canada), 1969, by permission of the author.

You were right to be worried, for you are one more victim of pollution, the modern plague that manifests itself in ways so numerous that many of them are still not known. Medical men know some of the effects of pollution, they can guess at others, they see many more as amorphous threats to society and are worried too. And though at last these worries have become communicated to the various forms of Canadian government, though some plans are now being made and some movements effected towards an attack on pollution, governmental action is still sluggish, like the writhing of some giant kraken inching into wakefulness deep within the bowels of the sea.

Ironical, isn't it? We live in a plush world of plenty and of scientific genius; a world in which medical men have found ways of defeating the majority of man's most dreaded epidemics, in which, if we could take advantage of the opportunity, we could even increase our span of productive life. Are we then living a healthier, happier life? Will our bodies be able to take advantage of the gift of longevity? Or are we, by our own hand, reducing our life expectancy to a level lower than it was during the Middle Ages?

You live in this 20th Century in a privileged land; you are more informed and better housed and more protected and better fed than any other generation of man. And yet you are abysmally ignorant of the world around you, of the *natural* world that you are helping to kill with the waste gases from your automobile; with the exhaled fumes of tobacco; with the filth you excrete into your drinking water; with the garbage that you strew indiscriminately across the surface of the land.

You release these killers with equanimity and you stand by passively while the makers of your social comforts discharge poison gas into your atmosphere, dump uncounted gallons of liquid poison into your water and strew killer wastes upon the very soil of your nation.

Thus, at the beginning of this tragic record of waste and destruction and death, I say to you: *You* are one of The Poison Makers. You are the embodiment of the fourth horseman of the Apocalypse, who, mounted on a black charger, spread pestilence, famine and death upon the world.

*   *   *

... it is my hope, you will be saying to yourself: Something should be done! And in this chapter I am going to outline some of the things that *can* be done to at least curb some of the major sources of pollution. But before we get into that, there are two graphic examples of the dangers of pollution and of the attitudes toward it that I want to detail here. The first concerns you and cancer. It is detained in a report originating in Denver, Colorado, in the *Toronto Star* of July 23, 1968. It reads as follows:

> *Denver.* – An association between air pollution and stomach cancer was reported here yesterday.
>
> Although most medical research in air pollution centres on diseases of the lungs and respiratory tract, more attention is being given other illnesses, including heart disease.
>
> Also under scrutiny is the possibility that dirty air is a factor in the high infant mortality rates in urban poverty pockets.
>
> Those were some of the highlights of the opening session of the American Medical Association's second medical research conference on air pollution.

Dr. Warren Winkelstein Jr., of the State University of New York at Buffalo, reported that the death rate from cancer of the stomach is almost twice as high in areas with large amounts of air-borne dust than in neighbourhoods with cleaner air.

On the basis of a three-year study conducted in the Buffalo area, Winkelstein reported that in areas with the highest amount of dust suspended in the air, the stomach cancer death rate for men and women in their 50s and 60s was 31 per 100,000 population.

In the areas with the least dust in the air, the comparable death rate was 16 per 100,000.

Winkelstein pointed out that his findings were consistent with the fact that deaths from stomach cancer have been declining in recent years as air pollution controls have succeeded in lowering the amounts of industrial dust in the air.

The researcher pointed out, however, that such air pollution remains high in certain areas and that gastric cancer continues to rank among the first four causes of death from cancer in American men.

Winkelstein also pointed out that two other independent studies have come up with similar indications of air-borne agents capable of producing cancer. Organic fuels such as soft coal are often mentioned as the most likely sources.

Winkelstein's survey did not show, however, an association between air-borne dust particles and lung cancer, although it did show a relationship to other respiratory diseases.

Some researchers theorize that breathing through the mouth rather than through the nose may be a factor in stomach cancers.

Another speaker, Dr. Seymour I. Cohen, of the California State Department of Health, said he believes "an association could exist between myocardial infarction [heart attack] fatality rate and atmospheric carbon monoxide pollution."

Car exhaust is the chief culprit in carbon monoxide air pollution.

Cohen said that inhaling carbon monoxide decreases the capability of the blood to deliver oxygen to the vital organs.

It is Cohen's theory that excess inhalation of carbon monoxide could "give rise to events" that would signal a heart attack in "susceptible" persons.

He said that blood studies of patients who have died from heart attacks show higher rates of carbon monoxide assimilation than similar studies of patients who died of other diseases.

Cohen also said that a survey of 18,500 Los Angeles hospital patients admitted with the diagnosis of myocardial infarction showed the same patterns.

The link between air pollution and infant deaths in slum neighbourhoods was suggested by Dr. Ruth M. Hagstrom, of Vanderbilt University School of Medicine in Nashville, Tenn.

Dr. Hagstrom reported that an extensive air pollution study in Nashville showed "sufficient indication of an association between levels of air pollution and certain categories of infant and fetal mortality to justify further investigation."

The study showed that air pollution levels were higher in areas where lower-income families lived.

Dr. Hagstrom also noted that the commonest cause of infant deaths during the first years of life is "influenza and pneumonia, categories of deaths which show a significant association with air pollution."

The report originated with the Chicago Sun-Times Services news agency and I quote it here in full because it substantiates some of the claims that I have already made and because it is of paramount importance to every one of us. Significantly, the report shows that medical men as yet know very little about the effects of pollution on the body and perhaps of even more significance is that as research progresses in this field, more and more frightening associations between sickness, death and pollution are being revealed. So far we are just scratching at the surface, as the report indicates; and the question remains: What is to come next?

The second report that I wish to mention shows the strange kind of thinking practised by some of our public health officials. This one deals with the pollution of the Rideau River, in Ottawa, where the bacterial count in the water was 40 times higher than the levels considered acceptable by the authorities. Beaches were closed as sewage flowed over them.

Officials pondered. Obviously the source of contamination – sewers in the area – could not be quickly eliminated, but if the bacterial count was allowed to continue its upward spiral, the Rideau would produce odours that even the politicians on Parliament Hill could not help but notice. And then somebody came up with a bright idea! Why not divert some of the pollution into the Ottawa River and thus, cut down contamination in the Rideau?

It was a case of reducing contamination in one river, only to poison a second one. An incredible situation, but one which received official approval. Of course, it was not a cure and I am sure that none of the people involved attempted to suggest that a cure was intended.

The Rideau River case is just one of many similar occurrences in Canada and the U.S. and it is precisely this sort of frantic bumbling that bears much of the responsibility for the pollution that is now within our midst. But how do we set about to change these attitudes? What can be done to eliminate the present dangers and to ensure that pollution is kept down to a minimum, that our land is not allowed to lie fallow or to be eroded? I do not have all the answers to these highly complex questions. But I have some which I shall now relate.

When a nation is subjected to dangers so widespread and severe that they affect all of its people, a state of emergency is declared and the central, or federal, government takes over, instituting defence measures for the national good. Such action invariably follows an outbreak of war, when, for the duration of the hostilities, the central government becomes the supreme authority and state or provincial governments become subordinates who follow the directives issued from the capital. We in Canada and the U.S. have seen this happen in our countries so often during the last two centuries that we accept such supreme authority without real objection. Indeed, we expect it, for we realize that without full federal control we would become a series of disorganized units that would quickly fall to enemy attack.

We know this, for our school books have impressed it upon us from the earliest grades and, what is more, we have amongst us a people who failed to operate under a centralized high command and became quickly defeated in consequence – the North American Indians.

But before we will readily submit to the regulations imposed upon us by this form of government, we have to see the danger that threatens us; we have to know that unless we allow "Big Brother" to take over, we shall succumb to the inroads of the enemy. War is a pretty obvious danger and when we see it coming our way we just naturally turn to our national government for guidance and instructions.

Pollution is not obvious. We don't see it in a shape awesome enough to inspire us with fear. We don't even smell it when its advance tendrils creep upon us. Indeed, we have come to accept pollution as inevitable. We know it is here, but we don't think it matters much. The fact is, we have been brainwashed into accepting it; we have been led to believe that at present the dangers of pollution are not all that serious and that the "authorities" will find a magic solution to the problems it creates in time to save us from suffering any real discomforts.

This is why we are not now waging all-out war against the harmful elements that have been loosed upon us. This is why federal authorities are not in full control of a problem that is national both in scope and importance.

Ultimately the formation of a central authority will provide the only sure way of combatting the effects of pollution and of preventing the poisons of mankind from devastating the world. Such an authority should be under federal direction and it should have branches within each state or province. But it should go further. It should work in close cooperation with its counterparts in neighbouring nations. A Canadian federal pollution control directorate, for instance, should work in partnership with a similar body in the United States, and the latter should team up with a like administration in Mexico.

I am aware that such an authority would very likely not meet with the approval of some state and provincial governments, which would claim that the national government was usurping local powers. Such objections would have to be put aside, for, I insist, pollution is national and international in its spread and effects. Pollution does not recognize geographic boundaries; it cannot be stopped at a frontier or a border. Unless there exists a central control, those states or provinces that keep a clean house will continue to be infected by neighbours who are careless with their poisons.

In like manner, particularly in North America, the international aspects of pollution cannot be ignored any longer. We in Canada cannot build a sterile curtain around and over our nation; the U.S. cannot do this either. We cannot isolate the Great Lakes; we cannot order the citizens of Detroit, Chicago or Buffalo to stop polluting Lake Erie, Lake Huron or Lake Michigan. Two nations share these inland seas; it is logical that both should see to it that they are kept clean. Many of our rivers and streams are shared, too, and whereas at the present time U.S. pollution is more common in our waterways than Canadian pollution in U.S. waters, there could come a time when the opposite might be true.

Nothing illustrates this better than the affair of the Presque Isle River, which flows into the Province of New Brunswick from Maine. In July 1968, the people of Centreville, N.B., took the law into their own hands when pollution from two processing plants in Easton, Maine, became too much for them.

Rightly or wrongly, the villagers of Centreville threw up a temporary dam to block what used to be a good trout stream in an effort to stop pollutants coming into Canada from the Maine plants. It was an act of open defiance, taken after all else had failed and after the people of the village had become sick and tired of the thousands of dead fish that washed up on the river banks, there to rot and stink out the area.

New Brunswick's Natural Resources Minister, William Duffie, said the act was "unnecessary as well as illegal". Illegal it was, but unnecessary it was not. Mr. Duffie, of course, does not live in Centreville and thus he does not have to smell and see the rotting fish, even though one might expect the province's Minister of Natural Resources to entertain more positive feelings about a matter that was devastating one of his charges. The pollution was obviously serious, to judge from Mr. Duffie's own comments on the affair, but until the citizens of Centreville rose in anger against the filth that was invading their village, both the Maine and New Brunswick governments did nothing to clean up the mess.

There were bland official explanations, of course, but these did not bring back to life the dead fish nor clean up the polluted water. Mr. Duffie told the press at the time the problem had been caused when the two processing plants had stepped up their production and thus created more wastes which they dumped, as was their habit, into the river. The New Brunswick Minister then said that "action" by the New Brunswick and Maine governments had resulted in cuts in production by the potato plant and the sugar factory that were to blame. But the pollutants continue to be released by both firms and although one of them, the potato plant, is no longer dumping its muck into the river, it is dumping it instead into a lagoon which, a Maine Air and Water Improvements Commission inspector said, will take 60 days to fill. Nobody explained what the firm was going to do when the lagoon was filled.

The Centreville affair is further noteworthy in that it shows the weaknesses that exist in the present systems for policing the spread of pollution in both the U.S. and Canada. The State of Maine has an Air and Water Improvements Commission, the Province of New Brunswick has its own pollution control system. Yet, despite the "watchdogs" on both sides, the water was polluted, the fish were killed, and the situation reached alarming, dangerous, and disgusting proportions before it was brought out into the open.

It took an outraged citizenry before a partial solution was found and a promise was made by the Maine Attorney-General, James S. Erwin, that the matter of the polluted river might (only *might*, mind you) be dealt with as a civil rather than a criminal matter by asking the courts to declare the river a public nuisance.

Continuing to use water pollution as our example (simply because the poisoning of water is more physically apparent than the insidious and probably more dangerous pollution of air) it should be noted that a Canadian consulting engineer, J. W. MacLaren, of Toronto, urged the adoption of one agency to combat pollution of the Great Lakes.

Mr. MacLaren addressed the Great Lakes Water Resources Conference that took place in Toronto in July 1968, and explained to some 300 delegates that the system which involved many governments in the development of the lakes was a piecemeal approach that failed to control the spread of pollution, which has killed most of the fish in the lower lakes. Mr. MacLaren noted that the problems of pollution control are too complex to be left in the hands of existing agencies.

At present, whereas the United States formed the Great Lakes Basin Commission three years ago and united the federal government and the governments of eight states bordering on the lakes in an attempt to control pollution and Great Lakes development, these problems in Canada are left entirely in the hands of the Ontario government. Although that province is leading the way in matters of pollution control, the enormity of the Great Lakes problem is such that federal participation is necessary if those huge bodies of water are to be saved.

Of course, the same applies to our air and our soil. At present there are literally hundreds of different agencies involved in pollution control and while these are making some progress, they are unable, either singly or collectively, to get the better of the pollutants. This is because most agencies work on their own, despite frequent joint meetings and talks. Often there is professional rivalry between them and frequently the interests of one clash with the interests of another.

For instance, perhaps a water conservation agency finds that some insecticide is affecting a lake or river under its control. It looks for the source, probably having the powers to halt the use of the insecticide upon its shorelines. Then it discovers that the source of contamination is several miles away, inland, resulting from the spraying of forests or farm fields. What can the water agency do? More often than not, it has no power to halt the spraying of inland plantations, so it approaches the people who are doing the spraying and a conference results. The forestry people, or the farm group, maintain that the spraying is necessary to save the crops (be they timber or produce) from this or that insect pest. The water agency makes suggestions. Perhaps it urges another kind of chemical, perhaps it suggests some different method, but at best it can only obtain a modified program of spraying, at worst the forestry programmers or the farmers say, in effect, "To heck with you, Charley, my cabbages (or trees) come first"; and the spraying continues. Throughout Canada and the U.S. farmers are allowed to spray their crops with deadly poisons whenever they feel this is necessary. Indeed, they are encouraged to do so by their state or provincial departments of agriculture and by the manufacturers of pesticides.

Now and then some province or state passes a realistic law, such as that drafted in 1967 by Ontario, which tied some important strings on the use of DDT. But let there be no mistake about it, what action has been taken so far in this regard is not nearly good enough! DDT is a deadly poison, we all know this; no sane government will deny the charge against this chemical. Yet it is still being widely used. It is only one of many deadly poisons that are being freely broadcast, and our governments know this also. Why, then, are these poisons sanctioned? Are the people of this continent to fall victims to diseases such as cancer because vested interests in both our nations insist that the use of these poisons is necessary for economic reasons?

July 1968 was a red-letter month in the matter of pollution and poison. Here is another example of this, which was unfolded in mid-month at Honey Harbour, Ontario, during the annual Canadian Cancer Research Conference.

At that time and in that place, Dr. John Higginson, of the International Agency for Research on Cancer, said that DDT had been linked to cancer in laboratory mice by researchers in Russia and Hungary. He said, further, that on the strength of its preliminary research, Hungary had banned the use of the chemical! But we in "enlightened" North America continue to use it in the home and outside!

Dr. Higginson explained that researchers in Budapest had found that mice exposed to DDT were 40 times more susceptible to cancer than mice not so exposed. This was bad enough; it startled the scientists, but what horrified them was the fact that the descendants of the mice exposed to DDT were even more susceptible to cancer, indicating that the genetic damage done to the original mice was not only being passed to their offspring, it was gaining strength with each succeeding generation! And we are still using DDT! Not that we are alone in this, for the chemical is used all over the world and is a major weapon in the fight against malaria and other diseases that are carried by insects. Its indictment as a cancer agent will undoubtedly pose a nasty problem in this regard, but it may be that if we evaluate the evils, the problem may not loom so large. Cancer is a killer; any chemical that has the ability to induce it, and is also able to increase its occurrence in unborn generations, is surely far more dangerous than any of the known insect-borne sicknesses!

The responsibility of our governments is great. Pollution transcends boundaries and reaches out to the far corners of the earth. Yet our politicians do not seem able to grasp this. Instead of tackling the problems of pollution quickly and positively, they allow political expediency to influence action. Instead of enforcing existing anti-pollution laws and drafting new, stronger ones, they resort to wheedling, offering rewards for efforts towards the control of pollution by companies and individuals, when instead they should be dealing out punishments.

During the spring of 1968 the then Finance Minister of Canada, Mitchell Sharp, told the Commons that the Federal Government was considering tax write-offs in order to encourage homeowners to install anti-pollution devices on their home furnaces, while similar (but naturally larger) tax incentives might be offered to industry to install water pollution control devices; and he told M.P.'s that he had been urged to provide similar inducements for the treatment of air and soil pollution.

These rewards for the makers of pollution will probably never come about, but they make good political copy. On the surface a government that says it is considering such inducements appears to have the interests of its people at heart. But dig deeper and you will find that such offers are made because they are the most politically attractive. It takes guts and determination to punish offenders when these are often subscribers to party funds. It takes guts to tell the voter that he must install anti-pollution devices on his furnace. It takes guts to make mandatory the installation of anti-pollution devices on automobiles. It takes guts to frame laws which will provide heavy punishments for those guilty of the indiscriminate use of dangerous pesticides. It takes guts to levy heavy fines from shipping companies when their vessels discharge oil in our lakes and rivers and along our coasts. It takes guts to close up an industry that is spewing poison into our air or our water. Tax write-offs in the matter of pollution control are like offering your small son a reward if he does not break a window; they are akin to offering a potential killer a pension if he refrains from murder. Tax write-offs do not solve pollution.

The defeat of pollution – *all* pollution – in the future can only come through central control, but before such control is put into effect our politicians must realize that pollution is not a minor nuisance that can be used on occasion in order to curry favour with the electorate. Politicians and senior civil servants must be made aware of the dangers of pollution and they must be made to realize that the voter – *you* – wants action. If enough citizens demand action, they will get it, for no government will risk the concerted wrath of its people.

At the present time, in both Canada and the U.S., there are many anti-pollution laws already in effect, but these, when they are enforced, often carry a ridiculously low penalty and, more often than not, enforcement does not come until the people involved have been warned several times. Often a company would rather pay the nominal fines imposed (which seldom exceed $500) than spend half a million dollars or more in order to control the pollution it is creating. Just as often, when large companies such as public utilities are involved, no action at all is taken on the premise that the company is too large and the problem too expensive to tackle now; the only promise of hope is a tenuous undertaking that future expansion of the facilities will include anti-pollution devices. In the matter of air pollution, for instance, it is frequently stated that it is far too expensive to install anti-pollution controls on industrial furnaces and that the problem can be solved by building chimney-stacks so that the smoke and its poisons are pumped high into the sky. This, it is felt, removes the pollution from the area. And so it does – by sending it off to settle on some other unsuspecting community miles away.

The control of pollution is a complete labyrinth of technical and legal problems, all of which are affected by the weather, the topography of the land, the immediate and future effects upon people and animals, and the *lack of experience* with the pollutants released.

At the present time these factors are being further complicated by the large number of pollution control agencies that have arisen and by the lack of co-operation that exists between many of them. If man is ever to banish the spectre of pollution, there is a mammoth job to be done and a great deal of money will have to be spent both on control devices and on research. It is difficult to say which of these is the more important. Right now, I suppose, control should come ahead of research, but ultimately research must be the more important of the two, for it is out of research that the right controls will come. Research will tell us what chemicals we can use in safety and what must be discarded as too dangerous to use. Research will also provide us with answers for the biological control of pests; it will give us new cars and new furnaces and even new bathrooms. Research will teach us how to lick the farm manure problem and it will tell us how to repair the great damage that has already been done to our world.

In the meantime we should do the best we can with the little knowledge that we have and the first item on this particular agenda is enforcement. Provincial, state and municipal governments must begin to enforce rigidly their existing anti-pollution laws. If there is a law that says no industry may discharge its poisons into our waters and if an industry is found contravening this law, the offender should be punished severely. New laws should be drafted allowing the authorities to close up companies that are fouling our air or our water, or contaminating our soil.

We have weaseled around long enough; let us have some action now, right away, under the present statutes. There are enough laws on our books, if they are effectively enforced. The time has gone when the people of this continent can continue to accept sweet words of hope instead of action from their elected representatives. While provincial and state governments deal vigorously with those who are rapidly poisoning our land, water and air, let the federal governments lead the way towards comprehensive, central control of pollution, backed by a massive research program aimed at all phases of the problem.

More specifically, much ground may be gained if it becomes mandatory for *all* automobiles, trucks, buses, aircraft and trains to have anti-pollution devices installed in their engines. And I don't just mean new (1969) cars, as is the case in the U.S. I mean *all* vehicles presently burning gasoline or any of its by-products. Certainly the U.S. law is a great step in the right direction, but it will not eliminate carbon monoxide pollution. At best it can only hope to hold the present level for about ten years, then the poison will start gaining ground again, for more vehicles will be on the road and present anti-pollution devices are not 100 percent effective.

The effects of pollution are drastic. It will require drastic measures if they are to be eliminated. Perhaps it is high time that we looked towards electricity as a means of eliminating at least two major sources of pollution. Electric cars, for instance, are already available, though at the present time they have three strikes against them: they cannot yet go as fast as we would wish them to go; they have complicated battery-charging systems; and they are a very serious threat to the oil industries. But this does not mean to say that, with more research, sufficient refinements cannot be built into these prototypes to produce a vehicle that will be safe, fast enough to suit us, and incapable of emitting pollutants into our atmosphere.

Likewise, the electric toilet, already on the market, can completely eliminate pollution from domestic sewage. About the only thing against electric toilets right now is their cost (they retail, installed, at about $500), but here the governments *could* step in with subsidies, for it will be cheaper to give every home an electric toilet than to install the complex and expensive sewage facilities that are now needed in urban North America. In Canada, for instance, urban populations constitute 74 percent of the nation and it is estimated that this will climb to 80 percent in ten years. And *that* means a lot of toilets and a lot of sewage.

The electric toilet functions simply, by incinerating the wastes. The slight residues of this incineration are trapped in a container and can then be used by the home owner as organic fertilizer for his garden. Here is an answer to pollution by sewage. It is functional, clean, efficient and relatively inexpensive. Electricity can drive much pollution out of our lakes and rivers through this means, and eliminate the need for expensive sewer lines and sewage treatment plants.

In the matter of garbage, we could quickly reduce this to more manageable levels if our governments had the courage to frame laws that forbade the sale of non-degradable products, such as glass, and if the manufacturers of the many goods that we buy daily cut out the "new, giant economy size" packages that are full of air. But *that*, after all, is up to *you*, the buyer. If you refuse to purchase these come-on packages, if you will not allow yourself to be wooed by the tinsel and the appeals to your something-for-nothing instincts. Believe me, you just don't get something for nothing! That big, big box of soap powder, now, – don't ever think that you got that for free, friend, because you didn't. You paid for every bit of pulp that went into that container, you paid for the privilege of lugging home a useless piece of cardboard that had to be burned after its meagre contents were used up.

Daily the science of packaging becomes more complex as you, the buyer, become more confused. Today we take for granted the half-empty boxes, the non-returnable bottles, the toss-away cans. And we don't stop to consider that these completely unnecessary items are not only costing us our hard-earned money, they are also contributing to the destruction of our environment, wasting our raw materials and eventually leading to an increase in the taxes that we pay, for, as additional garbage is created, municipal disposal costs go up. *You* pay for this, but you don't seem to appreciate it. Ask yourself: Do you *really* want those big boxes? Do you *really* insist on drinking your beer out of a gaudily-decorated can? Do you *really* want to pay good money for the fancy wrapping that is placed around your meat? Does that piece of cardboard that your meat sits on *do* anything for you? It should, you know, because you are paying for it.

In the matter of pesticides the problems become far more complex, for you have been well and truly brainwashed into believing that you just cannot survive without DDT, DDD, malathion, aldrin, dieldrin and the thousands of other poisons that are being sold daily on this continent to unsuspecting buyers like you. If we listened to the pesticide lobbies, we would be tempted to believe that the world would come to an end tomorrow if these deadly chemicals were never used again. Well, think a moment. . . . What year is this? . . . In what century are we living? . . . Right! Then how did we manage to survive, and thrive, for all those years prior to 1940 when the wonder poisons were discovered? How on earth did *Homo sapiens* manage to climb out of the tree without DDT?

I am not here advocating a complete ban on all pesticides. I most definitely *am* advocating far more caution in their use and far, far more research into the damage that they can cause. Today you may press a super-spray and kill a dozen mosquitoes at your cottage, tomorrow your children may be sterile, or, worse, they may give birth to tragic malformed babies, produced by the refinements of civilization.

Is a perfect cabbage worth these dreadful risks? Can you not settle for a fruit or vegetable that may have a blight or two but which is free of a chemical that can destroy your ability to breed? The producers blame you. They say you won't settle for anything less than perfection. You know and I know that this is not true. It is not true because by the time these perfect fruits and vegetables reach your neighbourhood they have been in transit for days, perhaps even weeks, and by the time you place them in your table the best has gone out of them. How often have you lamented the passing of *fresh* vegetables? So, if you are prepared to accept natural foods that have passed their peak of freshness, would it be too much to ask you to accept slightly flawed fruit and vegetables which were both fresh and cheaper (because the wholesale application of pesticides costs money) and which, in addition, were completely safe to eat! I think you would, if you realized that you were dicing with the lives of your children and their children!

In the final analysis, you should by now realize that you are responsible for the mess of pollution. *You* are one of the Poison Makers. Your wastes pollute the waters; your car pollutes the air; your garbage desecrates the land and sends up streamers of black, poisonous smoke. You are the one, we are told, who demands perfect produce that requires the drenching of the land with deadly chemical poisons. You are the one who continues to overpopulate the world, crowding yourself and your family into unsightly, unhealthy urban developments from which you constantly long to escape.

Does this make sense to you? Do you honestly believe that man can go on in this manner without destroying himself and all other living things?

Already it is as though the fourth horseman was amongst us. The macabre figure rides the yellow horse of famine, pestilence and destruction.

If you look closely, you will recognize the rider. It is *you*!

Who Will Save the Great Lakes?*

Ti Estin

"When I lived in Chicago during the summer of 1967," says Michael Doran, lecturer in Music at McMaster University, "my apartment was situated about seven blocks from the shores of Lake Michigan (otherwise known as Gitchy-Gooey).

"Most days the smell of dead fish penetrated into my living room, even when the windows were closed.

"Turning on the hot water tap one was invariably greeted by the smell of dead fish competing with that of chlorine. It was possible to make coffee and tea, but the stuff was undrinkable.

"From within a stone's throw of the lake one could survey the magnificent solid silver band of rotting fish which lined the shore at the exact formal distance of five yards. Ah, Chicago! Ich habe lust vor dich!"

During the summer of 1967, as well, the Chicago lake front was graced by an oil slick that extended for some 75 miles.

The Cuyahoga River, flowing through Cleveland into Lake Erie is usually covered by a coating of petrochemical wastes averaging two inches in thickness. The river is considered a fire hazard. Last year an arsonist set it ablaze and two bridges were seriously damaged.

Indeed, Cleveland's two fireboats wash oil from docks and pilings at regular intervals to minimize the risk of fire.

Cleveland is also one of the few cities which chlorinates its lakefront beaches in order to render them safe for swimming.

Meanwhile, the Great Lakes are dying.

Lake Erie has had it. In the last fifty years the effect of human waste and alterations in the environment has aged the lake 15,000 years.

*Jelte Kuipers and BA Veldhuis. Reprinted by permission. Originally published in the *Silhouette* (*Ti Estin* Special Edition on Ecology, Pollution, and Conservation), McMaster University, November 28, 1969.

Lake Michigan is perilously close to the point of no return. Its southern stretches are heavily polluted and contaminated, and this destruction is steadily spreading northward.

Lake Superior remains the purest of the lakes, while pollution in Lake Ontario is rapidly attaining to critical proportions. Lake Huron and Georgian Bay stands [*sic*] as something of a halfway house between the purity of Superior and a cesspool that is Erie.

Taken together the Great Lakes drainage system constitutes the largest single body of *fresh* water in the world, containing better than one-fourth of the world's supply.

In this case the word *fresh* is used only to distinguish the water from ocean brine, since in many cases the water in the Great Lakes is no more palatable than ocean water, and considerably less pure.

The entire Great Lakes basin supports a population well in excess of 30 million, compared with fewer than 300,000 early in the nineteenth century. This figure represents about one in eight Americans and about one in three Canadians.

By 1965 the water level of all five lakes had dropped to their lowest levels in recorded history. Erie and Huron were some five feet lower than during the early fifties.

This does not mean much until one realizes that a drop of one foot in the Great Lakes water level results in a loss of some 2.75 trillion cubic feet of water.

This loss and all other changes which have taken place in the Great Lakes are attributable to a single cause: man. However, what man has done to the lakes, and what he continues to do at an accelerating rate involves many complex questions. Of these, we shall select a few examples.

While Lake Superior is the largest and the purest, as well as the deepest of the Great Lakes, with a surface area in excess of 30,000 square miles and a maximum depth of 1,333 feet, it is also the most delicate of the five.

Being relatively cold and pure, the lake is more drastically affected by even small increases in pollution.

Hence, while remaining *pure* by human consumption standards, fish catches have declined drastically since World War II. The annual catch is now about one third of what it was in 1941.

Because the water of Lake Superior is soft, heavy metals such as copper, iron and zinc are highly toxic in low concentrations. Fish species in the lake are sensitive to metals and could be seriously affected in terms of behavior and reproduction if exposed to even minute levels of pollution.

Further, the lake's purity and coldness means that it reacts more slowly in recovering from pollution damage than might, say, Lake Erie (were it not for the fact that Erie has been subjected to immense pollution). The self-purging rate of Lake Superior has been estimated at well over 500 years – i.e. that is how long it would take for the lake to clean itself naturally.

Pollution in Superior now results from about four major sources: oxygen depletion in tributary rivers (associated with serious tributary pollution); wastes from shipping; industry along the lake; and urban municipal waste.

Because of the relatively small population along the lake municipal waste is a more or less negligible problem as yet.

Because a number of tributaries are deteriorating increasing amounts of sediment, mostly the result of erosion, are entering the lake. This is especially evident along the south shore where large quantities of red clay enter annually.

Sediment increases turbidity in water, thereby cutting off light penetration and decreasing the ability of plant and animal organisms to feed and reproduce.

The increase in shipping on the Great Lakes increases the amounts of oil and petrochemical pollutants spilled into the water. Again, the relatively small tonnage shipped over Lake Superior is offset by the lake's greater susceptibility to pollution.

Two examples of industrial pollution will suffice to indicate the great danger these present to Lake Superior, as well as to all drainage basins. They are the refining of low-grade taconite iron ore and the pulp and paper industry.

Taconite refining is a complex procedure of crushing and grinding the ore into fine particles and magnetically separating the iron from the residual dust and concentrating the iron into pellets of magnetite.

In the process some ten thousand gallons of water are used in order to produce a single ton of iron pellets. The waste residual of dust, or tailings, is produced at a rate of about two million tons per million tons of pellets.

The Reserve Mining Company, at its Silver Bay plant on Lake Superior discharges some 500,000 gallons of water per minute as part of its taconite refining process.

By December, 1967, twelve years after it had begun its operations, the Reserve plant had produced a delta stretching more than a mile out into the lake which was composed entirely of such waste *tailings*. This delta included only about 45 percent of the total waste debris of some 175 million tons produced by the one plant in a dozen years – the rest having been dispersed into the lake.

These tailings included a variety of dangerous metals, such as zinc and cadmium.

A study on this sediment made by the U.S. Department of the Interior in 1968 reported the following: "Using the estimated annual sediment yield of 10 tons per square mile as representative for all the drainage area into Lake Superior from Minnesota, then nearly 68,000 tons are discharged into the lake each year by tributary streams entering the lake from Minnesota. This is about equal to the quantity of taconite tailings discharged each day from the plant at Silver Bay, Minnesota."

When the Ontario Water Resources Commission laid charges last week against Domtar Ltd., Canada's second-largest pulp and paper producer for polluting Lake Superior's Nipigon Bay, it struck at one of the major polluting industries in Canada.

Pulp and paper plants are spread roughly evenly along the North Shore of Lake Superior, each one discharging its wastes into the lake.

The plant charged by the OWRC is located at Red Rock, some 65 miles east of the Lakehead. It employs some 1,200 men in four round-the-clock shifts who live in what amounts to a company town.

This plant is a major producer of Kraft containerboard.

It is also apparently a major polluter of Nipigon Bay.

At one time Nipigon Bay possessed some of the finest and widest beaches along Lake Superior. Today these beaches are covered by a heavy layer of bark and wood debris. Large quantities of lime and acid are inevitably discharged into the bay daily.

The process of destroying the environment in order to produce paper begins with the cutting of logs. Even assuming that a given woodlot is *farmed* – that is, replanted and not recklessly mowed down – the shipping of logs to the mill entails considerable destruction. Rivers are bulldozed so that the logs will not be caught by obstacles on the way to the mill.

This bulldozing of river beds certainly removes rocks, branches and other obstructions. It also destroys the spawning grounds for sturgeon, trout, and salmon.

Once the logs reach the mill they are cut into four to six foot lengths, then sent into a barking drum which strips the bark from the logs. This bark is sometimes blown into a boiler and burned, but a good deal of it simply escapes into the sewer and ends up in the lake. (The practise of burning bark is a recent one at the Red Rock plant, and was begun in answer to complaints about pollution.)

Once stripped of bark the logs are chipped in a large fan-like device which breaks them into small bits. In this form they enter the digesters where they are mixed with a cooking liquor produced on the premises.

This liquor consists largely of caustic soda, sodium- or potassium-hydroxide and lime. This liquor breaks down the fibres in the wood and makes it suitable for paper-making.

Subsequently the liquor is washed out of the stock for chemical recovery. An Evaporator removes the water; what remains is a heavy viscose compound somewhat resembling tar. This is burned to recover a *green liquor* which in turn is recirculated to a causticizing plant where it is clarified into a new batch of cooking liquor.

It is the pulp mill part of the process which is a major polluter of water, and the chemical recovery process which is a major polluter of the air.

Domtar's Red Rock plant is surrounded by a belt of dead or dying trees, mostly because of the gases produced in chemical recovery. These same gases and the particulate matter which accompanies them sometimes turn snow black before it reaches the ground.

Formerly waste sewage was dumped directly into Nipigon Bay; now it is left for a time in settling ponds so that some of the lime and other chemicals are precipitated.

Since most pulp stock is a bright red colour after being cooked, vast quantities of chlorine are used to bleach it to the consistent brown colour characteristic of Kraft stock.

It takes some 700 gallons to make a ton of paper stock. In 1965 alone nearly three million tons of paper were produced along the Canadian side of the Great Lakes basin.

The pollution problems that begin in Lake Superior are duplicated in **Lake Michigan**. There heavy concentrations of industry produce vast quantities of chemicals and sewage the better part of which are dumped raw or only partially treated into the lake.

Chicago draws vast amounts of water from the lake in order to dump its sewage effluent into the Ohio River, from where it enters the Mississippi – the trunk sewer of America.

This withdrawal of water by Chicago has as one effect that of robbing power plants as far downstream as Massena, on the St. Lawrence River, of sufficiently high water levels for the production of hydro-electricity.

There are more than twelve major fossil and nuclear-fuel thermal power plants along Lake Michigan. These produce what is called *thermal pollution*. As part of the production of electricity these plants must use vast quantities of water as coolants.

A fossil-fuel plant wastes about 1.5 units of heat for each equivalent unit of useful energy output; a nuclear-powered plant wastes, for comparable output, about 2.25 units of heat energy.

This heat is carried off by coolant water into the lake and significantly raises local lake temperatures, and, more imperceptibly, general lake temperatures.

As water is heated it loses its ability to hold oxygen, thereby making it more difficult, for example, for fish to breathe. The heated water also promotes the growth of filamentous algae (Cladophora), found throughout the lower lakes, especially in Lake Erie. This algal growth further chokes off the water.

Fish are especially vulnerable to thermal changes in water. Their greatest susceptibility is during reproduction, when their range of permissible temperatures is quite narrow.

One of the most important effects of a thermal rise in a lake area is that of synergistic action. Synergism is defined as the simultaneous action of separate agents which together have a greater total effect than the sum of their individual effects.

A temperature rise in water increases the lethal effect of toxic substances, such as potassium cyanide and O-xylene upon fish. Since domestic and industrial wastes are numerous in the Great Lakes, the likelihood of synergistic effects is common under any circumstances, and seriously aggravated wherever there is thermal pollution.

Similarly, as the water temperature rises, the metabolic rate of fish rises as well. Hence the need for oxygen increases as the available oxygen decreases.

Equally important, while fish can often live in relatively high temperatures, those temperatures frequently make it impossible for the fish to seek food or behave normally. Thus, fish are not so much killed outright as rendered incapable of survival.

All heavy industries, as well as thermal electric power stations, use vast quantities of water. Steel, automaking, petrochemicals, metal refining, textiles – all require vast amounts of water for cooling and cleansing purposes. Much of this is discharged back into the lakes as effluent. Some is lost as evaporation.

Annual use of water along the Great Lakes runs at approximately 60,000 cubic feet per second, for industry, municipalities and agriculture. Of this amount, some 2,300 cubic feet per second are used up – i.e. do not return to the lakes.

The accelerating growth of industrialization, of industrial populations, of irrigation in agriculture, and of thermal electric power stations entails a rapid increase in water usage. Water that is already polluted can, we expect, only be polluted more.

The use of pesticides has been so loosely controlled over the last few decades that these now permeate the environment. Some 60 percent or more of DDT used in Ontario is used on the tobacco farms along Lake Erie, from which it finds its way into the watershed.

(The new provincial and federal ban on DDT does not cover tobacco farming.)

Similarly, the large fruit belts around Lake Michigan, Western Lake Erie, and the Niagara region off Lake Ontario, are major sources of pesticides which end up in the lakes.

In the Green Bay area of Lake Michigan agricultural soils tested for chlorinate pesticides were found to contain concentrations as high as 7,800 micrograms per kilogram. Maximum concentrations found in bottom sediments approached 3,000 micrograms per kilogram – more than two million times that of the overlying water. The algae contained still greater amounts than did the bottom sediments.

The eggs of Coho salmon introduced into Lake Michigan were found to contain pesticides.

Lake Erie constitutes a sad, sad story. The central core of the lake is dead, a desert which cannot support any kind of aquatic life.

The lake is over-enriched with so-called nutrients, which includes a daily contribution of more than 137,000 pounds of soluble phosphorus per day from sources within the Lake Erie basin, most of it from municipal wastes. Two-thirds of this municipal-waste phosphorus content comes from detergents.

These wastes are, surprisingly, still being held somewhat in check by an iron compound called ferric iron or Iron III.

Iron III forms insoluble precipitates with various phosphates which thus settle to the bottom sediment and remain inert. This is possible, however, only so long as there is sufficient oxygen present in the water above the bottom mud.

Now however, there is occurring a serious oxygen-depletion in Lake Erie over the summer months. As a result the Iron III compound is beginning to break down, releasing the nutrients in the sediment. These nutrients are particularly welcome to algae which thrive upon them.

If the process of oxygen depletion continues it is quite conceivable a catastrophic bloom of algae will, within a few years, turn Lake Erie into huge swamp, rendering it unfit for recreation, navigation, and as a source of water.

The recent International Joint Commission Report on Lakes Erie and Ontario points out that "of the total input of phosphorus entering Lake Erie only 16 percent leaves the lake through the outlet; and of the total nitrogen entering Lake Erie only 44 percent leaves the lake."

It also reports the following:

> Major waste loads are carried to Lake Erie by the Detroit, Maumee, and Cuyahoga Rivers. The Detroit River introduces 83 percent (29,000,000 tons per year) of the dissolved solids, 74 percent (3,300,000 tons per year) of the chlorides and 58 percent (17,600 tons per year) of the total phosphorus and 65 percent (126,000 tons per year) of the nitrogen from all sources discharging into Lake Erie.
>
> The Maumee River is the largest source of suspended solids accounting for more than 40 percent (2,000,000 tons per year) of the total tributary inputs to the lake.
>
> It is estimated . . . that during the period January 7, 1966 to January 7, 1967, approximately 71,000 short tons of volatile solids, 18,000 tons of oil and grease, 2,000 tons of phosphorus, 2,000 tons of nitrogen, and 60,000 tons of iron were transferred to Lake Erie from Cleveland Harbour by dredging.

The usual practice of dredging is to take material from the bottom of a given harbour and dump it in the middle of the lake, away from shipping lanes.

But, then, this is quite a normal practice. Dump the problem somewhere else and hope that it will go away by itself, or at least that somebody else will have to worry about it.

Lake Ontario is rapidly following Erie in terms of phosphate pollution. Excess nutrients already have turned many popular beaches into ghastly spectacles of rotting scum and algae, unfit for any kind of human use. Oil and chemical spillages and seepages are inexorably destroying the wildlife in this lake as in all the others.

At present rates of destruction we will not have long to wait before the limit will have been reached and passed, as it has been reached and passed in Lake Erie, when remedial action will have come too late.

Like all natural resources the water we use is not exclusively our own to dispose of at will. It belongs as well to our descendants who must likewise depend on it for survival.

We hold the lakes in trust; so far we have failed that trust.

There are ample studies available to tell us what is wrong. The knowledge and technology is available to set right what has gone wrong. The evidence is before us. The time to act is now.

Pollution of Rainy River and Lake of the Woods[*]

Report of the International Joint Commission

Description of the Area

The Rainy River and Lake of the Woods are boundary waters located in western Ontario and north central Minnesota. Rainy River links Rainy Lake and the Namakan Chain of Lakes with Lake of the Woods. Figure 1 is a map of the area.

This report is confined to the Rainy River and that portion of Lake of the Woods south of a line drawn between Long Point, Minnesota and Hooper Point on Bigsby Island, Ontario.

Rainy River drains an area of 20,850 square miles, divided almost equally between Ontario and Minnesota. Two-thirds of the watershed lies above the outlet of Rainy Lake.

The average discharge from Rainy Lake into the Rainy River is 8,000 cfs (cubic feet per second); however, twenty percent of the time the flow is less than 5,000 cfs. At the mouth of Rainy River the average flow is over 10,000 cfs.

The outflow from Rainy Lake is controlled by the Minnesota and Ontario Paper Company at a dam at International Falls, subject to the terms of an Order issued by the International Joint Commission dated June 8, 1949 which prescribes the levels to be maintained on Rainy Lake. The outflows reflect the operation of the dam to achieve the lake levels prescribed in the Commission's Order. During periods of low water supply when the paper mill is operating only five days a week, the discharge from Rainy Lake on weekends is less than half of the weekly mean.

Rainy River is about 86 miles long with an average width of 600 feet. It has few meanders. The mid-channel depth varies from 10 to 20 feet. The average water surface gradient between Fort Frances and Baudette is one and a half inches per mile except at Manitou and Long Sault Rapids. Below Baudette the drop is one inch per mile. The result is a slow to sluggish current. Generally rounded, smooth, grass-covered banks abruptly rise 25 to 35 feet on both sides of the stream. The river has a narrow flood plain.

The southern portion of Lake of the Woods is shallow, generally free from islands and bounded by low, sandy or marshy shores with gently curving outlines.

The predominant industry in the area is the manufacture of pulp, paper and associated products, and related operations. The paper plant at International Falls is owned by Minnesota and Ontario Paper Company.[1] The plant at Fort Frances is owned by Ontario and Minnesota Paper Company Limited, a

[*]Report of the International Joint Commission, United States and Canada on The Pollution of Rainy River and Lake of the Woods, p. 2, Figure 1; pp. 8-14 with the exception of the subheading, "The Investigation" on pp. 9-10, 1965. Reproduced with the permission of Information Canada.

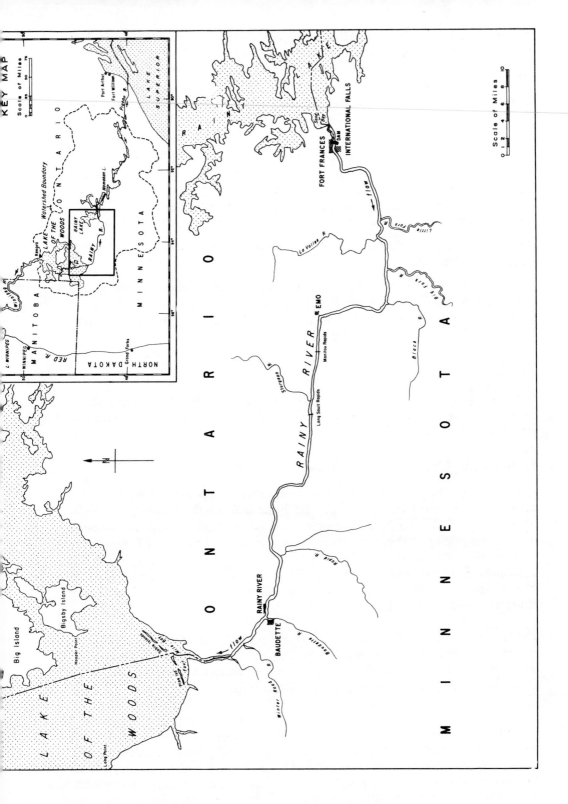

Figure 1
International Joint Commission Map of Rainy River
November, 1964.

121

wholly owned subsidiary of Minnesota and Ontario Paper Company. The manufacturing processes at both plants are integrated to such an extent that they operate in effect as one mill. The production of pulp is based on the groundwood, sulphite and kraft processes. In 1961 the average wood consumption was approximately 1,530 cords per day. At that time the average daily production was 730 tons of paper and 710 tons of insulite board and about 670 persons were employed at Fort Frances and 2,200 at International Falls.

Agriculture is the second most important industry with some 2,235 farms in the Rainy River drainage basin. Approximately 213,500 acres in Minnesota and 90,300 acres in Ontario are cultivated. Livestock is of prime importance on most farms. The principal crops are hay, grain and potatoes. Many farmers supplement their incomes by cutting pulpwood or timber during winter months.

Recreational facilities have been developed along the Minnesota side of the river between Baudette and Lake of the Woods.

According to the 1960 census, approximately 47,000 persons live in the watershed. About 9,500 reside in Fort Frances, 9,300 in International Falls and South International Falls, 1,100 in Rainy River, Ontario and 1,600 in Baudette, Minnesota. Fifty-eight percent of the population is rural.

Findings

After considering the results of the investigation, the evidence presented at the Public Hearing and subsequent briefs, the Commission arrived at the series of findings outlined below.

1. Multiple Uses of Rainy River

(a) *Domestic Water Supply:* Three communities obtain their domestic water supply from Rainy River. International Falls and South International Falls procure processed water from Minnesota and Ontario Paper Company's modern purification plant just above the International Bridge. The town of Rainy River obtains its domestic supply from the river. The only treatment given is chlorination. The estimated high cost of constructing and operating a suitable filtration plant forced Baudette to change its source of water supply from Rainy River to a *hard water* well.

(b) *Industrial Water Supply:* The pulp and paper mills at Fort Frances and International Falls use 83 million U.S. gallons (69 million Imperial gallons) per day, Minnesota and Ontario Paper Company has capacity to use up to 10,500 cfs for the generation of power at International Falls.

(c) *Domestic Sewage Disposal:* Sanitary sewage from four of the five sewered communities is discharged to Rainy River for final disposal. International Falls has secondary treatment facilities. Baudette provides primary treatment. The town of Rainy River has only sedimentation facilities. Fort Frances completed the construction of primary treatment works subsequent to the investigation. The fifth community, South International Falls, discharges its effluent into Rainy Lake.

(d) *Industrial Waste Disposal:* Industrial waste and sewage from the pulp and paper mills are discharged directly into Rainy River. Facilities to permit diversion of all domestic sewage from the paper mills to municipal systems are now under construction.

(e) *Recreation:* Most of the recreational developments are located in the section of Rainy River adjacent to Lake of the Woods. This resort area attracts those interested in fishing and boating. In 1959 vacationers spent an estimated $480,000 in this area.

2. Transboundary Movement

The currents of Rainy River cross and recross the international boundary. Observations on the movement of 72 floats released in the upper reaches of the river established the transboundary movement of these waters. Conductivity studies confirmed the results of the float tests. The constituents in these waters are thoroughly mixed at Manitou and Long Sault Rapids, about 30 miles downstream from International Falls.

3. Extent of Pollution

The quality of the waters under reference, after receiving domestic and industrial wastes, is discussed hereunder in relation to five indicators: coliform concentration, biochemical oxygen demand, dissolved oxygen, suspended solids and lignin. . . .

(a) *Coliform Concentration:* The coliform group of bacteria is used as an indicator group because these bacteria are the normal inhabitants of the intestines. The coliform group when found in water indicates that the water may have been contaminated with human or animal excreta. Fecal material contains a large number of coliform bacteria which are usually associated with the pathogenic group, a class of bacteria harmful to man. It would be impracticable to examine each water sample for all known pathogens since each identification would require a separate analysis. Hence, if the coliform group is present, it is assumed that the pathogens which represent a public health hazard are also present.

Raw sewage contains 10 to 25 million coliform organisms per 100 ml (millilitres). The median coliform count was less than 35 per 100 ml in Rainy Lake above the known sources of pollution. The word median in the term "median coliform count" is used to designate that value which is so related to the other values in a given set of samples that exactly as many values exceed it as fall short of it. An average value is the arithmetic mean of a number of samples.

Three miles above the dam at International Falls at the outlet from Rainy Lake, the median coliform count in Rainy River varied from 8 to 44 per 100 ml. Immediately below Fort Frances near the Ontario shore the coliform count ranged up to 147,000 per 100 ml. The median count in 1960 was 47,000. About a mile below International Falls near the Minnesota shore the median coliform count was 66,000; near the Ontario shore, 3,900. The median coliform concentration remained high for the next twelve miles downstream. Twelve miles below International Falls it varied from 7,200 to 15,000 per 100 ml. This is at least four hundred times greater than the count above the dam. Ten miles below Long Sault Rapids the median coliform count ranged between 4,600 and 6,700 per 100 ml. The concentration of coliform bacteria gradually decreased as the water progressed downstream. Near Baudette, in 1961 the median coliform count was 2,000 per 100 ml. In Lake of the Woods the average coliform count was only 7 per 100 ml.

(b) *Biochemical Oxygen Demand:* Aerobic decomposition of organic matter requires oxygen. The amount of decomposible matter contained in the water can be estimated by determining the amount and rate of oxygen utilization. This determination is called the biochemical oxygen demand or BOD and is the amount of oxygen consumed over a 5-day period at a constant temperature of 20°C. A British Royal Commission on sewage disposal to river systems suggested with respect to BOD levels, the following river classification based on the standard 5-day BOD test: BOD-1 ppm *very clean*, 2 ppm *clean*, 5 ppm *doubtful*, and 10 ppm *bad*. One ppm (part per million) is equal to one mg/l (milligram per litre).

At the outlet from Rainy Lake the BOD varied from 0.9 to 2.6 mg/l. Near the Ontario shore immediately below Fort Frances the BOD increased to 6.1 mg/l. About a mile below the mill at International Falls the average BOD near the Minnesota shore was 15.8 mg/l, in the middle of the river 3.5 mg/l, and near the Ontario shore 3.4 mg/l. Twelve miles below the pulp and paper plants the BOD varied from 4.0 to 7.4 mg/l – four times greater than the concentration above the dam. Ten miles below Long Sault Rapids biological stabilization reduced the BOD to 2.0 mg/l. In the Baudette–Rainy River area a slight increase in BOD was noted. In Lake of the Woods the average BOD was 1.7 mg/l.

(c) *Dissolved Oxygen:* A drop in the dissolved oxygen content indicates the presence of organic pollution. The point of maximum de-oxygenation may be some distance down river from the point of pollution, because the de-oxygenation of water by industrial wastes and sewage is a comparatively slow process. The oxygen deficiency is replaced by acquisition of oxygen from the atmosphere and by photosynthesis.

A substantial reduction in dissolved oxygen causes suffocation of fish. The second edition of Water Quality Criteria by the California State Water Quality Control Board cites the conclusions of M. M. Ellis that under average stream conditions, 3.0 mg/l of dissolved oxygen, or less, should be regarded as hazardous, and to maintain a varied fish fauna in good condition the dissolved oxygen concentration should remain at 5.0 mg/l or higher. The Aquatic Life Advisory Committee of the Ohio River Valley Water Sanitation Commission recommended that the minimum dissolved oxygen concentration for a well rounded warm water fish population should not be less than 5 mg/l during at least 16 hours of any 24 hour period and at no time should the dissolved oxygen content be less than 3 mg/l.

About a mile above the dam at International Falls the average DO (dissolved oxygen) concentration varied from 7.7 to 8.2 mg/l; the DO saturation varied from 85 percent to 90 percent. Twelve miles below the paper mills the average DO varied from 5.1 to 6.4 mg/l – a drop of 2.0/1; the saturation varied from 58 percent to 73 percent – a drop of 25 percent. Ten miles below Long Sault Rapids the minimum DO value was 3.9 mg/l while the average value varied from 5.4 to 5.8. As the water progressed downstream the average DO dropped to 4.1 mg/l or 47 percent saturation near Baudette. In 1961 the minimum values in the reach of the river near Baudette varied from 0.9 to 1.1 mg/1 or 10 percent saturation. Below Baudette the DO concentration began to recover due to algae in the slow moving water. In Lake of the Woods the average DO rose to 7.7 mg/1 or 88 percent saturation.

(d) *Suspended Solids:* The concentration of suspended solids indicate the extent of pollution due to the discharge of solids into the river. All settleable solids are suspended solids until they have settled on the bottom of the water course. Dissolved or colloidal solids, such as sulphite waste liquors, may be synthesized by bacteria in the stream to form suspended and settleable sludge. Turbidity is attributable to suspended and colloidal matter. The analytical data on the concentration of suspended solids excludes floating masses and bottom deposits.

In general the standards for water quality for most States require substantially complete removal of suspended solids attributable to sewage, industrial or other wastes.

At the outlet of Rainy Lake the average suspended solids concentration for each of the four sampling points was relatively low, varying from 4.2 to 7.1 mg/l. Immediately below Fort Frances near the Ontario shore the concentration of suspended solids was as high as 87.0 mg/1 with an average value of 31.9. About a mile below International Falls near the Minnesota shore the concentration was as high as 212.8 mg/1 with an average value of 36.8. The concentration of suspended solids in the middle of the river was 14.2 mg/1 and near the Ontario shore 12.3. Twelve miles below International Falls the average concentration varied from 11.0 to 20.8 mg/1 – a threefold increase over the levels found at the outlet from Rainy Lake. Below Long Sault Rapids the average suspended solids varied from 9.9 to 15.1 mg/1. In this reach of the river about half of the suspended solids were of organic origin. Immediately below Baudette the average suspended solids varied from 7.9 to 15.7 mg/1. In Lake of the Woods the average was 10.0 mg/1.

(e) *Lignin:* Wood is made up of cellulose combined with lignin, a substance related to carbohydrates. Lignin degenerates very slowly. It is a common constituent of water flowing through wooded and swampy areas and is usually associated with a brown color in water. The pulping process liberates the lignin from the wood fibres. Thus the lignin concentrations identify the type of waste being discharged into the Rainy River.

At the outlet from Rainy Lake the average lignin concentration varied from 0.6 to 1.2 mg/1. Near the Ontario shore immediately below the Fort Frances plant the average lignin concentration was 2.2 in 1961. About a mile below the International Falls plant the average lignin concentration in 1961 was 9.5 mg/1 near the Minnesota shore. The maximum concentration was 27.0. Twelve miles below the paper plants the average lignin concentration varied from 1.8 to 4.5 mg/1 – a threefold increase over the values at the outlet from Rainy Lake. In the reach of Rainy River between Emo and Lake of the Woods lignin concentration was fairly uniform. Average values ranged from 1.4 to 3.1 mg/1. The average lignin concentration in Lake of the Woods was 1.5 mg/1.

Water of good quality entered Rainy River from Rainy Lake. Significant changes in water quality were found immediately below Fort Frances and

International Falls. The strong wastes from the domestic and industrial sewer outlets were concentrated near each shore. Twelve miles downstream from International Falls the wastes had spread across the river. Essentially complete mixing of the wastes was attained by the time the water reached Long Sault Rapids about half way between the source of Rainy River in Rainy Lake and its outlet into Lake of the Woods. The effects of sedimentation and biological stabilization became more evident as the water progressed downstream. Serious pollution . . . existed throughout the Rainy River from Fort Frances to Lake of the Woods. The waters of Lake of the Woods showed a remarkable recovery when compared to the contaminated condition in the upper reaches of Rainy River. The water quality of Lake of the Woods is satisfactory.

4. Sources of Pollution

The water quality of the streams entering Rainy River below International Falls was determined. The median coliform count on the ten tributaries was relatively low, varying from 70 to 1,200; the average BOD ranged from 1.2 to 4.5 mg/l, a range from *clean* to nearly *doubtful*; the average dissolved oxygen varied from 4.4 to 6.9 mg/l; the average lignin concentration ranged from 1.4 to 3.9 mg/l; and the average suspended solids varied from 6.3 to 41.7 mg/l. Furthermore, since these ten tributaries contribute only fifteen percent of the total flow of the Rainy River, they cannot be regarded as a major source of pollution.

The estimated BOD load due to domestic wastes was 2,800 pounds per day. International Falls, with secondary treatment, contributed only 9 percent of the entire domestic waste load; Baudette, with primary treatment, contributed 18 percent; Rainy River, with only sedimentation, represented 5 percent; and Fort Frances, with no treatment at the time of the investigation, was responsible for 58 percent. The remaining 10 percent of the domestic BOD load was contributed by villages on the tributaries. The entire domestic BOD load discharged to Rainy River is about one percent of the combined domestic and industrial BOD load.

The major source of pollution was found to be the sewer outlets of the Minnesota and Ontario Paper Company's plants at Fort Frances and International Falls. All wastes from these plants, with the exception of 60 percent of the domestic sewage from the International Falls plant, were discharged to the Rainy River without treatment.

The sewer outlets at the International Falls plant discharged screened overflow from the pulp thickener, waste from the woodroom and bark recovery plant, overflow from the ash pond which receives the main boiler plant ashes, waste water from the sulphite screens and wet room, diluted spent sulphite liquor, bleach plant wastes, kraft mill wastes including lime sludge, wastes from the insulite mill, sewage wastes from the paper mill, backwash from the filtration plant and cooling water from the asphalt rodding mill. The Fort Frances plant discharged waste from the rotary bark screens, waste from the Tyler screens, waste from the sulphite deckers, lean white water overflow and sewage from the paper mill.

The mill surveys in 1960 and 1961 found the waste waters carried a high bacterial content. The BOD load contributed by the two plants was approximately 255,000 pounds per day. This is equivalent to the oxygen demand of the domestic wastes from a city of one and one half million people. Despite the effectiveness of the bark pond, before it washed out during the high water of 1962, the suspended solids load, including bark, fibre, chips and lime sludge, discharged to the Rainy River from the mill outlets exceeded 100 tons per day. Of this total the woody materials amounted to 61.5 tons per day. The lignin content of the waste was consistently high.

The Minnesota and Ontario Paper Company's brief of August 1964 confirmed the results of the Board's survey. The Company estimated that their overall daily discharge into the river included 57.2 tons of fibre and 60 tons of calcium carbonate (lime sludge).

5. Effects of Pollution

The discharge of untreated domestic wastes into Rainy River is a danger to health since the sewage contains organisms of diseases transmittable to humans. The coliform bacteria count in the first sixty miles below International Falls exceeded 6,000 per 100 ml. Thus, the river cannot be used safely as a source of drinking water unless there is auxiliary pre-treatment in addition to conventional purification. The waters of Rainy River, according to health authorities, are unsuitable for bathing.

The discharge of wastes from the pulp and paper mills has limited the development of river property between Fort Frances and Baudette. The unsightly and often odorous deposits along the shorelines and river bottom caused by suspended solids such as bark, fibre, chips and lime sludge has lessened the attractiveness of waterfront areas. The nutrients in the industrial wastes promoted the prolific growth of Sphaerotilus, a filamentous bacterium, in the upper reaches of the river. These slime masses attached to submerged or largely submerged obstructions and trapped fresh fibres have an objectionable appearance especially when the water level in the river recedes. The presence of suspended solids and slimes in the river has increased the cost of obtaining a satisfactory water supply at Baudette.

Biologically, Rainy River was most affected by wood fibres and associated wastes discharged from the pulp and paper mills. Benthos (the flora and fauna found at the bottom of streams, lakes and oceans) development was impeded. A number of the more desirable fish food organisms could not contend with the river environment during the summers with normal flows. In Four Mile Bay, at the outlet of Rainy River, the distribution of benthic animals was markedly affected by the pattern of sedimentation of wood waste materials. The condition of the river imposed limitations on the number of fish species in the upper eleven miles. Younger age groups of game fish were less numerous than normally anticipated. The fish population, according to witnesses at the Hearing, has been drastically reduced over the past twenty-five years.

The majority of organisms avoided fresh wood fibre deposits. Fresh wood fibres served as a nucleus for Sphaerotilus growth. The wood sugars (Xylose, Dextrose, and Fructose) from the pulping process not only have a high oxygen demand but also encourage the growth of Sphaerotilus which has a deleterious effect on fish propagation and fish food organisms.

Research studies established that survival conditions for Walleye eggs in Rainy River below International Falls were poor in 1961 and 1962. Survival to fry (the first stage of a fish after the egg) was less than one percent in 1961 and varied from 0.02 to 6.0 percent in 1962. Survival in controls from the same lots at the Waskish State Hatchery were 69.6 percent in 1961 and 41.4 percent in 1962. The principal cause of low survival was Sphaerotilus, a bacterium slime, covering the eggs during incubation. This prevented successful emergence of the fry.

The sulphites in the mill wastes readily become oxidized by removing the dissolved oxygen from the receiving waters. The fish population was jeopardized by dissolved oxygen levels being below 4 mg/l for appreciable periods in the ten mile reach of the river above Baudette.

The waters of Rainy River are polluted to such a degree that they are unsatisfactory for recreation. Sludge banks and floating islands of bark, fibre and chips, floating scum from lime sludge wastes, and malodorous conditions caused by bottom deposits has adversely affected the aesthetic value of Rainy River. The deposits of woody materials are over three feet thick in some areas of its outlet in Four Mile Bay. The river is unsafe for recreational bathing due to its polluted condition. Fibre and slime entanglement on fish lines is so serious that sport fishing is limited to the fast waters of the Sioux and Manitou Rapids and the lower ten miles of the river. A witness testified at the hearing that outboard motors become so clogged with fibres that they have to be overhauled every two weeks. Fishermen who formerly used the resort facilities in the lower reach of the river have, in recent years, gone to other places because they did not like fishing under such conditions.

6. Effects of Weekend Flow Reduction

During periods of low inflow into Rainy Lake the weekend discharge from the dam at International Falls was reduced to less than half of the weekday average. This lowered the water level in the upper half of the river above Manitou Rapids, exposing unsightly banks and part of the river bed. As a result, bottom animals and fauna on the exposed areas were destroyed and malodorous conditions developed.

7. Remedial Measures Constructed or Planned

The Ontario Water Resources Commission in 1964 completed the construction of a pollution control plant with facilities for primary treatment of sewage from Fort Frances. It is operated by the Ontario Water Resources Commission under an agreement with the City of Fort Frances.

The pulp and paper companies are in the process of completing the connection of their sanitary sewers in the Fort Frances and International Falls mills with the respective municipal treatment plants. The companies have also announced that they plan to complete some of the necessary in-plant waste segregation and recovery projects by 1967. These projects include bark burning facilities in the new steam plant, improved bark and waste wood recovery facilities at the Fort Frances plant, better recovery of fibre at the insulite mill, and modification of the sulphite chemical-cooking plant to utilize half of the calcium carbonate now being wasted. These in-plant improvements will be an initial step towards reducing the pollutants in the mill wastes and as such will be helpful in improving the quality of the waters of Rainy River.

Air Pollution*

Conservation Council of Ontario

Our stone-aged ancestors, huddled over a smouldering fire in a cave, were probably the first men to suffer from air pollution. Through the seventeenth and eighteenth centuries Europe coughed and spluttered over smoky fireplaces, and the industrial revolution brought in its wake the black cities of Europe where buildings, vegetation and humanity alike were covered with soot. But it is small consolation to the city-dweller of today, his eyes watering and his throat sore, to be told that the problem is an old one.

In any case, not all of our air pollution problems are very old. Automobile exhaust fumes are no older than the motor car itself, and some of the more complex industrial pollutants appeared even more recently. Radioactive fall-out is the best publicized and one of the potentially most serious forms of new pollution. Wherever man converts energy he produces air pollution, and the pollutants are many and varied.

The Kinds of Pollutants

Only a few groups of substances, however, form the great bulk of wastes that we pour into the atmosphere. The two commonest occur in the air naturally. Most abundant is water vapour, and next in line is carbon dioxide. Recently scientists have found that the carbon dioxide-oxygen balance of the atmosphere is changing, as our energy uses increase, and in the long term the growing amount of carbon dioxide in the atmosphere may have profound influences on world climate. Until this was known the gas was not considered a pollutant, and in its immediate impact on our air it is quite harmless.

A group of dangerous gases are present in automobile exhausts, and they are also produced in some industrial processes. Carbon monoxide is an odorless gas which is very dangerous to most people over a period in concentrations of 100 parts per million or more. That is not much: a good-sized car ashtray could hold enough carbon monoxide to endanger the people in the car! Nitric oxide is more poisonous, and may change to the even more deadly nitrogen dioxide, a reddish-brown gas, in the atmosphere.

Then there are gases such as ethylene, and other hydrocarbons of the same type. Ethylene itself will damage plants, but in the so-called "Los Angeles smog

Air Pollution by the Conservation Council of Ontario, Toronto, 1970. Postal address is Suite 604, 11 Adelaide Street West, Toronto 1, Ontario.

reaction" it and other hydrocarbons, with nitrogen dioxide, react together in sunlight. They form a complex mixture of ozone, aldehydes and other chemical compounds which irritate the eyes and nose, and can seriously damage plants and insects.

The burning of coal and of oil yields a second major group of pollutants. Sulphur dioxide is the most serious of these, and even a few parts per million of this gas are highly irritating to breathe. In the atmosphere the oxygen and water vapour in the air change some of it to sulphuric acid mist, which can be carried deep into the lungs. Soot is the product of inefficient combustion: it consists of chains of finely divided carbon, which can absorb hydrocarbons and carry these into the lungs. Some of the compounds carried in this manner have been shown to cause cancers; however, no direct relationship between general atmospheric pollution and cancer has been demonstrated.

Hydrogen sulphide is the "rotten eggs" gas; it is also poisonous, but its foul smell ensures fairly prompt attention. Stagnant waters containing industrial wastes often produce hydrogen sulphide.

A Multitude of Others

Among the multitude of other pollutants some are particularly important. Hydrogen fluoride is produced in the manufacture of phosphate fertilizers and in manufacture of some metals; it is extremely poisonous, and can seriously damage plants and livestocks. Pesticides and herbicides in the atmosphere are now known to have far reaching effects on the environment as a whole.

Figures on the amounts of urban air pollution differ with place and time; in Canada we might expect that winter would be the period of greatest pollution, and that the heavily urbanized areas of Ontario and Quebec would yield the highest concentrations. Figures are scarce, but a report on the Greater Detroit-Windsor area in 1959 quoted a total of 5270 tons of pollutants each day, with roughly 30 percent of this consisting of hydrocarbons, 25 percent various solids, and some 20 percent sulphur oxides. Coals and oil yield 60 to 120 pounds of sulphur oxides for every ton of fuel burned, and an automobile accelerating from a standing position to 25 miles per hour will emit half a pound of carbon monoxide per mile travelled. Diesel trucks smell unpleasant, but they emit only about ten percent of the hydrocarbons and one percent of the carbon monoxide emitted by automobiles per pound of fuel burned.

What To Do?

It is much easier to identify the air pollution problem than it is to solve it. We have relied on the ability of the air to cleanse itself. Air movement spreads out the pollution, and the pollutants react with one another and with the oxygen in the air to form less harmful compounds. Rain and snow dissolve many of these impurities in the atmosphere; the air is cleansed at the expense of our water courses, which receive the polluted rainfall. But this easy solution is now failing us. We are pumping too many pollutants into the air all at once and the impurities are not being carried "away", but just over to the next town or city, where they add to the problems already there.

The best solution to air pollution is to eliminate it at the source. Much industrial pollution can be controlled in this manner, although the equipment to do this work is sometimes very costly. In some cases, however, there may not be adequate technology to remove all pollutants in this manner; for example, when an industry's emissions consist of very small quantities of a wide range of different chemicals, the costs of removing them all might be very difficult to meet.

Other approaches to lightening pollution loads include such measures as locating industries down-wind of urban centres and increasing the height of smoke stacks. These have a legitimate place in pollution control; although they have justifiably raised the anger of conservationists because they have sometimes been used by industries to avoid the costs of installing available, but more expensive, control equipment.

The atmosphere has tremendous powers to dilute, disperse and destroy pollutants, and locating industries downwind or increasing the height of smoke stacks should allow pollutants to be dispersed or destroyed before they reach the ground. The difficulty is that winds do not always blow in the same direction and that down drafts can occur, thus bringing heavy loads of damaging pollutants to the immediate vicinity of the industry. Such measures can also be self-defeating if used too extensively: too many high smokestacks in extensive urban areas simply increase the overall level of pollution. The warm pall of air over large cities can stimulate *inversions*, where the polluted air is trapped over the area for days at a time.

Solutions Need Research

Solutions to automobile pollution, and to the pollution from domestic heating installations, are even harder to find. Until recently there has been little incentive for anyone even to try, but with the growing recognition of the problem pressure for research on improved equipment and on possible alternatives is gaining impetus.

While Canada was mainly rural air pollution did not represent a real problem, and this has been reflected in the relative lack of legislation. For many years air pollution was considered a very local matter, chiefly one of smoke abatement, and penalties at worst entailed a small fine. To polluting industries such fines were little more than a licence to pollute.

Recently Ontario has brought air pollution under Provincial jurisdiction, and appears to be moving towards a broad programme of control. Such action reflects the growing recognition that air pollution has not only impact on health, but has serious economic and social effects as well. Those polluting can now be held responsible for the pollution they cause. However, the existence of laws does not ensure their enforcement, and a strong and continuing pressure of public concern will always be needed if clean air is to be achieved.

The Quality of Our Environment

The problems of air pollution, and of pollution generally, are part of a broader, forbidding picture which includes our growing mountains of trash and garbage, our sprawling cities with their perennial traffic jams and ceaseless noise, and the gradual disappearance of our open green spaces with the overcrowding of those that remain. The picture is an increasingly unpleasant one: in spite of our technology and our growing affluence, the quality of our lives has begun to deteriorate.

The problem is two-fold: first, our numbers are increasing everywhere, putting more and more pressure on resources, such as land, that are only available in limited or fixed amounts. Second, our inventiveness is constantly producing new materials, new approaches, and new techniques, many very useful and desirable in themselves, but often inadvertently adding wholly new problems to the serious ones already existing. Pesticides, in their subtle, long-term build ups, threaten animal populations and even life itself. Radioactive wastes from nuclear power installations present largely unknown hazards. Overabundant plant nutrients upset the ecological balance of our lakes.

Ecology—Hope for the Future

Ecology, perhaps, is the key word. Ecology, the study of the natural systems and communities, has revealed what many early conservationists had sensed intuitively for many years: that our piecemeal, short-term approaches to using our natural resources are now seriously disrupting these subtle, but vital, interrelationships. We are only now beginning to realize that our environment is a complex system: a system in which air, water and soil, and the myriad kinds of life they support, interact together to produce a harmonious whole.

Possibly to many it will seem that not very much is wrong: they will not notice the disappearance of our birds-of-prey, they will accept that the local beach is no longer a suitable place from which to swim; and they will regard air pollution as the necessary product of being able to drive downtown. Besides, without reflection these are small matters, and surely they cannot really imply mankind itself is in some way threatened. The condition has been well named "the Quiet Crisis", for in fact it is now clear that these local, small-scale problems are not local at all, but on a global scale their impact on our world is shattering. Very soon it may be too late.

Disastrous Rate of Change

The world is not static, and change is inevitable. It is the rate of change today which is so potentially disastrous. We cannot turn the clock back and we really do not wish to do so, but we must bring these rapid and sweeping changes under control. We are living in a highly complex world and the answers we will find will entail difficult choices, and they will cost money. The cries of destitution from polluting industries are unconvincing, but we should still recognize that we must balance our need for clean air and water with the production of needed goods. We have to balance the need to preserve our natural lands with food needs of the growing world population. And we must also recognize that our burgeoning populations themselves, continuing unchecked, will in time defeat much of our efforts to achieve these balances. Conservation is a matter of intelligent choices which will benefit mankind's own long-term interests and be in harmony with his environment. But we must choose, and we cannot afford not to pay the cost. Economic yardsticks can no longer be the major criterion in our decisions.

Talk Louder, I Can't Hear You[*]

Ti Estin

The average person never stops hearing: he may want to, but it is very difficult to do. What makes this situation bad is the fact that the air is constantly filled with noise.

A certain amount of noise is unavoidable: but the amount of noise we hear daily is becoming more and more dangerous. It is a well established and well known fact that the longer we are exposed to loud noises, the less acute our hearing becomes. The acuteness of our hearing, however, depends not only on the loudness of sound or noise, but also its quality: the more frequencies a noise contains (especially higher frequencies) the more dangerous it is to our ears.

Noise does more than merely make us a bit hard of hearing. Prolonged exposure to noise can permanently shift our threshold of hearing: if this threshold is shifted far enough, we become deaf. Among the less serious effects we have auditory fatigue, a phenomenon which has many aspects; shifts in pitch, loudness and timbre of above-threshold stimuli, disappearance of a sustained tone initially above the threshold and ringing in the ears. Neither growth nor recovery of temporary threshold shift is influenced by drugs, medications, time of day, hypnosis, good thoughts or extra-sensory perception.

Further, noise inhibits speech intelligibility. Besides the obvious factor of loudness, there is a factor of the bandwidth that is passed for the ear to listen to. The wider the range of noise, the more it inhibits speech intelligibility.

Noise also has an adverse effect on non-aural sensory functions. Accommodation (the act of shifting the focus on the eye) is inhibited in the presence of loud noise. High level noise reduces the speed with which the eye can move through certain angles of focus clearly on near and distant objects.

Also, the quality of work, especially calculation, decreases as noise increases: noise has no apparent effect on the number of responses made, only on the number of errors.

Certain noises disorient us, not so much by their loudness as by what they symbolize. Sirens and approaching airplanes can cause apprehension and have adverse effects on our dispositions.

Loud noises, even noises to which we are accustomed, can bring about effects of which we are completely unaware. Among these are disturbances in the vegetative nervous system. Besides the above mentioned effects on accommodation (occasioned by an involuntary dilation of the pupil and loss of control of the muscles which focus light by contracting the lens), there also occurs a reduction of the blood volume in the skin. Often there also accompanies this an increase in diastolic blood pressure.

[*]BA Veldhuis. Reprinted by permission. Originally published in the *Silhouette* (*Ti Estin* Special Edition on Ecology, Pollution, and Conservation), McMaster University, November 28, 1969.

As is the case with auditory damage, disorientation of the vegetative nervous system is more serious if a broad bandwidth of noise is heard.

While it hasn't been established that meaningless noise disturbs sleep to any great degree, neither has it been proven that the noise of cars, car horns, sirens (plain or oscillating), airplanes, or screeching tires are meaningless noises.

How close are we, then, to dangerous noises?

Damage to the ear (especially the threshold of hearing) begins at 85 decibels (A). (dB (A) represents decibels on a scale (A) which has an upper range of about 10,000 Hz and discriminates against frequencies lower than about 400 Hz.) The average decibel count in urban areas is about 75. It is increasing at the rate of one decibel per year. This means that everyone will be completely deaf by the year 2000. The vegetative reactions listed above begin at ratings of 70dB (A) and higher.

Not only do these noise hazards apply to any person who happens to be taking his daily constitutional, they apply, with much greater danger, to industrial workers of all kinds. Also, the community aspect of excessive noise not only causes much damage but also affects the psychological and physiological well-being of its members and affects their interaction.

Certain highway authorities prohibit vehicular noise in excess of 88 dB (A) at a distance of fifty feet from the highway. At about 100 feet from the highway (the distance of the nearest houses) the decibel count has dropped to about 83. Certainly no one living at that distance from the highway is going to be deafened; neither are they, through the somewhat deficient solicitousness of the traffic authority, going to be able to talk.

One can easily dismiss (on the plea of progress) the fact that our threshold of hearing soon will run the risk of permanent dislocation: perhaps it isn't even too difficult to console oneself that everyone in America will be as deaf as posts by 20-0 [sic] A.D.: we can all take in stride the fact that the present noise level is having adverse psychological and physiological effect upon us: but can we, with the amount of trust we put in our behavioural psychologists, lightly dismiss the facts that guinea pigs, exposed to short periods of above normal but supposedly tolerable noise, have developed swollen inside-the-ear membranes and had vital inner ear hair cells (upon which they rely for equilibrium) destroyed? And can we dismiss the implications of the fact that rats, under prolonged exposure to noise, have turned homosexual?

Noise Pollution in Modern Day Society*

John E. K. Foreman

The detrimental effects of air, water and soil pollution, which have been steadily invading our society over the years until they have reached almost insurmountable proportions, are now becoming well documented. The press, radio and

*Mimeographed paper from the Faculty of Engineering Science, University of Western Ontario.

television are continually noting that much is currently being done to combat this growing problem, as evidenced by governmental and community action, international agreements and exchange of information, and, more close to home, programs at universities and community colleges aimed at air, water and soil pollution control . . . . Less well documented, however, are the serious consequences of the insidious advance of another form of air pollution in our daily lives – NOISE.

Pollution problems have certain common characteristics: usually they involve not one but many sources of pollution; usually they develop gradually and become well-established before the problem is recognized; the individual contributor to pollution is generally harmless, but the sum total of many contributors becomes a serious hazard – and so on.

The problem of noise in our modern day society certainly appears to fit the general pollution pattern. And, the idea that noise is a necessary price of industrial and economic progress is as antiquated as is the belief that contaminated waters and a polluted atmosphere must also accompany civilization's material advances. Noise pollution is only now beginning to receive a proper share of public attention.

Looking back in history, Juvenal bemoaned the all night cacophony of Imperial Rome, observing that "most sick people perish for want of sleep." To Schopenhauer, a nineteenth-century German philosopher, it was clear that the "amount of noise that anyone can bear undisturbed stands in inverse proportion to his mental capacity, and may therefore be regarded as a pretty fair measure of it." Now, however, noise-hating is suddenly becoming the in-thing. Many conscientious communities are beginning to treat noise as a public concern. A few cities are passing ordinances to control it. Sound engineers and acoustical experts are making strenuous efforts to understand the problem and to take corrective action. But a growing consensus holds that modern man must eventually be forced to attack noise in the same way that he attacks the contamination of his air and water – through enforcement. Engineers, though, are frequently in a position to help combat this growing nuisance because of their key role in the design of equipment and facilities, in operation, and in construction, and the initiative to alleviate noise problems by those who can do so may, in fact, head off this inevitable public clamour for enforced control as has happened with air and water pollution.

The development of noise pollution is symptomatic of our modern infatuation with mechanical gadgets. Our ears are continually being harassed by a growing range of roaring, buzzing, beeping, grinding, howling, jangling, blaring, booming, screeching, whining, gnashing, blatting, and crashing. And it seems to be getting worse all the time. Many militant anti-noise pollutionists blame this racket for such woes as heart disease, ulcers and sexual impotency. In a more positive sense, correlations have been established between noise and loss of hearing, nervous disorders, irritability and inefficiency, and even hypertension and high blood pressure.

Psychological effects are another serious consequence of noise. Some psychiatrists state that when noise interrupts a person's sleep, he is prevented from dreaming, which may result in such symptoms as paranoiac delusions and hallucinal and suicidal impulses. Certainly, this nocturnal invasion interrupts the "deep" sleep which is so necessary for physical and mental health.

Much of our man-made noise is intentional. Italians have put Alfa-Romeo horns on Fiats, and sometimes honk until the battery goes dead. The deep-throated, powerful roar which emerges from the unmuffled exhaust of a sports car or motor cycle is calculated to set off these particular vehicles as items of prestige. The modern highly-amplified beat music of the younger generation, the ever-present blaring of transistor radios, and the steady diet of Muzak, to which we are exposed no matter where we go these days, seems to indicate that our generation runs the risk of becoming habituated to noise.

Moreover, much of what irritates modern man is simply new noise traded in for old. The ear that now flinches at the blat of a diesel bus might well have recoiled as much from the clang, rattle, crash of the old street trolley. The whine of rubber tires on our modern day cars replaces the bang and screech of unsprung cartwheels on cobblestones. As a further tradeoff, I suppose that one could say that the back-fire of today's engines supplants the ringing hooves of yesterday's dray horses.

What is noise? Simply defined, it is unwanted sound. Subjectively, noise is something we hear and recognize, such as a train whistle or an alarm bell. Objectively, it is an energy wave transmitted to the air by vibrating air molecules. Most commonly, noise is measured in decibels. Abbreviated "d.b.", the decibel is a dimensionless number that describes levels of acoustic pressure, power or intensity. For example, it is a logarithmic ratio between two sound pressures: the actual pressure being measured and a reference standard pressure. The variation in range of acoustical power between a soft whisper and a modern turbo-jet engine is something of the order of 10^{15} or 10^{16}. The logarithmic ratio of decibels allows these wide ranges to be more conveniently handled. On the decibel scale, normal breathing measures 10 decibels, leaves rustling in a breeze score 20, a quiet restaurant or private business office 50, busy traffic at a hundred feet would be 70, Niagara Falls or inside a motor bus 90, inside a DC-6 airliner 105, engine room of a conventional submarine at full speed about 120, a jet at takeoff 140 and a space rocket 175. The threshold of hearing is 0 decibels, and the pain threshold is about 135 d.b.

So delicate an instrument is the human ear that at certain frequencies it can discern sound that moves the ear drum a distance of only 1/10 the size of a hydrogen atom. Sound vibrations are transmitted by the ear drum and ossicle bones to the inner ear, a bony and membranous structure lined with tiny cells. These cells, which respond to the various amplitudes and frequencies of sound vibration as detected by the ear drum, are connected to the brain's auditory nerve. It is these cells that are damaged most in noise-induced deafness. The ones that pick up the high frequencies are the first to be damaged, and as the noise bombardment continues, the destruction continues to nerve cells of lower frequency – all without the hearer being aware of damage. According to reliable estimates, about 18 million Americans suffer total or partial deafness; among working males, two out of three cases of deafness are caused by noise. Presumably similar percentages apply to Canada as well.

Noise in heavy industry – such as metal cutting, drilling, air blasting, riveting, drop forging, metal stamping, high speed paper rolls – has contributed over the years to the hearing loss of countless numbers of employees. As a result of compensation claims for industrial hearing loss, which have been decided in recent years by the courts in favour of the plaintiff, many industries have become more aware of the dangers of noise induced hearing loss, and have started noise abatement measures and regular tests of workers' hearing. Several states in the U.S.A., and several countries in Europe, have enacted or are currently in the process of enacting noise control legislation in industry.

A significant example of noise legislation passed in recent years is contained in the amendments to the Walsh-Healey Public Contracts Act in the U.S.A. . . . . These amendments establish limits on noise exposure for employees of companies with federal contracts of at least $10,000 annually. The exposure limits are based on data, accumulated over many years, relating occupational noise exposure to eventual hearing loss. The amendments set a limit of 90 d.b. (on the A-weighted scale[1]) for continuous noise exposure during an 8-hour working day, if ear protection is not used. Over a period of 10 or more years, this restricted level will prevent hearing loss in about 80 percent of those exposed. The impact of these amendments has been significant in industry because, in the vast majority of instances, present noise levels exceed this limit. Furthermore, the presumption of the regulations is that ear protection will be provided as a substitute *only* when a noise reduction program is clearly not feasible. There is no similar legislation in Canadian industry – yet.

But industrial workers are not the only people who are literally being deafened by the din of the technological age. Most of us are all too ignorant of the hearing hazards in everyday life. The suburban power lawn mower, the noise of a Honda exhaust, the high-pitched whine from a modern dish washer, the noise generated by diesel engines, air compressors, common pneumatic drills and other construction equipment, the sightseeing helicopters flapping overhead at Niagara Falls, the continual din of heavy traffic in urban areas (the noise level in cities has risen an estimated 1 d.b. a year for the last 30 years) – these are all examples of intensely dangerous hazards to one's hearing.

By contrast, quietness seems to save the ears. Doctors Bergman and Rosen of the Hunter College Speech and Hearing Centre in the U.S.A. tested hearing among the Mabaans of Sudan, a tribe so primitive that they do not even beat drums, and found their hearing pin-drop sharp. However, when subjected to loud noises, these gentle Mabaans suffered spasms of their blood vessels.

Even in the luxury apartments of the upper living class, there is little protection against noise. Unseen, but all too perfectly heard, are domestic strife (and bliss), telephone bells and door knockers (is it ours or theirs?), new hi-fis, and old TV commercials. Pounding on the wall is no solution; it is all too likely to collapse.

Poor walls, or no walls in fact, are partly responsible for the intrusion of noise upon our private lives. Urbanization and the consequent spurt in apartment living, together with high construction cost, has forced the developer to use smaller rooms, lower ceilings, cheaper materials. And the modern vogue for the light and glassy, rather than the solid and massive, seems to have little basis on function. Spaces are not isolated but continue without barrier through glass, grills and gardens. But continuous structures and the open plan are inimical to quiet living. From one room to another flow the sounds of whirring mixers, vacuum cleaners and garbage grinders, babbling radios and television sets, humming refrigerators and air conditioners. The air conditioner's incessant hum, in fact, is one of the important new sounds in North America. Recent noise ordinances which have been adopted in Florida have set the allowable loudness for air conditioning appliances so low that contractors are hesitant about installing any more air conditioners until the manufacturers have managed to reduce the noise. This, however, is becoming a real problem; the mechanical and electrical conveniences which accompany our technological growth are increasing in both speed and power, and, as a consequence, there is inherently an increase in sound energy associated with these units.

The irony of the air conditioner uproar is that, however unwanted the sound it makes on the outside, the hiss of air on the inside can be used to advantage. Sound engineers refer to it as "white noise" or "acoustical perfume", and they use it widely – especially in offices, to blanket distracting sounds which spring out of silence into disconcerting acoustical relief.

Noise abatement is probably most immediately on the minds of those whose homes are within a five-mile radius of a jet airport. A few years ago, Newark airport was closed as a result of complaints by a fearful and hostile community. In one of Manhattan's high-rent areas, residents have been up in arms about the heliport which has been located on top of the Pan American building. Seattle residents a short while ago concluded a successful lawsuit against the nearby airport by arguing that the airport authority was using their property in overflying it. This has raised fears that similar damage suits will be initiated elsewhere.

In his transportation message to Congress in 1966, former President Johnson directed the Federal Aviation Agency and NASA, along with the Secretaries of Commerce and Housing and Urban Development, to formulate a program to combat aircraft noise. Under increased pressure, aircraft manufacturers are designing for increased noise suppression in the aircraft itself. As an example, the 490-passenger Boeing 747 was designed to produce less noise than the 707, even though the newer model's engines will produce 40,000 lb. of thrust as compared to the 707's 15,000 lb.

Another instrument for any nation's attack on airplane noise is legislative action, which to date has hardly been employed at all. Perhaps the most striking illustration of the effectiveness of the use of legislation was at Dulles Airport in Washington D.C. There, a zoning law established 10,000 acres as a large buffer area around the airport, and housing developments were kept even further away by strict zoning regulations.

The bone-jarring sonic boom, however, which will accompany the advent of the supersonic age, will pose a threat of an entirely different dimension. These shock waves, which stretch out as much as eighty miles in width beneath a supersonic transport, can no longer affect only residents located near an airport. In 1964, a study of the effects of sonic boom on people revealed that 25 percent of them could not possibly learn to live with this peculiar thunder. How this undisputed fact will be reconciled with the supersonic airplane project has not yet been made clear – other than to curtail supersonic speeds over heavily populated land areas.

Examples of other noises are those that come from the electrical/mechanical appliances that serve the housewife every day and from industry whose manufacturing activities disrupt residential neighbourhoods. To combat noise from these appliances, the consumer himself should include "quietness" as a criterion for purchasing these items. Sufficient demand for quiet performance will spur manufacturers to produce less noisy equipment or to provide muffling devices where noise reduction cannot be further designed into a product. To prevent industrial noises interfering with the serenity of community living, noise experts have suggested that modern zoning ordinances include measured decibel limits at property lines as legal protection against noise-producing industries. Here again, we have an illustration of a potential power of legislative enactment, particularly zoning requirements. Certain cities in Canada have recently enacted noise control and zoning by-laws to offset these growing noise hazards.

The National Research Council of Canada, in conjunction with the manufacturing and construction industries, with universities, and with other institutes such as the Ontario Research Foundation, is taking the initiative in defining allowable noise levels and standards for Canada, and in rating (for acoustical quality) materials and design in, for example, the building industry. Other research, such as at the University of Toronto Institute for Aerospace Studies, is centred on studies of turbulent (or jet) noise. Still other research is directed at the study of bio-acoustics, the response of biological systems to various sound stimuli.

As a society and as individuals, we need, however, to give greater recognition to the deterioration of our environment; although we may not be conservationists, we do believe that the environment as it is now constituted is a precious, if already somewhat tarnished, treasure to be cherished and preserved – and possibly nursed back to a healthier state. Even though we cannot restore it to the state that we once knew, we should nevertheless set our goals in terms of some long term quality of life which we seek as a nation in the world community.

We need, moreover, to further emphasize the training of scientists and engineers in the fundamentals of acoustics and its application to sound analysis and noise abatement. A few years ago, the American Society for Engineering Education and the Acoustical Society of America conducted a survey to determine the need for acoustically-trained scientists and engineers, together with the potential resources to fill these needs. The result of this study showed that the demand for this type of trained individual exceeded the supply, and that this imbalance would become worse in the future. As a consequence, programs of study in acoustics and noise abatement have developed at many leading universities in the U.S.A..

Although a similar study has not been conducted in Canada, the conclusion which was reached by ASEE and ASA can be used as a guide for those who are concerned with technological education in Canada. The Faculty of Engineering Science at the University of Western Ontario has, for several years, given an introduction to the study of acoustics and the problem of noise to senior mechanical and environmental engineering students (and the Faculty is well-equipped to conduct comprehensive noise studies and analyses in industry and in urban communities). The subject of acoustics and its application to the study of sound analysis and noise abatement is as important as are many of the other basic engineering science subjects which we teach in our contemporary curricula – especially where the student is concerned with the design of mechanisms and machinery, buildings and structures, manufacturing plants or transportation systems and where he is likely to be involved in urban and regional development.

There may be yet other solutions to our noise problems – such as an ecological one, as was pointed out in a recent *Time* magazine essay. Studies have indicated that rats, exposed to loud noise, exhibit a marked decline in pregnancy rate although they copulate as zestfully as ever. Or perhaps the racket will drive men underground as in the case of a junior high school near Carswell Air Force Base outside Fort Worth, Texas. Or, yet again, mutation may be the answer. The big sound which is so favoured by discotheques may be the beginning of the New Man, who is thoroughly conditioned to equate a high decibel output with a high old time. Personally, rather than experiencing these drastic solutions, I hope that we can counteract the noise problem by the judicious use of our technological knowledge and the application of common sense.

Footnote

1. A measuring standard to conform to the psycho-acoustic response of the human ear to a wide spectrum (or range of frequencies) of sound.

References

Time Magazine, August 19, 1966.
The Engineer, Engineers Joint Council Inc., 7, No. 3, Autumn, 1966.
U.S. Federal Register, 34, No. 96, May, 1969 (revised July, 1969).

The People vs. Pollution*

Courtney Tower

Prince Rupert, British Columbia, is beautiful to see but it reeks from end to end. Three fish plants dump offal over the ends of wharves, where it simmers and stews. Stinking pulp-mill effluent fills a shallow Pacific bay. Smokestacks belch acid clouds across a mountain scene. "On warm days, hardy fishermen in the area vomit," says Dr. Donald Chant, pollution-fighting chairman of the University of Toronto's zoology department. "But when I asked a resident how he could stand that smell, he looked me in the eye and said, 'I kind of like it.' Another man said, 'Yes, it's the smell of money!'"

Across Canada, the fight goes hard against such a pioneer belief that our land, sky and water are infinitely able to absorb poisons in the name of progress. But public outcry is making itself felt. And Dr. Chant, leading a Toronto citizens' group called Pollution Probe, has shown what aroused people can do: they won the national 90 percent ban on DDT, which begins this month.

The group, one of many forming in a riled-up Canada, held its own public inquiry last summer into the spray-poison death of ducks. It sought injunctions against the Metro Toronto Parks Department's use of Diazinon, a member of

*"The People vs. Pollution" in *Maclean's*, January, 1970, pp. 1, 3, 5, 7. Reprinted with permission from *Maclean's*.

the DDT family. It peppered the Ontario government with scientific data and expert opinion. Resources Minister George Kerr received 3,000 letters.

Ontario soon joined three countries and three American states in a fairly extensive ban on DDT (although the tobacco lobby won some exceptions, which perhaps makes a cancerous kind of sense). Quebec followed.

Probe then lobbied intensively in a reluctant Ottawa. Probe member Marshall McLuhan dined with Prime Minister Trudeau. And Dr. Chant slyly let it be known that the U.S. intended to announce a big DDT ban (it later announced a small one). That did it, a federal source admits: "John Munro (health minister) had just said the Ontario ban on DDT was premature. If the U.S. was then going to ban it, we would look awful. So we decided to one-up the Americans."

However ludicrous the reason, there is now a Canadian ban on DDT, which kills fish and wildlife and retards the photosynthesis in ocean plants that produces 70 percent of the world's free oxygen. The ban was achieved by public anger, which rises now from fear. Eminent scientists talk soberly of the end of Man in perhaps 20 years if he continues pouring death into the air and the exhaustible seas. The scientists say that an exploding world population could use up food and oxygen supplies, while destroying the waters, forests and fields that produce the food and oxygen. What Dr. Chant calls "the red signs of danger" are evident – algae chokes waters; fish, animals and birds are disappearing; carbon monoxide fills the air from automobiles, planes, power plants and heating.

The Canadian Society of Zoologists says bluntly: "The very survival of mankind is at stake."

Montreal's poisoned smog is often so thick that only the tips of skyscrapers point through it, like grave markers. The acid rains from stacks in Sarnia and Sudbury are no better, although Ontario is stiffening controls. Montreal dumps 500 million gallons of raw sewage daily into the St. Lawrence, which still carries cargo but is unpleasant for anything else.

One of the world's great salmon rivers, the Fraser, is an open sewer at Vancouver and far up into its spawning beds. Alberta preaches precaution, but opens a fifth of Willmore Wilderness Park to mining operations. Lake Erie is in large part dead and Lake Ontario is dying of wastes from the U.S. and from a Canada that creates 1,500 pounds of garbage per person each year – four billion cans and two billion bottles and jars. St. John's, Newfoundland, and Victoria, British Columbia, dump raw sewage into the sea. More than a quarter of the shellfish in beds along New Brunswick are made inedible by the offal of fish-processing plants. Young salmon die within minutes of being placed in the St. Croix River below a New Brunswick pulp mill. Under scant control, the 170 pulp mills are Canada's biggest, most persistent and least apologetic polluters – they dump more than half the decomposable material that goes into our water courses each year, and threaten to leave if they can't play dirty.

Even parts of our allegedly protected parks are foul, from logging and over-crowded campsites. The Lake of Two Rivers in Ontario's Algonquin Park last summer tested at 150 times the unsafe bacteria level for swimming. "Algonquin Park was set up primarily to protect the headwaters of five river systems," says Patrick Hardy, managing director of the Canadian Audubon Society. "It seems too bad to start our water off that way."

But politicians and industrialists admit there never has been such public pressure about pollution. Ontario controls are beginning to bite, and the giant Domtar Ltd. was charged in court last month with polluting Lake Superior. A Toronto think tank, Systems Research Group, is preparing strategies for all Canadian governments to use against pollution. Industry's spending on pollution is steadily rising, although government sources say it is not as high as is often claimed. The business of producing anti-pollution equipment is worth perhaps $70 million a year and is touted as the coming glamour industry. But public heat must be sustained – some ways of doing this are shown on the following pages. Serious enforcement of the laws is the crux, or Canada will continue to be a paradox of law and ordure.

George Kerr opened his eyes in his bedroom in Burlington and a black monster leaped at him from an Ontario Hydro smokestack. Since Kerr is in effect the new pollution minister of Ontario and is responsible for Ontario Hydro, he could have felt his work had come home to haunt him. But it was an attack from within. His daughter Margo, 12, and son Jamie, 10, had stuck on his door a full-page newspaper ad protesting a 700-foot Hydro smokestack intended for Toronto.

The ad included a coupon to mail to Energy and Resources Minister Kerr, complaining of the sulphur dioxide being loosed upon everyone. He got 3,000 of them. It was the work of Pollution Probe, the citizens' group based at the University of Toronto.

Probe's membership of 500 students, professors, housewives and businessmen is expert at tackling issues such as dying ducks, the smokestack and the incredible state of Toronto's Don River (where coliform counts, the measurements of impurity in water, run from 14,000 to 61 million per 100 millilitres: safe swimming count is 2,400). It also has lawyers helping with suits against polluters. Advertising man Terry O'Malley (the Red Cap beer song) wrote the smokestack ad because "I have a couple of nice kids that I want to see live more than 10 years."

Joe Montgomery is chairman of the Committee of 1,000, in the Niagara peninsula. The group sends reports and samples of polluted air or water to the responsible authorities if it has made no headway with the offending firm or individual. "A year ago you could drive down any road in the peninsula and see pile after pile of garbage," Montgomery says. "Now you can count them on one hand." But the Committee watches helplessly as the city of Niagara Falls, New York, dumps 72 million gallons of raw sewage daily into the Niagara River and on into Lake Ontario.

Universities across the country have pollution-protest groups. Membership is soaring in save-our-parks, bird-watchers' and anglers' clubs – precisely because the parks get dirtier, the birds and fish fewer. The Ontario government pays attention to such groups, but not the regimes of Quebec and British Columbia. "I wonder whether it is useful or necessary to impose rigid punitive laws on industries," says Resources Minister Paul Allard of Quebec, which is spending $1.5 million this year fighting water pollution, compared with Ontario's $42 million. A citizens' group called the Expollution Committee took samples from 150 lakes in southern Quebec last summer. It found the water unsafe to drink in 92 percent of the lakes and unfit for swimming in 70 percent.

SPEC (Society for Pollution and Environmental Control) doesn't receive answers from the BC government of Premier W. A. C. Bennett. SPEC is composed of scientists, sportsmen, students and others – 2,000 in Vancouver and 28 branches being set up throughout the province. SPEC makes films, agitates, exposes pipes that dump raw sewage into the Fraser River. Various conservation groups oppose the coal strip-mining operation in the East Kootenays, which kills fish and game and rains acid into the waters.

Across Canada, the media have been increasing the pressure. "Everyone is starting to realize that lives are at stake," says Toronto *Telegram* outdoors writer Tiny Bennett. Larry Gosnell, award-winning CBC TV producer of the savagely superb "Air of Death" documentary and of "Our Dying Waters" last fall, worries that the pressure will not be kept up: "The politicians have really resisted, dug in their heels, until they were forced to act by public opinion."

Cleaner Than White

Housewives across Canada have been writing and telephoning Jerry Flynn, saying white will do just as well for their husbands' shirts as whiter than white. That could make him a myth-destroyer at a crucial time. Flynn, a 30-year-old University of Toronto graduate student, has developed a detergent that gets clothes clean – without defiling lakes and rivers.

Detergents are the single biggest pollutant of water in Canada. The phosphates in them, expelled in sewage as wastes, are not broken down by treatment. They so over-stimulate plant life that the next-to-lowest form, algae, bloom in choking abundance. The algae use up so much oxygen that higher levels of plant life die, fish die and the water itself dies under green slime.

But the detergent companies say they cannot do without phosphates, which act essentially as water softeners, because housewives demand that zingy glistening white action. The companies say they spend millions to seek alternative materials, so far without success.

Working in a U of T laboratory and using only $250 worth of materials, Flynn produced in about four months a laundry detergent that works without phosphates. He called it Formula N. He says lab tests show it cleans not quite so well as commercial detergents, but not with a difference that can be discerned by the unassisted eye. It does not pollute. His wife Yuttah uses it now, as do several of their friends, and "none has had any of those supercilious looks over the backyard clothesline from neighbors."

Flynn and his Formula N have appeared on TV and radio shows and in newspaper articles. Hundreds of Canadians have written to him. "Many, or most, have been housewives," he says. "They don't want to pollute the environment. They're concerned for their kids.

"They say they resent stupid advertising that makes them appear birdbrains demanding the last bit of whiteness. And they resent being forced to pollute."

Flynn received no response from the detergent companies.

Flynn's detergent might not work commercially. But scientists know that acceptable alternatives to phosphates in detergents could be found in a hurry.

They might increase the price of a box of detergent by a few cents. But the housewives' response to Flynn shows that, contrary to accepted myth, they can see what is happening to the environment and will pay to preserve it.

To allow them to do that, governments will have to ban phosphates in detergents. Ontario Resources Minister George Kerr says he may do that – after giving detergent companies perhaps a year's deadline to get rid of them voluntarily. The other provinces, and Ottawa, don't say anything. They should.

I See What We Breathe and It Scares Me

Maybe two or three days a month – no more – Vern Redmond can see across Toronto from the 56-story Toronto-Dominion Centre while he washes its windows.

"But mostly it's very smoggy and it's very hard to breathe," he says. "Most days I can taste the sulphur from the smokestacks. My eyes sting. It makes me and my two men groggy and lazy-feeling. We yawn a lot. It builds up inside you until you feel your chest is being squeezed and you can't get enough breath."

Sulphur dioxide assaults Vern Redmond and two million Torontonians – 80,000 tons a year of it from the five stacks of the coal-burning Hearn generating station. Across Canada, chimneys pump 10,000 tons of SO_2 into the air daily.

Carbon monoxide from 800,000 cars is in the Toronto air. Canada's eight million automobile exhausts produce almost 21,000 tons of carbon monoxide a day. They pour out tetraethyl lead and cancer-causing nickel additives; more deadly, 32 million tires vaporize minute particles of rubber; lethal asbestos particles rise from brake linings. As the cities develop more expressways, the intensity of pollution multiplies. Montreal Health Department reports a carbon-monoxide level high enough to damage Montrealers' sight, hearing and brain cells.

"When I see what people are breathing on the ground it scares heck out of me," Vern Redmond says. "I'd like to take my wife and seven-year-old boy out of the city. But I'm still here. And I worry."

Can't We Stop That Terrible Din?

The five phone-in lines to Vancouver radio station CKNW were jammed for the two hours that Arthur Lancaster acted as a sort of everyman's oracle on the pollution of big-city noise.

Lancaster, vice-president of Cowl Industries of Toronto, a new firm that controls industrial noise, had won local television, radio and newspaper headlines for silencing the outdoor din of an especially unpopular planing mill in suburban North Surrey at the request of its owners. Callers asked what they could do about the noise from a 24-hour glass-bottling plant (organize and agitate for anti-noise laws). They protested against aircraft noise, the racket on buses and the loudness of TV and radio commercials. Masters and mates told of engine-room noise levels in new diesel tugs of 115 decibels (the sound of the coming new supersonic transport jets is only 15 decibels more). Workers in one ear-splitting factory told of being offered earmuffs, which they rejected. "It's absolutely predictable that a person would go deaf in 10 years in that factory," says Lancaster. "They don't stand a chance."

Noise causes frustration, fatigue, emotional instability, hearing loss. United States Senator Mark Hatfield says it costs U.S. industry two million dollars daily. He says major culprits are jet aircraft, traffic, poorly constructed modern buildings, rock-music bands and factories. The noise level in the North American home has more than doubled in the past 40 years. The general din of urban life is doubling every 10 years.

The Urbanization of Canada[*]

Leroy Stone

Canada at the Forefront of World Urbanization Since the Early 1800s

A cursory review of the relevant historical data suggests that from the earliest phases of the relatively short history of European settlement in Canada, a marked tendency was shown toward the concentration of the colonial population in centres. However, no centre of population concentration was over 1,000 in population when the first census of New France was taken in 1666. The colony had two cities of over 2,000 in population (Montreal and Quebec) by the first quarter of the nineteenth century, and the available data indicate that these centres contained more than five percent of the colonial population of British North America in 1825, which suggests that Canada may be placed among the world's more highly urbanized regions by 1825. British North America was among the principal world regions in regard to the level of urbanization in the decade after Confederation, when it began a *take-off* toward high levels of urbanization. By 1961, Canada was firmly among the top one fifth of the world's most highly urbanized countries. Together with the United States, it formed one of the three most highly urbanized of the world regions. Around 1961, the levels of urbanization in Canada and the United States were very similar – at least 70 percent in both countries.

In 1851, 16 years before Confederation, the population of British North America was approximately two and one half million (Camu, Weeks and Sametz, 1964, Table 3.1). Roughly 13 percent of these persons resided in urban centres. Since 1851 the urban population has grown much more rapidly than the rural population.

Between 1851 and 1961 the urban population occupying the area of the three oldest major regions of Canada (the Maritime provinces, Quebec and Ontario) has increased at least 28-fold, while the rural population has been increased by at most twofold. It is notable that the population classified as rural in the area

---

[*]Leroy Stone, "Summary of the Main Findings and Interpretations," selected paragraphs from Chapter 10 of *Urban Development in Canada*, Dominion Bureau of Statistics, 1967. Reproduced with the permission of Information Canada.

of these three major regions was about two million in 1851 and was only about three and one half million in 1961. Between 1901 and 1961 the urban population in Canada (excluding Newfoundland, Yukon Territory and Northwest Territories) has increased at least sixfold, while the rural population has been increased by at most threefold.

No marked trend is observed in the decennial rates of urban population increase from 1851-61 to 1951-61 in Canada. What . . . shows predominantly is a pattern of prominent *upswings* and *downswings* in the intercensal rates of urban population increase. There are very high peaks for 1851-61 and 1901-11, less prominent peaks for 1871-81 and 1951-61, and troughs in 1861-71, 1891-1901 and 1931-41. The 1851-61 and 1901-11 peaks are equal (62 percent). These peaks are nearly twice as high as the median decennial rate of increase (34 percent) in urban population from 1851 to 1961, and they are more than three times as high as the low point (18 percent) of the above-mentioned rate, which was attained in 1931-41.

Doubling the Level of Urbanization Since the Turn of the Century

The marked urban-rural differentials observed in intercensal rates of population increase imply continued advances in the percentage of population that is urban. Between 1851 and 1961 that percentage (used here as a measure of the level of urbanization) increased at least fivefold in Canada . . . . Between 1901 and 1961 the degree of urbanization in Canada doubled from 35 percent to 70 percent.

The level of urbanization in Canada has advanced in every decade since 1851. In eight of the eleven decades from 1851 to 1961, the degree of urbanization increased by at least five percentage points. The three exceptional decades include two periods preceding the *take-off* of industrialization in Central Canada (1851-61 and 1861-71) and a period containing much of the Great Depression (1931-41). In 1851 the level of urbanization in Canada was less than 15 percent; it increased by about three percentage points in 1851-61 and in 1861-71, accelerated in the following decade and recorded an intercensal percentage point increase very near five percentage points from 1871-81 to 1891-1901. By 1901 the degree of Canadian urbanization was about 35 percent and by 1931 it had passed 50 percent. Although the increase in urbanization decelerated sharply in the generally depressed 1931-41 decade, urbanization markedly increased its rate of advance from 1931-41 to 1941-51, and in the periods 1941-51 and 1951-61 showed two of the three highest decade increases since 1851; an increase of seven percentage points is shown for 1901-11, 1941-51 and 1951-61. Obviously, since the 1961 degree of urbanization had reached 70 percent, a decade increase of seven percentage points could be maintained for at most four more decades.

Identity of Most Highly Urbanized Regions Unchanged Since the 1880s

There are very significant differences between Canadian regions in regard to the level and historical pattern of urbanization. These differences reflect the regional concentration of industrial activity and regional disparities in economic development. Five major regions of Canada (based on provincial boundaries) are widely recognized: (1) Maritimes (Nova Scotia, New Brunswick and

Prince Edward Island – Newfoundland being excluded here because of the lack of appropriate historical data for this province), (2) Quebec, (3) Ontario, (4) Prairies (Manitoba, Saskatchewan and Alberta), and (5) British Columbia. Each of the five major regions of Canada was at least 50 percent urbanized in 1961 – Ontario 77 percent, Quebec 74 percent, British Columbia 73 percent, the Prairies 58 percent, and the Maritimes 50 percent.

Ontario, Quebec and British Columbia have been the most highly urbanized of the five major regions in every census since 1881. Before 1881 the Maritimes were more highly urbanized than British Columbia. Since 1881 the differential in level of urbanization between that of the group of Ontario, Quebec and British Columbia and that of the Maritimes has widened. The differential in the level of urbanization between the Ontario-Quebec-British Columbia group and the Prairie region widened from 1901 to 1941 but has narrowed markedly since 1941 as a result of the sharp upturn in the advance of urbanization in the Prairies since the 1941 Census.

Urban Sex-Age Structure Is *Female-Dominant* and *Mature*

In regard to the relative numbers of males and females, the urban population of Canada in 1961 may be characterized as *female-dominant*. Females outnumbered males in the whole urban population and in the segment of persons aged 20-34, as well as in the older age groups where females tend to be predominant because of their lower mortality. In 1961 the urban age composition for Canada was that of a *mature* population. The urban age composition had been *rejuvenated* markedly by the postwar upswing in birth rates and this *rejuvenation* overshadowed the impact of net migration upon the age composition of the Canadian urban population.

Urban-rural differentials in the sex-age composition of population are basic indicators of the major divergences between urban and rural communities. In Canada, one finds that the rural areas were markedly *male-dominant*, while urban areas were slightly *female-dominant* in sex composition in 1961. The urban population was clearly an *older* population than the rural population, mainly due to the high *youth dependency* ratio in the rural population.

There are marked contrasts between the Canadian urban, rural non-farm and rural farm age pyramids in 1961. The portion of the age pyramid containing the survivors of the postwar baby-boom is considerably larger in the rural non-farm age pyramid than in that of the urban population. In regard to the urban-rural farm differentials, the ages zero to 19 contain a much larger portion of the rural farm age pyramid than of the urban age pyramid. The rural farm age pyramid shows a striking *trough* in the female side of its age pyramid from ages 20 to 39. This observation reflects the relatively high rates of age selective net migration losses from farms, which have been sustained for several decades. In regard to the masculinity ratio, to the median age, and to the general contour of the age pyramid, the rural non-farm population showed patterns intermediate to those of the urban and the rural farm populations.

The general pattern of urban-rural differentials in the sex-age composition of population as observed in 1961 seems to be traditional in Canada. At least since 1911, the urban population has tended toward *female-dominance* in sex composition while the rural population has tended toward *male-dominance*.

Since 1911 the urban age composition has been *older* than the rural, and the urban age pyramid has shown a more persistent tendency toward a bulge between the ages 20 and 39 than has the rural age pyramid.

Implications of the Age Distribution Patterns

The persistent *female-dominance* in the sex composition of the Canadian urban population is another confirmation of the viewpoint that, in Canada, urban development is an aspect of the spatial concentration of economic opportunities and changes. As Cameron and Hurd (1935, p. 229) have suggested, a surplus of rural population in Canada has been particularly evident among females, for whom there are relatively few, as compared with males, opportunities in primary economic activities such as agriculture. With the advancing industrialization of Canada since Confederation, more and more job openings have been available to females in service activities and, to a lesser extent, in light manufacturing. This long-standing urban-rural differential in the share of economic opportunities for females has probably been a major factor behind the sustained female-selectivity of the net migration gains to urban areas . . . . The data suggest that the *female-dominance* in the urban population since 1911 would have been even higher had it not been for periodic waves of male-selective immigration to Canada.

The *female-dominance* in the urban population and its likely relation with economic opportunities for females in industry is generally known. What may not be readily appreciated, however, is the likely impact of the long-standing net migrational flow of females on urban birth rates. On the whole, urban age-specific fertility rates have been lower than rural age-specific fertility rates over the past half-century at least (Charles, 1941, c. VII). By continually adding to the size of female urban population in the most fertile ages, the sustained net migrational flows of females into urban areas have probably kept the urban natural increase rates above the levels they would show in the absence of such flows. Thus, through its impact upon the age distribution of population, migration has contributed indirectly to urban natural increase rates.

In the light of the preceding observation, the recent downturn in the rate of growth for females aged 20-39 in the population of incorporated cities of 30,000 and over takes on added significance. Population growth rates in the traditionally core areas of Canadian urban development may be coming under an increasingly dampening influence from an unfavourable age distribution.

The decreasing weight of young adults in the age pyramid for the population of large incorporated cities is partly a result of the concentration of in-migrational flows upon the outer edges and fringes of these cities. In addition, much of the rural non-farm population is concentrated in and near counties and census divisions containing the larger cities. These two points suggest that the populations with the highest concentrations of persons in the most fertile ages are increasingly being located on the outer edges of, and in the areas near to the largest cities. In decades gone by, the farm populations contained the highest concentrations of persons in the most fertile ages (Charles, 1941, p. 147).

Thus, the areas of highest *youth dependency* are no longer the farms but are instead the non-farm areas on the edges of, and near to the larger urban centres. No doubt this century has seen marked increases in the demand for educational, recreational and health facilities for youth in such areas. While the financial burden of a high *youth dependency* load in these fringe areas may not be borne to any great extent by the income from economic activity within those areas, the location of educational, recreational and health facilities will increasingly be oriented toward obtaining close proximity with those fringe areas. The location of such facilities near the fringes of urban centres may act as an additional magnet drawing young families into those areas.

As the most fertile segments of the population tend to decrease their concentration in the core parts of the larger cities, the *old-age dependency* ratios in these areas tend to increase. More and more the core areas of these cities may tend to contain increasing concentrations of aged, middle-aged and unmarried persons, with some effects on the structure and volume of demand for goods and services in local areas.

Increasing Number of *Urban Complexes*

. . . each 1961 Metropolitan Area (MA) and Major Urban Area (MUA) is treated as a single complex of closely related centres. Thus the incorporated centres within any 1961 MA or MUA are not recognized as separate units of observation.

Canada had 190 urban complexes of 5,000 in 1961 . . . . This figure represents a tenfold increase in the number of such complexes since the 1871 Census, and a more than threefold increase since 1901. Since 1871 the number of urban complexes has increased in every intercensal period, with the decennial increases tending to be larger after the major decade of western expansion (1901-11) than before this decade. The largest intercensal increase in the number of these complexes since 1871 took place in 1951-61, when 53 units were added to the total of 1951; the smallest increase (nine) took place in 1891-1901.

Stability of the Size Distribution

The Canadian urban complexes of 5,000 and over are heavily concentrated in the lower end of this range of population sizes. In 1961, 87 (46 percent) of the 190 Canadian urban complexes of 5,000 and over were less than 10,000 in population, 32 percent had populations less than 30,000, about 13 percent were in 30,000-99,999 size group, and 10 percent in the group of 100,000 and over. Although this rank ordering of the four size groups in regard to their shares of the total number of Canadian urban complexes (of 5,000 and over) has been virtually unchanged since 1871, the shares of certain size groups show definite trends. The share of the 5,000-9,999 size group shows a generally downward trend over the period from 1871 to 1961. Generally, the percentage concentrated in urban complexes of 5,000-9,999, among those of 5,000 and over, was slightly higher than 52 percent from 1871 to 1911 and was somewhat lower than 50 percent in most of the 1921-61 period. A distinct upward trend is shown for the share of the 100,000-plus size group in the total number of urban complexes of 5,000 and over. Generally, the share of this group has increased from approximately four percent in the latter third of the nineteenth century to about 10 percent in the past two decades. No distinct trends are shown in the corresponding shares for the size groups 10,000-29,999 and 30,000-99,999.

The data for incorporated urban centres of 5,000 and over fail to show a consistent tendency toward direct association between the decennial population growth rate and urban size group (as defined at the beginning of each decade). Thus there was no consistent indication of an increasing concentration of population in the larger cities independently of the shift of urban centres into the larger size groups. However, the data for 1951-61 suggest that the failure to take into account the population in the urbanized fringes of incorporated cities may seriously bias the observation of urban size-groups differentials in population growth rates at least in the more recent decades. This qualification seems to have an important implication for the analysis of the growth rates of large cities. If the urban population growth associated with changes in the economy of a city is reflected largely by growth in the areas adjacent to the city (particularly its suburbs), the demographic data for the city alone may seriously bias the observed association between economic changes and urban growth.

Increasing Concentration of Urban Growth Outside of Incorporated Centres

Although 86 percent of Canada's 1951 urban population resided in incorporated cities, towns and villages, these areas accounted for just 55 percent of the urban population increase over the 1951-61 decade. A large portion of the 1951-61 urban growth must have attributed to the *explosion* of population in areas which are within daily commuting distances of the larger cities, this statement applying particularly to Ontario and British Columbia.

In every decade since 1871, population growth within incorporated urban centres (as defined at the beginning of each decade) has accounted for more than one half of the urban population increase in Canada. Generally, at least two thirds of the decennial urban population increase is attributable to population growth within the incorporated centres. The principal exceptions to this generalization are found near the end-points of the 1871-1961 period. In 1871-81 and 1891-1901 more than one third of the urban population increase took place outside of the incorporated centres (those existing and classified as urban at the beginning of each decade), largely due to the number of localities reclassified from the rural to the urban categories over each of these decades. Again in 1941-51 and 1951-61, less than two thirds of the urban population increase took place within the incorporated centres (existing and classified as urban at the beginning of each decade), largely due to the mushrooming of urban population in unincorporated areas (particularly those within daily commuting distances to the larger cities).

Net Migration Is One Third of the 1951-61 Growth of *Urban Complexes*

The component analysis of urban growth involves the consideration of demographic processes as well as the attribution of growth to different types of area. Mainly attributable to the fact that urban growth involves expansion in the territory of urban settlement (through urban-rural reclassification of localities and annexation of rural territory by cities), the demographic analysis of urban growth is beset with knotty data processing problems. The data needed for routine resolution of these problems are scarce. Because of these difficulties, the writer has prepared an analysis for the 1951-61 decade only, confining the coverage of the data to the urban complexes of 5,000 and over.

Over the 1951-61 decade the population in the Canadian urban complexes of 5,000 and over increased by 52 percent. Some six tenths of this increase may be attributed to demographic growth in the area classified as urban in both 1951 *and* 1961 and and an additional one tenth to demographic growth in the area *added* to urban territory between 1951 and 1961. Together these two sources comprise the *total* demographic growth. Some 43 percent of this total demographic growth may be attributed to net migration (the remainder being attributed to natural increase), and three fourths of this contribution of net migration pertains to the area classified as urban in both 1951 *and* 1961. Some 33 percent of the whole 1951-61 urban population increase may be attributed to net migration.

Among the five major regions, the relative importance of the direct impact of net migration on the total demographic growth for the urban complexes varies widely, it ranged from 11 percent in the Maritimes to 52 percent in the Prairies; in British Columbia it was 50 percent, in Ontario 47 percent, and in Quebec 35 percent.

Migration Retards *Ageing* of Population in Cities

Estimates prepared for six of Canada's largest incorporated cities suggest that in the absence of migration between 1901 and 1961 the population of these cities would have *aged* at a much faster rate than it actually did. These estimates also show clearly that the persistent *female-dominance* in the urban sex-age structure may be attributed largely to the influence of migration.

Metropolitan Growth, A New Focus for Migration Studies

The data . . . indicate that the 1961 Census Metropolitan Areas (MAs) increased their share of the Canadian population by five percentage points from 1951 to 1961. This increase was much larger than those shown for the 1961 Census Major Urban Areas (MUAs) and for other selected categories of areas. With the exception of the 1931-41 decade, the areas closely approximating the 1961 MAs (which may be viewed as the principal regions of metropolitan development in Canada) have increased their share of the Canadian population by roughly four percentage points in each decade since 1901-11.

In regard to the components of population growth in the Principal Regions of Metropolitan Development (PRMDs), the estimates indicate that the direct influence of net migration was more important than natural increase in 1921-31 and 1951-61. Only in 1931-41 was the direct impact of net migration markedly less important than natural increase in the population growth rate for the PRMDs. Since the 1921-31 period the PRMDs have consistently had much higher crude net migration ratios than other areas (taken as a whole). The findings on areal net migration ratio differentials since 1921-31, which are presented for the five major regions as well as for Canada, suggest a relatively new focus for migration studies in Canada – the gravitation of population into metropolitan areas.

Recent Acceleration of Population Redistribution Within Metropolitan Areas

[This section] . . . indicates that in Canada as a whole there were marked intra-metropolitan differentials in the growth rate of population over the 1951-61 decade. Generally, the lowest growth rate was attained in the central cities (24 percent). Among the other incorporated centres of 10,000 and over the 1951-61 population growth rate was 36 percent. In sharp contrast, the population in the parts of the 1961 MAs outside of incorporated centres of 10,000 and over more than doubled between 1951 and 1961, growing at a decennial rate of 118 percent.

Intra-metropolitan redistribution of population at the expense of the central cities is by no means a peculiarity of the 1951-61 decade. A DBS report (DBS, 1965b, Table VII, p. 2-14) indicates that the population in 15 1951 Census MAs grew by 27 percent over the 1941-51 decade. The central cities of these 15 MAs grew by 15 percent, while the remaining parts of the MAs grew by 64 percent. However, the intra-metropolitan redistribution of population redistribution took place at a faster rate in 1951-61 than in 1941-51 and the data also suggest that it may have accelerated sharply from 1931-41 to 1941-51.

Very Large Areal Differentials in Net Migration by Age Within Metropolitan Areas

Net migration is considerably more important than natural increase in accounting for the marked rate of intra-metropolitan population redistribution over the 1951-61 decade. The central cities sustained a net migration loss which was one percent of their 1951 population, while the remaining parts of the 1961 MAs had a net migration gain which was 69 percent of their 1951 population. The differential in net migration ratios between the central cities and the remainder of the 1961 MAs was very much larger than their natural increase ratio differential. Some 86 percent of the differential in population growth between the central cities and the remainder of the 1961 MAs may be attributed to the direct impact of net migration.

For each MA, the portion outside of the central city had a crude 1951-61 net migration ratio of over 25 percent. This means that through net migration alone each of these *non-central city* parts of the MAs would have grown by one fourth over the 1951-61 decade. The crude net migration ratio exceeded 50 percent in nine of the 14 MAs. In the *non-central city* parts of the Calgary, Edmonton, London and Hamilton MAs the crude net migration ratio exceeded 90 percent. These are phenomenal ratios of net migration for a decade, and they probably produced rapid changes in the economic and social conditions of the respective areas and have led to serious problems in the provision and co-ordination of municipal services.

The foregoing observations suggest that the 1951-61 migrational flows into the metropolitan areas were concentrated heavily upon locations outside of the central cities, while an increasing proportion of former central city residents may have relocated to the *suburbs* of the central city. Common observation suggests that an atypically high proportion of these relocators consisted of families with two or more children for whom the increasingly congested central city was undesirable.

References

Cameron, Jean C. and Hurd, W. Burton, "Population Movements in Canada, 1921-31," *Canadian Journal of Economics and Political Science*, 1, May, 1935, pp. 212-245.

Camu, P., Weeks, E. P., and Sametz, Z. W., *Economic Geography of Canada*. Toronto: 1964.

Charles, Enid, *The Changing Size of Family in Canada*, 1941 Census Monograph No. 1. Ottawa: 1948.

Stone, Leroy O., "Application to Canadian Data of a Method for Evaluating the Accuracy of Net Migration Estimates," paper presented at the Annual Meeting of the Population Association of America, New York, 1966.

Proceedings of the Special Senate Committee on Poverty[*]

The Honourable David A. Croll, Chairman
November 12, 1970

Evidence

Hon. Mr. Croll: . . . As we moved around the country we kept our eyes and ears open. When we returned to Ottawa we had had a good look at the bitter face of poverty in its many forms: rural, urban, metropolitan, Indian and Métis. We did not like what we had seen.

During our meetings, which were always open and available to anyone who wanted to attend, we made it a point to make the poor feel that somebody cared about them and that not everybody was against them. Whatever other message we may have put across, that one we did get across to them. I believe we have been successful in holding out hopes and expectations to the poor across the country and in showing them that they must involve themselves in solutions, thereby helping us to help them.

We gave some particular attention to Newfoundland and New Brunswick and were very fortunate in having on the committee Senator Cook and Senator Carter from Newfoundland, and Senators Fergusson, Fournier (Madawaska-Restigouche) and McGrand from New Brunswick. This house little appreciates the prestige and respect which these senators command in their home provinces – just as they do among us.

Senator Carter took a small committee up to Labrador. What a trip! It is worth taking a look at the four or five pages of our Minutes that he wrote on the trip.

*Proceedings of the Special Senate Committee on Poverty, The Honourable David A. Croll, Chairman, "Progress Report," pp. 12:5-12:9, The Senate of Canada, Third Session, Twenty-eighth Parliament, Thursday, November 12, 1970. Reproduced with the permission of Information Canada.

You will find them very interesting. Senator Cook shepherded us to Fogo Island and other parts of Newfoundland, and that too was an interesting trip. It was an eye-opener for me, of course, because I had never seen that part of Newfoundland. One comes in contact with a sturdy, independent people there – a carefree sort. The coves and the little fishing villages and out-of-the-way places are fascinating. You see a country poor in resources but rich in values.

We in Canada have for a little over 100 years been trying to redistribute wealth, and we must realize that they have only really tried to do that in Newfoundland for the past 20 years. They need our massive help and we ought to be generous to them; they are trying to help themselves, and it is a struggle.

New Brunswick also received a considerable amount of our attention. I suppose that was mainly because of the three members of the Senate to whom I have already referred and who, I might point out, never missed a meeting and were perhaps the hardest workers.

New Brunswick is a province that tries hardest, particularly in the social welfare fields. Senator McGrand had been talking endlessly about the natural resources of New Brunswick, but until we saw them we did not really appreciate them. In the company of Senator Fergusson and Senator Fournier (Madawaska-Restigouche) we finally saw the great natural forest wealth of the country. It is rich land. And yet the people are poor. You wonder why that is so until you find out that those natural resources belong to the great pulp and paper corporations, and what they do not own they control, and what they do not control they influence. With equal impartiality, they pollute everything. It is not hard, then, to realize that New Brunswick has a special problem.

The young people of New Brunswick, just like the young people of Newfoundland, venture out, go back again and venture out again. When you do some thinking you realize that there in New Brunswick the way of life is one that is perhaps preferable to the asphalt jungles these people would have to face in other parts of the country. They lead their lives as they see fit, and they lead full lives. It is our business to make sure that we give as much assistance as we can to assure an adequate level of life there.

I will say little about the west other than to suggest that the developing parts of the country around Edmonton and Calgary are exciting, as are Saskatchewan and the Yukon. Those senators from the West who are on the committee were always present when the committee was in their provinces. Of course, they were present on other occasions as well.

I would point out that on occasion we were joined by persons who were not members of the committee. The Leader of the Opposition (Hon. Mr. Flynn) came and sat with us when we were in Quebec; Senator Michaud sat with us when we were in Moncton; Mr. Bell was with us in Saint John and Mr. Fairweather and the former leader of the provincial government in New Brunswick sat with us on one very eventful day – I believe it was in Bloomfield – when we stopped at a beautiful old church. It was a venerable place, and its minister had ideas. I believe he was called the *Pulpwood Padre*. He impressed upon us the natural wealth of the province and what we ought to do about it. I was happy when the ladies finally brought in cookies and doughnuts. I think he might still be speaking, had he not been interrupted. But I must say he was an interesting person. You will find his brief on record – it is a good one.

Honourable senators, let me say something about the senators who came with us on this odyssey and joined in the work. The three ladies on the committee were a particular delight; they gave us tone and they added greatly to the respect accorded to us. Other honourable senators referred to them as the *Senate sirens*. But, as I say, honourable senators, they were there, tremendous respect was shown for them, and they made valuable contributions to the work of the committee.

I come now to the matter of public hearings. We held hearings here in Ottawa — and in passing I might mention that we had hearings yesterday, this morning and hope to hold one tomorrow morning. We plan to continue until the first week in November to complete our hearings schedule. Our research staff has been preparing studies and material for our consideration. The kind of report that we have to prepare cannot be hatched — it has to be sweated, and the sweating has already commenced.

Honourable senators, I have some other points to make. You may of course come to the conclusion that the chairman has made up his mind about some matters, and you may not be wrong. But I ask you to make allowances for the fact that the chairman wants to be fair. He gives expression to his views — and it would be something new if he sat on the fence. While his opinions may not always be the best or may not always be right, he usually expresses them anyway. I would ask you to make allowances for that today, even if you do not agree with the views expressed.

Honourable senators, there are about 4½ million people considered poverty-stricken, according to the definition of the Economic Council. They are not hard to find nor are they hard to identify. Half of those 4½ million people are what we might define as the disadvantaged, the aged, the disabled, the handicapped, female heads of families with children, relief-ites. These are all people who are no longer in the labour force as such. Then, the other half constitute what we call the *working poor*. These are the unskilled, the unlettered, people working full time, part-time or broken time, who are on and off unemployment insurance, working at minimum wages or worse, and never earning enough money to get by on. There is considerable movement between these two groups. The disadvantaged are served by the welfare system which has just grown and grown and grown.

Those appearing before us were unanimous in the view that the public welfare system has broken down, mired in bureaucracy and suffering from lack of leadership. It has failed in its ability to achieve humanitarian ends, and the public capacity to finance it in its present form is in question. The welfare system has failed for another reason, that is because it was considered a supplement to the economic system to provide for marginal people. It was never designed to supply basic needs for a large number of Canadians. I have been quoted as saying that the welfare system is a mess. That was some months ago, and now on reconsideration I think it is an impossible mess! It is too late for reform — it is beyond reform. It is too late to apply poultices or bandages or even to attempt to modify it. It is useless to try to make changes in the system because of citizen hostility and recipient anger. Its situation is now such that efforts to change it, even if such efforts should result in its betterment, are no longer possible and just would not be believed. It has infected generations of Canadians and plagues our society. I think we have to face up to that situation.

We have been considering this situation in committee, and so far as I am concerned I think the only solution is to scrap it. We must start all over again. We must begin anew. Then the question arises, do we have an alternative in the interim? I think we have.

Hon. Mr. Choquette: What is your alternative?

Hon. Mr. Croll: I will get to it. I would not leave you without one.

Hon. Mr. Choquette: I should think not.

Hon. Mr. Croll: I have just expressed my views about the system, but what do others say about it? What do people who are more knowledgeable about the system than I am think of it, and what do they say about it?

Some time ago the Department of National Health and Welfare appointed a National Council on Welfare. It is a newly constituted body of 21 private citizens to advise the Minister of National Health and Welfare on matters relating to welfare. In that group there are six categories with representation as follows: the low income groups, six; disadvantaged minorities comprising the black community, one; the Acadian community, one; the Métis community, one; the Indian community, one; social work educators, three; social service delivery system, one. Then there is the chairman, and five members interested in social service volunteer activity. These are the guests who came to dinner and this is what they had to say in a statement issued on October 7.

> The National Council of Welfare feels strongly that the provision of income support by way of needs tested public assistance programs is inherently degrading, stigmatizing and destructive of self-respect, having a debilitating effect upon the recipient and upon the children of the recipient families.

Those are their words.

> We look forward to the Federal Government's White Paper on Income Security, to the Report of the Special Senate Committee on Poverty and to what we hope will be a far-reaching national discussion which will encompass not only alternative mechanisms of income distribution, but the social values inherent in each of them.

Then they go on to say:

> At present, however, persons in need are dependent upon programs of public assistance administered by provinces and municipalities and supported by the federal Government through the Canada Assistance Plan. Recognizing both the inherent inadequacies of this approach to income support and its being all that presently exists to meet the urgent needs of all those Canadians who suffer poverty in an affluent country, the National Council of Welfare has resolved as follows:

Then they discuss the costs and continue:

> AND WHEREAS these conditions include that the province provide assistance to any person in need *in an amount or manner that takes into account his basic requirements,*

AND WHEREAS *basic requirements* are defined by the act as *food, shelter, clothing, fuel, utilities, household supplies and personal requirements,*

AND WHEREAS various provinces and municipalities would appear to have adopted policies and practices in clear violation of this condition, such as the exclusion from receipt of assistance of certain categories of persons in need, limits on the duration of receipt of assistance by certain categories of persons in need, and provision of assistance to certain categories of persons in need in amounts or manners which take into account less than all the basic requirements set out in the act,

We have been saying that across the country, in a gentle sort of manner, pointing it out as we visited each province, that a gap exists between the laws that guarantee the meeting of needs and their actual application. Failure to implement the legislation has weakened the very fabric of the system. Laws that are enacted and not enforced can only result in three things: militancy, protest and action.

Then they go on to say:

The existence of laws on the statute books does not ensure their compliance. Rights are established by law but defined and enforced by courts. Until recently, however, there has been virtually no use of the courts in Canada to ensure that the application of our welfare laws protects the rights established in them.

That is a statement made by a committee appointed by the Government, and I gave you their qualifications.

Federal Government money is spent on what we call basic needs, and they have been defined. These needs should be able to be met on the same terms and conditions in all parts of Canada. That raises the question of a uniform standard of basic needs across the country, as uniform as income tax. That in itself will involve the realistic distribution of Canada's wealth, which has not been the case for almost 20 years in so far as the poor are concerned.

We have always talked about the gap between the rich and the poor. What we are having to talk about in this country is the gap between the poor and the middle class. That is getting wider; that is something new and something that most of you can appreciate.

We had presented to us the view, and I think it has merit, that the basic needs of a family in Campbellton, New Brunswick, should be the same as those of a family of the same size living in Toronto or Vancouver; and that should no longer be a dream but a reality. There is not the slightest reason for continuing to justify the geographic inequities in the present system. There are provinces in Canada that say: "We will pay so much – period! It does not make any difference how many children you have in the family. Whistle for the rest from your municipality." I am not laying the blame on the provinces. The fault lies with the federal Government, and I will indicate why.

As we travelled throughout the country the only real difference in the cost of living, as we saw it in the cities, was that of rent. That could have some effect but, really, if we were a little more generous to some of the outlying districts the rest of us would not be greater hurt.

I said earlier that I thought we ought to be able to scrap the system completely. We could actually repeal every one of our social measures, with the exception of the Canada Assistance Act, the Canada Pension Plan and the unemployment Insurance plan, and meet every requirement under the basic definition of *need* in the Canada Assistance Act, modifying it to some slight extent. So, it would all fit under an umbrella rather than as now under a tent with 200 or so measures.

Hon. Mr. Connolly (Ottawa West): Would the honourable senator repeat that statement? It seems to be an important one. I did not quite catch it.

Hon. Mr. Croll: What I said was that the Canada Assistance Act provides for need, for basic need. It defines it. With a slight modification in the definition of need in the Canada Assistance Act we could repeal the welfare measures because they are basically for need, with the exception of the Canada Pension Plan and the Unemployment Insurance plan. They are contractual obligations, if you appreciate the difference.

That is a change, and when one talks about "change," the remarks of the Prime Minister in the Throne Speech debate come to mind, when he said:

> The challenge today is not simply change – it is more the pace and the scale of the change. We must adapt now as never before. I believe strongly that no country is better able to do so than is Canada, for no country is more fortunate in its basic attributes.

What is the alternative? Well, I will start by saying what the alternative is, and then I will explain it in a few minutes.

The alternative is adequate basic income, a national minimum level of income. What do the 4½ million working poor need? The vice-chairman will have something to say about that when he speaks. They need employment. When they cannot get it, the alternative is income. They need services and incentives to continue to work. What is more, the provision of income should come from the federal Government, and the provision of services from the provincial Government. We have a vehicle for delivery of services in the Canada Assistance Act. Income and services must be completely and totally separated.

I have a few more statements here that are worth thinking about. They have come out of presentation from the committee. I said that the working poor number about two million Canadians. All honourable senators will agree that the head of a family who is working full time but earning minimum wages, or poverty-level wages, needs help. He has earned the right to some help. He is a producer, yet we have so structured our welfare system that it provides help for those who do not work, and denies help to equally needy working people.

I can see that that is sinking in. I can see that honourable senators appreciate the implication. There are thousands of people who see their neighbours drawing more for not working than they receive for working. That is a colossal injustice. We know that what we are doing is wrong, and yet we keep on doing it.

We have at the present time 250,000 heads of families who could qualify for welfare but who choose not to do so. The majority of them could not only qualify for welfare but they would be better off on welfare. For how long do you think that is going to continue? Welfare allowances have grown relative to the minimum wage to the point where for a family of average size the welfare system is directly in conflict with the economic system, in that the individual could rationally choose the welfare system.

Some qualified and excellent welfare workers from Winnipeg appeared before the committee the other day. I should like to read to the house part of the record of what was said on that occasion. The witness was Mr. Clark Brownlee, Chairman of the Social Action Committee of the Manitoba Association of Social Workers, and he was talking about the welfare system and the working poor. He said:

> If that system can give him the supplement to his income or a guarantee of an income, or whatever it takes to bring him up to a level, I do not see it is necessarily a bad thing.

Senator Hastings then said:

> What you are doing is giving that man a guaranteed annual income through the welfare system with all the stigma that goes with it. . . . Isn't that what we are doing?

And Mr. Brownlee answered:

> In the present system, yes, but I would rather do that than see them starve. We are not omnipotent. We cannot change it under the present system.

And then the chairman of the committee put in his two cents' worth and said:

> We are thinking of how it can be done.

We are now, of course, on the verge of committing yet a greater blunder, something that I think will blight our future. I ask honourable senators to think about it. We have begun in a mini way to assist fully employed persons, the working poor, through the welfare system.

The welfare people find themselves in a very difficult situation. A man may be working and earning $300 a month, while a man on welfare is receiving $290 a month. But, the man on welfare is receiving medical care, dental care, drugs, and other things, which to a family of four are worth $40 a month across the board. The working man is sitting there and considering the fact that he is out the difference of $30 or $40 a month by not walking over and qualifying for welfare.

What happens is that that man goes to the welfare department and says: "I cannot get by. I shall have to quit my job and go on welfare." The welfare worker says: "Take it easy. I want you to go on working at your job, while I see if I can get authority to help you out." He then has to go back to the board to obtain authority to pay that man something, and the board says: "If we open this door, where are we?"

One province has opened the door, but that province is often accused of having money to burn. It is burning some of it very acceptably. The Province of Alberta is the only province that is going out to do a bit of a job in this respect. The provinces of Ontario and Quebec can afford to do the same thing, but they are not doing anything at all. Provinces are doing such stupid things as putting a man on welfare and spending $270 a month, instead of helping him out by giving him an extra $50 or $70 a month. This is being done. I am not overdrawing the picture.

If we start to supplement wages then we will engulf the working poor into the mystic web of welfare, and these people will start a journey without end. It will then be, of course, not just a blunder; it will be a monumental mistake. This committee has come on the scene just in time, and it will enable the Government and the country to reassess our position and to understand what we are getting into.

How we got where we are, I do not know. I should know, I suppose, but we have all got to put our heads together and see how we can get out of it. The working poor are producers and they have got to be kept away from the welfare system. If we are not able to accomplish that then we shall have opened up a Pandora's box. If the working poor can be kept working for minimum wages or less, and they can obtain some help from the welfare system, then the minimum wage will be meaningless. We will be back to sweatshop wages or worse, because the worker will know that he can get at some other place whatever the boss does not pay him. And the boss will also know it. That is the kind of situation we are facing. If we allow that to happen we shall have taken a long step into yesterday, yet we cannot and we must not deny these people whatever help they require.

I said earlier that about 250,000 persons could qualify for help. To give those people the incentive to stay away from that system we have to erase somehow the present invidious line between the working poor and those who are totally dependent upon public assistance. We have given the matter much thought. Each member of the committee has been thinking and talking about it. I think there is only one course open, to broaden the base for adequate basic income. Now, when I say broaden the base, there is another statement that would be interesting: 1,250,000 Canadians are drawing the guaranteed income in Canada today. We talk about it as though it was something new, something that is revolutionary. I will tell you where you can find them. There are 1,600,000 people on old age security. Half of them fill in income tax forms, negative income tax method, and in that way get their supplements. That is a guaranteed income. That is the way we wrote it. There are 1,400,000 on public assistance in this country. Four hundred and fifty thousand of those are on long term assistance.

All I am suggesting is that we broaden the base and include some of the others, the 1,250,000 receiving an inadequate basic income, 800,000 of them under the device which collects money from the affluent and pays out money, negative income, to the poor with no means test, an income test contained in normal income tax form which the 800,000 have filled in for three years. It has not always been 800,000. The numbers have grown.

Four hundred and fifty thousand are receiving inadequate basic income through the welfare system. They are long termers who have been receiving it for over three years.

This Too is Canada[*]

The Special Planning Secretariat, Privy Council Office

In 1965, one building in Montreal cost $80 million; another, in Toronto cost $60 million. *In 1965, spending for public housing in Canada was about $45 million* – just under one third the cost of those two buildings.

In an average year Canadians spend:

> $500 million on travel abroad
> $1 billion on alcohol
> $400 million at the race tracks
> $200 million on candy
> $30 million on dog and cat food

By international standards most people in Canada are well housed but 300,000 housing units are needed to replace substandard, unsanitary housing and to relieve overcrowding. While there were 134,000 housing starts in 1966, poorer Canadians still cannot afford to buy or rent decent housing at market prices. Publicly-assisted housing is needed. Until recently, Canada was starting such housing at the rate of 1,000 units a year. This has since stepped up to the point where, in 1966, nearly 6,000 units were started. There is still a long way to go.

Yet, if you are like most Canadians, you probably own a home or are thinking about buying one; for six out of ten Canadians do have their own homes – Canada is a very rich country.

And most persons who do own homes have a few standard things in them, things like electricity, hot and cold running water, central heating, a bathroom. Most homes also have a telephone: Canadians are the biggest telephone talkers in the world.

Some Canadians have very nice homes; others don't.

Take Mrs. E. Her home has a hot water heater – although it hasn't worked for three months and it is clean too, not "infested with cockroaches and bedbugs like the other places," where she lived.

Or look at Mrs. G. She has no heater – not even one that doesn't work. And her mailman will not deliver the mail. Small wonder – her home has been classed as unfit for habitation.

Then there's George P., his wife and three children. They have the advantage of living out in the country in a home with two bedrooms, one bathroom and nothing else of course. Calling their bathroom a bathroom is probably a little pretentious: it has no bath, no hot water, just a bucket which has to be carried out and dumped, somewhere.

Another Canadian family – a man, his wife, and their four school-age children – live in a seven-room frame house heated by a box stove, the kind of stove that gives little warmth except when it starts a fire. In their home, the water supply

[*]The Special Planning Secretariat, prepared by the Privy Council Office, "This Too is Canada," Ottawa, 1967. Reproduced with the permission of Information Canada.

comes from a hand pump. The nearest toilet is just down the path; in winter it's the other side of the nearest snowbank.

This home has no electricity, no refrigerator, no washing machine, no television, no telephone – and no dishwasher. It isn't very comfortable.

Why do persons live like this? Partly income, of course. Partly because we haven't built enough decent houses for those with little money to spend on housing.

If you earn less than $3,000 a year there is one chance in three that you will have more than one person per room in your house.

If you earn at least twice that much – $6,000 a year – you will probably have at least as many rooms as there are family members.

Of course, if you are a Canadian Indian, there is only one chance in 11 you will have an indoor bath, one in 10 you will have sewers or a septic tank, one chance in five you will have running water.

Mathematical averages are made of many individual cases. There are working girls in Canada happily sharing a bachelor apartment. There are elderly couples feeling rather lonely in the sprawling houses where their children grew up. But there are also many, many overcrowded dwellings. The average Canadian has one and one-third rooms to himself. George P. and his family, the ones mentioned above, have less than half a room apiece.

There are some charming homes in Canada. There are also some ugly, squalid slums.

This is Canada.

Canadians are pretty well educated. Not all of us get to college but at least we can read and write and – or can we?

There are still more than one million Canadians who are to all intents and purposes illiterate. They may have spent three or four years in school and they may be able to write their names or read a *STOP* sign but they are not capable of reading this pamphlet.

In this automated age, these persons are unfit for all but the most menial jobs. They can't help their children with their homework: they can't do it themselves.

Of course, their children will be better educated than they are – for education is free, open to everyone. At least, that's the Canadian myth.

The fact is that schoolrooms for the very young in Canada are equipped with books and toys and crayons and chalk and paints. Canadian poverty studies have turned up countless homes where none of these things exist. Youngsters from these homes never see a toy until they get to school.

Youngsters from most Canadian homes learn a great deal from their parents before they start school. They learn about our folklore, our literature, perhaps even about science. They have good toys to play with. School, to them, is just a home with more children in it.

Poor kids don't find it this way. They may never have seen a piano before the one in kindergarten. They haven't had any picture books to look at or fancy toys to play with. They are miles behind, before they begin.

To many children from Canadian city slums or backward rural areas, the classroom is a strange, frightening and disturbing place. To a child from a crowded, noisy home, even the quiet of the classroom is unfamiliar.

The child of poverty has other problems. He has no place to study. He has no one at home to help him or even prod him on. His attendance is bad because his health is bad. He feels out-of-place because his clothes are poor – children can be very self-conscious.

Of course, if he stays in school he will find that education can be extremely beneficial.

A man in Canada who has been only to elementary school can expect to earn $130,000 between 25 and 64. If he makes it through high school, his expected earnings rise to $200,000. If he completes university, he will earn $350,000 – nearly three times as much as the man who dropped out after grade school.

Most parents know this – and even the poor parents want their children to have a better education than they got.

The general level of education is rising.

But can you really expect a child of poverty who is often hungry, cold and ill-housed to fight all the odds for some vague, future reward when he can get a job now and escape from his school, his home, from the whole damned system?

Can you really expect a poor child to go to university when the cost of a single year would take half or more than half of his family's annual income?

Of course, you can't.

Today's average income job calls for more than eight years schooling. Yet, today, 30 percent of young Canadians, between 14 and 24, have left school with grade 8 or less and with no thought of returning.

What will happen to them in tomorrow's automated society? Already there are not enough Canadians to fill all the skilled jobs. We have to import skilled workers from abroad to keep our economy in high gear.

Untrained Canadians today mean unemployed Canadians tomorrow. Human intelligence, energy and character are being wasted on a gigantic scale by these massive dropouts.

This, too, is Canada.

When Canadians get sick, they call their family doctor. They go to hospital, when need be. They have specialists to help them when they are required. They have at their command medical facilities of the highest order. Or some do.

Others, who get sick too, seldom get to see a doctor. He may be a hundred miles – or a hundred dollars – away. Many just can never afford a dentist, or an optometrist, even if he is handy. Handicaps stay just that – handicaps. And miracle drugs only produce miracles if you use them. But first you have to have them prescribed and then be ready and able to pay the pharmacist. And we all know wonder drugs are expensive in anybody's terms.

And so it goes. Your chance of survival – let alone good health – depend in large measure on where you live and what you earn.

If you are born in Ontario, your chances of surviving your first year are fairly good: only 23.5 infants out of every 1,000 die in the first year of life in Ontario.

If you are born in Newfoundland, your chances of surviving the first year are also fair, but not as good: 37.5 infants out of every 1,000 die in the first year in Newfoundland.

What if you are a Canadian Eskimo?

In that case, you have about one-eighth the chance for survival as the young Ontarian; 193 of every 1,000 Eskimo children die in their first year of life.

Why is this rate higher for Newfoundland than it is for Ontario? Why is it so much worse still for Eskimo children?

Mostly, it's poverty.

Ontario has the highest income levels in Canada; it has the lowest infant mortality rate.

Newfoundland has the lowest income levels for a Canadian province; it has the highest infant mortality rate.

This pattern exists all the way down the line: if you know where your region stands in terms of income you also know where it stands in terms of infant mortality.

This too, is Canada.

Of course, you don't have to be an Eskimo to see that income and medical attention are related.

A federal survey found this about medical care being provided to children under age 15:

> 3 out of 10 in the low income group received care;
> more than 4 out of 10 in the middle income group received care;
> almost 5 out of 10 in the high income group received care.

If you are under 15, the more money your parents have, the more likely you will receive the medical attention you need.

Yet ill health is more common among poor Canadians. They live in conditions that encourage illness. Ill health is one of the reasons why Canadians become poor and stay that way.

A study of poor families in four Canadian cities found health problems in 50 percent of the households and chronic physical problems in 43 percent.

Health or ill health and poverty are very closely linked.

Studies have also shown this: poverty and sickness in childhood are definite, contributing factors to ill health in old age.

In other words, if you are poor when you are young you are likely to be sick when you are young and this means you are also likely to be sick in old age.

And sickness in old age is perhaps worst of all.

Expenses can mount at an alarming rate. A weekly visit from a nursing service can cost $3.75. Some pills cost $1.00 each. A 10-block ambulance ride can cost $26. A nursing home could cost $350 a month.

For an older person, such expenses can not only mount alarmingly, they can also destroy the peace of mind that may be needed for recovery.

The average age at death in Canada, today, is 59.7 for males and 63.1 for females. [editor's note: Estimates for 1971 are 69 years for men and 75 years for women.]

In the Northwest Territories, where many Eskimos and Indians live, it's 26.0 for males and 21.5 for females.

This, too, is Canada.

If you are an average Canadian family – and you do not live on a farm – your family income is about $5,500 a year.

You use a fair chunk of this money – but less than half – for food and housing.

The rest goes to items like clothing, health, education and recreation. You may even put a little aside as savings.

Of course, very few persons earn precisely the average, and it varies from city to city and province to province.

But most of us know persons who earn close to this – say, $4,500 to $6,500 a year – roughly $90 to $125 a week.

We know, no matter how well they manage, they never have much to spare. We know any appreciable cut in income will make things very difficult.

Well, for many Canadians, things are different.

The 1961 census showed that 23 percent of Canadian families – roughly one family in four – have an annual family income of less than $3,000 a year.

About half a million families have annual incomes below $2,000.

This means these families have less than $40 a week to pay the rent, feed themselves, clothe themselves and pay any other bills that might come along.

But these are only income figures: what do they mean to the people, themselves?

They mean that family income is completely tied up with the bare necessities of life. A study of families living in poverty in Canada suggests that these families spend 70 percent of their income on food and housing.

These persons can't plan their budgets; they have no money to plan.

These figures mean that opportunity is limited.

Low income can stifle initiative.

Poverty breeds poverty.

Of course, if you are like most Canadians, you never see these people.

One third of Canadian families live in Ontario where incomes, on the average, are high. More than eight out of ten Ontario families have an income over $3,000 a year.

About one fiftieth of Canadian families live in Newfoundland. Less than half the families in Newfoundland have an income over $3,000 a year. There, four out of ten are under $2,000.

This may be hard to digest.

Think of it this way: if you live in Ontario, the chances are 4 to 1 your family income is over $3,000 a year; if you live in Newfoundland the chances are 4 to 4 your income is below this level.

This, too, is Canada.

We have tried to isolate the various aspects of poverty – housing, education, health, income.

It really does not work.

If we draw a profile of a Canadian living in poverty, he looks like this:

> He lives in a substandard, crowded home;
> He has a poor education;
> His health is bad;
> His income is low;

And as for the stream of Canadian life – socially, economically, politically, culturally, he's not with it.

His living conditions are bad because his income is low. His education is poor, probably because he came from a poor home. His health is bad because his living conditions are bad and always have been bad. His income is low because he has poor health and a poor education.

And he, too, is a Canadian.

A Social Development Approach to Poverty*

A Brief presented by the Government of Manitoba to the Special Senate Committee on Poverty

1. Introduction

The Government of Manitoba wishes to use this opportunity to present, and to discuss, its views on the nature and causes of poverty and the directions we, federally and provincially, must take if poverty is to be eliminated. We admit that existing policies and programs, at all levels, are inadequate. Thus it is not our intention to describe or defend Manitoba's present policies and programs. Rather, we seek to present new conceptual perspectives and directions to inform and guide the efforts of all levels of government to achieve the goal of social development for all Canadians. It is an attempt, not to prescribe detailed policies and program plans, but to set forth a philosophic and methodological approach which we believe is essential to any effective solution to the poverty problem.

*"A Social Development Approach to Poverty," a brief to the Special Senate Committee on Poverty by the Government of Manitoba, The Honourable David A. Croll, Chairman, pp. 9:28-9:35, The Senate of Canada, Wednesday, November 4, 1970. Reproduced with the permission of Information Canada.

2. The Nature and Causes of Poverty

In examining the nature and causes of poverty the practice has been to analyze the poor individual, the poor family and the poor community. This approach has provided a good deal of information about the social characteristics of the poor. Such information has been useful in the development of programs to assist the poor in re-entering, or adjusting to the existing social order. However, this type of analysis cannot give a comprehensive understanding of the nature and causes of poverty for it assumes, through its focus on the poor, that poverty is solely a function of poor people and their immediate environment, rather than a function – partial or total – of the larger social system.

The Government of Manitoba believes that the nature and causes of poverty can only be fully understood within an examination and analysis of the total social order. From this perspective we see poverty as a function of the dispersion range in the distribution of both wealth and power in today's society.

Poverty is not simply a matter of some absolute level of income, for what constitutes an adequate income to the individual or family is defined by social conventions and by the social pressures of the larger society. Such pressures have been universalized and intensified through the mass media and the advertising industry. Thus to have adequate food, clothing and shelter – basic standards we have not yet been able to guarantee – is not enough in a society which defines and ranks people in terms of their consumption so that the individual must always consume increasing numbers of goods just to maintain his relative position. Added to this, there is the fact that transportation, communication, education and entertainment are all increasingly important variables in the quality of life which people experience in a society where the self-sufficiency of the individual, family and group has been replaced by the impersonal, complex interdependence of a large scale, urban, market society.

More than this, though, an adequate attack on poverty is not simply a matter of providing some sufficient income (considered in relative as well as absolute terms) but is very much a question of the manner or process by which such a sufficient income is provided. If its provision is seen as an act of benevolence, even though it is the impersonal benevolence of the state, it will support the largely false assumption that poverty is the fault of the poor, and will reinforce the feeling of *recipients* that they have no rights of their own and no control over their own lives. Their well-being depends on others. There develops a state of helplessness, powerlessness, alienation and cynicism, moderated only by a benevolence that is insufficient to offset these strong, destructive forces.

This condition of powerlessness and alienation is prevalent among much of society today, including many who have a sufficient income without direct government assistance. It illustrates an often ignored dimension of poverty which a wholistic, societal approach makes clear – namely the dispersion range in the distribution of power. Some people may object to poverty being defined, even partially, in terms of power, preferring to maintain a strictly financial or income conception of the problem. We wish to point out to such people that they can so limit the definition of poverty if they wish, but in so doing they do not eliminate the problem of a growing sense of powerlessness, alienation and cynicism, nor the necessity for any solution to the poverty-income problem as they define it to be accompanied by a consistent solution to the problem of poverty-power. Moreover, there is a clear connection between the distribution of wealth and the distribution of power. Today's economy is characterized by *market imperfections* and concentrations of *market power* in the form of monopolies, and oligopolies, all of which form a self-reinforcing cycle, concentrating control over the productive processes of society in ever fewer hands. This has led to great inequalities in the distribution of both wealth and power. Redistributing wealth without dealing with market imperfections and market power aspects of our economic system will leave the distribution of power largely intact. The dynamics of the economic system which incorporates these concentrations of power are such that they may well mitigate some of the effects of redistributing wealth, through a general price increase, and/or a further decrease in the quality of production. Without a conscious redistribution of power, we cannot even guarantee the effectiveness of any substantial income redistribution, let alone solve the problem of powerlessness.

It is in this light that the Government of Manitoba believes that poverty is fundamentally a problem of inequality in the distribution of both wealth and power. The eradication of poverty thus requires simultaneous action to redistribute both wealth and power. Such action will involve changes in the existing social order – in those institutions and mechanisms which distribute wealth and power in ways that maintain and reinforce the vast inequalities of today. Changes in financial assistance and social services are necessary, but alone will have very limited effects in eliminating poverty. Assisting the poor to re-enter or adjust to the existing order, while it may be beneficial for the individuals involved, will not prevent the continued existence of poverty, and particularly its powerlessness dimensions, for social order to which such programs help people adjust is the ultimate generator of poverty in all its dimensions.

What this means at the operational levels of policy and administration is that poverty cannot be eradicated by the actions of any particular government department, but rather must be the focus of a governmental approach spanning all departments. Further, the redistribution of power that is required for success broadens the scope of the problem so that poverty is best tackled within the context of overall social development, a context concerned with the quality of life of all Canadians and the egalitarian aspects of Canadian public policy.

3. Some Principles of Social Development

The Government of Manitoba is presently attempting to establish a social development approach to government programming. What follows are some initial principles of social development which we believe provide a guide for government decision-making. Specific *anti-poverty* programs should incorporate these principles; in addition, the principles, if applied broadly, would constitute an attack on the power dimension of poverty.

(a) *Social Development Is the Goal – Economic Development Is One Means to That Goal*

It is imperative that the social needs of the individual, family, community and society should be the basis of government policy. This means that the priority traditionally placed on economic policy will have to give way to the fact that economic development is only a means to the end of social development and not an end in itself. Prime emphasis on economic development has not solved our social problems. Policy can no longer be evaluated by its contribution to economic development alone, but must be evaluated on its overall contribution to social needs broadly considered.

(b) *The Well-Being of People Is the Goal of Policy, and Implies the Well-Being of Business*

A social development approach operates on the assumption that whatever is good for the social and economic well-being of Canadians is also good for the development of business and industry. This is a reversal of the traditional position, which has failed in as much as the well-being of all Canadians has not been realized by an emphasis on business and industrial development, even when that emphasis has been supplemented by government and private social services. Economic structures which are compatible with the social and economic well-being of Canadians will have to be developed where such structures do not now exist, or where the present structures prove incompatible with the public interest.

(c) *Economic Justice Must Become an Operational Concept*

Social development, in addition to establishing non-economic criteria for evaluating policy alternatives, also requires a concept of economic justice involving the principle that the costs of economic *progress* must be covered by the benefits derived from such *progress*. As one example, this would mean that persons displaced by technological change – whether their marginal farm has become obsolete, their small enterprise can no longer compete, or their skills have been made obsolete – are entitled, by right, to appropriate dislocation assistance to cover the costs of change which they bear – unemployment, retraining, relocation, disruption of family and community life and so on. The costs of this assistance should be paid as directly as possible by those who benefit from such changes. This type of reconciliation of the costs and benefits of economic decisions is essential to economic justice and thereby to a comprehensive social development approach.

(d) *Equality Is an Important Criterion of Successful Policy*

Greater equality in the social and economic relations of society is an important criterion of social development policy. It emphasizes the need to narrow the dispersion range in the distribution of wealth and power. In so doing, material comfort and accumulation is de-emphasized as the sole, or even major, human need and motivational force in an affluent society. Other human needs and motivations – such as social interaction, having common purposes with others, being a part of and contributing to a larger entity than oneself or even one's family, self-confidence, recognition, and personal intellectual and spiritual fulfilment – are allowed greater recognition and satisfaction in a more egalitarian social order. Thus, a criterion of greater equality is crucial to the development of whole individuals, the development of fully human persons.

(e) *Individual Freedom Is to be Stressed*

Social development policy must counter the fact that citizens today, who could be freer than any people in history, increasingly feel constrained and manipulated by the social and economic forces of modern society. To counter this requires that individual freedom be stressed in policy decision-making. Education, information, and product or service quality grading and control must be used as an alternative to restriction of individual freedom of choice wherever possible. The social, cultural and economic options open to people should be actively expanded in order to broaden the scope of individual choice. In addition, vehicles for citizen involvement in decisions which affect them will have to be developed in order that there might be a proper balance of responsibility and freedom for all persons involved. Controls, as far as possible, should be exercised over social and economic forces and institutions, rather than over individuals. Such an emphasis is part of a dynamic, rather than a static, approach to social problems.

(f) *Democracy Must Be Emphasized*

A renewed effort to make democracy meaningful and operational *at all decision points* is crucial to social development. This means re-evaluating and revising the present political processes so that there are more decisions made with direct citizen involvement, greater opportunities for citizen input into higher level decision-making, and better access to decision-makers and the processes of decision-making. It also means extending the principles of democracy from the political system to the economic system as well.

If such social development principles are adopted by all levels of government and applied to all programming and decision-making, poverty can, we believe, be successfully attacked and eventually eliminated.

4. Social Development and Specific Anti-Poverty Approaches

There are some specific anti-poverty policy and program directions which we wish to present. However, it should be repeated that these points are presented within the context of a comprehensive social development approach to government programming designed to allow the maximal development of all citizens: only through such a comprehensive approach, and not by any anti-poverty policies and programs alone, can poverty in all its dimensions be eventually eradicated.

In order to understand the shortcomings of present programs, and as a prerequisite to the development of effective programs, it is essential to distinguish between *preventive* anti-poverty measures and *ameliorative* anti-poverty measures. Preventive measures change the nature of the existing social order which maintains and reinforces wide inequalities in the distribution of wealth and power. Ameliorative measures focus on assisting persons already caught in the poverty trap. Past programs have been mainly directed to the poor and to their environment, on the assumption that the causes of poverty were among the poor. Failing to distinguish between the social causes of poverty and the individual symptoms (effects), such programs simultaneously sought to assist the poor and eliminate poverty. As a result they were able neither to prevent the continued growth of poverty, nor provide effective assistance to the victims of poverty. By recognizing the need for both preventive and ameliorative programs within a broad social development context, it is currently possible not only to eventually eliminate poverty; but to more fully assist those who are presently poor.

We offer, now, some examples of specific anti-poverty preventive and ameliorative policy and program directions which could be adopted as part of a total social development approach:

(i) Preventive Policy and Program Directions

(a) *Investment Policy*

A comprehensive investment policy is necessary if economic development is to serve as a means to social development. Investment is one of the key generators of economic activity. It is crucial in decisions about what is to be produced and how it is to be produced. What is produced affects the material dimensions of our lives. How it is produced affects the material dimensions of our lives too, through industrial location, plant design, pollution and so on, but it also determines, in part, the nature of on-the-job social relations of workers to each other, and to their work effort. Past and present investment decisions have tended to reproduce the American economy *in miniature* in Canada. This has resulted in inefficient production and either higher prices (protected by tariffs) or an inability to compete with foreign competition. Thus the Canadian consumer, including the poor, have paid more for some goods than need be, while Canadian workers have been rendered inefficient and uncompetitive by the structure of investment in Canada.

It is clear then, that investment decisions affect all Canadians. They share our daily lives, and our society. Past investment decisions have built, and present investment decisions maintain, a social order which produces poverty. Thus, even in the context of poverty, or perhaps we should say, especially in the context of poverty, a comprehensive investment policy is necessary for at least three reasons:

First, to maximize the social benefits of investment such as jobs, training, community involvement, and to minimize corresponding harmful external effects (*diseconomies*) such as pollution, congestion, noise and so on; second, to rationalize the Canadian economy in terms of realizing economies of scale, thereby maximizing efficiency and reducing some consumer prices; and third, in order to allow for the development of democratic methods by which decisive choices about what is to be produced can be returned to the population at large. (Investment decisions, particularly in new enterprises, are often little influenced by simple market forces, for planning and economies of scale require large investment decisions to be made by managers, even before a product is on the market, and then sold to the public.)

At present there is no comprehensive Canadian investment policy, only a series of partial, and mostly indirect, instruments for effecting investment decisions, for example, CMHC mortgages, tax incentives, tariffs, industrial loans, and special area agreements. Such instruments tend to reflect the old emphasis on economic development and the old assumption that what is good for business and industry is necessarily good for the social and economic well-being of Canadians, rather than reflecting a social development perspective which subordinates economic development to social prerequisites and priorities.

A first step towards an investment policy based on social development programming would be to redirect the existing instruments which affect investment. Factors such as employment of minority group members, employment of women, job training, provision for Canadian participation in management (where foreign ownership is involved), input prices (where the supply sources are vertically integrated), output prices or pricing formulae (where marketing and distribution outlets are artificially controlled), profit calculation as between head office and subsidiaries (where foreign ownership is involved), reinvestment policy, pollution standards (including noise levels), safety standards, the provision of related social overhead capital, tax policy at the local level and other such concerns, must be established concurrently with any incentives, loans, tariff advantages, or government provision of social overhead capital. Under-developed countries have found it imperative to negotiate items such as the above in order to maximize the social and the economic benefits of industrial development. We must do the same if we are to seriously assist the disadvantaged areas and people, and maximize the social development opportunities for all Canadians.

Nonetheless, such provisions are only partial measures; a comprehensive investment policy based on social development principles and coordinated by the federal government will still be necessary. It should be noted that such a policy need not imply state control of investment. What it does require is a joint re-appraisal by business and government of present growth and investment policies, and their cooperative charting of new policies and investment criteria which more fully incorporate social development concepts. Such an approach will be particularly necessary if overall government policy is to encourage rationalization of the Canadian economy, for such a move, while more efficient in terms of production, will involve increasing monopoly/monopsony, oligopoly/oligopsony power within the Canadian economy.

In addition to the above, we must attempt to develop mechanisms for public expression regarding general investment priorities. This means providing information to the public about new investment possibilities, public discussion of investment alternatives, support for citizen research efforts and developing specific mechanisms for citizen input to both business and government.

(b) *Alternate Economic Instruments*

In view of the continued increase in foreign ownership of Canadian natural and industrial resources with all of the socio-economic and political implications that such takeover implies, there is a growing urgency to develop new instruments for mobilizing and applying Canadian capital in lieu of foreign capital. Such instruments should provide exemplary models of socially conscious investment criteria, and resource development based on social development principles. Two instruments seem particularly appropriate here:

1. The formation of a Canadian Development Corporation which would muster savings of Canadians for large economic and social development programs. For example, if the necessary funds had been available through such a corporation, our Northern pulp reserves could have been developed by Canadians rather than through foreign involvement as witnessed by Churchill Forest Industries and Prince Albert Pulp Mill.

2. The use of Crown Corporations by provincial and federal levels of government to develop our natural resources, particularly those in the North. The constant drain from Canada of cash and dividends generated from exploitation of our resources makes the introduction of this instrument of high priority.

(c) *Industrial Democracy*

Preventive programs to deal with the power redistribution aspects of poverty should include the democratization of the work place. This means support for, and efforts to create an environment wherein workers can participate directly in the management and decision-making of their plant. Such a direction can not only enhance the power of the worker over his own life, but thereby can also, in many cases, improve the efficiency of the industrial process.

(d) *Governmental Democracy*

Government power must be made more responsive and accountable to the Canadian people if they are to regain a sense of self-control, self-direction, and self-determination. This requires operational decentralization of government whereby decisions, given their particular nature and scope, are made at the lowest level possible and with maximum feasible participation. Thus decisions affecting the administration of services in a particular region should be made within that region and with local citizen participation. Improving the quality and effectiveness of government democracy will also necessitate a far greater information and communication flow so that citizens can more easily inform themselves about issues and impending policy decisions. The development of instruments by which citizen knowledge and inputs on an issue-by-issue basis can be effectively gathered and incorporated into the governmental decision-making process is, likewise, of crucial importance.

(e) *Community Development*

Community Development services are perhaps the most effective means for encouraging meaningful citizen participation and self-help efforts. They are of crucial importance to any substantive redistribution of power policy in as much as they help build the capacity of disadvantaged individuals and groups and the general public to take an active role in directing their own lives, and shaping their society. In addition, community development directly assists those who presently suffer the hardships of poverty, by making maximum use of available programs and resources, and by bringing people together to meet their common needs.

(f) *Income Distribution Policy*

A preventive anti-poverty approach needs an income redistribution policy. This requires the establishment of a truly progressive taxation system. The present system must be reformed so as to fully and progressively apply the concept of *ability to pay* across the entire tax structure. Tax credits which take into account the relative as well as absolute requirements for an adequate standard of living in today's society, should be adopted, including allowance for the actual costs of child care services, education related expenses, employment expenses and other expenses which have a relatively greater impact on the poor and disadvantaged. The transfer of wealth between generations is a matter of urgent social and economic importance also. There is a need to assure that undue concentration of wealth will not inhibit progress toward income redistribution and this requires uniform, national taxation of estates to achieve a more equitable distribution of wealth. In addition, expenditure decisions should be based, in part, on their distributive effect in making income, goods and/or services more available to the lowest income quartile.

(g) *Public Goods and Services*

The provision and use of public goods and services can be utilized effectively both to redistribute wealth and also as a means of recognizing some of man's non-material needs and motivations. The provision of goods and services which are particularly needed by the disadvantaged – meals through school or community based breakfast and/or lunch programs, public transportation, work clothes, child care including day-care and after school services, school texts and so on – help to redistribute wealth by augmenting the income of the poor. Such programs only redistribute wealth, of course, if they are not paid for by taxes on the poor. Public goods and services which focus on collective use such as parks, cultural events, film services, playgrounds, and even public transportation and community based child services encourage positive social and cultural interaction, and provide opportunities in some cases for active involvement and identification. Such public goods and services must be consciously made accessible – geographically, technically and in terms of public information – to poor communities if they are to be of service to poor people.

(ii) Ameliorative Policy and Program Directions

(a) *Separation of Financial Assistance and Social Services*

The Separation of financial assistance from the provision of other social services demonstrates the application of a social development perspective to ameliorative programs. At the present time we submit an applicant for public assistance to a long, degrading application and interview process before granting financial assistance. The purpose of this procedure, in addition to establishing need, is to determine what social services such as personal or family counselling, health services, employment assistance, vocational retraining or other rehabilitative services, are required by the applicant. The acceptance of these services is then established as a pre- or co-requisite to the receipt of financial assistance.

This approach fails to recognize two important facts. First, not all persons who require financial assistance also require social services. This point follows directly from a recognition of the societal causes of poverty. Second, social services are of minimal benefit if entered into under compulsion. Voluntarily accepted social services are much more likely to assist the individual person.

Thus, the separation of financial assistance and social services helps establish the right of the individual to financial assistance solely on the basis of need. It makes financial assistance more readily available, and removes the necessity for submission to sometimes unnecessary and frequently inffective *treatment and rehabilitative* services which too often invade the privacy and degrade the dignity of the consumer of financial assistance programs. As a result of separation, and the consequent time saving, social services could be provided on a more intensive and personal basis to those who desired to use them, thereby improving the quality of assistance provided to the consumer of social services.

The separation of financial assistance and social service delivery systems will necessitate the development of new *outreach* programs for the delivery of social services. Such *outreach* will involve informing the community and particularly the disadvantaged about the availability of social services. It will include preventive measures which seek out early problem symptoms and encourage the use of appropriate social services in problem prevention. And it will require outreach counselling, on a voluntary client basis, as to which services might be helpful to a particular individual. Such new practice could very well improve the overall usefulness of the social services package.

(b) *A Self-Declaration Application for Financial Assistance*

The right of the individual citizen, and the dignity of the financial assistance applicant, can be further supported by the adoption of a simplified, self-declaration application procedure for financial assistance. The self-declaration procedure has been applied and has proven its worth and effectiveness in a number of areas, such as unemployment insurance, financial assistance for the aged, income reporting for taxation purposes, and more recently in the New Jersey Experiment involving a guaranteed annual income. Moreover, the self declaration procedure would free up significant amounts of staff time which would be directed to the improvement of non-financial social services, and the establishment of *outreach* programs. At the same time, honesty and accuracy can be adequately assured by means of a random sample post audit.

(c) *Incentive Scheme*

A social development approach to financial assistance programming requires that the individual be encouraged and supported in efforts to improve the social and economic environment he, his family and his community face. Present practices which remove, through decreased assistance, 100 percent of the earnings of a consumer of financial assistance programs once those earnings exceed some minimal amount are, to some extent self-defeating. An incentive scheme which encourages financial assistance recipients to develop supplementary income leading to economic self-sufficiency is needed. In this way persons on financial assistance will be able to contribute to their self-development and to the social development of the larger society.

(d) *Cost of Living Escalator Clause*

An automatic, cost of living escalator clause built into our financial assistance programs will protect the real value of the assistance provided. We consider such protection to be an important tenet of social justice.

(e) *Broader Eligibility for Assistance Programs*

Eligibility for financial assistance and all social services should be broadened in order to allow all those in need to be assisted, thereby contributing to the fuller realization of the social development potential of all Canadians.

(f) *Access to Health Care and Integration with Social Services*

Health is crucial to everybody's quality of life; thus health care services are essential to social development. While financial barriers to health care for the poor have been minimized, other barriers remain. Health care must be more directly extended into poor communities through the provision of neighbourhood health and social development centres. The provision of health care in isolated areas must be improved and extended. Also, increased information and understanding, decreased waiting time and red tape, continuity of services and perhaps most important, a more personal, less intimidating health care process must be developed. Health and social services need to be closely integrated so that the total needs of consumers of both health and social services are more easily and fully provided for. In the area of health care, the middle class often fare little better than the poor. For them, significant financial barriers remain to comprehensive health care. If a social development programming approach is to become a serious reality, these barriers must be removed by the extension of universal medical insurance coverage.

(g) *Preventive Health Care*

Preventive health care services must be given higher priority, particularly, in poor communities, if the health programs of the poor are to be ameliorated. The integration of health and social services will help public health personnel assist families to meet their preventive health needs through a closer association with the provision of special financial assistance, and other social services.

(h) *Educational Opportunities*

Education is a crucial way of helping people break out of the poverty cycle, but to date we have been unsuccessful in extending full educational opportunities to poor and disadvantaged citizens. To do so will require high quality teachers, modern educational resources, after-hour study facilities, community outreach programs, new adult education approaches and so on, all specifically oriented to, and located in, poor and/or disadvantaged communities. To ensure this orientation, poor communities must be given a greater role in the policy and operation of local schools.

In addition, if post-secondary education is to be accessible to poor and disadvantaged citizens, new student financing programs will have to be developed which take into account the reluctance of students from poor families to go into debt. This reluctance, based on the experience of their family and friends, is all too often justified. Credit and debt instruments are no friends of the poor. Moreover, student financing must take into account the foregone earnings of the poor student; these are often very necessary in a poor family.

In making education a vehicle for overcoming the poverty trap, it will be increasingly tied into the community, and into other government efforts. Federal assistance may well be needed, particularly in the area of student financing.

(i) *Housing*

Good housing is an essential means of fostering the fullest possible development of the family unit. As such, it must be related to the changing nature of the family unit and the corresponding needs of the family with regards to health and social development.

Housing policies must be designed to optimize the total costs including the social costs of residential services and provide highest performance of the total residential services package. Housing policies must be related to new kinds of social and economic activity and improved journey to work patterns particularly for the no car and one car households.

Housing policy must include taking responsibility for those elements of the residential environment which the private sector cannot or will not provide, as well as those areas of the urban milieu which have direct bearing upon the future breath of the urban complex.

Public transport services and community facilities, such as nursery schools, tot lots and parks ultimately affect the total residential environment, and legislation exists which if appropriately applied can give the public its rightful share of value added from new public improvements.

Housing is a major subset of any effective social development policy; therefore housing must be given a high priority in any attempt to ameliorate poverty and social disadvantage.

Housing policy must include alternatives which transcend the classic stereotypes of public housing and private homes. A variety of rental policies and ownership programs can be applied to achieve a wider range of choices in particular for the lower and moderate income groups.

(j) *Ecology*

Concern with man's physical environment is another aspect of social development. Pollution has become a major problem affecting us all; but it often affects the poor more acutely. They live in the most congested areas of our cities; they work in our most polluted factories; and in rural areas their water may be polluted and untreated because their homes lack municipal services. It is no longer sufficient to abate (or minimize) pollution, certain types of pollution must be prevented entirely if adverse long-term accumulative effects on health are to be avoided, and if the esthetical [*sic*] and recreational qualities of our society are to be adequately protected. Thus concern with pollution, which can result in ameliorative programs, can also expand into substantial preventive programs based on concern for human ecology, or the total human environment. Such concern and programs feedback into other programs providing, for example, a set of criteria as an input for investment policy.

(k) *Other*

Many more ameliorative anti-poverty policy and program directions could be presented – transportation, legal services, retraining, consumer education, recreation and on and on. All could be elaborated on in much more depth than we have done here. But our point, we hope, is clear; both preventive and ameliorative programs are needed – and both must be undertaken within the concept of a more comprehensive social development framework for all government programming and decision-making if poverty is ever to be eradicated from the Canadian social order.

5. Comments on the Guaranteed Annual Income

At this stage of your deliberations, given the importance you have attached to the concept of the Guaranteed Annual Income (G.A.I.), it would be inappropriate for us not to comment on this topic. Therefore we present a few, very limited comments about the G.A.I, considering it from a comprehensive social development perspective.

It should be clear from what we have already said about the separation of financial assistance from social services, the adoption of a simplified self-declaration application procedure for financial assistance and the need for an incentive scheme, that the Government of Manitoba supports the basic concept of the G.A.I. We believe that the G.A.I. is an important element in an overall social development approach.

However, we wish to caution that the G.A.I. is only one element in an effective fight against poverty. By itself, it is not a remedy for poverty; it is not even sufficient, on its own, to fully assist those presently caught in the poverty cycle. To suggest that the G.A.I. is an effective solution to the poverty problem would be irresponsible and dangerous. It would be irresponsible in that it could delay the adoption of a much needed, comprehensive social development framework for government programming and decision-making at all levels; it would be dangerous because it could arouse false hopes and ultimately result in frustration and desperation.

We must recognize that the G.A.I. is not an adequate instrument of redistribution policy. It does not significantly redistribute power; nor is there any assurance that it will even effectively redistribute financial resources. Rent and price increases could absorb any benefits of redistribution via the G.A.I. unless the supplies of housing and other goods now in greater demand were expanded. Moreover, there could be a tendency generated for wages, within a certain range in the non-unionized sector, to fall to the minimum level prescribed by law (this is known as the Speenhamland effect). Employers would profit; the G.A.I. would cover some portion of the drop in income, and workers would continue to work at their jobs unless they could find higher paying ones, which is quite unlikely.

Finally, we wish a word about the cost of the G.A.I. It is our firm belief that the G.A.I. will cost more than existing financial assistance. If an incentive scheme is built on a guaranteed base approximately equivalent to existing financial assistance payments, a great number of persons presently earning more than this amount, but less than the amount at which all assistance is eliminated under an incentive scheme, will become eligible for partial financial assistance. The exact amount involved will, of course, depend on the incentive rate incorporated into the G.A.I. plan. Nor, can we see a lower guaranteed base level of financial assistance than that presently provided; if anything, we believe that an emphasis on redistribution, and considerations of social justice in terms of a minimal standard of life, require a higher guaranteed income level. Further, recognition of the right of all citizens to a G.A.I., the simplified application procedure, and the separation of financial and social assistance will, in all likelihood, increase the number of applicants as those who previously felt harassed, intimidated, or simply frightened by the old administrative and punitive measures, claim the assistance to which they are entitled.

These cost increases associated with the G.A.I. are necessary if it is to be effective even within its limited scope. They must be openly discussed and accepted if we are not to be caught in a political trap where it becomes necessary to implement G.A.I. without any increase in financial assistance expenditures. To do so would mean that some people – those most adversely affected by poverty – would end up in a position far worse than at present. The assistance provided them would be reduced from that which they presently receive. To accept this, or to stumble into such a political trap, would make a fraud of the G.A.I. for it would then become a guarantor of poverty, not an element in its eradication.

It is therefore necessary to support the G.A.I., while admitting both its limitations and its cost implications.

6. Conclusion

The Government of Manitoba is attempting to move in new directions, seeking new ideas and new answers for the solution of long-standing problems. We are moving toward the type of wholistic social development approach to governmental programming and decision-making which is presented in this brief. We believe that this is the only effective way to tackle the structural origins of problems such as poverty, while at the same time exercising our responsibility for the social and economic well-being of all Manitobans.

But poverty is a national problem. It requires a national solution. We therefore hope that the federal government will also move towards a comprehensive social development approach, including both preventive and ameliorative anti-poverty policies such as those put forth for discussion here. This is the direction we hope the Senate Committee will urge.

"Their Own Fault"*

Albert Rose

Canadians are inordinately proud when they hear or read that their country enjoys *the second highest standard of living in the world*. This assertion, so often and widely made at the time of national elections, has taken on additional force in the years following the close of the Second World War, years in which Canada has experienced tremendous physical and economic growth.

It does seem to be true in the latter years of the 1950's that very few Canadians are without food or clothing or even lack the income to purchase food and clothing of adequate quantity and quality. Evidence of serious need for these elements of the standard of living is largely confined to specially disadvantaged groups – the aged, widowed mothers with children, the chronically ill, the disabled, the unemployables.

To some extent physical and economic growth has been accompanied by a significant expansion in the social services. There are, nevertheless, a number of areas of great social need which have scarcely been touched in Canada's great expansion. The need for housing, particularly homes for rent or for sale at prices which those in the lowest two-thirds of the income scale can afford, is one of these unmet needs.

If we judge housing accommodation by the criterion of *absolute lack* it is probably correct to say that very few Canadians are without shelter. If the criterion of *adequacy* is introduced, however, there can be little doubt that a substantial number of Canadians are without housing. *Adequacy* implies that each family shall be housed in sufficient space to maintain a happy family life and that this housing shall be of sound construction properly maintained. "The essential purpose of housing," writes Dr. J. M. Mackintosh of the University of London, "is to provide so far as structure and equipment can do so within defined limits of cost in capital and maintenance, the conditions of comfort, health and enjoyment that are needful for the making of a home and the nurture of a family. . . . A 'home' in the proper sense of the word is a family living in a separate dwelling as an organic unit of society and permeated with human feeling."[1] Moreover, the accommodation must be provided with adequate heat in winter and ventilation in summer, suitable natural and artificial light, and a modern sanitary plumbing system. Kitchen facilities must include a sink with hot and cold running water, a stove suitable to the needs of the family, and proper storage space and refrigeration for food.

Adequacy thus has both social and physical implications. But social and physical adequacy are not always found in conjunction. A dwelling may provide sufficient space for a small family but be quite inadequate for a family with several children. When, as frequently happens in the substandard neighbourhoods or slum areas of our cities, several large families crowd into the same unit of housing, accommodation which was formerly quite adequate for one family or household deteriorates to the point where it is no longer safe, sanitary or decent housing for anyone.

It is, of course, futile to discuss social and physical adequacy if much of the housing which meets acceptable standards is beyond the capacity of a substantial proportion of the population to own or rent. In Canada this is and has been the case for several generations.

A tenant selection officer (investigator) of a public housing project devotes most of his regular work to the investigation of inadequate housing conditions. Examples selected at random from the experiences of one such official in Toronto will illustrate the general point that is being made.

The houses on many of the streets in Toronto are typical of those built in a number of Canadian cities in the decades immediately before and after the First World War. These are solid houses, semi-detached, brick-veneered, with a good-sized veranda across the front to the left or right of the front door. The veranda, approached by three or four wooden steps, is protected by a wooden railing, usually painted white, and surmounted by a cross-bar, usually painted green. With the addition of a standard expandable gate at the head of the stairs a rather large play-pen for children can be created quite easily. The buildings are set back about twenty feet from the sidewalk and the intervening areas are a more or less successful piece of green lawn, depending often on the presence or absence of a maple or elm tree. These dwellings of six rooms, three of which are bedrooms, can, if properly maintained, be quite comfortable for one family. Obviously they are not so comfortable if they must be shared by two or more families.

It was to this type of house that an official of the Housing Authority of Toronto paid a visit in midsummer 1954. The house was on a street in West Toronto and there was nothing special about it except for the fact that a family living in it, which shall be called Gordon, had applied for an apartment in the Regent Park (North) Housing Project located nearly five miles to the east. Their application was one of more than five thousand on file at the time in the office of the Housing Authority of Toronto which administers Regent Park. As it happened, this was the nicest house into which the official of the authority was invited during several weeks of visits to applicants.

The purpose of these visits was to examine the housing accommodation of those families whose applications indicated on paper the greatest need. A twenty-minute visit would usually be sufficient to enable verification of the information concerning space and income, although the latter would be checked with the prospective tenant's employer. It would also provide an opportunity for an appraisal of the quality of the accommodation and a chance for the applicant to give additional information in support of his case for rehousing. The official reports of several hundred such visits would be of crucial importance to the authority in selecting the tenants of some 168 apartments which were expected to be ready for occupancy in October or November 1954.

The application signed by Mr. Gordon, a veteran of the First World War and currently employed by a veterans' organization, provided some of the information required and indicated that the Gordon family, composed of two adults and two male children of working age, was living in three upstairs rooms. This was *prima facie* evidence of overcrowding. As well, Mr. Gordon's income was reported as $50 a week and the weekly rental was reported as $17. The expenditure of a third of a man's income on shelter is certainly excessive.

Mrs. Gordon, a pert little woman whose tight gray-brown curls were held carefully beneath a hairnet, answered the doorbell and in response to the official's quiet introduction, "I'm from Regent Park, Mrs. Gordon," displayed the familiar nervous gestures of those in whose faces show a combination of distress and relief. The first view of the interior of the house revealed what appeared to be an extremely clean and well-kept home. The front hall and the stairs to the second floor were carpeted and on the right, at the head of the stairs, could be seen a modern bathroom tiled in black and white. The carpeting continued along the hall to the front bedroom.

The interview began and ended in the upstairs kitchen. For more than one reason there seemed no need to see the other two rooms. Mrs. Gordon stood with her back to the small stove and refrigerator (the first electric refrigerator seen by the visitor in a week of calls). The conversation proceeded smoothly. The Gordon family occupied two bedrooms and the kitchen and were not required to share the bathroom with the family of the owner (a newcomer from Europe four years before) except as a matter of courtesy by Mrs. Gordon to help with the toilet training of the landlord's youngest children. The owner and his family used a washroom in the basement. It was not clear whether they had a bath available.

The applicant's family found the kitchen a little small for dining purposes when three grown men and the mistress of the house sat down to meals. They greatly felt the need of a living room since the boys had no place to bring their friends. The front bedroom was ostensibly a bed-sitting room, but it was rather chilly in winter and, in any event, was the parents' bedroom. The kitchen occupied the space provided for a third bedroom.

Her husband earned $45 or $50 a week, continued Mrs. Gordon, depending upon his hours of work. The rent was $17 a week. One son was working, earning $50 a week and paying $10 a week for room and board. The second son was "laid off" just at the moment and was asleep in the smaller bedroom. It was nearly eleven o'clock in the morning.

When the visitor from the Housing Authority had asked the necessary questions, he began to arrange his papers and to say what must be said in terminating each interview.

"We cannot promise anything, Mrs. Gordon. There will be some apartments ready in October or November. But we have five thousand applications and we must visit all those which seem urgent and give preference to those with the greatest need."

Mrs. Gordon showed irritation. "We were promised a place a year ago by the Housing Manager," she said sharply. "My husband is a veteran and has been in touch with the office many times. You can see our need. This isn't living, it's just existing. Isn't there a preference for veterans?"

"I doubt very much that the Manager is in a position to promise you, Mrs. Gordon. We have five thousand applications. The people who lived in Regent Park were given priority. Now we can consider other people. Other things being equal, veteran's status is given some consideration but the need must be established."

"Others have been getting in," she said.

"Yes, Mrs. Gordon, but you must realize that when you say that you and your family are not living but just existing, we see families every day who are not even existing, let alone living – families in terrible conditions, with two to six children, all sleeping in one room – "

"That's their own fault!" Mrs. Gordon's interruption was almost hissed. Her left arm shot out, palm down, the fingers spread apart in an angry gesture.

"Surely, Mrs. Gordon, you would give preference to a family with one wage earner making $45 or $50 a week with two or three children in two attic rooms. You should see some of the families – "

"That's their own fault!" shouted Mrs. Gordon. Her arm shot out once more.

Perhaps three times, perhaps six times, the angry words and gesture were repeated as the visitor sought to explain. Mrs. Gordon did not accompany him downstairs.

A few days before he met Mrs. Gordon, the *tenant selection officer* of the Housing Authority of Toronto had paid a visit in East Toronto. The house was, as far as he could judge, fairly sound structurally. But the two attic rooms in which resided a family of two adults and five children (the Justice family, it will be called) were obviously inadequate on physical grounds, not merely for this family but for any family. Seven people slept in one attic room under an inverted V-shaped ceiling. They shared the second floor bathroom with two other families. The owner and his family occupied the ground floor. In all, nineteen persons lived in this house.

The space used by the Justices was grossly insufficient for living, eating, and sleeping, and there was apparently no refrigeration or other food storage facilities. A two-burner electric plate served as a stove for seven persons. One unshaded light bulb hung from the ceiling of the combined kitchen, living and dining space. There could be little argument about social inadequacy, not merely for one but for all three families.

On the same street, on the same day, arranging calls for the sake of time, the interviewer visited the Oxton family which had also applied for accommodation in Regent Park. The Oxtons, with their two boys and four girls (aged 3 to 14), lived in a five-room, one-storey, stucco cottage along with Mrs. Oxton's parents, who owned the house, and her father's brother. The two principal families had once occupied a seven-room house but an industrial accident to Mrs. Oxton's father and the consequent reduction in his income had forced the purchase of a smaller dwelling in 1948. At the time of the visit, Mr. Oxton, who worked nights as a porter for a department store and earned $45 a week, was asleep in his family's bedroom. Five nights a week the remaining seven members of his family slept in this room and on weekends the father was home as well.

Human ingenuity knows few bounds and the visitor was greatly interested in the arrangements whereby eight people managed to sleep in one bedroom measuring about nine by eleven feet. Fortunately the door had been placed in the middle of the room along the centre hall wall. Inside to the left of the door stood a bunk bed. Two boys slept on the upper portion; three of their sisters slept below. The baby of the family slept with her mother in a larger bed to the right of the door on five nights of the week and with both parents on the weekend.

Two days before these calls, the officer had talked to some of the Douglas family, who lived in a fairly good house, one of a group built thirty or forty years ago on a street which has been greatly widened and has become a well-travelled thoroughfare in the heart of the city. The street-cars passed only about forty feet from where the Douglases slept. The family occupied what is known as two and half rooms: a kitchen and a moderate-sized bed-sitting room off which an alcove had been converted into a second bedroom. This family was small – just two adults, a girl of 12 years and a boy of 8 years. These four shared the only bathroom with five other persons, certainly a more fortunate situation than some families experience. The parents slept in the larger portion of the bedroom on a sofa-bed, separated from their two children by a curtain. When their daughter wished to dress or undress, her brother departed for the kitchen, or took advantage of an empty bathroom.

There was nothing physically inadequate about the Douglas's dwelling. It simply did not fit the family. This lack of fit meant a social inadequacy of considerable importance to the Douglases, and particularly to their daughter.

These are not case descriptions specially selected for their horror or their *shock* value. Similar, and sometimes worse, situations exist in large numbers in a great many Canadian cities and to some extent in our rural slums. They were *all in the day's work* for the official of the public housing project.

Why do not families like the Justices, the Oxtons, the Douglases, and even the Gordons do something about their housing problem? It is often said that there are a great many opportunities for every Canadian family to better its housing accommodation if it will only put its collective mind and resources to the task. Literally hundreds or thousands of new houses have been built on the fringes of most Canadian cities during the past ten years. New apartment buildings with a hundred or more units each seem to spring up like vast mushrooms in our cities, and once erected are quickly occupied.

In Mrs. Gordon's view, the reason her husband and two sons did not combine their incomes and rent the space they required and wanted was because "boys today seem to want their money for themselves." At no time, however, would the Gordons consider that their situation was *their own fault*. It would be the fault of the government or the community, for not providing sufficient homes for old people, or for old veterans, or for old taxpayers.

Who then is at fault when inadequacy is obvious? In some cases it is *their own fault*. Some families have simply not learned to budget their modest or average incomes properly, with due attention to their health and all their physical and emotional needs. In these families an excessive proportion of income is devoted to recreation, or to clothing, or to alcoholic beverages, or to the purchase of an automobile, a television set or some other durable consumer good, the desirability of which is hurled at them continuously from every medium of mass communication. But a great deal more study than we have as yet undertaken in Canada needs to be done, and a great many more facts would need to be gathered, to pinpoint the critical time in a family's life at which their housing dilemma becomes *their own fault*.

The fact is that most of the families who apply to a public housing authority for a dwelling have made an effort to solve their own housing problems but their incomes are insufficient.[2] Alternatively, it might be said that their families are too large, but this is just another way of stating that their incomes are insufficient. The residue or *hard core* of families who simply do not care has been found to be an infinitesimal proportion.[3]

There is a significant pattern in the stories which families with small children tell. When they were first married the young couple rented one or two rooms. The husband earned a modest wage, perhaps $30 or $35 a week. The first child arrived and the family felt somewhat crowded. For a long time the mother, when she could go out with her baby in the daytime, and the father in the evenings, looked for more suitable accommodation. Ultimately they decided that they could afford two or three rooms.

In due course a second child was born and remained in its crib or in a carriage in the parents' bedroom. Most often all four slept in the same room. Within a short time the sense of crowding and the inadequacy of facilities became more than the family could bear. Once again the search for more adequate housing commenced, if it had ever ceased. Perhaps the father's weekly earnings were then $45 or $50 a week. If the family were extremely fortunate a partially self-contained flat of four rooms was located. The bathroom must be shared, of course, with other families.

The birth of each additional child brought such a family to a new level of difficulty. Invariably the purchase of a home was desired. Most older houses in the city were far too costly; others were inadequate. The new small two-bedroom bungalows and three bedroom one-and-a-half-storey houses in the suburbs offered some hope for a time although these locations greatly increase the cost of transportation to employment.

Yet even these houses at the lowest prices prevailing in the postwar period were beyond the capacity of most of the families at this income level. They had literally no savings in the form of cash or bonds or insurance policies, or, at the most, had savings of a few hundred dollars. The smallest down payments required were beyond their capacity to save. Even with a down payment, many families found that they could not qualify for homes financed through the most favourable mortgage terms since those institutions best able to judge had decreed that incomes of less than $3,000 or $3,300 or $3,600 per annum would not be sufficient to enable the family to carry the monthly payments successfully.

Since these families could not buy homes they returned to the tiresome search for rooms for rent. Apartments, flats, and duplexes are usually renting at far more than they can afford. And so the tenant selection officer finds them – in two rooms, in three rooms, in four rooms – without proper kitchen services, sharing minimum bathroom facilities with large numbers of other people, raising children who must sleep two and three to a bed, four and eight to a room: living their lives in the most inadequate physical and social circumstances.

Is it possible to identify in the history of these families factors which make their housing dilemma *their own fault*? It would seem more accurate to state that the housing conditions under which thousands of Canadian families live today, and in which many have lived all their lives, are the fault of everyone. For the most part, it is the community which has failed.

Footnotes

1. J. M. Mackintosh, *Housing and Family Life*. London: Cassell and Co. Ltd., 1952, pp. 10-11.
2. This is borne out in the experience of tenant selection officers in many cities on this continent. When prospective tenants who applied some months or a year before for accommodation are sought for interview, a substantial proportion are found to have moved. They have not advised the Housing Authority. Presumably they have improved their situation, although the reverse may be true.
3. Mackintosh, *op. cit.*, p. 26.

Impressions*

Federal Task Force on Housing and Urban Development

The Task Force began its public hearings in Ottawa on September 15th and concluded them in Hull on December 4th. In the intervening 80 days the Members consumed mounds of reading material, travelled more than 25,000 miles, and met many hundreds of Canadians. It was an exhilarating and informative experience. But it was a hectic schedule as well, an always-on-the-go kind of inquiry in which time and circumstances often prevented the Task Force from digging as deeply as it might have wished into some of the issues before it.

The Members regret that this was so, that too often where basic data was lacking they were left without time and resource to undertake or commission the kind of research needed to fill the information gap. From the outset, however, the Task Force felt that the urgency of many of the problems before it out-ranked the undoubted benefit of exhaustive research into some of them. The goal was to produce a report by early 1969 including at least some recommendations capable of implementation in time to affect the spring construction season. This meant compressing into four months travel and hearings which might have

*Report of the Federal Task Force on Housing and Urban Development, Paul Hellyer, Chairman, "Impressions," pp. 7-21, 1969. Reproduced with the permission of Information Canada.

taken six months or more and accepting, as a price of meeting that urgency, some shortfall in investigative techniques.

Having said that, however, the Members offer no apology for the fact that some of their comments and conclusions stem as much from mental note or emotional impression as they do from proven fact. Indeed they believe that the impressions formed during their too-brief journey across urban Canada are in many cases just as important as the tables of statistics and the background papers which clogged their brief cases. Housing and urban development are, after all, people problems, tied every bit as much to human desires and prejudices as to scientific graphs and calculated logic. As noted Greek planner Doxiadis so aptly put it to the Task Force, "a planner who is unable to sell his plan to the people and their politicians has no plan at all – just a piece of paper."

In setting forth its comments and recommendations then, the Task Force has tried to supply supporting statistical data or empirical evidence to the extent that such data and evidence could be assembled during the life of its inquiry. In some cases, the Members feel the data and the evidence so assembled are sufficient to prove the point. In other cases they are not as sufficient and the Members in some instances have had to rely as much on their impressions and their instincts. If this procedure leaves a gap for the urban scientist, the Task Force hopes that it might be a positive benefit to the urban dweller in putting at least some of these problems in the kind of human, emotional terms in which he so often sees them and in making this Report more than *just a piece of paper*.

The first and major impression of the Task Force – and one on which abundant statistical data exists – is that Canada is increasingly and rapidly becoming an urban nation. The statisticians say that seven out of every ten Canadians now live in urban areas and that more than eight out of ten will do so by 1980, most of them in 29 major urban centres across the country. If the statistics are impressive in themselves, even more so is the physical effect which this massive migration, equal in scope to the first settlement and development of Canada, has had and is having on the national landscape.

That landscape remains one of remarkable physical and human diversity. To travel Canada is to view a wide range of both geography and human experience. From mountain to prairie, from lush forest to barren rock, from quiet countryside to throbbing metropolis, from historic site to overnight boom town – Canada is all of them. Its people are varied as the land itself, each wanting to share in something *Canadian* and yet each seemingly intent on retaining something special of his own. Such was the paradox of submissions and requests from various regional, ethnic and social groups across the country. All want to share in Canada's material abundance, but many are reluctant to pay a social or cultural price for it. All want to be good citizens of the Canadian community, but many wish to preserve their community of ethnic heritage as well. A Canadian mosaic indeed.

The scene in rural Canada can be both confusing and contradictory. On the one hand, one finds the giant farm complexes, every bit as much an *industry* in organization and technique as their urban cousins, developing and marketing the produce of the land in a supply so bounteous as to be the envy and hope of a hungry world. No great lure of the city here amid people who are able to reap economic gains equal or more to their urban neighbours while retaining at least some of that independence of spirit and tranquillity of mind which seems to rise from the land itself. The agricultural giants are a part of rural Canada. But so, too, are the others, the small farms and the large families which industrialization too often has swept aside, leaving them to scratch the most meagre of existences from land often capable of different and more productive use. In most cases the physical setting reflects the economic barrenness. Houses are old and dilapidated. Gardens and lawns have become muddy bare patches intermixed with weedy scruff. In a few exceptions the landscape belies the overall economic problem. Here one finds well kept houses and neatly tended fields to disguise the facts of low income and economic under-development. But these are the exceptions and not the rule.

As a sort of half-way house between rural Canada and the burgeoning urban areas lie the small communities which dot the landscape, particularly across the prairies. They are a mixed bag. In regions where agriculture is strong, one finds prosperous and growing service communities, meeting the needs of the surrounding population, generating a growth factor of their own and seemingly on the verge, in a few cases at least, of that *great leap forward* into full urban status. In areas where the rural economy is weak, so are the towns, many of them struggling with local industries of varying relevance to ensure that a baby born or a new resident acquired is a net population gain and not merely an offsetting factor against the drain to the city.

Then there are the cities themselves. Whether urbanization is *good* or *bad* for humanity may be a debate without limit; why it is acquiring a certain inevitability is a more definable issue. For here truly is *where the action is*. Economic action in the manifold educational and employment opportunities, in the generation of industrial and manufacturing wealth, in a service-oriented urban marketplace which seems capable of adding new economic growth even as it serves existing economic demand. Social and cultural action in the diffuse and diverse mixture of backgrounds, personalities and talents caught in the continuing urban process of human exchange and inter-change. Size undoubtedly breeds problems, but it brings benefits, too, and there was little evidence among Canadians in 1968, as worried as many of them were about the problems, that they were prepared to try to halt the benefits of urbanization.

Within these urban areas, the Task Force was struck by the impression that much of what was happening was as much self-generated as controlled, more determined by raw interaction than by carefully-conceived plan. Even in the best of situations urban planning was a reactive and not a pre-emptive process. People often came to the city without a job or a house or both. They either found employment or the ever-growing welfare rolls added a new name. They found some kind of accommodation within the existing stock or, if their finances could withstand the shock, they paid the price to add yet another box to the sprawling suburban dormitories which devour so much of the surrounding land with so little apparent plan or direction. Children are born and grow – and the city struggles to find schools and playgrounds and recreation centres to fill their needs. Automobiles are purchased in almost direct confrontation to the lack of adequate transportation routes to carry them at more than a snail's pace. New industries create jobs – and water and air pollution, too.

Here, too, is poverty in its rawest and ugliest form. No pretty gardens or painted cottages here to camouflage economic depression. Poverty in the worst areas of the city core is abundantly visible in the decrepit structures which form its housing, the cracked pavement of the streets which are its recreational area, and the rodents which are its wild life. This poverty you can see – and hear – and taste – and smell. Its residents are not simply families struggling to catch up to the average national income; too often they are people fighting to retain a vestige of human dignity and self-respect. No Task Force impression is more vivid of mind or depressing of spirit than those formed amid the blight and slum of Canada's larger cities.

In some cities the conglomerate effect of all these problems can stretch the hope and confidence of the most optimistic urbanite. As each year thousands more Canadians seek city space and service to work and live and play and drive, one must wonder whether the existing metropolitan structure in some areas at least can even meet the additional pressure, less [sic] make any noticeable inroads in the backlog of problems confronting it. It can be argued that some of the factors at work and destruction in the major urban centres of the United States are unique to those centres. But it can be questioned, too, whether Canada's largest metropolitan areas are that far removed from the level of human frustration at which emotional violence threatens logical compromise. Even in cities where the powers and problems of urbanization are less developed and less drastic, there is an urgent need for quick, decisive and imaginative action.

Urgency. That certainly is among the strongest of the Task Force impressions. The need to act while reasonable action is still possible. Many Canadians, whose needs are of yesterdays, want adequate housing today and not tomorrow. Theirs is the voice of frustration that no longer will accept the explanation that it is *that other* government's responsibility to act. Theirs is the growing anger of people who, amid the material plenty around them, refuse to wait that *little bit longer* for their minimal share. In a world of rising need and increasing expectations, a bit more and a bit better are not good enough. Our cities must come to grips with their major problems now. With pressures so large and problems so complex, tomorrow will not do.

The Task Force is convinced that Canada has the resources, material, techno-logical and intellectual, to meet these needs and problems. To believe otherwise is to despair and surrender to the inevitable. But it is equally convinced that, if these resources are to achieve their most productive and imaginative potential, far-reaching changes are required in the attitudes, organization and effort of all those involved in the urban process. And *all those* in this context is an embracing phrase. It means governments at all levels. It means industrialists and academics and professionals in various fields. And, far from last, it means the people of Canada themselves who in the end will decide the kind of country and society this is to be.

Lest there be a misunderstanding, the Task Force did find planning at work in urban Canada. But it frankly was disappointed and discouraged by it. So much of it was concerned with minutiae while the need for a grand urban design goes begging. So much of it was a negative scripture, written in *thou shalt not's*, when the situation cried out for positive thought and initiative. The Task Force found rules upon rules to establish the widths of streets, yet it uncovered hardly a single community with a long-term plan and design for basic transportation corridors. It found a multiplicity of regulation at all levels to set minimum requirements and hardly anyone to spell out maximum objectives. Some planners and officials had an economic term of reference; hardly any seemed to have given much thought to the broader ecological or sociological issues. The urban scene seemed to abound with bureaucrats – but to be sadly lacking in dreamers.

If there was a common theme of tomorrow across Canada, it seemed to lie with that wondrous potion called urban renewal. One had to look to find a community that did not have at least an urban renewal study somewhere in the municipal works. In some cases, it was only half a joke to wonder what might be *renewed* – short of painting the general store. To the Task Force, it seemed urban renewal, with its standing offer of federal dollar bills for locally-raised quarters, was becoming as much a matter of municipal financing as municipal planning. Certainly in most schemes witnessed by the Task Force the accent seemed as much on altering assessment ratios as on renewing or adding to existing housing stock. In the best of circumstances, it was a process of physical renewal without sufficient accent on new social or cultural factors.

If the municipal politicians indicated they had caught on at least to the financial implications of urban renewal policies, the programs remained a source of continuing puzzlement to the people directly involved in them. Urban renewal, the Task Force might fairly comment, can serve as a successful example of neither public dialogue nor participatory democracy. In a number of areas actually visited by the Members, local residents seemed to know little more than that they were living in an *urban renewal area* and that this designation should not be interpreted as a compliment to their neighbourhood. What exactly was to be *renewed* and how, not to mention what would happen to them as individuals and families, were facts locked securely within the minds and filing cabinets of the bureaucracy.

It was, in all too many instances, a classic example of what befalls the *disorganized* in an organized society. Lacking an effective vehicle through which to assemble their collective problems and express their collective will, these people seemed totally unable to penetrate the bureaucratic mass. Instead, they were left amid their anxieties and their resentments to await the inevitable eviction or expropriation notice and the promised guarantee of *suitable alternate accommodation*. That the proffered accommodation was rental where home-ownership had existed before or might be in a suburban area for people accustomed and desirous of downtown living seemed irrelevant to its classification as either suitable or alternate.

Within the more limited context of the housing supply itself, the Task Force found ample evidence of imperfection within the existing market mechanism. Housing is a universal need, yet the private market on which Canadians have relied is anything but universal in its present scope and application. Housing, in a word, is too expensive for too many Canadians. If it is not true, as popular charge would have it, that any Canadian earning less than $8,000 a year cannot buy a home in today's market, it is true that this statement does apply in some metropolitan areas, while in many others *average* income will not buy a family an *average* home.

The Task Force found a variety of explanations for this situation, some of them applicable across Canada, others of a more regional or local nature. There are three main components in the cost of a house – the land it is built on, the structure itself and the loan on which it is financed – and all three have contributed to the escalating cost structure in both the home-ownership and rental markets. Unquestionably the largest single factor, in recent months at least, has been the cost of money, as reflected in spiralling interest rates. If this is the problem most easily identified, however, it also in many respects is the most difficult to deal with because of its undoubted connection with general international monetary conditions. The cost of land, while not a universal problem in Canada, is a severe one in some areas, such as Metropolitan Toronto where the cost of serviced lots has reached $15,000, and a growing one in others. As for the cost of buildings themselves, this factor undoubtedly has been at work, too, particularly within the context of even-larger houses with ever-more luxurious – and costly – fixtures and services within them.

That the costs of shelter have risen so rapidly during the past 30 months is serious enough in itself. But the Task Force found that these cost pressures were at work in, and indeed were intensified by, a Canadian housing market suffering from a basic shortage of stock. By CMHC estimates, there are about 5,500,000 housing units in Canada to serve a market of some 5,700,000 family and non-family users. Again according to Corporation figures, at least 500,000 of those existing units are in a substandard condition. The Task Force heard testimony that some Canadians accept, by choice, to *double up* in their accommodation. But even taking that fact into account, the Members readily came to understand why so many groups and individuals talked of a *housing crisis* in Canada.

This was particularly true in certain areas, for the distribution of housing stock and population is in anything but perfect harmony across Canada. In rapid growth centres such as Yellowknife and Thompson, Manitoba, the problem encountered by the Task Force was not a lack of land or even money as much as a simple case of too few housing units for too many people. In communities such as this, it was not unheard of to uncover cases of people sleeping in basements, kitchens or even automobiles, not out of poverty, but because there simply was nowhere else to go. These are the extremes, to be sure, but it is worth noting that of the major centres only Montreal has even a minimal vacancy rate for residential units.

Such was the general housing shortage, in fact, that the Task Force came to look upon it as an important cost factor in itself. To leave a general price structure to the mechanics of the private market is to expect that the normal competitive forces within that market will act as a cost control. Or to put the housing proposition in simpler terms, build enough housing units so that there is a surplus of supply over demand and prices will have to be affected as builders and developers compete to ensure that their units are not the surplus ones. This supply-demand factor may not be an overriding consideration in Canadian housing costs, but the Task Force acquired a growing impression that it was an important one. To test this theory, it had commissioned under CMHC's auspices a preliminary study of price-vacancy relationships. The study, done by Kates, Peate, Marwick and Company of Toronto, offered at least tentative confirmation that a very real relationship does exist between these two factors. . . .

This housing market of relatively short supply and relatively high cost has made the quest for adequate accommodation a major problem for more than the lowest income groups. They have a problem, to be sure, but so do those in the next income brackets, the *average* wage earners of the $5,000 to $7,500 range who in most cases do not qualify for public housing assistance and who should not have to seek such assistance in any case. With the general level of living costs what it is and with single-family dwelling prices what they are, the home-ownership dream of many of these Canadians is just that – a dream. Instead they are left to scramble in the rental market to obtain accommodation, much of it ill-suited for family living and most of it renting at monthly rates well beyond the 27 percent of income the CMHC handbook says is acceptable for a family budget. This is the group who, in many urban centres are increasingly earning the designation of the *affluent poor*.

For those in the lowest income levels, the alternatives are simple: life in one of the 500,000 units officially described as *in defective condition* and more popularly known as slums, or, if they are able to crack the lengthy waiting lists, tenancy in *public housing*, the government initiated and operated low-income accommodation which now numbers close to 40,000 units across Canada. With the possible exception of the *sweat equity* co-operative housing program in eastern Nova Scotia, the Task Force could find no effective or organized system in Canada whereby lower-income families could aspire to home-ownership.

That they do aspire to it – as indeed do most Canadians – was one of the more unanimous impressions the Task Force evolved from its cross-country tour. It was enlightening, if not humorous, for the Members to hear a continuous flow of *expert* testimony that future housing policies must be directed to the provision of multiple-unit accommodation, largely on a rental basis, while group after group of ordinary citizens voiced a deep yearning to own a single-family dwelling of their own. It became the practice of the Task Force, at its public meetings with various groups, to seek a show of hands on this question. Invariably the response indicated that at least 80 percent of those present wanted to own their own home, the same figure incidentally which Professor Edward Michaelson of Toronto obtained in a more scientific sampling.

Given the various factors which condition attitudes, the Task Force was only mildly surprised to have such a high proportion of real and potential home-owners within the Canadian populace. In searching for reasons for it, one could go back almost to Canada's beginnings and its attraction to new arrivals, particularly from Europe where private land ownership is a rarity, as a place where a man and a family could acquire their own piece of land. There seems little doubt that this same attraction and desire still are alive in this country, even if that piece of land is becoming ever more expensive to acquire. It should be added, too, that there continues to be widespread, if not universal, support for the time-worn concept that a home-owner is a better citizen of his community and his country than a tenant and that to have one's roots in the soil of home-ownership is to be stabilized against the vagaries and pressures of modern society.

In present circumstances, there are other factors at work, too, in encouraging Canadians to purchase a single family dwelling. One is the relative absence of any suitable alternative to it as an environment for family living. Certainly the kind of *high rise* apartment blocks which continue to burgeon upward in the major urban centres are no alternative, at least as they are presently designed – and priced. Tentative beginnings have been made in the field of row housing, but these styles still receive less than widespread acceptance. And condominium arrangements, under which families can acquire ownership of such multiple units, have been introduced only very recently into the Canadian housing market. They are not even generally known, less accepted, at this point in time.

Yet another reason can be found within the general economic conditions prevalent in Canada during recent years. The Canadian economy has been subjected not only to inflationary pressures, but to an inflationary psychology as well. People seem almost to have accepted continuing inflation as a way of economic life and, having done so, they are looking more and more to investment sources for their earnings and savings which seem to offer protection against declining purchasing power. In the recent years at least, there have been few better such sources than single family dwellings, prices of which generally have been rising in a supply-short market at rates sufficient to cover off even the worst inflationary loss. Single-family dwellings then increasingly have become not only a place to live, but a good investment as well.

With factors such as these at work, there does seem a definite *philosophy of home-ownership* among the Canadian people. Whether there should be such a philosophy is another issue. The Task Force, for its part, can understand why the philosophy exists under present circumstances. At the same time, it can wonder whether, in an increasingly mobile society, it would continue to exist, at least to the same degree, should more suitable alternate forms of living be developed within the Canadian marketplace.

One of the few places, in fact, where home-ownership is not king is within the National Housing Act itself. Its provisions dealing with the purchase of a house are strictly business. There are no NHA subsidies for home-ownership and its insured lending provisions have proven actuarially sound and then some. In contrast, it offers a wide range of federal special-rate loans and even outright grants for the provision of rented accommodation. In terms of the National Housing Act a least, the federal government cannot be accused of foisting home ownership on a reluctant or even an open-armed public.

If most Canadians seem attracted to home-ownership, many thousands of them, by attraction or otherwise, live in rental accommodation. Whether they are there by choice or by income limitation, whether they are paying their own way or receiving some public assistance, many tenants and tenant groups expressed dissatisfaction to the Task Force in regard to their relationship with their landlord. Their complaint, in a word, was that the relationship in most cases was heavily unbalanced in favour of the landlord. He could raise rents without being required even to explain, less to justify, the amount of the increase. He could set rigid rules as to pets and social activities without regard to what the majority of tenants might wish. He could demand advance deposits against possible damage to rental units while, in many cases, showing an extreme reluctance to refund them where no damage was caused. The tenant, for his part, seemed to have little alternative in these issues except to pay up, abide by the rules – or move out.

As in many other cases, the Task Force cannot help but believe that a significant increase in housing supply would do much to correct the imbalance. It is one thing to set unreasonable rental conditions where no alternative accommodation is available; it is another to be so unreasonable where tenants, in fact, can pack up and move to accommodation where the rates and the rules are more acceptable. But there are other aspects of the landlord-tenant relationship which might be improved, regardless of the adequacy of supply. The Task Force does not believe, for example, that it is unreasonable to ask landlords to recognize tenants' organizations and to give them an effective voice in deciding how their building or buildings are administered and serviced. And while the Members have strong doubts that rent control is any effective answer, they do believe that a landlord should be required to justify, certainly to his tenants, any rental increases which go beyond the amount needed to cover increases in taxes, servicing and other operational costs. Tenants do have some rights; landlords certainly have some responsibilities.

Of all the NHA provisions for subsidized rental accommodation, none engendered more debate than public housing itself. Like most Canadians of average or above income, few of the Task Force Members began the inquiry with intimate or expert knowledge of this program. They had seen these spanking new structures rising within the urban community and had felt, as most Canadians probably do, that the least society was doing for its under-privileged was to provide them with better housing than they had before.

To enter these gleaming new buildings, however, and to talk to the people who actually live inside them is to encounter a far different reaction. Problems unapparent on the surface are readily visible underneath it. Whenever the Task Force descended on a public housing project – and it visited close to 20 individual projects across the country – it encountered an almost steady barrage of complaints and criticisms from those within. Not every public housing tenant complained; there were some who expressed satisfaction with what was provided. But the satisfied residents were a definite minority. In the larger projects in particular, the near-unanimous view was that public housing was anything but satisfactory. Projects were ghettos of the poor; people who lived in them were stigmatized in the eyes of the rest of the community; social and recreational facilities were inadequate or non-existent; privacy was lacking and vandalism present. These were the views the Task Force heard repeated time and time again by those who live in public housing. Whether each complaint was factually accurate was one thing; the very fact they were repeated by so many people in so many projects was in itself enough to force the Task Force to wonder whether the present form of public housing was any answer, least of all the only one, to the accommodation needs of Canada's low-income families.

Within the overall tapestry of Canadian housing needs, the Task Force encountered many individual threads, many particular needs and situations apart from or beyond the general problems. Needs like those of Canada's elderly citizens who, if they seek a quiet place of their own in later life, indicated they still wished to remain a part of the community and to retain physical and social contact with it. Like those of the Indian, Eskimo and Metis peoples many of whom face all the problems of poverty atop the special cross of racial intolerance. The needs of students who arrive in ever-increasing numbers at Canada's universities and colleges to face an ever-increasing problem of obtaining living accommodation on or off the campus. Like the people of the Canadian north – whites who live in housing surprisingly identical to that in the south (except it generally costs more) and non-whites too many of whom, despite some noticeable progress in recent years, continue to live in *housing* which represents a national shame. All of them special problems and needs requiring special programs and effort.

On each of these issues, the Task Force received a multitude of comment and recommendation. It received submissions from national associations and regional groups, governments and private industry, university professors and housewives. Housing and urban development clearly are subjects on which there is no shortage of experts.

While there were some exceptions, the Members were struck by the common themes which ran through most of the submissions. Some clearly were statements of proven fact; others struck the Task Force, however, as being more in the nature of conventional wisdoms, sort of hand-me-down *truths* traceable probably to some bygone newspaper item or speech or academic paper and then blossomed into general acceptance through some osmotic process without their fundamental premises being subjected to any serious or continuing challenge. The result, in the experience of the Task Force, was that too many groups and individuals offered comments and recommendations without indicating that they had ever stopped long enough to really think through the import and implication of their proposals. Without attempting to minimize the importance of the submissions received or to sound ungrateful for them, the Task Force would suggest to some groups and individuals that they might well place under serious scrutiny some of the propositions too generally accepted as basic fact and truth.

In this context, the Task Force feels justified in pointing a particular finger at the academics and professionals who, one might have thought, would be in the forefront of testing conventional wisdoms, of pinpointing urban concerns and of seeking new guidelines and solutions. Some of the briefs and comments received from Canada's schools of urban studies, from other academics, from professional planners and architects, did attempt to offer new insights and break new ground. But too many of them fell short of such expectations. Too many echoed the call for more urban research without identifying the form or thrust it should take. Too many stressed the complexities and uncertainties of urban development without indicating much prior effort to unravel these problems. Too often the Task Force heard reference to the need for inter-disciplinary research, while hearing too little of constructive efforts to bridge the faculty gap within the university structure. It is to these groups, with their special knowledge and expertise, that not only the Task Force, but the community at large, should be able to look for guidance and leadership. On the basis of the Task Force's experience at least, not all of those involved can be said to be fulfilling that necessary role.

The Task Force, for its part, makes no claim that the recommendations which follow, necessarily flow from a fountain of infinite wisdom. They do hope, however, that, having presented their program for an urban Canada, they may at least be adjudged to have gone deeper than mere conventional wisdom in their search for the truths of housing and urban development.

Recommendations[*]

Federal Task Force on Housing and Urban Development

Social Housing and Special Programs

In offering its various comments and recommendations to governments and others concerned, the Task Force seeks as its basic aim to establish housing policies in Canada which, in company with rising incomes, will permit all but the most deprived families to select and finance accommodation of their own choice within the private market. This is, of course, a long-term goal. Until it is realized and even when it is realized, there remain and will remain many Canadians who for reasons of income or other factors require assistance in obtaining the warm clean shelter to which they are entitled.

To be numerically precise in terms of this group is difficult. Economists often refer to the *lower third* of the income scale, although this includes incomes as high as $5,300. CMHC estimates indicate there are at least 500,000 *defective* dwellings in Canada, most of which undoubtedly are inhabited by lower income families. The Fourth Report of the Economic Council of Canada suggested that at least 1 million Canadians live in substandard housing, while the Council's Fifth Report estimated that 29 percent of the entire population, including 4.2 million urban residents, were living in what is defined as a low-income situation.

There are other groups within the Canadian family who require assistance either apart from income limitations or for factors in addition to them. There are, for example, the Indians, Eskimos and Metis, Canada's *citizens minus*, as the Economic Council has termed them, who have income problems, to be sure, but who face social and psychological difficulties as well. There are the country's elderly citizens whose housing needs often require special physical facilities, but who still wish to retain, as they should retain, physical and social contact with the remainder of the community. There are the nation's university students who arrive at college campuses in ever increasing numbers and must somehow find living accommodation, be it on or off the campus. And mention should be made, too, of Canada's northland where all these special housing requirements exist and where residents face the additional task of adjusting to a different life style.

All these groups require assistance and all deserve assistance. All of them indeed are receiving it. The 1968 CMHC budget allocated $200 million for public housing, currently the major form of assistance for low-income groups, $75 million for the limited dividend and non-profit sections mentioned previously, and $85 million for student housing. Special housing programs for Indians and Eskimos, administered by Indian Affairs and Northern Development, account for another $15 million.

All of these needs will continue to make demands upon the public purse. Before commenting on any of the existing programs, the Task Force feels it should first make clear its own order of priority. All of these programs, after all, may be said

Report of the Federal Task Force on Housing and Urban Development, Paul Hellyer, Chairman, "Social Housing and Special Programs" and "Urban Development," pp. 52-70, 1969. Reproduced with the permission of Information Canada.

to be competing for the same tax dollars; value judgments and orders of importance will continue to be required. In the view of the Task Force, there is no question that first and most urgent priority must be given to the needs of the lower-income groups, whatever their racial origin or geographical situation. That is not to suggest that other programs are not worthy and worthwhile, but it is to comment frankly that, given the backlog of need in other areas, the allocation of $85 million or more than 20 percent of the total CMHC funds available in 1968 to student housing represents a misguided sense of priority. That is a view, by the way, shared not only by the Task Force, but indeed by some students themselves.

As has been indicated in a previous section, no single issue or program aroused more concern within the Task Force than the present scheme of public housing whereby the federal government, in co-operation with a province and/or municipality, finances the construction and subsidizes the operation of often large-scale, multiple-unit rental projects for use by low-income groups. Public housing is in a sense an *imported* concept in Canada. While it is a widely used approach in many European countries, it runs counter to the general Canadian concept of social welfare and security. In most areas this concept revolves around attempts to provide needy Canadians with sufficient income or assistance, via subsidy or insurance, in order for them to use the same services which exist for the population at large. There are no *public* groceterias or clothing stores in Canada; nor are there transportation systems or hospitals or doctors reserved solely for lower-income families. In the field of housing, however, the approach has been not to assist those in need to compete in one way or another in the private market, but rather to build special projects designated and reserved specifically for their use.

Public housing in North America drew its real strength from the policies of Franklin D. Roosevelt during the depression years in the United States. Anguished that one-third of his nation was "ill-housed, ill-clad and ill-nourished," the late President held out the promise of "decent, safe, and sanitary dwellings within the financial reach of families of low-income." So in 1937 began the rush to public housing in the United States. More than a decade later, following the veterans' housing program, it came to Canada.

Public housing can be said to have kept FDR's promise. It has provided, in the physical sense at least, *decent, safe and sanitary dwellings*. Roofs don't leak in public housing; the plumbing works; and the rats are gone. In that sense, it has been an improvement on the slums. More and more, however, the issue has become the exclusivity of public housing as the only method of meeting the accommodation needs of low-income groups and, equally important, the psychological and social issues just as crucial to the well-being of these groups as their needs for safety and sanitation. Yet amid these growing issues, public housing continues in Canada to stand alone and almost unchallenged as the sole answer to the problems of low-income housing.

One might have assumed the explanation for this situation lay with the economics of public housing, that it was in some way less costly and more efficient for governments, by proposal or tender, to have housing units built under their auspices and, once built, placed under their operational control. The Task Force, in its exposure to public housing projects across the Country, was unable to find any such economic justification. At best the per-unit cost of public housing was comparable to that of similar apartments or row housing constructed in the private market. At worst, as in such cases as Toronto's Regent Park and the public housing under construction as part of Montreal's La Petite Bourgogne urban renewal scheme, the per-unit cost of public housing far exceeds the comparable figures for the private market. One can argue, as some CMHC officials do, that the same private enterprise is building public housing as is constructing private dwellings. That being so, the Task Force can only conclude that the system itself seems to encourage a high degree of cost inefficiency. It should be noted, too, that the per-unit costs given for most public housing projects do not include a wide range of administrative expenses and in some cases exclude even the full costs of land acquisition.

But the Task Force's criticism of current public housing policies is not based solely – or even primarily – on a cost-benefit analysis. Its main complaint lies rather in the fields of sociology and psychology.

When the Members began to encounter widespread criticism of public housing among its residents, their initial reaction was tinged with skepticism. It was convenient, if not natural, to wonder whether they were hearing the representative voice and opinion of public housing tenants or merely, as is often the case, the continual bickering of the chronically disenchanted minority. That view may still be voiced by supporters of public housing. However, having heard the same complaints raised at virtually every project across the country, whether in the course of an organized meeting or an unexpected call at a public housing door, the Task Force has concluded that the dissatisfaction is indeed widespread and, further, that the grounds for such dissatisfaction, particularly in the largest projects, are genuine.

The big housing projects, in the view of the Task Force, have become ghettos of the poor. They do have too many *problem* families without adequate social services and too many children without adequate recreational facilities. There is a serious lack of privacy and an equally serious lack of pride which leads only to physical degeneration of the premises themselves. The common rent-geared-to-income formulas do breed disincentive and a *what's the use* attitude toward self and income improvement. There is a social stigma attached to life in a public housing project which touches its inhabitants in many aspects of their daily lives. If it leads to bitterness and alienation among parents, it creates puzzlement and resentment among their children. Or as the teenage girl so plaintively and graphically put it in Toronto, "all I know is that I live in Regent Park."

While the Task Force accepts full responsibility for its findings, these criticisms of public housing are not its alone. As a check against its growing impression that public housing was adding to the inherent social and psychological problems of lower-income families, the Members asked CMHC to commission an independent study of some of these issues. Such a study was done by Martin Goldfarb Consultants Limited of Toronto. While limited in scope by time and resources, the necessary research did involve in-depth interviews and group discussions with residents of five major public housing projects in Toronto. The major conclusions of this study were remarkably akin to those of the Task Force.

Mr. Goldfarb's interviews with public housing tenants confirmed that these people do believe they face a *range of negative stigmas* in dealing with the community around them. He, too, found a lack of community spirit and individual self-discipline. His study also scored the present rent-geared-to-income system as one which elevates "successful cheating to a symbol of success." He reports that teenagers are "looked at with a jaundiced eye," while children in large public housing projects are left to play without any supervision or direction in a confined area. He suggested that the problems of living in public housing were "akin to those experienced by some Indians who are on reserves."

The Goldfarb study concludes:

> The overall assessment from the study completed is that public housing cannot be a solution for a conglomerate of social and economic problems. It has produced a new, unique, complex conglomerate of social and psychological concerns.

> Public housing as it is presently structured does not appear to be *a place to stand* or *a place to grow*.

Public housing supporters may decry these criticisms as over-generalizations or as symptoms not of public housing, but of poverty as a more basic problem. They may point to many public housing tenants, particularly recent arrivals, who profess to be more than happy with their new surroundings. The Task Force would reply that, if the criticisms are over-generalized to some extent, they are nevertheless generally applicable. It would agree that many of the problems stem from a lack of income rather than merely a form of housing, but it would add that every sign indicates that public housing does nothing to reduce the root problems of poverty, while increasing many of them and adding new ones of its own. As to those tenants of public housing who seem satisfied with it, the Members could comment only that exceptions to universality neither prove general conclusions nor do they invalidate them.

The Task Force is tempted to cry *away with all public housing*. But it does realize that there are exceptions to the general rule, both in terms of groups of tenants and individual projects. Projects, for example, like Ottawa's Blair Court, Montreal's Jeanne Mance and Saint John's Courtenay Place where conditions seemed more favorable than the general rule. In the circumstances, is has decided to adopt a more moderate course at this stage and to strongly urge the federal government not to approve or assist any large new public housing projects until the whole range of issues, economic, social, psychological, raised by its investigation and the Goldfarb study are thoroughly researched by competent teams of social scientists. If any public housing projects are to be commenced before such research is completed, the Members would urge that they be severely limited in size in order at least to minimize the problems which seem to be compounded once a certain number of units is exceeded. The Task Force therefore recommends:

The Federal Government initiate a thorough research program into the economic, social and psychological issues of public housing. Until such a study is completed and assessed, no new large projects should be undertaken.

While urging such a review of the very basis of public housing, the Task Force also would hope that urgent consideration could be given to improving the operation of those projects already in existence. There are obvious limits as to what can be done by way of physical restructuring. But the Members would suggest that every effort be made to utilize vacant or redevelopment space within the immediate area to relieve some of the present shortcomings for recreational facilities and open space. They wonder, too, whether it might not be possible with a minimum of cost and inconvenience, to introduce at least a small part of the mixed-use concept mentioned in the previous chapter. While agreeing that rent scales must bear some relationship to income levels, they question whether changes cannot be made to at least relieve the present feeling among public housing tenants that there is no use trying to make an extra dollar because the public landlord is going to take 50 cents of it. And they would suggest, finally, that a conscious effort to erase the kind of lord-and-master relationship which now tends to exist between tenants and their public supervisors could well produce a greater sense of community involvement and participation among public housing residents.

Whatever the outcome of the review of large-scale public housing, the Task Force believes there are other and even better housing options which should be available to lower-income groups as they are to other Canadians. Indeed as the review is being carried out, these other options can be tested on a trial basis. Even within the term *public housing*, Members believe that efforts should be made to provide dispersed single dwelling units for subsidized rental by needy families in addition to multiple unit facilities. The benefits of such a program, a small start on which already has been made in some cities, are clear. Families are able to regain the privacy which they too often lose in large multiple-unit projects, parents and children alike have a backyard of their own, a garden to care for and, yes, even grass to cut and snow to shovel. But most important from a psychological viewpoint, they have an opportunity to shake their obvious *label* as semi-wards of the state. They gain a street address in place of a caste-like project name. The Task Force believes that federal loans should be available to municipalities, to assist in the acquisition of dispersed existing dwellings for this purpose.

Possession of such a supply of existing housing could be of considerable use to the municipality. It would, for instance, ensure at least a small stock of temporary or hostel accommodation for low-income or welfare families faced with a housing emergency. Over the long run – and this should be looked upon as a side benefit and not a primary goal – ownership of such housing might well simplify municipal planning and implementation of redevelopment schemes involving changes in land use patterns.

The Task Force believes further that policies beyond public housing in any form are possible and worthy of implementation, at least on a trial basis. It would suggest that, rather than only providing subsidized housing for low-income groups, governments also might subsidize the income themselves so that such families have sufficient finances themselves to compete in the private market. The Members believe that such assistance can be provided in a way which will allow these families, within practical limits, to rent or even buy the home of their own choosing.

The basic approach in either case would be to subsidize incomes rather than houses. In the case of rental accommodation, income supplements in the form of rent certificates could be provided on an appropriate scale so that the recipient could rent housing in the private market according to his individual or family need. Such an approach in a somewhat modified form was tried, in fact, for a brief experimental period under the Ontario Rent Certificate Scheme in 1961 in Toronto. As CMHC was not empowered to share in the cost, the province was forced to drop the program.

Given the fact that there is sufficient housing stock to make units available at reasonable rents, the most common objection to the income supplement approach is that, barring some form of control the scheme represents a too-open invitation to unscrupulous landlords to make large profits at public expense. The Task Force acknowledges that control of rental levels does present a potential problem, but it does not feel that it need be an insoluble one. It might even dare to hope that there are landlords in Canadian society whose sense of social responsibility might move them to offer any public authority administering such a program a number of units with the rent fixed against all but reasonable operating increases. The landlords, after all, would be receiving a virtual guarantee of continuous occupancy.

When compared to the present costs of public housing, a program of rental supplements is anything but uneconomic. A comparative cost study in the United States disclosed that the same amount of public revenue expended on 28,000 public housing units would be sufficient to enable 42,000 families to compete in the private market with income supplements – with some money even left over to rehabilitate some of the private properties they might occupy. As for Canada, it might be noted that federal operating subsidies for public housing under Sections 35A and 35E of the National Housing Act amounted to $7 million in 1968. Even at a supplementary rate of $50 a month or $600 a year, this same amount of money would permit more than 11,600 families to rent their own accommodation in the private market.

The provision of subsidized home ownership is another possible and worthwhile alternative to the present total reliance on public housing. Given, as recommended previously, a gradual reduction in down payment requirements to a point where home ownership could be acquired on a lease-purchase basis without any initial equity, this program would require little more than an amendment to the rental supplement scheme to permit payments to be converted at some stage to a mortgage loan. While the Task Force has stated its opposition to a general program of interest subsidization, it acknowledges that this approach might be applicable in bringing the opportunity of home ownership to the low-income groups. Income supplement or interest subsidy, the precise method could be determined by time and individual circumstances. Again there is no reason to believe the costs would be beyond reason, certainly not in the long term. Indeed one could argue not entirely facetiously that in cases where public housing has cost up to $40,000 a unit, it would have been more efficient simply to purchase homes for low-income families involved and turn them over on a pay-as-you-can basis.

There are several basic benefits to the income supplement approach, be it for rental or home ownership. It allows the recipient to exercise, at least to some degree, his own freedom of choice as to the style of housing in which he wants to live. By allowing each recipient to make his own choice, it disperses the lower-income groups, including those problem families, within the general housing population, thus eliminating the conglomerate pressures which large public housing projects seem to generate. And by no means least important, it would mean that subsidy recipients would be less easily identified or identifiable than they are in public housing, thus lessening much of the social stigma from which they currently suffer.

Regardless of the outcome of its recommended review of public housing, the

Task Force believes other options should be available to those Canadians in need of housing assistance. It therefore recommends that:

The Federal Government should make loans to municipalities to acquire dispersed existing housing for use by low-income groups.

As a further alternative to public housing, serious consideration should be given to a program of income supplements to permit low-income families to rent or even purchase housing according to their own needs in the private market.

Canada's Indians and Eskimos face not only the general problems of low-income groups, but a number of particular problems of their own as well. The result, as shown in a 1965 study which estimated that 90 percent of all housing on Indian reserves was "substandard by any reasonable criteria," is to make the housing problem faced by these indigenous peoples that much more severe – and that much more untenable within a country of Canada's wealth and development.

During the past three years in particular, the federal government has begun to make the kind of concerted effort which need and justice demand. A variety of programs are now well into their initial five-year trial period. In most of them, the Task Force is pleased to note that the accent is away from paternalism and toward schemes designed to permit Indians in particular to help themselves in improving their housing and environment.

There is, for example, a direct subsidy program under which reserve Indians can obtain grants of up to $7,000 per unit. In addition, government-guaranteed loans are available either to supplement these grants or to aid those who for one reason or another fail to qualify for subsidies. Similar funding is available to Band Councils themselves to develop community housing programs with a long-term goal of producing self-sustaining housing programs on the reserve.

Eskimos and off-reserve Indians can qualify for first mortgages under the National Housing Act plus second mortgages of up to $10,000 carrying with them a forgiveness clause provided payments are maintained on the initial loan. In the northern Territories a program is underway and on schedule to produce at least 1,100 single-family rental units by 1970. Initially designed for Eskimos, this program was broadened in 1968 to cover Indians as well and the Government of the Northwest Territories is considering the introduction of similar provisions in 1969 to embrace low-income whites, Metis and non-Treaty Indians.

Most of these programs are on a scale to offer some hope of significant progress. Since 1965, for example, some 9,000 houses have been built under the Indian reserve program. The problem, however, is that, despite this record, the initial backlog of housing requirements has not been reduced below its 1965 level of more than 6,000 units. Officials of the Indian Affairs Branch informed the Task Force that, in order to erase this backlog during the next five years, an additional $4 million a year is required beyond present budgetary projects. The Task Force believes these funds should be provided.

During its Winnipeg hearings, the Task Force learned of some initial research work which had been done on the concept of providing transitional or *half-way* housing for Indians seeking to make the difficult adjustment from life on a reserve to the demands of a large urban community. Members were sufficiently

201

impressed with this proposal to suggest that further research effort, including possibly the provision of funds for pilot projects, be undertaken.

Particular mention should be made of the plight of Canada's Metis population. Barred by present legislation from participating in special Indian-Eskimo housing programs, the Metis are anything but barred from the problems of poverty and discrimination which afflict these other groups. Indeed some of the housing conditions witnessed by the Task Force in Metis areas around Winnipeg ranked with the very worst one could encounter anywhere in Canada. These people require special assistance and should receive it. Members take some hope from the pilot projects currently underway in Manitoba and Saskatchewan. Under these programs modest two and three-bedroom frame houses are being built under federal-provincial partnership at a cost of less than $5,000 per unit. Metis purchasers are required to make a minimum downpayment of $200 and to repay the balance of the capital cost over 15 years in monthly payments related to their incomes. To date 94 such units have been built in Saskatchewan and agreements have been signed for a further 300 units in that province and 100 houses in Manitoba. The Task Force trusts that, should these projects prove satisfactory, they will form a basis of a larger and more general housing program for the Metis people.

In general, the view of the Task Force is that at least a start finally has been made on alleviating the decades of appalling disregard and worse suffered by Canada's native peoples. Members feel it is too early at this point to offer any judgment on the success or failure of the programs currently underway. Thus it will limit itself to recommending that:

Special housing programs and pilot projects for Canada's Indian, Eskimo and Metis peoples be carefully evaluated after a fair trial period and, if found successful, be vigorously pursued to meet the special needs of these groups.

While the main thrust of the Task Force's comments and recommendations have necessarily been directed toward urban Canada, mention should be made of the special housing needs of rural residents. The Members wish to make it clear that their proposals in such areas as improved mortgage finance are by no means limited to the city, but should be available equally to Canadians wherever they may choose to live.

Basically, rural Canada does not appear to face the same shortage of housing supply as one finds in the urban areas. With the heavy migration of Canadians to the city, most rural areas find themselves with a surplus of residential stock. There is, however, a shortage in many non-urban areas of private capital necessary to finance both the construction of new units and the rehabilitation of existing ones. CMHC has been attempting to fill this gap with a direct lending program under Section 40 which amounted in 1967 to almost 5,000 loans totalling more than $87 million. The Task Force feels this is both a legitimate and important role for the Corporation. Thus, as has been noted previously, it recommends that:

Central Mortgage and Housing Corporation, in its direct lending activity, should exercise particular care to ensure that adequate mortgage funds are available both for new and existing dwellings in rural areas.

202

As has been stated in a previous section, the Task Force believes that the provisions of Section 16A of the National Housing Act provide an efficient and effective method of meeting the particular needs of elderly citizens and recommends the maximum possible utilization of them. Beyond that, the prime concern of the Members in regard to housing for elderly Canadians is that effort be made in both site selection and operating program to ensure that these people are able to maintain contact with the community around them and to feel that they are still a very real part of it. From its visits across Canada, the Task Force feels that progress is being made in this area, but it notes that there still are too many *county* homes, built in almost isolated areas well away from the community-at-large and even transportation to it and conceived apparently on the notion that once one reaches a certain age, he should be neither seen nor heard within society. The Members believe that the aged can make a continuing contribution to society, that the vast majority of these people want to remain at least semi-active members of their community, and that they should be ensured an opportunity to do so. Thus it is recommended that:

Special care should be taken in the selection of sites for projects for elderly citizens to ensure that these people are able to retain physical and social contact with the rest of their community.

In commenting that student housing may have claimed an unreasonably large proportion of available public funds in 1968, the Task Force would not wish to imply that it lacks either sympathy for or appreciation of the needs of this particular group. Neither the Task Force nor any other responsible Canadian would wish to discourage young Canadians from pursuing their academic potential to the maximum and certainly not on grounds of inadequate housing accommodation. But the Members are concerned, as they feel they must be, with priorities and they are uncertain as well as to the form in which student housing might best be provided. During their public hearings, conflicting views were voiced by student representatives themselves, some urging even greater financial support for campus residences, others arguing that students should not be segregated from the community, but should reside within it. Even those favoring residences seemed unhappy with what they called the "long and sterile corridors" of existing dormitories.

The Task Force would hope that, in the long term at least, students, like any other element in the population, will be able to exercise an increasing freedom of choice as to where they live while attending university. A general increase in the housing supply, particularly in rental units, will give students greater access to the private market. Continuing funds should be and can be made available, if not on a first priority basis, to the construction of student residences. It might well be that, particularly if the school year becomes a 12-month affair, private enterprise would be interested and able to provide such residences under such programs as the limited-dividend provisions of Section 16.

While mention has been made of northern housing problems in respect of special programs for Indians and Eskimos, the Task Force feels some further comment is required in regard to the general situation in Canada's two northern Territories. While wishing that its schedule had permitted more than a day in each of the Territorial capitals, the Task Force came away from its tours of Yellowknife and Whitehorse both impressed and disappointed – impressed by the drive and spirit which motivates many of the Canadians seeking to develop these vast territories and disappointed at the general state of housing development facing white and non-white alike.

Reference already has been made to the abysmal conditions under which most of the indigenous peoples of the north are forced to exist. So, too, has the Task Force noted, at least briefly, the obvious lack of research and imagination which to date at least has gone into the design and construction of housing in the north. Cost is a major problem, too, both in terms of the price of a home and the monthly charges to heat it and to service it. Particular mention should be made of the effect of having to transport building materials long distances from southern Canada. A brief submitted by the Yukon Builders Exchange pointed out, for example, that a bag of cement costing $1.75 in Vancouver sold for $3.65 once it was transported to Whitehorse, while the price of asphalt shingles differed by almost $8 per 100 square feet between the same two points. The Task Force would hope that additional research could be undertaken with a view to reducing these transportation costs. Part of the cost problem, as well as the need for more imaginative and indigenous housing forms, might be met through increased research on the use of building materials available in the Territories themselves.

A more general recommendation raised in many submissions received in Yellowknife and Whitehorse was the need for more co-ordination among existing housing programs in the two Territories. Under the present system, a wide variety of agencies, including the Territorial governments, municipalities, Indian Affairs and Northern Development, CMHC and the Department of Public Works, all play some role in providing housing for one group or another. Such a system tends to produce administrative duplication and inefficiency, but, even worse, it seems to have led to social cleavage among northern residents based on housing programs. Whites who receive one form of housing subsidy live apart from other whites who receive different assistance. And neither have much contact with still other whites who do not qualify for housing subsidies or with the indigenous peoples, be they subsidized or not. The Task Force feels that improved co-ordination, possibly in the form even of a single housing agency for each Territory, would be a step in the direction of more effective regional planning.

There is one other group who have special housing needs and to whom particular reference should be made. There are some 55,000 Canadians receiving assistance under the Disabled Persons Act and relevant provincial statutes and many more who do not receive assistance, but who suffer from some physical handicap or disability. In their representations to the Task Force, spokesmen for handicapped groups did not ask for subsidies or other special financial treatment to meet their housing needs. What they did request was some consideration in the design and construction of housing, particularly multiple-unit complexes, so that at least some units would be available with widened doorways, ramps and other facilities to accommodate their needs. The Members feel this demand is a reasonable one and would hope that developers would make provision for it.

Urban Development

The recent report of a National Commission on Urban Problems in the United States commented that much of the urban crisis in that country "springs from using 19th century controls and attitudes in an attempt to mold and contain 20th century cities faced with 21st century problems." Much the same comment could be offered in respect of several elements within the Canadian urban structure. In no field would it be more applicable than in regard to the kind of political structures on which we currently rely for the planning and development of our urban areas. They are indeed 19th century structures attempting to deal with 21st century problems.

Almost all studies in the relevant fields of economics, sociology, ecology, and the like recognize that the process of urbanization is a regional one, operating on a relatively broad geographical basis stretching out from the core of the country's major urban conglomerates. Even the popular jargon of the day, in referring to *metropolitan* this and *greater* that, acknowledges that a city may well be one thing and an urban area another. In terms of political organization, however, Canada, 1968, seems closer to the walled city concept of ancient Greece than to the urban world of the 20th century. To visit urban areas across this country is to find the essential powers of planning and development in the hands of not one, not two, but up to 10 or 15 local governments, each of them ready to admit that its problems and concerns do not end at its municipal boundaries, but each of them reluctant to cede to a larger government sufficient authority for it to exercise the necessary overview. The Task Force strongly believes that this situation must be altered if urban Canada is to be effectively planned and developed in the years immediately ahead.

In stating its recommendations in regard to the assembly and servicing of land, the Task Force attempted to make clear its view that urban planning and development are dependent on control of the land itself. It would stress here its view of the essential need to ensure that the amount of land subject to the planning process – and the jurisdiction of the planning authority – bears some realistic relationship to the urban area. Urbanization, in short, is a regional process. It demands regional planning. And regional planning demands regional government.

To find justification for these contentions, one need look no further than the emerging development patterns in the present major urban areas of Canada. The pattern so offered is one not of cohesion, balance and order, but of confusion, imbalance and disorder. Growth lines reflect as much the vagaries of a speculative and uneven private land market as the logic of an orderly and comprehensive public plan. In place of positive zoning requirements to serve public need and interest stand an array of negative municipal restrictions ready in the name of *balanced assessment* to restrict housing development in favour of industrial growth and to duplicate, fragment or exclude, as whim would have it, needed public facilities. Where there might be cohesive urban areas, there are a dislocated series of commercial centres, industrial parks and dormitory suburbs. In total, they represent balkanization at its inefficient, illogical and intolerable worst. The Task Force believes that improvement is urgently required.

Its brief is not for the elimination of local government as it is presently constituted. If there are regional functions which demand regional authority, there are equally local concerns which can and should be handled at the local level. Centralization can be as unworkable in some contexts as can balkanization in others. The need is to delineate the proper division of functions between the two, and, in the case of Canada's current urban areas, to ensure that adequate political structures exist to perform those functions requiring greater centralization.

As has been indicated already, the Task Force believes that land use must be an area of centralized regional concern and control. Long-range development and redevelopment plans must be drawn on a regional basis, taking into account not only present areas of urban growth, but those into which it can reasonably be expected to extend in the immediate and less-immediate future. And having drawn such plans, regional governments must have the necessary authority to make them work. There must be regional authorities which define and control land use through its zoning, its assembly and its servicing. They must be the ones to plan and plot adequate transportation corridors and to select and preserve necessary land for parks and open spaces and for regionally-oriented public institutions such as hospitals. If they do not control property assessments directly, they must certainly possess powers of equalization to the point where there is no financial advantage or disadvantage in the relative location of industrial parks, residential developments and the like within the overall regional plan.

There is in this country today a limited number of metropolitan governments and, within Ontario in particular, a growing trend toward regional governments. Few to this point, however, seem to possess the full powers necessary to achieve effective regional planning. The Task Force believes this trend should be extended and accelerated and that, in both existing and future cases, care should be taken to ensure that regional authorities, in fact, possess the necessary powers to implement the tasks which should be theirs. This is strictly a matter of provincial jurisdiction and the Task Force's appeal for necessary action must be directed to that level of government. The Task Force does not recommend at this stage that Ottawa should tie a regional government *string* to its provision of funds for housing and urban development, although it does believe that, once effective regional governments have been created, action by them to establish long-range development plans should become, after due notice, a condition of the previously-recommended direct loans for the assembly and servicing of land. Most important, however, and at this stage the Task Force recommends that:

Since urban planning can only be done effectively on a regional basis, the provinces should establish a system of regional governments, equipped with adequate powers, for each major area.

If effective regional planning is essential to sound urban development, so equally is the adequate provision of urban transportation facilities. Indeed it can fairly be said that such facilities are at the very heart of effective urban planning. Transportation is the spine around which the urban area can and should grow and without which its inhabitants cannot effectively exist. It must be integrated within the urban plan. Indeed if one were starting from scratch to build a new city, transportation corridors would be among the first items on the drawing boards.

As anyone who lives in a city can readily attest, transportation is rapidly becoming one of the major problems of urban Canada. While one talks and reads of the marvels of space travel, most of the country's cities and citizens still are trying to come to grips with that 50-year-old marvel, the automobile. The Economic Council, estimating that Canada may well have 11 million cars on and off its roads by 1980, rightfully concluded that the problem so posed "ranks in economic importance with that of developing the national transcontinental transport system in the past."

Clearly the present system of trying to jam more and more automobiles into the same core area of the city will not work. What will work is less clearly defined at this time, although most transportation experts – and the Task Force was disappointed to receive so few submissions on this crucial topic – seemed to indicate that the probable answer lies in a balanced system of public and private modes. What is the proper balance for a given urban area and what those modes should be are subjects which clearly require more research. The Task Force believes that the federal government, which is beginning to show more interest in this field through both the Department of Transport and the Canadian Transport Commission, has a definite role to play in encouraging and co-ordinating, a broad program of practical research into urban transportation. It recommends that it do so, recognizing that such a program will be by no means limited to the federal level, but will and should involve other governments and the private sector.

It seems clear that, whatever the ultimate system, the cost of providing adequate transportation systems for Canada's growing urban areas will be considerable. The Economic Council projected a long-term investment of up to $4 billion. One witness before the Task Force said that the cost of underground transportation corridors – and greater use of them seems inevitable if cities are to avoid having half and more of their available land taken up with transportation routes – can run as high as $20 million a mile. If figures such as these represent the cost parameters, then certainly the development of urban transit systems cannot be left solely to local government, municipal or regional. It would seem to the Task Force that at some point a program of long-term federal loans will be necessary in order to finance the development of these systems. The Members do not feel that they can or should attempt to specify the size, form or nature of such loans, but they do recognize that these issues will have to be judged within the very real context of other federal spending priorities.

Insofar as urban transportation is concerned, while stressing its crucial importance to effective planning and development, the Task Force will limit itself to recommending that:

The Federal Government encourage and co-ordinate a broad program of practical research into urban transportation problems and consider, as other spending priorities permit, establishing a program of loans to municipalities for the development of effective urban transit systems.

Next to public housing, the issue which probably generated the most discussion before and within the Task Force was that of urban renewal. Not that the need to redevelop and renew urban areas was in question; it was not. But very much in doubt were both the present practices in this field and some of the principles which appeared to underlie them.

In terms of present practices, the argument revolved in the final analysis around the relative place and merits of demolition versus rehabilitation. One group of submissions leaned to the view that the only effective means to erase urban blight was to level it with a bulldozer and start over again. Others took the opposite line, going as far, in some cases, as to argue that almost no dwelling was so bad as to require demolition, at least without the willing consent of its owner and/or occupant.

The Task Force cannot agree that there is no such thing as a structure which has outlived its physical usefulness. But it did conclude from its cross-country journey that there was a tendency under present urban renewal policies to demolish dwellings which were not in this category. The Members noted, for example, CMHC's own table of urban renewal projects shows that the 48 schemes undertaken in the period 1948 to 1968 contemplate the demolition of 13,000 housing units and the construction of about 18,000, almost two-thirds of them in public housing projects. These projects involve a federal investment of $125 million for urban renewal alone, exclusive of the heavy additional cost of the public housing itself. While granting that the prime purpose of urban renewal policies is not to create additional housing stock, the Members do feel that these figures indicate a rather dubious investment of large sums of federal money at a time when the country is suffering from a continuing shortage of housing stock.

The demolition of any dwelling unit, unless it happens to be vacant (a rarity in Canada at the moment), means that some individual or family or group is forced to look elsewhere for accommodation. Indeed it is a fundamental requirement of existing urban renewal provision that groups so affected by these schemes be guaranteed alternate housing before any demolition takes place. The Task Force during its travels heard a number of complaints that this pre-condition was not being met in some cases. Whether these allegations were correct or merely a misunderstanding, two points are clear in this regard.

One is that the alternate accommodation which is provided often involves an abrupt and disruptive change in the living patterns of those involved. Families accustomed to living in a downtown area are offered housing in the suburbs; communities are dispersed and long-standing and vital social links shattered. Given the shortage of available housing in most urban areas, the problems of meeting the particular wishes of families caught in urban renewal may be understandable. But that does not make the disruptions and the difficulties any less severe or any more justifiable. The second problem in present renewal schemes strikes those who own their own home. Existing expropriation provisions in most provinces guarantee comparable rental facilities to those demolished; they do not promise *a home for a home.* Thus one finds in urban renewal projects, as the Task Force did, families, often elderly pensioners, whose main life saving, the home they own, is torn down in return for compensation which does not permit them in today's housing market any real opportunity to buy another house. Problems such as these demand solution in any event or circumstance; to pursue policies in a housing shortage, which makes them inevitable, makes no sense at all.

In short, the Task Force considers it a case of mixed priority to be demolishing even older housing units at considerable public expense at a time when some urban Canadians are without housing of any kind, new or old. It believes that on grounds of humanity, efficiency and plain good sense available public funds should be directed to creating a sufficient housing stock first and then – and only then – to destroying any numbers of existing stock. It therefore recommends that:

The wholesale destruction of older housing under urban renewal schemes should be suspended until the total housing stock has increased to the point where a reasonable number of vacancies exist.

In making that recommendation, the Task Force does not wish to imply that its only concern with the bulldozer technique is that its timing is bad in the present housing shortage. Rather the Members share the concern of many Canadians that greater selectivity be exercised and greater attempts at rehabilitation of stock be made, regardless of whether houses are in short or ample supply.

Successful rehabilitation can produce a number of very worthwhile benefits. For one thing, the cost in most cases is far less than destruction and replacement. But there are aesthetic and cultural benefits beyond that. In the Don Vale area which Toronto already has designated for urban renewal, for example, the Task Force visited a group of row houses which had been rehabilitated to produce a short street as attractive and enchanting as any new housing which might have followed the bulldozer. At sites like the Youville Stables in Montreal, Victoria's Bastion Square and Brunswick Street in Halifax, the Members saw rehabilitation programs not only pleasing to the eye, but worthy of preservation in an historical sense. The result in such cases is that people are able not only to live and look at housing forms of a bygone era, but the neighbourhood itself acquires a new variety and charm. The result, too, is a housing market in which the many Canadians who prefer to live in older housing can exercise that freedom of choice without fear of awakening to the sounds of a bulldozer on their front lawn. The Task Force then recommends that:

As a general principle, greater selectivity should be exercised in the demolition of existing housing within urban redevelopment projects.

If one is to seek greater effort to preserve existing housing stock, one also must be concerned that greater care be taken in preserving the state of it. The Task Force is in favour of maintaining good used dwellings, not of promoting slums or urban blight. Members recognize that the preservation of housing stock in adequate condition is anything but an automatic process, but indeed requires a conscious and continuing effort on the part of both government and the private homeowner. The Task Force believes that current policies in this area can and should be improved.

A starting point for such improvement might well be the enactment and strict enforcement of minimum standards by-laws by municipalities. Only a few municipalities currently have such by-laws requiring that property owners maintain their premises to established standards of health, fire safety and general appearance, and even those who do have shown reluctance in enforcing such by-laws to their full letter. It can be said, in fact, that the absence of such minimum standards and strict enforcement have played no small part in encouraging the degree of urban blight already present in many of the country's major centres. This is particularly true in areas designated for urban renewal where the non-enforcement of minimum standards coupled with the long delay – as much as five or even ten years in some cases – between designation of an area and actual implementation of a scheme permits and even encourages still wider and more general degeneration of the housing stock than might otherwise have occurred. The Task Force thus recommends that:

Municipalities should legislate and vigorously enforce minimum standards by-laws.

A second important point in regard to current municipal practices in this area lies with property assessment policies as they apply to home improvements. In a word, the present practice in most municipalities is to encourage home improvement with one civic hand and then penalize it with the other. To rehabilitate a private residence, even to improve its exterior appearance, is more than likely to result in a higher municipal tax bill. The Task Force wonders whether a more positive approach might not be possible. One possibility might be to at least offer an assessment tax holiday of, say, five years for home improvements. An even more positive approach would seem to be with the kind of provisions existing in the City of Montreal's by-laws which actually encourage owners to improve, rehabilitate or even replace sub-standard dwelling through a system of municipal subsidies. The Task Force recommends that:

Where necessary, municipalities revise property assessment practices to encourage, rather than penalize, the maintenance and improvement of residential properties by their private owners.

In considering the importance of maintenance, rehabilitation and, where necessary, replacement of existing housing stock, the Task Force felt it necessary to question not merely present procedures, but even the basic principles which appeared to underlie them. It found that, as a result of present urban renewal practices, there was widespread acceptance among the Canadian people of the principle that the state has a responsibility if not to share in the cost of maintaining privately-owned premises, then certainly to pay for the destruction of dilapidated buildings through financial compensation to their private owners. In the view of the Task Force, this is a questionable principle on which to base public policy.

Again it would appear to be a case of allocating to housing a status in terms of public policy and responsibility not applicable to any other major durable good. To repeat the analogy with the automobile, it is inconceivable that Canadians would expect to receive either direct subsidies from the state to maintain their cars in working order or public compensation for a vehicle which has outlived its physical usefulness. Indeed, insofar as automobiles are concerned, the state not only does not pay maintenance grants or replacement subsidies, but requires as a matter of law punishable in the courts that the individual car owner himself maintain his vehicle in good working condition or himself remove it from the road. The Task Force sees no reason why the same basic principles should not be applicable to housing. In its view, public policies should be based on the premise that it is the responsibility of the owner and not of the state to maintain houses up to minimum standards and, equally important, to demolish any housing which fails to meet such standards.

Houses have a certain physical lifespan as much as do automobiles and other durables. In the case of a well constructed dwelling, its lifespan can extend to 50 years and, in many cases, with proper care, to much more, certainly more than enough to amortize and depreciate its capital cost at a reasonable annual rate. Why should a property owner not accept such a concept of depreciation – and the responsibilities which it implies in a replacement sense – just as he does for his other physical possessions. The Task Force believes he should. Given the rapidly escalating costs of the demolition and replacement aspects of urban renewal, there is little question that acceptance of this principle will result in massive savings in projected public expenditures. But equally important it should help introduce into the Canadian housing market the much-needed concept of depreciated value, a concept which must become more effective in the market if the so-called *filtering down* process is to function effectively in regard to housing in this country.

When viewed over the long term, the Task Force frankly can see no possible alternative to this approach. Otherwise, the cost implications, when seen in the order of the 200,000 units a year now being constructed, are staggering. One wonders what the cost might be of replacing, at public expense, even half of these houses in the year 2019.

With such considerations in mind and because Members feel that housing should be looked upon as a physical possession subject to the same conditions as other durable goods, the Task Force recommends that:

As a matter of principle, property owners should be required to maintain their premises to approved minimum standards and, where and when necessary, to destroy them without compensation by the state.

The Task Force well realizes that one cannot alter the urban ground rules so basically without some period of transition from one system to another. In this instance, that is particularly true in areas already designated for urban renewal where, as a result of public policies, minimum standards have been relaxed and potential blight increased. In these situations, the Members accept that special programs involving public assistance in one form or another will be necessary to complete the already-initiated process of public redevelopment, be that by rehabilitation, demolition or a combination thereof.

With that major exception, however, the Task Force believes that the principle of owner responsibility can and should be implemented without undue delay. Municipalities can pass the necessary by-laws to establish minimum standards. In enforcing them, it can be made clear that the responsibility for maintenance and eventual destruction of individual units rests not with the state, but with the owner. It may well be that, for such a system to operate effectively, an improved system of home improvement financing may be necessary. The Task Force believes that some of the recommendations already outlined represent an improvement in this respect; it would suggest that further review of the existing home improvement loan provisions be undertaken to see what further alterations might be possible and advisable. The time to begin enforcing the concept of owner responsibility is now. The state may well be able to assist in the process or to improve the financial mechanics for it. But to resist its introduction, in the view of the Task Force, is to accept a bill for urban renewal certain to grow at a rate to frighten even the most avid spender of public dollars.

Given a system in which the responsibility for normal maintenance and demolition of houses or buildings rests with their owner, the whole concept of urban redevelopment, as a public undertaking, takes on a much more limited context. Rather than an expensive method of meeting the costs of normal wear-and-tear amid the urban landscape, publicly-initiated urban redevelopment becomes, instead, basically a planning tool limited to situations where governments decide that it is in the public interest to change land use patterns. In these cases, to meet transportation needs or to increase public facilities such as schools or hospitals, demolition may well be required if the land involved currently is in use for other purposes. And just as the bulldozer is justified in these cases, so, too, is a program of adequate compensation by the state to the owners of private properties which are affected by the redevelopment. This redevelopment, after all, does not arise from any individual negligence on their part, but rather from the fact that the community collectively feels that the land involved should be put to a more effective use for the common good.

Here certainly the residents and property owners affected are entitled to know what is planned and to have their *day in court* if they oppose those plans. And if the plans proceed, those whose lands are expropriated or whose accommodation is disrupted should receive full and adequate compensation and relocation assistance. The Task Force believes the federal government should continue to provide loans to local authorities to assist with genuine redevelopment plans of this kind. Whether municipalities also will require outright grants or subsidies in such cases and, if so, from which senior government are issues which the Members feel should be resolved in a more general agreement among governments as to revenues and responsibilities.

The Task Force wishes to offer one more comment in regard to urban renewal practices as they might apply to projects already in one stage or another or to new ones within the redefined limits of changing land use patterns. It is to suggest to all governments that they cease to designate or require the designation of broad urban areas as *urban renewal areas*. From the experience gathered during its cross-country tour, the Task Force feels that such public designations on such a broad basis can have near-catastrophic effects on the area and the people involved.

As has already been mentioned, the time gap between initial designation of an area and actual implementation of a scheme can be considerable. During that period, the situation can only be described as depressive. In most cases, even the most minimal health and safety standards no longer are enforced within the area. Its residents, in many cases cognizant of very little more than that they live in an area about to undergo major change, quickly lose any incentive to maintain their properties. Community spirit ends and community uncertainty and, in most cases, resentment begins.

At least part of this problem can be rectified by more effective communication between public officials and the people involved. But the Task Force feels that part of the difficulty comes from the very act of circling entire neighbourhoods with an urban renewal pencil, when the real concern, in fact, is with one or two blocks or a single street or even a group of houses on one street. If this is the case, why stigmatize the entire area. If public designations are necessary at all, they should be more carefully defined to cover the dwellings or groups of dwellings which really are at issue. The Task Force therefore would recommend that:

Where possible in the case of existing schemes and in future ones involving changes in land use patterns, the present practice of designating wide areas as urban renewal areas *should be discontinued in favour of policies and plans based on a more precise and effective scale of redevelopment.*

In setting out its comments under the general heading of *urban development*, the Task Force believes it should make at least brief reference to the relationship which it feels exists between urban growth and regional development. Much is being said and done in the field of regional development these days and it is clear that the federal government, in particular, is committed to large expenditures in this field. The Members have no quarrel with that; indeed they agree wholeheartedly with the Prime Minister and others that the continued strength of Canadian unity rests to no small degree upon the need to ensure as far as possible that all regions of Canada and all Canadians have a fair opportunity to share in the nation's material wealth.

The Task Force would wish, however, to underline its concern that, in devising programs for regional development, full weight and recognition be given to the essential requirement within any such region for a strong and large urban growth centre. Without such centres, the Members fear that Canada could find itself investing large amounts of public capital without realizing the desired gains in regional productivity and wealth.

The fact that the most prosperous regions of Canada are those surrounding the country's major growth centres is no accident of geography. The city has become *the* key source of economic growth, not merely as a focus of regional economic activity, but as an organism capable within its own powers of mass production and marketing of generating and sustaining enormous productivity and wealth. The city no longer is merely a marketplace for the products of rural resources. Rather it has acquired tremendous resources and productivity of its own which have long since surpassed those of the rural areas around it. The starting point for a strong and healthy regional economy is a strong and healthy city and not the reverse. Thus the Task Force believes that in the long term successful policies of regional development will be policies which stimulate the creation of urban growth centres of sufficient size to add to – and not be merely supported by – the economic strength of the region at large.

To argue this thesis is hardly to argue that what Canada's underdeveloped regions require is a large dose of Canada's urban ills. The Task Force is concerned enough about the problems of inadequate planning, insufficient facilities and inordinate poverty within existing urban centres without seeking to export them to new growth areas. But to look at a Toronto or a Montreal only through the negative eyes of its unquestioned problems is to be blind to its unquestioned power and benefit as an economic stimulator, as an employment and income generator, as a place of wealth and opportunity. It is these plus factors which the Task Force feels must be brought to bear within the confines of regional development. Hopefully, with some learning from past errors, this can be done without necessarily duplicating all the minus factors which unfortunately have accompanied the economic wonder of the city as it has emerged to date.

The Task Force itself had neither the time nor the mandate to explore this urban-regional relationship in any depth. It does feel, however, that a full understanding and adequate recognition of it are crucial to a successful federal program to stimulate regional development. It thus recommends that:

The Federal Government should undertake in-depth studies to determine the explicit relationship between urban growth and regional development.

Unemployment in Canada[*]

Sylvia Ostry

Introduction

The broad outline of the course of unemployment in Canada since the end of the War is well known and there is no need for recapitulation here.[1] In Table 1 and Chart 1, it may be observed that while overall levels were generally low for the first postwar decade (averaging less than 3½ percent for the period 1946-56) there was a sharp increase in rates after 1957 which persisted well into the 1960s. The deterioration of employment conditions after 1957 generated a lively debate in both Canada and the United States (where similar conditions prevailed) over the source of the higher level of unemployment and the most appropriate policy measures which should be adopted to combat it.[2] A survey of the literature suggests that the theoretical controversy is by no means settled, although public interest in the debate dwindled as unemployment levels moderated.

TABLE 1

Unemployment Rates, Canada, 1946 to 1966, Annual Averages

Year	Unemployment Rate	Year	Unemployment Rate
	%		%
1946	3.8	1957	4.6
1947	2.6	1958	7.0
1948	2.6	1959	6.0
1949	3.3	1960	7.0
1950	3.8	1961	7.1
1951	2.6	1962	5.9
1952	3.0	1963	5.5
1953	3.0	1964	4.7
1954	4.6	1965	3.9
1955	4.4	1966	3.6
1956	3.4		

Notes: Rates from 1946 to 1952 inclusive have been adjusted for inclusion of Newfoundland and timing of the Labour Force Survey which was conducted quarterly before November 1952.

Rates from 1956 to 1966 are based on estimates revised to take account of 1961 Census population counts.

Source: Based on data from *Labour Force Surveys*.

* Sylvia Ostry, *Unemployment in Canada*, selected portions of Chapters 1 and 2, "Introduction" and "The Characteristics of the Unemployed," pp. 1-28, Dominion Bureau of Statistics, 1968. Reproduced with the permission of Information Canada.

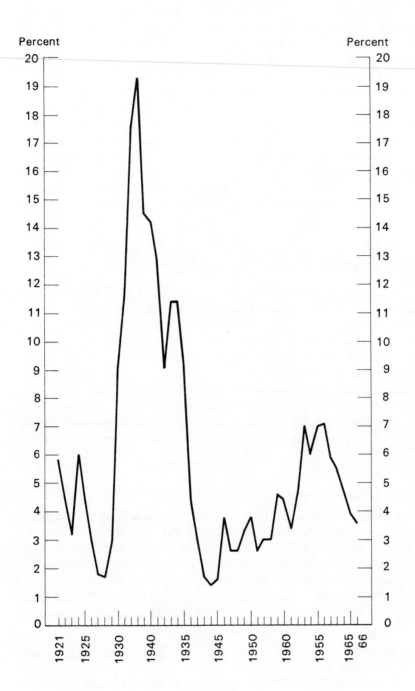

CHART 1.

Unemployment Rates in Canada: 1921 to 1966

The Census year, 1961, was one of high unemployment – by postwar standards (see, however, the period of the 1930s in Chart 1 for a longer-run view). The average annual rate, as measured by the Monthly Labour Force Survey, was just over 7 percent. Of course, at the time of the year at which a census enumeration is taken – largely during the first two weeks in June – unemployment would be lower than this, for seasonal reasons. The 1961 Census recorded a figure of 251,000 persons *looking for work* or 3.9 percent of the current labour force. However, the May-June average rate from the Labour Force Survey in 1961 was 6.2 percent, considerably higher than the Census figure. *Appendix A* outlines the main reasons for the difference between the Census and Survey counts but it is apparent that, when all factors have been considered, there is some degree of understatement in the Census total of *persons looking for work*. This, unfortunately, limits the analytical usefulness of the Census data and for this and other reasons the writer draws on a variety of other sources when preparing portions of this Study.

The Characteristics of the Unemployed

In discussing unemployment, as in discussing all economic phenomena, it is important to look behind the total figure or summary rate. Whether unemployment is high or low, its incidence is always uneven by personal or social characteristics of individuals or by economic or regional characteristics of groups. To some degree, the incidence is related to the level of unemployment.[3] But it is, in fact, a matter of *degree* and the *main* features of the *profile of unemployment* within a given country do not change radically except under conditions of profound institutional or economic transformation. What follows is for the most part a description of the characteristic profile of unemployment in postwar Canada because the lack of firm historical data precludes any intensive analysis of earlier years. . . .

Age and Sex

Age and sex are major correlates of both the rate and, as will be seen later, the duration of unemployment. As Table 2 indicates, the rates for males over the years have always been a good deal higher than for females, although the disparity between the two worsens as the general level of unemployment rises. That this relationship between the unemployment rates of the two sexes is a long-standing one in Canada is attested by the fact that in June 1931, during the depression, the percentage of males not at work was 21 percent, of females 9 percent.[4]

This variation of unemployment by sex is observed in all countries for which comparable information is available. But what is peculiar to Canada is the *direction* of the variation. The "Gordon Committee" in the United States (the President's Committee to Appraise Employment and Unemployment Statistics) in the course of a careful appraisal of comparative levels of unemployment in industrial countries, remarks that while unemployment rates are generally higher for women than for men, "Canada is a striking exception".[5]

The lower unemployment rates for women (relative to men) in Canada undoubtedly stem from a number of factors. The female labour force is concentrated in those sectors of the economy (white collar work, tertiary

TABLE 2

Unemployment Rates, by Sex, Canada, 1946 to 1966, Annual Averages

Year	Unemployment Rate Males	Unemployment Rate Females	Year	Unemployment Rate Males	Unemployment Rate Females
	%	%		%	%
1946	4.2	2.4	1957	5.3	2.3
1947	2.9	1.7	1958	8.1	3.6
1948	2.8	1.8	1959	6.9	3.0
1949	3.6	1.9	1960	8.1	3.6
1950	4.2	2.4	1961	8.4	3.7
1951	2.8	2.1	1962	6.9	3.3
1952	3.2	2.2	1963	6.4	3.3
1953	3.4	1.6	1964	5.3	3.1
1954	5.1	2.6	1965	4.4	2.7
1955	4.9	2.6	1966	4.0	2.6
1956	3.9	1.9			

Notes: Rates from 1946 to 1952 inclusive have been adjusted for inclusion of Newfoundland and timing of the Labour Force Survey which was conducted quarterly before November 1952.

Rates from 1956 to 1966 are based on estimates revised to take account of 1961 Census population counts.

Source: Based on data from *Labour Force Surveys.*

industries) which are generally less susceptible to unemployment. But the female unemployment rate, occupation by occupation and industry by industry, is usually lower than the male rate, so that the compositional factors cannot provide the full answer. (Moreover, the American pattern of female employment is very similar to the Canadian, but the over-all unemployment level of women in the United States has been consistently higher than that of males.)

Another possible background condition explaining the sex differential in unemployment rates in Canada vis-à-vis the situation in the United States and other advanced industrial countries is that Canadian women are less fully *committed* to labour force activity than are women in these other countries. Thus, when they lose a job they are less likely to remain in the market looking for work, but instead return to some non-labour force activity. Many desire only intermittent employment and will take a suitable or convenient job when it becomes available without any preliminary period of testing the market. Consequently, to a far greater extent than do men or, evidently, women in many other industrialized countries, Canadian women tend to *by-pass* unemployment when both entering and leaving employment. If, as appears to be likely, Canadian women become more firmly attached to labour force activity in the future, then the sex differential in unemployment should narrow.[6]

TABLE 3

Unemployment Rates, by Age and Sex, Canada, Average 1961 to 1964

Age	Males	Females	Age	Males	Females
	%	%		%	%
14–19	14.3	7.9	45–54	5.3	2.0
20–24	9.8	3.8	55–64	6.6	2.4
25–34	6.1	2.5	65 and over	4.9	2.4
35–44	5.0	2.2			

Source: Based on data from *Labour Force Surveys.*

From Table 3, it is apparent that unemployment rates are generally very much higher among younger persons than among mature workers. The lowest rates are found among males in the *prime ages* 35-44 and among females 45-54. Males between the ages of 45 and 64 are the group often referred to as *older workers*[7] and the rise in unemployment for these men, especially after they have reached their mid-fifties, may be evidence of market difficulties which are related to their lack of educational qualifications, relative to the younger 35-44 cohort.[8] The lower rate for males of 65 years and over undoubtedly reflects both voluntary and perhaps, in years of high over-all unemployment, *forced* labour force withdrawal.[9] Yet it is of some significance to note that the fall in the unemployment rate profile of males, at age 65 and over, is a postwar phenomenon. In 1931, during the Great Depression, the unemployment rate of male wage earners over 65 was almost 50 percent higher at the census date than was that of workers in the prime age groups.[10] The creation and expansion of private and public social security benefits has clearly played a dominant role in changing the unemployment picture for these senior workers.

The age pattern of male unemployment shown in Table 3, for the years 1961 to 1964, is also characteristic of the period since 1950 (Table 4) and indeed probably for the postwar period as a whole[11] although age detail is lacking for the earlier years. Teen-age unemployment has been more than double the over-all unemployment rate throughout the entire period (Table 4). (Further, there has been some upward trend in the teen-age rates relative to the over-all rate.[12])

Teen-agers and younger workers in their early twenties are just beginning their working lives and have little or no job seniority to protect them. They tend, also, to *shop around* in the labour market, moving from one job to another to a far greater extent than the more mature worker with greater family responsibilities. Although, on the average, the young worker is somewhat better educated than the prime age worker (and much better off, in terms of years of formal schooling, than the older worker[13]), he lacks the experience derived from on-job training and for this reason is often at a competitive disadvantage in many types of production jobs. There is evidence to suggest that younger men, in addition to experiencing higher rates of frictional unemployment, also suffer relatively more from seasonal fluctuations than do mature workers.[14] Further, as observed below, the extent of long-term joblessness among younger male workers is also distressingly high.

Finally, it should be noted that there has been a decline in the *relative rates* of unemployment of workers of 65 years and over as shown in Table 4, although there has been no long-run falling-off in their recorded rates of unemployment. As has already been mentioned, there may have been some involuntary labour force withdrawal of these older men in the post-1957 years of unemployment and to the degree this was so there has been a certain amount of *hidden unemployment* among workers in this age category.

Marital Status

The total count of the unemployed at any given time is an undifferentiated aggregate which includes everybody from the family breadwinner to the teen-age baby sitter so long as they are seeking work at that time. Clearly, from both a welfare and a policy point-of-view, the unemployment of some groups is

TABLE 4

Unemployment of Males, by Age, Canada, 1950 to 1966

Sex and Age	1950	1951	1952	1953	1954	1955	1956	1957	1958	1959	1960	1961	1962	1963	1964	1965	1966
	%	%	%	%	%	%	%	%	%	%	%	%	%	%	%	%	%
ANNUAL AVERAGE RATES																	
14–19	7.4	5.8	6.3	7.2	10.0	10.1	8.1	11.2	16.6	14.3	16.4	16.4	14.4	14.0	12.3	10.2	9.7
20–24	6.0	3.6	4.7	4.9	7.6	7.2	5.7	8.2	12.7	10.5	12.2	11.8	10.0	9.6	7.9	5.7	5.3
25–34	3.4	2.1	2.7	3.2	4.9	4.4	3.4	5.0	7.7	6.5	7.6	8.1	6.1	5.6	4.5	3.6	3.1
35–44	3.0	1.8	2.4	2.5	3.8	3.7	2.9	3.9	6.1	5.1	6.2	6.5	5.2	4.6	3.8	3.2	2.7
45–54	3.1	2.0	2.5	2.8	4.3	4.2	3.2	4.2	6.7	5.8	6.8	6.8	5.6	4.9	4.1	3.5	3.3
55–64	3.4	2.5	2.9	2.9	4.4	4.3	3.4	4.3	6.7	5.8	7.2	8.1	6.9	6.2	5.2	4.4	4.3
65 and over	3.8	2.5	2.5	3.1	3.7	4.2	2.9	4.3	5.0	5.2	4.7	5.8	5.4	4.6	3.9	5.1	4.5
14 and over	3.9	2.5	3.1	3.4	5.1	4.9	3.9	5.3	8.1	6.9	8.1	8.4	6.9	6.4	5.3	4.4	4.0
RELATIVE RATES[a]																	
14–19	211.4	241.7	217.2	240.0	227.3	229.5	238.2	243.5	233.8	238.3	231.0	224.7	236.1	250.0	256.2	255.4	263.2
20–24	171.4	150.0	162.1	163.3	172.7	163.6	167.6	178.3	178.9	175.0	171.8	161.6	163.9	171.4	164.6	142.4	145.0
25–34	97.1	87.5	93.1	106.7	111.4	100.0	100.0	108.7	108.5	108.3	107.0	111.0	100.0	100.0	93.7	88.5	83.4
35–44	85.7	75.0	82.8	83.3	86.4	84.1	85.3	84.8	85.9	85.0	87.3	89.0	85.2	82.1	79.2	79.8	74.7
45–54	88.6	83.3	86.2	93.3	97.7	95.9	94.1	91.3	94.4	96.7	95.8	93.2	91.8	87.5	85.4	88.3	89.1
55–64	97.1	104.2	100.0	96.7	100.0	97.7	100.0	93.5	94.4	96.7	101.4	111.0	113.1	110.7	108.3	109.0	116.1
65 and over	108.6	104.2	86.2	103.3	84.1	95.5	85.3	93.5	70.4	86.7	66.2	79.5	88.5	82.1	81.2	126.7	121.8
14 and over	111.4	104.2	106.9	113.3	115.9	111.4	114.7	115.2	114.1	115.0	114.1	115.1	113.1	114.3	110.4	110.2	109.5

[a] The male age-specific unemployment rate divided by the over-all unemployment rate standardized by seven age groups and by sex on the basis of 1956 composition, and expressed as an index.

Note: Rates from 1956 to 1966 are based on estimates revised to take account of 1961 Census population accounts.

Source: Based on data from *Labour Force Surveys*.

more serious than is that of others. However, as noted previously, it is possible to distinguish a number of groups within the total unemployed on the basis of personal characteristics such as age and sex. Further classification detail – on marital status – is also of direct relevance in this context. Married males represent a critical group in the working population, since most of these men have family responsibilities and their unemployment affects not only themselves but also their families. (See below for discussion of family patterns of unemployment.)

TABLE 5

Unemployment Rates, by Sex and Marital Status, Canada, Annual Averages, 1959 to 1966

Year	Single	Married	Other	All Status
		MALES		
	%	%	%	%
1959	12.0	5.2	(7.2)	6.9
1960	13.9	6.1	10.0	8.1
1961	14.3	6.4	10.8	8.4
1962	11.9	5.2	(9.5)	6.9
1963	11.6	4.6	(8.4)	6.4
1964	10.2	3.7	(7.3)	5.3
1965	8.2	3.2	(6.2)	4.4
1966	7.6	2.8	(6.1)	4.0
		FEMALES		
	%	%	%	%
1959	4.1	1.9	(3.1)	3.0
1960	5.0	2.1	(3.4)	3.6
1961	5.3	2.3	(3.4)	3.7
1962	4.7	2.2	(3.4)	3.3
1963	4.8	2.2	(3.2)	3.3
1964	4.6	2.0	(3.1)	3.1
1965	4.0	1.9	(2.6)	2.7
1966	3.8	1.7	(2.5)	2.6

Notes: Rates from 1959 on are based on estimates revised to take account of 1961 Census population counts.

Rates calculated from unemployed estimates of less than 10,000 are shown in brackets.

Source: Based on data from *Labour Force Surveys*.

From Table 5 it is apparent that the rate of joblessness among married men is consistently lower than among the male labour force as a whole and very much below that of either single men or males who are widowed or divorced. The same relationship, though less marked, is also characteristic of females, the unemployment rates of married women being lower than those of the other marital status groups. The lower unemployment rate of married persons is in part attributable to the age composition of the group; in particular there are relatively fewer teen-agers than among the single and relatively fewer older persons than in the widowed and divorced groups.

However, as Table 6 demonstrates, the same pattern of unemployment by marital status group is evident for all age categories within the male labour force: there is clearly some association between marital status *per se* and unemployment for males. However, such is not the case for females. In each age

TABLE 6

Unemployment Rates, by Sex, Age, and Marital Status, Canada, June 1961

Sex and Age	Single	Married	Widowed and Divorced
	Marital Status		
	%	%	%
MALES			
15–19	12.1	8.0	—
20–24	7.2	4.2	7.4
25–34	6.0	3.0	6.3
35–44	6.0	2.7	5.8
45–54	5.9	2.9	5.2
55–64	6.0	3.2	4.7
65 and over	3.8	3.2	3.2
Total, 15 and over	7.9	3.0	4.7
FEMALES			
15–19	7.5	8.3	6.1
20–24	2.2	4.7	3.2
25–34	1.5	3.0	2.7
35–44	1.2	2.2	2.8
45–54	1.1	1.9	2.3
55–64	1.1	1.7	1.9
65 and over	1.0	1.7	1.7
Total, 15 and over	3.4	2.7	2.2

Source: Based on data from *1961 Census of Canada.*

category the unemployment rate for married women is somewhat higher than that for single women and, except for women between the ages of 45 and 64, higher than that for the widowed and divorced as well.[15] Thus the lower unemployment rate for married women as a whole – when compared, in this instance, with single women – is entirely due to the age structure of the married work group. If one re-weights (standardizes) the unemployment rate for married women by the age composition of the single women's labour force, the rate becomes 4.7 percent, which is higher than the rate for single women. A comparable calculation for the male rate, however, yields 4.6 percent which, although naturally higher than the recorded rate, is still lower than the rate for single men.[16] Thus the *age effect* has some importance, but clearly cannot explain away the lesser degree of joblessness among married men. . . .

It is of some interest to note that married men are more likely to be in the labour force than are single or other males and these data on unemployment suggest that, age for age, married men have lower unemployment rates. Whether or not there is some connection between marriageability and employability is a subject for speculation, more appropriately conducted by psychologists and sociologists than economists. But at least it seems plausible to argue that when a man is married, he is under strong pressure – because of greater responsibility than the bachelor, at least – to find and hold a job.

Educational Attainment

The type of work people do is largely governed by the amount of formal schooling and training they have. Unskilled and semi-skilled jobs, sporadic and intermittent work in seasonal industries and occupations, are the only non-farm jobs usually available to persons without high school education and these are generally the jobs which are subject to relatively high unemployment and underemployment. Further, in a relatively loose labour market an employer can afford to be more selective in his hiring requirements and the simplest rule of selectivity (though not always the most relevant) is the level of formal education of the applicant. In most white collar work, the most rapidly expanding sector of the economy, a completed high school education is a *sine qua non* of employment and the same condition appears to be developing in some of the skilled manual job markets as well. For these and, no doubt, many other reasons, there is a close relationship between the education of workers and their unemployment experience.

From Table 7, the relationship between educational attainment and unemployment is clearly seen for two recent years, 1960 and 1965.[17] The unemployment rates of workers who failed to complete primary school education are more than six times those for workers with high school graduation or better and workers who dropped out of high school before graduation were more than twice as likely to become unemployed as were high school graduates.

TABLE 7

Unemployment Rates, by Sex and Level of Education, Canada, February 1960 and 1965

Level of Education	1960			1965		
	Both Sexes	Male	Female	Both Sexes	Male	Female
	%	%	%	%	%	%
Some primary school or less[a]	18.7	20.6	7.8	12.8	14.3	6.2
Completed primary school	9.6	10.9	4.3	6.6	7.5	3.4
Some high school	6.7	7.7	4.1	5.1	5.6	3.9
Completed high school education or more	2.7	3.4	1.6	1.9	2.3	1.3
Totals (all schooling)	8.9	10.7	3.7	5.8	6.9	3.1

[a] Includes a few persons with no schooling.
Source: Based on data from *Labour Force Surveys*, February 1960 and 1965.

Although the over-all negative relationship between schooling and unemployment applies to both male and female workers, there appears to be some difference in the pattern of the relationship for the two sexes. Among women, unemployment rates decline markedly with completed primary school and again when the level of high school graduation (or better) is reached. For men, however, sharp step-like declines occur at each successively higher level of the educational ladder.[18] Further, it may be noted that the general improvement in economic conditions which took place between 1960 and 1965 was not reflected evenly among the groups of workers represented in Table 7. The most marked decline in unemployment occurred among the least educated and among those with high school completion or more. In each case the decline in unemployment rates was more marked for men than women.

Finally, as Table 8 demonstrates, at each age group unemployment rates were higher for those with less education than for the better educated.[19] It is also interesting to observe from these data that the age differentials in unemployment noted above, in particular the high unemployment rates of the younger workers relative to the more mature labour force, are revealed at each educational level. However, a far larger proportion of the older than of the younger unemployed have relatively little education so that the lower average educational level of older workers does contribute to their unemployment experience.[20]

TABLE 8

Unemployment Rates, by Age and Level of Education, Canada, February 1960 and 1965

Level of Education	14-19	20-24	25-44	45-64
1960				
Some primary school or less[a]	32.4	28.4	19.3	14.1
Completed primary school	21.1	17.5	8.4	6.9
Some high school	13.6	9.2	4.7	4.9
Completed high school education or more	(5.6)	4.1	2.2	2.5
1965				
Some primary school or less[a]	21.8	16.6	13.3	10.8
Completed primary school	16.8	10.2	6.4	4.8
Some high school	8.4	7.2	3.8	4.0
Completed high school education or more	(4.6)	2.7	1.5	(1.4)

[a] Includes persons with no schooling.
Note: Rates calculated from unemployed estimates of fewer than 10,000 are shown in brackets.
Source: Based on data from *Labour Force Surveys*, February 1960 and 1965.

Although there is a close association between educational attainment and the *incidence* of unemployment, this is apparently not the case so far as the *duration* of unemployment is concerned. Thus, in February 1965, the percentage of the male unemployed who had been looking for work for four months or longer (the *long-duration* unemployed) was almost the same at each educational level. The relevant figures were 27 percent for those with primary school or less; 25 percent for those with some high school and 29 percent for those with high school completion or better. A man with a better education is less prone to unemployment, but once he loses a job he is likely to take as long – or perhaps even longer – to find another job as is the worker with much less formal schooling.[21]

Occupation

An individual's work, in the sense of his function or what sort of job he does, is a factor of some importance affecting his risk of unemployment. Thus, for example, much of the supervisory, professional and clerical staff in industry is regarded almost as *fixed capital* and employers will lay off production workers much more readily than they will these white collar workers. Further, the *skill* of a worker – skill used broadly to encompass education, training and experience in work performance – also affects his risk of joblessness. An employer, faced with a cutback in production, will be more inclined to discharge an unskilled worker since he has less *invested* in his training. On the same grounds he will try to retain his more skilled workers to avoid both the loss of training costs and the added burden of hiring costs when conditions improve and such workers are likely to be in relatively short supply. Further, a skilled worker can, if the alternative is unemployment, do the work of an unskilled or semi-skilled man, whereas substitution in the opposite direction is not usually possible.[22] Moreover, institutionalized protective devices – especially in collective agreements – are likely to apply more to skilled than unskilled workers, although this is less true today than it was in the 1930s. For these and other reasons, the less skilled are more prone to unemployment.[23] Thus, job function and worker skill, which are of course related, are both factors affecting unemployment.

The industry in which a worker is employed also influences his *propensity to be unemployed*. Not all industries are equally responsive to declines in demand since not all goods and services exhibit identical income elasticities.[24] Thus, for example, construction, consumer durables and durable goods manufacturing generally are much harder hit in a recession than are light manufacturing or service industries. Workers in mining and logging are much more vulnerable than those in agriculture. Further, average annual unemployment rates in some industries may be high also because of a high seasonal component: logging and construction are examples of such activity. Finally, longer-run structural changes in patterns of consumer demand, in technology and in resource exploitation may raise the unemployment risk in particular industries.

Unemployment rates classified by occupation and industry have to be used with considerable caution as indicators of the *source* of unemployment. This is so partly because of deficiencies in classification: these are particularly acute in the case of occupations, where notions of *skill* or varying levels of job content and worker requirements are not revealed by the present system and industry-oriented groups have by no means been eliminated.[25] Also, the occupation or industry referred to in the current labour force statistics is the occupation or industry of last employment. Workers displaced in a given industry who find intermittent employment in another will be attributed to the latter industry. This will, although probably not to any significant degree, mask the extent to which certain industries *generate* unemployment. Workers are less likely to shift occupational attachments (particularly among broad occupational groups) so that this criticism is less applicable to the occupational data.

Table 9A shows unemployment rates for major occupation groups from 1961 to 1966 (such data, based on the 1961 Census classification of occupations, are not available from current survey statistics for any year earlier than 1961). It may be noted that the lowest rates throughout the period are those of the white collar group. From Table 9B, based on the 1961 Census data, it is evident that there is some variation in the incidence of unemployment within the white collar sector as a whole. Clerical and sales occupations in 1961 experienced a rate several times as high as those of managerial and professional workers and this probably reflects a typical pattern of rates with the white collar division and not simply that prevailing in 1961.

Among manual workers, the unskilled have much higher unemployment rates than the semi-skilled and skilled who are classified together in the category "craftsmen, production process and related workers." This contrast may also be clearly seen in Table 9B: the rate for craftsmen, production process and related workers is less than half that for labourers. These blue collar occupation groups are drawn from a variety of industries although they are more heavily represented in manufacturing and construction than in others and their unemployment rates also reflect conditions in these industries. This is true to an even greater degree for the transportation group of occupations which is heavily concentrated in the transportation industry.

TABLE 9A

Unemployment Rates, by Occupation, Canada, Annual Averages, 1961 to 1966

Occupation (As of 1961 Classification)	1961	1962	1963	1964	1965	1966
	%	%	%	%	%	%
White collar occupations[a]	2.5	2.0	2.0	1.8	1.4	1.3
Transportation	10.2	7.9	7.8	6.0	5.1	4.5
Service and recreation	5.6	4.9	4.7	4.2	3.5	3.1
Primary occupations[b]	6.8	6.1	5.6	4.5	4.0	3.9
Craftsmen, production process and related workers	9.2	7.2	6.7	5.5	4.5	4.3
Labourers[c]	21.7	19.3	17.2	15.1	13.4	11.8
All occupations[d]	7.1	5.9	5.5	4.7	3.9	3.6

[a] Includes managerial, professional and technical, clerical, sales and communication occupations.

[b] Includes farming, fishing, trapping, logging and mining occupations.

[c] Includes labourers and unskilled workers not farming, fishing, logging or mining.

[d] Includes a few persons who never worked but were seeking work. These rates have been revised to take account of 1961 Census population counts.

Source: Based on data from *Labour Force Surveys.*

TABLE 9B

Unemployment Rates, by Sex and Occupation, Canada, June, 1961

Occupation (As of 1961 Classification)	Total	Male	Female
	%	%	%
Managerial	0.7	0.7	0.6
Professional and technical	0.7	0.8	0.5
Clerical	2.2	2.7	2.0
Sales	2.6	2.6	2.8
Service and recreation	2.9	3.2	2.7
Transport and communication	4.1	4.3	2.3
Farmers and farm workers	1.0	1.0	0.6
Loggers and related workers	16.2	16.2	—
Fishermen, trappers and hunters	5.5	5.5	—
Miners, quarrymen and related workers	4.9	4.9	—
Craftsmen, production process and related workers	4.4	4.5	3.5
Labourers n.e.s.	10.2	10.5	4.9
All occupations	3.3	3.7	2.2

Source: Based on data from *1961 Census of Canada.*

Finally, the census information presented in Table 9B shows that, with very few exceptions, the unemployment rates for women are lower than those for men in the same occupation. Thus, as was mentioned earlier in this discussion, the sex differential in over-all unemployment rates is not simply the result of a compositional effect due to the concentration of women in low-unemployment occupations, but reflects a genuinely lower female unemployment *propensity*. It may be observed from Table 9B that the relative advantage in female unemployment rates tends to be somewhat smaller for white collar than blue collar and transportation occupations. In the case of sales occupations, indeed, the female rate is a little higher than the male. This pattern is strikingly similar to that observed in the 1930s, when the authors of the Census *Monograph on Unemployment* observed that "clerical and commercial occupations have very small differences between the sexes. Manufacturing and service show considerable difference, all in the same direction (i.e. lower female rates) while male labourers' and transportation workers' unemployment is out of all proportion to that of females."[26]

Duration

The average duration of unemployment varies with age, sex, industrial and occupational attachment and from region to region. There are several ways of looking at this varying incidence. A good deal of the literature has focused on the long-term unemployed.[27] By estimating long-term unemployment *rates*, i.e. the numbers unemployed in excess of a given number of weeks as a percentage of specific labour force groups, one may observe the differing impact of this type of unemployment on various segments of the working population. Another measure, which provides further insight into this aspect of unemployment, is the average number of weeks of joblessness experienced by specific groups of unemployed persons. The first measure reflects the *risk* of long-duration unemployment in a given sector of the labour force, the second is an estimate of the probable *duration* of unemployment once the worker loses his job.

An annual work pattern survey shows the total number of persons unemployed during the year and the total amount of unemployment they have experienced, counting all spells of joblessness.[28] Because people move into and out of the unemployed group over the year, the total number who experience some joblessness during the course of a twelve-month period is considerably higher than the twelve-monthly average of the unemployed estimated by the Monthly Labour Force Survey. Similarly, the average duration of unemployment measured by an annual survey will be higher than the average of the monthly figures not only because all stretches of unemployment over the year are included, but also because the current data relate to the duration of seeking up to the time of the survey and not to total duration during the year. In a sense, then, a more *complete* picture of unemployment is provided by these annual data. Hence the analysis of duration which follows is based on the annual patterns derived from the January 1965 survey of work experience in 1964. Table 10 contains the basic information.

As one would expect, a larger proportion of unemployed men than of unemployed women experienced lengthy unemployment in 1964. Thus both the long-term (14 weeks and over) and very long-term (27 weeks and over) unemployment percentages as well as the measure of average duration of unemployment were higher for men than for women. As was mentioned above in connection with over-all unemployment comparisons, this sex differential reflects differences in occupational and industrial patterns between the two sexes and also fundamental differences in the degree of labour force attachment between men and women.

Among both men and women there was a distinctive age pattern evident in long-term unemployment. For males, the impact of long-term joblessness was lowest for prime age workers (25-44). The younger worker (14-24) and the

TABLE 10

Summary Statistics on Unemployment Experience During Calendar Year, 1964

Labour Force Group	Long-term Unemployment rate[a]	Very Long-term Unemployment rate[b]	Average Weeks Unemployed[c]	Unemployed Experiencing 2 or More Stretches	Total Unemployment rate[d]
	%	%	Man Weeks	%	%
Males					
14–19	13.5	7.2	18.1	42.7	27.1
20–24	11.7	5.1	15.6	47.8	26.2
25–44	6.9	2.5	15.3	43.9	15.7
45–64	8.4	3.7	20.0	48.2	13.5
65 and over	8.2	4.1	23.1	42.1	11.5
14 and over	8.6	3.7	17.1	45.5	17.3
Females					
14–19	8.8	4.3	13.8	26.8	23.7
20–24	5.7	2.4	14.0	24.0	14.4
25–44	4.7	2.4	15.9	27.6	10.7
45–64	4.2	2.0	18.9	37.4	7.8
65 and over	2.5	1.5	19.5	37.5	5.2
14 and over	5.3	2.6	15.4	28.3	12.6
Industry					
Agriculture	3.3	1.5	19.2	50.2	6.1
Other primary	26.5	11.8	19.6	57.9	41.8
Manufacturing	6.4	2.5	13.6	39.5	16.6
Construction	21.9	7.5	17.2	55.4	39.1
Transportation	7.5	3.0	17.6	44.8	13.6
Trade	5.0	2.2	14.4	31.7	12.1
Finance	2.7	1.3	11.7	12.7	8.7
Service	5.1	2.5	17.0	35.2	10.4
Public administration	5.8	2.7	17.5	45.4	11.2
Occupation					
Managerial	1.7	0.8	15.9	28.6	3.6
Professional and technical	1.7	0.9	14.8	22.6	4.3
Clerical	3.9	1.6	12.6	23.3	11.5
Sales	4.9	2.1	15.2	29.2	10.9
Agriculture	3.5	1.5	18.1	50.6	6.3
Other primary	32.1	14.3	20.7	61.6	47.3
Service	7.1	3.6	17.1	36.7	14.3
Transportation and communication	10.0	3.4	15.7	45.0	20.2
Craftsmen, production process and related workers	8.6	3.1	14.1	45.9	20.6
Labourers n.e.s.	22.9	10.3	30.1	52.7	36.8
Regions					
Atlantic	15.7	8.0	21.7	47.0	23.5
Quebec	10.1	4.3	17.7	44.8	18.7
Ontario	5.1	2.2	14.4	36.7	12.9
Prairies	5.3	2.3	15.8	39.3	11.9
British Columbia	6.4	2.4	14.7	36.2	16.0
Canada	7.6	3.3	16.7	41.1	15.6

a Number of persons unemployed 14 weeks or more as percentage of number of persons in labour force during 1964.

b Number of persons unemployed 27 weeks or more as percentage of number of persons in labour force during 1964.

c Total number of weeks of unemployment experienced by unemployed in 1964 divided by number of persons with some unemployment experience during 1964.

d Number of persons with some unemployment during 1964 as percentage of number of persons in labour force during 1964.

Source: Based on data from *Annual Work Pattern Survey*, taken in conjunction with *Labour Force Survey*, January 1965.

older worker (45-64) showed evidence of somewhat greater difficulties in finding work once separated from a job. Average duration was highest for workers past the customary retirement age. Although some proportion of men in this age group may leave the labour force rather than continue to look for work, those who maintain a labour force attachment evidently suffer very extended periods of unemployment once they become jobless.[29] The higher average duration of unemployment of the older worker was evidently not due to repeated spells of unemployment over the year since the difference in the proportion of the unemployed with two or more stretches of work-seeking during 1964 were not very marked among men of different ages (see column 5).

For women, the rise in the long-duration unemployment percentages after middle age was not apparent: both long-term and very long-term unemployment declined steadily with increasing age. But there was a quite marked rise in the average duration of job-seeking for the unemployed woman over the age of 45. Again (as was the case for the oldest male worker) older women who do not exercise the option of labour force withdrawal evidently experience greater difficulty than do younger workers in regaining employment once separated from a job. In some degree, the longer average duration of unemployment experienced by these women who have passed their mid-forties was accounted for by recurrent unemployment over the course of the year. Thus, as may be observed from Table 10, the proportion of unemployed with two or more stretches of joblessness during 1964 was considerably higher for women over the age of 45 than for the younger female worker.

The incidence of long-term and very long-term unemployment among broad industry and occupation groups appears to be roughly similar to the incidence of over-all unemployment. It was lowest for agricultural workers and workers in service-producing industries and very marked in construction and in primary industries other than agriculture. In construction and in the primary industry sector as a whole, recurrent unemployment was particularly troublesome and contributed to the higher-than-average duration of unemployment which characterized these industries.

Among occupations it is evident that long-duration unemployment was especially severe for unskilled workers who not only found it very difficult to regain employment once they lost their jobs but, apparently also had less steady jobs, i.e. were more subject to recurrent unemployment during the year than most other groups of workers. An interesting contrast between the white collar occupations and the skilled and semi-skilled manual group (craftsmen, production process and related workers) emerges from Table 10. The incidence of long-duration unemployment was very much higher for the blue collar worker, but once unemployed, his average duration of work-seeking did not differ greatly from that of the white collar worker. In fact, the higher incidence of long-term unemployment in the manual as compared with the white collar work-force, was mainly the result of a much greater frequency of repeated stretches of unemployment during the course of the year (column 5). These recurrent spells of unemployment resulted in a larger proportion of the craftsmen and semi-skilled work-force experiencing fourteen or more cumulative weeks of unemployment over the year.

Finally, it may be observed that there were some rather marked differences in the incidence of longer-term and over-all unemployment among the five main regions in Canada in 1964. Thus, the impact of longer-duration unemployment was especially severe in both the Atlantic region and Quebec. In both regions, but particularly in the Atlantic Provinces, the *differential* in the long-term rate (when compared with the Canada rate) was very much higher than in the over-all rate. Part of this difference in incidence was undoubtedly due to the greater frequency of repeated unemployment in these two areas (column 5), a condition which, in turn, is probably linked to the industrial composition of the regions' labour force (see below for a discussion of industrial structure and provincial unemployment patterns). A contrasting situation was apparent in British Columbia where the risk of unemployment was somewhat above that prevailing in the country as a whole but the risk of a worker experiencing long-term joblessness and the average duration of unemployment were well below the Canada average. Thus, unemployment in British Columbia was much more clearly of a short-term (and non-recurring) nature than in, say, Quebec which had a similar over-all level of unemployment in 1964.

Geography

Another Study in this Series examines the changing provincial distribution of employment over the past intercensal decade and notes some tendency to convergence of industrial and occupational structures in the provinces as well as some decline in the inequality of distribution of unemployment. None the less, wide inter-regional and interprovincial differences in the level of unemployment persist as a characteristic feature of the *unemployment profile* in this country. This is clearly evident from the rates presented in Table 11 for the years 1946 to 1966.

TABLE 11

Unemployment Rates by Region, Annual Averages, 1946 to 1966

			Region			
Year	Atlantic	Quebec	Ontario	Prairies	B.C.	Canada
	%	%	%	%	%	%
1946	7.7	4.3	2.8	2.4	4.2	3.8
1947	6.5	2.7	1.8	1.8	3.1	2.6
1948	6.2	2.5	1.7	1.7	3.5	2.6
1949	6.9	3.6	2.3	2.2	3.9	3.3
1950	8.4	4.6	2.5	2.2	4.4	3.8
1951	4.7	3.2	1.8	1.8	3.7	2.6
1952	4.6	3.9	2.2	1.9	4.1	3.0
1953	5.5	3.8	2.1	1.9	4.0	3.0
1954	6.6	5.9	3.8	2.5	5.2	4.6
1955	6.5	6.2	3.2	3.1	3.8	4.4
1956	6.0	5.0	2.4	2.2	2.8	3.4
1957	8.4	6.0	3.4	2.6	5.0	4.6
1958	12.5	8.8	5.4	4.1	8.6	7.0
1959	10.9	7.9	4.5	3.2	6.5	6.0
1960	10.7	9.1	5.4	4.2	8.5	7.0
1961	11.2	9.2	5.5	4.6	8.5	7.1
1962	10.7	7.5	4.3	3.9	6.6	5.9
1963	9.5	7.5	3.8	3.7	6.4	5.5
1964	7.8	6.4	3.2	3.1	5.3	4.7
1965	7.4	5.4	2.5	2.5	4.2	3.9
1966	6.4	4.7	2.5	2.1	4.5	3.6

Notes: Rates from 1946 to 1952 inclusive have been adjusted for timing of the Labour Force Survey which was conducted quarterly before November 1952. Newfoundland is included in estimates for the Atlantic Region.

Rates from 1956 to 1966 are based on estimates revised to take account of 1961 Census population counts.

Source: Based on data from *Labour Force Surveys*.

In the postwar period the absolute differences among regional unemployment rates have been greater in years of low economic activity than in periods of prosperity. Indeed, an index of dispersion based on (weighted) percentage point differences between the regional rates and the Canada average moves closely in accordance with the over-all unemployment level, rising when unemployment increases, diminishing when it declines.[30] In other words, as economic conditions in Canada worsen (improve), the absolute increases (decreases) in unemployment tend to be greater in the high unemployment regions like the Atlantic Provinces, Quebec and British Columbia than in the more favoured Prairie Provinces or Ontario. Further, there has been very little change in the ranking of regional unemployment rates over this period: only Quebec and British Columbia have, from time to time, exchanged places as the province with the second highest rates in the country.[31] (See Table 11.)

The regional differences in unemployment levels reflect for the most part differences in regional labour market conditions, i.e. greater or lesser degrees of structural maladjustment,[32] and – of considerable importance in the Canadian context – greater or lesser seasonality of employment. (See Table 12, which indicates the severity of seasonal unemployment in the Atlantic Region and Quebec compared with Ontario and the Prairies.) But unemployment rates across Canada also reflect regional differences in labour force composition, in respect to the personal characteristics of workers (age, sex, marital status, education) as well as deployment by industry and occupation.

TABLE 12

Unemployment Rates, by Region, Months of Lowest[a] and Highest[b] Seasonal Unemployment, Four Month Averages, 1953 to 1966

Year	Region									
	Atlantic		Quebec		Ontario		Prairies		B.C.	
	Low[a]	High[b]	Low[a]	High[b]	Low[a]	High[b]	Low[a]	High[b]	Low[a]	High[b]
1953	3.5	7.5	2.6	5.0	1.5	2.7	0.8	3.2	2.6	5.8
1954	3.9	10.2	4.6	7.8	3.2	4.7	1.3	4.0	3.4	7.7
1955	4.2	10.2	3.6	10.1	2.2	5.0	1.3	5.5	1.9	6.4
1956	2.9	10.2	2.7	8.2	1.8	3.4	0.7	4.3	1.4	4.0
1957	5.8	11.8	4.0	8.3	3.0	3.8	1.2	4.1	3.6	5.8
1958	8.3	17.8	6.2	12.3	4.3	7.0	1.9	6.9	6.5	11.5
1959	7.0	16.8	4.8	12.1	3.2	6.4	1.7	5.1	4.5	8.7
1960	6.5	16.2	6.5	12.9	4.8	6.2	2.5	6.1	7.3	9.6
1961	6.9	17.3	6.3	14.0	3.9	8.0	3.0	7.0	5.8	12.2
1962	6.6	16.1	5.5	10.4	3.4	6.1	2.1	6.4	5.2	8.4
1963	5.7	15.1	5.5	10.6	2.8	5.4	1.2	5.9	5.1	8.5
1964	5.0	12.8	4.8	8.8	2.6	4.3	2.0	4.9	4.1	6.9
1965	4.0	12.4	4.0	7.5	1.9	3.4	1.5	4.2	3.3	5.5
1966	4.2	10.1	3.7	6.2	2.3	2.9	1.4	3.1	3.8	5.3

a July, August, September, October.

b January, February, March, April.

Notes: The months were selected on the basis of an examination of the seasonal adjustment factors (Census Method II). Although these particular groupings of months are not, in every year and in every region, invariably those with the lowest or highest deviation between adjusted and unadjusted unemployment rates, they generally prove to be so and provide a better comparison than, say, the third and first quarter.

Rates from 1956 to 1966 are based on estimates revised to take account of 1961 Census population counts.

Source: Based on data from *Labour Force Surveys*.

Footnotes

1. See, for example, *The First Annual Review of the Economic Council of Canada.* Ottawa: Queen's Printer, December, 1964, Chapter 2.

2. Cf. bibliography cited in Frank T. Denton and Sylvia Ostry, *An Analysis of Post-War Unemployment,* Economic Council of Canada, Staff Study No. 3, Ottawa: Queen's Printer, 1964, p. 6. Also Barbara Berman and David E. Kaun, "Characteristics of Cyclical Recovery and the Measurement of Structural Unemployment," Washington, Brookings Institution, mimeographed, no date. For most recent review of the literature in the United States, see Eleanor G. Gilpatrick, *Structural Unemployment and Aggregate Demand.* Baltimore: 1966.

3. Denton and Ostry, *op. cit.,* pp. 6-18.

4. Canada, Dominion Bureau of Statistics, *Census of Canada, 1931,* Volume XIII, *Monographs, Unemployment.* Ottawa: King's Printer, 1942, p. 235.

5. *Measuring Employment and Unemployment.* Washington: 1962, p. 260, f.n. 40. The higher rates for women in the United States and elsewhere are attributed to higher levels of frictional, short-run unemployment due to voluntary turnover or *job shopping.*

6. Another factor which may account for some of the difference between the Canadian and American situation is a difference in the wording and ordering of questions on the labour force enumeration schedules. These differences, though apparently minor, do suggest that the Americans tend to *probe* a little more and perhaps pick up more women in both the employed and, more especially, the unemployed counts.

7. Cf. Sylvia Ostry and Jenny Podoluk, *The Economic Status of the Aging.* Ottawa: 1965.

8. *Ibid.,* pp. 46-52.

9. *Ibid.,* p. 24.

10. *1931 Census Monographs, op. cit.,* calculated from Table LXXVII, p. 183.

11. This is also true of female unemployment. But since the numbers involved in many of the age groups are so small and subject to substantial sampling variability, these data are not separately shown here.

12. Cf. Denton and Ostry, *op. cit.,* p. 14 and Table B-1.

13. Ostry and Podoluk, *op. cit.,* pp. 46-50.

14. Denton and Ostry, *op. cit.,* p. 32, Table A-4.

15. These Census data show that the over-all rate for widowed and divorced women is lower than that for married women, a reversal of the relationship revealed by the Labour Force Survey statistics. Considering the difficulties of accurately measuring unemployment by means of a decennial census, one is more inclined to accept the Survey information in this case.

16. Reweighting the unemployment rate for married males by the age distribution of widowed and divorced males produces a rate of 3.0 percent, again somewhat higher than the recorded rate but still below the rate for *other* males.

17. These data relate to February in both years and, hence, would be affected by seasonal unemployment. For this and other reasons, the 1960 data will differ from the June 1961 statistics derived from the Census. For a further analysis of these data on education see Dominion Bureau of Statistics, Special Labour Force Studies No. 1, *Educational Attainment of the Canadian Population and Labour Force, 1960-65* by Frank J. Whittingham, Ottawa: Queen's Printer, 1966.

18. More detailed data on educational levels than that presented in Table 7 show this even more clearly.

19. The sample estimates for the unemployed in many of these categories were small and, given the extent of sampling variability, not considered sufficiently reliable for analytical purposes if disaggregated by sex. Further, the estimates for persons 65 years and over were omitted for the same reason.

20. Whereas 76 percent of the unemployed male workers aged 45 years and over had only a primary school education or less in 1965 the comparable figures for 20-24-year-olds was 48 percent and for 14-19-year-olds, 50 percent.

21. Of course, the same conclusion emerges from an examination of the educational composition of unemployment of differing duration: there are no marked differences in the average level of schooling of the short, medium or long-term unemployed.

22. Cf. Walter Y. Oi, "Labour as a Quasi-Fixed Factor," *Journal of Political Economy,* December, 1962; Melvin Reder, "Wage Structure and Structural Unemployment," *The Review of Economic Studies,* October, 1964.

23. Concern here is with demand-induced unemployment. Whether or not a given occupational group is more strongly affected by structural unemployment than another group

depends on the nature of the structural change and the speed of adjustment to that change in the given labour market.

24. Cf. Frank T. Denton, "Some Calculations Relating to Trends and Fluctuations in the Post-War Canadian Labour Market," Canadian Political Science Association Conference on Statistics, 1961, *Papers*, edited by Wm. C. Hood and John A. Sawyer, Toronto: Printed in the Netherlands, 1963.

25. In respect to the first criticism, the difference between the 1961 and 1951 Census occupational classification system is negligible although the former is preferable to the latter because industry orientation has been somewhat reduced.

26. *1931 Census Monographs, op. cit.*, p. 236.

27. The United States Department of Labor's Bureau of Labor Statistics, for example, issues, periodically, Special Labor Force Reports on the Long-Term Unemployed. See also Walter H. Franke, "The Long-Term Unemployed," in *In Aid of the Unemployed*, Joseph M. Becker, (editor), Baltimore, 1965.

28. Two such surveys have been carried out by the Dominion Bureau of Statistics, one in January 1962 for the calendar year 1961 (see *Canadian Statistical Review*, November, 1962) and the other in January 1965 for the calendar year 1964. The results of these surveys have been more fully analyzed in Dominion Bureau of Statistics, Special Labor Force Studies No. 2, *Work Patterns of the Canadian Population, 1964*, by Frank J. Whittingham and Bruce W. Wilkinson, Ottawa: Queen's Printer, 1967.

29. The 1931 Census data showed that average weeks lost per wage-earner losing time fell to a minimum for the prime age category but then continued to rise steadily with advancing age.

30. The index was calculated as follows: the regional unemployment rate was subtracted from the Canadian rate and the absolute differences multiplied by the regional share of the Canadian labour force. Cf. Denton and Ostry, *op. cit.*, pp. 9-11. See also Frank T. Denton, *An Analysis of Interregional Differences in Manpower Utilization and Earnings*, Economic Council of Canada, Staff Study No. 15, Ottawa, 1966.

31. In the 1930's, however, unemployment rates were lowest in Quebec and Ontario and highest in the Western Provinces. The Maritimes were in an intermediate position in respect to unemployment levels. Cf. *1931 Census Monographs, op. cit.*, p. 243.

32. Structural unemployment arises not from a deficiency of aggregate demand but from structural changes in the character of the demand for labour which require transformation of labour supply, usually a time-consuming process. Major shifts in consumer demand, exhaustion of natural resources, changes in the organization of ownership of industry that result in the closing down of plants are examples of structural changes which can reduce job opportunities for workers in a specific local area or region. Technological changes, within a given industry or industries, which reduce the demand for particular groups of workers, will also have a differential regional impact insofar as the affected industries are concentrated geographically. The ease and rate of adjustment to structural change may also vary regionally since it will be affected by, among other factors, the personal characteristics of the individuals concerned and the institutional environment.

3 Minority Groups

What is a minority group? A complete definition of the term might vary according to the context in which it is used, but always implicit in its use are the notions of subordination and superordination. Louis Wirth once wrote that "a minority status carries with it the *exclusion from full participation* in the life of a society"[1] (emphasis ours). Thus, a minority group may be large numerically in relation to the dominant group (blacks in South Africa represent 70 percent of the total population), but the minority is always a subordinated segment of the population in relation to power and influence in the society. In one way or another, minority groups are singled out for differential and unequal treatment by the majority. A minority group by definition is disadvantaged.

Within the framework described here, does Canada have minority groups? Does Canada embody identifiable groups of people who are excluded from full participation in the society and who do not enjoy equal opportunities to exercise power and influence relating to that participation? Or does Canada consist of various groups of people who are identifiable, but who are not in subordinated positions in the society? That is, groups that are different and recognized as such but have equal access to power and influence with any other group. Such collectives of people we might term *parallel groups*.

Usually, in this type of a discussion, minority groups or parallel groups are subsumed under the more generic label, ethnic group. These are groups of people who display a sense of *peoplehood* and have specific physical or cultural traits in common such as race, religion, or national origin. However, these criteria of physical or cultural traits that identify ethnic groups are not the only possible minority of parallel aggregations. Sex, social class, life style, etc. may be distinguishing characteristics used for the evaluation of minority or parallel group status. Throughout this section, we have focussed primarily on ethnic groups to determine whether minority or parallel structures (or some combination of the two) are the prevailing patterns in Canada. The last article in this section is an exception; it examines the status of women in Canada.

The Eskimo population of this country numbers something over 12,000. As Musson's article "Infant Mortality in Canada" demonstrates, general mortality levels for Eskimos are higher than those found in other ethnic groups. Generally speaking, the standard of living and the access to influential decision-making is so limited that the Eskimos can easily be labelled as a minority group. We have used a section of Vallee's study of Eskimos in the Central Keewatin called "Kabloona and Eskimo: Social Control" (Kabloona here meaning European-Canadian) to illustrate how social control is maintained in this minority population. From childhood, the Eskimo is taught "the tendency to appease and the desire to be appeased; the abhorrence of violence in manner or deed; an admiration for adult-like achievement in the appropriate skills – hunting, fishing, sewing, and so on." Thus, rebellion is unlikely and the Eskimo accepts his place in the society, no matter what that place turns out to be. The Eskimo believes that conformity is the right way, and thus control by the Kabloona is made easy. Eskimos as a group remain unorganized, have the use of only limited resources, and the prospect of complaints or threats from the community is not likely. As Vallee states: "No Eskimo is in a position to give orders to a Kabloona." Finally, Vallee contends that the Kabloona will retain their decision-making prerogatives, although the Eskimos will begin to have some say in the process.

The position of the Indian in Canadian society has been studied extensively over the past five years. The government has issued a White Paper (1969) which describes policy changes in the Indian Affairs Branch and the ultimate phasing out process of the Branch. In addition, the White Paper intimated that integration of whites and Indians must ultimately be the answer to the Indian problem. In response to this proclamation, several Indian leaders issued a Red Paper (1970) that stated Indian Affairs must remain a viable organization in order to give the Indian an official means of communication at the federal government level, and that the Indian must decide his own participation in Canadian society – whether it be integration or separation. Perhaps the most articulate spokesman for the Indian has been Harold Cardinal, the president of the Alberta Indian Brotherhood. A selection from his book *The Unjust Society* provides information on the Indian as an ethnic *minority* group, people without equal access to power in the society.

Cardinal claims that the federal government has always betrayed the Indian trust and that the White Paper is just another example of the government trying to rid itself of the *Indian Problem*, this time by the tactic of cultural genocide. He cites the socio-economic deprivation statistics that are indicative of minority group status – high unemployment, substandard housing, high welfare costs, low incomes, and minimal education. He finds prejudice and discrimination on the part of the larger society toward the Indian as the major factors responsible for the minority position of the Indian. Cardinal says that Indians must break away from the domination of outside forces through indigenous organization in order to help themselves: "We will not trust the government with our futures any longer. Now they must listen to and learn from us."

Cardinal goes on to discuss the problem of Indian identity. Who is an Indian? Does one become an Indian by a decree from the government, by the logic of the Indian Act? What is a Métis? Cardinal says that ultimately the Indian must define himself, and in the definition regain the pride and sense of heritage of a strong, self confident people. The challenge of the Indian people "is to redefine that identity in contemporary terminology."

At this point we turn from an examination of Canada's native people to an analysis of one of the charter groups of Canadian society, the French. People of French descent compose slightly less than 30 percent of the total population of Canada, most of whom live in Quebec. The Commission Report on Bilingualism and Biculturalism, "Socio-economic Status and Ethnic Origin," describes data obtained in the 1961 census that show disparities between English and French descendants on important standard of living variables. In general, the incomes of people of French origin are less than those of British origin; the French descendants are not educated to the same level of training; and "the British Origin Labour force is more strongly concentrated in the high-income occupations than that of French origin." British people are more likely to be in professional occupations while the French are more likely to predominate at the blue-collar level. These relationships hold even within Quebec, where 80 percent of the population are of French descent. The report also documents how the ownership of productive industry in Quebec is usually concentrated in the hands of people of English origin or in foreign-owned establishments.

In the next article, "Quebec Since Duplessis," Robert Cliche describes the change that he feels is taking place in Quebec, at least as it relates to pride and identity. He says that Quebec is undergoing a revolution that is *not* quiet, and people are more aware of themselves and feel that they can accomplish constructive changes in the society. According to Cliche, the people of Quebec will take their place along side other people of Canada in solidarity and in strength. This article was written in 1968.

The year 1970 brought a different kind of response from elements within Quebec society – the culmination of distrust and frustration – the FLQ. The article by the *Montreal Star* documents the socio-economic and political disparities between people of French and English origins in Quebec: "Whenever the interests of Anglo-Saxons and Quebecers come into conflict, Quebec's interests are inevitably discounted." The *Star* then discusses this inequality as one of the principal factors in the rise of an organization like the FLQ. There are groups of men and women who are so dissatisfied with existing conditions – "Look," says one, "they can't even fire me in my own language" – that any activity is seen as legitimate in trying to bring about social change in the structure, even kidnapping and murder. Implicit in this article is the notion that the formation of an organization such as the FLQ is made inevitable by long standing and seemingly indestructible social, political, and economic inequalities.

By the time the Canadian Census is taken in 1971, blacks living in Canada will probably number close to 100,000, with about 30 percent of them residing in Toronto. Martin O'Malley, in his article "Black, White, and Canadian," describes the situation of blacks living in Toronto. Most blacks who spoke with him said that Canada is a racist country and that prejudice and discrimination against blacks is very real. However, O'Malley sees progress in race relations in Canada, with organizations such as the Ontario Human Rights Commission leading the way.

Whereas the black people living in Toronto have only recently come to Canada (Toronto had only 3,000 blacks in 1961), Nova Scotia has had a substantial black population for some 200 years. It was estimated in the 1961 census that 12,000 blacks were living in Nova Scotia out of a total of 32,000 blacks living in Canada as a whole.[2] Clairmont and Magill "Nova Scotia

Blacks: Marginality in a Depressed Area," discuss marginality in terms of poverty and they feel that blacks in Nova Scotia are marginal in the fullest meaning of that term: "Blacks have had their freedom, but little else." Throughout their history, Nova Scotia blacks have been concerned with their survival. Blacks have always been divided into small sub-groups and as a result have never had a collective identity or power base. Now however, there is a black cultural revolution going on in the province through community organization and self-pride. In time, blacks may take a more equal part in the total society, but as of the present they find themselves in a minority position.

Immigrant groups have always played an important role in the history of Canada, and even in 1961 foreign-born people accounted for nearly 15 percent of Canada's total population. Kalbach, in his selection "The Evolution of an Immigration Policy," indicates that although Canada has been dependent upon an immigrant population to help in the settling and developing of the country, it has been extremely selective as to the kinds of people allowed into the country. There has never been a formal quota system, but the English and French have been given preference at the expense of non-European applicants. The current immigration policy judges immigrants on the basis of acquired education and skill which the Canadian economy can absorb easily.

The second article relating to immigration is from the Commission Report on Bilingualism and Biculturalism and refers to "Social Patterns of Immigrant Groups." It describes the importance of the family, marriage patterns, religion, educational attainment, and voluntary organizations of the various large immigrant groups in Canada. The voluntary associations of these immigrant groups are important for cultural survival, and such associations have proven to be relatively short-lived in other countries. The B and B Commission indicates that it is too early to know if these associations in Canada will prove to be exceptions, but currently many groups have 50 or more such organizations in operation. In general, it was found that the Ukrainians seem to have the most viable intergenerational organizations, but other groups may also continue to exist. This article indicates that colonies or ghettos do form (often self-imposed), but that in time they tend to break down. Thus, although perhaps originally without equal access to power and privilege, the majority of immigrant groups slowly assimilate into the larger society, and cease to exist as minority groups.

Kelner's article "Ethnic Penetration into Toronto's Elite Structure" shows that immigrant (ethnic) people are still relatively underrepresented in the power positions of the society, but she makes some distinctions between types of elite structures. For example, she says "the proportion of non-Anglo-Saxon corporate leaders living in Toronto is still very small, approximately 7 percent. . . . The labour elite was more receptive to non-Anglo-Saxons than the corporate. Approximately 21 percent of the labour elite in Toronto were not of Anglo-Saxon origin. . . . In the political sphere, 19 percent of those in elite positions were non-Anglo-Saxons." However, Anglo-Saxon domination is still clear in the core of the elite system. Penetration into other types of elites such as real estate and academic leaders (strategic elites) is on the increase, and there are some differentials depending on which ethnic group is being examined. In general, ethnic penetration into the various elite structures is on the increase, but "the shift from criteria based on ascription to those based on achievement is far from complete."

To this point, it would appear that immigrant groups are usually in a minority position at some stage, but in time the immigrant population has influence on and access to the decision-making process in the society. This of course varies by the particular immigrant group and by the goals and objectives of the members of the group. Ben Tierney's article on the Hutterites shows that when such a group desires to remain separate and autonomous, it may find itself subject to what it defines as harassment and discrimination.

The Hutterites first came to North America in the 1870's and settled in colonies in the Northern United States and Canada. Today there are nearly 20,000 members of this group and the number of colonies has increased to 180. The Alberta Communal Property Act (which was recently upheld) forces the Hutterite group to apply for land through the provincial government before a new colony can be undertaken. The Hutterites claim that the Property Act interferes with their freedom of religion and is thus discriminatory. Historically, there has always been bitterness between the Hutterites and other people in surrounding communities, and at least portions of this resentment are related to the enclosure and autonomy of the Hutterite Brethren.

The last article in this section examines not an ethnic group, but women as a minority group. This selection is from the Royal Commission Report entitled "The Status of Women in Canada," and takes the position that prejudice and discrimination against women in Canada is a very real issue. Occupational type-casting, income differentials for the same work, lack of access to certain professions – all lend support to the notion of the woman as a minority. In addition, the report describes the *cultural mold* that socializes women into thinking that only certain behaviour patterns are *feminine*. Such a socialization process does not present women with the full range of alternatives necessary to achieve maximum personal goals, objectives, and satisfactions. Stereotypes of the woman as a sex object are perpetuated by the mass media, and ultimately, women are afraid to step out of the *character* that has been defined for them. According to this report, the role of the woman is changing and there will be agitation to achieve the opportunity for women to realize their full capabilities.

The issue of minority groups in Canada is a very real one. Native peoples, French-Canadians, blacks, immigrants, women – all have, in varying degrees, unequal access to the power and privilege which our society has to offer.

Footnotes

1. Louis Wirth, "The Problem of Minority Groups," in Ralph Linton (ed.), *The Science of Man in the World Crisis*, Columbia, 1945, p. 347.
2. Census of Canada, "Population: Ethnic Group," Vol. 1, Part II, No. 5, Dominion Bureau of Statistics, Ottawa, 1962.

Kabloona and Eskimo: Social Control*

F. G. Vallee

Social control is one of the broadest topics handled in sociology. In popular usage the term control connotes a process of deliberate and calculated manipulation of self and others so that certain aims are achieved, or certain happenings avoided. In sociological usage, however, social control has broader application, particularly since the impact of Freudian psychology made itself felt in social science. In its broadest sense, social control refers to that process whereby order is maintained in social systems, the maintenance of order in turn depending on an optimum level of conformity to the important social norms; the preventing of deviance from these norms and the adequate checking of deviance once it occurs; and the co-ordination of activities in the society. There are regular ways of maintaining social order in any society, no matter how primitive, and these are *social* ways. That is, tendencies to conformity and to check deviance are not biological: they are not inherited in the genes, they are not *instinctive*.

By and large the ways in which social order is maintained operate without people being conscious of them. Deliberate and calculated ways of control, through command, bribery, law, force, and so on, present only the top of the social control iceberg. One becomes keenly aware of this in groups where there is no codified law, no police force, no structure of formal authority, and yet where things get done, where people intermingle without much noticeable conflict, where deviance is kept at a minimum.

Such is the situation in a typical Eskimo camp. The fact is that the Eskimo had no codified law, no political structure, no specialized institution to exert authority is so well known as to make comment on it superfluous. Van den Steenhoven (1957) and others who have studied social control among the Eskimos in this region call attention to the lack of authority based on force and to the importance of informal means of social control, such as gossip, ridicule, ostracism, often subsumed under the general term *public opinion*. For instance, Birket-Smith (1959:151) states that, among the Eskimos, ". . . it is (public opinion) . . . on which social control really depends, and not on application of physical force in threat or in fact".

The effectiveness of public opinion presupposes that the individuals identify with the public whose opinion influences his behaviour; that the individuals respect the values and rules upon which the opinions are based; that it is more rewarding to conform to the opinion of this public than it is to challenge it. Identification with others and respect for values and rules are generally assumed to be the outcome of what we call the socialization process, or, in the vernacular, the outcome of a person's bringing up. The rewards and punishments con-

---

*Article taken from *Kabloona and Eskimo*, 1967, pp. 187-208. First published in 1962 by the former Department of Northern Affairs and Natural Resources and the former Northern Co-ordination and Research Centre (now the Northern Science Research Group). The monograph was republished in 1967 by the Canadian Research Centre for Anthropology in co-operation with the present Department of Indian Affairs and Northern Development.

nected with conformity and deviance are more a function of the situation a person is in, whether or not, for instance, the person needs help, food, recognition, approval, and so on. Let us look first at the matter of early socialization.

Although opinions differ as to the degree of significance, no student of human behaviour would attribute only a small significance to what happens during infancy and childhood in determining the individual's adult approach of life. It is during that period that the foundations of personality are laid and basic response patterns set. Among the outstanding features of child care among the Eskimos in this region, we comment on the following: the constant tending of infants and young children, who are seldom out of contact with some other person; the provision of nurturance on demand, particularly during infancy; the lack of a corporal punishment and of angry reactions to childish deviance; the stress on control over aggressive impulses; the gradual edging of the child into an adult role, beginning at a relatively early age.

The majority of mothers carry their infants snuggled in a pouch which is suspended from the shoulders of their *atigis* (outer robes). They take their infants with them wherever they go: to church, to dances, movies, fishing trips, visiting, shopping, and so on. Until the infant can walk and even for many months after that, it is hardly ever separated from the mother or from some mother substitute, for Eskimo children are mothered by any woman or man or child who happens to be around when the true mother cannot handle the infant. In the dwelling the infant is placed on the bedding, but outside the dwelling it practically lives in its pouch on the mother's back. When awake it is placed in a kneeling position so that its head grazes the nape of the mother's neck; when asleep it is eased downward so that the head disappears along with the rest of the body into the mother's clothing. If in this position the baby awakes and begins to cry the mother will either give it the breast immediately or, if not in a position to do that, she will reach behind her and jiggle the baby gently up and down with a steady rhythm to soothe it. The infant's crying is never simply ignored. Babies are constantly fondled and caressed by all manner of people indoors and outdoors.

Most women breast feed their children until the age of about two or until the next one is born. Nowadays the switch is from breast to bottle, although the two-year old is given soft food to eat also. We have seen children of three years bottle feeding. The principle established during infancy is continued through childhood; the child is fed or allowed to take food whenever it is hungry.

We have never seen an Eskimo parent strike a child, although two mothers told us that they had slapped their children lightly on rare occasions. All other parents consulted claimed that they did not strike their children, even lightly. Children are restrained from doing things which the parents consider to be improper or dangerous by gentle constraint or murmured remonstrance, not by sharp and loud commands. The parent lets the child know that the offensive action would hurt the parent's feelings and make it difficult for the parent to go on helping and nurturing the child. If the child shows aggression against another, he is again gently restrained and reminded that others will shun him if he continues to act in that way.

Eskimo toilet training discipline is not severe, although the child is restrained from eliminating just anywhere. From the age of about six months it is regularly potted, usually on some empty tin which had previously contained powdered milk or some such food. The child is never punished for mistakes in elimination. The attitude here is similar to the one applied with respect to other demands on the child: no one should expect a child to be able to exceed its capabilities. Compared to the Kabloona child, the Eskimo one does not have to be constantly restrained within and without the household for the protection of himself and of the costly objects within the household. Fewer and less stringent demands are put upon him.

We have noted earlier that the Eskimo child graduates unselfconsciously from stage to stage, taking on responsibility for an increasing number of tasks appropriate to the person's sex, until by the late teens the person is expected to take over the responsibilities of full adulthood. This pattern is changing, primarily because of the establishment of the school, with the result that the person is regarded for a longer period as a *child* and the transition to adulthood is more abrupt and discontinuous. However, it is still true that boys and girls are expected to make significant contributions to the household – through domestic work, fishing, tending younger children, and so on – from the age of about six or seven.

We emphasize that we had neither the competence nor the time to carry on a full-scale study of the relation between child-training and personality or *ethos* and that we offer little but speculation and suggestion on this important matter.[1] It is suggested that the kind of child-rearing practices outlined above bring out the following traits and encourage their development: an unwillingness to postpone gratifications; the assumption that help will be given when required without having to please; the tendency to appease and the desire to be appeased; the abhorrence of violence in manner or deed; an admiration for adult-like achievement in the appropriate skills – hunting, fishing, sewing, and so on.

The least likely trait to emerge from such rearing, we suggest, is rebellion. To borrow the terminology of Parsons (1950) the *conformative* need dispositions prevail over the *alienative* need dispositions. Without going into the exhaustive and intricate detail of his analysis we point out only that where the person is swayed more by the conformative than the alienative need dispositions, he is likely to conform conspicuously and, if he does deviate, is likely deviate by *over*-conforming, for instance, by becoming a ritualist or by exerting himself to pander to others. Where the alienative need dispositions hold sway, the person is likely to deviate in ways which *cut him off* conspicuously from others, for instance, by violent aggression, outright rebellion, or complete withdrawal, which usually takes the form of retreat but which may also be manifested in suicide.

What can we say about deviance among the Eskimos in this region? Overt aggression as a response to frustration is certainly not unknown. The resort to force in order to gain something which was being withheld is reported in several places in the literature and by older informants, but as a thing of the past. Rasmussen (1927:80) tells of a man who killed an entire family in order to procure a wife he greatly desired, and Hanbury (1904:46), who relates a similar story of a man resident near Baker Lake who also killed six people in a dispute over a woman. The use of force is nowadays definitely condemned and from what we can gather it never was approved, but people seemed to recognize that an individual could be driven to desperation and was not entirely to blame if he lost his head when severely frustrated, which, incidentally, would be a strong reason for not frustrating him, that is, for conforming to his desires.

All of the incidents involving the use of violence known to us saw men fighting or killing in order to get a woman whose relatives did not want her to go with the assaulter. Another point: although the numbers of people murdered in a given period might seem impressive, this does not mean that there was a tendency to murder among large numbers in the population, for the pattern seems to have been for a few murderers to kill many victims. That is, if a man gave vent to aggressive impulses, he would likely overdo it once the irrevocable act had been committed. Thus we have the *amok* pattern, familiar in the literature. The important point for our consideration here is that few people ever gave vent to aggressive impulses in the first place. In the past twenty years there has been no clear-cut case of murder in the region, although in one *accidental* death murder was suspected. Fighting is extremely rare and informants were hard put to recall incidents involving fighting.

As for open rebellion, the only illustration we could find of this involved the defiance of parental authority by two girls who did not want to marry the men to whom they were promised. These were cases of rebellion against persons. Rebellion against norms and values, such as we find among delinquent gangs in the south, is unknown in this region among the Eskimos.

Where deviance which alienates the deviant from others does occur it usually takes the form of simply going away from them, withdrawing in some cases from contact with all other humans for a period. There were too few incidents of this kind to justify generalization, but it is interesting to note that within the past five years there have been at least four cases of girls leaving the households where they lived and wandering out over the land for periods averaging about two days and nights, causing much alarm. Three of these girls were orphans who had been passed from family to family. We were also able to record several cases where children and adults simply withdrew from the households in which they were residing and turned up in other households, but without having spent a long interval of solitude on the land.

Perhaps the most spectacular form of withdrawal or retreat is that of suicide. In the twenty-year period from 1940 to 1959 there were four suicides which we know about. Unfortunately we could get very little background information on these suicides. The most recent one involving a person from this region was that of a 45-year-old woman, the mother of three teen-aged children, who hanged herself in a sanatorium where she had been confined as a serious T.B. case. We know of an attempted suicide by a woman in recent years after she had received news that one of her sons had been killed accidentally. This woman had lost three other members of her family in three years and, as she put it after her unsuccessful sucide attempt, "I want to go away."

The alienative forms of deviance described have the effect of making people feel sorry for the deviant and, except for the suicides of course, arouse from them all kinds of appeasing responses, so that the deviant is absorbed back into the group and into the network of mutual help and affection. That people need one another's help and affection is self-evident to someone reared in the way described. If it does not become self-evident in childhood, it certainly should by the time the person reaches adulthood, particularly if he lives on the land, for conditions there make it obvious that people are profoundly interdependent. According to older informants, one of the worst punishments meted out in the past was that of ostracism.

We do not suggest that the obvious need for help of others in sheer physical survival and the dependence on others for nurturance, which is always forthcoming during childhood, provide the underlying cause for the readiness to conform to the wishes of others. People come to depend on others for esteem, affection, and approval and these needs may press insistently for satisfaction, just as do those for food, sexual gratification, and so on. In his discussion of child-rearing and ethos among an Eskimo group from the Eastern Arctic, Honigmann (1959:111) states that,

> The baby in the Eskimo household is a cynosure, a focus of pride and pleasure, but he is also considered to be helpless and dependent. Therefore, it is felt that he deserves nurturance and devotion. *The parents' and relatives' adoration and pride become components of this attention.*[2]

It is suggested that the person's stake in keeping attention and devotion flowing his way is sufficiently strong to inhibit him from risking the alienation of others by displeasing them too much. Observation of everyday behaviour in the community lends support to this view. On numerous occasions when a person has aroused another's displeasure, he has been observed to appease the other and restore the harmony between them. This appeasement technique is especially evident among children. Teachers and others who have had experience with Kabloona and Indian children commented on the remarkable tendency for Eskimo children to win back their approval after losing it for even a slight misdemeanour by bringing some object to the person or by offering some service. Honigmann (1959:113) also comments on this appeasement technique, after describing how the infant and young child is constantly appeased by the parents and others: "Accustomed to being appeased the child becomes an adult who is able to appease and expects appeasement." It will be recalled that appeasement of the spirits was a highlight of the traditional religion among the Eskimos.

What we are emphasizing in this discussion of the relevance of socialization for social control, is that the socialization process during infancy and childhood impresses on the person the notion that conformity pays. In a positive sense, the practice of conformity brings in ever-increasing rewards of care and affection. In a negative sense, deviance turns people away: they withdraw their affection and care, and may possibly withdraw their help when this is sorely needed. To be alone and abandoned in this environment for an indefinite period is a terrifying prospect. Needless to say, in both traditional times and at present, religious teaching also gets across to the growing person that deviance results in the withdrawal of protection against harmful spirits, in the modern situation personified as Satanasi.

Recent studies of child-rearing (Henry, 1956; Sears, 1957; Whiting and Child, 1953) indicate that where children are not subjected to strict discipline, and particularly to corporal punishment, they will develop the tendency to blame themselves when things go wrong; children who are strictly disciplined and punished physically will develop the tendency to blame others when things go wrong, to find scapegoats and to attack the scapegoats. It is reasoned that such children have learned that aggression pays: the evidence in their eyes is that their own deviance was halted – at least temporarily – by parental aggression in the form of corporal punishment. Some support for part of this hypothesis is to be found in the Baker Lake region, for not only is there little overt aggression between individuals, there is a readiness to accept blame which is noticeable enough for teachers and others to comment on it. Perhaps aggression is turned inwards. This would appear to fit with some of the traditional religious attitudes . . . [which indicate] . . . the importance of suffering, confession, and expiation.

We have been discussing the building up of predispositions to conform to the social norms which is, of course, only one aspect of social control. In fact, we have been emphasizing not so much conformity to norms as conformity to what people want one to do. In the socialization of Eskimo children, the emphasis is not on sets of rigid norms of conduct, etiquette, convention, and so on, although a concentration on the normative is being demanded of children in school and in church which is a departure from tradition. The child who is pressed into conformity with such codes of behaviour as those contained in the Commandments, Emily Post, the Boy Scouts, and so on, is likely to put a considerable unconscious investment of his emotions into these norms and to either conform to them or break them no matter what people think. The informal organization of Eskimo life did not have as one of its features a multiciplity of carefully spelled-out norms to which the individual was expected to adhere no matter what people thought. There were, as we saw, an abundance of sacrosanct rules pertaining to production and domestic life besides a few fundamental principles relating to kinship, sharing, and sexual prerogatives, but even these latter were not invested with supernatural support, were not perceived as eternal verities. Although norms were and are part of every social situation, the focus in conformity and deviance was on persons rather than on norms.[3]

Another aspect of social control has to do with situational pressures. Elsewhere we have mentioned the lessening of interdependence among the Eskimos, particularly in the settlement. The threat of withdrawal of support is not as effective where a person can get along easily without the help of others as it is where the support of others is absolutely essential.

An even more significant feature of the contemporary situation as far as conformity and deviance are concerned is the presence of opportunities – in the environment – what Roman Catholics would call *occasions of sin* – to satisfy the new wants which are being generated among the Eskimos. We have in mind specifically one kind of deviance, in fact the only kind which seems to arouse much apprehension in the region: that of theft, which by all accounts was extremely rare in the past but which is becoming, if not common, at least less rare. In a one year period ending in September, 1959, there were four separate thefts reported in the settlement. In all but one of these thefts, young men in their middle teens are suspected or have been found guilty. This matter of theft was brought up at two meetings of the Eskimo Council where the older men expressed their indignation and alarm but were unable to suggest a course of action, even where the identity of the thief was known. The Eskimos claim that traditionally theft was so rare that they had no special way of dealing with it once it occurred.[4] If someone took something which did not belong to him, it was assumed that he must be in dire need and that he would replace it quietly whenever he could do so.

People often overlook the fact that the process of assimilation to what they regard as a desirable way of life involves the taking on of undesirable modes

243

of conduct, at least among some in the assimilating group. If the Kabloona society is made up of admirable features such as material affluence, educational opportunities, marvels of technology, and so on, it is also made up of abnormally high rates of alcoholism, divorce, criminality of various kinds, and so on. As far as the Baker Lake population is concerned, the mechanisms of social control have so far been more than adequate in nipping deviant tendencies in the bud.

Information from researchers, police and other officials and our own observations lead us to conclude that forms of deviance endemic in the south, such as vandalism, alcoholism, prostitution, assault, and so on, are much more common in such settlements as Churchill, Great Whale River, Frobisher Bay, and Inuvik than in Baker Lake. A number of reasons may be considered for Baker Lake's record of comparative conformity. As we have seen, all Eskimos at the settlement are full members of one or the other religious congregation and are therefore subject to internal and external conformative pressures from this source. Then, at Baker Lake the population is smaller and more homogeneous than it is at the other Arctic settlements mentioned, so that informal control by ridicule, gossip, ostracism and other pressures usually subsumed under the heading of *public opinion*, is more workable there. We must remember, too, that at Baker Lake there are few realistic opportunities for inhabitants to procure alcohol, smash up automobiles, or gang-up with like-minded deviants. Finally, the Kabloona element at Baker Lake is made up entirely of professional, managerial, clerical, and technical workers, many of them married and with a vital stake in respectability. In the other places mentioned among the unattached Kabloona males in construction work, in mining, and in the forces, there are many who prey upon the Eskimo women, providing the latter with opportunities to prostitute themselves, this exploitation of the women giving rise to tension between Eskimo and Kabloona males. In fact the presence of large numbers of unattached Kabloona males, some of whom have only a feeble stake in respectability, provides justification for mining, military and government officials to insist on non-fraternization and to maintain a high degree of public segregation between their Kabloona employees and the Eskimos in the interest of social control. This segregation has the unintended consequence of raising the level of tension between the two ethnic groups, tensions which are sometimes worked off in assault, heavy drinking, and other forms of deviance.

Although the Baker Lake population boasts low rates of conventional deviance, we expect these rates to increase in the future. As we mentioned, new wants are being generated among the population and they are not being provided with the facilities and means to satisfy them. As the amount of felt deprivation increases, it would be surprising if people did not seek other, illegitimate, means of getting what they want or if they simply accepted the deprivations without hitting out in some way at the system, certainly one of the motivating elements in much vandalism. One of the few safe wagers to make concerning the Arctic as a whole is that the enforcement functions of the R.C.M.P. will increase greatly in significance within the next decade or so.

Having considered some of the highlights of conformity and deviance in this region, we turn to another aspect of social control: the organization of activities which are important to the group. In discussing this matter we pay special attention to power, authority, and decision-making.

When we say that a person has power, we mean simply that he can will that certain actions should take place and that either he or others then carry out these actions. Where power is legitimate we call it authority. For instance, a factory owner has the authority to shut down his factory. If he does so, no one else can open it, unless they do so on superior authority (i.e., that of the state) or unless the owner transfers his authority to someone else. A workman in the factory may have the power to close it – for instance, by blowing it up or setting it on fire – but this is not authority, it is simply the illegitimate use of power.

As Bierstedt (1950) points out, there are three sources of social power: numbers, organization, and access to resources. All other things equal, the majority is more powerful than the minority. Where two or more groups are equal in number and resources, the one which is organized is more powerful than the other. A well organized minority can control an unorganized majority. Where two organized groups are equal in number, the one with the most control over resources is more powerful than the other.

What resources are significant depends on the situation in which a particular group finds itself. In one group, access to the spirit world may be a resource which is limited to only a few people; if the spirit world is of outstanding significance in that group, those with a monopoly of access to it are very powerful indeed. Among other resources which may be of significance power-wise are money, property, skill, and knowledge. In no society are all resources distributed at random; in no society does every person have equal access to all resources. Of course, in our society money is the key resource, because access to so many different things can be bought with it: information, knowledge, skill, the labour of persons, property and so on.

In the context of Canada as a whole the Eskimos are a tiny, unorganized minority with very limited access to significant resources. In the context of the local region and community in the Arctic, the Eskimos outnumber the Kabloona, but they are comparatively unorganized and, by and large, have access only to subsistence resources. There is nothing which they can withhold which would cause the Kabloona acute discomfort, except their services and their co-operation in helping the Kabloona achieve their goals.

The role system in the Baker Lake region accentuates the difference between the Kabloona and the Eskimos in terms of the distribution of power. No Eskimo is in a position to give orders to a Kabloona. No Kabloona needs to get the sanction of an Eskimo in order to receive purchasing power in the form of wages, relief, or credit. Hiring, firing, lending, giving, teaching, commanding – all of the functions which put a person or a group *one-up* over another person or group in the power market are Kabloona prerogatives.

Not only do the Kabloona exercise power in the specific ways listed, but whether they like it or not the Eskimos impute to them a kind of diffuse, generalized power. Kabloona at the settlement claim that the Eskimos over-estimate fantastically Kabloona power, both in the mass and personally.

> Some of these people figure all I have to do is write a few lines on a paper and a plane comes, or the boat brings eight houses. It's like magic. Somebody does some work for us and he comes in the office. I get out this blue slip of paper and scrawl a few hieroglyphics on it and the Eskimo goes to the Bay and buys and buys until the clerk tells him – "you only have about thirteen cents left" – and the Eskimo doesn't

question this, he just looks around until he finds thirteen cents worth of something which will exhaust the magic of the blue piece of paper. Maybe it will be thirteen hunks of bubble-gum!

They think we're millionaires and they think there's absolutely nothing we can't do if we really want to.

The other day X came in and asked if we would get him a canoe or a plane to take him back to his camp because he had a lot of supplies to take back. I thought, what the hell do you think we have here, a taxi service? But I tried to explain to him that I just couldn't get planes and boats and all kinds of things just when I want them. We always try to get across to these people that the government isn't made of money, that there's a limit to what we can spend, but I guess they don't believe us or they don't understand.

It is hardly surprising that the Eskimos do not understand the logic of the Kabloona system of allocating facilities and wealth, for the logic is not at all self-evident. To clarify this point, let us look through Eskimo eyes at the following events. One day they see a small plane land on the lake. Later they learn that the two Kabloona in the plane come from a place in the United States about 3000 miles away, and that they have come all this way to go fishing! A few days later another plane lands with a party of men who go round examining the tiny flowers and taking samples of the soil, placing it carefully in boxes. Then, from still another plane emerges a man of solemn appearance who rushes from tent to tent recording stories from old ladies, flying off again within two days.

These arrivals and departures are capped by the arrival of a planeful of government dignitaries and their wives, civil servants, newspaper men and other unidentifiable Kabloona, all elaborately equipped with cameras, a few with portable recorders. After visiting the interior of several Kabloona installations, they emerge and scatter, wandering around the settlement, patting children on the head, asking people to "say a few words – anything – as long as it's in Eskimo," into their portable recorders, taking pictures of old shacks and tents, before re-entering their plane and disappearing forever from the community. The Eskimos remember that for days prior to the arrival of this party considerable sums of energy and wages were channelled into cleaning up the settlement, collecting and burning garbage, straightening out uneven rows of oil drums and generally tidying up.

We do not suggest that there is no logic or rational purpose to these happenings. Nor can we report that the Eskimos are baffled or disturbed in the slightest by them. The point we make here is that the Eskimos can only attempt to understand this logic on the basis of their experiences or the evidence of their eyes, having no precedents in their own society for such goings-on, and their experiences are confined to the externals of the happenings. They are like people who see only small, unconnected parts of many plays and who therefore cannot be expected to understand fully the plots or the roles. To continue the analogy, they are excluded from the vantage point of back-stage, which is in the south, a vantage point from which many of the happenings described above make sense. None of this would matter if the Eskimos were always in the audience, but they too have been drawn into the play, in most cases without the benefit of rehearsal.

It is one of the most difficult features of the N.S.O.'s job to persuade the Eskimos that there are indeed limits to what can be done and to explain the rationale for what is and is not done. Part of the difficulty has its sources in the existence of evidence to the contrary of what the Officer says, evidence, that is, in the eyes of the Eskimos.

For instance, an Eskimo couple and their child of the Back River group have not been seen for several months. Rumour has it that they are moving north towards King William Island. The N.S.O. and the R.C.M.P. expect to hear from an administrator in that area, which is outside the E2 district, that this family has arrived there. Months pass, summer arrives, and they hear nothing. They become concerned and ask pilots who happen to fly over that general region to keep an eye out for the Eskimo family. Still there is no word. Finally, at the end of the summer, an R.C.M.P. plane comes to the settlement with patients from the south. The pilot agrees to take the N.S.O. on a quick search of the Back River district, and they eventually spot a tent about 100 miles from the settlement. Landing on a lake nearby, they find the family they are seeking, in good health, doing quite well as far as caribou and fish are concerned. Does the family want to be flown to Baker Lake? No, they see no reason for going there. There is a friendly parting, the Kabloona get into the aircraft and fly away. How does the Eskimo perceive this incident? He does not define himself as lost or in trouble, but nevertheless an aircraft makes a special trip just to ask him how he is and if he wants to go to the settlement. Is it surprising then that this Eskimo, and others who learn of the incident, ask for a plane at a time when they feel they need it?

The evidence of unlimited power arbitrary wielded – in the eyes of the Eskimo, that is – is not confined to the use of transport. The Kabloona try to convince the Eskimos that their decision-making powers are limited, that they are really only cogs in a machine, small bosses. But what do the Eskimos see? They see the Kabloona making decisions every day which are of the most crucial importance to the Eskimos. The Kabloona try to convince the Eskimos verbally that their own purchasing power is narrowly limited, that they (the Kabloona) are really poor. But what do the Eskimos see? They see people living in what to them are immense houses, the smallest of which is many times bigger than the average Eskimo tent or igloo or shack; surrounded by an incredibly opulent array of red maple furniture, radios, tape recorders, beds, movie cameras and projectors, any one of which objects is worth more than the entire estate of some Eskimo families. The Eskimo women who mind the Kabloona children and keep the Kabloona domiciles free of dust and grime report on the fabulous stocks of foodstuffs, extra blankets, toys, and cupboards full of clothing common to these homes.

The conclusion which an Eskimo is likely to draw from the protests of the local Kabloona that he has limited decision-making and purchasing power, is that those in the South must have infinite powers of this kind. Knowing the Kabloona have bosses in the South does not appear to diminish their awe of the local Kabloona's powers; rather it seems to magnify their awe of the powers of the bosses outside, and they are *the government*. Indeed, we have seen that they have evidence of the wondrous powers of the bosses outside: not only do local officials defer to them, but when they come to visit, all the garbage has to be concealed and a special impression created.

If the Eskimos do not understand the logic of Kabloona life this does not mean that they have no rational ways of dealing with the Kabloona. Actually, over the decades they have developed formulae which they apply in their dealings with Kabloona, formulae which seem to work. One is reminded of persons who learn formulae for the solution of certain problems, say, for instance, the problem of finding the area of a parallelogram, without knowing the logic upon which the formula is based, without knowing the underlying theory. As far as the topic of this chapter is concerned, a few of the relevant formulae may be stated as follows:

(1) Let the Kabloona person initiate action. Except when on the land, the Kabloona know best, so always let them lead.

(2) Never displease a Kabloona by open resistance to his suggestions or commands. If you do not want to do whatever it is he wants his way, say you do not understand or, better, go away and do it your own way and hope that the results are so satisfactory that the Kabloona will be pleased.

We could list many other informal rules of behaviour which have in common the underlying theme of pleasing the Kabloona, or at least, not arousing his ire. It is interesting to note that when a rule does get established there is a tendency to overdo the observance of it. For instance, in the settlement the *thank-you* ritual which is so vital a part of Kabloona folkways is taking hold and with some people is applied in matters which Kabloona themselves think inappropriate. At a recent meeting of the Eskimo Council, one man arose and thanked the government for giving his mother a pension. The woman is not only sixty-five years of age: she has been blind for thirty years. This illustration points up a salient feature of present-day attitudes of Eskimos to *the government*. As far as we could determine, most of them have no idea of citizenship rights which are established and guaranteed by the government, although the teachers and N.S.Os. take special pains to explain the theory and practice of government to them. The government is partly a vague abstraction, partly an aggregation of bosses which makes rules concerning a variety of things, such as hunting and fishing, lights on boats after dark, where one can and cannot put up a shack, and which dispenses wages for labour and other monies – for instance, for having children – according to some formula which is not clearly understood. Thus if one receives something from the government, it is appropriate to thank it.

It is certain that as the Eskimos learn more about the Kabloona world their appraisal of the Kabloona, and by implication of themselves in relation to the Kabloona, will become more realistic. In the meantime, we have the unusual situation in which D.N.A. officials (who are all-powerful in the eyes of the Eskimos) try to force a definition of the Eskimos on themselves in which they as Eskimos have rights as citizens, in which they have the power to initiate changes which even the Kabloona themselves could be committed to follow. Before taking up this feature of the situation, let us shift the focus of our attention from the Kabloona and his world and back to the Eskimos. What can we say about power among the Eskimos themselves?

As in traditional times, in the camps today the exercise of authority is based on familial roles: parents can tell children what to do; older brothers can tell younger brothers, and so on. Where the father is infirm or the older brother grossly incompetent, some other person will be in charge. In camps which are not complete kinship units, leadership is taken by some person who by common consent is a successful hunter and who knows best the terrain in the vicinity, provided that the person is not conspicuously younger than the other men, although he does not have to be the oldest of the group. The process of selecting a leader in these camps is not a formal, deliberate one: leaders emerge from the give and take of interaction in such camps. The word for leader is *isyumatah*. It is customary for the *isyumatah* to speak on behalf of the camp, when a spokesman is required, in short, to represent the members of the camp. This aspect of the *isyumatah* role was accentuated after the establishment of the fur trade, for the traders preferred to deal with one person on behalf of the entire camp. To some extent the government officials and policemen have given support to this tendency, for they have normally operated through the *isyumatah* also.

We cannot overemphasize the fact that what authority there is among the Eskimos is domestic and informal and not backed by the ultimate use of force. Authority is exercised in a muted fashion, for the Eskimos are averse to giving orders. Most decisions affecting the camp as a whole appear to emerge from quiet discussion and the exchange of views. The leader is the one whose views are given more weight than those of other people in the camp. There have been and are exceptions to this rule. For instance, in a large camp where the leader was not only a great hunter and trapper but also a powerful *angakok*, it is reported that he gave commands and reached decisions without much or any consultation with others. But according to the literature on this region and according to older informants, this was certainly not the typical arrangement, and today it does not occur at all, except in a mild form at one camp where a vigorous grandfather of 53 years of age rules over his wives, sons, and their families with unquestioned authority.

Thus the basis for decision-making among the Eskimos is informal consultation, with the domestic leader exercising slightly more influence than the others. Another important feature of authority and decision-making in the camps is that the domestic authority is limited to the one camp. The *isyumatah* can speak only for those in his camp; decisions arrived at by the group are binding only on members of that group. It is of crucial importance to remember this feature of Eskimo social organization when considering problems of Eskimo leadership in Arctic communities today. The idea of someone in authority speaking on behalf of and giving orders to large numbers of people to whom they are not related by kinship or camp membership is a completely foreign one for which there are no precedents in Eskimo history or culture in this region.[5]

It is not difficult to see why there were no such precedents. We expect to find clear lines of authority and the vesting of authority in specified offices where the group is large; where there is a very complex division of labour required to do the job of the group; where the people in the group are heterogeneous with respect to kinship affiliation, social class, culture, etc.; and where there is decidedly unequal access to resources so that some people control the access of others to whatever crucial resources there are. A group or society in which these conditions prevail is one which requires clear lines of authority, vested in offices (such as general, mayor, chief, councilman, etc.) and having the backing of force. On none of these counts did the traditional Eskimo society need such an element in its organization. There were simply no large residential groups; the division of labour was relatively simple, based on sex and age; the members of the residential groups were homogeneous with respect to kinship, social class, culture; and there was equal access to resources within any given camp and between camps – except for the one resource of contact with the supernatural, and it is in connection with the latter that we find the closest approach to the exercise of both naked power and formal authority among the Eskimos.

Of course many Eskimos are now living under conditions in which the traditional organization of activities and use of domestic authority based on camp conditions, are not at all adequate. We refer here to the settlement, where the permanent and semi-permanent Eskimo population numbers about 160, from mixed kinship backgrounds, from different parts of the Arctic, already stratified to some extent according to social and economic class. In some measure the spontaneous and unplanned emergence of the Kabloonamiut at the settlement is filling the organizational and leadership gap, although this process is only getting under way.

The process of which we speak is being propelled by the delegation to Eskimos of some authority formerly wielded only by Kabloona. We give a concrete example of this from the work sphere, although it happens also in the religious sphere where the catechist is delegated some of the authority formerly exercised exclusively by the missionary. As the installations of D.N.A. continue to expand, the number of man hours required for maintenance and repair multiply accordingly. By 1960, the D.N.A. installations included: three school buildings, two warehouses, a workshop, an office, and eight dwelling units for teachers, N.S.Os, Wildlife personnel, and Eskimo employees of D.N.A. Each day these buildings must be supplied with stove oil and water, which is pumped into tanks or delivered in buckets; chemical toilets emptied; garbage collected and burned; schools swept out; besides the performance of innumerable seasonal jobs, such as the installation of screens and double windows, paintting, and so on. At first one Eskimo janitor carried out these tasks, aided by one or two part-time helpers. However, when it was found that this janitor worked about twelve hours per day, it became clear that a more systematic arrangement would have to be adopted. More help was hired, but it was many months before the Eskimo janitor assumed a purely supervisory role, letting the Eskimo helpers do the manual jobs and telling them what to do. In brief, it was some time before the man could bring himself to wield authority in an impersonal way, as a boss.[6]

It appears that those Eskimos who wield over their fellows authority which is delegated to them by Kabloona will be the first to take on diffuse leadership functions in the community, that their limited authority in one sphere (that of the job or of the chapel, as with the catechist) will spill over into the community. Whether or not this leadership will engender enthusiastic followership on the part of other Eskimos it is too early to say.

D.N.A. is the only agency in the community which is deliberately trying to foster Eskimo participation in the affairs of the region and of the settlement in particular. This is part of a deliberate plan to discourage the attitude of dependence on Kabloona which has prevailed since the latter settled in this region. Obviously, one root of this dependent attitude is fed by the ever-increasing economic succorance required to raise the standard of living and to lower the excessive death rate. Until stable employment in the settlement or elsewhere for many people is available and until a more rational and profitable exploitation of land resources than the present one is pursued, one cannot expect a dramatic change in the attitude of dependence. In the meantime direct assaults on this attitude are confined to citizenship education in the setting of Eskimo Council meetings where, as we noted earlier, it is the aim to involve the Eskimos in community decision-making.

In the absence of a community-wide organization of Eskimos (apart from the Eskimo Council) and in the absence of leadership which covers the whole community, this is not an easy task. It would be made easier if the Eskimos had concrete problems of some moment to themselves to grapple with in meetings, and if it were probable that their decisions and representations would be influential in solving these problems, for the pragmatic Eskimos are not given to discussing problems unless the discussion itself leads to concrete action to solve the problem.

At the moment, most community-wide problems are those which are formulated by the Kabloona and those which affect them as much as or more than the Eskimos: for instance, adequate teaching facilities for Kabloona school beginners who do not have to master the language barrier; a community deep-freeze for storing frozen foods; adequate playgrounds for the children; the zoning of new dwellings; the pollution of drinking water; the disposal of garbage; the establishment of an adequate power plant; and so on. These are problems the solution of which requires the concerted discussion and action of Kabloona as community members or residents rather than as the personnel of this or that agency and there is a pressing need for some kind of association of residents to cope with these problems. However, the Eskimos on the whole do not share the Kabloona concern for such problems and, in fact, some of them have diametrically opposed interpretations of what the problems are. For instance, where the Kabloona are concerned about the mushrooming of shacks built out of scrap materials, because of their shabby appearance and unhygienic conditions, the main problem for several Eskimos is how to get scrap material to build more shacks!

The attemps [sic] at something like local government in the Baker Lake settlement were initiated by the Kabloona in the fall of 1960 when they established a Residents Association which will, in the words of one Kabloona, "represent the interests of the people here as members of a community rather than as civil servants, missionaries, merchants, and so on." How the Eskimos will link up with the Kabloona residents in such an association has not been worked out definitely, there being a lack of consensus among the Kabloona on this question.

At one extreme is the view, apparently held by only one Kabloona couple, that every adult in the settlement, Eskimo and Kabloona, should be full members of the projected association from its inception, with equal voting rights, and that all meetings should be open to every resident. The majority of Kabloona consulted feel that, apart from the great technical difficulties of holding such meetings and particularly the difficulty of constant interpretation, it is premature to set up an undifferentiated association. One person put it this way:

> What would happen if we had just the one big association? We would invite the Eskimos and they would all come, because they usually take an invitation as a command, even if you don't mean it that way. Then at

the meeting none of them would open their mouths, only the whites would talk. How do you think this would make the Eskimos feel? They would feel even more controlled than they are now. It would only confirm their feeling that the whites run everything anyway.

Only two Kabloona were against any Eskimo participation whatsover. A few expressed the opinion that the Kabloona should get the association started, then invite those settlement Eskimos who understand English to become members, thus holding out membership as a reward for learning English. However, the majority opinion among the Kabloona was that initially there should be two associations linked together by a committee consisting of both Kabloona and Eskimos. One association would be formed by the present Eskimo Council, augmented by the adult women of the Eskimo community, in itself quite a departure. The other would be made up of Kabloona men and their wives. Each association would elect representatives to a committee which would span both. The committee members would attend both Eskimo and Kabloona meetings and try to articulate the agenda and decisions of both. This solution was discussed at a special meeting of Eskimos in the settlement and received a favourable reception. At this meeting, the Eskimos elected a Kabloonamio[7] man with a fair command of English and a woman, a widow who speaks no English and who is the mother of four marginal Kabloonamiut sons, as their representatives on this committee. Incidentally, the election of this woman is a singular precedent, not at all predictable from a knowledge of Eskimo culture, and baffling to the Kabloona in the community who had assumed that two men would be named to the committee.

Whatever the final structure and procedure of the Residents Association, it is the first approximation of a local government body in the region, although its powers will be quite limited. It would be naive to assume that the community power structure will suddenly shift and that the Eskimos will presently acquire the same decision-making prerogatives enjoyed by the Kabloona. Major decisions affecting the population will still be made mostly by Kabloona in their capacities as representatives of national institutions, influenced partly by the Kabloonamiut of the settlement. . . . Nevertheless, given the aim of reducing the dependence of the Eskimos and of encouraging them to speak for themselves, the projected arrangement described above should be a step toward its fulfillment.

To the author's knowledge, the Baker Lake Residents Association is the only institution of its kind in the Arctic. Eskimo Councils exist in other communities, but from what we have been able to learn, their value to the Eskimos is primarily educational: at the meetings the Eskimos learn something of the Kabloona way of life, their plans, and so on; these meetings also provide the Eskimos with opportunities to exercise the formalities of parliamentary procedure. To take one community as an illustration, the Dailey's (1961) observations about the Eskimo Council at Rankin Inlet, observations which we were able to confirm, are that Council meetings there are primarily occasions when messages from the Kabloona mining and government officials are transmitted to the public, advising them of new community or work regulations, exhorting them to keep their dogs tied and their life-belts on when afloat, ordering them to burn their garbage, and so on. The outstanding sociological feature of the Rankin Inlet community is that it is a company town. Its residents are directly or indirectly dependent on the mining company. Compared with

Baker Lake, the Rankin Inlet community is much more ethnically and class segregated, at least formally, and is integrated much more along authoritarian lines. There is little likelihood that its Kabloona and Eskimo residents would form an association to further their interests as community members.

If we regard the local grouping of adults of all ethnic groups and classes into community associations as an index of social assimilation, the Eskimo element at Baker Lake has a higher social assimilation score than the Eskimo element at Rankin Inlet, although the latter is culturally more assimilated to the dominant Kabloona way of life.[8] We do not yet have sufficient data from Arctic communities to permit systematic comparison of how the different Eskimo elements fit into the community decision-making process, but the data on hand suggest the hypothesis that the Eskimo element in a community has the minimum say in those places which are dominated by a single agency, such as a company, a branch of the armed forces, or a mission station. No one agency dominates the Baker Lake community; the social structure there is comparatively propitious as a setting in which the Eskimos may develop a stepped-up rate of involvement in their own destiny, at least at the local level.

Footnotes

1. The only systematic study of personality among the Eskimos was undertaken by Margaret Lantis (1953) among the Nunivak of the Bering Sea region.
2. Italics supplied.
3. Cf. Parsons (1951) for this distinction between focus on norms and focus on persons and its significance.
4. Not the least interesting feature of traditional Eskimo social organization in the Keewatin District is that they had no definite course of action which people were expected to take in certain cases involving deviance which in so many parts of the world bring on sanctions which are not only definite but almost automatic, particularly in cases of murder and theft (cf. Steenhoven 1957).
5. Cf. Balikci (1959, 1961) for a discussion of leadership and organization in Eskimo communities.
6. It is noteworthy that this man still feels some discomfort about wielding impersonal authority. At a meeting of Eskimo residents he was asked to address the group on the subject of Eskimo participation on a Residents' Committee. He began by explaining at some length that he could not do any heavy work because he had a sore back, describing in detail his ailment and how he had contracted it, although all this had nothing whatsoever to do with the business of the meeting. "If it were not for my sore back," he explained gravely, "I would be working too and not just telling men what to do and watching them."
7. The *mio* suffix is the singular form for *miut*.
8. For a discussion of the difference between social and cultural assimilation, see Vallee et al., (1957).

References

Balikci, Asen, "Two Attempts at Community Organization Among the Eastern Hudson Bay Eskimos," *Anthropologica*, 1, 1959, pp.122-135.

Balikci, Asen, "Relations Inter-éthniques à la Grande Rivière de la Baleine, Baie d'Hudson, 1957," Canada, *National Museum Bulletin*, 173, 1961, pp. 64-107.

Bierstedt, Robert, "An Analysis of Social Power," *American Sociological Review*, 15, 1950, pp. 730-738.

Birket-Smith, Kaj, *The Eskimos.* (2nd Edition), London: Methuen, 1959.

Dailey, Robert C. and Dailey, Lois, "The Eskimo of Rankin Inlet: A Preliminary Report," Canada, Department of Northern Affairs and National Resources, *Northern Co-ordination and Research Centre Report, 61-7*, 1961.

Hanbury, David T., *Sport and Travel in the Northland of Canada.* London: Arnold, 1904.

Henry, Andrew F., "Family Role Structure and Self Blame," *Social Forces*, 35, 1956, pp. 34-38.

Honigmann, John Joseph and Honigmann, Irma, "Notes on Great Whale River Ethos," *Anthropologica*, 1, 1959, pp. 106-121.

Lantis, Margaret, "Nunivak Eskimo Personality as Revealed in the Mythology," *Anthropological Papers of the University of Alaska*, 2, 1953, pp. 109-174.

Parsons, Talcott, *The Social System*. Glencoe, Ill.: Free Press, 1951.

Rasmussen, Knud, *Across Arctic America*. New York: Putnam, 1927.

Sears, Robert R. et al., *Patterns of Child Rearing*. Evanston: Row, Peterson, 1957.

Steenhoven, Geert van den, "Legal Concepts Among the Netsilik Eskimos of Pelly Bay, N.W.T., Canada," Department of Northern Affairs and National Resources, *Northern Co-ordination and Research Centre Report 59-3*, 1959.

Vallee, Frank G. et al., "Ethnic Assimilation and Differentiation in Canada," *Canadian Journal of Economics and Political Science*, 23, 1957, pp. 540-549.

Whiting, J. W. M. and Child, I. L., *Child Training and Personality*. New Haven: Yale University Press, 1953.

The Unjust Society*

Harold Cardinal

The history of Canada's Indians is a shameful chronicle of the white man's disinterest, his deliberate trampling of Indian rights and his repeated betrayal of our trust. Generations of Indians have grown up behind a buckskin curtain of indifference, ignorance and, all too often, plain bigotry. Now, at a time when our fellow Canadians consider the promise of the Just Society, once more the Indians of Canada are betrayed by a programme which offers nothing better than cultural genocide.

The new Indian policy promulgated by Prime Minister Pierre Elliot Trudeau's government under the auspices of the Honourable Jean Chrétien, minister of Indian Affairs and Northern Development, and Deputy Minister John A. MacDonald, and presented in June of 1969 is a thinly disguised programme of extermination through assimilation. For the Indian to survive, says the government in effect, he must become a good little brown white man. The Americans to the south of us used to have a saying: "The only good Indian is a dead Indian." The MacDonald-Chrétien doctrine would amend this but slightly to, "The only good Indian is a non-Indian."

The federal government, instead of acknowledging its legal and moral responsibilities to the Indians of Canada and honouring the treaties that the Indians signed in good faith, now proposes to wash its hands of Indians entirely, passing the buck to the provincial governments.

Small wonder that in 1969, in the one hundred and second year of Canadian confederation, the native people of Canada look back on generations of accumulated frustration under conditions which can only be described as colonial, brutal and tyrannical, and look to the future with the gravest of doubts.

*"The Buckskin Curtain," pp. 1-17 and "Red Tape," pp. 18-26 presented here are taken from *The Unjust Society: The Tragedy of Canada's Indians*, 1969, published by M. G. Hurtig Ltd., Edmonton, Canada.

Torrents of words have been spoken and written about Indians since the arrival of the white man on the North American continent. Endless columns of statistics have been compiled. Countless programmes have been prepared for Indians by non-Indians. Faced with society's general indifference and a massive accumulation of misdirected, often insincere efforts, the greatest mistake the Indian has made has been to remain so long silent.

As an Indian writing about a situation I am living and experiencing in common with thousands of our people it is my hope that this book will open the eyes of the Canadian public to its shame. In these pages I hope to cut through bureaucratic double talk to show what it means to be an Indian in Canada. I intend to document the betrayals of our trust, to show step by step how a dictatorial bureaucracy has eroded our rights, atrophied our culture and robbed us of simple human dignity. I will expose the ignorance and bigotry that has impeded our progress, the eighty years of educational neglect that have hobbled our young people for generations, the gutless politicians who have knowingly watched us sink in the quicksands of apathy and despair and have failed to extend a hand.

I hope to point a path to radical change that will admit the Indian with restored pride to his rightful place in the Canadian heritage, that will enable the Indian in Canada at long last to realize his dreams and aspirations and find his place in Canadian society. I will challenge our fellow Canadians to help us; I will warn them of the alternatives.

I challenge the Honourable Mr. Trudeau and the Honourable Mr. Chrétien to reexamine their unfortunate policy, to offer the Indians of Canada hope instead of despair, freedom instead of frustration, life in the Just Society instead of cultural annihilation.

It sometimes seems to Indians that Canada shows more interest in preserving its rare whooping cranes than the Indians. And Canada, the Indian notes, does not ask its cranes to become Canada geese. It just wants to preserve them as whooping cranes. Indians hold no grudge against the big, beautiful, nearly extinct birds, but we would like to know how they managed their deal. Whooping cranes can remain whooping cranes, but Indians are to become brown white men. The contrast in the situation is an insult to our people. Indians have aspirations, hopes and dreams, but becoming white men is not one of them.

Indifference? Indians have witnessed the growing concern of Canadians over racial strife in the United States. We have watched the justifiably indignant reaction of fellow Canadians to the horrors of starvation in Biafra. Television has brought into our homes the sad plight of the Vietnamese, has intensified the concern of Canadians about the role of our neighbour country in the brutal inhumanity of war. The Unitarian Service Committee reminds us of the starving conditions of hundreds of thousands of Asians. Canadian urbanites have walked blisters on their feet and fat off their rumps to raise money for underdeveloped countries outside Canada.

We do not question the concern of Canadians about such problems. We do question how sincere or how deep such concern may be when Canadians ignore the plight of the Indian or Métis or Eskimo in their own country. There is little knowledge of native circumstances in Canada and even less interest. To the native one fact is apparent – the average Canadian does not give a damn.

The facts are available, dutifully compiled and clucked over by a handful of government civil servants year after year. Over half the Indians of Canada are jobless year after year. Thousands upon thousands of native people live in housing which would be condemned in any advanced society on the globe. Much of the housing has no inside plumbing, no running water, no electricity. A high percentage of the native peoples of Canada never get off welfare. This is the way it is, not in Asia or Africa but here in Canada. The facts are available; a Sunday drive to the nearest reserve will confirm them as shocking reality.

Bitgotry? The problem grows worse, not better. A survey by the Canadian Corrections Association, entitled *Indians and the Law*, reveals some of the problems that the native person faces in the area of prejudice and discrimination. The survey reports bluntly: "Underlying all problems associated with Indians and Eskimo in this country are the prejudice and discrimination they meet in the attitudes of non-Indians. The result is a conviction on the part of the Indians and Eskimo that they are not really part of the dominant Canadian society and that their efforts to better themselves will fail because they do not have an even chance."

Probably the most perceptive statement of the report observes: "Few non-Indians will admit to feelings of prejudice against the Indian and Eskimo people because such views are no longer acceptable, but the façade often vanishes when problems arise."

Many Canadians, however, have always claimed and continue to assert that Canada has little racial difficulty. Statements of this nature are just so much uninformed nonsense.

In any area where there is a concentration of native people there exists racial tension. Urban centres with their multiplicity of attractions and opportunities are drawing more and more natives who come in hope and stay in misery. These migrants, with little financial security, all too often with insufficient job training and nearly always with terribly inadequate knowledge of white mores, inevitably jam into ghettos, increasing not only their own problems but those of the city. The people of the city answer with bigotry, wrongly atributing the problem to colour or race rather than to any inadequacy of opportunity and social response.

As Indian people attempt to organize and as Indian leaders become more vocal and articulate, the shades of bigotry which now appear in pastel with show up in more vivid colours. People who are tolerant of a problem which hasn't touched them are put to the test when the problem moves next door.

As an ethnocentric society, the Canadian non-Indian society puts its own peer group at the centre of all things desirable and rates all other cultures accordingly. It is an assumption, quite often becoming a conviction, that the values, the ways of life, the whole culture of one's own group must be superior to those of others. Tell a person long enough and often enough that he is inferior, and likely he will eventually accept the false image you thrust upon him.

An Indian leader in the Northwest Territories, asked why his people couldn't do a certain job for themselves, wisely and sadly observed, "They could, but they have been told for so long by the white man that they can't that now they don't think they can." Indians long have been victims of this sort of conscious and unconscious downgrading pressure from the non-Indian.

Ignorance? It thrives on the incestuous mating of indifference and bigotry and in turn breeds more of the same. Ignorance is irretrievably locked in with prejudice. How often have you heard a white man say, "Indians are lousy workers," or, "Indians are shiftless" or "dirty" or "lazy," or "Indians are drunken bums"? I have seen in numerous cities across the country non-Indians engaged in excessive drinking, making drunken fools of themselves. In these circumstances, what do you hear? "Well, isn't he having a ball," or "He's just letting his hair down," or, perhaps, "Boy, isn't he a real swinger!" Let native people be seen in similar conditions and what do you get? The comments are more in the nature of epithets: "Worthless drunks!" or "Drunken bums!"

This double standard has stereotyped the native people as a whole as people who can't handle liquor. More damaging is the fact that similar double standards are applied to nearly every aspect of native life. Typically, the Indians-can't-hold-their-liquor theory is inexcusably used by church groups or church leaders to try to force governments to accept the churches' views on liquor. And employers, like the churches, use this stereotype as a lever against government enforcement of fair employment standards. Let a white man get drunk and miss a day of work . . . his boss may fire him, but he gets another white man for the job. He doesn't say, "All white workers are drunken bums and too shiftless to hold a job." If the Indians misses a day, the entire race is condemned and categorized as no good; the next worker hired is not likely to be an Indian.

If more of these church groups, more of these employers and more of the other pressure groups who make opportune use of this handy double standard were honest with themselves and with government, they would quit using the Indian as an excuse to foist their own beliefs on the rest of society.

It can be argued that ignorance in some segments of society is understandable if not excusable, but ignorance at higher levels is neither. Political leaders must have, at the very least, a working knowledge of the particular constituencies they represent. They must know the people who elected them to represent their viewpoints; they must know the problems, the needs, the desires of *their* people. Particularly is this true when a politician is named to higher office, for example, a ministry.

Ministers of the crown have a large bureaucracy available to inform, advise and help them in the discharge of their responsibilities. They have almost endless resources upon which to draw. Nor are they dependent entirely upon such official and hired help. Their constituents also, for the most part, have resources. They have their own organizations or lobbies; they may have financial resources which can be utilized and will most often be respected. They have the means and the talent to present to the minister their own viewpoints and they can bring sufficient pressure to make certain *their* minister or *their* representative listens. Furthermore, the news media, because of their responsibility to look at both sides of the picture and to bring balanced views to bear on current problems, help elected representatives of the people discharge their duties properly and in an informed manner.

All of this theoretically works fine as a system of checks and balances, providing the necessary background knowledge and understanding of a situation to ensure proper and fair legislation . . . except that none of the above applies to Indians in Canada.

Throughout the hundreds of years of the Indian-government relationship, political leaders responsible for matters relating to Indians have been outstanding in their ignorance of the native people and remarkable in their insensitivity to the needs and aspirations of the Indians in Canada. More often than not, government people simply do not know what they are doing, and if they show any evidence of caring, it usually is in direct proportion to political pressure and political expediency at the time.

The question of paramount importance in the minds of successive ministers responsible for Indian Affairs appears to have been and to remain the defence of the gross ineptitude of their department. Any attempt to uncover the actual state of affairs and do the necessary housecleaning appears to have been either beyond them or of no interest to them.

Two factors play a part in the seemingly endless state of ignorance displayed by most federal politicians about native people. Too many are content to close their minds to any but the stereotype images so easy to pick up in Canada. They make little or no effort to go to the people and find out firsthand what is really happening. Secondly, until very recently, the question of Indians had never been a major political issue. The people of Canada simply have not been moved by the problem. Consequently, members of Parliament haven't felt it worth their time to investigate the Indian situation.

Historically, the question of Indians has been one raised by politicians for some purely ulterior motive, perhaps to create an image of social awareness or compassion. The concern has been passing, viable only when the image was politically attractive, usually forgotten as soon as the votes were counted or the winds of change blew from another quarter.

Most politicians and, as far as that goes, most Canadians, tend to plead ignorance as a defence for the inexcusable treatment of the native people of this country. One should keep in mind that ignorance is not acceptable in law as a defence, even in the case of a violated local ordinance, nor is it acceptable in international courts passing judgment on crimes against humanity.

However, even more reprehensible than the man who does not act because he is ignorant is the man who *does* know the situation but fails to act. I can only label this type of performance *gutless*. When I talk of a gutless person, I am talking about a human being who does not have the courage to try to change an unjust situation. I call gutless a person who, rather than change an indefensible state of affairs, tries to sweep the mess under a rug. I call gutless the politician who stalls, procrastinates and tries to perpetuate the antiquated systems and attitudes which have produced injustice, in order to try to maintain his own positive image. When I look at the existing situation among the natives of Canada, I cannot help but assume we must have a hell of a lot of gutless politicians in this country.

In 1969 it is true that there are some notable exceptions on the political scene: Robert Andras, minister responsible for Housing; Martin O'Connell, a Liberal backbencher from Toronto and a member of the House Standing Committee on Indian Affairs; Gerald Baldwin, a Conservative member from Peace

258

River and Frank Howard, the New Democratic party member from British Columbia. While a few men like these have worked to build up Indian competence and leadership qualities, many more through the years have contributed to a disastrous and calculated programme of leadership destruction.

The white man's government has allowed (worse, urged) its representatives to usurp from Indian peoples our right to make our own decisions and our authority to implement the goals we have set for ourselves. In fact, the real power, the decision-making process and the policy-implementing group, has always resided in Ottawa, in the Department of Indian Affairs and Northern Development. To ensure the complete disorganization of native peoples, Indian leadership over the past years and yet today has been discredited and destroyed. Where this was not possible, the bureaucrats have maintained the upper hand by subjecting durable native leaders to endless exercises in futility, to repeated, pointless reorganizations, to endless barrages of verbal diarrhoea promising never-coming changes.

Indeed, the real tanners of hides for the Buckskin Curtain are these self-same bureaucrats. To gain insight into the Indian problem, a basic understanding of the group of people known as bureaucrats, civil servants or mandarins working in the Department of Indian Affairs and Northern Development (formerly the Indian Affairs Branch of the Department of Citizenship and Immigration) is necessary.

These faceless people in Ottawa, a comparatively small group, perpetually virtually unknown, have sat at their desks eight hours a day, five days a week, for over a century, and decided just about everything that will ever happen to a Canadian Indian. They have laid down the policy, the rules, the regulations on all matters affecting native peoples. They have decided where our sons will go to school, near home or hopelessly far from home; they have decided what houses will be built on what reserves for what Indians and whether they may have inside or outside toilets; they have decided what types of social or economic development will take place and where and how it will be controlled. If you are a treaty Indian, you've never made a move without these guys, these bureaucrats, these civil servants at their desks in their new office tower in Ottawa saying "yes" . . . or "no."

And, you know something? It would almost be funny if it weren't so pathetic. In the latter part of 1968, a government official suggested publicly that the mandarins in Ottawa would probably not even recognize an Indian if they met one on the street.

These are the people who make the decisions, the policies, the plans and programmes by which we live, decisions made in almost total isolation from the Indians in Canada. Their ignorance of the people whose lives and destinies they so routinely control perpetuates the stereotype image they have developed of the native people.

Through generations of justifying their positions to the Canadian public and to Canada's political leaders, the bureaucrats within the department have come to believe their own propaganda. They have fostered an image of Indians as a helpless people, an incompetent people and an apathetic people in order to increase their own importance and to stress the need for their own continued presence.

259

Most of their action stems from their naïveté and a genuine belief that their solutions are necessary to ensure the survival of Indians. For the most part they are not really evil men. They have evolved no vicious plots intentionally to subjugate the Indian people. The situation for the Indian people, as bad as it is, has resulted largely from good intentions, however perverted, of civil servants within the Department of Indian Affairs. However, one cannot forget the direction usually taken by roads paved with nothing but good intentions.

Small wonder that the report on *Indians and the Law* notes: "Many non-Indians believe that nothing better can be expected from the descendants of Canada's original people, and many Indians and Eskimo oblige by acting in a way that confirms this expectation."

I have talked with many Indian people. I have had the opportunity to discuss our situation as a people with affluent Indians who have it made and with Indians living in the worst state of deprivation. I have met my fellow Indians of all generations, in all walks of life and from nearly every part of Canada.

Always I find that as Indian people, we share hopes for a better Canada, a better future and a better deal. We share hopes that Canadian society will accept us as we are and will listen to what we have to say.

One of the most difficult challenges our people face comes with this question of acceptance by non-Indian society. Certainly it means that on both sides we must change misconceptions about each other. It means that we must have the intelligence and the courage to set aside the old stereotypes on both sides. It means that we must change negative attitudes, shrug off bigotry, overcome the accumulated effects of generations of isolation from each other. It means honest-to-God intellectual and emotional effort by Indians and non-Indians.

Acceptance of the Indian in non-Indian society must mean acceptance as an individual in his own right, as a fellow human being. I emphasize the need for acceptance on an individual or personal basis. As members of a minority group we sometimes are bemused by the attitude of non-Indian people who meet us. Sometimes we literally can see the expression on their faces saying, "How do I approach this Indian? Can I go over and say hello? Will he be offended if I do this or say that? How should I act?" No problem, really. Be yourself. If you are a snob, you aren't going to make it with us anyhow. If you are a phoney, we're going to sense it. If you are okay, then there will be no problem. Just don't try to fake it. Be yourself. Now and then Indians run into a situation where a non-Indian makes his presence obnoxious by attempting to show that he feels you are no different that he is. He may think this is a great compliment, but you know damned well you *are* different from him – and, as often as not, you are glad of it.

Is it, then, too much to ask that we be accepted by the larger Canadian society as individuals in our own right, who can and will work with members of that larger society without first being required to become brown white men or white-washed brown men?

Talking and listening have been one-way streets with white men and Indians. Until very recently white men have expected Indians to do all the listening. Indians, on the other hand, have felt that the white man just couldn't shut up long enough to listen. For many years now our people have talked about what concerned them most, have suggested solutions to our problems as we see them, have talked generally about our hopes for a better future. Some have talked articulately and with eloquence, some less lucidly; some have spoken with great intensity and emotion, others with objectivity and almost passively. But all talk, brilliant or dull, visionary or cautiously realistic, remains futile when the people you talk to simply won't listen. We want the white man to shut up and listen to us, really listen for a change. Some Canadians listen but they wish to hear Indians say only what white people want to hear. They like to hear an Indian tell them what a good job government is doing and how the lowly Indian would have vanished if not for the white man's help. Such people quit listening when an Indian tries to tell them the hard facts of Indian life in Canada.

The Indian people are now impatient with the verbal games that have been played. We want the beginnings of a real and purposeful dialogue with non-Indian people and government representatives in order to get on with the business of solving some of the most basic difficulties that we face. When we enter into a dialogue, we wish to have the respect and the courtesy of the non-Indian society in their recognition that we are talking sense, that we have the intelligence and capacity to judge for ourselves what is good or bad for us. When we offer suggestions, we expect those suggestions to be given the attention they deserve, instead of the usual brush-off. Are you familiar with that brush-off? It goes, "Well, boys, what you have to say is good and you must be commended for the intelligence you have shown through your extremely good presentation," and, subsequently, the inevitable, "but we know your problems and what should be done, and we're certain that you will be pleased with our carefully considered decisions."

We want to be heard as reasonable, thinking people, able to identify with our own problems and to present rational solutions. We want to be treated as human beings with the dignity and equality we feel is our right. We ask the non-Indian society to wake up to things the way they are, to see us as a people with needs, emotions and untapped potential. These are the hopes of the present generation of Indian leaders. Surely these cannot be unreasonable hopes. They must not be.

We listen when Canadian political leaders talk endlessly about strength in diversity for Canada, but we understand they are talking primarily about the French Canadian fact in Canada. Canadian Indians feel along with other minorities, that there is a purpose and a place for us in a Canada which accepts and encourages diversified human resources. We like the idea of a Canada where all cultures are encouraged to develop in harmony with one another, to become part of the great mosaic. We are impatient for the day when other Canadians will accord the Indian the recognition implied in this vision of Canada.

The vast majority of our people are committed to the concept of Canadian unity and to the concept of participation in that unity. The Indians of Canada surely have as great a commitment to Canada, if not a greater one, than even the most patriotic-sounding political leaders. More truly than it can be said of anyone else, it is upon this land that our heritage, our past and our identity originates. Our commitment to Canada exists because of our belief that we have a responsibility to do all we can to ensure that our country is a nation with which we can proudly identify.

To fulfill our dreams for participation in the greatness of Canada, we must be able to contribute to Canada. We invite our white brothers to realize and acknowledge that the Indian in Canada has already made a considerable contribution to the greatness of our country, that the Indian has played a significant role in Canadian history. Our people look on with concern when the Canadian government talks about "the two founding peoples" without giving recognition to the role played by the Indian even before the founding of a nation-state known as Canada.

However, Canada's Indians look to the future as the greatest period for participation. Our contribution will be based upon what we are as a people, upon what, as a culture, Indian society will add to the mosaic and upon what we can accomplish as individuals to add to our country's total potential.

Here there is a lack, glaringly obvious. Our people lack the skills through which we might best contribute as individuals. If the Indian receives no training as a doctor then he cannot add to Canada's potential in medical advances. If he does not acquire the skills of a politician, he cannot hope to advance Canada politically. The Indian people must realize their greatest contributions to Canada's potential through whatever skills they may be able to add to Canada's pool of know-how. This is why Indians include in their aspirations better training in skills at all working levels, from professional to technical, to make it possible for each of us to work with our fellow Canadians so that the sum total of our efforts as Canadians results in the growth and expansion of the land we call our home.

No one realizes better than the Indian that the road ahead is long and hard going. There exist more than two thousand reserves across Canada, situated in every geographical area of our immense country, some actually within the boundaries of major cities (in Vancouver, Winnipeg and Toronto), some deep in the underdeveloped northern wildernesses, many isolated not only from the mainstream of society but from one another. The needs and the problems of Indians living in such diverse circumstances vary widely and, of course, the environment influences greatly their desires and ambitions.

The language barrier has isolated our people as truly as the geographical barrier. There are eleven different major language groups among the Indians of Canada with scores of dialects changing from band to band. Only recently has English become universal enough among Indians to serve as a medium of communication. And, even today, the most articulate (in English) Indian will confess readily that he still feels more at home in his mother tongue.

Nationwide Indian unity represents a dream long held by Indian leaders well aware of the divisive influence of the emphasis upon individual bands and tribes. Only recently, with the growth of strong provincial organizations in turn leading to the creation for the first time of a viable national organization, the National Indian Brotherhood, has this dream shown signs of realization. When our people begin to call themselves Indians instead of Crees or Saulteaux or Mohawks, when intertribal cooperation no longer allows the government to threaten our individual treaties, then we will have the strength of unity, the power to help make some of our other dreams come true.

Canada is an enormous country. Even within a single province such as Alberta, conditions vary so widely from reserve to reserve that common needs, aspirations and goals that can be attributed to the entire Indian people are often difficult to determine.

Perhaps our most persistent dreams stem from our most insistent reality – poverty – the one reality most Indians share. Perhaps because the Indian people face the most difficult and demoralizing situation in Canada, our aspirations are the more intense. We face the greatest challenge and, at the same time, the greatest threat.

Indians gladly accept the challenge – to become participating Canadians, to take a meaningful place in the mainstream of Canadian society. But we remain acutely aware of the threat – the loss of our Indian identity, our place as distinct, identifiable Canadians.

However idealistic some Indian dreams may be, there remain everyday hopes that come right down to earth. Indians are like anyone else. We look around and see a very affluent society. Just like our non-Indian neighbours, we want a share, a new car, a well-built home, television. These represent surface things, but it hurts deeply to see the affluence of our country and not be allowed to benefit from it. We want better education, a better chance for our children and the option to choose our own pathway in life. If we are to be part of the Canadian mosaic, then we want to be colourful red tiles, taking our place where red is both needed and appreciated.

Our people wish to become involved in all aspects of the professional community, but how many Indian doctors, Indian lawyers, Indian community planners, Indian engineers, artists, writers, professors do you know in Canada? While we see the white society training its young people for life in the professional and technological world of the space age, we find the government attempting to train our people in skills that have not been required since the Industrial Revolution.

If we as a people are to assume a purposeful role in our own lives, if we are to become truly involved in today's and tomorrow's society, then we must be given the opportunity of controlling our own future. Indians resent eternal overprotection. How can we take our place in the world, ever hope to make the right choices, if we are denied the opportunity to choose at every remote chance of peril? Have no white men ever failed? Have no white men ever risen above failure, the wiser for the experience?

An aspiration that seems to puzzle and disturb the white man remains common to every Indian I have ever talked to who is on welfare. This aspiration is simply to get off relief. You'll never find a prouder Indian than one who can say, "I've never been on welfare." The fact that such a high percentage of Indians are on welfare at any given moment only sharpens the point. Indians realize that social assistance is part of the white man's world, that many white families must accept welfare. Indians accept the fact that now and then circumstances may dictate to any man that he must accept temporary help in clothing and feeding his family but, and this seems to surprise the white man, the Indian by nature finds acceptance of welfare demeaning. It is not so much the giving as the implication. When that man looks at you as he hands over the check and you reach for it, you know what his look means. It means that you aren't man enough to make your own living; it means that you aren't man enough to feed and clothe and house your own wife and children. That's when an Indian hates welfare. That's why a common dream among Indians coast to coast and border to pole is to get off welfare.

We want to get involved, but we have had only a gutful of vague philosophical government commitments to give us opportunities for involvement. To us involvement remains meaningless without the money to make it work. It's just so much Ottawa doubletalk to tell us to go ahead on any programme without proper provision for the financial, human and physical resources that are required. Involvement must mean enough money to enable Indian people to hire the professional consultants and experts necessary, without regard as to whether they are red, white or yellow. It means money to buy equipment and facilities and it means access to years and years of accumulated research documents buried deep in dusty files in the Indian Affairs offices. Only when the government is willing to back up its lip service to the ideal of Indian involvement with the necessary resources will we be able to talk in terms of a meaningful role for Indians in charting a course for our future. Until then, all statements by the federal government about involving Indians are hypothetical exercises, irrelevant, academic and utterly useless to the Indian.

We have charted the difficulties ahead; we know the obstacles. No matter how concerted an effort we make, we realize that many problems will fall only to combined Indian and non-Indian assault. We point out that to begin, some problems must be faced up to as government responsibilities.

One such major problem arises from the refusal of our present Canadian government in its most recent white paper, and of Canadian governments in the past, to honour commitments for treaties signed with the Indians. Coupled closely with this is the unwillingness of successive governments to recognize the aboriginal rights of our people.

Government after government has, in some way or another, vaguely committed itself to native rights but no government, including and particularly the one in power today, has yet committed itself to the simple honesty of fulfilling its obligations to our people as outlined in the treaties . . . . it can be noted here that as far as the Indians are concerned, there is not one treaty that has not been broken by the white man, not one treaty fulfilled.

Positive steps by the government to fulfill its treaty obligations represent one aspiration common to all Indians. It was for this reason that our people were encouraged by Prime Minister Trudeau's call for the creation of the Just Society. This brief, dazzling flare of hope, however, quickly fizzled out when Mr. Trudeau publicly announced that the federal government was not prepared to guarantee aboriginal rights and that the Canadian government considered the Indian treaties an anomaly not to be tolerated in the Just Society.

We will not trust the government with our futures any longer. Now they must listen to and learn from us.

Canadians worry about their identity. Are they too English? Are they too American? Are they French or some other kind of hybrid? Indians worry about their identity, too. For the most part they like to think of themselves as Canadians. But there are towns and cities in Canada, in every province of Canada, where an Indian dares not forget his identity as an Indian. There are towns and cities in Canada where a Canadian Indian simply dares not go.

If that seems a shocking statement to the non-Indian, it shocks Indians even more. There are towns and cities in Canada where simply being an Indian means getting a beating. Indians in such towns and cities have even been dragged out of restaurants into the streets and beaten. In such cases an Indian foolish enough to attempt to bring charges finds *himself* charged with creating a disturbance. No citizen is likely to forget his identity under such circumstances.

For the Canadian Indian the question of identity bears heavily on the kind of life a native may lead. Under Canada's mixed-up legal definition, full-blooded Indians may be classed non-Indian, and full-blooded whites can legally be Indians. The *Indian Act* defines an Indian as "a person who pursuant to this Act is registered as an Indian or is entitled to be registered as an Indian." This simplistic legalism, however, eliminates roughly 250,000 native people who, under the American system, would be recognized as Indian.

This *Indian Act* definition has been and continues to be a divisive force among Canada's natives. If you are legally an Indian, then you and your family can live on reserves and are entitled to certain limited rights. No matter how full-blooded you may be, if you are not a legal Indian, you can forget the reserve. You can't live there.

The whole silly bit about who is an Indian and who isn't came about as a result of the treaties. On the Prairies, the native people were given a choice at the time of signing as to the status they wanted. If they chose to be Indians under treaty, native people were promised certain treaty rights, including land on a reserve, perpetual hunting and fishing rights, along with myriad lesser pledges, but they were denied the right to vote or access to liquor.

The alternative was to choose script, a legal piece of paper proclaiming the victim's citizenship, providing a sum of money (it varied in different treaties) and a piece of land (the area varied). This choice gave access to liquor and the vote, the same privileges accorded any citizen of Canada.

If a man chose to give up his Indian status, he never could reclaim it. But if a native chose to become a registered or treaty Indian, he still retained a sort of horrible option. He could enfranchise. This meant and still means that a treaty or registered or legal Indian still could and still can give up his special status by applying to Ottawa for enfranchisement. This remains a pretty drastic decision for an Indian. He gains full citizenship rights, the vote, liquor (which he now can get as an Indian, anyhow) and, in theory, becomes a Canadian like anyone else. But he renounces his Indianness: he loses all treaty or aboriginal rights; he gives up forever his right to membership on a reserve and all title to his portion of resources or reserve land. He cannot return to the reserve to take up residence where the rest of his family, his relatives and his friends live.

If the parents make this choice or if an entire Indian family enfranchises, then the children of that family and all subsequent grandchildren and direct heirs lose forever the right to claim title to being Indians, at least legally. The only exception to this loss of identity occurs in maternal lineage. If any woman, Indian or non-Indian, marries a treaty or registered Indian, she automatically becomes a legal Indian; no matter whether she is red, white, yellow or black, married to a legal Indian she becomes one, too. However, it doesn't work the other way around. If an Indian woman marries a non-Indian man, she automatically forfeits her claim to be an Indian.

Just to make it more confusing, when a white or non-Indian woman becomes by reason of marriage legally an Indian, this does not mean that her children necessarily will be Indian. Under section 12, subsection (a) 4 of the *Indian Act*, effective in the 1970s, a person whose mother and paternal grandmother are non-Indian (except by right of marriage) also loses his claim to be an Indian.

This legal hocus-pocus has created many problems for the younger generation. In some instances, where full-blooded Indian families have for one reason or another enfranchised, they and their children are, in the eyes of the law, non-Indian, Métis or even white – in theory. At the same time, in the case of a white woman marrying a registered Indian, she and her children suddenly, in the eyes of the law, are Indians. Among the younger generation where pride of race once again is growing, Indians in all but law have found themselves classed as non-Indian no matter how much they want to be Indians, because parents enfranchised. Many young Indians today are being denied their birthright because someone else decided to renounce his legal claims to being Indian. They have no recourse; they never legally can reclaim their birthright.

Stan Daniels, president of the Métis Association of Alberta, puts the problem this way: "The question of my identity is hard for me to understand; on one hand, when I consider myself an Indian, and I say this, the Indian says, 'Who do you think you are: you are nothing but a white man.' And when I consider myself a white man, talk or act like one, the white man says to me, 'Who in the hell do you think you are?' You're nothing but a damned Indian.' I am a man caught in the vacuum of two cultures with neither fully accepting me."

Legalities continue to play a divisive role among Canadian Indians. Even among those who have a legal right to be Indian, further classifications complicate the matter. There is, for example, a distinction between treaty Indians and registered Indians. A treaty Indian is one whose ancestors signed a treaty with the representatives of the queen and ceded some land rights to the crown in return for specific rights. Treaties have been signed with Indians in Ontario, Manitoba, Saskatchewan, Alberta and portions of the Northwest Territories. A registered Indian is one whose ancestors signed no treaties, such as Indians in the Maritimes, in Quebec, in portions of the Northwest Territories and in British Columbia, but who did choose under the *Indian Act* to be registered as legal or registered Indians. Maritimes Indians signed *pacts of friendship* with the representatives of the queen. Many treaty Indians fear that association with Indians from non-treaty areas will jeopardize their claims to their treaty rights, while Indians from the non-treaty areas are concerned that association with treaty Indians will compromise their requests for settlement of aboriginal claims. In some cases, even minor differences between treaties can confuse and worry Indians as to their rights when they intermingle. Treaty Six carries a medicine chest promise, which in present-day usage can be considered the right to paid-up medicare. Treaties Seven and Eight, although the question of medical treatment was promised verbally, never followed through on this issue in writing. A Treaty Six Indian conceivably could lose her claims to medical care by marrying a Treaty Seven man.

Sneakier things than that have come from government offices. In fact, the government, specifically the Department of Indian Affairs and Northern Development, seems to enjoy this divisiveness and even, in many cases, to encourage it. Anything that divides the Indians makes the department stronger. No wonder no Indian in his right mind trusts the department.

Some progress is being made towards unity among Canada's native people, but much work remains to be done to tear down the inner Buckskin Curtain. It is self-definition, not this network of inhuman legalities or the recently proposed alternative of assimilation, that will foster Indian unity. All the legal definitions fail to accomplish one thing — they fail to solve the real, human problem of identity. Identity means as much to an Indian as it does to the Québecois in Trois Rivières or the Icelander in Gimli. Obviously this has no meaning for many people. They are the sort who feel that the only future for the Indian lies in assimilation. Such people see all residents of Canada as Canadians, without regard to ethnic background. As far as we are concerned these melting-pot advocates don't understand the nature of our country, let alone the nature of the native. To all too many, being Canadian simply means, *white is right*, or *be Anglo and you'll be happy*, or *be like me and all your problems will vanish*.

Other people, both Indian and non-Indian, seem to feel that being Indian means being some sort of relic out of the past, a guy with a feathered head-dress and beaded buckskin clothes, a buffalo hunter. They feel that Indianness is a thing of the past, with no relevance today. Indians who feel this way can be spotted quickly. They continually apologize for being Indian. They may be extremely successful in the white man's world, perhaps even in Canadian legislative bodies, but they always apologize for being Indian. You don't hear a man like Lincoln Alexander, MP for Hamilton, apologize for being a Negro.

Such Uncle Tomahawks have a compelling urge to go around telling other Indians to pull up their bootstraps. Once they have it made, they seem to develop a case of very bad memory as to how it was with them on the way up. They lose touch and become blind to the circumstances under which their *brothers* are living. They don't command much respect from their own people for very long. Indians can be fooled once, like anyone else, but don't try it twice.

When I attended a white school, there were a very few Indians there. None ever wore articles of Indian apparel. When winter came, I put on my mukluks. Some of the other Indian students came to me and suggested I shouldn't wear them. My mukluks called attention to the fact that I was an Indian. But I continued to wear them, not as any sort of hollow protest and not feeling particularly self-righteous — just warm. The next year more Indian students found the *courage* to wear Indian clothing in which they felt comfortable. By my third year, even the white students who could get them were wearing mukluks.

Now Indian clothing is acceptable. In fact it has become high fashion in some quarters. The only problem now is that an Indian runs the risk of being taken for a hippie if he wears his ordinary clothing.

I wear a buckskin jacket today and have for many years. I wear it first of all because it is one of the most comfortable garments I have, but I also wear it as an example to young Indians. One other reason: I got tired of being asked if I were from China or Japan or India or somewhere like that. I got tired of having people jump to the conclusion that, just because I was educated and could talk like a white man, even though I obviously am not one, that I must be an Asian. I wear my buckskin jacket because it says, *I am a Canadian Indian.*

For a long time many, many Indians accepted the white man's evaluation of them as a race and as individuals. So often were they told openly and brutally that they were no good, that they were nothing, that they came to accept this negative image. "What can we do?" one hears an Indian say. "We are just Indians." Or, "How can we talk of equality? We will always be Indians no matter what we do. The government can't just suddenly rule that we are equal and make it a fact. Will the person who hated us yesterday because we are Indian love us tomorrow because the government says he should?"

Young Indians who went off to residential schools were obviously at a disadvantage. The missionary teachers soon made them aware of it if they didn't know it when they came. It doesn't take many times being called "an ungrateful little savage" to impress your difference upon you. And those who went into the white man's schools to be integrated found their little white friends brought their homes to the classroom: "My father says all Indians are drunks; my mother says Indians are dirty and I can't play with you." Indians who went to the cities to try to make their way found themselves isolated, pointed out, penalized for being Indian. Small wonder many Indians sought to hide their Indianness. They had lost their pride. They had overlooked the one thing they had that no white man had or has or can have – Indianness.

Today the trend is the other way. Young Indians are proud of their heritage and are learning more about it. During and after World War II many of our people crossed the colour line. It was a status thing to do. They had lived in a white world; they had fought as well as the white soldier. They were accepted for the time being, at least. Many married across the colour line. Now social pressure swings the other way with Indians, and is against marrying into white society.

Of course no one can deny there still are many negative factors relating, if not to actual Indian identity, then to the popular image of our identity. Indians are sensitive. We know that we may be turned away from the odd hotel because of our colour. We know that available suites at good highrise locations suddenly are taken when we show up. We are careful about the kind of restaurant we go into. But we also know that more and more Indians are suddenly standing straighter, walking with a firmer step and finding a new pride in being Indian.

The political aspect of our identity causes misunderstanding. In a meeting with the National Indian Brotherhood, Prime Minister Trudeau seemed concerned that a possible growth of separatism might exist among Indians. It is necessary to emphasize that the question of establishing a positive Indian identity does not mean political separatism – not yet, at least, not if the white man will agree to be reasonable – nor does it mean a desire to return to the days of yesteryear. The fact remains, however, that most Indians firmly believe their identity is tied up with treaty and aboriginal rights. Many Indians believe that until such rights are honoured there can be no Indian identity to take its place with the other cultural identities of Canada.

Our identity, who we are; this is a basic question that must be settled if we are to progress. A native person in Canada cannot describe himself without basically talking about himself as a Canadian. Being Canadian is implied and understood. To an Indian, being Indian in Canada simultaneously and automatically means being Canadian. The German Canadian has a homeland called Germany; the Ukrainian has a homeland; even the French Canadian, although he may have ancestors going back three hundred years in Canadian history, has a homeland called France. The Indian's homeland is called Canada.

The challenge to Indians today is to redefine that identity in contemporary terminology. The challenge to the non-Indian society is to accept such an updated definition.

If I were to accept the bothersome term *Indian problem*, I would have to accept it in light of the fact that our most basic problem is gaining respect, respect on an individual basis that would make possible acceptance for us as an ethnic group. Before this is possible, the dignity, confidence and pride of the Indian people must be restored. No genuine Indian participation in the white world can be expected until the Indian is accepted by himself and by the non-Indian as an Indian person, with an Indian identity.

As long as Indian people are expected to become what they are not – white men – there does not and there will not exist a basis upon which they can participate in Canadian society.

Before we can demand acceptance by the white man, we must earn his respect. Before we can take our place in a larger society, we must regain our own confidence and self-respect. To do this we must be allowed to rebuild our own social institutions, torn down by their white counterparts. We must rebuild our structures of social and political leadership, demoralized and undermined for a hundred years by the Department of Indian Affairs; we must restore our family unit, shaken and shattered by the residential school system; we must rebuild communications between the younger and older generations of our people. We must recognize that the negative images of Indianness are false; the Canadian government must recognize that assimilation, no matter what they call it, will never work. Both Indian and non-Indian must realize that there is a valid, lasting Indian identity.

We are not interested, therefore, in the government's newest definition of who and what an Indian is, or must be. We have ceased to allow our identity to be a paperwork problem for members of the Department of Indian Affairs. Our people are now in the process of discovering what they are in a positive sense; Canadian society must accept us in a positive way before there can be an identification of common purpose and before true citizenship can develop. It is only when men are able to accept their differences as well as their similarities and still relate to each other with respect and dignity that a healthy society exists.

Socio-economic Status and Ethnic Origin[*]

Royal Commission on Bilingualism and Biculturalism

Income

The material advantages stemming from a high income are as obvious as they are sought after. Few indeed are those to whom money is a matter of indifference. It follows that, if there is a substantial disparity between the incomes of two groups, the less fortunate will generally have strong feelings of resentment and grievance. In most modern societies, serious income disparities figure among the prime causes of social unrest; with this in mind, we compare the positions of Canadians of French and British origin on the income scale.

Let us first consider the relative participation by Canadians of various origins in the country's total male labour force in 1961.[1] Those of British origin formed the largest proportion – 44 percent[2] of the total; Canadians of French origin were in second place with 28 percent; those of German origin made up a further 6 percent, those of Italian and Ukrainian origin approximately 3 percent each, and those of Jewish origin about 1 percent.[3] These proportions should be borne in mind in order to keep in proper perspective the relative importance of Canadians of various origins in any income, educational, or occupational category. For instance, while 23 percent of those of Ukrainian origin were farmers, only 5 percent of all farmers across Canada were Ukrainian.

We discovered a very noticeable disparity in income between Canadians of French and British origin. If the average income of the total male labour force in Canada is expressed as 100 (Table 1), those of British origin stood 10 points (110) above the national average in 1961, while those of French origin fell 14 points (86) below it. All in all, then, 24 points divided the two groups.

Comparing only the non-agricultural workers (Table 1),[4] the disparity between the income indices for those of British and French origin remained much the same as that in the total labour force, falling only slightly, from 24 to 22 points. Canadian men of British origin earned on average nearly $1,000 more in 1961 than those of French origin – $4,852 compared with $3,872.[5] Thus, in 1961, those of French origin were effectively earning about 80 percent as much as those of British origin. But the British and the French did not quite form the extremes of the income scale, despite the disparity between their average incomes; the French stood higher than those of Italian origin and the income of the British was substantially lower than that of Jewish men. Nevertheless, the gap separating those of French and British origin was much wider than that separating the French from the Italians.

[*]*Canadian Royal Commission on Bilingualism and Biculturalism Report*, Book III, Part 1, Chapter 1: "Income," pp. 16-17, Sections 36-39; "Education," pp. 25-27, Sections 60-67; "Occupation," pp. 35-36, Sections 88-92; "Ownership of Quebec Industry," pp. 53-56, Sections 121-130, 1967. Reproduced with the permission of Information Canada.

TABLE 1

Average Total Income

Average total income of the male non-agricultural labour force and of the total male labour force, by ethnic origin—Canada, 1961

	Non-agricultural Male Labour Force		Total Male Labour Force
	Dollars	Index	Index
All origins	4,414	100.0	100.0
British	4,852	109.9	109.8
French	3,872	87.7	85.8
German	4,207	95.3	103.1
Italian	3,621	82.0	81.0
Jewish	7,426	168.2	166.9
Ukrainian	4,128	93.5	86.8
Others	4,153	94.1	98.2

Source: André Raynauld, Gérald Marion, and Richard Béland, "La répartition des revenus selon les groupes ethniques au Canada."

Education

Education plays a key role in economic development. In an economy as advanced as Canada's, simple literacy is no longer enough. Rather, the minimum requirement for any person in the labour force is a good, all-round education; he must have the general knowledge and flexibility of mind to cope with the increasingly rapid changes produced by modern technology in both types and methods of work. For this reason, more and more stress is being placed on keeping students in school for a longer period of time. This trend is manifested by the recent recommendation of the United States National Commission on Technology, Automation, and Economic Progress that 14 years of free public schooling be the minimum standard henceforth.[6]

Modern industry also requires a ready supply of workers with a specialized technical education and the necessary skills to employ the latest advances in scientific method. Indeed, the writing is on the wall for the unskilled labourers. Forming 13 per cent of the male labour force in Canada in 1931, this proportion had fallen to 7 percent by 1961.

Modern industry also needs a properly trained managerial and administrative staff. The upper ranks of today's corporations include not only lawyers, engineers, and accountants, but also physical and social scientists, as well as increasing numbers of graduates in business administration. There is little room for the untrained at these levels.

If the economy of a country is dependent for its continued development on the existence of such academic qualifications as these among the labour force, then any group which is cut off from attaining these qualifications will share only marginally in the social advantages stemming from industrial progress. The key positions will not be open to them; the possibilities of developing their own cultural potential will be lessened; and material affluence will most definitely not be theirs. In other words, the socio-economic conditions for equal partnership depend in large part for their fulfilment on equality of schooling. Thus, when we compare Canadian Francophones and Anglophones on the scholastic scale, we are dealing with a matter that profoundly affects their relative positions in the Canadian society and economy, both now and in the future.

Table 2 summarizes the level of schooling for the male labour force of various ethnic origins in 1961. It shows that 54 percent of those of French origin had not passed beyond the elementary level, but for those of British origin the proportion was 31 percent, while the national average for all origins was 42 percent.

TABLE 2

Schooling

Percentage distribution of the male non-agricultural labour force, by ethnic origin and level of schooling—Canada, 1961

Ethnic Origin	None	Elementary	Secondary 1–2 years	Secondary 3–5 years	University	Total
British	0.3	30.6	25.2	31.4	12.5	100
French	0.7	53.5	21.4	18.1	6.3	100
German	*	40.1	21.8	28.5	9.2	100
Italian	*	71.0	12.8	11.9	3.0	100
Jewish	*	26.8	15.2	31.5	25.5	100
Ukrainian	*	46.7	21.3	23.0	7.9	100
Others	1.5	42.6	19.3	25.7	10.9	100
All origins	0.6	41.0	22.5	25.8	10.1	100

*Statistically insignificant.
Source: Raynauld, Marion, and Béland, "La répartition des revenus."

If Canadian men of other origins are ranked according to the proportion of those having only elementary education, their relative positions exactly mirror the ranking by average income. The men with the highest average income, those of Jewish origin, had the lowest proportion of those with no more than elementary schooling. Next were those of British origin, followed by the Canadians of German, Other, and Ukrainian origins. Those of French origin were second from bottom, outranking only those of Italian origin.

Substantially the same order is apparent if the labour force is ranked by the proportion having a university education. A very high percentage of Jewish people had a university education. In effect, one person of Jewish origin in four had been to university, while for those of British origin the ratio was one in eight, for those of French origin it was one in 16, and for those of Italian origin it was one in 32.

In the United States, the level of education is higher than in Canada. For example, at the beginning of 1965, 52 percent of the U.S. population 18 years and over had completed high school education. For the Canadian population aged 17 years and over, the proportion was only 26 percent.[7]

Occupation

The kind of work a man does to earn his living provides a good measurement of his socio-economic status. It determines in large measure the monetary rewards he receives, and it indicates whether or not he is in a position to influence the lives of others. A comparable distribution of Francophone and Anglophone Canadians along the occupational scale would reflect the existence of an equal partnership; a greater concentration of one group in the low-paying, less influential occupations would be a symptom of inequality.

However, the existence of equal partnership does not demand that the two groups be identically distributed in the occupational structure, nor does it require that there be no differences between them. In fact, at each level of the social structure there can be differences which simply reflect the preferences and cultural characteristics of each group. The absence of distinctive occupational patterns does not necessarily signify the existence of an equal partnership, just as the existence of differences is not necessarily a proof or a cause of inequality. Differences at comparable levels of the social scale do not seem to us to be very significant, but the concentration of one group in the occupations at the top of scale, and the concentration of the other group in those at the bottom, is an indication of a real socio-economic inequality.

The rapidly changing occupational structure of the country is an important factor in this analysis. The relative importance of the various occupations in an economy centred on agriculture is obviously very different from that in a largely industrial economy. As Canada moves through the stages of economic development, some occupations are declining in significance while others are rising. If one section of the population is disproportionately clustered in the declining occupations, while another group is well to the fore in the expanding occupations, then any present inequality in the sharing of wealth and influence will become much more acute, unless some remedial action is taken. The distribution of occupations between Canadians of French origin and those of British origin is, therefore, a measurement of both the existing and the likely future state of the partnership.

A broad picture of the occupational distribution can be obtained by means of an index expressing the distribution of the labour force among various occupational categories ranked according to the average income they command. Table 3 gives the indices for Canadians of different ethnic origins in the male labour force.

TABLE 3

Occupational Status
Indices of occupational status[a] for the male labour force, by ethnic origin— Canada, 1961

British	1.000	Jewish	1.312
French	0.925	Ukrainian	0.892
German	0.913	Others	0.933
Italian	0.892		

[a] For the purposes of calculating this index, 13 occupational categories were identified.
Source: Raynauld, Marion, and Béland, "La répartition des revenus."

The table shows that the labour force of British origin is more strongly concentrated in the high-income occupations than that of French origin: if the index for the British is taken as 1.000, that of the French is 0.925. The position of the French is above the levels for the Canadians of German and Ukrainian origin, although the French rank lower on the income scale than these two groups.[8] The labour force of French origin, in other words, ranks higher on an occupational scale than it does on the income scale. The occupational index for those of Jewish origin, like their income index, is exceptionally high – about one-third again as high as the index for those of British origin.[9]

As Table 4 shows, the Canadian male labour force was essentially an urban one in 1961. Farming occupations accounted for only 12 percent of the labour force, having shrunk from 34 percent in 1931 and 20 percent in 1951. Another diminishing category was that of unskilled labour; it accounted for 13 percent of the labour force in 1931, but only 6 percent in 1961. The proportion in the craftsman category rose from 17 to 29 percent between 1931 and 1951, but this increase slowed down to less than 1 percent between 1951 and 1961. Two categories which are clearly expanding are the managerial, and the professional and technical. Between 1931 and 1961, the former rose from 6 to 10 percent and the latter from 4 to 8 percent. In order to show more clearly the part played by Canadians of various origins in the country's transition to an advanced industrial society, we shall omit farming from the following discussion and concentrate on the four trend-setting occupational categories: managers, professionals and technicians, craftsmen and production workers, and labourers.[10]

In occupational distribution, the differences between those of British and French origin are quite substantial. In 1961, 21 percent of the British, compared with 14 percent of the French, were in the top occupational brackets (professionals and managers); in the two blue-collar categories (craftsmen and unskilled labourers), those of French origin had the larger proportion: 39 percent, compared with 30 percent for those of British origin.

In [Table 4] . . . we have presented the proportions which Canadians of six different origins formed in these four occupational categories. The most noticeable item is the consistency of the order formed by the six with respect to their concentrations in each category. In both of the high-paying, expanding categories,[11] those of Jewish origin had the highest concentration, followed serially by the British, Germans, French, Ukrainians, and Italians. The concentrations were reversed in the blue-collar categories, with the Italians considerably the highest, followed by those of Ukrainian, French, German, British, and Jewish origin.

Thus, in the expanding professional and managerial categories it was those of British and Jewish origin who enjoyed the greatest advantage. In comparison, the French and Italians did poorly in these occupations; indeed, these groups had been losing ground over the past three decades.

John Porter[12] has shown that, between 1931 and 1961, the positions of Canadians of French and Italian origin decreased respectively from 0.8 to 1.9 points and 3.3 to 5.2 points below the national average in the professional and financial category.[13] Men of British and Jewish origin also moved further away from the average, but in the opposite direction. Thus, Canadians of British origin progressed slightly from 1.6 to 2.0 points above the national average, while those of Jewish origin advanced more strongly, moving from 2.2 to 7.4 points above the national average.

Much the same pattern can be observed in Quebec, but in a more striking form.[14] Quebec residents of British ancestry were only 3 points above the provincial average in the professional and managerial categories in 1931; by 1961 they exceeded it by almost 9 points. Those of French origin were 1 point below

TABLE 4

Occupational Structure

Percentage distribution of the male labour force, by ethnic origin and occupation—Canada, 1961

	All Origins		British	French	German	Italian	Jewish	Ukrainian	Other
	Number	%							
Professional and technical	356,578	7.6	9.3	5.9	6.1	2.8	13.7	5.8	6.9
Managerial	481,379	10.2	12.1	7.6	8.3	6.6	39.4	7.1	9.5
Clerical	324,811	6.9	8.2	6.7	5.0	3.7	6.8	5.7	5.1
Sales	263,229	5.6	6.6	5.2	4.4	3.2	14.1	3.5	4.2
Service	400,399	8.5	9.2	7.7	6.4	8.5	2.6	7.3	9.6
Transport and communications	354,736	7.5	8.0	8.9	6.2	4.7	2.8	6.4	5.5
Craftsmen and production workers	1,354,594	28.8	25.5	31.4	32.5	43.7	15.6	29.6	29.8
Labourers	294,059	6.2	4.6	7.5	5.6	19.2	1.1	6.9	6.8
Farmers	573,098	12.2	10.8	10.8	21.0	2.7	0.5	23.0	15.8
Other primary	179,593	3.9	3.1	5.3	2.3	2.3	0.0	2.5	4.6
Not stated	123,042	2.6	2.6	3.0	3.0	2.6	3.4	2.2	2.2
All occupations		100.0	100.0	100.0	100.0	100.0	100.0	100.0	100.0
Number	4,705,518		2,071,417	1,303,280	297,003	137,071	49,820	135,987	710,940

Source: Census of Canada, 1961, Cat. 94–515.

average in participation in 1931 and 2 points below average in 1961. At the other end of the occupational scale the positions were reversed. In the same 30-year period, the British moved from 6 to 9 points below the average in the skilled and unskilled labour categories. Those of French origin, on the other hand, remained at less than 1 point above the provincial average.

In each of the provinces, the 1961 distribution according to ethnic origin among the occupations was much the same as at the national level. For instance, in Ontario – the most highly developed province – those of French and British origin in each of the occupational categories had approximately the same positions as they had in Canada as a whole. The only large discrepancy appeared among those of Ukrainian origin; because of their heavy concentration in the Prairies and on the farms, their positions in Ontario and in the country as a whole were quite different.

Ownership of Quebec Industry[15]

The individuals and groups who own or control industrial enterprises play a vital role in the economy. Generally, these are people of high income and a fair degree of economic power. Owners of business constitute an élite group, in which Canadians of both official languages should be represented if equality in the economic field is to be achieved. We have singled out for consideration the industries of Quebec because – given the composition of this province's population – it is here, more than in any other part of Canada, that French-speaking Canadians should be most in evidence as participants in this economic élite.

The business establishments in Quebec were classified according to whether the owners were Francophone Canadians, Anglophone Canadians, or foreigners.[16] The main body of the analysis will focus on the manufacturing sector, but we will begin by considering the whole of Quebec industry. One measure of the relative status of the three ownership groups is a comparison of the numbers of workers employed by each group.

Taking all the nine industrial sectors listed in Table 5 together, establishments owned by Francophone Canadians employed nearly half (47 percent) of the provincial labour force in 1961. However, if the individual sectors are examined, it will be seen that the distribution was very uneven, with a heavy concentration in two areas. Roughly half the labour force working for Francophone Canadian interests (24 percent of the total Quebec labour force) was concentrated in agriculture and service industries, the other half (23 percent of the total labour force) being divided among the remaining seven industrial sectors.

This concentration in two sectors becomes even clearer when it is seen that 91 percent of the total agricultural labour force and 71 percent of that in the service industries were employed in Francophone Canadian establishments. The other seven industrial sectors had much lower proportions. In the mining industry, less than 7 percent of the labour force worked for Francophone Canadians. A fifth of those engaged in manufacturing were employed in Francophone establishments, a quarter in financial institutions, a little more than a third in transportation and communications and in wholesale trade, and about a half in retail trade and construction.

276

Only the establishments in the manufacturing sector will be studied in terms of output, number of employees, productivity, size of payroll, and value of sales outside Quebec. This sector accounted for 27 percent of the total Quebec labour force and is thus the largest of the industrial sectors.

TABLE 5

Ownership of Establishments

Size of establishments owned by Francophone Canadians, Anglophone Canadians, and foreign interests in selected industrial sectors, measured by numbers employed—Quebec, 1961

| | Employees | Percentage of Labour Force in Establishments Owned by | | | |
	Number (thousands)	Franco- phone Canadians	Anglo- phone Canadians	Foreign Interests	Total
Agriculture	131.2	91.3	8.7	0.0	100
Mining	25.9	6.5	53.1	40.4	100
Manufacturing	468.3	21.8	46.9	31.3	100
Construction	126.4	50.7	35.2	14.1	100
Transportation and communications	102.4	37.5	49.4	13.1	100
Wholesale trade	69.3	34.1	47.2	18.7	100
Retail trade	178.7	56.7	35.8	7.5	100
Finance	62.2	25.8	53.1	21.1	100
Services	350.9	71.4	28.6	0.0	100
All industries[a]	1,515.3	47.3	37.7	15.0	100

Source: Raynauld, "La propriété des entreprises au Québec."
[a] Excludes forestry, fishing and trapping, the public sector, and unspecified industries.

Industrial output is measured by the statistical concept of *value added*. This is the value of the produced goods less the cost of energy and raw materials: it represents the transformation wrought by an establishment upon the products or materials it purchases. Table 6 presents the value added in each manufacturing sector, distributed according to the categories of ownership that we have established.

Table 5 showed the weak position of Francophone Canadian manufacturers: they employed only 22 percent of those working in manufacturing industries. Table 6 shows that these same establishments accounted for a still smaller proportion – only 15 percent – of total value added in the manufacturing industry in Quebec. In the establishments owned by Anglophone Canadians, 47 percent of the labour force produced 43 percent of the value added. In contrast, establishments under foreign ownership employed only 31 percent of the manufacturing labour force but produced 42 percent of the value added. Francophone Canadians predominated in only one sector – the wood industry; they also accounted for nearly half the value added of the Quebec leather industry.[17]

In contrast, there were nine sectors – including the clothing, textile, printing and publishing, and beverage industries – in which Anglophone Canadian interests accounted for 50 percent or more of the industrial output. In another nine – including the industries manufacturing petroleum products, non-ferrous metals, transportation equipment, and chemical products – the foreign interests had a comparable representation.

Francophone Canadian establishments produced an average value added of $790,000 a year, those owned by Anglophone Canadians $3,310,000, and foreign-owned establishments $5,640,000. The value added by a Francophone Canadian establishment was thus on average a quarter the size of that added by an Anglophone Canadian establishment, and one-seventh of that for a foreign establishment. In all manufacturing sectors, the value added by a Francophone Canadian establishment was smaller than that for a foreign-owned establishment and, with the exception of the leather industry, than that for an Anglophone Canadian establishment as well.

When the number of employees, rather than value added, was used as a measurement of size, the typical Francophone Canadian manufacturing enterprise was again smaller than its Anglophone Canadian or foreign-owned equivalent. In fact, the average number of employees was 94 in Francophone Canadian, 145 in Anglophone Canadian, and 332 in foreign-owned establishments. In average number of employees, Francophone Canadian establishments were below foreign-owned establishments in all sectors, and above Anglophone Canadian establishments in only four of the 22 sectors for which information was available.

TABLE 6

Ownership of Establishments in the Manufacturing Industry
Size of manufacturing establishments owned by Francophone Canadians, Anglophone Canadians, and foreign interests, measured by value added—Quebec, 1961

	Percentage of Total Value Added in Establishments Owned by			
	Francophone Canadians	Anglophone Canadians	Foreign Interests	Total
Food	30.9	32.0	38.1	100
Beverage	4.7	64.9	30.4	100
Tobacco products	0.9	31.2	67.9	100
Rubber	8.0	37.5	54.5	100
Leather	49.4	46.3	4.3	100
Textile	2.1	68.3	29.6	100
Knitting mills	24.7	53.2	22.1	100
Clothing	8.2	88.6	3.2	100
Wood	84.0	13.2	2.8	100
Furniture and fixtures	39.4	53.6	7.0	100
Paper	4.8	53.3	41.9	100
Paper products	22.0	41.2	33.8	100
Printing and publishing	28.2	65.7	6.1	100
Iron and steel	11.7	28.9	59.4	100
Non-ferrous metals	3.7	11.6	84.7	100
Metal fabricating	23.7	35.9	40.4	100
Machinery	18.3	17.0	64.7	100
Transportation equipment	6.4	14.4	79.2	100
Electrical products	6.6	58.0	35.4	100
Non-metallic mineral products	14.8	51.2	34.0	100
Petroleum and coal products	0.0	0.0	100.0	100
Chemical and medical products	6.5	16.4	77.1	100
Precision instruments	4.6	23.5	71.9	100
Miscellaneous	24.5	41.3	34.2	100
All industries	15.4	42.8	41.8	100

Source: Raynauld, "La propriété des entreprises au Québec."

Footnotes

1. We generally consider only the male labour force because of difficulties in interpreting the income statistics for the female labour force.

2. Throughout the text, percentages have been rounded to the nearest whole number.

3. Those of German, Ukrainian, and Italian origin were selected for individual study because they formed the next three largest segments of the Canadian population after those of British and French origin. Canadians of Jewish origin were included because they constituted one of the larger groups in Quebec and particularly in the Montreal metropolitan area.

4. The average income of the total male labour force naturally includes those incomes derived from agricultural occupations. However, because of the techniques employed by the Census of Canada, the data on agricultural incomes are not strictly comparable with those for incomes received by the non-agricultural labour force. Consequently unless otherwise stated, we have not considered the agricultural labour force.

5. There is limited data available on median as opposed to average, incomes. (The median is the value in the exact centre of a scale of values ranked according to size.) The median incomes of the two groups are $4,300 and $3,600 respectively. The disparity is now only $700, or 16 percent, while the disparity in their average incomes is $980, or 20 percent.

6. *Technology and the American Economy*, Report of the National Commission on Technology, Automation, and Economic Progress, I, Washington, D.C., 1966, p. 110.

7. Canada, Dominion Bureau of Statistics, *Educational Attainment of the Canadian Population and Labour Force: 1960-1965*, by Frank J. Whittingham, Special Labour Force Studies, No. 1, Cat. 71-505, Ottawa, 1966. On page 18 the study cautions that "Because of data limitations it was necessary to compare the educational attainment of the United States population 18 years and over as of March, 1965 with the Canadian population 17 years and over as of February, 1965. . . . This comparison should also be treated with caution because of differences in the educational systems between the two countries and differences in the questions used to ascertain level of education in the two countries."

8. *See* . . . Table 1 [in Income section].

9. B. R. Blishen, using 1951 census figures, ranked the various occupations according to income and level of schooling and obtained results similar to ours. In the upper-levels occupations, those of Jewish origin had an index decisively above the levels for the rest of the labour force. They were followed in order by those of British, French, German, Italian, and Ukrainian origin. *See* B. R. Blishen, "The Construction and Use of an Occupational Class Scale," *Canadian Journal of Economics and Political Science*, XXIV, No. 4, Toronto, 1958, pp. 519-25.

10. The service occupations—whose rapid expansion is considered a prime characteristic of the post-industrial society—include in this context all people not directly engaged in producing goods. For example, medical and legal occupations would fall into this broad definition of services. The census occupational category of services is far narrower, covering only such people as policemen, firemen, waiters, entertainers, barbers, and funeral directors. Because of the restricted and unrepresentative nature of the census category, we have limited our analysis to four census categories: managerial occupations, including managers in specific functions such as advertising, credit, and purchasing, and owners and managers classified by industry; professional and technical occupations, including engineers, teachers, health professionals (physicians, nurses, etc.), artists, clergy, social welfare workers, photographers, librarians, etc.; craftsmen and production workers, including blue collar workers identifiable by function, such as bakers, shoemakers, bookbinders, welders, painters, etc.; and labourers.

11. In 1961 the average incomes of managers and professionals were $6,833 and $6,578 respectively. At the other end of the scale, the craftsmen were earning $3,723 and the unskilled labourers $2,257.

12. *The Vertical Mosaic: An Analysis of Social Class and Power in Canada*. Toronto, 1965, p. 87.

13. The figures in this and the next paragraph should be treated with caution since occupational categories vary slightly from one census to another.

14. Yvon Lussier, "La Division du Travail Selon l'Origine au Québec, 1931-1961," unpublished M.A. thesis, University of Montreal, 1967. The author does not explain how he overcame the difficulties of comparing data from different censuses.

15. This chapter is based on Andre Raynauld, "La Propriété des Entreprises au Québec," a study prepared for the R.C.B.&B..

16. For definitions of enterprises and establishments, and an explanation of the method used to place them in these categories, *see* notes on the Reynauld study in Appendix VII, [not presented here].

17. The wood industry is largely made up of sawmills and *sash and door* factories; the leather industry includes tanneries and factories producing shoes, handbags, and the like.

Quebec Since Duplessis[*]

Robert Cliche

When Quebec awakened from its long slumber in 1960, there were explosions in all fields of our province. It is said that when someone is sleeping, his brain keeps working sub-consciously. Upon reflection, it is evident that this was the case with Quebec. For twenty years, our subconscious mind worked and on the day when the quiet revolution started, the province of Quebec was no longer *unanime*. The explosions touched all fields, and we finally became aware that the French fact had been contained within a specific geographic area, yet had become a nation.

In the field of the arts, our painters have rapidly gained recognition. Our song writers perform on stages all over the world, singing Quebec. Our writers have their books published in Paris in ever-increasing numbers. These books are translated into several languages and prove that the written language of Quebec can contribute to contemporary French literature. Using Quebec as a backdrop, our artists are able to attain universal scope.

In the field of politics, Quebec discovered that its best tool was the provincial government. The word Socialism, long taboo, was no longer feared as the government moved to the left by socializing certain key industries. We were generally becoming aware that our problems could be solved by our government, our social values could be protected, and our desire for *épanouissement* could be developed and translated into reality by parliamentary institutions controlled by ourselves.

However, I would not like to fall into the error that many commentators have perpetuated, in talking of a quiet revolution. First of all, it is not so quiet. Every morning when I wake up, I wonder what kind of a bomb, political, social or even a real bomb, may possibly explode. I believe there is an ever-present element of potential violence, as is always the case wherever there is radical social change. By this, I wish merely to point out that the phrase *The Quiet Revolution* is more obscuring than illuminating.

The complex, evolving reality of present-day Quebec does not fit easily into one formula. There is not just one change going on, there are several, and our future depends on the way these changes interact with each other. If we have to reduce this reality to a few categories, I will speak of two revolutions, one national and one social. We might have to make room for a third, for beyond these two lies a crisis in our fundamental beliefs in that which has been the very bedrock of French-Canadian society. It is now being called into question. We used to think of ourselves as a stable society, but we are a society ridden by doubt and even anguish as we search for a new road.

The revolution, about which we hear most often, is a national one. It is true that there has been a national reawakening in Quebec, which has surprised all observers. But I prefer to speak of a reawakening because we are not witnessing simply another wave of old-style nationalism. On the contrary, the new national consciousness represents a break with the past, or at least, with the primary traditions of French-Canadian thought.

Formerly, many English Canadians thought that our nationalism was a product of our backwardness. We were nationally sick because we were an isolated society, partly cut off from the great movements of North American society and from its intellectual and political currents, resisting those developments, where we could not totally avoid them, as we tried to resist organization. It is true that traditional nationalism was a product of that society. However, our national consciousness is a dimension of our existence as a group. It will not disappear as long as we flourish, a community of people, of French language, afloat in a sea of English speakers.

That nationalism, the traditional type, disappeared because it was based on an illusion which held that French Canada already had all the crucial things which counted – the French language, the sophisticated culture, the true faith. It was felt that all we needed to do was to preserve these values from the contamination of materialistic North America, from that race of shop-keepers which was busy making money and acquiring the real power to shape our destiny.

It is with a sense of bitterness, of betrayal, that French Canadians look back now on the purveyors of these myths. This fact can help to explain the third revolution to which I alluded, the reversal of our traditional beliefs.

These illusions have something to do with our present plight, together with the economic domination which English-speaking people attained in Quebec itself. In the past the big argument has been as to which factor was the more responsible, French-Canadian illusions, or Anglo-Saxon prejudice, but today this debate would be sterile and futile. Our present national consciousness is not interested in this endless obsessional autopsy of the past.

We have discovered that the two main forces which are presiding over the emancipation of a group are socialism and nationalism. What interests us are today's facts and they reveal French Canada as a developing society. What does this mean? This means that more and more of our people are working in cities, in industry, in commerce, in communications, or in some occupation that is integrated into the larger economy of North America.

French Canada is ceasing to be a separate society, living according to its own rhythm outside the mainstream of world history. This development is desired by our own people. They are working to further it, and yet, until recently it has been carried on in conditions which demanded from us a virtual cultural extinction. The English-speaking establishment of central Canada, for the promotion of whose interests this country has been run for the last century, has had such control over the economy of Quebec that they could extort a condition of virtual assimilation from all those who aspired to enter any position of responsibility. Since no one speaks English better than those whose native tongue is English, there was a time when a French Canadian had trouble getting a job even of foreman. There was time when all union negotiations and political contracts in many industries were carried on and drafted in English, even though all the workers were French-speaking.

These things are rare today, but we still have companies, like Noranda Mines, to remind us what bigotry and small-mindedness can do to procure the frustration of a whole people. If French Canada is to realize its full potential it must be possible for our people to undertake this development in their own language. This means not only the end of discrimination against French Canadians. It also means the making over of an industrial economy in Quebec so that it reflects, not the language of the few owners (many of whom are still not Canadians), but rather the language of the majority of our people. It is absurd that a French-Canadian engineer working in Montreal should have to make out his plans and write his reports in English. It is absurd that a French copywriter should draft advertising copy which is the simple translation of lines drafted on Madison Avenue. All this is worse than absurd. It is, in the long run, fatal to our culture.

You can see, therefore, why the facts reflect themselves in national consciousness, a consciousness of the great backwardness of our society in many respects, our need for development, coupled with determination that this development will be our own, and will allow us fuller self-expression and not cramp us into still narrower cultural margins. It must contribute to that contemporary collective culture, without which the lives of millions of our people will remain stunted and incomplete. In taking up this task, you must realize that we are not looking backwards over our shoulders. It is not just to be true to our fathers that we do this but to be true to ourselves and to our children.

The only creative response to our present predicament is one which allows the national and social aspirations into one coherent charter for progress for French Canada. This means a progressive Quebec, but this goal also demands a progressive Canada that must become a genuine instrument of both of the great nations which made up the country. This indicates the need for basic change. The federal government must become genuinely bilingual, in the sense that French-speaking people can work there as easily as the English. The position of French Canadians outside of Quebec must cease to be that of second-class Canadians.

I've spoken up to now of the aspirations of Quebec. What are those of Canada? To put it another way, what does the true revolution in Quebec mean for Canadian solidarity? This is a strange country. We are not naturally united by race, language, or geography as some countries are. We can find our unity only in common purposes. We started out with a common negative goal of not being Americans, but not just any purpose will do.

In the past, Canada has been run only to promote the interest of the financial and industrial establishment of central Canada, mainly located in Ontario, with the result that it is just not our province which has felt alienation. The Prairies and the Maritimes also feel exploited and neglected by the power at the centre of Canada. To correct this alienation, we need a new alliance among the progressive elements of this country, which you find only in scattered socialist movements.

Personally, the answer to all our problems is based on the principle which unites those who believe in socialism. Then, we will be able to rally around common purposes, then our functions will be united by common denominators, then will we know that Canadians speak the same language. This can be the basis for a new unity, for real solidarity which touches the people of the country, one which does not need to be supported by the empty rhetoric of politicians, and a unity which does not rob us of our different identities but which makes them more real. This is the kind of unity we are fighting for.

The F. L. Q.*

The Montreal Star

A Federal Royal Commission Examined Canada's Two Founding Peoples and Diagnosed A Crisis

The B and B Commission (sometimes called the Bye and Bye Commission because of the duration of its study) held hearings in all parts of Canada and ordered original research into unknown aspects of language, living standards, education, and ethnic income.

The Commission rushed out a first, preliminary report in February 1965. "Canada," it said, "without being fully conscious of the fact, is passing through the greatest crisis in its history."

In a succession of reports since then the B and B Commission has produced documentary evidence for nearly all the intuitive grievances that impelled the FLQ towards its desperate course.

The French-Canadian, it discovered, was near the bottom of the income ladder, even in his own province of Quebec where he is in a majority. In 1961 unilingual English-speaking Quebecers had an average income of 5,502 dollars; bilingual Quebecers averaged 4,772 dollars; unilingual French-speaking Quebecers averaged 3,099 dollars. The only ethnic groups with lower average incomes than the French-Canadians were the Italians and the native Indians.

French language and education had been discouraged and suppressed in other provinces. No province offered its French-speaking minorities anything like the rights and privileges Quebec offered its English-speaking minority.

The status of French in the federal capital explained much of the distrust and disinterest of French-Canadians towards Ottawa. Government business was conducted almost entirely in English. French school and cultural facilities were lacking. The best posts in government, the best jobs in industry, even in Quebec, were virtually closed to anyone who could not speak English well.

French-Canadians, for a number of complicated reasons, many of their own making, were not in fact Canadian citizens of the first order. Collectively they were and still are disadvantaged.

Still, the Commission thought it was not too late for changes which would make French-Canadians feel at home in Canada and make equality of opportunity something more than an election slogan.

*"Seven Years of Terrorism – The FLQ," by James Stewart in *The Montreal Star*, 1970. Reprinted with the permission of *The Montreal Star*.

The FLQ, in those early days when independence rather than the world Marxist revolution was its motive force, thought it was already too late. For them, independence was the only answer, and violence and terror were the means to awaken a sleeping population to awareness of its servility and alienation.

In circulation that summer of 1963 was "A Message from the FLQ to the Nation." It contained the customary revolutionary call to arms and the independence or death slogans. But it also contained a polished review of Canadian history and the current status of French-Canadians. The federal government, it pointed out, had jurisdiction over all the vital political levers – the economy, foreign trade, defence, banking, immigration, criminal law. In the federal parliament, English-speaking Canadians, it was claimed, had a constitutional majority which they used to maintain and accentuate the inferiority of Quebecers.

> Whenever the interests of Anglo-Saxons and Quebecers come into conflict, Quebec's interests are inevitably discounted. Whether militarily through conscription, demographically through assimilation policies, or internationally through the total supremacy of the English-speaking in diplomatic fields, always, without exception, the Ottawa government has acted in the interests of Anglo-Saxons to the detriment of Quebecers. At times, even force has been used. The blood of our people has been spilled for the benefit of colonial finance.

The message noted that eighty percent of the Quebec economy was controlled by foreign interests. "We supply the labour, they bank the profits." The author of this message saw the whole history of Canada as a long process of assimilation of the French, a process which could only be stopped now by revolution and independence.

> Even socially Quebec is a colonized country. We are eighty percent of the population but the English language dominates practically everywhere. Little by little French is being relegated to the realm of folklore while English is becoming the working language. . . . The colonialists consider us to be inferior beings and they do not hesitate to tell us so.

In rather less heated language, the B and B Commission would soon be saying very similar things. These are grievances lying in the hearts of many French-Canadians. The people shared at least that much with the FLQ, even if they could not condone the resort to terror.

The Story of a Canadian Revolution

Hardly anyone was prepared for the quantum jump in terrorism that electrified Quebec and all Canada in October 1970. Perhaps we should have been prepared. If you write down, one after another, all the deeds and declarations of the Front de Libération du Québec over the past seven years, you compile a catalogue of violence that recognizes no conventional limits.

But it would be no more than a catalogue, a selection of half-forgotten products of seven years of blasting, robbing, and raiding by the FLQ in the name of Quebec independence and the global socialist revolution: seven people dead, many injured: a bomb planted, on the average, every ten days.

A record of systematic violence, yes, but not a reign of terror, never an irreversible challenge to peace and order: to most Montrealers, in fact, not much more than intermittent spasms in the slow current of getting and spending, living and loving.

Everything changed with the kidnapping of James Cross and Pierre Laporte; changed utterly when Laporte was strangled with the religious chain he wore around his neck.

The taking and killing of hostages is an act of war and rebellion at least as old as civilization. The FLQ, impelled by God knows what psychic charges, was in full rebellion against the lawful governments of Quebec and Canada. A few desperate men had a fatal grip on a society that by almost any standard is as free, open, and politically advanced as any in the world.

For better or worse, the governments of Quebec and Canada refused to meet the FLQ's demands for the release of twenty-three "political prisoners."

The FLQ answered in a note found on the evening of October 17: "Pierre Laporte, Minister of Unemployment and Assimilation, was executed at 6:18 tonight by the Dieppe Cell (Royal 22nd). We Shall Conquer. FLQ."

The body was found a short time later, stuffed into the trunk of the car in which Laporte, Quebec's Minister of Labour and Immigration, had been abducted exactly a week earlier.

The FLQ was born in late 1962 out of the socialist and separatist ferment in Quebec colleges and universities. It attracted young French-Canadians impatient to separate Quebec from the rest of Canada, and it drew inspiration from the FLN in Algeria and the Cuban revolution.

Loosely organized, cellular, clandestine, apparently without a permanent active leadership, the FLQ has been difficult to contain, but has often been crippled by arrests. Each time it has found new recruits, not only dedicated to independence, but increasingly committed to the international theology of revolution.

The FLQ is and always has been more a community of instincts and ideas than a tight organization. It is secret, yet open to almost anyone who cared to bomb or smash in its name. Wherever two or three were gathered together, there a new cell could be born. One cell would not necessarily know what others were doing. There seems never to have been any real hierarchy or coherent conspiracy. Most members of the cell alleged to have kidnapped Pierre Laporte, for example, were in Texas when James Cross was kidnapped. They rushed back to carry out the Laporte abduction in haste and apparently on their own initiative. The members of the FLQ shared not so much a plan of action as a system of action and a general attitude.

The FLQ gets intellectual nourishment from the standard international sources – Marx, Marcuse, Mao, Che, and Carlos Marighella. It also has its own dangerously brilliant Marxist theoretician in Montreal-born journalist Pierre Vallières, even though he has spent most of the last four years in jail.

In ransom notes following the October 5 abduction of British trade commissioner James Cross from his Montreal home, the FLQ trumpeted its solidarity with the world's liberation movements – the Black Panthers and the Weathermen, the Palestine commandos, Viet Cong, Latin American guerrillas, and the Catholics of Northern Ireland.

Along with the declarations of solidarity came the FLQ's seven demands to be met in exchange for the life of the forty-nine-year-old British diplomat: release of twenty-three prisoners; transportation to Cuba or Algeria; $500,000 in gold bars; reinstatement of postal drivers who lost their jobs when the Post Office took over a private contract; broadcast and publication of the FLQ manifesto; cessation of police activity; identification of a supposed informer who led police to another FLQ cell.

Authorities rejected these demands, offering instead safe conduct from Canada for the kidnappers if they released their hostage. Another FLQ cell then intervened, apparently on impulse (they purchased their weapons only that day). The Chénier Cell kidnapped Laporte to reinforce the full ransom demands of the first cell.

Quebec authorities called in the Canadian Army, rejected the ransom demands, then on October 16 asked the federal government to proclaim the War Measures Act to meet a state of apprehended insurrection. The proclamation outlawed the FLQ and suspended many civil rights.

Laporte was killed the following day.

At the time of writing, James Cross was still missing but believed to be alive and well. The government offer of safe conduct for his kidnappers was still available whenever they chose to release their hostage. Police issued warrants for six men for the kidnapping of Cross and Laporte but only one – nineteen-year-old Bernard Lortie, a student – had been arrested. Lortie gave an inquest a full account of how he, along with two brothers, Paul and Jacques Rose, and Francis Simard, kidnapped Laporte and held him in a house at St. Hubert, near Montreal. Lortie testified he had no personal knowledge of the death of Pierre Laporte or of the kidnapping of James Cross.

Shakespeare Non, Molière Oui

Those days in October traumatized the Canadian people. The FLQ had committed an act of pure revolution. The country stood firm against it, but at great cost.

Some civil liberties were suspended, dozens of people arrested, held without charge, and then released. One man had been murdered. Another might meet the same fate at any moment.

After the horror came a train of guilt. The FLQ had fed on grievances deep in the consciousness of most Quebecers. Had everything possible really been done to make the French-Canadian as secure in his life and language in Quebec as, for example, the English-Canadian is in Ontario? Had everything possible been done to alter those old conditions which burden Quebeckers with a higher than average share of poverty and unemployment, a lower than average income?

In all the heave and tumble of Quebec's quiet revolution, its sudden awakening and search for collective identity, these questions have often been lost in the fog of rhetoric. No one, least of all the FLQ, has been called upon to be precise, to give clear definitions of words and goals.

Some of this was unavoidable. Quebec and Canada were groping towards a new relationship which no one could define in advance. The air was full of words with little meaning, or with so many meanings that it amounted to the same thing: revolution, biculturalism, one Canada, two nations, special status, national unity, co-operative federalism, constitutional reform.

It was all one piece, a seamless garment of rhetoric. Not much distinction was made between children shouting "Shakespeare Non, Molière Oui," and the pledge to eliminate all collaborators, made in the FLQ's very first "Notice to the Population of the State of Quebec," in 1963.

It was like a giant community quilting party, with everyone adding bits of colour and strips of cloth, but no one paying much attention to the design that was emerging.

It is easy now to look back seven or eight years and trace the strand of blood and violence that was being woven so diligently into the design. We think of the silent throttling of Pierre Laporte, and hear again in the mind the bombs or guns that killed Jeanne St. Germain, Jean Corbo, Thérèse Morin, Alfred Pinisch, Leslie MacWilliams, Wilfred O'Neil.

At the time it was less easy to put it all in context. Quebec, after all, was asserting itself in every way. Montreal was full of life and excitement and new architectural splendors. It was civilized, prosperous by world standards, tolerant, creative, opening itself to all the nations at Expo 67, the world exhibition in Montreal. A good many people in the early sixties tried to channel this evolution towards an independent Quebec. A handful of impatient young people in the independence movement decided they couldn't wait for electoral sanction.

They became the FLQ.

"Look, They Can't Even Fire Me in My Own Language!"

The death in 1959 of the authoritarian Quebec Premier Maurice Duplessis had released the pent-up energies and emotions of the Quebec people. The following year Jean Lesage and his Liberals won the provincial election and the province plunged into a furious transformation of its ancient social and political forms. With the general awakening came the re-awakening of the movement for separation of Quebec from Canada, a movement that had sometimes slept but never died in the two centuries since the British conquest of Quebec. At least three formal separatist parties were in being in the early sixties, one of them headed by Marcel Chaput, a former chemist at the Defence Research Board in Ottawa. Chaput became a temporary folk hero when he was fired for taking unofficial leave to make speeches in favour of independence. As he left his post, Chaput waved a letter at waiting reporters and said, "Look, they can't even fire me in my own language." His letter of dismissal was in English.

The first popular protests against federal institutions were made against the state-owned Canadian National Railways. The CNR had erected a new hotel in downtown Montreal and had obtained permission from Queen Elizabeth of Canada and the United Kingdom (Canada's head of state), to name it the Queen Elizabeth Hotel. CNR President Donald Gordon had also made some unfortunate remarks about being unable to find competent French-Canadians to fill senior positions on his railroad.

Separatists took to the streets in the first major demonstration Montreal had seen in years. They marched in front of the hotel shouting independence slogans, burned a Canadian Red Ensign, and an effigy of Donald Gordon. It felt good, but not good enough for some.

At the end of October 1962, a small group of separatists formed a revolutionary committee to speed independence by strategic violence and if necessary by arms. Recruitment was slow, and there was more talk than action. The Réseau de Résistance, named after the wartime French resistance group, was organized to stock arms and explosives and plan for several months before acting.

Even this was too slow for some of the hasty hearts, especially the young men who later claimed to be the founders of the FLQ. By the end of February 1963, these men had decided it was time to act. They broke away from the Réseau and the FLQ was born. A little more than a week later, on the night of March 7-8, the new terrorists blazed into action. They hit three Canadian Army military establishments in Montreal with Molotov cocktails. The mysterious letters *FLQ* had been painted on the walls before the bombings. The FLQ had launched three rather damp squibs against the armed forces, but its propaganda effect was considerable. The next day the news media got copies of the FLQ's first notice to the population, entitled, "Revolution by the People for the People."

Notice to the Population of the State of Quebec

The Quebec Liberation Front (FLQ) is a revolutionary movement of volunteers ready to die for the political and economic independence of Quebec.

The suicide-commandos of the FLQ have as their principal mission the complete destruction, by systematic sabotage, of:

a) all colonial (federal) symbols and institutions, in particular the RCMP and the armed forces;

b) all the information media in the colonial language (English) which hold us in contempt;

c) all commercial establishments and enterprises which practise discrimination against Quebecers, which do not use French as the first language, which advertise in the colonial language (English);

d) all plants and factories which discriminate against French-speaking workers.

The Quebec Liberation Front will proceed to the progressive elimination of all collaborators with the occupier.

The Quebec Liberation Front will also attack all American cultural and commercial interests, natural allies of English colonialism. All FLQ volunteers have on their persons during acts of sabotage identification papers for the Republic of Quebec. We ask that our wounded and our prisoners be treated as political prisoners in accordance with the Geneva Convention on the rules of war.

Independence or Death

The dignity of the Quebec people demands independence.
Quebec's independence is only possible through social revolution.
Social revolution means a free Quebec.
Students, workers, peasants, form your clandestine groups against Anglo-American colonialism.

After this bit of breast-beating, the FLQ fell silent for three weeks. Still inexperienced with explosives, the group realized it would have to perform acts more in keeping with the high standards of its propaganda. Dynamite had to be found, bombs made, targets selected. (A ready source of explosives was available from construction sites for the new Montreal subway.)

On March 29 someone knocked over the Wolfe monument on the Plains of Abraham at Quebec City. (British General James Wolfe defeated the French defenders of Quebec under Montcalm in 1759. The following year the French garrison at Montreal capitulated and the top half of the continent became British North America.) The monument caper was apparently the work of free-lance nationalists in Quebec City. But the FLQ in Montreal welcomed it as moral support and launched a wave of bombing attacks that lasted two months and abated only with the arrest of a score of suspects. One man died and another was maimed for life as the suicide-commandos attacked federal symbols.

On April 1 a bomb exploded in the federal government's National Revenue building at Montreal. Another was found in a corridor at Central Station. Another bomb blew up a section of track on the CNR's main line between Montreal and Quebec City a few hours before Prime Minister John Diefenbaker's campaign train was to pass. The break was repaired in time.

A few days later a twenty-four-stick bomb was discovered beside the television transmitting tower on Mount Royal. The now familiar letters *FLQ* had been painted on the tower. The bomb was dismantled. It would probably have disrupted most broadcasting in the city, including broadcasts of the federal election results a few days later.

On April 12, in what became known as the Good Friday raids, police rounded up fifteen suspects, questioned them, searched their premises, and then had to release them. A few days later the FLQ announced Operation Lesage, and said their next actions would be in honour of Quebec's premier. They described him as a traitor and a collaborator for his denunciations of terrorism and of the independence movement.

On April 20 separatists and activists marched to RCMP headquarters in Westmount to protest police state methods in the Good Friday raids. There were some fights and arrests, and the burning of the Canadian Red Ensign. Later that night a bomb was thrown at a window at RCMP headquarters. It fell to the ground and exploded. Someone called Canadian Press and said that Operation Lesage had started.

Later still that night, sixty-five-year-old Wilfred Vincent O'Neil, night watch-man at the army recruiting centre on Sherbrooke Street, went out to the back alley to empty a wastebin. At that moment a bomb exploded in the garbage container. O'Neil dropped to the ground, dead instantly from massive wounds to chest and face. The death released shock and outrage. Virtually everyone in the province, including the three major separatist parties, denounced the FLQ. "In all civilized countries, to kill in such circumstances is murder, and it is no exception in Quebec," said Guy Pouliot, president of the RIN (Rassemblement pour l'Indépendance Nationale), the most important separatist party.

Marcel Chaput, leader of the Parti Républicain, put forward the idea that the FLQ had been founded by English elements to discredit honest separatists like himself. It had then been taken over by Communists both French and English. If that was so, it had worked in Chaput's case. He was thoroughly discredited.

Both Premier Lesage and the opposition leader Daniel Johnson denounced the terrorists. Lesage blamed publicity given to separatist parties as an "encouragement of terrorism." André Laurendeau, editor of *Le Devoir*, described the O'Neil bombing as "the fireworks of hate." The proud nationalist and gentle intellectual added that "French-Canadians are on the side of the victim."

The O'Neil death apparently disturbed some members of the FLQ as well. From the beginning the bombers had agreed that innocent people should not be harmed. Now that a man had died some members were ready to quit. They were talked out of it by others who argued that it had been an unfortunate accident, that these things happened in a revolution, and that after all, O'Neil was not a French-Canadian.

"A Revolution, Alas, Can Not Be Achieved Without the Spilling of Blood."

Throughout the month of May the bombing attacks continued at a furious rate. On May 3, a bomb exploded under the steps of the Canadian Legion Hall at St. Jean; another was dismantled after an FLQ caller warned of its whereabouts in a Place d'Armes office building housing Solbec Mining Company. This was apparently a warning to Solbec to settle its differences with its striking miners. On May 10 a bomb exploded at the Black Watch Armory in Montreal; on May 13 there was a blast at RCAF technical services in the Town of Mount Royal; and on May 16 an explosion against an oil tank at an east end refinery, potentially the most dangerous explosion to date.

The FLQ meanwhile had been reading descriptions of its members as murderers and assassins, and decided to set the record straight as they saw it. In a message to newspapers on May 9, the Front accepted responsibility for the bomb at the recruiting centre which "resulted in the accidental death of an anglophone." The message continued: "But a revolution, alas, can not be achieved without the spilling of blood. . . . In the death of O'Neil, the guilty ones are not The Patriots. They are the collaborators, the low exploiters who have forced Quebec Patriots to take up arms for the liberty of the nation."

The message announced formation of the FLQ's Revolutionary Tribunal which would judge foreign criminals and Quebec traitors. Only two sentences – exile or death – would be carried out on those found guilty. The FLQ also announced it had recently acquired the sum of 35,000 dollars, which would advance the cause of the revolution "instead of being used to pay vile mercenaries." This was an apparent reference to an army payroll robbery on April 30, in which paymaster Marcel Ste. Marie had been wounded. The Front also claimed responsibility for the bomb at the Canadian Legion in St. Jean, "the servile appendage of the British Imperial Legion which invariably adopts every possible position in favour of Anglo-Saxon colonialism."

On May 17 the FLQ struck at what it considered the heart of Anglo domination and exploitation – Westmount, a city separate from but virtually surrounded by Montreal. FLQ members walked through Westmount in the middle of the night, dropping dynamite bombs in fifteen streetcorner mailboxes. Five of them exploded. Police and army experts rushed in to find the others and dismantle them. Sgt. Major Walter Leja, forty-two, neutralized two bombs. As he carefully removed another from a third mailbox, it exploded in his hands. Leja hovered near death for days. But he survived, maimed for life.

On May 20 Premier Lesage called a meeting of representatives of all police forces in the Montreal area with the Canadian Army to plan an anti-terrorist strategy. After the meeting he announced a 50,000 dollar reward for information leading to the arrest of those responsible for the bombing attacks. The City of Montreal also put up a reward of 10,000 dollars.

On that same weekend the FLQ delivered what turned out to be the parting shot, at least for the main body of the group. In honour of the Victoria Day holiday, the Front placed a large bomb against the wall of the Army Engineers armory on St. Grégoire street. The spectacular blast shattered windows, damaged walls and four cars parked nearby.

The FLQ apparently spent the last weekend of May reorganizing and developing its cell structure for better protection. But the group never had time to take the protective measures, or conduct any of the para-military operations it was apparently planning.

On June 21 plainclothes police dressed in *beat* attire stopped a car on St. Catherine street and took its occupants to headquarters. Either from these men or from someone else, the police obtained information. Arrests on warrants followed swiftly. Nine FLQ suspects were arrested by noon the next day. A score of persons in all were held and sixteen were finally convicted of offences.

Again acting on information, police raided a summer cottage of one of the suspects at St. Faustin in the Laurentians. There they found arms and explosives at what presumably was a training camp for the FLQ. Said Montreal Police Director Adrien Robert: "I would say the FLQ has been broken. We know it was a small group."

Out of the Mix of Separatism and Socialism, Three Founders of the F.L.Q.

The suspects were not immediately charged. Instead they were held incommunicado as material witnesses in the inquest into the death of O'Neil, questioned, and denied legal counsel for several days. This aroused heated protest from lawyers, newspaper editors, political parties, and civil rights organizations. That tactic, though a normal practice under the then existing Quebec Coroner's Act, also created sympathy for the thin, youthful but defiant prisoners, many of them students or just out of school, who were to be accused of acts of terrorism. Most were under twenty-four years of age.

The oldest, and apparent leader, was Georges Schoeters, thirty-three at the time, the Belgian-born co-founder and co-ordinator of the FLQ. The two other founders and main operators were Gabriel Hudon, then twenty-one, an industrial draughtsman, and Raymond Villeneuve, nineteen, a school drop-out.

Schoeters, abandoned by his parents during World War II, witnessed Nazi atrocities and at thirteen was a courier for the Belgian resistance. After coming to Canada in 1957 he married a French-Canadian girl and got caught up in the mix of separatism and socialism at the University of Montreal. He later went first to Algeria and then to Cuba to observe revolutionary strategy, and was able to provide the first FLQ with some technical expertise as well as ideology.

Alternately weepy and arrogant at the hearing, Schoeters confessed his terrorist activities. He refused to name his partners but a statement he allegedly made to police gave a complete account of the founding of the FLQ, the names of participants, and the criminal acts that had been carried out to speed the independence of Quebec.

Others were equally open about their bombing attacks. A few young witnesses claimed they were in the FLQ for excitement rather than ideological reasons. "Je faisais ça pour les kicks," said eighteen-year-old Yves Labonté. He said he and nineteen-year-old student Jacques Giroux had taken a bomb to downtown Dominion Square intending to blow up the John A. Macdonald statue. When they saw too many policemen in the area they dumped it instead in the garbage cans behind the recruiting centre. It was this bomb that killed O'Neil.

Schoeters said the Front laid down three rules in its attacks to stimulate Quebec independence: (1) there were to be no victims; (2) no member was to be caught; (3) establishments to be attacked were to be federal or establishments that symbolized the exploitation of Quebecers.

Eighteen persons, including Schoeters' wife Jeanne, were sent to trial on 165 different counts related to that first wave of terrorism. Two were later acquitted.

At the subsequent trials, most of the defendants wore an air of arrogance. They characterized themselves as political prisoners, patriots, prisoners of war, and frequently refused to co-operate on the grounds of their *political principles*. All but three of the eleven who pleaded guilty (after a deal with the Crown reducing the major charges from murder to manslaughter) were allowed to read a prepared statement before sentences were passed.

It said: "I do not recognize the foreign law under which I am charged. However my lawyers advise me that this law applies in this case. I acknowledge the facts mentioned in the indictment. It is true that I committed these acts but I surely committed them because I believe that this is the only attitude that can free the people of Quebec from the colonial domination and yoke which burden them."

Hudon and Villeneuve pleaded guilty to a reduced charge of manslaughter in the bomb death of O'Neil, and were sentenced to twelve years in prison. Also, for manslaughter in the O'Neil death, Jacques Giroux was sentenced to ten years, and Yves Labonté to six years. Georges Schoeters was sentenced to ten years for five offences of placing bombs and causing explosions. For the maiming of Sgt. Major Leja in his attempt to dismantle a bomb from the Westmount mailbox, Denis Lamoureux was sentenced to four years. François Gagnon to three years. Others received lighter sentences, or, like Mrs. Schoeters, suspended sentences. Five accused who had been granted bail failed to appear at their trials.

Some followed the lead of eighteen-year-old Richard Bizier, who created a delicate international incident by going to St. Pierre and Miquelon, French islands off the coast of Newfoundland, and asking for political asylum.

Canada's relations with France were becoming tense at the time, and would get worse, but Bizier was not granted asylum. He returned voluntarily in time for his trial and was sentenced to six months for placing explosives which caused damage.

The five others who skipped bail did not return in time for trial. Gilles Pruneau, in fact, who was twenty at the time, never did return. He went to Algeria where, it is said, he runs a souvenir shop. He is believed to be in regular contact with Arab revolutionaries and New Left groups in Quebec. Another accused returned voluntarily, but late, and was given a suspended sentence.

The three others skipped to St. Pierre and Miquelon. From there they chartered an aircraft to the United States where they were quickly picked up in Boston. Two of them waived deportation hearings and returned to Montreal voluntarily. The third stuck it out, fighting deportation, and suffered for it with a stiff sentence when he was brought back to Montreal.

One of those who returned voluntarily was Mario Bachand, then twenty, who was sentenced on return. He later joined the Company of Young Canadians. In 1969 he was helping to organize the McGill Français protest march when he was arrested on a charge of stealing police tape recorders and cameras. (The equipment was apparently left behind when police made a hasty departure after being discovered in the projection room of a hall in which the organizers of the march were meeting.) Bachand skipped bail on that charge and is now reported to be in Cuba.

By the end of 1967, all those who had been convicted in the first wave of FLQ bombings had been released. Of the three founders, George Schoeters was paroled in December 1967 on condition he leave Canada. Back in his native Belgium he has said nothing would induce him to return to Quebec, even though the woman he married and his two children still live here.

Raymond Villeneuve was nineteen when he was sentenced for manslaughter. He was paroled in 1967 after serving four years of his twelve-year term. Villeneuve enrolled in a business administration course at the University of Montreal when he was released, but was drawn inexorably towards the heady contestation of sociology. His revolutionary juices began to flow again and at the beginning of 1969 he left for Cuba, via Mexico. He has said he will never return until Canada becomes a second Cuba. If he does come back before that, he will have to serve the remainder of his prison sentence.

The third member of the FLQ founders was Gabriel Hudon, who like Schoeters and Villeneuve was active in the separatist movement before forming the FLQ. Hudon, now twenty-eight, was also paroled at the end of 1967. An industrial draughtsman, he apparently studied sociology and politics while in prison and seemed to be observing the conditions of parole. Earlier this year however, Hudon was arrested in connection with armed robberies in the Laurentians and is back in prison. He is one of the prisoners listed by the FLQ kidnappers for the exchange of British diplomat James Cross.

In that summer of 1963, with the original FLQ ringleaders in jail, the police could say they had broken the FLQ, but they probably didn't believe it themselves.

The FLQ had been a radical and clandestine derivative of the legitimate separatist parties. Its founders had first met at open meetings of the RIN.

Even before the first FLQ suspects had been tried, a defiant message had been received by newspapers declaring that the FLQ had been reorganized and would "continue our victorious march." "Neither the incendiary statements of our national traitor Jean Lesage, nor the stupid cash rewards and the thousands of vile mercenaries sent in pursuit of us will prevent our increasing action."

In truth, however, there was not a great deal of FLQ action until late in the year. On July 13 Queen Victoria's statue at Quebec City was blown up. On August 22, while a number of the accused were on bail, a bomb exploded on a railway lift bridge over the St. Lawrence Seaway.

The Lesage Government Went From Strength to Strength on its Slogan — Masters in Our Own House

It was by no means only the FLQ that was causing concern in Canada. The whole of Quebec society was bubbling with self-awareness and self-determination. The old educational system was being painfully transformed into a modern instrument for personal and collective development. Militant trade unions were moving into formerly untouched areas, such as the teaching profession and the public service. The Quebec government pressed boldly forward towards a degree of state direction of the economy, taking over private power companies, setting up investment and financing boards, research and development corporations. Health services, welfare, pensions, were being overhauled, and Quebec's young new technocrats were producing social and economic concepts more inventive and progressive than those in other parts of Canada.

The government of Quebec is the only one in Canada controlled by a French-speaking electorate. That is and always has been a source of pride and at the same time an inevitable cause of tension within Confederation. Two centuries ago, when this part of the world came under British control, only 60,000 of the citizens were French. Now, in a remarkable feat of survival, there are five million French-Canadians in Quebec, representing eighty percent of the population of the province. Close to a million people of French origin live in other provinces where many have been assimilated into the English-speaking environment. In all, French-Canadians represent twenty-eight percent of Canada's total population.

In the early years of this decade, that often dormant pride of language and survival, was in full flower. The government and all political parties took an increasingly nationalist stance. The federal government, which had its hands on a lot of the tax funds Quebec needed for its social transformation, was considered an obstacle.

During the Second World War and in the heady economic boom afterwards, the federal authority had invaded areas of provincial jurisdiction like social welfare. It had the power, the money, and the ideas to do so – attributes that were distressingly absent in provincial administrations of the time.

But now the provinces were pushing back, reclaiming their lost authority and tax resources. The push coincided with dramatic political realignments at the federal level where a divided Canadian electorate was unable to give either Diefenbaker or Pearson a strong mandate. Diefenbaker's massive 1958 support melted away in the 1962 election and left him at the head of a minority government. Liberal leader Pearson won the April 8 election in 1963, but he too failed to get a majority of the parliamentary seats.

While the Lesage government was going from strength to strength on a reform program and its slogan of "Masters in our own House," federal governments could not mobilize a Canadian consensus. Too many people were worried about economic stagnation and excessive unemployment; about the rightness or wrongness of obtaining warheads for Canada's nuclear weapons under the command of NORAD and NATO; and about the political future of Canada.

What had become known as the *Quebec question* was central to these federal elections. Many English-speaking Canadians were convinced Lesage was breaking up Canada and that Pearson was unwittingly helping him. Others believed the breakup was inevitable unless some quick and important accommodations were made for the French fact in the federal system. There was hostility and suspicion east, west, and centre. For most of the sixties, no federal political party could convince a majority of voters that it had the policies to save Canada.

Pearson's sympathetic attitude won his additional support in Quebec. But even there economic unrest and discontent with federalism denied the Liberals the complete victory they had expected. Réal Caouette's protest party, the Créditistes, ran off with 26 of Quebec's 75 seats in 1962, and held on to 20 of them in the 1963 election.

Events were moving so quickly in Quebec that many federal observers feared the Lesage government was bound for technical if not official independence. The political climate in Quebec did little to remove those fears. Pressures coming up from party ranks forced adoption of nationalist programs. Leaders outbid each other in their claims for autonomy.

Voices raised on behalf of federalism in the province were few. The tone of debate was often ambivalent but at no time did either major party take decisive steps away from Confederation.

In Ottawa, it became Prime Minister Pearson's chief task to contain Quebec's ebullience within the federal framework. He did this by yielding to many of the fiscal and jurisdictional demands of Quebec, and by devising formulas applicable to all provinces. At the same time the federal government sought to meet some of French-Canada's more obvious grievances by increasing bilingualism in the public service and by encouraging acceptance of Canada's French fact right across the country.

The federal government did one other thing at that time. It appointed a Royal Commission on Bilingualism and Biculturalism to recommend "what steps should be taken to develop an equal partnership between the two founding races."

Black, White, and Canadian[*]

Martin O'Malley

A study titled "Perception of Discrimination among Negroes and Japanese Canadians in Hamilton" has a rather broad category called "differential treatment." Besides such things as a clerk keeping a Negro waiting beyond his turn, the study says, "it includes a landlady stealing a respondent's mail and spitting in her soup. . . ."

Despite extremes, black militants and even moderates see us as polite racists. Like Canada itself, they say, our discrimination is cautious and somewhat reserved. "Like a hair across the cheek," a Negro woman told a Toronto audience, "you can feel, but can't see." Most annoying, especially to the militants, is that we insist we are so damn *tolerant*.

"The fundamental difference between Canada and the United States vis-à-vis the black man is not that you are less prejudiced – you just have fewer black people," says an angry West Indian.

The militants are a vociferous minority within a minority, but their influence is growing. Some read discrimination into the most innocuous instance of human frailty; like the Jew who applied for an announcer's job and complained he wasn't hired because of "p-p-p-prejudice." The housing problem, for example, which hits everyone, is a frequent source of racial bitterness.

There is no black ghetto in Toronto, although blacks refer to a *green banana belt* in the west-central section of the city. Many West Indians are scattered throughout the metropolitan area. Few are unemployed. Many have well-paying professional and managerial jobs.

The militants say these are blacks who have been bought off by The System. Many of the slogans have been imported from the United States. When some Detroit Black Panthers visited Toronto last December, one of them, Len Brown, "the deputy minister of education," complained on C.B.C. radio's *Don Sims Show*, "I can bet the police – the pig department – in Canada, in Toronto, is sitting around saying, 'We don't want to spark up anything.' And there are apathetic blacks sitting around thinking the whole situation is taken care of. They don't understand what's really happening. Canada is under a farce, a façade. It's a façade of being liberal. She's at the forefront of exploitation just like all the rest."

And yet at a Black Panther rally later that night, only about 100 blacks showed up – and about 500 white radicals. A *New York Times* reporter at the rally told me, "I would have been much more impressed if there were not so many whites."

This is not saying that there is no racism in Canada. If the black militants err in exaggerating, the whites err in underestimating the extent of Canadian discrimination.

[*]Reprinted with the permission of *The Globe and Mail*, Toronto. First appeared in *The Globe Magazine*, February, 1969.

Typical is the case of Myrtle Yearwood, a young Trinidadian girl who came to Toronto in 1965. On February 21, 1967, she had a co-worker, May Bothwell, phone an apartment building on Bathurst Street to ask about vacancies. She said she was calling on behalf of a coloured girl and asked if that mattered. A man told her it did not and asked her to call back next morning.

She called back, identified herself, and was told there were no vacancies. Another friend, Susan Gibson, called five minutes later and was told a bachelor suite would be available on March 1st.

Miss Yearwood visited the rental office that night and asked if there were any vacant bachelor suites. A woman said no. She asked about one-bedroom suites, and the woman said not until April 1st. Could she see a suite? The woman said it was too late. She left.

Two minutes later, Susan Gibson arrived and asked about vacancies. The woman took her to see two one-bedroom suites, one of which would be available March 1st, the other April 1st.

Hundreds of examples like this are on file at the Ontario Human Rights Commission.

In 1963-64, the second fiscal year of operation for the Commission, it received 284 complaints. In 1967-68, it received 3,673. Much of this simply reflects an increased awareness of the Commission. From April to December of 1968, however, there were 4,477 complaints, already substantially higher than for the entire 1967-68 fiscal year.

Dr. Daniel Hill, the forty-three-year-old, Missouri-born director of the Commission, does not deny that there is discrimination against Negroes in Toronto. About 50 percent of the complaints involve Negroes, who make up only 1.5 percent of Metro Toronto's population. But he says it is ridiculous to regard this minuscule percentage as a serious threat to law and order.

He believes Canadians should be able to cope with an increasing black population because they did not respond negatively to the 50,000 refugee slaves who fled here in the mid-nineteenth century. (His Ph.D. thesis was on Negroes in Toronto, 1793-1865.) Besides, he says, human rights legislation in Canada, particularly Ontario, is much better than similar U.S. legislation.

Not all Canadians are so calm.

On the CBC-TV program *Viewpoint* last month, a Toronto newspaperman, Peter Dempson of *The Telegram*, reacted almost hysterically to what he said would be about 18,000 black immigrants to Canada in 1968. He warned that Canadians will find disturbing an increase in immigration from Africa, Asia, and the West Indies and a possible decrease in immigration from Britain and Western Europe.

"As long as we are selective and admit only the educated and skilled," he concluded, "we have no problem. But if the doors are opened to the riff-raff, then heaven help us. Watts, Cicero, Newark would be on us in no time."

Black militants say this is no way to improve race relations. "Take the bone with the meat," they argue. Jan Carew, a Toronto novelist and playwright who once was Guyana's director of culture, says Canada is in almost a unique position to do something constructive in race relations. "You are not going to solve the problem by shutting out immigrants."

He sees Canada as a wide-open country without the inherited problems of the United States or Britain. He finds healthy the self-deprecating, non-chauvinistic attitude of Canadians, as well as their apparent espousal of multi-nationalism.

So far, as with other ethnic groups, Toronto has only gained by its black culture. Our biggest Centennial event, for example, with the unlikely exception of the mayor's beard-growing contest, was a lively carnival week called Caribana '67. A week of uninhibited dancing, games, and colour added some bezazz to a generally complacent summer.

West Indian restaurants and groceries offer such specialties as curried goat, okra, saltfish, jack fruit, cho-cho, passion fruit, bread-fruit, yams, mango nectar, papaya, and avocados. We can enjoy West Indian music (*rock steady*) in West Indian night clubs and record stores. Toronto has black barber shops, beauty salons. People from Guyana, Jamaica, Grenada, Trinidad, Tobago, Aruba, and Saint Kitts have formed associations that make Toronto different from, say, Winnipeg. There is even a West Indian market in Scarborough run by an Italian.

Most Toronto Negroes are not militant. And they seem to prefer the terms Negro and coloured to black and Afro-American, especially the native-born. To a militant, black is a political term. Generally, it means an advocate of Black Power. (Some conservative West Indians will distinguish between black, brown, and coloured, all of which have specific meanings back home.)

Never call a militant coloured.

Despite the preponderance of non-militants, there is a growing awareness of blackness. Even whites admit black is in. Afro-wigs. African boutiques. Soul music and soul food. Eldridge Cleaver for President.

Sometimes it is clumsily expressed. A West Indian newspaper in Toronto ran an editorial last fall eschewing the word Negro, arguing it was created "by the white slave masters to separate the black race around the world," and that "it is suggestive of a head scratching, grinning, inferior black man who lives in America." It was followed by a notice from the Negro Women's Association.

And in a corner of the front page was an advertisement for Norem Hairstylists – specialists in hair straightening.

Moderate blacks eye suspiciously attempts to "do a story on the black community" (which might "stir up trouble") or compare the black situation in Canada with the black situation in the United States. Some deny there is racism here. Others say they are simply tired of reading about it.

"The minute one begins to talk in Canada about race, they say you stir up racialism," says Carew, a tall, muscular man who runs three miles a day, winter and summer, and has a karate black belt. "I say I *expose* it. It is there. You expose it, you put it out for scrutiny and begin to dismantle it. You don't go through the hypocrisy of saying you don't have it."

Even the moderates, if you talk with them long enough, will give you examples of discrimination. Sociologists say blacks feel the brunt of whatever racism exists here because of their *high visbility factor.*

298

Accurate statistics are not available, but Canada's Negro population probably exceeds 60,000. Toronto has about 22,000 Negroes. In 1961, according to the census, Canada had 32,000 and Toronto only 3,000. Dr. Hill says it is important that a better count of ethnic groups be taken.

The main source of black immigration is the West Indies, but more Negroes are coming here from Britain and the United States because of increased racial tension. More are coming to Ontario, too, from the Maritimes. Negro immigrants to Canada in 1968 numbered more than 15,000, and final figures may show about 20,000.

Dr. Hill urged the Personnel Association of Toronto last fall to take definite action "to forestall the racial strife and divisiveness" of the United States. He was speaking to them as employers. Housing is another crucial area, he said.

Don't panic at Black Power. Some militants say Black Power, in the sense of black awareness, is what prevented any serious racial outbreaks in the United States last summer. Frustration has been channelled more constructively into black identity. But others will tell you it is merely the calm before the revolution.

More emphasis on black (and Indian) history in the schools would help. Denny Grant, a Halifax West Indian, complains bitterly of his Anglo-Saxon textbooks: "In botany, I had to study British plants which I had never seen. The plants I knew by sight and touch (mango, guava, sugar apples) were not even mentioned. I wrote poems about the oak, the elm, the pine tree, and the birch, which I knew only by imagination and picture."

José Garcia, secretary of Toronto's Afro-American Progressive Association, came to Canada from the West Indies island of Aruba in 1965. A stocky young man, he speaks in a deep, husky voice and lives in a small walk-up flat on Bloor Street West with his white wife and their pudgy two-year-old daughter. Canadian society, he says, is "racist to the core." Despite his militant posture, he has a rather warm, engaging personality.

Is the A.A.P.A. some sort of Canadian chapter of the Black Panther Party for Self-Defence?

"We're part of the same political line, which is a Marxist-Leninist line. Why call it a Black Panther Party? It's a nationalist thing. The struggle internationally takes different phases. Like in Vietnam. We identify with the Vietnamese. They're struggling for us. . . ."

He had never lived in an Anglo-Saxon society before coming to Canada. "I wasn't prepared for this Anglo-Saxon . . . *thing*. Christ, I used to get on a bus, and I could feel it in the air, the tension. I've been through all the stages – where the man says the room has just been rented, where the job has just been taken."

A friend of his, a young black social worker who was born and raised in Toronto, said he did not want his name mentioned because he might lose his job. Both men said Toronto has the beginning of a black ghetto, and they drew up a map of an area bounded by Queen, Bathurst, Harbord, and University.

Garcia's friend says Toronto is a great place to live, but he finds a special warmth when he visits the black ghettos in the United States. His father was a barber. He has many white friends outside the ghettos, however.

They both agree there is not enough oppression in Toronto to unite the blacks. "The general feeling of blacks here is, 'I'm all right, Jack,' " says Garcia's friend. "The quantity of blacks here isn't a threat," adds Garcia, "but it has grown five times (more like 10) since 1957. It's not a threat yet, like in England."

Like in England. Many see a resemblance.

In 1956, the *London Observer* did an article on West Indians after 17,000 had come to Britain in the first seven months of that year. It ended by saying they "tend to keep later hours than their British neighbours and landladies, particularly on Saturday nights, but they are hospitable and have found it sometimes works wonders to invite their neighbours and the landladies to join in. In short, the West Indians long ago won British affection."

On September 2, 1958, the *New York Times'* Drew Middleton began a dispatch from London: "Shouting, 'Down with the niggers,' rioters swept through the Nottingham district of London late tonight in a renewal of race riots."

At the Black Panther rally in Toronto last December, 600 jammed the Ontario College of Education auditorium on Bloor Street West. A pretty, mini-skirted girl dispensed red Che Guevara flags in the lobby. A huge, moustached Negro sold books at a table (titles: Honky-this, Whitey-that, sex, and racism). Slogans represented the latest ideological hemlines.

Three Black Panthers from Detroit sat at a long table in front of the stage. They wore khaki jackets, khaki pants, black tams, and black sweaters. Burnley (Rocky) Jones of Halifax was there. And Jan Carew. And Garcia, of the A.A.P.A., a Black Power group that is so exclusively black he is not even permitted to bring along his white wife. (About 100 show up at weekly A.A.P.A. meetings.)

Garcia opened the meeting with a short speech and the clenched-fist Black Power salute.

Rocky Jones stopped his speech once to lecture the largely white audience, which was applauding him furiously. "You're damn fools to applaud me when I call you racists." (The applause ceased.) "You're a symbol of what has happened to me. Every cop I ever came across, every teacher I ever knew, was white. . . ." (Rocky is not overly fond of white radicals.)

Ron Scott, deputy minister of justice for the Panthers' Michigan chapter, said, "They saw Watts and they saw Detroit, but they haven't seen Toronto yet." (Cheers.) "Canada has become a left-hand lackey of America," said Leonard Brown, deputy minister of education. "They get together collectively, and they become partners in crime. International thieves and thugs." (Cheers.)

After the speeches, a scratchy film on Huey Newton. Bullet holes in walls. There's Huey. (Chants of "Hugh-Eee . . . Hugh-ee.") There's Cleaver. (Cheers.) A quick shot of Stokely Carmichael. The whites don't seem to know whether he is still worth a cheer. (He is.)

A fat white policeman waddles from a building to the rear of a cruiser, amply stocked with rifles, helmets, tear gas grenades, and other riot-fighting equipment. (Snickers.) "Honky Power," grunts a voice from the balcony.

The white radicals are almost sadly alienated. They watch the black militants stroll through the crowd, and they listen to the hearty, slapping sound whenever two of them embrace. Their whiteness, unfortunately, is indelible.

While the militants blame capitalism for all racist evils, Wilbert Richardson, a successful black businessman in Toronto, sees employment opportunities in Canada as the reason for our relatively tranquil atmosphere.

"I live in a world where monetary remuneration is a driving force," he says in his office at Wayne Distributors and Advertising on Queen Street East. While he does not accept the A.A.P.A.'s Marxist-Leninist philosophy, he can understand why its members think and feel that way.

"Black militancy is misunderstood. You need some degree of militancy in any revolution. It adds impetus to the movement."

He came to Toronto from Pennsylvania in 1947, worked at Massey-Ferguson as a welding inspector, then went into advertising with Mercury Distributors, now one of his competitors. He has seven Negroes on his staff of forty-eight. His firm's annual gross is $2 million.

He once tried to buy a $45,000 house on Parkdale Road, and the real-estate man said the other homes on the block would depreciate by $20,000. Richardson went to newspapers and television for help, and the man eventually went out of business. But he never did buy the house.

"Most Negroes in Toronto would be hard-pressed to find any incidents," says Dr. Joseph Alban Liverpool, a West Indian who came to Canada in 1941. He admits that he might have had it soft as a doctor. He directs a $250,000 medical clinic on College Street, surrounded by corned-beef-and-pastrami signs, tiny real-estate offices, and the smell of warm, crusty bread. When he began practicing medicine in 1956, he was the only black doctor in town.

He was called to a house in Toronto's west-central section one Saturday night by the Academy of Medicine. He knocked on the door, a white man opened it, then slammed it in his face. He knocked again, said he was the doctor, and told the man he might as well let him in because he would be charged for the call anyway.

The man's brother was lying on the floor with a stroke. Dr. Liverpool took him to St. Joseph's Hospital, and he eventually recovered – and became one of Liverpool's patients until he died a few years ago. The man who slammed the door in his face is still a patient.

At his clinic, six black G.P.s, six specialists (two black), and a black dentist handle an average of 130 patients a day, 35 per cent white. He says the racial situation in Canada has improved greatly in the past fifteen years. "The Panthers would be hard-pressed to convince the average Negro in Toronto that he hasn't any rights."

Some accomplishments of the Ontario Human Rights Commission are impressive, especially when you consider it has hardly any legislative teeth. The Ontario Human Rights Code provides for a maximum fine of only $100. Most of the Commission's work is done by persuasion, and its most effective weapon is exposure. "People in Canada do not like to have their prejudices made public," Dr. Hill said.

Six Toronto West Indians complained in 1966 that a U.S. firm discriminated against them when it was hiring men for an Iowa construction project in the city. The Commission prepared to hold a formal enquiry at Queen's Park, and the company made a settlement with the men before the hearing. It paid them $28,600 for wages they would have earned had they been hired. Few formal hearings are required.

A formal enquiry was held into a complaint from Allen Eugene Walls, a twenty-year-old Essex County Negro who said he was denied accommodation at a Windsor apartment because of colour. He said he phoned the proprietor last April after reading an advertisement for a suite. The man told him to come and see him. Walls later phoned to ask if the fact that he was Negro made any difference.

"You know how coloured people are," the man said. Walls hung up when the man began telling him about all the trouble Negroes were getting into. He wanted a suite in Windsor because he had a job there. He finally managed to get one eleven weeks later, and he submitted an expense account of $153 to the Commission for travel costs to and from work.

The man testified at the hearing that when he said "nigger," he did not mean Negro. He meant a "destructive person" or "a person who does not live within the law." But he signed a statement that read: "I would prefer to have an empty house rather than rent to coloured people and have it destroyed." Enquiry Chairman Horace Krever recommended that the man pay Walls the $153. The man said he would appeal the decision; the appeal has yet to be heard.

Another file at the Ontario Human Rights Commission describes an incident in which a Hamilton landlord repeatedly called a dark-skinned tenant a "God-damned Gypsy Armenian Turk," slapped him in the face, twisted a towel around his neck, and tried to bite him.

Dr. Wilson Head, born in Atlanta, Georgia, came to Canada nine years ago and says he has not come up against a single case of overt discrimination. He does not say there is no discrimination in Canada, just that he hasn't met it head-on.

He worked in Windsor five years before coming to Toronto, and now he is research director of the Social Planning Council of Metro Toronto. "I was surprised to find how little discrimination there was here. The difference between Detroit and Windsor? You can almost feel it in your hands."

Despite all this, he sees racial violence as inevitable, even in Canada. He said it will probably come from Canada's Indians. (The A.A.P.A. is considering opening its black-only meetings to the Indians in order to help them organize as part of the *oppressed* Third World.) Negro racial violence is unlikely because of the small numbers, he said, but something like the housing shortage could prompt lower-income whites to strike out against such *high visibility* targets as the blacks.

Historically, there were a few hundred Pawnee and Negro slaves in Canada in the eighteenth century, primarily in the Niagara district. In 1793, the province passed An Act to Prevent the Further Introduction of Slaves and to Limit the Term of Forced Servitude Within This Province. It provided that the children of slaves be set free at age twenty-five. In 1834, the Emancipation Act abolished slavery in the British Empire.

William Lyon Mackenzie once told a meeting in Philadelphia that equality could be seen in all its glory in Upper Canada. He was referring to a coloured man named Butler in the town of York who had a white man and women servants from Europe looking after him and his black children.

Today as then, though, looking for bad examples in other countries seems rather futile. Dr. Eugene Carson Blake, then secretary-general of the World Council of Churches, said in 1963, "It is always easy to point to a worse situation somewhere else: in the United States we could always point to South Africa, and in the North to Mississippi and Alabama. I will not draw the lesson there may be for Canadians in this regard."

Militant blacks do draw the lesson: if their population is too small to be a threat, the Indian-Eskimo population is not. And they are living in conditions often worse than in some Southern states. And they numbered 125,000 in 1941, 220,000 in 1961, and about 250,000 now.

Nova Scotian Blacks: Marginality in a Depressed Area*

Donald H. Clairmont and Dennis W. Magill

Introduction

Marginality, in a sociological sense, refers to a lack of influence in societal decision-making and a low degree of participation in the mainstream of political or economic life. Usually it turns out that a social group designated as marginal is, also, economically disadvantaged. In modern mass society the economic factor appears to be, indeed, the most important criterion in terms of which marginality is defined. Consequently, marginality in a sociological sense tends to be identified as economic marginality or poverty.[1] In the fullest sense of the word, Nova Scotian Blacks can be classified as marginal.[2] Many Canadians probably were unaware, until recently, of the historical presence of Blacks in Nova Scotia. Few studies, historical or otherwise, have *placed* the Blacks in Canadian society and described adequately their ecological distribution and their socio-economic conditions. In a brief presented to the Special Senate Committee on Poverty,[3] we have documented Blacks' poverty and their valid sense of exclusion from the broader society. The marginality of the Nova Scotian Blacks may be explained by the following set of factors, organized in terms of basic and intermediate variables:

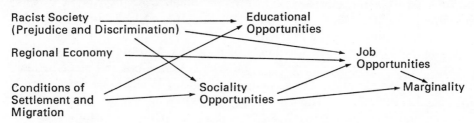

* Edited version of "Nova Scotian Blacks: Marginality in a Depressed Area," 1970, pp. 96-98; 109-120; 136-142, from *Nova Scotian Blacks: An Historical and Structural Overview*. Reprinted with the permission of The Institute of Public Affairs, Dalhousie University, Halifax, Nova Scotia.

303

In terms of the model diagrammed above, the basic factors accounting for the marginality of the Blacks are three: Nova Scotia has been historically a racist society; free Black migrants to Nova Scotia were settled, for the most part, on inadequate and barren lands outside the main centres of economic growth; and, the Nova Scotian economy has been sluggish and new economic opportunities which could channel the Black immigrants and their descendants into the economic mainstream have not developed. These three basic factors in turn produced, for Blacks, opportunity structures that appear to have accounted directly for their marginality in Nova Scotian society. The factors are discussed in detail in the brief. There we have shown particularly how prejudice and discrimination historically have affected, both directly and indirectly, the possibility of Blacks' obtaining their fair share of Nova Scotian wealth and have forced them to the status of marginals. It is this factor, especially, which differentiated Blacks from poor Whites, added considerably to the mobility obstacles which Blacks had to overcome, and generated among them a cycle of poverty.

Cultural Adaptation Among Nova Scotian Blacks

Blacks have lived in Nova Scotia for well over two hundred years. Prior to the early 1800's, a significant number of Nova Scotian Blacks were slaves. Slavery was institutionalized in Nova Scotia and the number of slaves had reached a significant proportion of the total Black population because of the migration to Nova Scotia of slave-owning Whites from the Thirteen Colonies, first in the middle of the eighteenth century and, later, during the American Revolution. Slaveholding in Nova Scotia began to disappear during the last years of the eighteenth century, and the process was accelerated in the early years of the nineteenth century. The majority of Black settlers came to Nova Scotia as free men, first as part of the Loyalist immigration and later as refugees during the War of 1812, enticed by the British Government's promises of freedom, land and wages. By the end of the first quarter of the nineteenth century, slavery was eliminated, Black settlement was essentially completed, and the basic patterns for the involvement of Blacks in Nova Scotian society were set for the next one hundred and fifty years.

The basic theme of the Black presence in Nova Scotia for the past one hundred and fifty years has been marginality. Blacks have had their freedom, but little else. They were scattered throughout the province in small clusters, usually on barren and rocky lands "removed from both coastal fishing commercial centres and from inland centres."[4] For Blacks in Nova Scotia, life has been a constant struggle for subsistence, a struggle which was observed with some indifference by their White neighbours. Although most Black settlements were, in effect, appendages of White towns and villages, the pattern of relationships and everyday expectations was such that Blacks were acknowledged marginals,[5] people who were *all right* in their own communities and place.[6] Blacks were excluded informally but systematically from White schools, churches, and social organizations. Their relationships with Whites were typically of the dominant-subordinate type. Blacks depended on Whites for employment as domestics and casual labourers, and on government (identified by them as White) for minimal assistance that sometimes was necessary in order to avoid starvation.

Many of the conditions necessary for the development of a distinctive sub-culture existed among the Nova Scotian Blacks.[7] Free Blacks were settled in groups;[8] their settlements have had a long history; Blacks were compelled to develop their own institutions and parallel structures; and Blacks were re-moved, for the most part, from the centres of growth and commerce. But the Blacks were not economically and socially independent of the larger society. Their lands were neither sufficiently fertile nor plentiful enough to enable them to avoid having to cast themselves in roles subordinate to the Whites. Indeed, even in the more isolated rural areas, there was often greater regular contact among neighbouring Blacks and Whites than among Blacks in different settle-ments. Economically marginal, Blacks tended to assume, nevertheless, the occupational specializations characteristic of the respective regions of the province in which they resided.

Free Blacks who migrated to Nova Scotia during the American Revolution and during the War of 1812 appear to have had many of the same aspirations as White migrants to Nova Scotia. They came for the freedom, land and wages that the British Government promised runaway slaves and free Blacks. When the promises were reneged upon (or at least fell short of expectations), Blacks protested and petitioned. Initially, many sought integration with Whites in the churches and schools. When integration did not take place and when they could not afford their own churches and schools, they responded readily to the assist-ance offered by White church organizations and philanthropic societies and built their own, less viable, parallel structures. Many Blacks became disgusted with the nominal freedom and the racism that they found in Nova Scotia and migrated whenever the opportunity presented itself. Thus more than one-third of the Nova Scotian Black population migrated to Sierra Leone in 1792;[9] addi-tional migrations took place in 1800 (to Sierra Leone), in 1821 (to Trinidad), and in the last half of the nineteenth century, even back to the United States.[10] Blacks who remained in Nova Scotia (they tended to remain not only because they were locked into the countryside by land and home ownership but, also, because often they had inadequate information about conditions in the receiving societies[11]) continued to protest quietly against the prejudice and discrimina-tion directed against them. They took advantage generally of whatever oppor-tunities they had to advance their socio-economic status and to overcome their marginality. Opportunities were not numerous, given the racist culture and the sluggish regional economy. Some Blacks did become mill operators and skilled coopers in Halifax County, in the days when there was substantial demand for barrels to contain fish and fresh produce; others responded quickly to the demand for porters, which came with the growth of railway passenger service; still others migrated, in the early part of the twentieth century, to burgeoning centres of industry and mining within the province, at places like Cape Breton, New Glasgow and Springhill.

Since there have been no in-depth studies of the Nova Scotian Blacks (of the sort called for by Valentine),[12] it is difficult to ascertain the extent and depth of any Black Nova Scotian subculture. To the extent that a subculture existed, it would have been organized and transmitted through the church. A large majority of Blacks in Nova Scotia have been Baptist. The Loyalist Black settlers apparently had not been church affiliated priod to their immigration.[13] Their mass conversion to the Baptist denomination was partly the work of an escaped Virginian slave, David George, who reached the province during the

Loyalist exodus from the rebellious American colonies. George's evangelism was part of the 'Great Awakening', centered largely in the Baptist and Methodist churches, that swept the North American colonies during the latter part of the eighteenth century. The ranks of Black Baptists, depleted by the subsequent migration of George and numerous Black Baptist congregations to Sierra Leone, were replenished twenty years later through the conversion of many of the Refugee Blacks by the English evangelist, John Burton. Burton and his successor, Richard Preston, a former Virginian slave, were responsible for the organization of the African Baptist movement. In 1854, representatives of all the Black Baptist churches, meeting in convention, formed the African Baptist Association of Nova Scotia. One hundred years later, the Association encompassed twenty-two congregations and its *preaching stations*, some ten thousand members and adherents.

Throughout the history of Black settlement in Nova Scotia, the churches provided the indigenous leadership in the Black community. Black leaders and spokesmen, vis-à-vis the wider society, usually were the religious leaders[14] and the Association was the base for unity and contact among the isolated Black communities. Within the Black communities, the church provided a variety of services and organizations, and social status was associated intimately with participation in church activities.[15] The Association was active on a number of fronts, struggling to keep schools open, founding the Nova Scotia Home for Colored Children, and funding the travelling pastors or circuit preachers. Its leaders engendered reform organizations such as the Nova Scotia Association for the Advancement of Coloured People (NSAACP) and the Urban and Rural Life Committee. The African Baptist Association and the local church leaders were looked upon, by the official societal power structure and by voluntary organizations representative of the official morality, as the representatives of the Black population. Official communiques were transmitted usually through the church leaders and it was through these leaders that White do-gooders entered the communities.

Church leaders were in a position to conserve and enrich any distinctive Black subculture in Nova Scotia. Most of the Black schoolteachers were children of ministers in the Association.[16] The well-educated Black in Nova Scotia usually had strong links with the church. But both church leaders and schoolteachers were trained by Whites in White institutions. Deprivation in the Black communities was such that full attention had to be addressed to maintaining the Association's religious functions and its modest program of social welfare. Structural limitations imposed by the size of the Black population, its scattered distribution and the isolation of the region, contributed to the difficulties which the Association faced in unifying and giving direction to the Black community.[17] Moreover, with a few notable exceptions, Black Nova Scotian churches have not been known as repositories for *soul* in the fashion of American Black Baptist congregations.[18] Indeed, it may very well be that the salience of the Church in the Black communities and the community leadership of the church leaders, at least in recent years, have been over-emphasized. In the four Black communities that we have studied rather intensively, we found that the church leaders formed a small clique and had only limited general influence; most of the community residents did not attend church service and were quite cynical about the role of the church and the church leaders in effecting significant social change or in translating their high formal status into real power.

It would be easy to exaggerate the salience of the church in the Black communities, for usually the church has been the only formal organization and church leaders have been representatives acknowledged by the White power structure.

Probably because of the isolated, rural character of the Nova Scotian Black population, the *cool cat* or *sport* social type, which Finestone found to be common in American cities with large Black populations, has not been prevalent. Until the last few years, there were few, if any, Black social clubs which featured Black styles of music. In areas such as Guysborough, Annapolis, and Halifax Counties, *country and western* music, characteristic of the region as a whole, has been the popular style among the Nova Scotian Blacks. Neither has there been among Nova Scotian Blacks the separatist organizations with millenialist ideologies which have been a significant characteristic of Black response to racism and exploitation in the United States.[19] Although Garvey clubs (the Universal Negro Improvement League) were established in Ontario and Quebec in the period between two World Wars,[20] chapters were not organized in Nova Scotia. Similarly, the N.A.A.C.P., organized around the turn of the century and based in Washington, won some followers among Blacks in Ontario,[21] but a Nova Scotian parallel did not come into existence until 1945.

It appears then that Black cultural adaptation in Nova Scotia has been preoccupied, necessarily, with the problem of survival. Always marginal, Blacks have been ready to migrate and to take advantage of whatever local opportunities arose to improve their socio-economic status. They have gently prodded the White power structure in an attempt to negate the prejudice and discrimination directed against them. For clear structural reasons, apparently there did not develop among Blacks the kind of identity and militant collective consciousness which, given the racism and the generally depressed socio-economic conditions in the province, some see now as necessary for significant change. Blacks do not appear to have developed a distinctive Black Nova Scotian culture which contributed to their poverty and marginality. They have had the same values and aspirations as their White counterparts throughout the province, discounting of course for their marginality and poverty. Being Black in a White-dominated society, they obviously had some special coping strategies. It is both an indication of racial oppression and an indicator of dissatisfaction with marginality that many Nova Scotian Blacks came to deny their Blackness, often identifying the beautiful and socially rewarding with light skin and fair hair.[22] These observations are not meant to deny the existence of any "consciousness of kind",[23] but the latter cannot be identified with a significant, distinctive subculture.

Towards a New Subculture?

It may seem ironic to talk about the emergence of a distinctive Nova Scotian subculture in contemporary Nova Scotian society. We have argued that a significant, distinctive, Black Nova Scotian subculture does not appear to have taken shape over the past two hundred years. It would appear that now, Blacks are much more involved in Nova Scotian society. Segregated schooling has been almost eliminated (existing now only in a few primary schools); Jim Crow practices have either been eliminated or are under attack from a new Human Rights Act and a new Human Rights Commission; there has been a decline in the Black rural population and in the isolation of Blacks. But Blacks are still poorer than their fellow Nova Scotians and there is still the sense and the reality of marginality.[24] There is less discounting, among the better-educated Blacks, in the general values and aspirations which they share with their fellow Nova Scotians. There is still the large submerged half of the racist *iceberg* with which they must contend. Moreover, social conditions have changed in favour of the development of a new cultural style that can produce more effectively the basic structural changes necessary to alter the social position of Blacks. The Nova Scotian Black population is growing and becoming more concentrated in the metropolitan Halifax area. The Nova Scotian economy has become increasingly dependent upon governmental service expansion and subsidy of industry, altering the traditional modes of employment dependency and making more necessary and valuable the organization and unity of Blacks as an aggressive pressure group. Improved education and greater outside communication have sharpened the dissatisfaction of Blacks and have made them aware of new models of coping with the institutional life that has been organized for them.

A crucial variable in the changing cultural style of Nova Scotian Blacks has been the Black cultural revolution in the United States.[25] There has always been contact between Blacks in Canada and the United States. The early Black settlers in Nova Scotia, for the most part, emigrated from the United States and, during the latter part of the nineteenth century, many of their descendants returned to the United States. Three of the nine pastors (up to 1954) at the Mother Church of the African Baptist Association had been recruited from the United States. Nova Scotian Blacks seem always to have been ambivalent about their relationship to American Blacks and about American society. Similarly, there have been opposed interpretations concerning the similarity between American and Nova Scotian Blacks. The Black cultural revolution in the United States, beginning with the Civil Rights Movement, has encouraged a much closer relationship. Developments among American Blacks have been concurrent with the changing social conditions in Nova Scotian society, noted above, and with the increasing Americanization of Canadian society. Accordingly, many Nova Scotian Blacks over the past few years have looked to American Blacks for their identity and for strategies of overcoming poverty and marginality. Martin Luther King was virtually as much an inspiration to Nova Scotian Blacks as he was to the American Blacks. Black leaders in Nova Scotia now depend considerably upon American Black magazines and newspapers and American Black authors for ideas and interpretations about the White-dominated societies in which they live.[26]

The growing ties between developments in the United States and Nova Scotia strengthened and assumed greater substance, with the emergence of the Black Power Movement in the United States. The Nova Scotian visit, in the fall of 1968, of Stokely Carmichael, and subsequently a delegation of the Black Panther Party, made a tremendous impact and crystallized the development of the Black United Front (B.U.F.) and the manifestation of a new social and political consciousness. Carmichael's message was simple and straightforward: "We're with you; be Black and proud." The Panthers emphasized the development of Black, militant, organization and established communication with the younger and more militant local Black leaders. While the Black community in the Halifax area (where the visits were made) was divided in its assessment of the visits and of the appropriateness of *American tactics and strategies*, the visits did much to convey a sense of strength and universality to the Black struggle in Nova Scotia, to reinforce a budding cultural style among Nova Scotian Blacks and to stimulate ameliorative governmental response to Black marginality. One Black leader in Halifax observed: "The whole community, Black and White, were really shaken up by the visit of the Panthers";[27] another Black leader noted: "The visit of the Panthers helped me realize the universality of the problem of Black people and the importance of applying myself to try to understand the basic issues and try to do something positive, realizing that if I didn't, we too would have problems."[28]

The dimensions of the new cultural style that seems to be emerging among Nova Scotian Blacks include racial identity and pride, institutions to develop and revitalize Black identity and experience, organizations designed specifically to promote unity among Blacks and to effect social change, and a militant, confrontation style of combating racism. Such changes are the most evident in, but not restricted to, the Halifax area. Racial identity and pride is indicated in a variety of ways, through *Afro* dress, natural hair-styling, a song about Black pride developed by Black youths in the town of Truro, and the *we're Black and we're proud* chant of youth in the urban fringe community of Cherrybrook (in reaction to the use of the word *coloured* by their elders during a community meeting).[29] The self-designation as Black has, within the past two years, become common among the Black population throughout the province. One Black Haligonian indicated the importance of this designation in the following way:

> I like the word, Black; I used to use the word, Negro, and I think that used to be my favourite at one stage in my life, and I've used the word, coloured. But when I heard the word, Black, and learned why it was used – to make people aware of what they are and who they are and by using the word that they disliked most they condition themselves to think a little clearer – then logically this is then a good contention and I accept this one word . . . then we can become brothers among ourselves.[30]

Within the past two years several Black social clubs have been established in Halifax and Black study groups have been organized to explore Black Nova Scotian history. A Black-oriented publication is currently being prepared for use in the schools. The Black United Front, an all-Black and provincewide organization, is being established to develop social and political consciousness among Blacks at the grassroots, community, level. The change in cultural style from migration rather than confrontation and progress without antagonism, is evident in several demonstrations that have taken place within the past two years and in the recent successful opposition to the appointment of a City Manager (in Halifax) who was considered by local Blacks to be a racist.[31]

The future course of the budding new cultural style is difficult to predict. What happens in the larger, wealthier, American Black community will undoubtedly be significant. At the minimum, its enduring ideas for Nova Scotian Blacks appear to be those of community organization and an attack against the denigration of Blacks. Since the Black Nova Scotian population is still small and scattered, since the demographic structure of the non-metropolitan population indicates the predominant presence of young children and the aged, and since migration of young adults to Montreal, Toronto and other large centres will probably continue, the survival capacity of a separatist Black organization with a distinct cultural style in Nova Scotian society is problematic. Much of the contemporary poverty and marginality among Blacks is part of the general depression in Nova Scotia. Ultimately, the kinds of strategies necessary to bring about basic structural changes and new directions in government policy seem to entail a larger consciousness and a more broadly based concerted action. The new cultural style among Blacks may be important as a vanguard in this process and as assurance that Blacks will not be neglected or discriminated against. In this sense, the new Black cultural adaptation, like the old one, will be oriented to homogeneity rather than pluralism.

Footnotes

1. Norman Whitten, Jr., "Adaption and Adaptability as Processes of Microevolutionary Change in New World Negro Communities," a paper presented at the Annual Meeting, American Anthropological Association, 1967.

2. In discussing the institutionalization of slavery in eighteenth-century Canada, Ryerson observes: "The iniquitous institution of slavery was thus in effect in French and English Canada for at least two centuries. The stain of it is not so much to be measured by the extent of its application in the economy, as by its fostering of the bestial prejudices of 'White chauvinism' and deep-rooted delusions of racist superiority." Stanley Bréhaut Ryerson, *The Founding of Canada: Beginnings to 1815*. Toronto: Progress Publishing Co., 1963, p. 238.

3. A brief presented, November, 1969, to the Special Senate Committee on Poverty, in Halifax, by staff members and associates, Institute of Public Affairs, Dalhousie University, Halifax, Nova Scotia.

4. Whitten, *op. cit.*, p. 8.

5. Concerning race relations in the United States, Winks observes: "other ethnic groups, of whatever definition, passed through the traditional stages of assimilation in the United States, from first to second and ultimately third generation immigrants. The Negro remained always of the first generation, for however his cultural traits might in fact alter, his skin did not change and he remained instantly identifiable as a person apart." Robin W. Winks, "The Canadian Negro, Part One," *Journal of Negro History*, LIII, 1968, p. 286. Winks argues that this pattern was even more pronounced in Canada where there has been a greater pluralistic orientation.

6. G. Brand observed that the view that Blacks are *all right* in their own communities and place was still prevalent, in several counties of Nova Scotia, among Whites at each end of the social scale. G. Brand, *Interdepartmental Committee on Human Rights: Survey Reports*. Halifax, Nova Scotia: Social Development Division, Nova Scotia Department of Public Welfare, 1963.

7. William Yancey, *The Culture of Poverty: Not So Much Parsimony*, mimeographed, St. Louis, Missouri: Washington University, 1967, p. 13.

8. Black slaves were brought to Nova Scotia by numerous Whites. Smith observed that "the names of proprietors owning but one or two 'servants' are too many for repetition." T. Watson Smith, "The Slave in Canada," *Collections of the Nova Scotia Historical Society*, X, Halifax, 1899, p. 24.

9. "When the 1792 migration of free Negroes to Sierra Leone took place, this left more Negro slaves than free Negroes in Nova Scotia," Robin W. Winks, *The Negro in Canada*, Yale University Press, forthcoming.

10. One Black Nova Scotian religious leader noted this heavy migration to the United States "where whole families are continually moving every year, induced by higher wages for labor." P. E. MacKerrow, *A Brief History of the Coloured Baptists of Nova Scotia, 1832-1895*, Halifax, p. 87. Especially since the First World War, there has been considerable migration by Blacks to Montreal, Toronto and Winnipeg.

11. Much misinformation was fed Blacks, prior to the Sierra Leone migration in 1792. One Baptist leader at the time observed, "The White friends now were very unwilling that we should go, though some had treated us as cruelly as if we were their slaves. Many persuaded us if we went they would make us slaves again." MacKerrow, *op. cit.*, p. 13.

12. Charles A. Valentine, *Culture and Poverty: Critique and Counter Proposals*, Chicago, 1968.

13. Walker, interview cited.

14. Preston, a major Black Nova Scotian leader in the middle of the nineteenth century, was also prominent in the Abolitionist movement.

15. Whitten, *op. cit.*

16. W. P. Oliver, *The Advancement of Negroes in Nova Scotia*, Adult Education Division, Department of Education, Nova Scotia, 1949.

17. MacKerrow, *op. cit.*, p. 63.

18. Africville was one of the exceptions; see C. R. Brookbank, "Afro-Canadian Communities in Halifax County, Nova Scotia," unpublished M.A. thesis, University of Toronto, 1949. The comments about *soul* are supported also by the participant-observation of our staff and by the interviews conducted with several local Black religious leaders in the summer of 1969. Historical evidence is naturally hard to come by, but there are some indications that *soul* was not characteristic of Black churches in Nova Scotia, and that the style of service was much like that of White Baptists. For example, Boone came from the United States to assume the pastorage of the Cornwallis Street Baptist Church, but left after one year (1881), for he found the customs so different from those in the United States (MacKerrow, *op. cit.*, p. 37); MacKerrow (p. 53) also notes how the spirituals and songs composed in slavery sounded so quaint to Black Nova Scotian Baptists in the 1890's. It is relevant to note the observations of Arthur H. Fauset, who found in a 1925 study, that "the native Nova Scotian Negro knows little or nothing about the original folk-tales which are common property among Negroes of the South. Animal stories, so prevalent in the lore of Africa, are almost entirely lacking among these people." Fauset concluded that Nova Scotian Blacks shared with Whites the typical Nova Scotian folk-tales. See Arthur H. Fauset, *Folklore from Nova Scotia*, American Folklore Society, New York, XXIV, 1931.

19. See J. Howard, "The Revolutionary," in William Maxwell McCord *et. al.*, *Life Styles in the Black Ghetto*. New York: W. W. Norton and Co., 1969.

20. Harold Potter and Daniel Hill, *Negro Settlement in Canada*, A survey presented to the Royal Commission on Bilingualism and Biculturalism, Ottawa, 1966.

21. Robert W. Winks, "Negroes in the Maritimes: An Introductory Survey," *The Dalhousie Review*, XLVIII, 1968-1969, p. 453.

22. We found many instances of such remarks in our studies of the Guysborough Blacks and of Africville. Hair-straightening has been common in Nova Scotia. In Nova Scotia the term *four hundred* has commonly been used in the Black community to mark those who have higher status and enjoy better socio-economic conditions than other community residents. The *four hundreds* are the Nova Scotian equivalent of the Black bourgeoisie discussed by E. Franklin Frazier, *Black Bourgeoisie*, Collier Macmillan, 1962; like the latter, they tend to be more light-skinned than other Blacks and to dissociate themselves from the rest of the Black population.

23. In view of the lack of good contextualist studies of the Blacks in Nova Scotia, it would be foolish to discount certain indicators of Black consciousness over the years. For instance, little is known about the several Black newspapers that existed sporadically. Two events would be especially interesting to examine; namely, the reluctance of refugee Black settlers to accept a governmental plan in the 1830's which would have given them better lands but which, also, would have dispersed them throughout the province, and the successful opposition to the proposal in the 1880's which entailed the merging of the African Baptist Association with its predominantly White counterpart, the Maritime Baptist Convention.

24. There are insufficient data from which to determine whether the comparative position of Blacks has improved.

25. One of our student research assistants is currently examining the internationalization of the Black Power movement and, especially, its implications in Nova Scotia.

26. Based on interviews with twenty Black leaders in the Halifax area in the summer of 1969.

27. Interview, tape-recorded, September 1969.

28. Interview, tape-recorded, August 1969.

29. Reported by a participant-observer, Summer 1969.

30. Interview, tape-recorded, September, 1969.

31. Here Blacks *joined* with labour organizations in a kind of association that formerly was hindered by the racism of some unions.

The Evolution of an Immigration Policy*

Warren E. Kalbach

Unrestricted international migration is clearly a thing of the past. It is true that there are still large areas of the globe that are relatively under-populated, but these are not the rich virgin and unclaimed lands that attracted millions of migrants to the New World. While there are under-developed areas, they are no longer unclaimed and access is now more carefully controlled than ever before. Most countries in the world today that are attractive to potential migrants share a mutual concern over the problems posed by the influx of large numbers of aliens. Consequently, all countries receiving immigrants tend to impose restrictions on both the number and the kind of people permitted entry.

With a total area second only to Russia in size and containing vast natural resources, Canada with its twenty million people who enjoy one of the highest standards of living in the world presents a highly attractive picture of opportunity to thousands of underprivileged people throughout the world. Canada owes its very existence to immigration but its history of immigration, legislation and regulation points up the serious dilemma it has faced since Confederation in 1867. Canada has been dependent upon immigrants to help settle and develop its vast territory and resources. Yet, at the same time, it has jealously guarded its right to be selective with respect to the type of immigrant it will admit. From its very inception, Canada, like other *receiving* countries, has attempted to keep out the incompetent and socially undesirable along with the ill and infirm. Also, it has attempted to encourage the immigration of people similar in culture and language to those who initially settled the land in order to preserve its early cultural heritage. The difficulty has been that those who have been defined as most acceptable as immigrants in the past have had less need to migrate during recent times, while those from the less-developed areas of the world, whose cultures are most dissimilar and are commonly regarded as presenting the greatest difficulties with respect to assimilation, have experienced increasing pressures to migrate. For the most part, the post-war victims of the population explosion and inadequate economic development have not been found in Canada's list of *preferred* immigrants.

Canada has never imposed any general quota on the number of immigrants that may enter the country, but the effects of its immigration legislation and implementation of policy through Orders in Council have been essentially the same as if it had. Those permitted easy entry were clearly defined about the time of World War I and generally were limited to British subjects from the predominantly white Commonwealth countries and to citizens of the United States. The prohibited classes were gradually expanded from the physically, mentally and socially unfit to include various categories of racial and ethnic origins representing diverse cultural backgrounds, as it became apparent that the character of immigration was beginning to change. The control of Asiatic immigration has ranged from careful regulation to virtual exclusion since 1885.

*Warren E. Kalbach, *The Impact of Immigration on Canada's Population*, Chapter 7, 1.2, "The Evolution of an Immigration Policy," pp. 393-395, 1970. Reproduced with the permission of Information Canada.

Negroes from Commonwealth countries have also been carefully controlled since the early 1920s and the *non-preferred* immigrant classification was used during the 1920s to include central, eastern, southeastern and southern Europeans. During the depression years of the 1930s, immigration controls were again tightened and the flow of immigrants virtually ceased as Canada attempted to cope with the overwhelming effects of the economic doldrums and massive unemployment.

World War II and events of the post-war years again demonstrated the sensitivity of the country's immigration policy to national self-interests. Rapid economic development, shortages of labour caused by war-time mobilization, and low fertility of the depression years neatly coincided with the growing humanitarian desire to assist in the resettlement of refugees and displaced persons. The net consequence was the increasing liberalization of immigration regulations and more governmental assistance in providing transportation and in locating employment. The ultimate consequence of these trends was the emergence of an extremely utilitarian immigration policy in 1962 designed to control the size and quality of immigration in relation to Canada's economic needs and interests. Prospective immigrants were now to be judged solely on the basis of their *education, training, skills, or other special qualifications*, regardless of their race, origin, religion, etc. While this latest change occurred too late to affect the character of post-war immigration during the particular period of concern here, i.e., 1946-61, it reflected the extension of trends that developed during this period and perhaps represents a milestone in the evolution of Canada's· immigration policy. Its potential for altering the cultural characteristics of Canada's immigrants is very great, but the removal of the more obvious discriminatory clauses from the regulations did not loosen to any marked degree the Government's control over the character of immigration. This is quite obvious when one considers the fact that the kinds of skills in greatest demand in an increasingly industrialized nation such as Canada are still to be found most frequently in similar industrialized societies. Meeting labour shortages by encouraging the immigration of highly skilled persons from under-developed areas of the world poses a moral problem that has yet to be resolved. In addition, recognition of this problem by any *receiving* country entails the consideration of broader issues and concerns than its own immediate self-interests. Perhaps it is unrealistic to expect this of any country at this particular point in the evolution of human society.

Social Patterns of Immigrant Groups[*]

Royal Commission on Bilingualism and Biculturalism

Immigrants are under immediate and direct pressure to adjust to the economic, political, and legal structures of the country to which they immigrate but there

[*]*Canadian Royal Commission on Bilingualism and Biculturalism Report*, Book IV, Part II, Chapter IV. Selected portions of "Social Patterns," pp. 89-112, Sections 234-276 and 291-307, 1967. Reproduced with the permission of Information Canada.

are some areas, such as family life, religious belief and practice, and social and cultural associations, where society exerts less pressure and permits a wider variety of behaviour. As a result, immigrants may continue to follow traditional patterns in these areas. Society at large has tended to accept and even encourage this retention, but even so life in Canada has inevitably brought changes in the social patterns of all cultural groups, even the most isolated and self-sufficient.

A. The Family

1. Kinship

Many of Canada's immigrants came from societies in which kinship ties were very important, and where families were often linked into networks which would assist the young men of the families to emigrate. Once established in the new land they were in turn expected to help their kinsmen to follow them.

The role of kinship among immigrant Hungarian peasants provides an illustration.[1] Their basic kinship institution, called the sib, included a wide circle of relatives (aunts, uncles, cousins, sometimes of a very remote degree, in-laws and their families, and godparents and their families). Membership in the sib was not governed solely by blood relationship for some distant relatives might be strongly attached while nearer ones were excluded. Within the sib the separate families maintained independent households which were often scattered over neighbouring villages or, in the case of middle-class sibs, over the whole country. Marriage between members of the sib was common and often encouraged in order to keep the families' resources within the sib. The sib involved many unwritten customs and obligations of which the most binding was to help other members in every way – through assisting with labour, money, or moral support. "The lore of the sib system, its etiquette and genealogy made up a conspicuous part of the education every child received from his family. Such an education, together with certain familistic sanctions, were effective enough to keep up the system for many centuries." The sib played a crucial part in migration for members of the poor classes could never have financed the cost of emigration without the help of their relatives. "Sometimes five to ten families contributed to 'send out' one person to America." In return, the immigrant recognized his obligation to return the aid he had received. As soon as he found a steady job, he would start to send back money to help his relatives and in time to assist them to emigrate. Generally only one son from each family would emigrate, thus the original immigrant would normally not be joined by a brother but by a son of another sib family. This process was continued by each newcomer in turn. "It was a strict obligation upon sib members to guard the newcomer, to teach him Canadian ways and to provide him with quarters and a job."

The extended family seems to have played a role similar to that of the Hungarian sib for other ethnic groups from Europe. Many immigrants attempted to establish the kinship systems that had been important parts of their lives before migration, but these systems can exist only in a special set of circumstances. Among Polish peasants "the traditional form . . . can evidently subsist only in an agricultural community, settled at least for four or five generations in the same locality and admitting no important changes of class, religion, nationality, or profession."[2]

Kinship was also important among Asian immigrants. For example, Japanese families in the late 19th century were not limited to a single household but included the largest possible kin group as part of the family. Thus the Japanese concept of family "takes in the nation, for from a historical point of view the people consider themselves all of one blood."[3] The obligation of *mutual help-fulness* applied to all kin. The family was highly patriarchal and based on the theory of male superiority. Doctrines of filial piety, seniority, masculine superiority, and ancestor worship conditioned the roles of all members. "Marriage was contracted by family action for purposes of family continuity."[4] The family was also important for the Chinese. If a family had no sons to perform the filial duties towards the father, then it was considered necessary to adopt sons.

Since the 1920's, and especially since 1945, the role of the larger kinship network, as against the conjugal family, has been diminishing in Canadian society and it will probably continue to do so. This change is due to industrialization, urbanization, and increased mobility. These factors are reinforced by the increased proportion of urban, middle-class immigrants and a government policy of selecting immigrants on the basis of skills, education, and training.

There are a few exceptions to this trend, the most notable being among Italians.[5] Although the central institution of Italian society is the *nuclear family*, the larger kinship group is still extremely important in present day Italy, particularly southern Italy, and many Italian immigrants continue to maintain their kinship ties in Canada:

> each person stands at the centre of a vast network of individuals to whom he is related through both mother and father, and through marriage. . . .
>
> Thus the southern Italian divides the world around him into kin and non-kin. The former are allies with whom he shares reciprocal rights and obligations of mutual assistance and protection. The latter are either enemies or potential enemies, for each seeks to protect and improve the position of his own family, if need be at the expense of others.

Most Italians in Montreal have immigrated with the help of their kinsmen, and on their arrival they tend to settle near their kin. Many share their houses with close relatives. The ties of kinship are very strong among those of Italian origin born in Canada as well as among new immigrants. In the group studied in Montreal "a full two-thirds had close relatives living within five minutes, including over one-half who had relatives living in the same building, though not necessarily in the same dwelling area. . . ." Italians in other urban centres show similar residence patterns.

2. Marriage

Some immigrants married before coming to Canada, and either brought their wives and children with them or sent for them within a few years. Others left *fiancées* behind and later sent for them. Still others settled near members of their own cultural groups, and so tended to meet and marry members of their own cultural group in Canada. Ethnic endogamy, marriage within the cultural group, was highest among the immigrants whose lives and migration were inextricably linked with kinship.

Endogamy was particularly common among the sectarian groups with strong isolationist tendencies, such as the Mennonites in Manitoba.[6] As late as 1947, and in spite of many changes in their economic and community life, their education, and even their religious convictions, "the family remained the foundation and nucleus of the Mennonite group," playing the same role in the social structure as it had in 1877 when they arrived in Canada. The group was bound together by "countless blood ties and intermarriages. . . . The discussion of family trees was still one of the favorite pastimes at social gatherings. . . . A man without an identifiable genealogy was barely considered a true Mennonite."

Hungarian immigrants faced considerable difficulty in contracting marriages.[7] Most were not married when they arrived in Canada; some were engaged and when they had saved sufficient money would send for their *fiancées*, but this presented a considerable financial problem for many. "The great depression wrecked many marriage plans and when the economic situation improved, war stopped immigration from Hungary." In one group as many as 40 percent were estimated to have failed "to establish a normal family life within a reasonable time after immigration because special difficulties faced immigrants in contracting marriages." One solution, marriage outside the cultural group, was hindered by the language barrier and other national peculiarities. As late as 1931, nine of out ten marriages of those of Hungarian origin were within the cultural group, and the percentage was even higher for immigrants.

The problem of establishing families was especially acute for the Chinese. Between 1923 and 1947 they were not permitted to bring their wives or unmarried children under 18 years of age into Canada, unless they had obtained citizenship by a very difficult procedure.[8] Some illegal entry occurred, but the Chinese remained a largely male population. In 1931 there were 46,500 Chinese men and only 3,600 Chinese women in Canada. The Japanese were in a different situation. From 1885 to 1910, nearly ten times as many men as women had entered Canada but after 1910 the percentage of female immigrants was high. By 1921 there were 10,500 males and 5,300 females and, by 1931, 13,000 males and 9,200 females.

In many ethnic origin categories a substantial number of men did not marry. Some of these regarded their migration as temporary, and when they stayed in Canada permanently were unable to bring their prospective wives here because of immigration regulations or financial circumstances. In the Canadian population as a whole, the number of males per 100 females was 105 in 1901, rose after a decade of heavy immigration to 113 in 1911, was 106 in 1921, and 105 in 1941. Among the foreign born the number of males per 100 females was much higher than among the native born. It was 158 for the foreign born in 1911 and for certain groups it was particularly high.

Since World War II, the huge male surpluses of earlier years have disappeared. Male immigrants have more often been accompanied by their wives and children, or soon reunited with them. In fact, since 1931, Canada has admitted more women than men. Although in recent years more women than men have emigrated to the United States, the sex ratio in most groups has still tended towards a balance.

The degree to which the different origin groups are still endogamous indicates the extent to which they are still bound by their cultural heritages and social networks. In 1961, for eight European ethnic origin categories, the other European categories taken together, and the Asian categories, the proportion of endogamy was under 50 percent only for Scandinavians, Russians, and Poles. For the Germans and Dutch the proportion was between 50 and 60 percent; for the other Europeans and Ukrainians it was between 60 and 65 percent; for Italians, Asians, and Jews it was over 75 percent. In making comparisons with 1951, no figures are available for the Italians and Russians. But of the other categories, the percentages for the Dutch and Ukrainians were the only ones showing noticeably different proportions of endogamy. The Dutch had less than 45 percent endogamy in 1951, the Ukrainians over 70 percent.

Comparable figures are not available for earlier years but, in 1941, 29 *racial* origin groups were ranked according to an index of intermarriage and this ranking is strikingly similar to that noted above. The index was based on the percentage of fathers of legitimate children born in the given year married to mothers of the same *racial* origin.[9] The Scandinavian groups had some of the lowest indices of endogamy; the Polish, Dutch, Italians, Russians, and Germans had indices between 51 and 58; and the Chinese, Ukrainians, Jews and Japanese had indices ranging from 75 to 99.

The British and French groups appear to act as magnetic poles in the Canadian social structure. These groups are themselves highly endogamous, but they are large enough to account for much of the exogamy among the other origin groups. The British origin category makes up 44 percent of the population and has great economic power and strong cultural influence. It therefore exerts the strongest attraction for outmarrying members of other ethnic origins. The only exception to this rule is in Quebec, where the French exert a greater attraction for some groups. However, the proportion of immigrants who settle in Quebec is relatively small.

The massive post-war immigration to Canada did not result in significant changes in the exogamy/endogamy ratio between 1951 and 1961. The overall proportion of endogamous marriages was almost stable between the two censuses. Two factors have combined to produce this near stability: an increase in second- and third-generation exogamous marriages, and a large number of endogamous marriages involving post-war immigrants. But it appears there is also an increasing tendency for recent immigrants to marry outside their cultural groups. Reasons for this include their education and their dispersion residentially and occupationally, and more cosmopolitan attitudes both among immigrants and among middle- and upper-class Canadians. For example, the Hungarian immigrants who came to Toronto after 1945 showed a tendency to marry those of British origin.[10] In 1962 about 9 percent of the Italian immigrants marrying in Montreal married those of French origin and the rate was higher among Canadian-born Italians.[11]

Marriages outside their cultural group have been increasing even among the groups most strongly endogamous in earlier days, such as the Japanese. "Many Nisei[12] and Sansei favour this trend in principle on the grounds that complete assimilation is impossible without intermarriage. There are some (mostly Kika), however, who join many Issei in deploring the trend because 'it will spoil the purity of the Japanese blood.'"[13] Another argument is the difficulty which may face the offspring of such a marriage. Some Issei parents also fear that a Hajukin son- or daughter-in-law might not assume the traditional obligation of supporting his or her spouse's parents.

3. Generational Changes

The conditions required for perpetuating the old kinship systems did not exist in Canada, and the rise of a new generation often brought drastic changes. In any differentiated society there are differences and conflicts between generations; in an immigrant group, these tend to be increased. The transmission of a way of life depends upon acceptance of a total system of institutions and such a system can only rarely be transmitted intact to a new land. This transfer is most complete for such sects as the Mennonites and Hutterites, and the generational conflicts are therefore least severe within these groups.[14]

To the degree that the transfer of the traditional system is incomplete, the etiquette or ritual that governs relations between generations in the family and the community breaks down. The young may still be taught approved forms of behaviour by their parents, relatives, and other members of their cultural group; but their neighbourhood, school, and church may not reinforce this teaching.

The experience of the Japanese cultural group illustrates the effects of generational differences.[15] Whereas in Japan the schools reinforced the training given at home, helping the children "to chart their course properly through the rigid ceremony of every day behaviour," Canadian public schools did not fulfill this function. In fact they did just the reverse by stressing the values of democratic individualism, "which ill accorded with the authoritarian collectivism of the community." Thus the Nisei did not fit easily into the Japanese community. The discriminatory attitude of society as a whole, which failed to recognize "the Canadian orientation of the majority of the Nisei and directed its hostility at all Japanese, irrespective of place of birth," added to the problem. "Unable to prove they were 'good Canadians,' the Nisei were forced back into dependence upon the ethnic community and this made the cultural conflict more obvious."

The second generation of those of Ukrainian origin offer an example of generational changes in which a particular immigrant occupation played a part.[16] Young girls would often go into domestic service in the cities and thus come into contact "with new ways of living, new social relationships, a new language – in short, a new world." Some of the girls would marry within the families for whom they worked, and were quickly almost completely assimilated. Many of them returning to visit their families, would find their parent's modes of dress, language, food, and general way of life "uncouth and even 'foreign.'" The parents would then reproach their children for having "forsaken the old ways."

B. Religion

The relationships between religion and ethnic identity and religion and ethnic origin are complicated. Some religions, for example, Judaism, are explicitly ethnic. Christianity is not, although some Christian denominations are. Some cultural groups are almost entirely of one religious affiliation, others are spread among many different faiths. Within every cultural group there are people who practise no religion, although they may profess one to a census-taker, but who adhere to the ethic of the religion they inherited but have abandoned.

Many cultural groups shared a single religious affiliation when they first came to Canada. The Italians were almost all Roman Catholics; the Scandinavians Lutherans; the Japanese Buddhists; the Ukrainians either Greek Orthodox or Greek Catholic. The Jewish group in Canada was less divided than in the United States; few Sephardim or liberal German Jews came to Canada. For the Germans and Dutch, who were of many different religious affiliations, religion was not an important part of their ethnic identity.

Many problems confronted immigrants in setting up their religious organizations. Some religions are much less portable than others. The Doukhobors, Mennonites, and Hutterites had little difficulty maintaining their forms of worship on the Canadian prairies, and Jews could secure their religious accoutrements, at least in the cities. Those of other faiths were often less fortunate, particularly if they were dependent upon a highly trained priesthood. Often they did not bring priests with them to Canada and had little money to pay priests for their services here. For example, the Japanese Buddhist Church was not prepared to send priests to provide for the religious needs of immigrants.[17] Early Ukrainian settlers had great difficulty in transferring their religion to Canada because their attempts to interest priests in emigration failed. Josef Oleskow, who encouraged many early Ukrainian settlers to come to Canada, suggested one novel solution, but with no success:

> Oleskow wrote to the Minister of the Interior, H. J. MacDonald on May 16, 1896, urging that priests of the same faith and nationality as the settlers should be encouraged to emigrate, through provision of a nominal salary for them, until such time as the settlers were in a position to assume the financial responsibility. This was an unprecedented request, the Canadian government was not prepared to cope with it. . . .[18]

As a result the settlers were left very much alone, except for a few visits by guest priests (for example, N. Dmytriew and D. Polyvka), from the United States. This situation left many new immigrants susceptible to the missionary efforts of the more established denominations. The introduction of rival faiths in turn bred quarrels and divisions within the community.

Sometimes when clergy did emigrate, for example, Bishop Seraphim who came to Winnipeg to serve the Greek Catholic Ukrainians, they were unable to adjust to the new environment.[19] In other cases where religious leaders did adapt to Canadian conditions, they encountered resistance from more conservative church members or from church functionaries further from the scene. This resistance sometimes provoked one group to split off from the central church organization. Such a secession occurred among the Greek members of the Greek Orthodox Church in Toronto in the 1960's.

In cases where a suitable priest was secured, he frequently found that his position was undermined by several factors. The experiences of the laity in setting up a congregation and in seeking out a priest frequently made them more independent than they had been at home and less willing to accept the priest's authority. The necessity of constant fund raising also detracted from the priest's sacerdotal role.

The burden of setting up a religious organization and financing religious services, building for worship, and religious objects often presented further difficulties. In the homeland, the financial burden of upkeep was widely shared, especially in the established churches. Immigrants, already under financial stress, found the financial demands of their religion onerous, especially when they compared them to the costs of religions that rejected conventional church architecture and appointments.

Many new arrivals also found that earlier immigrants of different ethnic origins had already established churches of their particular religious denomination. In some cases, the new immigrants simply joined the existing parishes; the Dutch Catholics are one example. However, many others were disturbed by differences in belief, ritual, and language. Italian Roman Catholics in Edmonton, for example, had been accustomed to the cult of the Virgin Mary and lost some of their zeal when they encountered Canadian churches which instead stressed the Trinity and Christ in their services.[20] Where the church was hierarchical in structure, some found the problem compounded by the fact that the higher clergy were of a different background and often unsympathetic to their wants. For example, on occasion Irish bishops assigned Irish priests to Polish congregations, and bitter struggles ensued until Polish priests were provided.

Sometimes later waves of immigration brought groups who shared the ethnic origin of earlier arrivals but differed markedly from them in their religious beliefs and rituals.[21] The Jews who emigrated at the beginning of the 20th century were more aware of their ethnic, rather than their religious identity. But since World War II the Jewish cultural group has been augmented by small numbers of highly orthodox and Hassidic Jews who have influenced the rest of the Jewish cultural group. These later arrivals have attempted to transfer their traditional way of life, including their mode of dress, to their new home. They pose a threat to some members of the Jewish cultural group for they hinder the process of integration into Canadian society. At the same time other Jews, who have themselves given in to the forces of assimilation, welcome the orthodox arrivals because they seem to guarantee the survival of traditional Jewry in Canada, without demanding any sacrifices on the part of those with less strict devotion to the traditions of their religion.

The orthodox and Hassidic Jews make up a small percentage of the total Jewish community in Canada and have little connection with other Jewish groups. Even so, their presence has tended to reverse the normal pattern of integration:

> Canadian Jews were most highly acculturated in the very earliest period of settlement; between 1840 and about 1940 they were differentiated by ethnic characteristics . . . from the surrounding population, but there was much interaction between Jews and non-Jews, and a willingness to assimilate values of the new culture. Only now, in the latest phase of Jewish life in Canada do we have what usually comes at the beginning — enclavic groups, intent upon maintaining in unadulterated form their traditional mode of living.[22]

North African Jews from French and Spanish Morocco, who came to Montreal and Toronto in the late 1950's and early 1960's, also added variety to the Jewish religious community. Their Sephardic form of Judaism set them apart in ritual and custom from most of their co-religionists in Canada. They quickly began to hold services according to the Sephardic rite, and sought aid from the Jewish community in setting up their own synagogues.

The problem of strenuous missionary activity on the part of denominations already entrenched in the community has further confused new immigrants anxious to establish their traditional forms of worship. In downtown Toronto, in the years before World War I, the Methodists campaigned actively to convert Italian Roman Catholics through night schools, nurseries, and Italian-speaking ministers.[23] At the same time the Presbyterians devoted much attention to converting Jews in Toronto. These efforts were centred in the area known as *the Ward*, the district bounded by University Avenue, Queen, Dundas, and Yonge streets. Marked by overcrowding, poverty, poor housing, and disease, the area quickly developed the characteristics of a slum and by 1910 was considered a major social problem by the city. It was here that the evangelical sects and established denominations set up their churches and mission houses:

> Through the provision of various social services, some financial assistance, and mid-wifery all neatly packaged with the Gospel, a number of conversions of Jews did occur. By 1911, the members of Holy Blossom Congregation were seriously concerned. . . .[24]

While neither the Italian Roman Catholics nor the Jews proved to be ready converts, certain others, for example the Japanese, have joined the Protestant denominations in large numbers.

> During and after the evacuation crisis, missionaries and church groups in both Eastern and Western Canada worked extremely hard to ameliorate the severity of conditions in the camps and to give aid in the resettlement process. Many people, Issei in particular, became Christians quite frankly to express their gratitude for this help. The Buddhist efforts to help in this crisis were hampered by the Government's action in suspending the activities of all priests except the one Canadian. The latter worked very hard, cooperated with community organizations but of necessity his achievements seemed small when contrasted with the efforts of the organized Christian groups.[25]

The Roman Catholic, Anglican, and United churches made strong inroads and conversions have continued since the war.

Even without proselytizing campaigns, members of a particular religious or cultural group not numerous or wealthy enough to establish their own neighbourhood church have sometimes begun attending the existing church most congenial to them. Greek Catholic Ukrainians have attended Roman Catholic churches, Greek Orthodox Ukrainians, Anglican churches. In some cases it has later been possible for them to return to an ethnic church; in others, the transfer has become permanent.

A desire to preserve their faith has frequently strengthened the determination of members of a cultural group to maintain their language, for people are more ready to use an alien tongue for business or political activity than for worship or confession. Churches have tried to profit from this feeling and hold their flocks by offering language classes for children. In spite of these efforts transfers to Anglophone congregations tend to increase in the second and third generations.

The Protestant evangelical sects have attracted immigrants as well as the major established denominations. The rapid growth of such groups as the Pentecostals, Christian Missionary Alliance, Jehovah's Witnesses, and Seventh-Day Adventists has been in good part a result of their appeal to immigrants whose own religious faith and religious organizations seemed to fail them in their new land. In Alberta in the 1930's and 1940's such sects surpassed the major denominations in serving immigrants.

> For instance, the German Baptists, the Evangelical United Brethren, the Swedish Mission Covenant, and the World Alliance of Missionary and Evangelical Churches, by integrating numbers of German and Scandinavian immigrants into a religio-social community which preserved their old language and many of their old traditions and customs, served to protect these ethnic groups from social disintegration and to cushion the shock of their adjustments to a new culture. On the other hand, sects like the Pentecostal Assemblies of Canada, the Alliance, and the Prophetic Baptists aided greatly in the ultimate assimilation of people of European background by accepting them on equal terms with Anglo-Saxons.[26]

A study of inter-faith marriages found that there was a general trend towards increasing religious exogamy between 1922 and 1957 extending in varying degrees to all provinces and to all three of the major religious groups, Protestant, Catholic, and Jewish.[27] The continuation of this trend after 1945 gives further evidence of the fact that many post-war immigrants have been more cosmopolitan and hence less exclusive than earlier immigrants.

C. Education

The relationship between religion and education is close. In Canada the school one attends, the quality of instruction, the choice of programmes and subjects, and the availability of higher education are all related to the major religious division between Catholics and non-Catholics, as well as the main language division between Anglophones and Francophones. Ethnic background is also an important factor.

Levels of Education

The average level of education attained by the population has been rising over the last 80 years, both in Canada and abroad. In addition, Canadian immigration policy, which before World War II tended to give preference to agricultural immigrants and those willing to enter domestic service, has now been altered to give preference to those with education and training. The level of education among immigrants has therefore tended to be high since 1945, except among immigrants who are sponsored and need not meet these requirements.

The immigrant population taken as a whole has a lower educational level than the Canadian-born population, but it also has more members with university training. When the immigrant population is classified according to the time of arrival, those who came before 1931 predominate among those with little education; those who came after 1945 include a high proportion with university-training. Some of these immigrants have obtained or completed their education in Canada. The high proportion of recent immigrants who have settled in urban areas is also related to the high proportion with university training.

The total immigrant population includes a substantial proportion of British origin, and it is probable that many of them are highly educated. A study of

Ontario students showed that more parents of Anglophone students have university training than those of students from homes where the language spoken was neither English nor French.[28] However, students from the *other* language category, taken together, showed the highest yearly retention rate[29] and this could only be partially explained by such factors as the father's occupation, the size of the community, parental education, the geographical location of the school, or the size of the families studied. The future educational plans of the students and their attitude towards attending university seemed to be associated with their retention rate. This *other* language category presumably contained mainly immigrants and children of immigrants.

Immigrants from different countries are by no means equal in the area of education. Education levels have not risen at the same rate in all countries, and immigrants from different countries often come from very different strata within their homelands. When these variations are taken along with variations in the socio-economic positions of the ethnic origin categories in Canada, the result is a wide variation in the educational levels of members of the different ethnic origin categories.

Table 1 compares the educational levels of the members of six specific ethnic origin categories in the Canadian labour force and all others taken together. Jews have the highest average level of education, followed by the British, Germans, "others," Ukrainians, French, and Italians. The average level of schooling for Jews is 10.1 years, for Italians 6.2. The rank order of the groups varies somewhat for the four provinces of New Brunswick, Quebec, Ontario, and British Columbia, and for the three metropolitan areas of Toronto, Montreal, and Ottawa, but the Jewish, British, and German groups were consistently high, the Ukrainians, French, and Italian consistently low.[30]

D. Voluntary Associations

Many immigrants had little experience with voluntary associations when they arrived in Canada. The family, the kin group, and the church had provided their social structures in their homeland. Settlers in rural areas established few voluntary associations, but immigrants in towns or cities tended to organize associations, either to fill old wants or to meet new needs created by migration. Many of these voluntary associations were sponsored by the churches; some in turn became sponsors of part-time schools.

Ethnic associations are set up to meet those wants that people share with their ethnic fellows but not with the community at large. They are of many types: mutual aid or benefit associations designed to give assistance in crises such as unemployment, illness, accident, or death; philanthropic or social welfare associations through which the more successful and established members of the group may assist the less successful newcomers; associations with political aims, either in the homeland or in the new country; social and recreational associations; occupational and professional associations; research institutes and learned societies; women's groups; youth groups and coordinating bodies.[31]

Different types of ethnic associations have usually been characteristic at different periods, because of the different types of immigrants who came in each period and the different state of development of the Canadian communities in which they settled. Mutual benefit associations emerged first. Faced with few

TABLE 1

Levels of Education in the Labour Force
Distribution (in numbers and percentages) of the labour force, by ethnic origin, sex, and education level—Canada, 1961

Ethnic Origin	Sex	No Schooling		Elementary School		High School 1–2 Years		High School 3–5 Years		University Training		Total	
		Number	%	Number	%	Number	%	Number	%	Number	%	Number	%
British	Male	5,100	.3	535,500	30.6	442,400	25.2	550,300	31.4	219,000	12.5	1,752,300	100
	Female	600	.1	134,700	18.5	190,300	26.1	337,500	46.3	65,400	9.0	728,500	100
	Total	5,700	.2	670,200	27.0	632,700	25.5	887,800	35.8	284,400	11.5	2,480,800	100
French	Male	7,600	.7	584,300	53.5	233,400	21.4	197,900	18.1	68,900	6.3	1,092,100	100
	Female	900	.2	152,700	39.4	99,900	25.8	116,300	30.0	17,600	4.5	387,400	100
	Total	8,500	.6	737,000	49.8	333,300	22.5	314,200	21.2	86,500	5.8	1,479,500	100
German	Male	800	.4	88,400	40.0	48,100	21.8	62,900	28.5	20,300	9.2	220,500	100
	Female	100	.1	29,100	31.6	22,600	24.5	35,200	38.2	5,200	5.6	92,200	100
	Total	900	.3	117,500	37.6	70,700	22.6	98,100	31.4	25,500	8.2	312,700	100
Italian	Male	1,700	1.3	93,800	71.0	16,900	12.8	15,800	12.0	4,000	3.0	132,200	100
	Female	1,700	3.6	30,900	66.0	6,300	13.5	6,800	14.5	1,100	2.3	46,800	100
	Total	3,400	1.9	124,700	69.7	23,200	13.0	22,600	12.6	5,100	2.8	179,000	100
Jewish	Male	500	1.0	13,400	26.9	7,600	15.2	15,700	31.5	12,700	25.5	49,900	100
	Female	200	1.4	3,100	22.1	2,100	15.0	6,500	46.0	2,100	15.0	14,000	100
	Total	700	1.1	16,500	25.8	9,700	15.2	22,200	34.7	14,800	23.2	63,900	100
Ukrainian	Male	1,100	1.1	44,800	46.7	20,400	21.3	22,100	23.0	7,600	7.9	96,000	100
	Female	1,100	2.6	15,300	35.5	10,300	23.9	14,200	32.9	2,200	5.1	43,100	100
	Total	2,200	1.6	60,100	43.2	30,700	22.1	36,300	26.1	9,800	7.0	139,100	100
Others	Male	8,300	1.5	241,500	42.6	109,100	19.3	145,900	25.6	61,600	10.9	566,400	100
	Female	2,300	1.1	67,100	32.3	43,200	20.8	78,800	38.0	16,200	7.8	207,600	100
	Total	10,600	1.4	308,600	39.9	152,300	19.7	224,700	29.0	77,800	10.1	774,000	100
Total	Male	25,100	.6	1,601,700	41.0	877,900	22.5	1,010,600	25.9	394,100	10.1	3,909,400	100
	Female	6,900	.5	432,900	28.5	374,700	24.7	595,100	39.2	109,800	7.2	1,519,600	100
	Total	32,000	.6	2,034,600	37.5	1,252,600	23.1	1,605,900	29.6	503,900	9.3	5,429,000	100

Source: Raynauld, Marion, and Béland, "La répartition des revenus."

resources in a frontier society, immigrants banded together to provide the kind of help that the family or kin group had provided in their homeland. Sometimes these mutual aid societies became the forerunners of flourishing businesses. Often they were short-lived, because their members prospered and had no further need of them, because those who were entrusted with the funds lacked experience, acumen, or honesty, or because economic depressions prevented members from paying their dues while at the same time multiplying the number of claimants for benefits. Those that endured were often responsible for social and ceremonial occasions as well as for material aid. In recent years there has been a decline in mutual benefit associations for at least three reasons: the greater sophistication of many immigrants, the increased economic opportunities in an expanding country, and the growth of public welfare measures. In addition, credit unions established by earlier arrivals have been of considerable financial assistance to newcomers, meeting some of the needs originally filled by mutual benefit associations.

Among early immigrants, the sense of ethnic identity often did not extend beyond the kin group, or those from the same town, village, or region in the homeland. Therefore the associations that grew up tended to be small, and to unite only those from a particular region rather than all the members of a linguistic or cultural group. Among the Chinese cultural group, for example, clan and family associations and district associations were numerous. German, Italian, and Greek groups also had many regional associations. The list of *landsmanschaften*, associations of persons from the same place of origin, among the Polish Jews in Toronto was said to read like a gazetteer of the place names of central Poland.[32] Where religious affiliations were important, the associations were often confined to those who shared a faith as well as an ethnic identity; for example, many Ukrainian associations were sponsored by churches, and even nominally secular associations were composed of either Ukrainian Roman Catholics or members of the Ukrainian Orthodox Church.

In the inter-war period, ethnic associations tended to reflect the political divisions of Europe, and often to be affiliated with organizations there. The emergence of the U.S.S.R. led to the formation of many associations in Canada among the central and eastern European peoples, some favourable to the Soviet regime and others opposed to it. The Ukrainians in particular were divided into various political camps by the arrival of immigrants who had participated in the struggle for Ukrainian independence and in the short-lived republic of the Ukraine. The upsurge of Fascism in Italy and Nazism in Germany also influenced ethnic associations in Canada. Italian immigration was drastically curtailed, and through its consulates the Italian government began to play an active role in Italian ethnic communities, setting up a series of political associations that were the counterparts of those in Italy. Anti-Fascist organizations were then founded as a reaction to this activity. Within each ideological grouping consolidation took place, so that organizations tended to include all the members of a particular group who shared a political viewpoint, rather than simply those who came from a particular region.

Nationalistic associations that limited their sphere of interest to events in the homeland had particular difficulties in recruiting members. Life in Canada dulled the sharp edge of concern for European or Asian issues. These associations often turned to youth, and devoted considerable attention to building associations for young people. Immediately after World War II, as political refugees joined the various cultural groups already in Canada, concern with political issues related to the homeland reached its peak.

In the 1950's and 1960's the increasing social, educational, and economic differentiation, both in Canadian society as a whole and among most cultural groups, led to associations based more on occupational and professional interests, social status, or cultural interests than in the past. The ethnic dimension of social stratification in Canadian society and the social stratification of particular cultural groups are important phenomena meriting extensive research, which we were unable to conduct.

Cultural groups with elaborate networks of associations have established, or tried to establish, coordinating bodies for the city, province, or country. The initiative in the formation of these congresses or federations has not always come from within the group itself. For example, the Ukrainian Canadian Committee, although it had forerunners, was set up in 1940 on the suggestion of the Canadian Department of National War Services. The Canadian Jewish Congress, the Canadian Polish Congress, the Trans-Canada Alliance of German Canadians, the Czechoslovak National Alliance, and the National Japanese Canadian Citizens' Association are other examples of ethnic federations. Such federations may not enlist all the existing eligible organizations for a variety of reasons, including inability or unwillingness to pay the dues. Some of these federations exclude from membership those organizations that they consider to be left-wing or subversive.

Ethnic associations generally have not been long-lived, although coordinating associations may prove to be an exception to this generalization. Since virtually all of them were founded in 1940 or later, it is too early to know how durable they will be. The individual associations have been composed largely of immigrants, and have not usually been successful in enlisting either the native born or more recent immigrants as members. People who join ethnic associations indicate a sense of ethnic identity, and membership in such associations probably reinforces this sense of identity because participation in the association increases contact with other members of the same cultural group at the expense of contact with others. The fact that ethnic associations are composed mainly of immigrants, and that the ethnic associations with the largest proportion of native born are Ukrainian associations, confirms the important role of ethnic identity in voluntary associations. There are many other indications that those of Ukrainian origin in Canada have maintained a strong sense of ethnic identity.

In 1965, the Commission conducted a survey of the ethnic associations of the four cultural groups associated with some of the largest ethnic origin categories.[33] The study identified 105 German, 225 Ukrainian, 204 Italian, and 106 Dutch associations: 67 German, 225 Ukrainian, 129 Italian, and 66 Dutch associations finally reported either by mail or through field interviews. Interviews were held in metropolitan areas where there was a large number of associations. The small number of German and Dutch associations should be kept in mind where percentages are given.

The number of associations identified and reporting is itself an indication of the intensity of group consciousness among the different cultural groups. Although the Ukrainian ethnic origin category is less than half as large as the German, there were more than twice as many Ukrainian associations as German identified. Italians, too, seemed considerably more group-conscious than Germans.

The Dutch associations exhibited a pattern more like that of the German ones. Both the German and Dutch associations averaged more members who were more widely dispersed geographically than the Ukrainian and Italian associations. Nevertheless, the total membership of all these associations still reflected a preponderance of Ukrainians and Italians because of their larger number of associations.

In only 8 percent of the Dutch associations were more than 30 percent of the members Canadian-born, compared to 11 percent of the German, and 23 percent of the Italian associations. Even though post-war immigration of Ukrainians was small, only 41 percent of the Ukrainian associations had more than 30 percent of their members who were Canadian-born. The Dutch had the highest proportion (56 percent) of associations with exclusively immigrant membership. Most of these appeared to be local church groups.

Members of the executives of the associations frequently act as spokesmen not only for the associations but also for the cultural groups related to them. An even higher proportion of officers than of members were immigrants, particularly post-war immigrants. Eighty-nine percent of the Dutch associations had no officers who were Canadian-born, and 82 percent had no officers who had arrived in Canada before 1946. For the German associations the corresponding figures were 64 percent and 39 percent; for the Italian associations 39 percent and 42 percent; for the Ukrainian associations 36 percent and 43 percent.

The ethnic exclusiveness of the associations is as important an index of social integration as the proportion of immigrant members. The German associations were the only ones in which such exclusiveness was not predominant. Eighty-five percent of the Dutch, 82 percent of the Ukrainian, and 77 percent of the Italian associations were ethnically exclusive, compared to only 40 percent of the German associations.

Generally, it appears that the more an ethnic group finds its origin a handicap, the more likely it is to form a strong structure of ethnic associations. Thus members of the German cultural group, with a long tradition in Canada and close cultural affinities with the British, do not have as many associations that are exclusively German as do other cultural groups. The Dutch, also well established and sharing a northern European culture with the British, have had difficulty in maintaining and developing an associational structure.

The fact that there were few exclusively German associations could well be related not only to the general lack of barriers between those of German and British ethnic origin, but also to hostility towards the German language and culture during and after the two world wars. This provided a strong reason for taking advantage of the ease with which people of German origin could disappear into the population at large. Faced with similar hostility, members of the Japanese community in Toronto after World War II were reluctant to build up an ethnic association structure such as had existed in Vancouver in the 1930's, because of the resulting visibility of the Japanese cultural group.

A sense of ethnic identity and participation in ethnic associations are positively correlated in many instances. The correlation is not perfect, however, and this is of particular significance for recent immigrants. The tendency of immigrants to form colonies or ghettos has been diminishing as new immigrants have become less exclusive and more sophisticated. These same factors have probably decreased interest in ethnic associations. This may not necessarily indicate that new immigrants have become less eager to maintain their cultural heritage, but only that they wish to maintain it by other means. However, participation in ethnic associations is not purely segregating in its effects. Associations provide opportunities for their members to learn from one another the facts of Canadian life. This is of particular importance for immigrants whose communication with other Canadians is hampered by language and cultural barriers.

Footnotes

1. Kosa, *Land of Choice*, pp. 13-16. Quotations in this paragraph are drawn from this work.

2. William I. Thomas and Florian Znaniecki, *The Polish Peasant in Europe and America*, 2nd edition, New York, 1958, pp. 87 and 98.

3. S. F. Miyamoto, "Social Solidarity among the Japanese in Seattle," *University of Washington Publications in the Social Sciences*, II, No. 2, December, 1939, p. 60.

4. Leonard Bloom, "Familial Problems and the Japanese Removal," *Research Studies*, State College of Washington, XI, No. 1, 1943, p. 21.

5. Boissevain, *The Italians of Montreal*, pp. 9-11. Quotations in this paragraph are drawn from this work.

6. Francis, *In Search of Utopia*, p. 271. Quotations in this paragraph are drawn from this work.

7. Kosa, *op. cit.*, pp. 44-47. Quotations in this paragraph are drawn from this work.

8. This involved obtaining the consent of the Minister of the Interior of China and advertising in two local Chinese papers that one was renouncing one's Chinese citizenship.

9. Enid Charles, *The Changing Size of the Family in Canada*, Dominion Bureau of Statistics, Eighth Census of Canada, 1941, Census Monograph No. 1, Ottawa, 1948.

10. Kosa, *op. cit.*, p. 47.

11. Boissevain, *op. cit.*, p. 42.

12. Nisei are the generation born in Canada of immigrant parents; Sansei are the next generation born in Canada; Kika are the first generation born in Canada who were sent back to Japan for their schooling; Issei are first-generation immigrants, born in Japan; Hakujin are non-Japanese.

13. Wangenheim, "The Social Organization of the Japanese Community in Toronto," p. 32.

14. Francis, *op. cit.*, p. 272 and Willms, "The Brethren Known as Hutterians," pp. 394-405.

15. Wangenheim, *op. cit.*, pp. 36-38. Quotations in this paragraph are drawn from this work.

16. Vera Lysenko, *Men in Sheepskin Coats: A Study in Assimilation*, Toronto, 1947, pp. 238-239. Quotations in this paragraph are drawn from this work.

17. Wangenheim, *op. cit.*, p. 65.

18. Woycenko, *The Ukrainians in Canada*, pp. 76-77.

19. Lysenko, *op. cit.*, pp. 74-78.

20. Hobart, "Italian Immigrants in Edmonton."

21. R. R. Wisse, "Jewish Participation in Canadian Culture," an essay prepared for the R.C.B.&B.

22. *Ibid.*

23. Sidlofsky, "Post-War Immigrants in the Changing Metropolis," p. 36.

24. A. Rose, "The Price of Freedom," in *A People and Its Faith*, pp. 73-76.

25. Wangenheim, *op. cit.*, p. 70.

26. W. E. Mann, *Sect, Cult, and Church in Alberta*, Toronto, 1955, p. 154.

27. David M. Heer, "The Trend of Interfaith Marriages in Canada: 1922-1957," *American Sociological Review*, XXVII, No. 2, April, 1962, pp. 245-246.

28. A. J. C. King and C. Angi, "Language and Secondary School Success," a study prepared for the R.C.B.&B. by arrangement with the Ontario Institute for Studies in Education.

29. The proportion of those starting their school year together in a given year who survive at each succeding [*sic*] grade.

30. *Report of the Royal Commission on Bilingualism and Biculturalism*, III, Table 7.

31. See John Gellner and John Smerek, *The Czechs and Slovaks in Canada*, Toronto, 1968, a recent study of cultural groups in Canada which pays particular attention to voluntary associations.

32. Kayfetz, "The Jewish Community in Toronto," p. 23.

33. D. Sherwood and A. Wakefield, "Voluntary Associations among Other Ethnic Groups in Canada," a study prepared for the R.C.B.&B.

Ethnic Penetration into Toronto's Elite Structure[*][†]

Merrijoy Kelner

The elite concept has been interpreted in many different and often contradictory ways. One widely accepted usage focuses exclusively on the power held by elite groups (Mills, 1956). Another, somewhat related view stresses the functional importance of elites to society at large (Keller, 1963). A third view emphasizes the rewards that accrue to elites (Lasswell, 1958). Frequently overlooked by investigators of elite status is the element of *prestige*, that is, the social recognition and respect accorded to an individual by others who have power and have themselves already achieved high status.

In the course of a recent study of the ethnic composition of elite groups in the Toronto community, it became apparent that further refinement should incorporate considerations of *both* power and prestige, as well as functional importance to society.

For the purpose of the study, two distinct levels of elite status were delineated. The bottom level of the elite structure was seen to consist of persons who have achieved key functional roles in Canadian society. This level, which includes labor leaders, corporation presidents, cabinet ministers, and the like, was defined as the level of *strategic* elites, following Keller's classification. Members of strategic elites qualify for inclusion in these groups on the basis of their achievements, since it is their functional contributions to the society which are the crucial consideration.

The upper level of the elite structure, a much smaller group, was restricted to persons who not only filled key functional roles, but were also accorded high social status in the community. This select group, found at the apex of the elite structure, was defined as a *core* elite.

Members of the core elite form a socially homogeneous group which is distinct from, and superior to, the strategic elites from which it is drawn. It is, in short, more elite than other elites. High social-class position in itself is not a sufficient qualification for core elite status; it must be combined with the power and wealth

[*]Reprinted from *The Canadian Review of Sociology and Anthropology*, 7:2 (1970), by permission of the author and the publisher.

[†]Based on a paper presented at the Annual Meeting of the Canadian Sociology and Anthropology Association, York University, June, 1969.

that accompany functional leadership. The essential point here is that, unless members of strategic elites can use their power and wealth to win acceptance from the social leaders in the community, they will be relegated to the fringes of the elite structure, and can never win admission to the core elite.

Utilizing the conception of two distinct levels of elite status, a study was completed which analyzes the extent and methods of non-Anglo-Saxon penetration into Toronto's elite structure.[1] The primary aim of the study was to explore further Porter's conclusion that elite positions in Canadian society are held almost exclusively by Anglo-Saxons (Porter, 1965) by reference to developments in the Toronto community in the last two decades.

The city of Toronto provides an excellent setting for this kind of research problem: In 1961 close to 40 percent of its population was foreign born and indications are that this proportion has increased even further in subsequent years. The swift pace of development, together with the large influx of European immigrants, have transformed the social character of the Toronto community since the conclusion of World War II. The presence of so many people of various ethnic origins in a rapidly expanding urban centre has served to release new forces. The pace of technological development and the thrust of industrial expansion have brought new opportunities for advancement. It was postulated that these changes have resulted in alterations in recruitment patterns to elite positions and a weakening of the Anglo-Saxon monopoly of elite status, as access to positions of power and prestige widens and increases.

Data and Methods

Data for the study were acquired in a variety of ways. Detailed interviews were conducted with a representative group of 55 Torontonians occupying important positions in Canadian life. Informal discussions were held with a variety of informants, such as editors of daily newspapers and journalists writing for magazines of local interest. Listings of the boards of directors and top officials of leading companies and institutions were compiled and analysed.

Daily reading of the three Toronto newspapers for a period of two years, plus close attention to local magazines and journals, also provided useful source material. In addition, census figures for Metro Toronto, information concerning the immigration patterns of ethnic groups, old newspaper files, and the biographies of established Toronto families (Gillen, 1965; Wilkinson, 1956; Eaton, 1956; Harkness, 1963; Wilson, 1965) all contributed pertinent data.

Boundaries for the study were drawn with a view to encompassing a broad structure of power and prestige, while still limiting the number of people to be considered. The requirement for inclusion was that members of the study population live and work within the confines of Metro Toronto. No limits were placed on the scope of their influence and reputation, which frequently extended to the international scene.

Following the positional model used by Porter, Mills, and others, elite groups residing in the Toronto community were identified for each major institutional sphere. Such an approach assumes that elite groups consist of those who occupy key positions in major institutional hierarchies. It has been suggested that formal position does not necessarily imply that an individual actually exercises the influence conferred upon him by that position. He may, on occasion, be merely a figurehead for the real, if invisible, power behind the throne. Nevertheless, formal position at the top of a major institutional order is, in itself, an important social phenomenon, one which also has the advantage of providing systematic, codifiable, and verifiable facts.

Use of the positional approach in this study followed closely the pattern established by Porter in *The Vertical Mosaic*. A corporate elite, a labour elite, a political elite, a civil service elite, a communications elite, and an academic elite were delineated. All these groups clearly fit into the category of strategic elites, as defined above. Members of these groups were initially identified in the following way: (1) *The corporate elite* consisted of those residents of Toronto who were listed as directors of the 100 largest Canadian companies.[2] Added to this group were the Toronto-based directors of the major Canadian holding companies, such as the Argus Corporation, Power Corporation of Canada, and George Weston Limited. (2) *The labour elite* consisted of those residents of Toronto who were senior officials of the largest unions, plus those holding executive positions with organizations like the Ontario Federation of Labour, the Toronto Labour Council, and the Canadian Labour Congress. (3) *The political elite* consisted of all Toronto residents who had, since the inception of the study, served as members of the federal cabinet, the provincial cabinet, and the Metropolitan Council, plus all supreme court judges residing in the city. (4) *The civil service elite* consisted of senior provincial and municipal civil servants living in the Toronto area. (5) *The communications elite* consisted of the Toronto-based owners and directors of the major newspapers, book publishing firms, television networks, and radio stations. (6) *The academic elite* consisted of Toronto residents who had been elected by their peers as fellows of the Royal Society of Canada, an exclusive and self-selecting group of academic leaders which includes representatives from all disciplines of higher learning.

The total listings for each group were examined, in order to establish the ethnic backgrounds of those included. All those whose names did not appear to be clearly Anglo-Saxon in origin were followed up in biographical sources such as *Who's Who in Canada* (1967). In addition, personal interviews were conducted with other leaders in the field in order to obtain additional information regarding the ethnic origins of those included in the study population. This was necessary because names alone can be misleading as a guide to ethnicity, particularly since non-Anglo-Saxon names are often discarded along the road to leadership positions.

The aim of this systematic analysis was to assess the extent to which non-Anglo-Saxons have risen to functionally important positions during the past twenty years. It became evident that although non-Anglo-Saxon representation in elite groups has definitely increased since 1948, in no major institutional field has it reached the same level as non-Anglo-Saxon representation in the total community.

Findings

Investigation disclosed that the proportion of non-Anglo-Saxon corporate leaders living in Toronto is still very small, approximately 7 percent.[3] The 100 largest corporations listed only about 20 non-Anglo-Saxon businessmen among 325 Toronto-based directors, and only one of the 20 had multiple directorships in the leading corporations. None of Canada's major holding companies included non-Anglo-Saxons on their boards.

The labour elite was more receptive to non-Anglo-Saxons than the corporate. Approximately 21 percent of the labour elite in Toronto were not of Anglo-Saxon origin. The data also indicated that labour leadership at the local level was easier for non-Anglo-Saxons to achieve than at the national level, where few had succeeded in reaching executive positions.

In the political sphere, 19 percent of those in elite positions were non-Anglo-Saxons. Three of the 32 judges of the supreme court of Ontario were of non-Anglo-Saxon origin, as were two of the six provincial cabinet ministers residing in Toronto, and several of those involved in the municipal political structure. Again, non-Anglo-Saxon penetration into elite positions is shown to be easier to effect at the local level than at the national level; Toronto had no non-Anglo-Saxon federal cabinet ministers representing it at the time of this study, in spite of the ethnic diversity of its population.

The civil service was less receptive to non-Anglo-Saxons at the top levels than some other fields; approximately 10 percent of its upper-echelon jobs were held by people of non-Anglo-Saxon origin, and these were clustered mainly in the research branch. Only two non-Anglo-Saxon names appeared on the list of over 40 Toronto-based deputy ministers and assistant deputy ministers, while about 25 non-Anglo-Saxons were occupying positions as division or branch heads, out of a total of approximately 229 persons. At the municipal level, two of the 19 senior officials were of non-Anglo-Saxon origin.

Owners and directors of the mass media were still overwhelmingly Anglo-Saxon. All the major book publishers were Anglo-Saxon, as were their boards of directors. Some inroads had been made into top positions in newspaper publishing, however; one of the three daily newspapers had two men of non-Anglo-Saxon origins on its executive committee and another included a prominent non-Anglo-Saxon on its board of directors. One of the two major television networks had a non-Anglo-Saxon director, as did two local radio stations. These men represent only about 5 percent of the total list of owners and directors of the media, however.

Non-Anglo-Saxon members of the academic elite, i.e., Fellows of the Royal Society, included approximately 19 percent of the total list of Fellows living in the Toronto area. It is significant that a higher proportion of these came from the humanities and social sciences division than from the science division.

When Porter's model for identifying members of the elite was applied to the community of Toronto, there was clear indication that in no major institutional field had the proportion of non-Anglo-Saxons in the elite reached the same level as the non-Anglo-Saxon population in the community as a whole. However, comparisons with the ethnic composition of the elite structure 20 years earlier revealed that, in every case where comparable figures were available, non-Anglo-Saxon representation had increased considerably.

An Alternative Model

The Porter model emphasizes the importance of power and institutional position in determining elite status, but does not include considerations of prestige. For example, Porter deliberately excludes members of the Senate from the political elite on the basis that they have no real power. If, however, the concept of prestige enters into the definition of elite status, then senators must be included in the political elite. Warner, Baltzell, Hunter, and others have demonstrated that an individual's reputation in his community plays an important role in locating him in the social stratification hierarchy (Baltzell, 1964; Warner, 1949; Hunter, 1953). However, it is not always the people who hold top-level positions who acquire reputations for influence and achievement in their chosen fields. Just as different personalities realize the power potential of their positions in different ways, so certain individuals exert a significant influence on their society without the underpinnings of formal position to bolster their elite status. A reputation for outstanding accomplishment in a particular field can often bring membership in an elite group, even though the individual involved holds no position on any board of directors or executive committee. Writers and artists, in particular, base their claims to elite status on these kinds of considerations. The leadership group of each institutional sphere mentioned above was redefined utilizing the concept of prestige in conjunction with the concept of power, and the ethnic composition of elite groups was reassessed.

In this second overview, attention was also directed to the dynamic processes taking place in the community. In order to avoid a static approach to the issue of elite status, analysis focused not only on those who have arrived at the top, but also on those currently moving up from the middle levels of leadership.

Findings

This kind of perspective revealed new patterns, established within the past few years, which will eventually have a significant impact on the ethnic constitution of the strategic elites. For example, new trust companies and savings and loans associations have recently been formed or taken over by non-Anglo-Saxons. These newer financial institutions have not yet achieved the stature of the older, established corporations, *i.e.*, they are not included in the listing of leading financial companies, but they have already helped to facilitate the participation of non-Anglo-Saxon businessmen in ventures which might otherwise never have been funded. Other developments also point to gradual non-Anglo-Saxon penetration into important corporate roles. By 1969 two Jews had been admitted to the Toronto Stock Exchange, formerly an exclusive bastion of Anglo-Saxon power.

Real estate development in Toronto, which has enjoyed tremendous growth since the end of World War II, is a form of enterprise which has become vitally important to non-Anglo-Saxons as a way up the commercial ladder. The building business has offered fresh opportunities to many who found more established commercial fields, like banking and insurance, closed to them. It is a high-risk field which requires little equity to operate on a small scale. By borrowing from the banks on the basis of pledging their own personal worth, and by skilfully manipulating payments to the trades, many small-scale non-Anglo-Saxon builders, particularly Jews and Italians, dramatically widened the scope of their activities, moving from building a few houses to developing complete subdivisions and apartment complexes.

Similarly in other institutional spheres, non-Anglo-Saxons have been moving up toward positions of power and prestige. In the labour field, for example, the large number of Italian labourers has been reflected in the recent inclusion of Italians in the leadership of local trade unions. In the political field, non-Anglo-Saxons have been putting themselves forward as political candidates in increasing numbers. At present, 8 of the city's 22 federal members of Parliament and 7 of the 29 provincial members are of non-Anglo-Saxon origin. The first Jewish senator appointed in Canada also resides in Toronto.

Since the end of World War II, the proportion of non-Anglo-Saxon university professors has increased markedly, particularly in developing fields like the social sciences. Analysis of the ethnic composition of the faculty in the sociology department at the University of Toronto over the past 30 years clearly illustrates the changing patterns of recruitment. During the 1938-1939 university session, the four staff members were all Anglo-Saxons. Ten years later, the faculty consisted of five members, one of whom was non-Anglo-Saxon. During the next ten-year period, the department expanded rapidly, and by the 1967-1968 session, it had developed a faculty of 29 people, 11 of whom were non-Anglo-Saxons. Clearly, the rapid rate of growth imposed an urgent need for qualified personnel, and considerations like ethnic origin became increasingly irrelevant.

At the leadership level, changes in ethnic composition have been slower. More non-Anglo-Saxons have achieved top-level academic posts at York University, which, being newer, had to fill a large number of positions in a short space of time. Approximately 9 of the 20 departmental chairmen at York University were of non-Anglo-Saxon origin, while only one of the 19 chairmen of departments at the University of Toronto was not Anglo-Saxon.

The major thrust of upward mobility has taken place in the interstitial, innovative fields, which had no entrenched aristocracy in control, and in those fields which require a high degree of technical specialization. Some of the most dynamic spheres include mining, entertainment, construction, and psycho-analysis.

The rate of increase in the proportions of non-Anglo-Saxons admitted to strategic elites has not been uniform for all ethnic groups. To date, Jews have been more successful than other non-Anglo-Saxons in reaching leadership positions in major institutional hierarchies, due primarily to their urban back-ground, high educational level, and a generally longer period of acculturation to Canadian society. Variations were also found in the types of routes to elite status that were followed by members of different ethnic groups. The cultural sphere, for example, has drawn a significant proportion of its leadership from the Jewish group, while the labour movement is currently attracting Italians and Ukrainians to its top-ranking positions. A wide variety of non-Anglo-Saxon groups is currently represented in the research and planning branches of the civil service.

Analysis of the avenues of ascent followed by members of strategic elites reveals that in contrast to Anglo-Saxons, who rise within the bureaucratic structure, non-Anglo-Saxons typically achieve prominence outside it, through more individualistic and higher-risk paths. In other words, upward mobility is achieved by Anglo-Saxons through established, stable, corporate entities, while non-Anglo-Saxons have to achieve status as individual entrepreneurs.

In a society which is becoming more and more bureaucratically structured, this differential pattern of upward mobility has significant implications for non-

Anglo-Saxons. The bureaucratization of contemporary society has been recognized by many social analysts (see, for example, Bensman and Rosenberg, 1963:269). Today, every major occupation is increasingly organized and bureaucratized. Concurrently, opportunities for individual entrepreneurs to rise to positions of power and prestige are disappearing. Enterprise today requires large capital investments, and this requirement brings with it the necessity for large corporate structures. Thus, it appears that the individualistic, high-risk avenue to elite status that have typically served the ambitious non-Anglo-Saxon, are becoming less and less available to him. In the future, we can expect that non-Anglo-Saxons will increasingly have to make their ascent to elite positions *within* the bureaucratic structure; an accommodation which may well lead to considerable inter-group conflict. The usual pattern is to start one's own small business and to build it up into an important corporate structure, at which time it is customary to add some Anglo-Saxon names to the board of directors, to ensure legitimation.

The Social Elite

Omitted from the Porter study was consideration of leaders in several other major institutional fields, such as the celebrity elite, the cultural elite, the social elite, and the professional elite. The inclusion of prestige as an element of elite status raises the issue of the ethnic origins of social leaders. Social leaders are those who decide who shall be included in the membership of the *best* clubs and who shall be invited to the most exclusive social gatherings. Their position is based on their upper-class status, which derives from a composite of many factors, including old family prestige and a particular life style.

Analysis demonstrated that the social leadership of the Toronto community is still almost exclusively Anglo-Saxon. The city's high-status social clubs do not welcome non-Anglo-Saxon members either by expressed policy or by long-standing custom. The purpose of these clubs is to limit social interaction to the *right* people, the people *one knows*, and these are rarely members of non-Anglo-Saxon groups. Detailed interviews with high-status respondents revealed that Anglo-Saxon leaders rarely make close friends among people of other ethnic groups. Social relations between upperclass Anglo-Saxons and others in the community were found to be categorical and formal in nature, and restricted almost entirely to public occasions.

This social exclusion has important repercussions for the hierarchical structure of the society. Social restrictions have the effect of containing power and prestige within a select circle, even though this may not be the primary motive for exclusion. Membership in the leading men's clubs, for example, is a tacit prerequisite for advancement to top positions in many fields, particularly in the professions and in large corporations. It is in the relaxed club setting that many major decisions are made, and it is through the camaraderie of the club atmosphere that younger men are recognized and selected for future leadership roles. Personal relations are cemented in common social experiences and those who are excluded from them are at a serious disadvantage in their attempts to reach and maintain top positions.

It is important to note, however, that there are powerful forces within the various non-Anglo-Saxon groups which also act to limit social interaction. Their leaders encourage them to maintain a distinctive identity, and, in doing so, they discourage them from close social relations with members of the general community, thus imposing serious limitations upon the degree of upward mobility that can be achieved.

Exclusion from intimate social interaction with the Anglo-Saxon upper class imposes certain practical limitations on advancement into key functional positions, that is, into membership in strategic elites, in the ways suggested above. Such exclusion is also a crucial factor in restricting the entry of non-Anglo-Saxons into the small inner circle designated here as the core elite. This elite nucleus, whose members combine leadership roles in major institutional spheres with high social status, is the most powerful and prestigious group in the community, and it is this group which has proven almost impervious to non-Anglo-Saxon penetration.

Conclusions

The results of this study indicate that the growing need for skilled specialists and executive talent, occasioned by the increasing complexity of management and the constant development of new techniques, combined with the influx of New Canadians into the society, has resulted in freer access to membership in Toronto's strategic elites. Positions of power and prestige have become more accessible to qualified non-Anglo-Saxons as ascriptive criteria have become less important in recruitment.

This democratization process has been shown, however, to have definite limitations, contrary to Keller's thesis that, as industrialization creates large and more complex societies, ruling classes or core elites (as they are described here) will disappear and be replaced by strategic elites. The elite nucleus is still very much in evidence and is still almost completely reserved for upper-class Anglo-Saxons. In short, the shift from criteria based on ascription to those based on achievement is far from complete.

Within their own groups, the non-Anglo-Saxon members of strategic elites occupy positions of high social status and limit their friendships to others of their own socioeconomic class. They encourage their children to marry within the upper stratum of their group, in much the same way as the Anglo-Saxons. It is within the community at large that a lack of congruity exists between their wealth and power on the one hand, and their social status on the other, and it is this discrepancy which prevents non-Anglo-Saxon members of strategic elites from entering the core elite and, thus, from achieving the highest levels of power and prestige.

On the basis of this study it seems clear that a dual-level conception of elite status can be usefully applied to research in this area. Application to other settings is now required for its further refinement and development.

Footnotes

1. In this study, the designation "Anglo-Saxon" includes members of the English, Scots, Welsh, and Irish groups.
2. The 100 largest Canadian companies (in terms of assets, profits, and sales) were determined by a survey reported in *The Financial Post*, August 13, 1966. The directors were identified through *The Directory of Directors*. Toronto: 1966.

3. These figures should be regarded as approximations only, due to the difficulties involved in assessing ethnic origins.

References

Baltzell, E. D., *The Protestant Establishment*. New York: Random House, 1964.

Bensman, J. and Rosenberg, B., *Mass, Class and Bureaucracy*. Englewood Cliffs: Prentice-Hall, 1963.

Eaton, F. M., *Memory's Wall*. Toronto: Clarke Irwin, 1956.

The Financial Post, *The Directory of Directors*. Toronto: MacLean-Hunter Limited, 1966.

Gillen, M., *The Masseys*. Toronto: Ryerson Press, 1965.

Harkness, R., *J. E. Atkinson of the Star*. Toronto: University of Toronto Press, 1963.

Hunter, P., *Community Power Structure*. Chapel Hill: University of North Carolina Press, 1952.

Keller, S., *Beyond the Ruling Class*. New York: Random House, 1963.

Lasswell, H., *Politics: Who Gets What, When, How*. Cleveland: The World Publishing Co., 1958.

Mills, C. W., *The Power Elite*. New York: Oxford University Press, 1956.

Porter, J., *The Vertical Mosaic*. Toronto: University of Toronto Press, 1965.

Warner, W. L., *Social Class in America*. Chicago: Science Research Associates, 1949.

Who's Who in Canada, 1966-68. Toronto: International Press Limited, 1967.

Wilkinson, A., *Lions in the Way*. Toronto: Macmillan, 1956.

Wilson, A., *John Northway*. Toronto: Burns and MacEachern, 1965.

Hutterites Uneasy: Alberta May Provoke Exodus*

Ben Tierney

An exodus of Hutterites from Alberta is possible as a result of last week's Supreme Court of Canada decision upholding the constitutional validity of Alberta's Communal Property Act.

Max Moscovich of Lethbridge, one of two Southern Alberta lawyers who represented the two Hutterite churches which challenged the Alberta law, says he has been told that many of the Hutterites are considering pulling up stakes once again.

The Supreme Court unanimously rejected the Hutterites' contention that the Communal Property Act, which governs the size and location of Hutterite colonies, interfered with their religion, and was, consequently *ultra vires* of the province. The act, the court declared, clearly concerned the ownership of land and was therefore within the jurisdiction of the province under Section 92 (Subsection 13) of the British North America Act.

The Supreme Court decision brings to an end legal proceedings which began when the RCMP launched an investigation into reports that Hutterites were

* Reproduced with permission of Ben Tierney, Ottawa correspondent for Southam News Service. Reprinted from *The Globe and Mail*, Summer, 1969.

buying land in the Brant area of Southern Alberta to establish a colony without first seeking the approval of the Communal Property Board.

The RCMP investigation led to charges being laid against 15 people, six of them Hutterites. However, before the charges of violating the Communal Property Act (carrying a maximum fine of $500 or one year in jail) could be heard in magistrate's court, the two Hutterite Churches announced their intention of challenging the act in the Alberta Supreme Court and a stay of proceedings was entered at the lower court level.

Mr. Justice J. V. H. Milvain (now Chief Justice Milvain) heard the Hutterite case and, in November 1965, ruled the law within the jurisdiction of the province. His decision was taken to the Alberta Supreme Court Appellate Division, but it upheld the decision in a judgment handed down in December of 1966. This week's Supreme Court decision is a result of that verdict.

If, as Mr. Moscovitch suggests, the Hutterites move from the province, it will likely be in the direction of Saskatchewan.

Saskatchewan has about 20 Hutterite colonies (compared to 71 in Alberta) and each of these is a *daughter* colony of an Alberta colony.

Hutterite colonies (or *bruderhofs*) split once they grow to more than 100 people, and, according to E. F. Breach, chairman of the Alberta Communal Property Board, there have been one or two Saskatchewan colonies arising out of Alberta colony growth each year in recent years, and three in 1968.

Saskatchewan is attractive to the farming Hutterites because its Government's policies are not, at the moment, as stringent as Alberta's.

Alberta Hutterite colonies are restricted to 6,400 acres on good land, 10,240 acres on middle quality land, and 15,360 acres on poorer land (mostly grazing areas located in the southeastern part of the province). In addition, the Government maintains a policy of keeping colonies about 15 to 20 miles apart, and of encouraging their development in the northern rather than the central and southern sections of the province.

Another reason for Saskatchewan's appeal for the Hutterites is simply that their number there is not sufficient to have stirred the public resentment that has been felt in Alberta.

In Alberta, even a whisper that Hutterites are planning a colony is enough to send the district's farmers and merchants scurrying about with anti-Hutterite petitions. A recent Communal Property Board hearing into establishment of a Hutterite colony had placed before it 51 briefs, 47 of them opposed to the new colony.

In December 1967, the Alberta Association of Municipal Districts and Counties asked the Government to suspend approval of all further colonies until an extensive inquiry into their implications had been carried out. The Government has since approved another colony.

Resentment of the Hutterites is, to some extent, based on myth. It is often charged, for example, that the devout, German-speaking members of the sect won't pay income tax. In fact, the Hutterites were exempt [*sic*] as "a charitable organization of a religious nature" under Liberal legislation passed after the

Second World War, but this was changed by the Conservative Government in 1961.

Resentment also arises from Hutterite pacifism. Bitterness was extremely high immediately after the Second World War (the Communal Property Act was passed in 1947) when veterans returned to Alberta and found that their hopes of buying farm land were to be frustrated by the stay-at-home Hutterites, who had benefited financially from wartime demands and could offer top prices for land.

But, most of all, the basis of the resentment is economics. The average Hutterite colony, according to the Communal Property Board chairman, Mr. Breach, dislodges four to seven farmers. Thus, if four colonies were to establish around a small town, the resulting loss of 16 to 28 farmers from the district would affect local business because the Hutterite purchasing pattern is different.

Hutterites provide as much if not more business for local implement dealers, bulk oil dealers and other merchants of that kind, Mr. Breach says. But they are bad news for barber shops, appliance stores and the like.

Though not a great deal is said about it, the Hutterites are also bad news for Government liquor stores. The Hutterites make their beer and wine ("they make excellent wine," says Mr. Breach).

The Hutterite faith was founded by Jacob Hutter, a German, at the time of the Reformation. In 1874, 400 Hutterites settled in South Dakota, and the faith spread into Canada when the United States entered the First World War and the Hutterites were faced with conscription.

Today there are about 18,000 in 180 colonies in the northern United States and Canada (Alberta has 71, Saskatchewan about 20, Manitoba about 40, South Dakota about 25, Montana about 20, and Minnesota, North Dakota and Washington have one each).

Devout and Spartan in their ways, individual Hutterites take for themselves only what they need to survive and turn the remaining product of their labor over to the colony.

They are generally regarded as excellent farmers and each of the Alberta colonies is self-sufficient in food.

Though the Hutterites drink wine and beer in moderation, singing and dancing is forbidden by their 400-year-old anabaptist religion. Religion also limits the education of their children to Grade 8 or 9 at small schools within the colony.

"We would not allow our children to attend county schools," one Hutterite leader has been quoted as saying. "We want to keep them on the colony because we do not want them to come home with bad habits."

A. J. Hooke, the province's former Minister of Municipal Affairs, has predicted that the "Hutterite problem" will be "practically non-existent in 20 years" because the young people are gradually accepting non-Hutterite ways.

But economics rather than dissatisfaction among the young might be the major factor in limiting the growth of the Hutterites.

Professor Karl Peter, an authority on Hutterites, has pointed out that the Hutterite population doubles every 17.3 years (the average family has 10 children), and each colony splits after its number reaches more than 100. Consequently, the Hutterites are constantly in search of new land, land that is continually increasing in cost.

Professor Peter feels break-up is inevitable and he has suggested that "only the fear of losing salvation" is stopping some colonies from dispersing.

In the meantime, the Hutterites are faced with the problem of what to do about the Communal Property Act, a law which they feel interferes with their religion.

The solution, says the Hutterites' lawyer, Mr. Moscovitch, must lie in political action now that the possibility of further legal action no longer exists.

But hope for results from political action is hardly bright. Hutterites don't vote. Farmers do. And Alberta's Social Credit Government, as far as can be determined, is not giving any consideration to either repealing or substantially amending the act.

In lieu of action by the Alberta Government, about all the Hutterites can hope for its entrenchment of a charter of human rights, including property rights, in the Canadian constitution, thereby invalidating the Alberta act.

But that, like Alberta Government action, could be a long time coming.

The Status of Women in Canada[*]

Royal Commission Report

Criteria and Principles

In a dozen succinct words the Universal Declaration of Human Rights[1] has clarified the issue of the rights of women: "All human beings are born free and equal in dignity and rights."

Canada is, therefore, committed to a principle that permits no distinction in rights and freedoms between women and men. The principle emphasizes the common status of women and men rather than a separate status for each sex. The stage has been set for a new society equally enjoyed and maintained by both sexes.

But practices and attitudes die slowly. As we travelled across the country, we heard of discrimination against women that still flourishes and prejudice that is very much alive. It became abundantly clear that Canada's commitment is far from being realized.

We have been asked to inquire into and report upon the status of women in Canada and we have done so in the light of certain principles. A general principle is that *everyone is entitled to the rights and freedoms proclaimed in the Universal Declaration of Human Rights.* We have examined the status of

*Report of the Royal Commission on the Status of Women in Canada, "Criterion and Principle," pp. xi-xii and "Canadian Women and Society," pp. 1-18, 1970. Reproduced with the permission of Information Canada.

women to learn whether or not they really have these positive rights and freedoms both in principle and in practice. Some of our recommendations should establish a measure of equality that is now lacking for men as well as for women.

Explicit in the Terms of Reference given us by the Government is our duty to ensure for women equal opportunities with men. We have interpreted this to mean that equality of opportunity for everyone should be the goal of Canadian society. The right to an adequate standard of living is without value to the person who has no means of achieving it. Freedom to choose a career means little if the opportunity to enter some occupations is restricted.

Our Terms of Reference also imply that *the full use of human resources is in the national interest.* We have explored the extent to which Canada develops and makes use of the skills and abilities of women.

Women and men, having the same rights and freedoms, share the same responsibilities. They should have an equal opportunity to fulfil this obligation. We have, therefore, examined the status of women and made recommendations in the belief that *there should be equality of opportunity to share the responsibilities to society as well as its privileges and prerogatives.*

In particular, the Commission adopted four principles: first, that *women should be free to choose whether or not to take employment outside their homes.* The circumstances which impede this free choice have been of specific interest to our inquiry. Where we have made recommendations to improve opportunities for women in the work world, our goal has not been to force married women to work for pay outside of the home but rather to eliminate the practical obstacles that prevent them from exercising this right. If a husband is willing to support his wife, or a wife her husband, the decision and responsibility belong to them.

The second is that *the care of children is a responsibility to be shared by the mother, the father and society.* Unless this shared responsibility is acknowledged and assumed, women cannot be accorded true equality.

The third principle specifically recognizes the child-bearing function of women. It is apparent that *society has a responsibility for women because of pregnancy and child-birth, and special treatment related to maternity will always be necessary.*

The fourth principle is that *in certain areas women will for an interim period require special treatment to overcome the adverse effects of discriminatory practices.* We consider such measures to be justified in a limited range of circumstances, and we anticipate that they should quickly lead to actual equality which would make their continuance unnecessary. The needs and capacities of women have not always been understood. Discrimination against women has in many instances been unintentional and special treatment will no longer be required if a positive effort to remove it is made for a short period.

With these principles in mind, we have first looked at women in Canadian society. Within this perspective we have gone on to consider the position of women in the economy, the education they receive, their place in the family and their participation in public life. We have considered the particular implications of poverty among women, conditions of citizenship and aspects of taxation, and the Criminal Code as it affects the female offender.

Canadian Women and Society

The rapid changes which have taken place in Canada, especially during the last 30 years, have profoundly affected the lives of women. Technological developments, urbanization, industrialization and the progress of medical and other scientific research have altered the way they live today, and will continue to alter it.

New methods of communication, especially television, have shown Canadians themselves and people in other countries in a new perspective. These and other developments have led people of all ages, but particularly the young, to question long accepted beliefs and traditions. Our society has become more permissive as a new generation reacts, often violently, against the domination of established authority and the old way of life. There is a growing belief that many of our attitudes are based on traditions and myths which do not reflect the facts and realities of today.

Although a rigid definition of woman lives on today as a stereotype despite rapidly changing circumstances, a new consciousness and concern about the status of women are indicated by the creation of a number of national commissions to study and report on the matter.[2]

In the past, many thoughtful people have questioned women's place in society. Some men have realized that a world organized and ruled by men will be naturally inclined to keep women in subjugation. As John Stuart Mill put it: "Men do not want solely the obedience of women, they want their sentiments . . . not a forced slave but a willing one."[3]

Men are becoming more conscious of the unbalanced nature of a social order in which everything centres on one sex alone. "It is understood that they, men, essentially constitute Man, and that women's part in mankind is merely accessory. It is a purely subjective attitude raised on an immense intellectual apparatus that makes prodigious claims to objectivity. Men have scarcely ever been able to see the basic unreality of this structure . . . ."[4] This Canadian writer adds that "the profound result of feminism has been to set up a variety of mutations in man, for humanity will never be adult without the full presence of woman."

Through the years, some women have protested at length, though often unheeded, in a world still insensitive to the social problem created by their status. Over recent years, the number of books on the subject has increased rapidly. Many have been widely read. Two of these, which were in the vanguard and may have been the source of aroused interest, were *The Second Sex* by Simone de Beauvoir,[5] and *The Feminine Mystique* by Betty Friedan.[6] Both authors assail the traditional and contemporary myths that have tended to keep women in a dependent and subordinate position.

In the United States, the last four years have seen the rapid growth of increasingly diversified groups of women that try to improve their collective lot as well as to combat discrimination. In some ways they seem to be a resurgence of the early feminist movements which battled for woman suffrage. However, reformist feminist groups today question all aspects of society. Some of them are not merely reformist but revolutionary in their aims, seeking radical changes in the economic system as well as in the institution of marriage and the nuclear family. Others agree that economics plays a fundamental part in their problems but maintain that this only involves an equal right to work which, in turn, must rest on equality in the educational system.

Similar movements are growing in Canada. For example, as of March 1970, there were local units of the Women's Liberation Movement in 16 cities from Vancouver to Halifax. Their articles, studies and discussions examine all kinds of global solutions as well as specific reforms.[7] Other groups have been formed which are occupied solely with the status of women.

Women made use of the public hearings of this Commission as a vehicle to express their aspirations. In our search for ways to ensure for women real equality of opportunity in Canadian society, we heard women, and also men, from coast to coast, tell of their hopes and frustrations concerning the status of women. The main aspiration was for elementary human rights and genuine equality: ". . . we subscribe to the fundamental principle of equality of the sexes as human beings and as citizens and we believe that any action either legislative, corporate or individual which infringes on that equality violates a fundamental human right."[8]

Other briefs stressed that women's sense of personal dignity is not being respected by the present political, economic and social structures of Canada: "Our government bodies are not unlike stag parties but the stakes here are human dignity and social progress not plastic poker chips."[9] "It may not be the loss of dollars that bothers as much as the lack of dignity in not receiving recognition for labour willingly done."[10]

A woman suffers when she is not recognized as having an individual identity as a person with her own aspirations, strengths, weaknesses, tastes and ideas that are not necessarily those of all other women whether married or unmarried, whether wives at home or workers outside. She does not accept with good grace the easy generalizations, often accompanied by a superficial idealization of the concept of womanhood, that fill so much of the literature, thought and even languages of western countries. Many Canadian women protest against the stereotypes imposed upon them: "Women are not a homogeneous group, and their needs are variable in relation to their social and economic status, their role and contribution in employment, and their role and responsibility related to the needs of children."[11] "Changes would have to be in the direction of acknowledging women as individual human beings, even in marriage."[12] "Women are adults not children to be protected, pampered and adored."[13] "Manpower counsellors, most of whom are men, think that all women have the homemaking instinct. This is no more realistic than assuming all men are mechanically minded."[14] "(The married woman who works) is no longer regarded as the wife of Mr. X, but rather as Mrs. X, social worker, nurse, doctor, technician, or other specialist. When talking to her, one no longer feels obliged to begin by asking about her children, the subject that would previously have been assumed to be the centre of her life. One may speak to her of her profession since it is an open window, letting her look out on the world; one may also choose to talk with her about political, economic or social topics."[15]

Many women insist that it is not the traditional division of masculine and feminine roles alone which must change, but the conventional image of marriage and the family as well. The desire for this change was expressed in many briefs: "If women are to attain equality there must be a change in the whole expectations of husband and wife. Marriage must become a partnership where each is free to pursue a career and is equally responsible for the home and family. The family unit would become strong again because men and women would less often look on marriage as a trap."[16] "Just as we regard the terms *father* or *husband* as indicating a human relationship, so we should regard the terms *wife* and *mother*. It does not follow that women need to make a career or a whole way of life out of being wives and mothers – just as men do not make marriage and parenthood their whole way of life."[17]

Many women in briefs asked for the right to a degree of personal fulfilment. "To be a 'person in her own right' – not just a husband's alter-ego – a female child and teenager will have to be conditioned to regard marriage and child-bearing as a phase of life not the whole of it. Each female should be encouraged to discover her own particular gifts, talents, drives and to cultivate them for self-expression and for contribution to society. The Creator has endowed her with no less than the male. The mental climate in which she is reared should recognize and provide for her development to the fullest extent . . . ."[18] "Girls and women must be encouraged to seek self-fulfilment as human beings rather than merely as females."[19]

In other briefs women pointed out that these profound and earnest desires can be realized by women only if they are given help, whenever necessary, to achieve the balance between their life at home and their outside interests. They asked that society as a whole and its institutions recognize that women's minds are at least as important as their traditional domestic roles. ". . . (these roles) no longer express the profound reality of their lives. Women would, however, welcome a true understanding of their destiny and purpose in life."[20] "At the World Conferences of Churches in Geneva in 1966, Margaret Mead observed that the church has traditionally granted woman a soul. She pleaded to grant her also a mind. The plea should be directed to all men."[21]

Canadian Women in a Changing World

Canadian women have benefited, along with the rest of the population, from medical and social progress. Science has made it possible for both women and men to lead longer, healthier lives. At the end of the 18th century, the average life expectancy of both sexes was probably not more than 35 years. Since then, the toll of death through illness and epidemics has steadily declined. A decreasing number of women die in child-birth or are exhausted by numerous pregnancies. In 1931, the life expectancy of Canadian women was 62, compared with 60 for men. In 1968, in Canada, women could expect to live almost to the age of 76, and men to 69. (Life expectancy was approximately 66 years for Indian women in 1968 and 50 years for Eskimos – both sexes – in 1967.) In the Canadian population as a whole, there has always been a larger proportion of men than women but the ratio has steadily declined. In 1966, there were 101 males for every 100 females.

The fertility rate has been declining in Canada, as in many other western countries, owing to an increased use of birth control methods. In the middle of the last century, Canadian women who were still married at the age of 50 had borne an average of eight children. By the turn of the century the number had decreased to six, and, by 1961, three, even before the wide spread use of the contraceptive pill. This means that the reproductive function no longer dictates the destiny of most women as it did in the past.

There used to be two cycles in the life of most women; the pre-marital stage and the period given over entirely to child-bearing and the rearing of children. Today, most women can look forward to a third and longer cycle between the ages of 35 and 76 because the majority give birth to the last of their children around the age of 30. In comparison with the life span of their great-grandmothers, this represents for women the equivalent of a second life.

Progress in medicine is helping women of all ages. Developments in gynaecology and hormone chemistry ensure better control over menopause, which used to disrupt the psychological or physiological balance of about 85 percent of women – causing, for example, depression, insomnia, and troubles of the circulatory system and metabolism.[22] Today, doctors and psychologists report that the menopause is often followed by a period of renewed vigour. "Contrary to popular belief, aging does not start or speed up with the advent of the menopause. Ovarian function is a transitory phenomenon which is not essential to a woman's life, but rather additional to it."[23] Some physicians think that many of the symptoms associated with the menopause are psychosomatic. More knowledge and understanding are now alleviating or eliminating the cause of these symptoms.

The new life cycle for women makes it imperative that girls should be prepared for energetic usefulness in the later years of their lives. All girls should be made aware of the choices and diversity that life can offer them. They should not restrict themselves to short-range occupations as stop-gaps until marriage. Rather, in recognition of their own talents and interests, their plans should be long-range and their choice should include parenthood, outside work, other activities, or whatever combination of all three they prefer. "With each passing day, the part of life ruled by biological factors becomes smaller, and that left to free choice, larger."[24]

Effects of Technological Change

In Canada as elsewhere, one result of the industrial revolution has been that domestic production, part of which used to depend on women, is now carried out in factories. As this change occurred, women entered workshops and factories where they earned less pay than men. Many of the skills they had learned were rendered obsolete by the mass production of consumer goods. By 1891, one-eighth of the Canadian labour force was female. Women were a pool of cheap labour for industry. They were often exploited.

As the years went on, women were concentrated more and more in *traditionally* female occupations. Perhaps traditional attitudes about women's *place* in the home encouraged the idea that they did not really belong in the labour force. Even today, some people still consider women's work outside the home unnecessary; they are not yet fully aware of the need for two salaries in some households or of the number of women who are the sole providers for their families. Also often forgotten are some of the positive effects of women's paid work on society. The work women do for pay is essential work and the proportion of the Gross National Product and of tax revenues represented by women's participation in the world of work is substantial. Although labour unions have made contributions toward better working conditions for all employees, women

CHART 1

Life Expectancy at Birth, Canada, 1931-68, Total Canadian Population
and Canadian Indians by Sex and Eskimos

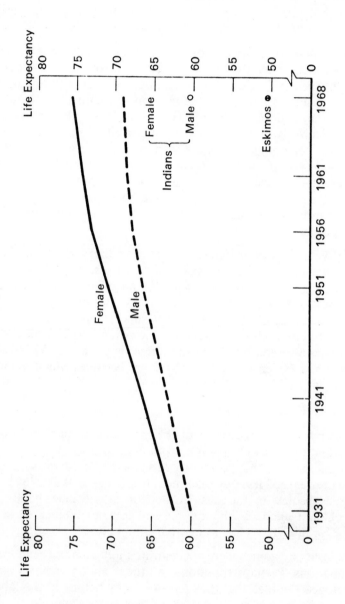

Source: Dominion Bureau of Statistics. Abridged Life Tables. 1968, Health and Welfare Division,to be publish
Unpublished data forwarded by the Dominion Bureau of Statistics to the RCSWC.
Department of National Health and Welfare, *Life Expectancy of Canadian Eskimos.* Canada, 1969.

have not as yet obtained equal opportunities with men at work in all sectors or acquired full representation in labour unions. According to a study prepared for the Commission: "when unionists discuss women at work, it is never in quite the same way they discuss men at work. There always seem to be implications, in the conversation, that woman's role is elsewhere."

Technological progress has transformed the familiar world of the home by eliminating or lightening many household tasks. Often, however, housework expands to fill the time available, as advertising exhorts women to add so-called refinements to housekeeping. Nevertheless, married women today have more time for outside activities than they ever had before.

In recent years, the increased participation of women, especially married women, in the labour force, has greatly changed their lives. In 1968, women workers accounted for 34.4 percent of the Canadian labour force. More than half of them were married.

Social Change

Recent decades have been characterized by shifting patterns of population distribution. In the 15 years from 1951 to 1966, an ever increasing number of Canadians moved to the cities.[25] The trend to urban living has seen the development of large cities surrounded by suburbs. City living, for women, has meant easy access to a variety of services and has given them greater freedom while, at the same time, creating new problems and conflicts such as separation from a larger family group and a familiar community. Suburban living has drawbacks for women since it often isolates them from the activities, community services and programmes found in the central city.

The industrial production of a vast array of household goods has turned women into consumers on a large scale. Much of the advertising of consumer goods is directed at women because they do most of the daily shopping for the family. Buying goods and services has become so complicated that the formation of governmental and private agencies has become necessary in order to provide consumers with information based on research.

In industry, the nineteenth century work week of 50 to 60 hours has now been reduced to 37 to 40 hours with the result that the leisure time of the worker has increased, allowing more time for amusements, community activity and family life. However, mothers of families who also hold outside jobs are often an under-privileged class as far as leisure is concerned. Canada, by signing the Universal Declaration of Human Rights, has accepted the principle that every person has the right to adequate rest and leisure but married women will not have that right until there are better community services, indispensable in an industrialized society, and until there is a change in attitudes concerning the responsibility of husband and wife for housework and child care.

Technological advance in the field of communications, especially in radio and television, has also brought about social change. It has been estimated[26] that, in 1969, Canadian adults spent an average of four hours each day watching television and about three and one-quarter hours listening to radio.

A nation-wide survey[27] has shown that newspapers reach as many Canadian women as men. Three-quarters of the women surveyed read the editorial page;

nine-tenths, the general news. They are less interested than men in the financial pages. The women's pages are read by 88 percent of women and 45 percent of men.

The democratization of education has greatly affected the aspirations and expectations of Canadian women. Little by little, the doors of nearly all educational institutions have been opened to them over the last hundred years. In 1967, female graduates made up about a third of the 27,533 Canadian graduates in arts, pure science and commerce, and more than half the 7,590 graduates in education, library science and social work. And yet many fields of learning still remain substantially male preserves with only token female representation; fewer than five percent of the 1,796 graduates in law and theology, fewer than 12 percent of the graduating medical doctors and about six percent of the graduating dentists in 1967 were women.[28] Moreover, institutions of higher learning have yet to adapt their general plans and structures to the needs of married women.

In the face of deep-rooted functional change, marriage and the family persist as an institution of particular importance to women. The importance of the family is due to the need of human beings, whether children or adults, to *belong* in a close social relationship with others. Functions of the family, however, which wives used to perform – such as the education of children, treatment of illness and care of the aged – are now undertaken increasingly by private or public institutions. Today 90 percent of Canadian women marry and live in families and, because of the longer life span, may remain married for an average of 40 years. Divorce is now increasing and many divorced women remarry.

The Cultural Mould

Contacts with people and with the world in general are affected by stereotyped images partly due to education and upbringing and partly to experience with other people. "The real environment is altogether too big, too complex and too fleeting for direct acquaintance. We are not equipped to deal with so much subtlety, so much variety, so many permutations and combinations. And although we have to act in that environment, we have to reconstruct it on a simpler model before we can manage it."[29] A fund of accepted notions promotes a certain degree of social balance and stability by enabling people to act in ways well understood by others. Nevertheless, very strict or out-moded mental stereotypes have a constraining effect that may interfere with personal liberty, since society will blame and reject those who depart from its usual standards. Consequently people gradually accustom themselves to conform to established rules. Society's ideas about them are made part of their own mental pictures of themselves, and in the end have a way of moulding their attiudes and their thoughts. All of this holds true for the stereotypes about women.

The traditional concept of the role of women probably began in pre-historic times when repeated child-bearing and inferior physical strength relegated women to a subordinate position which, centuries later, was rationalized in philosophical terms. Many philosophers and most theologians have consistently taught that the subordination of women to men is right and natural. Particular emphasis was put on the subordination of a daughter to her father and a wife to her husband.

348

They postulated the existence of an inferior feminine *nature*, in opposition to that of man. Aristotle's theory that a woman's role in conception is purely passive was accepted for centuries. It was not until the second half of the nineteenth century that scientists demonstrated that both parents made equivalent contributions to a child's biological inheritance.

The three principal influences which have shaped Western society – Greek philosophy, Roman law, and Judeo-Christian theology – have each held, almost axiomatically, that woman is inferior and subordinate to man and requires his domination. This attitude still persists today; for example, in most religions, a woman cannot be ordained or authorized to be a spiritual leader.

On the basis of ancient concepts, it has been all too easy to divide assumed male and female functions and psychological traits into separate, opposing categories. These categories, or stereotypes, have by no means disappeared from popular belief and thinking about the nature of women and men. Women are expected to be emotional, dependent and gentle and men are thought to possess all the contrary attributes: to be rational, independent and aggressive. These are the qualities assumed to be suitable for women in the closed world of the home, husband and children, and for men in the outside world of business, the professions or politics. The stereotypes and the models of behaviour derived from this assumption do not necessarily correspond to real personalities of a great number of men and women.

Each culture imagines that the qualities and functions it attributes to men and women are part of the natural order. Anthropologists, however, report that tensions and balance between the sexes result in very different ways of life and role divisions from one culture to the next. Margaret Mead has pointed out, for example, that feminine and masculine roles are interchangeable in New Guinea. It is important to recognize that psychological characteristics of either sex, often taken for granted as derived from nature, may be based instead on cultural habits which in some cases have developed into ideologies.

Even among industrialized nations, there are substantial differences in the occupations considered *feminine* or *masculine*. In the U.S.S.R., the majority of doctors are women; in Finland, most dentists are women and architecture is considered as suitable for women as for men. Until the development of obstetrics, only women assisted other women in childbirth; it would not have seemed fitting for a man to do so.

What then are the innate differences between men and women and what are the ones imposed by education and culture? Aside from physical differences, there has been no scientific proof of differences, either psychological or intellectual in the genetic inheritance of men and women.

And yet, women's child-bearing function and their physical differences have served as the basis for restrictive generalizations and overt discrimination. Regardless of age or circumstances, women are identified automatically with tasks such as looking after their homes, rearing their children, caring for others and other related activities. It is almost as if we were to say that it is man's nature to work in an office or factory, simply because most of the men we know in cities happen to do so. This time-honoured custom of identifying woman, more or less exclusively, in terms of her relationships and functions of wife and mother has solidified into a confining mould.

In Canada as elsewhere, the cultural mould has been imposed upon and accepted by many women and tends to confuse discussions on the subject of the status of women. Several briefs pointed this out: "Women, too, in large part still believe that a woman's place is in the home, at least while her children are young."[30] "The all-too-prevalent opinion, common amongst women as well as men, that women with the odd exception are less ambitious, timid, less capable, less well-organized than men, is fallacious, if closely examined."[31]

During the 1968 public hearings of the Commission, two Canadian daily newspapers published questionnaires "for Men Only"[32] in order to obtain a sampling of men's opinions on the question of women. Such surveys are usually affected by different kinds of bias: for example, the sampling might not be representative of the whole population. Nevertheless they are not meaningless even though the results have to be interpreted with care. In these samplings the results showed, generally, traditional opinions. Many of the respondents declared that women tended to find more discrimination than in fact existed and that Canada did not need a Royal Commission on the Status of Women. More than half the replies received by the *Toronto Star* declared that woman's place is in the home. In the survey by *Le Devoir* majority opinion favoured a male rather than a female superior on the job. Most respondents were of the opinion that women lack the emotional control demanded for combining a career with marriage and motherhood. On the other hand, the young men who responded to *Le Devoir*, and the husbands of working wives who replied to the *Toronto Star* were almost unanimous in their view that gainfully employed women should be legally responsible for the support of their families, and that they should be required, if necessary, to pay alimony in cases of divorce.

The feeling that women who have equal financial resources should have responsibilities equal to those of men may mark an important evolution of attitudes. The stereotype of the man as the sole breadwinner yields to the new picture of the wife as his economic partner. Yet woman remains mainly identified with her old role as a housewife. When people try to reconcile these two different images – the traditional woman and the actual woman who is many-faceted, as a man is, and who often works for pay – the stereotype is not always discarded.

Many women, conditioned to be acquiescent and passive, reflect traditional views on their status and role. Surveys have revealed that these attitudes are held even among highly educated women, including college and university students.

The effect of imposed stereotypes has been clearly demonstrated by experiments in the United States. In one,[33] a number of university women were selected to read six articles. Some concerned *masculine* subjects such as city planning, others treated neutral subjects such as the history of art, and still others were about such *feminine* interests as dietetics. In some booklets, three articles were signed with male and three with female names. In others, the male and female *authorship* was reversed. The women were asked to read and appraise each article, without having their attention called to the authors' names. In all cases, articles under male signatures received higher ratings. It was concluded, in the study, that the respondents' choices had been influenced by belief in the intellectual superiority of men.

Many women are afraid of not conforming to the subordinate role assigned to them by tradition. This can be so strong that it may make them belittle themselves. They have low expectations for their own achievement and, very often, accept work that makes far less than full use of their capabilities. In the words of a brief received by the Commission: "Too many of us were willing to accept a lower position and stay there, not even expecting or demanding to be promoted to a higher position, given that our training and experience and ability warrant it."[34]

Another brief[35] was based on a survey covering 11,153 English speaking readers of a Canadian magazine. It reported that 73 percent of the housewives and 54 percent of the working women who responded believe that men prefer a woman with little ambition for a career. Other figures from the same survey indicated that 59 percent of those questioned wanted to combine a career, marriage and motherhood; four percent favoured a career and marriage, and three percent preferred to remain single and have a career. Among the same group 44 percent thought that men and women should contribute equally to economic, household and family responsibilities, and 23 percent were in favour of totally interchangeable social roles for men and women.[36] In a study carried out for the Commission in Quebec, the results showed that out of the 2,000 female respondents, seven percent would choose a profession or responsible position such as that of school principal as their *ideal occupation*. Less than 25 percent mentioned work of a semi-professional nature. The remainder indicated that their ideal choices were jobs with less responsibility and authority.

The stereotype of the ideal woman has its effect upon Canadian women. It appears that many women have accepted as truths the social constraints and the mental images that society has prescribed, and have made these constraints and images part of themselves as guides for living. This theory could partly explain why some women are little inclined to identify themselves with the collective problems of their sex and tend to share the conventional opinions of society. Social scientists have noted a similar phenomenon in their study of certain minority groups,[37] or people treated as inferior. Their members often fail to identify with their own group. This is particularly true of individuals who cross the border separating them from the majority and who then adopt its attitudes and standards.

The concept of the psychological minority offers one possible interpretation of the effects upon women of stereotyping. Women do not, in fact, constitute a social group since they are found everywhere and in all classes. They cannot be isolated, as a collectivity, from the other members of society with whom they live in close relation. They cannot, moreover, be described as a demographic minority in society as a whole, though they are often a minority in the world of work and politics. But, according to some writers, a psychological minority group is an aggregation whose collective destiny depends on the good will or is at the mercy of another group. They – the members of a psychological minority – feel and know that they live in a state of dependency, no matter what percentage they may be of the total population.

Stereotypes are perpetuated by the mass media. Day after day, advertising reinforces and exploits stereotypes to achieve greater sales by repeating the idea that the *real* woman and the *real* man use this or that product. Although men as well as women are stereotyped, the results may be more damaging for women since advertising encourages feminine dependency by urging women not to act but to be passive, not to really achieve but to live out their aspirations in the imagination and in dreams.

Woman is often presented as a sex object, defined as a superficial creature who thinks only of her appearance, who sees herself mainly in terms of whether she is attractive to men. She conforms to the beauty and youth standards which men are said to want of her. In a study prepared for the Commission, it was found that over 89 percent of the women pictured in Canadian newspapers and magazines are less than 35 years of age. As presented by the advertiser, women are hardly ever associated with intelligence, sincerity, culture, originality or talent. Instead, they are depicted as being young, elegant and beautiful. "The mass media must in some way be encouraged to change their emphasis. . . ."[38]

At least 30 of the briefs received by the Commission protested against the degrading, moronic picture of woman thus presented. These briefs objected to woman, in advertisements, being shown as fragile, without depth or reality, and obsessed by her desire to please masculine hero-figures as artificial as herself. Repetition is a *hidden persuader* in advertising, an especially effective tool influencing children and young girls to aspire to constraining models and low ideals. When women are shown in active pursuits, these activities are in the order of polishing furniture and preparing food. Some women's magazines contribute to the exaltation of housework as a fine art and very often persuade women that to conform to the image of housewife *par excellence* is a duty and that not to conform signifies inadequacy. Housework is rarely viewed in these publications, and in advertising, for what it is; a necessary task that is performed in order to make the family comfortable.

Stereotypes pass naturally from one generation to the next. Whatever sex-linked biological determinants of personality there may be, no one yet seems to have isolated them clearly, or surely. However, the standards and models of behaviour taught either explicitly or by example in the family begin to affect boys and girls from their earliest childhood.

The spontaneous definitions of father and mother gathered in a Montreal kindergarten in 1969[39] revealed how effectively sex role stereotypes are passed on to very young children. As we point out in the Chapter on education, [not presented here] many of the images held by children are related to cultural habits and the traditional division of tasks in the home such as that mothers do the cooking and that fathers are always working. Children absorb a concept of the exclusive roles of men and women which may restrain and limit the development of both girls and boys. They show the impact of early family influences on the acquisition of stereotypes.

Older children continue to be influenced by the family. A study prepared for the Commission surveyed the opinions of 8,000 children of ages nine to 15 in Nova Scotia, Quebec, Ontario and British Columbia in order to ascertain to what extent and in what ways they differentiated between the roles of girls and boys, and men and women. The boys made more of a distinction than the girls. In this sample, the French-speaking differentiated less than the English-speaking children between masculine and feminine roles. Children acquire most of their ideas about their parents' tasks through simple observation. "If sex makes a difference in the organization of the family, then it will make a difference in the thinking of children."

This study indicated that girls who do well in school conform less readily to accepted ideas about their sex. "Doing poorly academically was an accompaniment of thinking in traditional terms about the sexes." "Girls who sex-typed were less likely to do well academically than those who did not sex-type." School-aged children who *go steady* with someone of the opposite sex, tend to imitate traditional adult patterns earlier than other teen-agers, as might be expected.

Another study prepared for the Commission, conducted in a few Canadian technical schools and universities, revealed highly conventional views about men's and women's functions in marriage. "Among men and women there is yet a strong feeling that the wife should continue to perform a traditional role obligation." Fifty-eight percent of those surveyed thought the woman should stop working after the birth of her first child. A higher percentage of girls than boys held this opinion, conforming to the expectations of society.

Expressed opinion is one thing – actual behaviour may be another. Despite their traditional point of view, as shown by these studies, young people are living lives that increasingly differ from those of their parents. Well over half the Canadian population is under the age of 30[40] and not all are conforming to all the old patterns. Some of them commonly express dissatisfaction with – and freely question – customs and institutions long taken for granted. And it cannot be assumed that the once accepted roles of men and women will be exempt. The behaviour of many young people, for example, in their choice of dress, music and life-style, may tell as much about their attitudes as their responses to formal surveys.

The role of women will necessarily change as society itself evolves. In making our recommendations, we have to take into account what may be in store for Canadians in the years to come. Predictions about what life will be like in the future are increasingly being used as tools for better understanding of changes in present society.

The psychologist, Carl Rogers, sees the man-woman relationship of the year 2000 as more enjoyable and less possessive, one which will be ". . . a potentially joyful and enriching part of a relationship. The attitude of possessiveness – of owning another person, which historically has dominated sexual unions – is likely to be greatly diminished. It is certain that there will be enormous variations in the quality of these sexual relationships – . . . It is becoming increasingly clear that a man-woman relationship will have permanence only in the degree in which it satisfies the emotional, psychological, intellectual, and physical needs of the partners. This means that the permanent marriage of the future will be even better . . . If a couple feel deeply committed to each other and mutually wish to remain together to raise a family, then this will be a new and more binding type of marriage. Each will accept the obligations involved in having and rearing children. . . ."[41]

Margaret Mead sees signs of a future in which there would be "an emphasis on very small families and a high toleration of childless marriage . . . parenthood would be limited to a smaller number of families . . . adults who functioned as parents would be given special forms of protection . . . There would be a growing disregard for sex as a basic mode of differentiation . . . Limitations on freedom would be removed from women as a social group. Boys and girls would be differentiated not by sex-typed personality characteristics, but by temperament . . . Over time there would be considerable individual rebellion against any form of social sex-typing that ignored personality differences."[42]

The future of our country will be determined substantially by the direction we Canadians choose to take now. If women are to be able to make full use of their capabilities, help is needed from the whole society. Even so, women themselves must work for change: ". . . women are the best helpers of one another. Let them think; let them act; till they know what they need. We only ask of men to remove arbitrary barriers. Some would like to do more. But I believe it needs that Woman show herself in her native dignity to teach them to aid her; their minds are so encumbered by tradition."[43]

Footnotes

1. U.N. General Assembly resolution adopted unanimously December 10, 1948.

2. Including the following: President's Task Force on Women's Rights and Responsibilities (U.S.), 1969-70. U.S. Status of Women Commission (1961-1963); National Commissions of Inquiry of France (1966- . . .), of West Germany (1962-1966), of Denmark (1965- . . .); National Study Committees of the United Kingdom, Finland, the Netherlands; Central Office of the Status of Women in Austria (1966- . . .); Advisory Committee (Department of Labour) Belgium; Report of the Norwegian Government (1966). (In 1935, the League of Nations set up the first international study on women's status; the United Nations set up a Commission in 1946.)

3. John Stuart Mill, *The Subjection of Women*. London: Oxford University Press, 1912, (first published 1896), p. 443.

4. Jean LeMoyne, *Convergence* (translated by Philip Stratford). Toronto: The Ryerson Press, 1966, pp. 99, 101.

5. Simone de Beauvoir, *The Second Sex*. Paris: Gallimard, 1949.

6. Betty Friedan, *The Feminine Mystique*. New York: W. W. Norton and Company, Incorporated, 1963.

7. Margaret Benston, "The Political Economy of Women's Liberation," Discussion Paper, Vancouver Women's Caucus, mimeographed, 1969-1970.

8. Brief No. 441.

9. Brief No. 194.

10. Brief No. 387.

11. Brief No. 70.

12. Brief No. 329.

13. Brief No. 279.

14. Brief No. 160.

15. Brief No. 349.

16. Brief No. 32.

17. Brief No. 279.

18. Brief No. 112.

19. Brief No. 373.

20. Brief No. 326.

21. Brief No. 7.

22. Dr. Robert A. Wilson, *Feminine Forever*. New York: Evans and Company, 1966.

23. Dr. Anne Denart-Toulet, "Les deux âges de la femme," *Esprit*, May, 1961, p. 791.

24. Suzanne Lilar, *Le malentendu du deuxième sexe*. Paris: P.U.F., 1969, p. 234.

25. In 1951, 31.4 percent of the total population lived in urban centres of 30,000 or more, while in 1966 the corresponding proportion was 54 percent. Dominion Bureau of Statistics, *Canada Year Book*. Ottawa: Queen's Printer, 1968, p. 194.

26. "Average Listening and Watching Time, Television and Radio, by Sex, Canada, 1969," *Coverage and Circulation Report*. Toronto: Bureau of Measurements, November, 1969.

27. *Newspaper Research*. Toronto: Canadian Daily Newspaper Publishers' Association, 1964, p. 4. Based on a national survey of 11 Canadian dailies.

28. *Op. cit.*, Dominion Bureau of Statistics, 1968, p. 337.

29. Walter Lippman, *Public Opinion*. New York: The Macmillan Company, 1922, p. 10.

30. Brief No. 64.

31. Brief No. 75.

32. *Le Devoir* (Montreal) and the *Toronto Star*, which received 492 and 739 completed questionnaires respectively.

33. Philip Goldberg, "Are Women Prejudiced Against Women?" *Trans-Action*, University of Washington, April, 1968, pp. 28-30.

34. Brief No. 279.

35. Brief No. 346.

36. The 3,245 additional answers from Quebec were roughly similar but indicated more personal independence.

37. Similartities [*sic*] between women and racial minorities have been studied by a number of persons. *See* Gunnar Myrdal, *An American Dilemma*, 2 Vols., Harper Brothers, 1944, p. 1077.

38. Brief No. 371.

39. Catholic School Commission of Montreal, May, 1969.

40. Fifty-six percent as of June 1969. Dominion Bureau of Statistics, *Estimated Population by Sex and Age Groups*, Catalogue No. 91-202.

41. Carl R. Rogers, "Interpersonal Relationships: USA 2000," *Journal of Applied Behavioral Sciences*, 4, 1968, pp. 270-271.

42. Margaret Mead, "The Life-Cycle and its Variations: The Division of Roles," *Daedalus*, Summer, 1967, p. 871 and following.

43. Margaret Fuller, "Women in the Nineteenth Century," *The Writings of Margaret Fuller*. Ed. Mason Wade, New York: The Viking Press, 1941, pp. 213-214. The article was originally published in 1845.

4 Canadian Identity

The concern over Canadian identity is chronic rather than new. Current concern is expressed primarily in terms of the danger of Canada losing or not maintaining her identity, her sense of being an entity that is separate, special, and independent of other national entities. Another view, not quite so widely held, is that Canada has been having difficulty in actually developing an identity of her own. The *causes* of Canada's identity crisis are sometimes seen as internal and sometimes external. Specific internal cleavages are religion, language, political parties, and regional disparity. External forces are seen by some as being the Commonwealth, by many, especially in historical perspective, as being Great Britain, and by most – in the present and for the foreseeable future – as being the United States.

It is probably a truism that no nation can make important decisions even in the domestic sphere that do not have some repercussions for other nations in the world. Nonetheless, Canada's history is one of having other nations – particularly Great Britain and the United States – looking over its shoulder and attempting to influence decision-making in a way that would not only avoid adversely affecting the great powers but frequently in a way that would benefit one or both of them, often at Canada's expense. Further problems result from Canada's subordinate position relative to more powerful and highly developed nations. These are some of the problems that are put into historical perspective and analysed in this chapter.

The first two arcticles in this section begin by indicating how some of Canada's ties with Great Britain have made it difficult for Canada to develop an independent identity and strategy toward world problems. Both go on to point out how Canada's gradual move away from Commonwealth influences was accompanied by a frequently unwitting shift toward greater influence by the neighbour to the south. In "Canadian Identity: Underlying Problems and Critical Influences," Mildred A. Schwartz discusses some of the internal cleavages that present major problems both for political stability and for identifying an unambiguously Canadian Nation." These are regional disparity of people and resources, differences in ethnic and religious groups and the effects of this diversity on the Canadian political system. She also examines the implications of political symbols, the intellectual elite, the military, the mass media, and education for Canadian identity.

Philip Resnick's, "Canadian Defence Policy and the American Empire," traces the shift in Canadian defence policy alliances. At the roots of such alliances which shifted from the British Empire to the American Empire, Resnick sees a "colonial mentality" and a "liberal ideology" on the part of "Canadian Capitalist elites."

Defence policy is not the only aspect of Canadian life to be influenced by the United States. Mel Watkins addresses himself to what is considered by many to be the single most important threat to Canadian Identity, the foreign control of Canadian industry. In "The Watkin's Report: Foreign Ownership and the Structure of Canadian Industry," he details several aspects of the current situation. For example, it is noted that more than 50 percent of many important Canadian industries are owned by non-residents, most of whom are Americans. The multi-national corporation clearly poses a number of threats to Canadian self-determination at the domestic level. Not only is there a lack of control over which industries are to be expanded or which natural resources tapped, but the profits are diverted from Canada. The report goes on to make both general and specific proposals designed to aid Canada in coping with the multi-national enterprise; for example, the formation of a Canada Development Corporation (which now has been accomplished) and more effective utilization of the system to protect Canadians from direct foreign investment.

There is considerable debate over how to handle problems stemming from foreign ownership of Canadian industry. One approach is suggested by Liberal M.P. Alastair Gillespie whose hope for the future and "a prescription for a Canadian identity" is based on moulding a vigorous group of Canadian capitalists: "an appropriate economic policy for Canada . . . should concentrate far more on adapting to the multinational form of corporate organization than resisting it; it should be concerned with converting Canadian entrepreneurs from a rather inward-looking group to an outward-looking group. It should commit resources to the building of Canada rather than buying it back." Mel Watkins disagrees and calls for the beginning of a move toward an "independent socialist Canada." A Canada that, through the process of nationalization, will eventually replace multinational corporations with a "publicly owned and democratically-administered economy."

While the issue of foreign ownership of Canadian industry poses the most important and pervasive threat to Canadian identity there is also considerable concern over the "takeover" or "de-Canadianization" of Canadian social and cultural institutions by foreigners. The battle over the use of non-Canadian textbooks has already been fought and partly won on the elementary and high school level. Concern is now focussed on Canadian universities. Robin Matthews and James Steele began the current round of debate in late 1968 when they charged that Canadian universities were being taken over by non-Canadians (especially Americans) who accounted for an increasing proportion of Canada's university faculties.[1] The final article in Unit 1, "Population," of this book, "The Universities: Takeover of the Mind," could just have well been placed in this section on Canadian Identity. Hence, the reader is again referred to it as it contains the major thrust of the arguments and data assembled by Matthews and Steele (1969). While Matthews and Steele have had some dissenters they have also received considerable support. Hugh MacLennan, in his "Address to the Montreal Symposium on De-Canadianization," praised Matthews and Steele for their dedication and courage in raising the issue central to de-Canadianization. He indicates that Canada must fill more of her academic positions with Canadians in order to avert "national suicide." As a way of achieving this he supports the idea of a quota system that restricts the rate of non-Canadian academics. A case study of de-Canadianization is provided by James MacKinnon and David Brown in "Political Science in the Canadian University, 1969." In 1968-1969 there were 378 political science professors whose nationalities were as follows: fifty-two percent Canadian, twenty-nine percent American, nine percent British, and ten percent of other nationalities. Their survey of 285 of these professors revealed that many of the Americans had maintained American reading habits, planned to return to the States, and taught few courses concerned with Canadian Government. However, they go on to find that the greatest problems faced by those who wish to study political science are not caused by the influx of foreign professors, but by a shortage of adequate or appropriate teaching materials such as books and research findings. This theme is picked up by Lewis Hertzman who, in "Canada's Lagging Quality," sees the principal problem stemming from "generations of neglect" of the Canadian graduate schools especially in social science and the humanities.

The Executive and Finance Committee of the Canadian Association of University Teachers developed a policy statement for consideration by its membership, "Canadianization and the University." This statement emphasizes not nationality but competence. It defines competence to include not only promise and ability as a scholar and teacher, but "also those qualities which affect his performance within the Canadian University Community" and this may require considerable "familiarity with things Canadian."

The university is hardly the only sector of Canadian society that is threatened by American cultural imperialism. The Davey Senate Committee Report on the Mass Media made it very clear that millions of Canadians are exposed daily to various aspects of the U.S. media. Although this includes books, magazines and newspapers, no facet of the media is likely to have so pervasive an influence as U.S. television broadcasting. Many Canadians receive U.S. signals without the aid of special receivers, but the Davey Committee Report was particularly concerned with the wholesale importation to all Canadians of American TV programming via cable. However, these U.S. influences on Canadian culture have not just been discovered by the Davey Committee. Rather, as the article by Singer on "American Invasion of the Mass Media in Canada" indicates, these are rediscoveries of concerns that have existed for some time.

Therefore, the establishment and maintenance of an independent Canadian identity is threatened on many fronts, domestic, political, economic, educational, and cultural to list some of the more important ones. The pervasiveness of outside influences on Canadian life is already well documented but the final article in this section gives it an added dimension. Bruce Kidd examines what has happened to Canada's *national* sport. Although some counter trends have taken place since the Kidd article was written, for example, Vancouver finally received an NHL franchise in 1970, Kidd's arguments are still valid. The commercialization of hockey rather than its professionalization has led to the takeover by U.S. economic interests. Kidd suggests that only through nationalizing hockey can Canadians expect to retain reasonable control over their national sport.

Footnote

1. Robin Matthews and James Steele, eds., *The Struggle for Canadian Universities: a Dossier.* Toronto: New Press, 1969.

Canadian Identity: Underlying Problems and Critical Influences*

Mildred A. Schwartz

National Problems

The problems common to all political systems are manifested in Canada, in some cases in a unique fashion, with external problems of independence and foreign commitments, internal problems of internal cleavages and the role of government, and symbolic problems. The elaboration of these should indicate both the general and the unique natures of the problems.

Independence

Independence has become basic to Canada's identity as a result of several historical factors. In the modern world the attainment of full citizenship has come about either by revolutionary breaks with past governments or by the development of self-government within a colonial empire. For countries which have followed the latter course, the empire has gone through a major transformation in character. At the present this is the development which is most prevalent as Britain continues to divest itself of its colonial domains, but when Canada attained self-government it was the first of the British possessions to follow this course. It set an example for the states and dominions that have followed, but its problems have also been unique: "Canada had not only to achieve autonomy inside the British Empire, but also to maintain a separate existence on a continent dominated by the United States. She thus has to come to terms with two imperialisms, real or potential."[1]

Dependence on Britain

Canada is, first of all, a political creation of Britain, brought into being by an act of the British parliament and, until 1967, still dependent on that country for constitutional amendments concerning the federal structure. Since Confederation, Canada has had almost complete control over all local affairs except for appointments of the Governor-General; suggestion, and hence really appointment of, the Governor-General became the prerogative of the Canadian government in 1926. Except for some Canadian participation in discussions, initially Britain alone formulated foreign policy, and in this way some

*Originally published by the University of California Press; reprinted by permission of The Regents of the University of California. Taken from Mildred Schwartz, "Canada: Promise and Disappointment," Chapter 3 of *Public Opinion and Canadian Identity*, University of California Press, 1967, pp. 25-56.

leaders saw Canada committed to the Boer War. This was the first occasion on which Canadians, particularly those of French origin, could complain about "entanglement in British imperialist wars."[2] British initiative again brought Canada into World War I, although, with the formation of the Imperial War Cabinet in 1917, the Dominion prime ministers were permitted to participate directly in policy-making. But this war also produced bitter feelings, and, in 1917, when the Conscription Act was passed, those French-Canadian Liberals who were opposed to it formed a splinter group of the party while the remaining Liberals joined Robert Borden and his Union government. With the Statute of Westminster of 1931, the self-governing dominions attained full autonomy if they wanted to exercise it. When war came in 1939, some dominions felt that Britain's declaration included them, but Canada waited seven days before declaring war. Again the Canadian government had to come to terms with the heritage of previous wars. In this instance, however, Prime Minister Mackenzie King was able to adopt a number of alternatives which avoided the breakdown in relations between French and English that had occurred in 1917.

Although for the American colonists British trade policies were a major source of grievance, since that time Britain's economic relations with her possessions have often appeared advantageous to the latter. The importance of trade with Britain is so crucial to some Commonwealth members that British politicians have had second thoughts about the value of joining the European Common Market. The Canadian government played a leading role in criticizing Britain's proposed membership in E.C.M. in the early 1960's, since as a leading trading nation, Canada was greatly disturbed by the prospect of losing traditional markets.

Among Canada's ties with Britain are those of population, and this has undoubtedly contributed to the continued development of Canada as an English-speaking country within the British Commonwealth. The largest group of Canadian citizens born outside the country come from Britain. Since the end of World War II about two million immigrants have been admitted, of whom about one-third are of British origin. While British immigrants have not been faced with the same discriminatory legislation passed at various times to curtail immigrants from other countries, a certain amount of ill feeling has been expressed against them. Unlike the objection against those from continental European countries, the objection against the British can never be made that they cannot speak the language or understand the basic political institutions. Opposition is less defined, expressing itself in feelings that British immigrants treat Canadians like colonials, or are always commenting on better ways of doing things.

Dependence on the United States

If relations with Britain, particularly those involving dependency, have been crucial in shaping Canada's existence, then those with the United States are at least equally important. Politically, the United States was an important example to the Fathers of Confederation in developing a system of federal government; in other respects, however, it served as an anti-model. Despite a famous unguarded boundary, fear of an invading army was an important impetus in bringing about Confederation in 1867, and attack seemed imminent as late as 1895.[3] In boundary disputes before Canada attained dominion status the disadvantages of being a small, powerless nation were consistently proved, for even Britain was not willing to antagonize the Americans. Since World War II, as new power arrangements have emerged, Canada and the United States have come to work together more closely in defence plans, to the resentment of some Canadians.

Materially and artistically, the United States has always served as a basis of comparison, and Americans have usually been the style setters. Robert Barr, a Canadian journalist who moved to the United States at the turn of the century, told his fellow writers to "get over the border as soon as you can. . . . Shake the dust of Canada from your feet, get out of the land that is willing to pay money for whiskey, but wants its literature free in the shape of Ayer's almanac."[4] Large numbers of Canadians study in the United States, and many of these, as well as others who have taken advanced training in Canada, often decide that opportunities are greater in the neighbouring country.

In the 1940's, the government appointed a royal commission to investigate the ways in which the United States was influencing Canada's cultural development, with a view to presenting proposals for confining some of these. Government agencies specifically designed to confine American cultural influences include the National Film Board, Canadian Broadcasting Corporation, Canada Council, and National Research Council, most of which existed even before the Royal Commission made its recommendations. Despite these measures, Canadians receive most of their news, television programs, movies, and magazines from the United States.[5]

Canada, rich in natural resources but always with a limited population, has depended on the nationals of other countries for its economic development. Resources have been developed mainly with foreign money. In some cases, particularly that of the United States, subsidiary manufacturing companies have been set up in Canada. Since 1939, the United States and Great Britain between them have made about 90 percent of the total direct investment in Canada, with the share of the former much greater than that of the latter.[6] Among the difficulties stemming from this extensive United States investment in Canada are those related to American foreign policy. Restrictions on trade with mainland China have been extended, for example, to Canadian subsidiaries who have been prevented from shipping automobile parts to China. While this incident aroused considerable resentment, particularly because of the size of the economic loss entailed, Canada's continued trade with Cuba after the United States broke with the Castro government did not appear to have an economic motivation, since trade never achieved a great volume, but rather an emotional appeal, as a way for Canada to show its defiance of American policy.

. . . Since about 1936, more amicable trade agreements have been worked out between Canada and the United States, but the issue of trade continues to be a source of dissatisfaction. With each passing year, the amount of American ownership of Canadian industry and resources grows, and, with it, the extent of Canadian resentment seems also to grow. But no matter how concerned Canadians may be about the economic influences of the United States, there are limitations to the amount of ill-feeling that can be expressed or the kinds of reprisals which may be taken: "Owing to the fact of North American civilization, Canadians who set store by material development – and most do – must inevitably be nationalists of a qualified type."[7]

Links with the Commonwealth

Another traditional tie is that with the British Commonwealth. The New Commonwealth which has emerged since World War II is neither a significant export market nor a major source of immigrants for Canada. But it is perhaps in less tangible ways that the Commonwealth has attained great importance in recent years. Herbert Spiro notes how present-day African nationalism differs from European nationalism of preceding generations in its *internationalist* character. Emerging African nations often seem more concerned with developing pan-Africanism than with uniquely national identities.[8]

There may be an analogy to this in the relations between the Commonwealth and Canada. At the same time that the United States has become an increasingly powerful neighbour, Britain has lost much of its power on the international scene. Meanwhile politicians of many countries have been concerned with the development of a third force that could somehow mediate between the United States and Russia. The Commonwealth has then appeared as one such alternative, where membership is a way of acquiring a greater voice in world affairs.

Other Foreign Commitments

In other international commitments Canada has tried even harder to establish for itself a unique role internationally. One of the primary facts of modern life is the division of the world into two main ideological camps. Nations then have the choice of identifying with one or the other of these blocs. (This identification is of course not always voluntary.) Another alternative is to stay aloof from political struggles and attempt to retain friends in both camps. For Canada, remaining apart from international conflicts and commitments has always been difficult. Canadian governments have never believed that such isolation is possible, and this is reflected in the views of the Canadian people. Canadians have always had economic, political, and commercial ties with Great Britain, the Commonwealth, and to a more limited extent with France, and there has always been the pervasive evidence of American influence and proximity. In the context of present international realities and the historic and economic ties which involve countries in each other's affairs, what can a country such as Canada do to establish its identity on the international scene? The solution that has become increasingly prominent is participation in international bodies. Through membership in such bodies single nations, by themselves of limited influence and importance, can attain support for national policies and enhance their status on the international scene. For example, the United Nations, through its formal commitment to values of nondiscrimination and self-government, the opportunities it provides as a world meeting place and forum, and its involvement in trusteeship territories, has become an important focus for the new African states eager to acquire stature and throw off colonial ties. In the same way Canada, through its international involvements, has attempted to control and mitigate the influence of the United States on its own affairs.

Canada has taken an active part in the United Nations and its specialized agencies from the inception of the parent body. But participation in international organizations does not necessarily contribute to a characteristic identity unless Canada at the same time pursues some distinctive policies. In particular there should be divergence, at least some of the time, from positions taken by the United States and Britain. Such differences have occurred in Canada's commitments to NATO, the concept of the role Canada should play in North American defence, its lack of participation in the Pan American Union, and reactions to British involvement in Suez. But in many cases Canadian international activities have been guided or at least influenced by the perceived interests of traditional allies. For example, while Canada trades with mainland China and has some cultural exchanges with that country, governments up to the time of writing have never pressed for United Nations recognition of the Chinese Communist government in the face of American opposition, although the British government has officially recognized that country. Up until about 1960 Canadian activities in the United Nations with respect to issues of colonialism were limited and relatively insignificant partly because of the lack of colonial experience and the limited popular appeal of this issue within the country. At the same time Canada's ties with countries which do have colonial and trusteeship experiences probably contributed to the minor role which Canada has played.

Internal Cleavage

The social and economic diversity within Canada presents major problems both for political stability and for identifying an unambiguously Canadian nation.

Unequal Distribution of People and Resources

Among the major internal differences is the unequal distribution of resources, both human and economic, and of allied rewards. Although Canada covers a land mass of more than three and a half million square miles, settlement has been concentrated only in certain areas, spreading along the southern border; the northern hinterland has few permanent residents. The centres of population have always been in the central provinces of Ontario and Quebec, but, since Confederation, other population centres have shifted from the Maritimes to the west (see Table 1). There is also a considerable difference in the extent to which different areas of the country have become urbanized. The most highly urbanized provinces are Ontario, British Columbia, and Quebec; the least urbanized are New Brunswick, Saskatchewan, and Prince Edward Island, in the order given. The proportion of those living in cities in the three highly

TABLE 1

Percentage Distribution of Population by Region, 1881-1961

Year	Atlantic[a]	Quebec	Ontario	Prairies	British Columbia
1881	20	31	45	1	1
1891	18	31	44	3	2
1901	16	31	41	8	3
1911	13	28	35	18	5
1921	11	27	33	22	6
1931	10	28	33	23	7
1941	10	29	33	21	7
1951	12	29	33	18	8
1961	10	29	34	17	9

[a] Newfoundland is not included in the Atlantic provinces until 1951. Percentages do not add to 100 because of rounding and the exclusion of the Yukon and North-West Territories.
Sources: Canada, Dominion Bureau of Statistics, *Ninth Census of Canada*. Ottawa: King's Printer, 1951; and *1961 Census of Canada*. Ottawa: Queen's Printer, 1962.

urbanized provinces is about twice as large as the proportion living in the least urbanized.

A limited number of staple products have always had overriding importance in the Canadian economy. Beginning with furs, the major wealth of Canada has also been derived from fish, lumber, pulp and paper, grain, and mineral resources. These products are related to particular regions, and provinces vary in their resource wealth. For example, the major part of the pulp and paper industry is concentrated in northern Ontario and Quebec, whereas the prairie provinces have become the main granaries for the world. At the same time provinces differ in their economic dependence on these products. In the trend toward modernization and mechanization throughout the world, increasingly smaller proportions of labour are required in agriculture. In recent years expansion has been in the tertiary sector of the economy, as the primary and secondary sectors become more highly automated; Ontario is the most modern, with less than 15 percent of the male labour force engaged in agriculture and more than 40 percent in tertiary industry. Ontario is followed in this respect by British Columbia. Prince Edward Island and Saskatchewan emerge as dramatic contrasts, with more than half of the male labour force still engaged in primary industry. There are even differences in the rewards received for similar types of work. For example, the highest median earnings in manufacturing are to be obtained in Ontario and British Columbia, those in the Atlantic provinces are considerably less. (See Table 2 for total provincial differences.) As a consequence, each region has a different standard of living. (See Table 3 for some examples.)

TABLE 2

Per Capita Personal Disposable Income, for Canada and Provinces, 1961

Provinces	Canadian Dollars	Provinces	Canadian Dollars
Canada	1,400	Ontario	1,640
Newfoundland	860	Manitoba	1,340
Prince Edward Island	920	Saskatchewan	1,080
Nova Scotia	1,130	Alberta	1,460
New Brunswick	990		
		British Columbia	1,640
Quebec	1,230		

Source: Financial Post, *1962 Survey of Markets and Business Year Book.* Toronto: Maclean-Hunter, 1963, p. 19.

TABLE 3

Indicators of Differences in Living Conditions by Region, 1941-1961

Region	Percentage of Labour Force Unemployed			Infant Mortality per 1,000 Live Births		
	1951-1955	1956-1960	1961	1941	1951	1961
Canada	3.3	5.7	7.2	61	39	27
Atlantic[a]	5.5	9.7	11.1	71	45	31
Quebec	4.5	7.4	9.3	76	48	31
Ontario	2.7	4.2	5.5	46	31	23
Prairies	2.2	3.3	4.6	52	32	26
British Columbia	4.0	6.4	8.5	37	30	24

a Newfoundland has been included in the Atlantic provinces for all years.

Sources: Percentage of labour force unemployed: Canada, Dominion Bureau of Statistics, *Unemployment in Canada,* Bulletin 71-503; Ottawa, April, 1962. Infant mortality: Canada, Dominion Bureau of Statistics, *Vital Statistics,* Ottawa, 1963.

Regional Differences in Ethnic and Religious Groups

The second important internal cleavage derives from the marked difference in social composition of the population in various regions. For example, Quebec has a heavy concentration of people of French origin; they also make up a sizable proportion of the population of New Brunswick, while all the other provinces have some representatives of French origin but in lesser proportions. At the time of the first census in 1871, people of European origin who were neither British nor French made up 7 percent of the total population. At the 1961 census the same group constituted 26 percent. Since the last decades of the nineteenth century, continental Europeans have been important in the settlement of the prairie provinces and in recent years their numerical significance has grown in Ontario (see Table 4).

TABLE 4

Percentage Distribution of Population of Non-British Origin, by Region, 1961

Region	Non-British and Non-French	French
Canada	26	30
Atlantic	9	19
Quebec	9	81
Ontario	30	10
Prairies	50	7
British Columbia	37	4

Source: *Census of Canada*, 1961.

The great diversity in settlement patterns of ethnic groups has been accompanied by a diversity in religious groups. As would be expected, Roman Catholics are dominant in Quebec because of their connections with the French, but they have also become an increasingly important denomination throughout Canada, making up, for example, the largest single group in Ontario. Fundamentalist groups are concentrated in the prairie provinces.

Related to origin and religion is the distribution of foreign-born Canadians. Since Canada has always been a country of immigration, the foreign-born have naturally contributed significant numbers to the population. Here again settlement has been unevenly distributed throughout the provinces. Since the postwar years Canada has accepted more than two million immigrants, and a sizable proportion, possibly half of these, have settled in Ontario, with major consequences for the composition of the population.

Effects of This Diversity on the Canadian Political System

The wide range of interest groups represented in the country and their unequal geographical dispersion present a politically volatile situation. If there is a complete coincidence between social and economic interests, and these are concentrated in particular geographic regions, the likelihood becomes great that they will find an outlet in united political action of a highly divisive sort. When Confederation was still in the planning stages, those concerned with creating a unified nation had already to contend with the varied character of Canada's resources and population. The existence of a French minority was an obvious problem. The Fathers of Confederation also had to come to terms with the prior existence of colonial legislatures. There were some who favoured a unitary system of government, as in Britain. But a more realistic policy had to take into account a French minority, which needed guarantees for its continued existence before it would give its loyalty to the new nation, and sectional interests which were represented by the existing legislatures. Already there was some rudimentary manufacturing industry in Ontario, and those engaged in these enterprises were anxious to have protection. This was the beginning of a conflict that would continue between the manufacturing interests in the central provinces, and those, first in the Maritimes and later in the prairie provinces, whose prime source of income depended on trade in unfinished resources, and who therefore benefited from the free movement of products. The solution to the problem of accommodating all these divergent interests was in a federal system of government.

The Canadian political system which has developed has therefore incorporated several devices to protect sectional interests. These include representation in the House of Commons and Senate, the continued existence of provincial governments, and judicial interpretations on the distribution of powers between provincial and federal governments. Another means of insuring sectional interests has come about through the development of Cabinet government. Although there is no official recognition in the British North America Act of a party system or a Cabinet, tradition, following that employed in the British parliament, has given Canada two or more political parties, a Prime Minister, and a Cabinet normally appointed from members sitting in the House of Commons and responsible to it. The desire for the representation of various interest groups in the Cabinet has grown as the Senate, the body originally intended to reflect regional interests, has shown itself less effective politically. It has become customary for an effective Cabinet to take into account the proportionate size of each province, special regions within the provinces, and various ethnic and religious groups in the country. The existence of major sectional, ethnic, and economic cleavages and the distribution of power, both actual and desirable, which should exist among interest groups based on these cleavages, become then other important determinants of Canada's identity and of the identities of its citizens.

The Role of Government

The role of government is important in affecting the definition of national identity because what government does is an important way of characterizing nations; government activities in the economic sphere have been significant instruments in nation-building; and government activities in the realm of ideas have aided in the development of national cultures.

One of the primary ways of characterizing modern nations is by the amount and kind of governmental participation. Whether they have socialist or free-enterprise systems is thought to have implications, not just for the economy, but for many critical social institutions. There are those who contend that issues pertaining to government activities are no longer significant today. But even if, as Dahl and Lindblom remark, "it has become increasingly difficult for thoughtful men to find meaningful alternatives posed in the traditional choices between socialism and capitalism,"[9] these choices refer to decisions between government policies and not to the ideological tone associated with particular forms of government. It is this tone rather than the concrete policies with which we are concerned here as a determinant, in part, of a country's internal character and thus its identity.

Related to this ideological content, the role of government has further relevance because of its connection with class-based appeals. For example, survey material from the United States reveals that those who identify with the working class tend to favour government action in the areas of social welfare, public ownership, and the regulation of economic activities.[10] Attitudes toward the role of government should then serve as an extension of the preceding discussion on cleavages by giving content to class-based appeals in Canada.

Secondly, and more important, however, is the fact that government economic activities have often been a conscious tool used to develop the nation. Part of the *national policy* of the first Prime Minister was the building of a transcontinental railway. Although this railway, the Canadian Pacific, has never been publicly owned, the government's generous assistance in funds and land grants has kept it in an enviable financial position to this day. The publicly owned Canadian National Railways have not fared as well financially, but they "are not to be judged merely by the test of profitable returns on investment, since, like other lines, they have been an instrument of nation-building, drawing together widely-scattered communities and making possible the exploitation of natural resources remote from the industrial heart of Canada."[11] The impetus for government economic activity and regulation has often come, not from organized labour, but from the business community. Thus, public regulation of hydro-electric power in Ontario was encouraged by manufacturers and merchants. For these groups in Ontario and elsewhere, government help was needed to protect business interests from American competition or domination. "The concept of Canadian nationality has lent coherence to the numerous claims of these interests for protection, and in public debate has given such claims a more attractive complexion."[12] The tradition of cooperation between private business and government has been an important aspect of the economic life of Canada since 1867, and indications remain that this will continue to be the dominant policy. In a statement made in 1958 a prominent Canadian businessman, R. M. Fowler, president of the Canadian Pulp and Paper Association, said that "the businessman does not, or should not, want to escape from public regulation of business practices and that such regulation is a proper and necessary function of the modern democratic state. Indeed, you will probably think – with some accuracy – that I am suggesting better control and regulation in the national interest than business has had under the present misconceived and misdirected effort."[13] The acquiescence of business interests to government regulation continues to be strongly motivated by a concern with countering American influences.

As a consequence of the way government is seen in Canada – as promoting the development of the nation and controlling competition from the United States – it has been a major participant in economic endeavors. Such varied activities as scientific research, communications, air and rail transport, development of products and resources such as synthetics and atomic energy, have all come under the aegis of government. While the federal government continues to play an important part in economic affairs, its concern in recent years has been more with social-welfare services. Welfare measures include unemployment insurance, family allowances, old-age pensions, and a hospital plan shared with the provinces. At this time the government's efforts at nation-building have been directed toward reducing economic inequalities.

Thirdly, the federal government has attempted to promote the distinctive character of Canada not only through its activities in the economic and social fields, but also in the realm of ideas. Mention has already been made of the creation of government cultural agencies. Since the time of Confederation, cultural domination from outside the country appears to have grown into an increasingly critical issue for many Canadian intellectuals and, through them, the government. For example, in the *Report of the Royal Commission on National Development in the Arts, Letters and Sciences*, the conclusions drawn were that something must be done to develop a unique and rich cultural life in Canada. The best course to follow appeared to be the provision of funds by the three levels of government, although recommendations concerned only federal expenditures.[14] Even in the newspaper and magazine fields, where the participation of government could be viewed as an infringement on freedom of the press, government protection is still seen as a critical necessity. The recent Royal Commission on Publications thought it necessary in order to have specifically Canadian publications, that the government take steps to enforce economic discrimination against American publications in terms of advertising and postage rates. . . .

In a report on the state of scholarly research in the humanities and social sciences in Canada, the author concluded that the only effective solution to the development of these fields in competition with those of the United States was through massive doses of government investment in universities and specifically in research opportunities.[15]

Political Symbols

Before looking at such Canadian symbols as flags, anthems, leaders, rules of government, and historical heroes and events, we must consider their nature and significance in general. The minimal attribute of political symbols is that they are easily recognizable communicative devices. More noteworthy is their peculiarly emotional content. Symbols also have some roots in the traditions of the people they represent, whether these nations are new or have existed for centuries. By their appeal to history symbols can help to enforce respect for authority and for existing institutions.[16] Through this link with the past, symbols also serve to legitimate new laws and practices. They acquire additional importance as they become the basis of some ideological elaboration. In this way, the American Constitution may be regarded as the basis of a relatively consistent system of beliefs in which particular events are always judged in terms of their constitutionality, regardless of the utilitarian value of such judgements. Monarchical institutions also take on this ideological character. A further characteristic of political symbols is their potential for serving as either unifying or divisive rallying points for the residents of a country. For example, in the United States, the refusal of Jehovah's Witnesses children to salute the flag brought forth a historic decision by the Supreme Court which stated in effect that certain aspects of national unity were more important than other constitutional guarantees such as freedom of religion.

In Nigeria the use by the British of legal forms and terminology linked with the Crown helped to mobilize national sentiments of Nigerians against British policies. Even before Bismarck added red to the black and white Prussian flag, the political and national aspirations of Germans were divided by loyalties symbolized by different flags. There are religious groups in both Turkey and Israel which do not accept some of the national heroes and which express their opposition in a variety of ways.

By enumerating the attributes of symbols in addition to merely communicative ones, attention is drawn to their political consequences. One view is that at least some of these symbols, notably national rituals and holidays, represent a "major test of legitimacy"[17] for the nation. Examples cited where symbols had divisive effects would be taken to indicate that some proportion of the population does not accord legitimacy to the state. This raises an empirical question of how critical this is for political stability. In the view of the Justices who ruled in the case of *Minersville School District* v. *Gobitis*, the uniform acceptance of symbols was essential for national unity, but the later ruling acknowledged that this was not in keeping with other values of the United States: "Freedom to differ is not limited to things that do not matter much. That would be a mere shadow of freedom. The test of its substance is the right to differ as to things that touch the heart of the existing order."[18]

But in countries such as Germany and South Africa, lack of approval of political symbols has been highly divisive. A major difference between these countries and the United States is that symbols in the former have served as focal points for public advocacy. Jehovah's Witnesses make up a small proportion of the American population, and their activities are primarily centred in the religious sphere, with only secondary implications for the polity. If, however, they should increase greatly in number and extend their activities to opposing other aspects of the state, then the danger to political stability could indeed be great. In Germany and South Africa differences in attitudes towards political symbols have been mainly related to political matters and have become associated with specific parties. Agitation then has been conducted principally in the political sphere, with important consequences for national unity.

In Canada, the provision o feither unambiguous or unifying symbols has been singularly lacking. At Confederation Canada was given permission to fly the Red Ensign, the flag of the British Merchant Navy. By 1891, the Commonwealth dominions were permitted to use either the Red or Blue Ensign with the addition of their coat-of-arms. Prime Minister Mackenzie King in 1925 attempted to introduce a new flag but dropped the idea in the face of strong opposition. A parliamentary committee met in the fall of 1945 to consider more than two thousand designs and select a new flag. Although the committee made a choice, the government failed to act on it because, for one thing, it feared that the continued inclusion of the Union Jack would be offensive to French-speaking Canadians. A uniquely Canadian flag was adopted in 1965, but not until great controversy had been generated about the design which most appropriately represented Canadian origins and loyalties.

The official national anthem of Canada is generally recognized to be "God Save the Queen," and it is this song which is most often played at public assemblies. After Confederation many felt that Canada needed a national song of its own. At that time English-speaking Canadians were singing "The Maple Leaf Forever," which Alexander Muir wrote in 1867. In it reference is made to the British victory at Quebec and it has never been acceptable to French Canadians.[19] In 1880 Calixa Lavallée wrote "O Canada," and although this has not yet been acknowledged as an official anthem, it is the most widely accepted national song in English- and French-speaking Canada today.

Canada is a constitutional monarchy, and the Queen does not share in any governmental activities except ceremonial ones. When she is absent from the Many outsiders still believe that Canadians support the royal family through country her representative, the Governor-General, carries out these activities. direct taxation. This is not the case, but it is understandable how such a misconception may persist in view of the widespread display of the Queen's picture on Canadian money and postage and in public places generally. Canadians apparently feel a real bond of affection for the royal family, as witnessed by the widely read magazine and newspaper articles about it and the warm welcome that accompanies its visits. Some commentators have considered this the Canadian equivalent to attitudes toward Hollywood stars, but the significance of the Queen as a unifying symbol for all Canadians is a topic which has never been publicly discussed.[20] The hostile reception which the Queen received during her 1964 visit to Quebec may then have come as a shock to many Canadians.

The Governor-General, like the monarch, has, over the years, evolved into a symbolic rather than an actual head. Appointment of the Governor-General as the Queen's representative had been interpreted by the British parliament as lying within their purview. After the Imperial Conference of 1926, the Governor-General was appointed only after consultation with the Canadian Cabinet, which meant in effect that the Canadian Cabinet decided on whom it wanted. In 1952, the first Canadian, Vincent Massey, was appointed. It has been questioned whether the Governor-General can ever attain the same emotional appeal as the monarch. Since he is nominated by the Canadian government and holds office for a relatively short period of time, it does not seem likely that he can build up the same prestige or inspire the same loyalty. But now, as a Canadian, his unifying potential is conceivably greater.

The British North America Act, though drawn up by Canadians from two major political parties and presenting a number of points of view, was never ratified by the Canadian people. Instead it was passed as an ordinary Act of the British parliament. In contrast, the Australian Constitution, which was drafted somewhat later, was passed by a direct vote of the people as well as by the British parliament. The British North America Act does not provide for amendment by Canadian authorities and full responsibility for this has yet to be settled. Many written constitutions contain formal guarantees of basic rights. The Canadian one has never had this, and it was not until 1960 that a Bill of Rights was passed by parliament. This is in striking contrast with the American Constitution in which the drama of the Bill of Rights and the preamble to the Constitution provide foci to which people can pay homage.

Although Canadian history seems short, it is certainly lengthy enough to have acquired historical heroes and dates of important events. But, lacking a revolutionary tradition, Canada has none of the dramatic heroes or historical occasions that are commemorated by other peoples. Politicians in Canada, because of the requirement of knitting together so many divergent strains, have been, where successful, experts at compromise, and as such they are often considered rather colourless individuals. National heroes inherited from earlier periods are marked by their divisive potential. If the English Canadians have General Wolfe, the French Canadians have General Montcalm. History has been taught in French Canada with an emphasis on past glory rather than on present conditions. But Canadian history often seems even more remote to English-speaking Canadians.[21]

Perhaps the most fitting summary of the state of Canadian symbols is contained in a verse by F. R. Scott,

> The Canadian Centenary Council
> Meeting in Le Reine Elizabeth
> To seek those symbols
> Which will explain ourselves to ourselves
> Evoke unlimited responses
> And prove that something called Canada
> Really exists in the hearts of all
> Handed out to every delegate
> At the start of proceedings
> A portfolio of documents
> On the cover of which appeared
> In gold letters
> > not
> A Mari Usque Ad Mare
> > not
> E Pluribus Unum
> > not
> Dieu et Mon Droit
> > but
> COURTESY OF COCA-COLA LIMITED.[22]

Influences on National Identity

Political Party

The political party plays a major role in influencing the character of the nation and the identities of its members. (See Figure 1.) Political party is defined here as made up of respondents who have indicated that they would vote for that party in a forthcoming election.[23] To suggest that party identification alone influences opinion would be to take an absurd position. It is rather the intention of this study to examine the *degree* to which parties have an impact on their supporters.

This may be taken as a further attempt to grapple with Lazarsfeld's statement that "a person thinks, politically, as he is, socially" as an explanation of political attitudes.

Before proceeding, some comments are in order about the nature of the Canadian party structure. Despite some changes in name, the national scene has been dominated by two parties, the Liberal and the Conservative. Along with this two-party dominance there have always been some splinter groups.

New alignments assumed importance in four federal elections: in 1917 as the result of the conscription crisis in Quebec, in 1925 during a period of agrarian

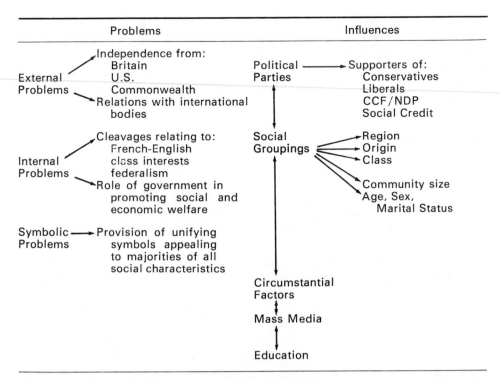

Problems		Influences

External Problems → Independence from:
    Britain
    U.S.
    Commonwealth
    Relations with international bodies

Internal Problems → Cleavages relating to:
    French-English
    class interests
    federalism
    Role of government in promoting social and economic welfare

Symbolic Problems → Provision of unifying symbols appealing to majorities of all social characteristics

Political Parties ⟶ Supporters of:
    Conservatives
    Liberals
    CCF/NDP
    Social Credit

Social Groupings ⟶ Region
    Origin
    Class
    Community size
    Age, Sex, Marital Status

Circumstantial Factors

Mass Media

Education

Figure 1
Canadian Identity: Underlying Problems and Critical Influences

protest, 1935 because of the depression, and in 1945 when conscription again became an issue in Quebec. In most cases dissident groups have been re-absorbed into the two-party structure. The election of 1935, however, resulted in some lasting changes. It was then that the Co-operative Commonwealth Federation (CCF) and Social Credit parties first appeared on the federal scene. These two parties both have their roots in the depressed conditions of western farmers, but they took different directions. The CCF began and has continued as a party of democratic socialism. In 1961 the party was reorganized, and its name changed to the New Democratic party (NDP) in order to broaden its base from agrarian support to that of organized labor. The Social Credit party was founded on the economic theories of Major Douglas, but with the passage of time these theories have been played down, and it has emerged as a second conservative party. While neither of these parties has attained a significant number of seats in the federal House of Commons, they both have had experience governing in the provinces, the CCF in Saskatchewan and the Social Credit in Alberta and British Columbia. In speaking of parties and party support in Canada the subsequent analysis is confined to these four parties.[24]

The public image of Canada can be further elaborated by taking into account the views of those whose social characteristics have been commonly found to have a bearing on political opinions. These are social groupings associated with region, origin, social class including trade union affiliation, community size, age, sex, and marital status.

Since this is primarily a study of public opinion derived from national polls, other influences on national identity cannot be derived from these same sources.

The activities of elites, the military, the mass media, and educational institutions and organizations cannot be extensively treated, but their consequences are at least partly manifested in the opinions of party supporters and other social groups. To expand our understanding of the Canadian setting, then, at least some brief description of these otherwise omitted agents for building national unity is necessary.

The Intellectual Elite

In speaking of elite groups and their role in the promotion of a distinct identity, we have confined ourselves to intellectual elites. When they have become self-consciously nationalistic, English-speaking Canadian intellectuals have often forcefully rejected American culture. In some instances they have preferred to look to Britain as a model. Some French-speaking intellectuals too have looked outside the boundaries of their society for a standard of comparison. For some, a completely separate identity for Quebec has become the favoured alternative.[25] But for many writers, artists, educators, and others concerned with the creation and dissemination of ideas, survival as Canadians is a crucial problem. The conditions of working in a country that has not as yet completely outlived its frontier tradition, where most things are judged by their instrumental utility, and where both official languages are used in more populous countries with richer cultural heritages have made Canadian intellectuals outspokenly nationalistic. In seeking to formulate a national identity both·for themselves and for others they have often looked to government to protect their indigenous market from outside competition. How successful these people have been in influencing the development of Canadian identity is not the task of this study to evaluate. For our purposes it is sufficient to say that the intellectual elite as a group is both concerned with the state of Canada's identity and often desirous of defining it as distinctly different from any other country.

Because of our major concern with the role of political parties, some brief comments are in order on the role of intellectuals in parties. Considering in this category educators, journalists, writers, scientists, economists, political scientists, and artists, these were represented to varying degrees among the candidates of the four parties in the 1963 general election. Of the four parties, the New Democratic party had the largest proportion of intellectuals (25 percent) among its candidates. The Liberal and Social Credit parties were similar with 12 and 11 percent respectively, and the Conservatives had fewest intellectuals (5 percent).[26] Yet, according to popular feeling at least, the parties differ considerably in their use of intellectuals as candidates and as contributors to policy-making. These differences, however, are based mainly on hearsay, and we have little empirical evidence. On such grounds, at least, the Liberals and CCF/NDP are considered to command allegiance of the majority of politically minded intellectuals and to use their training and ideas within the parties. . . .

The Military

The military probably plays a relatively minor part in the formation of an identity in a country such as Canada. Canada, lacking a revolutionary tradition, gives even less significance to the military than the United States. Still, veterans' organization such as the Canadian Legion may be important as pressure groups and do in fact present annual briefs to the Prime Minister and Cabinet, but little is known about their operation. The Canadian Legion was one organization, however, which came out openly for the adoption of the Red Ensign as Canada's official flag.

Mass Media

The mass media, as we have already indicated, have often been perceived as conscious tools for the formation and continuation of a national consciousness. This is true whether or not the media are controlled by the government. Despite efforts to provide a unifying system of national communication through the Canadian Broadcasting Corporation, regional sentiments may actually be strengthened because broadcasting is done in both English and French, allowing Canadians of either language to minimize contact with the other. But if the development of the broadcasting media has been guided by the need to establish some basis for national unity despite the limitations imposed by two official languages, this has been much less true of the printed media. The poor competitive position of Canadian magazines provided the major impetus for the Royal Commission on Publications.

> The desperate situation of the magazines . . . is due almost entirely to the tremendous competition of the so-called Canadian editions of American publications. *Time* and *Reader's Digest*, the two largest of these, dump their editorial material into Canada and then solicit advertising to keep the news pages apart. Since their editorial costs have already been paid in the United States, they can run a highly efficient and well staffed advertising department, and can offer combination deals to big international advertisers.[27]

At present at least, newspapers remain Canadian-owned, although Roy Thomson, the owner of one newspaper chain, lost his Canadian citizenship when he appeared on the 1964 Queen's Honours List. But, due to a number of factors, including the lack of a single national newspaper, the uneven dispersion of population, and the relative cheapness of syndicated services provided from the United States and Great Britain, a content analysis of major Canadian newspapers reveals that they tend to be filled with local news of a most restricted nature, and supplemented by national and international news and columns, often of foreign origin. According to Donald Gordon, political scientist and formerly London correspondent for the Canadian Broadcasting Corporation,

> I put it to you that our Canadian newspapers – those paragons who are doing all the shouting about Canadian identity these days – are in fact selling out on that very goal.
>
> For all their pretensions, they are actually – albeit partly unintentionally – the spotters for the barrage of American and British brainwashing that we have such cause to worry about right now. Through a sustained, substantial and significant pattern of coverage, they are managing to condition us daily to abandon our own real culture in favour of a blurred carbon of the two giants at our elbows.
>
> The basis of this indictment is straight forward: the *source* of most – around 80 percent – foreign news reaching us is basically American and British. An editing screen is maintained by the Canadian wire services (Canadian editors selecting and adjusting copies before relay),

but this cannot make up for the fact that alien eyes actually see and evaluate events as they occur.[28]

A great potential for national image-building lies with the mass media. While their actual effectiveness appears to be seriously hampered, we must keep in mind both their intentions and the conditions under which they operate as factors in the formation of opinions on national problems.

Education

The place of education in furthering national consensus is no doubt hindered by the constitutional provision that the provincial governments be responsible for education. Since each province may establish its own system of education and curricula, differences are found in emphasis on historical events and heroes and even on general social values. Integrative possibilities are further hampered by evidence of regional inequalities in educational opportunities. In addition, the operation of the educational system has helped to perpetuate social-class differences to an extent probably greater than might be imagined by those who see Canada as an approximation of the more equalitarian United States. That Canadian education is so bound up with social class is not in itself damaging to national unity. For example, in avowedly class-based countries mechanisms may exist whereby talented individuals of all social classes can be incorporated into the elite. Alternatively, and this is probably more characteristic of Canada where social class in itself is not a particularly salient characteristic, the perpetuation of class cleavages through the educational system is usually not perceived as a cause for resentment or disunity. Yet objectively the system of education does not provide the foundation for integration across lines of social class, region, or official language.

The preceding summary, brief though it is, of those factors, outside the scope of this study, but nevertheless influencing the development of national identity should contribute to extend our understanding of Canadian society and the conditions affecting public opinion.

Footnotes

1. Donald G. Creighton, "Nationalism in Canadian History," *Conservative Concepts*, 2, Spring, 1960, p. 6.
2. Frank H. Underhill, *The British Commonwealth*. Published for the Duke University Commonwealth Studies Center; Durham: Duke University Press, 1956, p. 32. See also W. L. Morton, *The Canadian Identity*. Madison: University of Wisconsin Press, 1961, p. 49.
3. This was related to the Venezuela boundary dispute with Great Britain, which President Cleveland saw as an infringement of the Monroe Doctrine.
4. Quoted in Alexander Brady, *Democracy in the Dominions*. 3rd edition, Toronto: University of Toronto Press, 1958, p. 37.
5. For evidence on the penetration of American mass media in Canada, see H. F. Angus, *Canada and Her Great Neighbor*. Toronto: Ryerson, 1938, pp. 124-172; *Report of the Royal Commission on Publications*. Ottawa: Queen's Printer, 1961. Other countries too receive much of the content of their mass media from the United States. But what has been especially troublesome for the Canadian mass-communication industry is the geographic closeness of the competition, the sameness of language, the apparent technical superiority of the finished product coming from the United States, and the economic advantages of Americans in competing for the same markets. The results have been, for example, that 92 of the 96 periodicals in Canada which sell more than 10,000 copies per month are American, that there are no nationally recognized newspaper columnists, and that almost the only Canadian films which have won international recognition are those

produced by the government-sponsored National Film Board. John A. Irving, "The Problems of the Mass Media," in *Mass Media in Canada*. ed. by John A. Irving, Toronto: Ryerson, 1962, pp. 221-235.

6. J. Grant Glassco, *Certain Aspects of Taxation Relating to Investment in Canada by Non-residents*. Royal Commission on Canada's Economic Prospects, Ottawa, February, 1956. This has been a continuing trend, which the present administration is attempting to limit.

7. Alexander Brady, "Nationalism and Democracy in the British Commonwealth: Some General Trends," *American Political Science Review*, 47, December, 1953, p. 1030. An economist who strongly argues against nationalistic economic measures such as protectionist tariffs and "forced insertion of Canadians into the ownership and management of American enterprises in Canada" is Harry G. Johnson, in "Problems of Canadian Nationalism," *International Journal*, 16, Summer, 1961, pp. 238-249.

8. Herbert J. Spiro, *Politics in Africa*. Englewood Cliffs: Prentice-Hall, Spectrum Books, 1962, pp. 12-23.

9. Robert A. Dahl and Charles E. Lindblom, *Politics, Economics, and Welfare*. New York: Harper, 1953, p. 3.

10. Heinz Eulau, *Class and Party in the Eisenhower Years*. New York: Free Press, 1962, p. 64.

11. Brady, "The State and Economic Life," in *Canada*, ed. by George W. Brown, Toronto: Toronto University Press, 1950, p. 357.

12. *Ibid.*, p. 354.

13. R. M. Fowler, "The Future of Competition in Canada: A Businessman's View," in *The Canadian Economy: Selected Readings*, ed. by J. Deutsch, B. S. Keirstead, K. Levitt, and R. M. Will, Toronto: Macmillan, 1961, p. 69. His derogatory reference was to the Conservative government of John Diefenbaker.

14. *Report of the Royal Commission on National Development in the Arts, Letters and Sciences, 1949-1951*. Ottawa: King's Printer, 1951, p. 272. See also the recommendations for government expenditures on pp. 276-382. See also Hugh MacLennan, in *The Price of Being Canadian*, ed. by D. L. B. Hamlin, 7th Winter Conference, Canadian Institute of Public Affairs; Toronto: University of Toronto Press, 1961, pp. 27-35.

15. Bernard Ostry, *Research in the Humanities and in the Social Sciences in Canada*, published for the Humanities Research Council of Canada and the Social Science Research Council of Canada, Ottawa: 1962.

16. Herbert J. Spiro, *Government by Constitution*. New York: Random House, 1959, p. 377. In relation to the British monarchy see Edward Shils and Michael Young, "The Meaning of the Coronation," *Sociological Review*, 1, December, 1953, pp. 63-81. The unifying potential of the monarchy is questioned by N. Birnbaum, "Monarchs and Sociologists: A Reply to Professor Shils and Mr. Young." *Sociological Review*, 3, July, 1955, pp. 5-23.

17. S. M. Lipset, *Political Man*. Garden City: Doubleday, 1960, p. 80. For an interesting discussion on the use of ritual in legitimating the identity of Yankee City, see W. Lloyd Warner, *The Family of God*. New Haven: Yale University Press, 1961, pp. 89-154.

18. *West Virginia State Board of Education* v. *Barnette*, 319 U.S. 624, 63 S. Ct. 1178, 87 L. Ed. 1628 (1943).

19. At the 1963 meeting of the Canadian Authors' Association, it was agreed that a contest be held to obtain new words for the music of "The Maple Leaf Forever," words which would be acceptable to all Canadians.

20. For the Queen's possible impact on non-British, non-French immigrants, see Mildred A. Schwarz, "Political Behaviour and Ethnic Origin," in *Papers on the 1962 Election*. ed. by John Meisel, Toronto: University of Toronto Press, 1964, p. 258. A Canadian TV star, now resident in the United States, raised an outcry from some segments of the public when she appeared on the Jack Paar show before a royal visit and said that most Canadians were *indifferent* to the Queen.

21. A Toronto newspaper reported how a group of children made elaborate preparations to enact the American Civil War. Questioned on the appropriateness of this battle rather than one more closely related to Canada, the children's teen-aged adviser answered, "We thought about that, but we seem to know so very little of our own history. The kids see Civil War scenes on television, and this is more interesting to them." *Toronto Star*, August 23, 1962.

22. F. R. Scott, "National Identity," *Maclean's*, June 1, 1963, p. 2.

23. In referring to party supporters it should be understood that the main unit and its constituent parts are only relative terms since many supporters will not vote and some may change their allegiance in a coming election. But the important thing is that at the

time of each survey respondents were willing to identify themselves as party sympathizers. It might increase the significance of this study if it were possible to discover how strongly partisan supporters were, but this information is not available. Still, as the subsequent analysis will indicate, this conception of parties is a useful device as long as it is recalled that parties are loosely organized and allow considerable shifts in composition over time. Even if we were concerned wth party membership we would still find major definitional problems. See Maurice Duverger, *Political Parties*. London: Methuen, 1954, pp. 61-64.

24. In June 1963, two months after a general election, thirteen of the twenty Quebec Social Credit members of parliament broke away from the national party, and formed a new party, Le Ralliement des Créditistes, under the erstwhile deputy leader of the Social Credit, Réal Caouette. But since we are concerned with party supporters, and the electorate had not yet had the opportunity to vote for this party, it is not necessary for our analysis that we distinguish between the two factions.

25. According to a survey conducted for the Canadian Broadcasting Corporation and *Maclean's* magazine, 29 percent of those interviewed who had technical training beyond the secondary level and 26 percent of those with classical college or university education were in favour of separation of Quebec from the rest of Canada. This compared with 11 percent for those with either elementary- or secondary-school education. Unpublished tables on separatism, Le Groupe de Recherche Sociale, Montreal, September, 1963.

26. Source: Canada, Chief Electoral Officer, *Report, 26th General Election, 1963*. Ottawa: Queen's Printer, 1963.

27. Arnold Edinborough, "The Press," in Irving, *op. cit.* (in n. 8), p. 27.

28. "Moulding the Canadian Mind Without Really Trying," *Saturday Night*, January, 1964, p. 17.

Canadian Defence Policy and the American Empire[*]

Philip Resnick

This paper[1] sets out to examine Canadian defence policy since the Second World War, with particular reference to the development of a continental defence alliance between Canada and the United States. I am concerned with relating Canadian junior partnership in defence to a larger process – the subordination of Canada to the American empire. For the acceptance by Canada's political and military élites of American direction in the period of the Cold War was linked intimately to the economic development of Canada along liberal capitalist lines, a process which turned Canada into a region in the continental and worldwide American economic system. Moreover, the colonial mentality which characterized Canadian defence and foreign policy vis-à-vis the United States was related in turn to the liberal ideology through which the Canadian capitalist élites viewed, and continue to view, the world. It was only natural that their support of liberal values and free enterprise, combined with their anti-communism, should have led them to define Canadian interests in terms of the American empire.

The colonialism of Canada's élites predates 1945. Ever since 1867 they have tended to look to the outside for direction and capital, and have identified Canadian nationhood with empire. There were no Noah Websters at the time

*Reprinted from *Close the 49th Parallel, etc.*: *The Americanization of Canada*, edited by Ian Lumsden, by permission of University of Toronto Press. © University of Toronto Press 1970.

of Confederation to declare in Canadian terms: "America is an independent empire and ought to assume an independent character. Nothing can be more ridiculous, than a servile imitation of the manners, the language, and the vices of foreigners."[2] Instead, Canada during the first fifty years of her existence was a staunch supporter of British imperialism, while national consciousness, with the exception of the Alaska boundary settlement of 1903, remained all but dormant. For the Canadian élites, a deferential, hierarchical society at home found its logical counterpart in deference to imperial policy abroad.

The First World War, with its large commitment of Canadian men and resources, brought foreign and defence policy home to Canada with a vengeance and served to tarnish the old imperial connection. Subsequently, Robert Borden was instrumental in pressing for the autonomy of the Dominions at the Imperial War Cabinet meeting of 1917, and in securing the admission of Canada to the League of Nations two years later.

It would be wrong, however, to think that the new emphasis on political sovereignty after the First World War meant the disappearance of a colonial attitude on the part of the Canadian political élite. Borden set forth the case for autonomy in the following terms: "I am beginning to feel that in the end and perhaps sooner than later, Canada must assume full sovereignty. She can give better service to Great Britain and the U.S. and the world in that way."[3] The dispatch of a Canadian force to Siberia in 1918-19, in support of the Allied intervention, was an early example of the autonomy Borden had in mind.

If the 1920s and 1930s witnessed growing disengagement of Canada from the British empire, it simultaneously brought an increased Canadian orientation towards the United States. In this period, American investment in Canada soared from under $500 million in 1910 to over $2 billion in 1920, and over $4 billion in 1930.[4] The development of hydro-electric power, pulp and paper, and minerals of the Shield area gave the Canadian economy a new continental direction and allowed American imperialism to dislodge the British. In Harold Innis's words, "Canada moved from colony to nation to colony."[5]

This shift was reflected in Canadian foreign policy. Mackenzie King's vacillation during what Eayrs, paraphrasing Auden, has called " a low dishonest decade" (that is, the thirties), represented more than a strong isolationism in Canadian public opinion. King appeared to be reacting to a rift in the North Atlantic Triangle, to a divergence of interest between the old imperial power and the new. The international crisis in liberal capitalism, but more particularly, the crisis in Anglo-American relations, lay at the root of Canadian indecision.

Although Canada entered the Second World War at Britain's side, Canadian foreign policy was to regain its equanimity only with the forging of a defence alliance with the United States at Ogdensburg in August 1940 and with subsequent American entry into the war. In its rush to commitments after 1945, Canadian policy sought both to compensate for its hesitations in the 1930s, and to align itself forthright with the United States.[6] The bogey of Soviet imperialism was to provide the excuse, and the post-war defence alliance the instrumentality. Liberalism would reinforce colonialism in making Canada a willing ally of the United States in the Cold War.

Thus it was not by accident that Canadian policy-makers ignored any threat which the overwhelming power of the United States might represent for Canada. In his important Gray Lecture in January 1947, Louis St. Laurent declared: "It is not customary in this country for us to think in terms of a policy in regard to the United States. Like farmers whose lands have a common concession line we think of ourselves as settling, from day to day, questions that arise between us, without dignifying the process by the word 'policy'."[7] And a year later Lester Pearson vouched for the beneficence of American power in these terms: "The power of the United States in the world, a power now decisive, was established against the will of the Americans, who were quite content without it. . . . It is in the hands of a people who are decent, democratic, and pacific, unambitious for imperial pomp or rule."[8]

When we compare this with the rhetoric which the American political élite used in defence of its empire, a rhetoric laden with liberal terms, the link between Canadian liberalism and junior partnership in the Cold War becomes clearer. Thus in 1967, in defence of US involvement in Vietnam, W. W. Rostow declared:

> The United States has no interest in political satellites . . . We seek nations which shall stand up straight. And we do so for a reason: because we are deeply confident that nations which stand up straight will protect their independence and move in their own ways and in their own time towards human freedom and political democracy . . . We are struggling to maintain an open environment on the world scene which will permit our open society to flourish and survive.[9]

It was this same *open environment* which the United States sought to maintain through its policy of containment of Russia and later China, and which Canada has supported since 1945. American leadership of the *free world* became the basis of Canadian foreign and defence policy.

Two symbolic dates mark the continental reorientation of Canadian defence policy in the 1940s, and Canada's entry into the American sphere of influence. The first is August 18, 1940, the date of the meeting between Franklin Roosevelt and Mackenzie King at Ogdensburg, at a dark moment of the war, which resulted in the establishment of a Permanent Joint Board of Defence between the two countries. This board was particularly important during the first two years of its operation, serving to mesh Canadian with American defence planning against an anticipated Axis attack. In practice, however, the board confined its activities to the northern half of North America; it involved the United States in the defence of Canada's eastern and western coasts, and in the later stages of the war, of the Canadian northwest. Canada, for its part, had only a minor influence on American and Allied policy and, in fact, became increasingly dependent on the United States for both trade and matériel. The Hyde Park Agreement of April 1941, which co-ordinated the mobilization of resources in both countries, was a corollary to the Ogdensburg Declaration and a portent of increasing economic integration between the two nations.

The second symbolic date is less well known than August 1940, but is in some respects more important. On February 12, 1947, Mackenzie King rose in the House of Commons to announce an agreement worked out in the Permanent Joint Board of Defence to extend Canada's wartime alliance with the United States into the post-war period:

> It is apparent to anyone who has reflected even casually on the technological advances of recent years that new geographical factors have been brought into play. The polar regions assume new importance as

the shortest routes between North America and the principal centres of population of the world. In consequence . . . when we think of the defence of Canada, we must, in addition to looking east and west as in the past, take the north into consideration as well.[10]

What his listeners did not know was that this agreement was the product of almost a year and a half of discussion in the joint board, and that ever since June 1945, the American military had expressed a strong interest in "the continuing value to continental defence of the facilities developed in northwest Canada during the war."[11] Fewer still were the Canadians who recognized King's sudden interest in the north for what it was – the first step in Canada's defence alliance with the United States in the Cold War.

There is no space here to trace the steps by which Canadian policy-makers yielded to insistent American pressure and in February 1947 accepted the five principles of defence collaboration.[12] Suffice it to say that at the war's end American military planners had already come to see the Soviet Union as a future enemy, and that American diplomacy both in Eastern Europe and over the A-bomb had largely set the stage for the Cold War.[13] Thus if the United States was insistent on defence collaboration with Canada, it was because of the new military strategy which containment of Russia dictated. As General H. H. Arnold declared in 1946, "If there is a Third World War, its strategic centre will be the North Pole."[14]

Canadian policy-makers, while initially wary of sacrificing Canadian sovereignty on the altar of a defence alliance, none the less came to support American military strategy. As early as August 1945, General Foulkes, chief of the general staff, speaking of defence research, had declared: "Canada's future commitments will lie either in fighting with Empire forces or with the forces of the United States of America . . .There appears to be no place in Canada's operations in the future for special Canadian equipment of which British or American commanders may not have full knowledge or experience."[15] To be sure, Foulkes still placed Britain and the United States on a par in his strategic planning in the summer of 1945. By July 1946, however, when Pearson in speaking of the Canadian North could claim that "there is no refuge in remoteness" and that "fear and suspicion engendered in Iran can easily spread to Great Bear Lake,"[16] the United States had emerged as the dominant post-war capitalist power. By November 1946 the principles of the February 12 agreement had been accepted, and Canadian defence policy was becoming aligned to that of the United States.

Mackenzie King in his Commons statement downplayed the importance of these new arrangements and stressed Canadian support for the United Nations. But the significance of the agreement had been underscored by A. R. M. Lower some months earlier: "If Canada wishes to become a subordinate state and even a more complete satellite of the United States than she is at present, the surest road for her to take is to accept American assistance in defending her own territories. Should Yugoslavia accept Russian assistance in defending her Adriatic coast line? We all know the meaning of the answer 'Yes' to that. It is the same with us."[17] Canada had become a fortress in the American chain of command in the Cold War.

It was only in the months following the February 12 agreement, after the Truman Doctrine and Kennan's containment policy had been unveiled, that the full scope of Canadian junior partnership in the Cold War became evident. In a speech in Quebec City in October 1947, St. Laurent openly revealed his Cold War liberal assumptions: "If theory-crazed totalitarian groups persist in their policies of frustration and futility, we will not, for much longer, allow them to prevent us from using our obvious advantages to improve the conditions of those who wish to cooperate with us."[18] In a major address to the House of Commons on April 29, 1948, he went even further in defining the principle of Canadian foreign policy: "Our foreign policy, therefore, must, I suggest, be based on a recognition of the fact that totalitarian communist aggression endangers the freedom and peace of every democratic country, including Canada."[19]

Nowhere at the time, in either St. Laurent's or Pearson's speeches, was there any question of the validity of identifying Canadian with American interests vis-à-vis the Soviet Union. Nor was any consideration given to a policy of neutralism, such as that which Sweden chose to pursue. Instead, the Canadian élite opted for the American camp, disguising behind the catch-word *internationalism* its subordination to American policy.

This rejection of Canadian independence in the Cold War becomes more understandable when one bears in mind the policy of continentalism in economics which Canada's political and corporate élites simultaneously began to pursue. The currency crisis of November 1947, in which Canadian reserves plummeted to a post-war low of $480 million, revealed the fragility of Canada's capitalist structure. The old Atlantic markets had dried up, and it was to the United States that Douglas Abbott, minister of finance, turned in announcing emergency measures.

Specifically, Abbott announced a temporary curb on imports from the United States and provisions for US Marshall Plan purchases in Canada. But more important, as a long-term policy he stated that the Canadian government would seek to develop natural resources, to reduce permanently the lack of balance in Canadian-American trade.[20] Thus the great resource give-away and inflow of American capital of the 1950s was heralded.

Hume Wrong, Canadian ambassador to Washington and one of the architects of the February 12 agreement, brought home the implications of this policy in an address in early 1948: "We certainly do not want to make the two figures of exports between the two countries equal or nearly equal, for that could only be achieved by a most extreme form of economic nationalism, which would gravely lower the Canadian standard of living."[21] Wrong implicitly rejected economic independence in favour of long-term American development of Canada. Canadian trade with the United States would be be balanced in the future by closer integration between the two economies.

Integration in defence policy became a logical counterpart to economic continentalism. Following the outbreak of the Korean War and the mobilization of the Canadian economy and Canadian resources in support of American containment of China, the two would in fact go hand in hand. As American strategy became global, so did Canadian. Brooke Claxton, minister of national defence, was quite candid when he stated " that the best place to defend Canada would be as far away from our shores as possible."[22]

The American involvement in Korea dated back to 1945. In November 1947, on US initiative, a UN Temporary Commission was established to supervise free elections in Korea, thus involving the United Nations in a matter involving post-war settlement among the great powers. Interestingly, Mackenzie King opposed participation by Canada on this commission, "conjuring up visions of Canada's being crushed in a conflict between the United States and the Soviet Union," but he was overruled by his *internationalist* advisers – that is, St. Laurent and Pearson.[23]

Although there had been indications of a slackening of American interest in Korea in late 1949 and early 1950,[24] the outbreak of war brought an instant American response. In particular, the United States turned to the United Nations, and pushed through the Security Council a resolution recommending intervention by UN members.[25] This became the ostensible basis for Canadian intervention, involving the dispatch of three Canadian destroyers and a special brigade to serve in Korea.

The real motivation of Canadian policy was made plain, however, in a statement by St. Laurent on July 19, 1950, in which he declared: "The attack of the North Korean aggressors on South Korea is a breach in the outer defences of the free world."[26] It was as a junior partner in the American empire that Canada was reacting to the Korean War and supporting the containment of communism.

In the fall of 1950, when American rearmament began in earnest, the Canadian government secured $450 million in supplementary defence expenditures from Parliament. At the same time, in the spirit of the Hyde Park Agreement of 1941, a Statement on the Principles of Economic Co-operation between the two countries was released in October, tightening Canada's economic ties with the United States.[27]

In January 1951 Brooke Claxton predicted a defence expenditure for 1951-2 in excess of $1,500 million (the final figure exceeded $2 billion) and listed a whole series of developments, ranging from manufacture of radar and electronical devices in Canada, to manufacture of the F-86 and CF-100, to an increase in military personnel to over eighty-five thousand men. "Defence has become today the biggest single industry in Canada," Claxton declared. In a period of only nine months, eighty thousand defence contracts were entered into by the Canadian Commercial Corporation. Canada's role on the production side was to concentrate on such basic materials as steel, nickel, and aluminum, in line with the needs which the 1952 Paley Report on raw materials and American industrial requirements had outlined for the United States.

Canadian junior partnership in defence was now more explicit. As Claxton stated:

> We are constantly reviewing our territorial defence with the U.S. services because the defence of the North American continent is a joint operation. Our security does not depend exclusively on what Canada does or what the Americans do, but on the sum of our joint effort. *Every cent spent in Canada helps to defend the United States and vice versa. We have the same interests in our common defence*, and from day to day we are making arrangements to strengthen that defence.[28]

In the first years of the 1950s, the Canadian political élite spent over $2 billion annually in support of these *common defence interests*. At the same time, the Korean War and the American rearmament programme sparked a boom in

Canadian economic growth between 1950 and 1957 unmatched in Canadian history.

> The stimulus for the boom of the 1950's came wholly from the United States, with the result that the east-west structure of the Canadian economy was fundamentally modified by an almost massive north-south integration. Toward the end of the period Canadian trade statistics revealed the emergence of almost entirely new exports to the U.S. of iron ore, uranium, oil, and nonferrous metals which rivaled and in some cases superseded in size the traditional staples which were sold in overseas markets.[29]

Junior partnership in defence thus reinforced continentalism in economies, for it was to US capital that the Canadian élites turned in "opening up Canada's treasure house of base metals, uranium, and rare metals needed for the jet age."[30] While helping to finance the defence of the American empire in both Europe and Asia through its own rearmament programme, the Canadian political élite simultaneously imported large quantities of US matériel and capital, until by 1956-7 approximately two-fifths of net capital formation was being financed directly by non-residents.[31] Even as decisions on Canadian resources and development came to be made most often in the United States, so too decisions on defence increasingly were made outside the country.

Canadian foreign policy over NATO and Korea had already shown the way. Only rarely did Canada seek to dissociate herself from American actions, as in a speech which Pearson made but two days before Truman's firing of Mac-Arthur: "The days of relatively easy and automatic political relations with our neighbour are, I think, over . . . Our preoccupation is no longer whether the US will discharge its responsibilities but how she will do it and how the rest of us will be involved." In the same speech, however, Pearson expressed the real substance of Canadian foreign policy, its underlying support for American actions:

> We should be careful not to transfer the suspicions and touchiness and hesitations of yesteryear from London to Washington. Nor should we get unduly bothered over all the pronouncements of journalists, and generals, or politicians which we do not like, though there may be some, indeed are some on which we have the right to express our views . . . More important, *we must convince the United States by deeds rather than merely by words that we are, in fact, pulling our weight in this international team.*[32]

Why show suspicion towards Washington when one shared the ideological outlook of American policy-makers, welcomed American capital to Canada, and defined Canadian interests in terms of American willingness to lead the free world? With brigades in Germany and Korea, with high defence expenditures, Canada was indeed pulling her weight in the defence of the frontiers of the American empire. Measures for continental defence would not lag far behind.

With the exception of several cold weather manoeuvres in the far north, the agreement of February 12, 1947, was not given immediate priority. The explosion of a Soviet A-bomb in September 1949, however, ended the American nuclear monopoly, and gave the defence of the North American continent, where the US nuclear force was concentrated, a new importance in American military strategy. Soon a new round of militarization of the Cold War began, leading to the installation of three radar networks in Canada between 1951 and 1957, and to total subordination of Canadian defence policy to that of the United States.

Discussions regarding the first of the radar lines, the Pinetree Line, began in the Permanent Joint Board of Defence in 1949. The line, to be built along the Canadian border, was equipped both to detect and to intercept approaching aircraft. The line would almost certainly have remained beyond the realm of military or financial feasibility, had the Korean War not broken out. In August 1951, however, an exchange of notes between the Canadian and American governments formalized the agreement to build the line at an ultimate cost of $450 million, split two-thirds – one-third between the United States and Canada.[33]

The second line, the Mid-Canada Line, was begun even before the Pinetree Line was completed. It was entirely Canadian in equipment and financing, to the tune of $170 million. The third and most important line, the Distant Early Warning Line (DEW), was entirely American in inspiration, and originated in a study carried out for the US Air Force at the Lincoln Laboratories of MIT in 1951-2. The explosion of a Soviet H-bomb in August 1953 triggered American action, resulting in National Security Council Minute 162 judging the Soviet threat to be total, and recommending much greater efforts to improve continental defence.[34] Eisenhower's first visit to Ottawa resulted in "complete agreement on the vital importance of effective methods for joint defence"; a year later, in November 1954, the decision was announced to proceed with the construction of a distant early warning line.

The costs of financing, about $450 million, were to be borne exclusively by the United States, and US personnel were to be stationed in the North. Elaborate provisions regarding Canadian sovereignty were included in the DEW Line Agreement, but in effect Canada was reduced to providing the real estate while the United States provided the policy.

Ralph Campney, the new minister of national defence, articulated a Canadian defence policy based upon protecting the American deterrent:

> . . . it becomes essential that greater efforts be put forward immediately in strengthening the defences of this continent because North America is the base from which operations for the defence of Europe can be supported and also because of the necessity of protecting the thermo-nuclear retaliatory capacity of the United States, which provides at the present time probably the greatest single deterrent to war.[35]

Canadian spokesmen refused to admit that the American deterrent was part and parcel of a forward strategy which the United States was pursuing around the globe. American concern with continental air defence became *ipso facto* a Canadian concern. The defence of the centre of the American empire was the defence of Canada. Well might Eisenhower declare in 1954: "Our relations with Canada, happily always close, involve more and more the unbreakable ties of strategic interdependence."[36] As the Cold War entered its second decade, interdependence led to integration of the RCAF itself into a USAF command.

The decision to establish NORAD, the North American Air Defence Command, in the summer of 1957, marked a high point in the loss of Canadian freedom of action in the military-strategic field. For by agreeing to an integrated head-quarters in Colorado Springs to plan and oversee continental air defence, Ottawa recognized that control over that air defence "had to all intents and purposes passed to the United States as the major partner in the combined command."[37]

The pressure for NORAD originated with the USAF, which had already set up a Continental Air Defense Command in September 1954 and naturally was eager to extend its scope to embrace the whole of North America. The Canadian military, especially the RCAF, had acquired the habit of working with the Americans ever since the Second World War; and they regarded the arrangements for Arctic defence worked out in 1946-7 as a "weak compromise" which had failed to come to grips with "the realities of a Soviet air attack on this continent."[38]

In 1956 a joint US-Canadian military study group was set up to prepare the groundwork for a joint command, and the recommendation of this body became in turn the basis for NORAD. By a quirk of electoral fortune, it was the ostensibly nationalist Conservative government of John Diefenbaker, newly elected in June 1957, which accepted the agreement on August 1.

General Charles Foulkes later confessed that the Canadian military had "stampeded the incoming government with the NORAD Agreement."[39] But Howard Green has admitted that although the new government might have taken a harder look at the proposed air defence command, in the end it would have been forced to accept it.[40] The Conservatives, no less than the Liberals, were opposed to a policy of neutralism for Canada. Diefenbaker was as insistent as Pearson in maintaining that "Canada by herself cannot provide adequate defence in a modern war. . . . Our close relationship geographically, with the U.S. makes it natural that we should join together."[41] Ideologically strongly anti-communist, and a firm supporter of a capitalist Canada depending on a massive infusion of American capital,[42] Diefenbaker was ill-prepared to reverse the pattern of junior partnership in Canadian defence policy.

Through NORAD Canada went beyond merely offering her territory for radar installations or communications facilities. The RCAF had in fact become "a colonial military instrument serving the nuclear strategy of the United States."[43] On the pretext of being consulted by the US officer commanding NORAD, previous to the interception of hostile aircraft, Canada ensured well-nigh automatic involvement in any American measures relating to continental defence.

The parliamentary debate of May 1958 failed on the whole to come to grips with the real implications of NORAD. Both Diefenbaker and Sydney Smith chose to emphasize the element of joint consultation which NORAD provided for, overlooking the fact that in an alliance between a great power and a small one, the power relationship, not the forms of sovereign equality, determines its real character. The opposition, for its part, argued strongly for the need to link NORAD to NATO, as though an alliance set up to foster the American military presence in Europe could somehow alter the subordination flowing from continental air defence.

Only Bert Herridge, CCF member from Kootenay West, drew attention to the future consequences of NORAD during the debate. He stressed the increased economic dependence of Canada on the United States that would follow in connection with the design and production of military equipment. He interpreted Sydney Smith's announcement of May 21, 1958, regarding surveys to establish Semi-Automatic Ground Environments (SAGE) in Canada to bolster radar defence, as pointing to the acquisition of Bomarc. And he foresaw the Defence Sharing Agreement of 1959 in his prophetic observation: "The future pattern may well be that Canadian industry, if it is to get any share at all in the production of new and complex equipment needed in the air defence of Canada, may have to be satisfied with participating as sub-contractors in large US production programs."[44]

NORAD, in effect, entailed the complete acceptance of American strategic doctrine, where Canadian defence policy was concerned. At the time of the NORAD negotiations, Tom Kent, future executive assistant to Lester Pearson, wrote: "The first essential interest of Canada in the world today is the security of the United States; that takes overwhelming priority over everything else in Canada's external relations."[45] On the military side, NORAD demanded a fairly high commitment of air defence forces by Canada in succeeding years. Not only would the radar lines have to be modernized, but also Canada would have to embark on costly arms purchases in the United States, necessitating, as Herridge had predicted, economic integration in defence production between Canada and the United States – that is, an end to independent Canadian production. At the same time, the new weaponry would require nuclear armament, forcing Canada in the end to compromise her concern for non-proliferation of nuclear weapons and disarmament, in the name of NORAD's nuclear strategy.

Between 1958 and 1961, Canada's continental defence alignment with the United States took shape. SAGE electronic equipment was installed in the Canadian air defence system to increase the efficiency of the Pinetree Line and to prepare for the introduction of Bomarc. The Bomarc itself was acquired, in line with American estimations of a manned bomber threat to North America, though a substantial body of opinion held that both SAGE and Bomarc would be obsolete by 1962-3, the dates they were scheduled to become operational. The Lockheed F-104F (Starfighter) and the Voodoo F-101 were acquired for the RCAF, both requiring nuclear weapons. While Howard Green was firm in his moral opposition to nuclear weapons, and Diefenbaker insistent that "Canadians wish to make their own decisions in international affairs,"[46] the government, by accepting NORAD and the nuclear weaponry to go with it, surrendered Canadian freedom of action in defence and painted Canadian defence policy into a nuclear corner.

The Cuban missile crisis was an acid test of the automaticity of NORAD. For, despite Diefenbaker's refusal for forty-eight hours to sanction the alert, he was powerless to prevent it. Five years later, an American official, recalling the crisis, admitted: "It wasn't as bad as it looked. This was because the Canadian forces went on full alert despite their government. But this is a hell of a way to operate."[47] The Canadian military, in the crunch, was prepared to accept its orders from Colorado Springs, rather than Ottawa.

The fall of the Diefenbaker government in February 1963 was itself a reflection of the constraint which NORAD had placed on Canadian policy. Once Lester Pearson had made his dramatic reversal of January 1963, and argued that the government "should discharge its commitments . . . by accepting nuclear weapons for those defensive tactical weapons which cannot be effectively used without them,"[48] Diefenbaker's procrastination became untenable. Unwilling to come out in support of a policy of neutralism, he fell victim to the logic of the State Department, arguing: "A flexible and balanced defence requires increased conventional forces, but conventional forces are not an alternative to effective NATO and NORAD defence arrangements using nuclear-capable weapons systems."[49] Given a policy of junior partnership, Pearson's position was the only logical one. Nuclear virginity was incompatible with continental integration around a nuclear strategy. NORAD led irrevocably to nuclear weapons.

Although the nuclear weapons question had generated much controversy in the early 1960s, most of the opposition died down once the Liberals returned to power in April 1963, and allowed nuclear weapons onto Canadian soil. Indeed, as the importance of bomber defence began to decline in the middle 1960s, with the advent of the missile era, there was less tendency in Canadian public opinion to see NORAD as a reflection of Canadian colonialism vis-à-vis the United States.

But there was no inclination on the part of the Canadian political élite to scrap NORAD when the agreement came up for renewal in May 1968. Although as early as 1965 US Secretary of Defense MacNamara had told a House of Representatives committee that the radar systems in Canada were either obsolete or of marginal value to overall American defence,[50] Canadian spokesmen continued to hold that the continental defence arrangements "provide security, which is the basis of independence."[51] The Americans for their part were prepared to continue NORAD as a hold-back line, and saw the agreement as providing the United States with a framework to continue overflights into Canada, and the use of Canadian facilities for testing and deployment. They found the Canadian government a pliant partner.

Paul Martin rationalized the renewal of NORAD "as the only option compatible with Canadian sovereignty."[52] Given this mentality, we can understand how Canadian foreign policy-makers could lend support to American policy in the Dominican Republic[53] and Vietnam, and continue to style itself independent. In defence, as in foreign policy, the colonial mentality is self-imposed. The Canadian political élite is prepared to give freely what in Czechoslovakia has to be imposed – fealty to imperialist power.

As General Foulkes expressed it: "Canada has not always agreed with U.S. strategic policies, but is usually frank enough to point out its views, and is staunch enough to support immediately any challenge to our North American way of life."[54] In this support of "our North American way of life" against Russia, against China, in the extension of the American empire in Latin America and in Asia, lies the key to Canadian junior partnership, and to her membership in NORAD.

NORAD represented the culmination of the process whereby Canada accepted American strategic and military direction in her defence policy. In turn, however, continentalism in defence policy reinforced continentalism in defence production and led to the Defence Sharing Agreement of 1959, entailing tight Canadian dependence on the American market in the production of defence commodities. This agreement, even more than NORAD, became in the late 1960s a symbol of Canada's growing involvement in America's imperialist policies through the mechanism of continental defence, and an acid test of the political subordination that follows in the wake of military and economic subordination to a great power.

Continentalism in defence production dated back, of course, to the Hyde Park Agreement of 1941, and was in turn reinforced after the outbreak of the Korean War in 1950. In the early 1950s Canada in fact developed a fairly sophisticated defence industry, so much so that she embarked on the development of the CF-105, a supersonic jet fighter, by herself in the early 1950s. The cost of the Arrow became prohibitive by 1958-9, and in the absence of American sales (reflecting the insistence of the American military-industrial complex on producing its sophisticated weaponry at home), Diefenbaker was forced to cancel production.

The Arrow had been designed to stave off a bomber threat to North America — that is, had been conceived of in terms of a continental, rather than a Canadian, strategy. With the establishment of NORAD, integration of defence policy had been carried a stage further, and it was only natural that the Canadian government, faced with the dislocation of its aircraft industry, should have seen integration of Canadian defence production with American as a veritable *deus ex machina*. In his statement cancelling the Arrow, Diefenbaker observed: "Under the irresistible dictates of geography the defence of North America has become a joint enterprise of both Canada and the United States. In the partnership each country has its own skills and resources to contribute, and the pooling of these resources for the most effective defence of our common interest is the essence of production sharing."[55]

From the American point of view, the Defence Sharing Agreement was a useful concession, greatly strengthening Canadian economic dependence on the United States. While tariffs and the Buy American clause were eliminated on Canadian bids for US military contracts, American policy-makers probably also saw in the agreement a check on any hypothetical bid by Canada for freedom of action in the foreign policy field. The Vietnam war was to bring this point forcibly home.

Elsewhere, I have dealt with the workings of the Defence Sharing Agreement in the 1960s, and Canada's increasing involvement in arms sales for Vietnam.[56] Here, it is enough merely to draw the implications of continentalism in defence production for Canadian defence and foreign policy.

Lester Pearson is himself the most damning witness in this regard. In his reply to the request by professors at the University of Toronto in January 1967 that Canada ban all further arms sales for Vietnam, Pearson made clear the overall continental framework within which Canadian policy operated:

> It is clear that the imposition of an embargo on the export of military equipment to the United States, and concomitant termination of the Production Sharing Agreements, would have far reaching consequences which no Canadian Government would contemplate with equanimity. It would be interpreted as a notice of withdrawal on our part from continental defence and even the collective defence arrangements of the Atlantic Alliance.[57]

In the context of the Vietnam war this meant that Canada would continue to support the United States and abstain from any measures which might detrimentally affect her long-term relationship with the United States; Pearson stated this on another occasion: "In concrete terms, and on the Canadian side, this means that we shall support the United States whenever we can and we shall hope that will be nearly all the time."[58]

Thus, the economic stake in continentalism served to reinforce the military one. The North American continent, one for purposes of defence since 1945, was no less one where defence production was involved. Canada could not disengage from integration in weaponry without grave consequences in the short run to her capitalist economy. Nor could she turn her back on the sophistication and expertise of the United States in military production, given her dependence for over twenty-five years on American research and development. The Swedish model of an independent industrial base and an independent defence industry was well-nigh unrealizeable in Canada in the late 1960s, short of a concerted national policy to Canadianize and socialize the economy. Despite Walter Gordon and the Watkins Report, the Canadian political and corporate élites were no more prepared now to support economic nationalism, even in a capitalist form, than they had been a decade or two previously.

It is here that we come to the roots of the whole process of continentalism in the post-war period, and to an understanding of Canada's position within the American empire. For unlike the sentimental nationalists who abound these days, not least within the ranks of groups such as the University League for Social Reform, I view the process of continentalism as having been unavoidable, once granted the premise of a liberal capitalist Canada.

Intellectually, Canadian liberals were incapable in 1945 of seeing liberal America, the source of their inspiration, as a rising imperial power. Economically, a capitalist Canada which was part and parcel of a world economic system dominated by the United States could not have developed on its own. The vision of its corporate élite was too narrow, its domestic market too small, to have a vibrant capitalism; only American capitalism, with its growing empire and dynamic military-industrial complex, could put to use the natural resources which became the basis of Canadian development. Politically, therefore, Canada's liberal élite had every reason to opt into the Cold War and to link Canada's interests to the American star.

To fail to see these connections is to blind oneself to contemporary reality. For the liberalism of a Trudeau can no more break with the American pattern than the liberalism of a C. D. Howe. The imperatives underlying foreign and defence policy are in Canada's case rational, not emotional. The interests of Canada's liberal élites continue to dictate an open capitalist society, closely linked to the United States. If here or there Canadian policy may show greater independence, on fundamentals her capitalist structure dictates junior partnership.

There is no point therefore in talking vacuously about an independent Canadian foreign policy[59] or neutralism in defence, unless one relates these structurally to the nature of Canadian capitalism. Nor does the *Americanization of Canada* mean anything unless one sees Canadian membership in the American empire and support for American imperialism as a reflection of her élites' liberal capitalist ideology.

The alternative to the empire, today as in 1945, is not sentimentalism but socialism. Only a socialist economy can avoid extreme dependence on the American market, both for trade and for capital. Without our underestimating the difficulties she would have faced, both within and from outside, a socialist

Canada could none the less have laid the basis for economic independence, the necessary precondition for political independence.

Moreover, revolutionary socialism alone would have provided the rationale for neutralism in the Cold War. Rejecting capitalism on the one hand, Stalinism on the other, a socialist Canada might have been able to play a vital role in the easing tension between the two blocs, by unilateral disarmament of the North, for example. At the same time, she could have been much more forward in her support of the liberation of the third world from all imperialism, including Canadian capitalism.

Whether neutralism would have allowed Canada to reduce her over-all defence expenditure is another matter. Much would have depended on the reaction of the United States. But armed neutrality in support of Canadian independence would have provided Canadian defence policy with a *raison d'être* quite different from continentalism in support of the American empire.

The real threat to Canada since 1945 has come from the south, not the north. And it is our liberal capitalist élites, in their pursuit of continentalism, who have let American imperialism into the gates.

Footnotes

1. The content of this article is in large part extracted from an M.A. thesis of the same title submitted by the author to the Political Science Deparment, McGill University, November, 1968.

2. Noah Webster, *Sketches of American Policy, 1785*. New York Scholars' Facsimiles and Reprints, 1937, p. 47.

3. *Borden Diary*, Dec. 1, 1918, cited in Gaddis Smith, "External Affairs During World War I," in Hugh Keenleyside, ed., *The Growth of Canadian Policies in External Affairs*. Durham, N.C., 1959, p. 57.

4. John Brebner, *North Atlantic Triangle*. Carleton Library Edition, Toronto, 1966, p. 244.

5. "Great Britain, the United States, and Canada," in Mary Q. Innis, ed., *Essays in Canadian Economic History*. Toronto, 1956, p. 405.

6. Pearson in a speech in 1944, cited in James Eayrs, "Canadian Defence Policy since 1867," *Studies for the Special Committee on Defence*, Ottawa, 1965, declared: "That collective system which was spurned in Peace [sic] has proved to be our salvation in war." When we bear in mind the passion which Pearson, Escott Reid, and St Laurent brought to the concept of collective security through an Atlantic Alliance a few years later, the internationalism of post-war liberal foreign policy, directed against communism, appears as the other side of the coin from the isolationism and appeasement that characterized that same foreign policy vis-à-vis fascism in the 1930s.

7. Department of External Affairs, *Statements and Speeches*, Ottawa, Jan. 13, 1947, p. 8. Referred to hereafter as *S and S*.

8. *S and S*, June 8, 1948. Address to the Kiwanis International, Los Angeles.

9. W. W. Rostow, "Guerilla War in the Underdeveloped Countries," in M. G. Raskin and B. D. Fall, eds., *The Vietnam Reader*. New York, 1967, p. 111.

10. *House of Commons Debates*, 1947, 1, p. 347.

11. General Henry, the Senior US Army member of the PJBD, at its June 1945 meeting. Cited in Stanley Dziuvan, *Military Relations between the United States and Canada, 1939-1945*, US Army History of World War II, Washington, 1959, p. 335.

12. There is a brief account of this process in the US Army history of Canadian-American military relations during the Second World War, *ibid*. But Canadian documentation remains under wraps, and the vital role played by such figures as Lester Pearson, A. D. P. Heeney, and Hume Wrong in fostering the Cold War defence alliance with the United States, is hidden from the public eye by External Affairs' fifty-year secrecy rule.

13. See Gar Alperowitz, *Atomic Diplomacy: Hiroshima and Potsdam*. New York, 1965, and Isaac Deutscher's "Myths of the Cold War," in David Horowitz, ed., *Containment*

and Revolution. Boston, 1967, to cite but two works, for an analysis of American responsibility for the origins of the Cold War.

14. Cited by James Reston, *New York Times*, February 13, 1947.

15. Cited in Captain D. J. Goodspeed, *A History of the Defence Research Board*. Ottawa, 1958, p. 22.

16. "Canada Looks 'Down North'," *Foreign Affairs*, 24, July, 1946, p. 644.

17. In reply to a questionnaire in the *Financial Post*, August 24, 1946.

18. *S and S*, 41/16, October 7, 1947, p. 3.

19. *Ibid.*, 48/23, p. 8.

20. *Ibid.*, 47/20, November 17, 1947, p. 9.

21. *Ibid.*, 48/3, January 30, 1948, p. 7.

22. *House of Commons Debates*, March 27, 1954, p. 3339.

23. See the account in Dale C. Thompson, *Louis St. Laurent: Canadian*. Toronto, 1967, pp. 222-4.

24. Dean Acheson, in a speech in January 1950, left Korea out in his discussion of those Asian countries covered by the American security umbrella.

25. George Kennan, in his *Memoirs, 1925-1950*, Boston, 1967, argues cogently against American use of the United Nations to legitimize its intervention, and scores the use of the word "aggression" in the context of the Korean Civil War.

26. Cited in F. H. Soward, "Have We Accepted Collective Security?" in *Twenty-Five Years of Canadian Foreign Policy*. Toronto, 1953.

27. *External Affairs*, Ottawa, 2, No. 11, November, 1950.

28. *Financial Post*, February 3, 1951 (Italics not in original).

29. John J. Deutsch, "Recent American Influence in Canada," in *The American Economic Impact on Canada*. Durham, N.C., 1959, p. 45.

30. C. D. Howe, cited in the *Financial Post*, March 14, 1953.

31. Irving Brecher, "The Flow of US Investment Funds into Canada since World War 2," in *The American Economic Impact on Canada*, p. 103.

32. *S and S*, April 10, 1951 (Italics not in original).

33. See R. J. Sutherland, "The Strategic Significance of the Canadian Arctic," in R. St J. Macdonald, ed., *The Arctic Frontier*. Toronto, 1966, and James Eayrs, *Canada in World Affairs*, 1955-57. Toronto, 1959, pp. 141-52 for an account of the construction of the lines.

34. Samuel Huntington, *The Common Defense*. New York, 1961, pp. 327-34.

35. *Ottawa Evening Journal*, January 29, 1955.

36. Cited in Richard Stebbins, *The United States in World Affairs*. New York, 1955, p. 406.

37. Melvin Conant, *The Long Polar Watch*. New York, 1962, p. 88.

38. Charles Foulkes, "The Complications of Continental Defence," in L. Merchant, ed., *Neighbours Taken for Granted*. New York, 1966, p. 111.

39. House of Commons, Special Committee on Defence, *Minutes of Proceedings and Evidence*, October 22, 1963, p. 510.

40. In an interview with the author, August 13, 1968.

41. *S and S*, 59/22, June 7, 1959.

42. *Ibid.*, 59/27, September 3, 1959.

43. Major-General W. H. S. Macklin, *Globe and Mail*, Toronto, October 28, 1958.

44. *House of Commons Debates*, 1958, 1, pp. 1020-1.

45. Tom Kent, "The Changing Place of Canada," *Foreign Affairs*, 35, July, 1957, p. 581.

46. *Canadian Weekly Bulletin*, July 12, 1961.

47. *Financial Post*, March 25, 1967.

48. *Globe and Mail*, January 13, 1963.

49. *New York Times*, February 1, 1963.

50. *Winnipeg Free Press*, Editorial, May 28, 1965.

51. Paul Martin, *S and S*, January 31, 1966.

52. *Ibid.*, 68/8, March 7, 1968.

53. Pearson, for example, shortly after American intervention in the Dominican Republic, declared: "We have received evidence that there are indeed communists in the directing group who are controlling that particular group seeking recognition" (i.e., Caamano). *House of Commons Debates*, May 11, 1956, p. 1152. Paul Martin, in response to criticism

of the US intervention from some NDP quarters, a few weeks later said: "It is easy enough to criticize countries which bear the brunt of responsibility when dangerous situations develop. Such criticism might best be directed at the imperfections in our international arrangements." *House of Commons Debates*, May 28, 1965, p. 1776. Of such legalism and moralism is the stuff of Canadian junior partnership made.

54. Foulkes, "The Complications of Continental Defence," p. 120.

55. *House of Commons Debates*, 1959, 2, p. 1223.

56. In my article "Canadian War Industries and Vietnam," *Our Generation*, 5, No. 3, in particular pp. 22-6.

57. *S and S*, March 10, 1967.

58. *Ibid.*, 65/6, March 5, 1965.

59. The majority of essays in S. H. E. Clarkson, ed., *An Independent Foreign Policy for Canada*, Toronto, 1968, do precisely this, avoiding any mention of the capitalist basis of continentalism and colonialism in Canadian foreign policy.

The Watkins Report: Foreign Ownership and the Structure of Canadian Industry *

Mel Watkins

Issue

The extent of foreign control of Canadian industry is unique among the industrialized nations of the world. Canadians are aware of the economic benefits which have resulted from foreign investment. They are also concerned about the implications of the present level of foreign control for Canada's long-run prospects for national independence and economic growth.

National economies are becoming increasingly interdependent. A world economy may yet become a reality. Canadians have a vital stake in these developments. Canada needs to attract and absorb capital and technology from abroad and to gain access to foreign markets. In the past, Canada has relied heavily on foreign direct investment to meet these necessities. This will continue. But there are other options as well, and more use could be made of these in the future. It is possible, to some extent, to acquire capital and technology without relinquishing control. It is important to devise national policies which will increase the benefits and decrease the costs of foreign investment.

The multi-national corporation is a growing feature of the embryonic world economy. Many industries, including those based on the new technologies, are characterized by large corporations whose operations span the globe. This international business integration adds new dimensions to national policies. Canadians are concerned that these corporations be truly multi-national, genuinely respecting Canadian aspirations, and that Canada's national policies ensure that their behaviour is fully consistent with Canadian goals.

*Reprinted from *Report of the Task Force on the Structure of Canadian Industry*. Privy Council Office, Ottawa: Queen's Printer, 1968. Reproduced with the permission of Information Canada.

It is the intent of this Report to analyze the causes and consequences of foreign investment, to assess actual benefits and costs, and to put forth proposals for legislative consideration.

National Goals

Two of the goals uppermost in the minds of Canadians today are national independence and a rising standard of living.

While recognizing the steady shrinking of the globe, it is important for Canada to maintain that degree of national independence necessary to undertake Canadian initiatives at home and abroad. Thereby, Canadian objectives can be pursued and the possibilities of self-assertion as a people enhanced.

The maintenance of steady economic growth, accompanied by an equitable distribution of income among regions and classes, is necessary to raise living standards generally and to provide job opportunities for an expanding labour force.

Maintaining national independence will increase the capacity of the Canadian economy, by both private and public initiatives, to grow and develop in ways determined by Canadians. Maintaining steady economic growth will increase the extent to which Canadians can pursue distinctive national and international policies.

Our Centennial has highlighted a national independence achieved by the activities of citizens and the policies of government. As our second century begins, new national policies are required to sustain that independence and enhance the welfare of the Canadian people.

Present Situation

In describing the significance of foreign capital in the Canadian economy, it would be useful to know what proportion of our total wealth is owned and controlled by foreigners. Because of statistical difficulties encountered in evaluating social capital, and in evaluating the assets employed in agriculture and certain services, this estimation cannot easily be done. Attention will be focussed upon those capital flows and industries for which official statistical information is available. These paint an approximate but revealing picture of where we have been and where we are today as a result of foreign investment in Canadian economic activity.

In 1964, foreigners owned $33 billion worth of assets in Canada, while Canadians owned $13 billion of assets abroad. Canada's balance of international indebtedness was therefore $20 billion; this compares with a postwar low of $4 billion in 1949. Since, over the same period, gross national product has risen from $16 billion to $47 billion, the percentage increase in net foreign debt has exceeded that of aggregate Canadian output. The major contributor to this increased indebtedness was the expansion in foreign long-term investments in Canada, which rose from $7 billion in 1945 to $27 billion in 1964.

The most significant increase in foreign long-term investment was in foreign direct investment. These, which are the primary concern of this Report, grew from $2.7 billion, or about 40 percent of foreign long-term investment, in 1945 to $15.9 billion, or about 60 percent of foreign long-term investment, in 1964.

Of this $15.9 billion, United States direct investment accounted for $12.9 billion or 80 percent while residents of the United Kingdom accounted for an additional $1.9 billion or 12 percent. The value of company assets controlled abroad is higher, since these figures represent only the part financed abroad.

Although direct investments accounted for most of the increase in foreign capital since 1945, in 1963 and 1964 direct investments grew less rapidly than in earlier years while portfolio investments grew more rapidly. This was largely a result of sales of new bond issues in the United States by provincial governments and municipalities. The sale of corporate bonds to non-residents also increased, while the federal government continued to sell almost all of its securities to Canadians. Non-resident ownership of Canadian long-term funded debt (excluding sinking funds) increased from $3.8 billion in 1954 to $8.2 billion in 1964, about one-third of which represented investment by United States insurance companies. In sum, non-residents owned 19 percent of all Canadian funded debt in 1964; the United States alone accounted for 16 points of this 19 percent.

As a result of the increase of direct and portfolio investments, the payments of interest and dividends to foreigners have risen substantially in absolute terms to more than $1 billion a year in recent years. Such payments abroad as a percentage of gross national product, however, have declined from 2.9 percent in the late 1920's and 6.4 percent in the depressed 1930's to 1.9 percent in 1957-65. As a percentage of the earnings available from foreign sales of goods and services, payments abroad of interest and dividends have fallen from 16 percent in the late 1920's and 25 percent in the 1930's to 9 percent in 1957-65. These payments of income include those by both resident-controlled and non-resident-controlled firms.

Payments to foreigners for business services (such as management fees, royalties, franchises, advertising, rent, professional services, annuities and insurance) are one of the direct effects of non-resident investment in Canada. Unfortunately, statistics on these payments have not been available until recently nor are they yet available for unincorporated branches. However, excluding unincorporated branches and certain other types of corporations, payments to non-residents for business services in 1963 totalled $245 million, a slight increase over the 1962 figure. The manufacturing industries accounted for most of these payments, insurance and management fees and royalties being the main items for which payments were made.

Foreign investment, portfolio as well as direct, has been and is an important source of funds for the financing of capital formation in Canada. Although Canada was a net exporter of capital in the years immediately following the war, in periods of rapid capital formation, such as from 1954 to 1957, Canada relied heavily on foreign financing. Canadian savings were adequate to finance 81 percent of net capital formation between 1962 and 1965, but because some of these savings were invested abroad or used to retire debts held abroad, Canadians relied on direct foreign financing for 40 percent of this capital formation. The use of foreign resources as a percentage of gross capital formation in the 1926-30 period was 25 percent compared with 20 percent in the 1962-65 period. The direct foreign financing of gross capital formation in the 1926-30 period was 50 percent compared with 33 percent in the 1962-65 period.

Foreign ownership and control of corporations located in Canada is concentrated in manufacturing, petroleum and natural gas, and mining and smelting. Foreign ownership of Canadian manufacturing industries has increased substantially from 38 percent in 1926 to 54 percent in 1963, and foreign control has increased even more, from 35 percent in 1926 to 60 percent in 1963. Foreign ownership and control of mining and smelting have similarly expanded considerably, from 37 percent in 1926 to 62 percent in 1963 in the case of ownership and from 38 percent to 59 percent over the same period for control. For these two important industrial sectors, there has been a clear tendency toward increasing foreign ownership and control. In addition, a substantial petroleum and natural gas industry has developed and has absorbed large amounts of foreign capital; in 1963, this industry was 64 percent foreign-owned and 74 percent foreign controlled. Foreign ownership and control have declined, however, in both railways and other utilities from 1926 to 1963, for ownership from 55 percent to 23 percent, and from 32 percent to 13 percent, respectively, while foreign control of these sectors is now less than 5 percent. Official statistics for the aggregate of these five industries and merchandising show that foreign ownership has declined slightly from 37 percent in 1926 to 35 percent in 1963 but that foreign control has risen sharply from 17 percent to 34 percent over this period.

Both ownership and control by United States residents have increased substantially since 1926 according to the official statistics. For the aggregate of the industries noted above, United States ownership has risen from 19 percent to 28 percent, while ownership by other non-residents has fallen from 18 percent to 7 percent. United States control of the group of industries has increased from 15 percent to 27 percent, while control by other non-residents rose from 2 percent to 7 percent.

Within the manufacturing sector, there are certain industries where foreign control is very high, and in all such cases ownership is predominantly by United States residents. In 1963, foreigners controlled 97 percent of the capital employed in the manufacture of automobiles and parts, 97 percent in rubber, 78 percent in chemicals and 77 percent in electrical apparatus. The corresponding figures for United States control were 97 percent, 90 percent, 54 percent and 66 percent.

Not only is foreign equity capital concentrated in certain industries, but also it is concentrated in large corporations. In 1963, for 414 corporations with assets greater than $25 million, it is estimated that $19.9 billion or 53 percent of the total $37.9 billion of assets in these firms were in firms more than 50 percent owned by non-residents. On the other hand, for firms with assets of less than $25 million, $10.7 billion or only 32 percent of the total $34.0 billion of assets in these firms were in firms more than 50 percent owned by non-residents.

Canadian private long-term investment abroad in 1964 totalled $5.3 billion of which direct investments abroad accounted for $3.4 billion and portfolio investments $1.9 billion. Canadian direct investments abroad have more than doubled since 1954, 60 percent of which are now located in the United States. It is significant, however, that non-residents have an important equity in Canadian direct investments abroad arising from foreign ownership in whole or in part of Canadian companies having subsidiaries or branches in other parts of the world. Foreign equity and control of Canadian direct investment abroad accounted for 47 percent and 43 percent respectively of the total. United States equity and control alone accounted for 39 percent in each instance.

At the same time as United States direct investment has been taking place in Canada, Canadian institutions and individuals, faced with a shortage of Canadian equities, have tended to be attracted to American equity securities. These investments are of a portfolio rather than direct investment nature, and do not result in control. In the last few years, Canadian purchases of foreign equity securities have been substantial, averaging $27 million a year from 1961 to 1964, rising to $92 million in 1963 and $245 million in 1966, and standing at $66 million in the first six months of 1967. Over the same period, there has been a substantial net repatriation of Canadian stock owned abroad: $117 million average for 1961-64, $242 million in 1965, $83 million in 1966 and $53 million in the first six months of 1967. While this repatriation reduced foreign ownership, its nature does not appear to have been such as to reduce foreign control to a corresponding extent.

Canadian Policy

While there has been concern among Canadians for some time about foreign, especially American, ownership and control of Canadian industry, it has, in general, been the policy of all levels of Canadian government not only to permit, but to actively encourage, foreign investment. Although Canadians have been anxious to maintain political independence, they have also wanted to maintain a high standard of living and develop the country's natural resources.

Unlike France, the United Kingdom and Japan there is no formal screening procedure for foreign investment and no governmental agency with which a foreign investor must consult prior to undertaking direct investment. While this absence reflects, compared to most countries in the world, a particularly liberal policy toward foreign direct investment, it does not mean that Canadian policy has been non-existent. In particular, the Canadian government has discouraged foreign ownership or control of certain key sectors and industries: American control of railways in the post-Confederation period; airlines, bus lines, and radio stations in the 1920's and 1930's; television stations and insurance companies in the 1950's; and newspapers and banks in the 1960's. Canadian ownership and control have been ensured by the setting up of Crown corporations, as in the cases of Air Canada and the Canadian Broadcasting Corporation.

The major deficiency in Canadian policy has been not its liberality toward foreign investment *per se* but the absence of an integrated set of policies, partly with respect to both foreign and domestic firms, partly with respect only to foreign firms, to ensure higher benefit and smaller costs for Canadians from the operations of multi-national corporations.

Objectives

Canadians want national independence and economic growth. They want to increase the benefits from foreign ownership and reduce the costs. They want a *national* economy that functions efficiently within the world economy. Canadian history bears witness to those aspirations.

It is a function of government to translate those aspirations into objectives for national policy. Those objectives can be stated as:

to require foreign-owned subsidiaries in Canada to behave as "good corporate citizens" of Canada, and to perform in ways that are fully consistent with Canada's economic and political interests.

to improve the overall efficiency of the Canadian economy, and the performance of Canadian corporations, Canadian-owned as well as foreign-owned, in ways which will facilitate the capacity to generate self-sustained economic growth.

to take positive steps to encourage increased Canadian ownership and control of economic activity, in ways that will facilitate the achievement of greater national independence and continuing economic growth.

These objectives should be pursued only in the context of the explicit recognition of the constraints within which policy is formulated by the Government of Canada. National policies with respect to foreign investment must take full account both of the constitutional rights of the provinces and the property rights of foreign owners. Canadian respect for these rights is deeply ingrained and they should not be violated.

Canadian Participation

Foreign ownership and control are not only pervasive in Canada but are likely to remain so. There is a need to ensure Canadian participation in the benefits of foreign direct investment and a Canadian presence in the decision-making of multi-national enterprises.

It is recommended that the Canadian tax system be used as effectively as possible to maximize benefits for Canadians from foreign direct investment. It has been recommended above that the special agency examine taxation procedures on an on-going basis to ensure that Canada gets its proper share of taxes paid by multi-national firms. Furthermore, it is recommended that Canadian tax authorities exercise caution in granting special tax arrangements to industries predominantly consisting of foreign-owned firms.

It is recommended that the Canadian Development Corporation be created as a large holding company with entrepreneurial and management functions to assume a leadership role in Canada's business and financial community in close cooperation with existing institutions. It would have the capacity to draw on the expertise of the financial community and to provide a focal point for the mobilization of entrepreneurial capital. Its size and its quasi-public character would enable it to make a unique contribution in organizing consortia of investors, domestic and foreign, thereby carrying out large projects beyond the capacity of a single institution and throughout maintaining a clear Canadian presence. The C.D.C. should be permitted and encouraged to be active in all sectors of the economy. Without limiting the generality of its operations, it should specifically be active in the areas of resource development and the rationalization of Canadian industry.

It is recommended that stronger incentives be considered to encourage large corporations, including foreign-owned subsidiaries, to offer their shares to Canadians, thereby increasing the supply of Canadian equities, facilitating disclosure, and providing levers for public regulation and for dealing with extra-territoriality. There are costs as well as benefits to this recommendation. For this reason, the use of Canadian capital for purely Canadian private ventures or for the Canada Development Corporation is preferable to its use for buying minority holdings in foreign-controlled subsidiaries to the extent that other recommendations for obtaining disclosure and dealing with extraterritoriality are implemented.

Each of these proposals should be considered on its own merits, and all do not require implementation at the same point of time. But these proposals, taken as a whole, are designed to be a comprehensive program which deals with foreign ownership in a way that is both economically and politically realistic and is in Canada's long-run national interest.

Conclusion

A New National Policy

The old National Policy served Canada in its day, as an instrument of nation-building and a means of facilitating economic growth. The challenges have changed and a new National Policy is required. The nation has been built, but its sovereignty must be protected and its independence maintained. A diversified economy has been created, but its efficiency must be improved and its capacity for autonomous growth increased.

It is this spirit which informs the present proposals. While each individual proposal deserves careful consideration, taken together, these proposals are designed as a program which is realistic and attainable both from an economic and political viewpoint. Increased economic interdependence among nations is recognized, but also that a stronger national economy is needed to function effectively in a global setting. The movement within Canada toward stronger provincial authority is also recognized, but this does not alter the fact that foreign ownership is a national issue that goes beyond regional concerns. The growing mutual dependence of nations today suggests finally that Canada's foreign policy and global responsibilities can be made more effective by sustaining a healthy national independence.

Toward Canadian Capitalism[*]

Alastair Gillespie, Liberal M.P.

What we need to do now is to place the problem of foreign ownership in perspective. We must see it as part of a larger economic policy, not an end in

[*]Reprinted from *Gordon to Watkins to You*, by Dave Godfrey and Mel Watkins, pp. 248-250, published by New Press, 1970. Reproduced with the permission of New Press.

itself. Such a policy must be designed to preserve our freedom to make political choices and to build our strength in support of them.

In trying to protect our markets from foreign products, we have encouraged the take-over of our own manufacturers. Now, ironically, we are dismantling much of the tariff apparatus which was erected to protect our markets without substituting any apparatus to protect the ownership of our industry. Is it already too late? If we do nothing in the next five years the process will be irreversible and the result inevitable.

Yet we can still build an independent-minded Canada for future generations.

An appropriate economic policy for Canada should emphasize our opportunities alongside the largest market in the world; it should concentrate far more on adapting to the multinational form of corporate organization than resisting it; it should be concerned with converting Canadian entrepreneurs from a rather inward-looking group to an outward-looking group. It should commit resources to the building of Canada rather than buying it back. It should place primary emphasis on new technology.

There are, in my opinion, five priorities for the 1970's:

1. We need new federal powers to regulate economic activities in the national interest. Specifically:

a) Legislation to provide that all future natural resource development in Canada will have a minimum 50 percent Canadian equity participation.

b) Creation of the Canada Development Corporation to provide the funds for such national resource development if private Canadian investors fail to meet the 50 percent yardstick, and to purchase large blocks of stocks in Canadian multinational corporations when they become available.

c) Protection of existing Canadian controlled multinational corporations from foreign take-overs by legislating that not more than 50 percent of the shares may be foreign owned and not more than 10 percent of the shares may be held by any one non-resident without federal approval.

d) Prohibition of any increase in foreign ownership of already foreign controlled Canadian corporations without prior federal approval.

e) Prohibition of foreign take-overs of existing Canadian domestic corporations with sales in excess of some minimum such as $10 million, prescribing not more than 10 percent owned by any one non-resident, without federal approval.

2. We must encourage Canadian firms to go multinational. The Canadian spirit will only thrive if we look outwards. We must accept and adopt the multinational corporation as the most important form of corporate organization in the future. We must protect our few existing multinational corporations from foreign take-over.

3. We need to eliminate the chronic deficit in our current account balance of payments. We must turn a $1 billion deficit into a $1 billion surplus by the 1980's. There is no assurance that foreign capital inflows will continue to finance such deficits into the 1970's, nor is it desirable that they should. A surplus position would give our policymakers new options to finance Canadian direct investment abroad, to underwrite foreign aid, and to deal from strength instead of weakness on foreign investment. We may have to settle for a slower rate of growth.

4. We need to increase both the quantity and quality of professional management and entrepreneurship. Colonial attitudes still prevail in much of our management thinking, and we graduate too few professionally trained managers. In 1965 U.S. business schools enrolled 40 times as many undergraduates as their Canadian counterparts. Why not federal grants to business schools here?

5. We need a policy to develop our own technology. When we import foreign technology we must do so without discouraging Canadian innovation. The manufacturing license agreements have for too long substituted for real Canadian research, development and innovation.

These priorities are more than a program for the 1970's: They are a prescription for a Canadian identity. Our success or failure in each of these areas will determine whether we exist as a country by the year 2000.

Toward Canadian Socialism*

Mel Watkins

We live today, in Canada, in a dependent capitalist economy. We can choose, with J. J. Greene, Stanley Randall and a host of others in high places, to stay that way. Or we can follow the Walter Gordon–Watkins Report approach. Or the Alastair Gillespie approach – which seems to be gaining ground in Ottawa, presumably to head off the new nationalism of the left – and try to build an independent capitalist Canada, with Canadian firms playing a more prominent role in the Canadian economy and themselves going multinational. Or we can follow the New Democratic Party, and particularly its leftwing Waffle group, and begin the struggle for an independent socialist Canada.

The resolution on foreign ownership which came out of the N.D.P.s Winnipeg Convention spells out the specifics of what must be done (in italics below), provides a useful framework for elaboration, and for a critique of what the Trudeau government may do in the near future.

Policy must be framed in terms of both immediate and ultimate needs. *The immediate necessity is to support policies that compel foreign-based corporations to perform in the Canadian public interest. The ultimate goal is to build an independent economy where the priorities of social development are set within Canada by Canadians.* On the first round, we must tame the multinational corporations. In the long-run, we must replace them by a publicly-owned and democratically-administered economy.

Concretely, this means:

Full disclosure and publication of financial data by corporations (Canadian-owned as well as foreign owned), [right parenthesis ours] and the immediate

*Reprinted from *Gordon to Watkins to You* by Dave Godfrey and Mel Watkins, pp. 250-255, published by New Press, 1970. Reproduced with the permission of New Press.

creation of a special agency to formulate policy toward multinational corporations.

These are modest demands and were set forth by the Watkins Report. Indeed, it is a striking commentary on the policy, or lack thereof, of the old parties that even such minimal policy does not yet exist. By permitting wholly-owned subsidiaries to masquerade as private companies, the Canadian public, and its civil servants and politicians, are denied even the limited financial disclosure which shareholders are accorded under company legislation in the case of public companies. D.B.S. and the tax authorities know, but only on condition that they don't tell the rest of us. To date, the Government has met this serious deficiency by sending out questionnaires to the larger firms to see if they are acting as good corporate citizens. But the questionnaire is voluntary, the data is collected on a basis that prevents it being related to other statistical series, and the published results and analysis based therein of little no [*sic*] value.

The Government has already brought forward amendments to the Canada Companies Act requiring disclosure from all firms but the very small ones. Unfortunately, this will apply only to federally-incorporated companies. In any event, it is not yet law and there are rumours of opposition from Liberal backbenchers. There has been some speculation in the press that the special agency will be created, but we would be well-advised not to believe it until it happens.

Until these things do happen, we are at the mercy of the corporations to volunteer information, with consequences nothing short of disastrous. When Dunlop of Canada announced on March 6, 1970 that it would close its Toronto plant in eight weeks and throw 600 men out of work because it was losing money, there was no way to check that assertion. The Canadian subsidiary being wholly owned by a British parent, we do not even know what the profit or loss is of the Canadian operations overall, much less of that one plant. Even the proposed legislation would not touch the problem; what is further required is for corporations to show cause when they engage in abnormal and socially costly activities.

The immediate creation of a government export trade agency to block the intrusion into Canada of American law prohibiting trade with certain countries through the medium of the American direct investment firm, and the extension of that agency to engage directly in international trade.

The first part of this proposal follows the recommendation of the Watkins Report for dealing with the extraterritorial application to American-controlled firms in Canada of American legislation prohibiting trade with mainland China, North Vietnam and Cuba. The problem has been somewhat alleviated – though not eliminated – by the recent relaxation of the Nixon Administration. It would seem in order to deal urgently with this problem or risk finding that we have recognized China but are free to trade with China only at Washington's whim.

The additional proposal of a state-trading agency comes to terms with the reality that, given the nature of Communist economies, this is the most efficacious way to trade with them. We recognize this in the case of wheat and have a Canadian Wheat Board, and in the case of armaments where we have the Canadian Commercial Corporation. What is good enough for those cases is worth extending generally at a time when Canada needs to diversify its trade by lessening its present dependence both on the United States and on a handful of primary staples.

There is no evidence whatsoever that the Trudeau government intends to do anything at all in this critical area.

Public control over foreign takeovers, so as to limit further loss of existing national firms, by the prohibition of foreign ownership in certain sectors (as in media and banking presently), by a strengthened anti-combines policy, and by Crown corporations.

An important means by which the Canadian economy has fallen under foreign control is the takeover of existing Canadian firms. The most obvious benefits alleged to result from foreign ownership, such as more jobs and more government tax revenue from newly created profits, presume that new investment is taking place and not simply a change in the ownership of existing investment. Indeed, the obvious results of a takeover are that there are fewer firms operating in the world and the presumption of consumer benefits from competition holds with less force.

To date, the Canadian government has dealt with this issue by one means alone – the so-called *key sector* approach. No overall policy has emerged applicable to all sectors and firms; indeed, no general policy has been formulated even in terms of key sectors, and the government has been properly accused of ad hoccery, as in the case of Denison Mines.

While the Trudeau government deserves credit for stopping an important takeover in the case of loan companies (Traders' Finance) and uranium (Denison) – but not in investment houses (Royal Securities) – two blocked takeovers hardly make a dent on the population of more than 7,000 foreign-owned firms in Canada. The apparent addition of uranium to the list of prohibited sectors – but not applied to existing foreign-owned firms nor even to firms that have begun exploration though not yet production – could be the thin edge of a wedge to cover resource industries generally. There is presently, however, no reason to believe that the government is sufficiently committed to such a policy to seek the provincial co-operation that would presumably be necessary in cases, unlike uranium, where federal power to legislate alone may not exist. And such a policy, in the absence of any intent to roll back, has limited relevance for the resource industries such as oil where foreign-based giants are in firm command.

And so bad has the record of Liberal governments been historically on foreign ownership, that it is not necessary to be a paranoid or a cynic to fear that the Trudeau government may make much of some new policy on ownership of resource industries while quietly acceding to a continental resource deal that will, on net, take us much further down the road to a fully dependent economy.

The case for extending the key sector approach to the resource industries in an unequivocal way is strong to the point of being compelling. That is where this country's comparative advantage in trade lies, that is where we have proven our competitive ability historically, and that is where the need to compete in world markets will ensure that we will remain efficient. No other step contains as much promise of increasing economic benefits for Canadians, of creating more jobs through further processing of resources, and of beginning to move toward a more planned economy by serious resource planning now.

Even were all of this to be done, there remains the need to have an across-the-board policy on takeovers applicable to all firms. This was what Walter Gordon's infamous take-over tax in the budget of 1963 was meant to deal with, and it can only be regretted that the fiasco which resulted has given this excellent idea such a bad name. An alternative approach would be to amend the anti-combines legislation in such a way that approval must be sought for all takeovers and that the criteria for determining which should and should not take place put a high priority on maintaining Canadian ownership. Certainly the present anti-combines policy is intolerable, with great tenderness being shown in its application to businessmen who plea [*sic*] that a hands-off policy is necessary so that large Canadian firms can emerge capable of competing with foreign giants, and then feel free to sell out to foreigners when they wish. E. P. Taylor and Canadian Breweries is instructive in this regard. Indeed, such is the attrition rate among long-established Canadian firms that urgent consideration needs to be given to passing a corporate equivalent of national monument legislation. What assurance do we have that Massey-Ferguson, whose predecessor firms go back more than a century, will not go tomorrow or Eaton's the day after? Only a fortuitous U.S. court order saved the venerable Labatt's.

The immediate creation of a Canada Development Corporation with full government ownership and control. It will be directed to pursue social, and not simply corporate objectives. It will also be an instrument of government planning and a means of increasing Canadian independence.

It is some years now since Walter Gordon first proposed the CDC and, in spite of a recent quip of Mr. Trudeau's to the effect that legislation to create it was 74th on a list of 74 priorities, the rumour mill in Ottawa has it that it will emerge soon and that former Power Corporation executive Maurice Strong, who originally came to Ottawa to head it and ended up running the Canadian International Development Agency, will at last get what he wanted. What kind of a CDC it will be remains uncertain, with possibilities ranging from the original Walter Gordon conception of a big mutual fund to buy back Canada to the Watkins Report's notion of a catalyst to mobilize entrepreneurial talents in consortia, in conjunction with the private Canadian sector and as an alternative to full foreign ownership. What does seem certain is that it will not be fully owned by the government.

A socialist conception necessarily differs in that respect. In a separate resolution, the N.D.P. calls for financing of the CDC through bonds, with financial institutions required to invest therein. It should play an entrepreneurial role, in developing industries on the frontier of technology and in rationalizing existing industry, along the lines envisaged in the Watkins Report. But as a first step toward socialism, it should not ape a private corporation but rather pursue such social objectives as balanced regional development and worker participation. So conceived, the creation of the CDC would be a large and potent first step of a democratic socialist government.

Expansion of public and co-operative ownership to promote ownership by Canadians of a larger sector of the economy and to halt and reverse the trend to foreign domination, particularly in new industry and development.

This is, of course, the classic but controversial insistence of socialists that ownership of the means of production matters. The rationale is neatly set forward in a separate Winnipeg resolution on Public Ownership:

> Promote an expansion of public and co-operative ownership not as a panacea, but as vital instruments with which to achieve these objectives:

(a) *reduce the concentration of economic power in the hands of the business community;*

(b) *halt the rapid Americanization of the Canadian economy;*

(c) *assist in effective comprehensive economic planning;*

(d) *ensure the development of industries vital to the future of our economy which neither foreign nor domestic private enterprise has developed;*

(e) *increase the amount of national savings available to the public sector to redirect resources and to create a balanced economic growth;*

(f) *create models of democratic decision-making in industry.*

This is hardly nationalization for its own sake but for very specific objectives. What is new, in terms of the conventional case for nationalization, is the realization that it is the most effective, and very possibly the only effective, alternative to foreign private ownership. No less a person than Tory historian Donald Creighton appears to agree: "Nationalization is about the only thing that might work – at least in the sense that it hasn't been tried yet."

And what should be made explicit is that new Crown corporations are effective ways to create new jobs and more creative jobs. When newly-elected democratic socialist governments are threatened, even blackmailed, by businessmen pleading lack of confidence, it should be made clear that if the private sector does not shape-up then the necessary employment and economic growth will be created by an expanded public sector, and it is clearly possible that what will result will be considerably more creative jobs, in terms of scope for managerial and research talents, than a simply branch plant economy can offer.

Some will argue that public ownership is unnecessary, that corporations can be made to heed the will of government by effective regulation and taxation. Certainly, as the resolution on Public Ownership points out, these instruments have been used "half-heartedly" by Liberal and Conservative governments, and it insists that "a New Democratic government will use them with effect." But it repudiates the view put forward by half-hearted social democrats that this would make public ownership unnecessary: "public regulation and taxation, by themselves, are inadequate tools to effect the changes that must be made. Regulations can be evaded; taxes can be passed on to consumers or back to the work forces." A case remains for public ownership.

The creation of an integrated set of national policies to stop the further slide of Canada into dependent status and to replace the present inefficient branch plant economy with an independent economy capable of generating its own growth and of being effectively controlled and directed by the national government.

The struggle to liberate our economy is primary, and without it, all else is pointless. Nevertheless, it is still only a part of the broader struggle to create a Canada controlled by the Canadian people. Americanization is presently pervasive and must be resisted on many fronts:

Proposals to continentalize our resources must be repudiated. If a resource deal of the Hickel-Greene variety goes through, there will be so little left of Canadian independence that even a committed socialist government might be unable to reverse the trend to North American integration. Which is not to say that socialism is autarchy, but only that the question of selling resources would be determined, under socialism, in the context of a broader plan of the national and public interest.

The present structure of branch plant unionism should be replaced by full autonomy for Canadian workers within international unions. It must be hoped that, in due course, the present fragmented structure with too many unions and too few Canadians unionized will give way to larger more comprehensive and fully Canadian unions.

The battle to protect the media must be continued, and the presently increasing commercialization of public, as well as private, broadcasting reversed. And we must join with Robin Mathews and James Steele in insisting that the Americanization of Canadian universities, indeed of our educational system in general, cease.

For all of these things to happen is to ask a good deal. Clearly it will require not only the repudiation of the present mainstream parties in favour of a socialist party, but a socialist party that is, in fact, genuinely committed to socialism with the support of a Canadian people that values independence and real democracy.

Address to the Montreal Symposium on De-Canadianization[*]

Hugh MacLennan

If I have ever accepted an assignment less congenial than my present one, I am unable to recall it. The title of this symposium speaks for itself and its implications are enormous and conflicting. They involve the individual futures of thousands of academics. They actually involve the viability of the Canadian nation, a commodity of which she has always been improvident, but now may have carried her pitcher one time too often to the well. Our conscience, our sensibilities, our notion of courtesy are deeply strained by this issue. I hate the idea that I may appear to be hostile to American friends of whom I am fond, or to American colleagues whom I esteem and know to be dedicated men. I am sure you all feel exactly the same about this aspect of today's symposium as I do myself.

Perhaps I should define my present assignment as I understand it. Though I am a member of the academic community, I would prefer you to think that I am speaking as an ordinary Canadian citizen. I have no expert knowledge to offer you. For basic information I have relied mainly on the facts and figures compiled by Professors Mathews and Steele. I am speaking now as I have often done in the past on the issue of the identity of our country, and identity is no abstraction. The instinct to assert and maintain it ranks second only to the

*Reprinted from *The Struggle for Canadian Universities,* by Robin Mathews and James Steele, pp. 141-151, published by New Press, 1970. Reproduced with the permission of New Press.

instinct to eat when you are hungry. The struggle to assert and maintain it has caused most of the wars and all of the triumphs of human civilization, and a man would have to be blind to the lessons of history and biology to pretend otherwise. Identity – we can add this, too – is almost as basic and essential to the human group as it is to the individual.

It seems to be grievous – something I never dreamed could ever happen in this way – that the unending struggle for the Canadian identity should once again find its arena in our universities. However, this is what has happened. Therefore it seems desperately important that this crisis, which has come upon us so suddenly that it was here before we even knew it, should be faced with the maximum of understanding and the minimum of prejudice. Above all it is vital that any measures taken to deal with it should be undertaken with the scrupulous care of a person who is handling a delicate, intricate and wonderful organism. For that is what a university is, and that is also what it is in danger of ceasing to be.

But having admitted this, let us not turn our eyes away from certain shameful, bitter facts. Suddenly, and everywhere, the university has become a battleground in which mysterious forces have exploded and which unscrupulous power-seekers have exploited. The atmosphere of many a campus today is poisoned with slogans which far too often are uttered as proven truths. Character assassination has become the routine weapon of too many student and faculty politicians. Reason and logic have been swamped by animal passions. Our natural unwillingness to believe that people would contaminate science and philosophy, to say nothing of the teaching of youth, with political propaganda has paralyzed the energies of many of us, and this paralysis may be partially a cause of the particular crisis we are met here to discuss. For a long time we failed to realize – and who can blame us? – what it means that the modern multi-university should have become the focus of some of the worst hatreds and passions which divide the post-war world. Yet this has happened, and if it has happened – with one notable exception – with less virulence than in Germany, Italy, Japan, France and the United States, there is no guarantee that Good Old Canada, trailing as usual behind the prevailing fashions, may not find herself a victim like the others. The atmosphere, we may as well admit, is polluted here, too. And it is in that atmosphere that we are met here today.

You know, and I know, what will be said about us for even daring to raise the subject of today's symposium. Professors Mathews and Steele have already had a nasty foretaste of this. And therefore I would like to say that never in the history of the Canadian academy has there been a finer example of just and dedicated courage than that displayed by those two men. I am sure they hated having to do what they had to do just as much as I hate having to face the implications of what they have told to us and to the nation.

If Kant was right when he said that duty can be recognized as something you do not do gladly, then we will seldom have a better chance of doing our duty than we have now. It is painful to be misunderstood and be quoted out of context, but we are certain to be misunderstood and quoted out of context. In some quarters we will be called parochial, illiberal and paranoiac. We will be accused of preferring nationalism to quality – but of that I intend to say more later. It will be said that we betray the ideal of the international university, although the international university as it existed in the Middle Ages disappeared in the nineteenth century. We will outrage more than one embattled idealist who refuses to face reality. Just as liberals a generation ago leaped to Wendell Willkie's One World slogan – and he meant this in the social sense – so do the idealistic successors of that earlier generation accept in a spirit of brotherhood McLuhan's assertion that we live in an electronic village. Therefore, so the emotional reasoning goes, there are no boundaries any more and anyone who acts as though they still exist runs contrary to progress.

However, there are boundaries a-plenty today, more than ever in human history. While Willkie toured the world hypnotizing himself with his own good will, Stalin, who had fixed him with his obsidian eye and told him how much he liked him, lost no time in establishing the Iron Curtain between Russia and the West, and included behind it some sixty million peoples of whom only a tiny minority wished to be there. And now, in the era of McLuhan, it is difficult to recognize the unifying effects of electronics in Nigeria, South Africa, South America, Cuba, Indonesia, the Russo-Chinese borderlands, or even the campus of a North American university.

Since this is so, what is the point in pretending it is not so, or of denying that the conception of a boundary lies so deep within the genetic inheritance that is probably ineradicable? Let me put the situation in a single sentence written by a brother novelist, Mordecai Richler, the current writer in residence in this university. Why does Richler's *The Apprenticeship of Duddy Kravitz* go straight to the core of the human experience? In many respects Duddy is one of the most disagreeable characters in Canadian literature, but he is nonetheless a character absolutely universal. The quest of this status-less, mannerless youth seeking a place of his own strikes a universal chord in all humanity. Duddy's inspiration came from a remark his grandfather kept repeating to him from his earliest childhood: "A man without land, Duddel, is nobody." And neither is a nation anything but a geographical expression unless it is able to control its own communications and above all to control its education and the service to which it enlists its universities in the moulding of its people.

For at least a century and a half this idea has been accepted in practice by every nation in the world. Paradoxically, the only way a modern university can truly serve the international community is by first serving its own community. This is true because it is out of its own community that it grows; because it is its own community that supports it; because no community on earth can be loved and understood by foreigners in precisely the same way as by those people who have been born and bred in it, or have elected to become permanent citizens of it because they love and understand it, too. Just as Shakespeare, the supreme world poet, was a profound Englishman, so are certain world universities the repositories and expressions of their nation's profoundest conscience and genius – Bologna in Italy, the Sorbonne in France, Oxford and Cambridge in England, Uppsala in Sweden, Heidelberg in Germany, Harvard and several others in the United States, the Hebrew University in Israel. The only way a university can become a harmonizer and a civilizer within the human chaos is by becoming harmonious within itself.

Surely what I have so far said is practically self-evident. Yet in the atmosphere now prevailing, I feel, and I am sure that you do feel, a very powerful inhibition. So many people everywhere are sniping at the United States that the word *anti-American* has an ugly sound, and deservedly so. Americans have been so well-meaning, so generous and efficient that they are naturally sensitive to any nuance of an attack on their good intentions, and we, their closest neighbours, are more sensitive than they guess about incurring the suspicion that we can be numbered among those who bite them. I think it a statement of simple fact that there is no anti-Americanism in Canada as this idea is understood elsewhere. Rather, there is a nervous unwillingness to protect and develop ourselves in all areas where we may even appear to be acting contrary to American interests. As I am a veteran in this dubious no man's land, and once again am making myself a target, perhaps I may be forgiven if I speak personally for a few minutes.

I am not now, and never have been, anti-American, but this does not commit me to the assumption that it is my duty to place American problems, upon which I can have no influence whatever, before Canadian problems which I may perhaps be able to influence a little. During our times of trouble at McGill, for instance, I know I have been called a reactionary by some ardent young American colleagues, recently arrived, for refusing to join with them and some of our internationally-minded student activists in a continuous assault on our Principal because, so they believed, he was serving an Establishment which in turn served the military-industrial Establishment of the United States. If Lester Pearson as Prime Minister was unable to influence ex-President Johnson's Viet Nam policy, I failed to see what chance poor Principal Robertson had of doing any better. Meanwhile in Canada we have had acute internal problems of our own which only we can solve, and in this spill-over of American griefs within our universities, however international those griefs may be in their implications, I must say with regret that our universities have had their native energies badly distracted. Why, I used to ask myself a few years ago, were Canadian students and teachers demonstrating for the civil rights movement and an end to the Viet Nam war – areas in which their activities could only arouse resentment in the bulk of the American people if for no other reason than that they were not Americans – while at the same time they did hardly anything to meet the racial and cultural divisions which threatened the existence of Canada, and which to some extent still threaten it? Emphatically, I am not anti-American when I think like this. As a novelist I have always had a warmer reception from American reviewers than from those in my own country, and for this I have been profoundly grateful. But I have always believed, probably by instinct, in the validity of the border, in the old New England maxim that good fences make good neighbours. Thirty-four years ago when I graduated with a Ph.D. from Princeton, it never occurred to me to think that the chairman of my department was unjust when he told me that he could make no effort to place me in a university in the United States, because at that time academic jobs were as scarce as snowballs in summer and his first duty was to graduates who were his own fellow-citizens.

But when I returned to Canada I encountered for the first time a Canadian attitude which makes us unique among the nations of the world. There was a vacancy in my field in Dalhousie, my old Canadian university, and I applied for it. I was then told by one of my former professors, who had become chairman of the department, that he was surprised that I had come to him. Did I not know that an Englishman had applied for this position and was sure to get it? I asked what the Englishman's record was, being perfectly prepared to give way if it was better than my own. I discovered that it was practically the same as my own had been at Oxford and that he had no advanced degree beyond that. Needless to say he got the job. Nor could I get a job anywhere in a Canadian university, and finally I settled for teaching school at $25 a week.

It seemed to me then, and it still does, that this was a curious attitude for my old teacher to have taken. But in those days it was a typically Canadian one.

Now I will come to the nub of this symposium. You all have the brochure furnished us over the signatures of Professors Beissel, Dudek and Gnarowski containing the figures researched, I presume, by Professors Steele and Mathews. For the record, let me repeat what seem to me the most important of these figures. In 1961, approximately 75 percent of faculty in Canadian universities were Canadian. In 1968, by September, this proportion had dropped to 49 percent and has almost certainly dropped further since then. This current year, Canadian universities made about 2,642 new appointments. Of these appointments 1,013 were Americans, 545 British, 722 others.

The truly devastating statistic is the one which indicates that only 362 were Canadians – *the smallest single group.*

I submit that within any nation in the world, with the possible exception of Nigeria and the Gold Coast before they became independent, figures like these would be regarded as beyond belief.

The question naturally arises, how did such an incredible disproportion come about? Earlier this week Opposition Leader Stanfield, referring to this situation as one of the gravest threats to Canada's future, implied that our universities had been unable to engage more of our own people because their expansion-rate, especially that of the new ones, had been so rapid that our own graduate schools were unable to graduate enough candidates to fill the positions. As I have not been able to obtain the complete text of Mr. Stanfield's speech – if speech it was – I may be misquoting him. But one thing at least is certain: there was no serious lack these past three years of adequately trained Canadians to fill many of our academic vacancies.

Looking once again at the figures in the brochure, we see that between 1965 and 1967, Canada produced a total of 14,151 individuals with advanced degrees, of whom 1,837 were Ph.D.'s and 12,312 were M.A.'s. And we note further that of this group only 1,320 found jobs in Canadian universities. The final statistic is the most shocking of all: last year Canadian universities engaged only 9.5 percent of the total Canadians available to fill academic positions.

If these figures are true, and I can only presume they are, I don't think I exaggerate when I say that they suggest a programme of national suicide.

The next question naturally arises: how did such a situation come about? It has been widely suggested that the American draft system has been the chief cause of Canada's sudden attractiveness in the eyes of so many of our young American academic friends, for we must presume that by far the largest percentage of these academic appointments have gone to young scholars and scientists and not to international specialists for whom the whole world competes. But after many conversations with American colleagues, I am inclined to doubt that this explanation is the basic one or even the right one. Quite possibly this sudden influx results from the overflow of a domestic American market already saturated. This is a new phenomenon. When I was a graduate student in the United

States in the 1930's, graduate student populations were extremely small. Moreover, there were no more than seven or eight universities whose graduate schools had great prestige all the way across the board. As a matter of fact these same universities still retain that prestige. Harvard, Yale, Princeton, the Hopkins, Chicago, M.I.T., Berkeley – the number of these élite institutions has been certainly increased, but I wonder how substantially it has been increased. And I cannot fail to ask myself the question why, if young Americans beginning an academic career could obtain a position in the United States, where they would be paid more than here, they should be crossing the border in such alarming numbers to work in another country which has never interested Americans before save as a source of investment and raw materials?

Another possibility is that our own graduate candidates are generally inferior to those in average or minor graduate colleges south of the border. In some subjects they may be – though I rather doubt it – but across the board I believe this a preposterous suggestion, because for decades the great lament in Canada has been the brain-drain that occurred automatically every year when we had far fewer universities than we have now, a much smaller population and were unable to furnish jobs for some of our best people.

The second reason for this overwhelming influx of foreign scholars has been, as usual, our typical Canadian casualness, our deplorable habit of never waking up to situations until they become desperate. And I suggest that our situation is going to become a good deal more desperate than it is now unless something is done about it very quickly.

At the moment the magic word in universities is *democratization*. I am not going to discuss the desirability or the undesirability of this development, but I am stating it as a fact we all recognize. Not only are students being admitted to senates, steering committees and departmental meetings; in many universities departments have become virtual parliamentary assemblies in which all colleagues, regardless of their age, experience and reputation, have equal voting rights in deciding academic policies and standards, which in turn influence the policies and standards of the university as a whole.

Since this is the case, it is idle to pretend that the preponderance of senior Canadians in the academic departments can keep our universities Canadian in character much longer. As more and more Americans enter the departments, as the balance swings more and more away from native teachers, this will mean only one thing – that the departments will be split down the middle with the Americans in control of the majority factions. I say this with regret and sadness, not only because it is human nature that this should occur, but because I have already seen it occurring with my own eyes, and have even seen some departments which are so entirely Americanized that they operate within the university as a whole as though they were still in the United States. This means that soon, and in some departments it has already happened, the dwindling number of Canadians in our faculties are being reduced to colonial status. It means more for the future. As like always tends to elect like, it means that in the future more and more Americans will be hired and more and more Canadians will have to leave the country or give up the academic life entirely.

This situation, which has come about as suddenly as the physicists' Big Bang, is bound to have catastrophic results both within the nation and within the delicate, nervous organism of our university system. It will not only make Canadian faculty members increasingly discontented and bitter; when its implications are known, it will outrage the Canadian taxpayer. He will ask, make no mistake about it, why he should finance the erosion of his own society, why he should pay out enormous sums for the training of his own people who are denied jobs in his own universities.

What can be done about this specifically is a complex problem, and I presume some solutions will be suggested this afternoon. I take it for granted that in the near future this crisis will become the subject of one of the most important national debates in our history, for the violence within universities, the changes within them, are now front-page news all over the world. The only possible solution here is the one suggested already by Professors Mathews and Steele – that a quota system be established and adhered to. What percentage that will be is of course subject to debate. And whatever quota may be decided upon, of this we may be certain, it will be far, far more generous to foreigners than any existing quota in any other nation. But a quota will have to be established if our universities are to remain Canadian, and my own suggestion is that it should be enacted by law passed by our provincial governments. They, after all, are the chief paymasters of the university today. I speak ruefully when I predict that the Canadian universities, if left to their own devices, would never under any circumstances, least of all existing ones, take a measure of this sort on their own initiative and make it stick.

Now, two more things must be said before I finish. Neither Professors Mathews and Steele, nor anyone of us here, in any way whatever wishes to refuse a warm welcome to American and foreign scholars within our midst. A university, to be a good one, must always have foreign scholars and scientists on its faculties. And when it admits them, it should treat them exactly as it would treat its own native teachers. But for this very reason it should be strong enough in its native majority to be able truly to welcome them, and that majority is what this nation must protect and if necessary create – a strong enough native majority on our faculties to guarantee both our control of policy and our grateful goodwill to those others we invite to work with us. If we fail to secure such a majority, and secure it soon, it takes no clairvoyance to foretell a disastrously unhappy situation for all concerned, for our visitors no less than for ourselves. For the territorial imperative will be sure to assert itself if it is excessively violated, and if it should come to that, then Canadians will behave as it has always made people behave when their own destinies have been taken out of their hands. The volume of ill-will that would then ensue would be something so unpleasant that I cannot bring myself to contemplate it.

Political Science in the Canadian University, 1969[*]

James MacKinnon and David Brown

Recently, there has been considerable discussion in the press and in academic circles about the influence of foreign professors in the Canadian university. Much of this discussion has been based on two opposing theories of knowledge. One contends that knowledge is universal, so that an influx of non-Canadian academics means an influx of academic excellence which can only serve to strengthen the Canadian academic community. The other contends that, while there may be general principles of universal applicability, these must be derived from and applied to specific circumstance. When foreign academics are unable or unwilling to relate their knowledge to the particular circumstances of this country, the argument continues, then they are not fully competent to teach in Canada.

The theories have been stated and their logical conclusions drawn; if further discussion is to be fruitful, there must be a thorough examination of the actual situation in Canadian universities. As well as varying from university to university, it is generally agreed that this situation varies from discipline to discipline. Before an overall picture can be drawn of the extent and effects of foreign influence in the Canadian university, each field must be studied individually.

As students in political science, we have attempted to find out what the situation is in this one discipline. Like the other social sciences, political science is a field in which the number of non-Canadians is rising rapidly. This has serious implications. The subject matter of social science courses is directly relevant to the student's conception of the society in which he lives. Therefore, what he learns in these courses greatly affects his understanding of the society, and consequently his future attitudes and behaviour toward it.

This would appear to be particularly important among students who take courses in political science, because it is likely that from this group will come a large proportion of the political elite of Canada a generation hence.

By *political elite* we are referring to the relatively small group in any society who have offices on the corridors of power: the politicians, the higher civil servants, many of the journalists and academics, some of the lawyers, and a certain number of representatives of economic and social interests. There can be no doubt that present members of this elite have had practical, if not formal, training in political science. And when one talks to political science students, and other students who take political science courses, one finds that a large proportion of them aspire to join this elite in one way or another.

It seems fair to conclude, then, that the political science courses being taught today are exercising some considerable, though largely indefinable, influence

[*]Reprinted from *The Struggle for Canadian Universities* by Robin Mathews and James Steele, pp. 151-162, published by New Press, 1970. Reproduced with the permission of New Press.

on the attitudes and abilities of those who will be playing an important role in governing this country in twenty years' time. If these courses are not oriented toward Canada and Canadian problems, are these future leaders being adequately prepared to understand and deal with the problems they will have to face? And can political science courses be oriented in that way if a large proportion of them are taught by non-Canadians?

In order to answer these questions, something more than a theoretical knowledge of the subject is required. Therefore, with the encouragement of a number of political scientists, chiefly at York University and the University of Toronto, we designed a questionnaire. This was sent to as many as we could reach of the approximately 425 professors who taught political science in Canadian universities in 1968-69. We received about 160 replies, mainly from English Canada. Because we do not consider our French Canadian results to be statistically significant, what follows relates only to political science as it is taught in English Canada, unless otherwise indicated.

In 1968-69, there were approximately 378 professors teaching political science on a full- or part-time basis in the 36 English-language universities which have departments of political science. Of these, 52 percent were Canadians, 29 percent Americans, 9 percent British, and 10 percent of other nationalities (mostly European). In addition, there were about 45 teaching in French-language and bilingual universities, over 60 percent of whom were Canadians.

Our assessment of citizenship in the above figures is based on the country in which the undergraduate degree was granted. All but six of the universities supplied us with complete lists of their political science staffs in 1968-69, including the degrees held by each professor and the universities at which they were granted; in the remaining six cases, figures have been estimated from published figures for earlier years. The results of our questionnaire indicated that place of undergraduate degree is a very accurate measurement of citizenship. Ninety-two point three percent of our respondents were citizens of the country in which they took their first degree. And for the most part the remaining cases cancelled each other out.

To be specific, for 132 out of 143 respondents, citizenship was the same as the country in which first degree was earned. Of the remaining 11 cases, seven were Canadians who had received their first degrees abroad, two were non-Canadians who had received their first degrees in Canada, and two were non-Canadians who had received their first degrees in countries other than Canada of which they were not citizens. It should be remembered that the seven Canadians who were granted undergraduate degrees abroad were for the most part naturalized citizens of this country. As Canadians, and particularly as naturalized Canadians, they are likely to have a greater than average interest in Canadian problems, and thus are likely to have responded in more than proportionate numbers (see below). Thus there is every evidence to indicate that the nationality of the first degree is a very accurate measurement of citizenship.

In our survey, conducted in March, 1969, we made contact with 285 of the 378 professors teaching political science in English-language universities, and had usable returns from 142 of them (or 49.8 percent of those contacted). Of these, 63 percent were from Canadians, 23 percent from Americans, 6 percent from British, and 8 percent from others. Thus Canadians were heavily over-represented in our replies. Although 58 percent of the Canadians we reached returned completed questionnaires, only 43 percent of the Americans, 32 percent of the British and 38 percent of others did so.

The low response rate by the non-Canadians strikes us as significant. There is probably no simple explanation. But one conclusion that is hard to avoid is that the non-Canadians who teach political science in Canada are less concerned with its problems than are their Canadian colleagues, and are less than willing to involve themselves in a controversy about their status in Canada. If this be true, it would seem logical that the non-Canadians who did reply are more concerned with Canadian problems than are their colleagues who did not. This should be borne in mind when looking at our results.

At this point it may be appropriate to note that aggregate figures such as those we have been quoting do not adequately reflect the situation in any given university, which is of course of greatest concern to the students. Political science departments tend to be either predominantly Canadian or predominantly non-Canadian. The large, old and established departments (and where political science is concerned, 25 years is old and established) tend to be heavily Canadian. Thus, if you omit Toronto, Carleton, Queen's and McGill from the list, Canadian professors are in a minority. Most departments are small; only five in Canada have more than 20 professors, and the median size is just eight point five. The newer departments, and those in the West, tend to be dominated by non-Canadians, most of whom are Americans.

The non-Canadians are recent arrivals. Only 5 percent of our sample had been teaching here for more than six years. Although Canadians were heavily over-represented in our results, only 44 percent of those who had been teaching here for less than three years were Canadians. On the basis of this and other information, we calculate that slightly less than 40 percent of the new teaching positions in political science in the past few years have gone to Canadians. A roughly equal proportion appear to have gone to Americans.

It is to be presumed that non-Canadians who come to Canada with the intention of becoming citizens of this country will gradually come to look at politics in ways that are relevant to Canadian students. But our results show that most immigrant professors do not intend to become Canadian citizens. Only 27 percent of the Americans in our sample believed that they would be teaching here in 10 years' time. Ninety percent did not intend to become Canadian citizens. By contrast, 42 percent of non-Canadians of other national groups had applied or intended to apply for citizenship.

If they do not want to become Canadians, why do these academic immigrants come here? Our survey, together with extensive interviews, showed that professors come here for two major reasons. Some come because they are unhappy with the situation in their country of origin. Perhaps the low number of Americans who intend to stay in Canada reflects the hope that the Vietnam situation and the domestic social crises in the United States will be improved in 10 years' time.

Others come here to further their careers. Canadian political science is smaller and less highly developed than American. Canadian universities tend to show a marked preference for graduates of certain American graduate schools. This means that it is often easier to gain recognition and rapid advancement in

Canada than in the States. Since, at the junior level, salaries and working conditions are usually comparable to or better than those in the United States, this tends to attract a number of capable, younger professors to teaching positions in Canada. At the senior level, however, American salaries tend to be much higher than Canadian, and research funds are more readily available on a larger scale. Thus those who have succeeded in establishing a reputation in Canada have a strong incentive to return to the United States.

By no means all immigrant political science professors come here with the intention of using a stay in this country as a shortcut to success in the United States or elsewhere. In recent years, Canada has suffered from a genuine shortage of political scientists, due mainly to the rapid expansion of Canadian universities, which has resulted in a net increase of some 50 political science professors annually. At the same time, there has been something of an over-supply in the United States. As a result, Canadian universities have in many cases been forced to hire professors who have had difficulty securing jobs elsewhere; 15 percent of the Americans in our sample admitted that lack of employment opportunities elsewhere was one of their reasons for coming to Canada.

Foreign professors come to Canada for numerous reasons beyond dissatisfaction with their home countries or career considerations. For many, the shorter academic year and the fact that the pressure to publish or perish is less provide strong inducements to take a job in Canada.

One way to measure an educated man's relationship to the society in which he lives is to analyse his newspaper and magazine reading habits. We found that American professors read considerably less Canadian material than did their Canadian or even their other non-Canadian colleagues. Fifty-five percent of the Americans read *The Globe and Mail* regularly, compared with 80 percent of the Canadians and 79 percent of the other non-Canadians. Only 9 percent of the Americans read *Le Devoir* regularly, compared with 30 percent of the Canadians and 16 percent of the other non-Canadians. By contrast, 67 percent of the Americans read *Le Devoir* regularly, compared with 30 percent of the the Canadians and 37 percent of the other non-Canadians. *Maclean's* claims to be "Canada's National Magazine"; approximately, 52 percent of the Canadians read it regularly. Only 15 percent of the Americans and 21 percent of the other non-Canadians did so. From these figures, it seems fair to wonder how well non-Canadian political scientists, particularly the Americans, are integrating into Canadian society.

Perhaps even more important than the professors, in terms of political education, are the courses they teach. Doubtless it is a good thing for Canadian students to be exposed to professors from other countries; the difficulty is that the subject matter and source material of most courses in political science are also heavily non-Canadian. As a second part of our questionnaire, we asked our respondents to send information on each course they taught in 1968-69; 117 did so. By a liberal definition, 19 percent of the 291 courses analysed were concerned with Canadian government. The others dealt with numerous areas, most notably the government of other nations, political philosophy, and international relations. Usually, a given university's course offering will cover two or three areas in some depth, and the rest superficially or not at all.

Most students who take courses in political science are not political science majors. Their exposure to the discipline is for the most part limited to two or three courses, usually of a general nature. On the basis of these courses, the students develop impressions of how politics (particularly Canadian politics) operates. These impressions will guide their attitudes and behaviour toward Canadian political problems, and strongly affect the way that they, as future leaders, propose to deal with them. Therefore, what is taught in these few courses assumes great importance.

By far the largest number of students is enrolled in introductory courses taught in the first year, or occasionally the second (as much as 35 percent of total enrolment in political science courses, according to estimates based on our results). These courses generally attempt to present an overview of the dimensions of political science, and would normally include some political philosophy, some methodology, and an introduction to the study of governments. Frequently, but not always, Canadian government is examined at least briefly. This is perhaps a concession to the traditional role of the Canadian government course as the general introduction to the study of politics.

In almost all cases, Canadian government courses now appear to be taught in the second and subsequent years. Our results show that, although the number of Canadian government courses offered is at least 50 percent greater than the number of introductory courses, the total enrolment in the former is no more than 60 percent of the latter. This is probably a function of the level at which the two types of courses are taught, since class size tends to get much smaller in the more senior years of university.

From our results it appears that about half the Canadian government courses are general in nature, serving as an introduction to Canadian government and politics. Beyond this introductory level, there appears to be no general pattern of advanced courses on various aspects of politics in Canada. Across Canada, not more than half a dozen courses appear to be offered in such important areas as the dynamics of federal-provincial relations, provincial politics, the political sociology of Canada, and the politics of French Canada.

Owing to a lack of suitable books and other material, many students find Canadian government courses less interesting than courses about other countries, for which more material is available. The study of Canadian government seems to be a victim of a *first-book syndrome* that is characteristic of Canadian scholarship in general; any moderately competent book on any aspect of Canadian government becomes a classic and remains unchallenged in its field, to be endured by generations of Canadian students. This is perhaps partially due to the small size of the Canadian market, which makes writing a book a financially unrewarding proposition. More important is a seeming reluctance to do research on a major scale, combined with a chronic lack of resources for research and publication. For every 10 dollars the federal government provides for scientific research, it gives only one dollar toward research in the social sciences and the humanities, although the number of professors teaching in the latter is at least as great as in the former. Political science gets only a very small slice of this very small pie.

Perhaps many of the inadequacies of courses in Canadian government are attributable to the fact that, according to our survey, some three-quarters of Canadian political scientists have gone to American or British graduate schools, where Canadian studies hardly occupy a prominent place on the curriculum. Thus many Canadian political scientists are not really qualified to teach courses

417

about Canada. Perhaps realizing this, 58 percent of the Canadians sampled were doing research on one or more aspects of politics in Canada. By contrast, only 27 percent of the Americans and 37 percent of the other non-Canadians were doing so. It has long been accepted practice for Canadian graduate students to go abroad. This may be partly owing to youth's natural desire to travel and see the world, but it is largely due to a serious lack of good graduate schools in Canada. In political science, there are few if any faculties that first-rate political science graduates would consider. As a result, the best Canadian graduate students in political science go abroad; and past experience has been that many of them have stayed there, especially among those who have gone to the United States. What has been happening in the past, then – and there is no reason to believe that the situation has changed substantially in the last few years – is that Canada has been losing many of those who are potentially her best political scientists, and having to replace them with immigrants who are not necessarily of equal calibre.

With courses other than those in Canadian government, the problem is slightly different. Thanks to the influx of foreign professors, there is no lack of professors competent to teach them. But virtually all the published material available is American or British in origin; and in most cases professors, even the Canadians, have been trained to regard their fields in American or British, rather than Canadian, terms. We believe that for this, the largest group of political science courses, to become relevant and useful to Canadian students, there must be reference to Canadian experience both in class and in the source material. Our respondents did not seem to disagree with this contention; 60 percent felt that a knowledge of Canadian history, politics and culture was either *essential* or *highly desirable* for the teaching of *any* course in political science. Yet foreign professors to whom we have talked have generally admitted that their inadequate knowledge in these fields has prevented them from including very much relevant Canadian material in their courses.

According to our survey, only a quarter of the books used in political science courses in Canada have been written by Canadians or published in Canada. The bulk of these are used in courses on Canadian government and in introductory courses. In courses not directly concerned with Canadian government, only 8 percent of the books can be liberally termed *Canadian*. Two-thirds of the remainder are of American origin.

This means that in most fields, Canadian political science students are studying from books that attempt to explain political phenomena in terms of American experience. For example, in a comparative politics course comparing French and Russian government, both systems will be analysed in American terms; it will be up to the student himself (often with little help from his professors) to relate what he has learned to the Canadian system. The result is that most political science students in Canada probably have a better understanding of the subtleties of the American system than those of the Canadian. They begin to think of the Canadian system in American terms, which may not be appropriate.

Many of the professors who replied to our questionnaire were unhappy with the books they were forced to use. In only 54 percent of the courses analysed did they indicate that the books available were satisfactory. This figure dropped to 29 percent in the case of Canadian government courses, and 26 percent in the case of introductory courses. In other words, in the two most important areas, those in which the largest numbers of students are enrolled, the material available is least satisfactory. In not a few introductory courses, professors indicated that all their material was adequate, except that dealing with Canada!

As a further indication of the problems faced by those who teach political science, 63 percent of our respondents felt that their university library facilities were inadequate for their own use; 45 percent felt they were inadequate for the use of their students. The younger professors were more dissatisfied with library facilities than were their elders, perhaps because in most cases they had recently been exposed to much better ones abroad.

One of Canada's basic problems is lack of communication and understanding between English and French. This is probably as true of Canadian academic life, and of political science in particular, as it is of the society as a whole. Of 50-odd courses on Canadian government and politics described by our respondents, only one dealt specifically with French Canada. A dismayingly low percentage of those sampled – 18 percent – claimed to be able to speak French well enough to teach a course in that language. It is notable that English Canadians claimed to be more proficient in this respect than the non-Canadians. The reading habits of the professors are perhaps indicative of their attitudes. Only 23 percent of them read *Le Devoir* regularly, compared with 47 percent who read *The New York Times* and 73 percent who read *The Globe and Mail*. We might add that, even among the Canadians, more read *The New York Times* (42 percent) than *Le Devoir* (30 percent).

If those who teach political science are not even enough in touch with the realities of French Canada to read French Canadian newspapers, it is unlikely that their students will develop more than a superficial awareness of one third of Canadian society. An English Canadian political science which ignores the facts of French Canada is not greatly more useful than English Canadian political science would be if it refused to study Canadian politics at all! The same would apply to the study of the discipline in French Canada!

The conclusion to be drawn from these results is that Canadian political science is failing to provide Canadian students with enough insight into the areas with which they will have to concern themselves in the future. Unless more research is done on Canadian politics and on other aspects of political science which should be made relevant to Canadians, and unless more of what is done is published and made widely available, Canadian students will to an increasing extent look at political problems through American eyes, by default.

A number of other things need to be done. Canadian graduate schools must be strengthened, so that they are capable of providing training which not only is of high quality, but is seen to be of high quality. Such strengthening would ensure that top Canadian graduates become more likely to remain at home and Canadian universities become more willing to hire their own products. This would involve larger expenditures, by both private sources and government, to improve library and research facilities. All this assumes that the political scientists in Canada will have enough interest in and concern for the future of their discipline to make these necessary changes worthwhile.

It seems, then, that the deficiencies of Canadian political science are not the result of an influx of foreign professors. This is merely a symptom of the problem and not its cause. The challenge is to develop the potential of political science in Canada so that it can competently perform its vital function of educating the future leaders of this country.

Canada's Lagging in Quality*

Lewis Hertzman

In recent weeks there has been disjointed discussion of the strong presence of Americans and American influences in Canadian universities. The question came up originally as one aspect of the current work of the University League for Social Reform, a group of young nationalists centred in the University of Toronto, and the news media have been echoing variations of the numbers theme. At best the topic can be described as an interesting non-issue. At worst, it is another revealing example of the chauvinism of a minority, a potential threat in itself to the free development of our intellectual life.

There have never been enough Canadians to fill out the faculties of our universities. Crude statistics suggesting otherwise simply do not show the discrepancy within fields and specialties. In colonial and post-colonial days large numbers of our faculty members came from Britain, and most of our advanced students studied there. Since then, in face of demographic pressures and the unparalleled expansion of Canadian educational institutions, even larger numbers of scholars and teachers have been recruited in the United States. Moreover, most Canadian students who study in the United States are there not merely because of the financial generosity of American universities, but in recognition of their scholastic excellence.

In Canada there are no institutions comparable to Harvard, Chicago, California or the Massachusetts Institute of Technology. We have no collections of books that even approach in size and quality what can be found in the Library of Congress, the Huntington Library in California, the Hoover at Stanford, and the Newberry in Chicago, to name a few. While such discrepancy of quality persists, it is right that our best students go where the quality is. Mobility of men and ideas is an essential mark of a free and open society.

If Canadian scholars seem to write and publish less than their counterparts abroad, there may be several reasons. During term their teaching duties are heavy. Great libraries are distant, and it is difficult to advance major work over distances despite the occasional assistance of travel grants and the long summer break. But even where a text or a monograph is completed, chances are it will be published abroad, and probably then come under the suspicion of our nationalists. The fact is that publishing is a precarious, not very lucrative field. There are few books than can be economically published in Canada for a primarily Canadian university market. There is some money to be made in

*Reprinted by permission of Lewis Hertzman. Article first appeared in *The Toronto Telegram*, April 17th, 1969.

a few areas like Canadian history or economics. But for the most part the only reliable market for Canadian texts is at the level of primary and secondary schools. To be sure, Canadian authors should be encouraged and assisted in finding markets in their own country as well as abroad, but only on the basis of competitive excellence.

The basic problem lies in the weakness of the Canadian graduate school, especially humane and social studies. Expansion has been unduly limited in comparison to need, and in marked contrast to the continued growth of undergraduate faculties. Clearly, growth in the graduate sector must now be accelerated to compensate for generations of neglect. To mention the area I know best, in most fields of historical study there has been little improvement since I obtained my first degree twenty years ago. Canadian historiography, while showing a few signs of new life, is still backward compared with the lively intellectual advances in other parts of the English- and French-speaking worlds. In Ontario any university department anxious to inaugurate an advanced studies program must go through a tedious and unsatisfactory procedure of outside appraisal that is calculated more to discourage than encourage initiatives. Even with approval of a given project, financing from public funds is likely to remain problematical. In Ontario that is particularly true at this present juncture of government austerity in most areas of health, education and welfare.

Given such limitations of both human and material resources at the local and national levels, we are fortunate that we are still able to attract foreign scholars, teachers and other highly skilled individuals. If we insist on hiring the best, we can only benefit until we are able to supply most needs from among our own graduates. There will in fact never be a time when we would not benefit from the infusion of new blood and ideas, regardless of national frontiers. Indeed, the university is one institution in our society that will suffer severe decline if it is not in immediate contact with the streams and currents of the entire intellectual and scientific world. There is a danger in the present situation in Canada that needs emphasizing – the danger that universities will hire second-rate people, whether for economy or because of inability to find more qualified persons. But again, if blame is to be assigned, it falls on us and not on some sinister plot of foreign imperialism.

It would be a sad day if we were forced to apply a citizenship test to professors, or even perhaps a quota on foreign books in order to check *Uberfremdung* in the universities (a frequent pejorative word in the German fascist vocabulary on undesirable alien presence). Even if it were possible, that is not likely to occur in this country. The ultra-nationalists and would-be purifiers of our education and culture nevertheless should be answered. In Quebec, for all the pathos in some circles, the intellectual aim has been enrichment through wider contact with the world of *francophonie*. But anglophone nationalists in the rest of the country too easily equate pro-Canadianism with a know-nothing anti-Americanism, though they might argue the benefits of associations throughout the non-U.S., English-speaking world. A better range of goals for Canadians, of whatever language, might be through intellectual cosmopolitanism, to evolve in this country newer concepts of international nationhood uncomplicated by traditional notions of sovereignty and autarchy.

421

"Canadianization" and the University*

The Executive and Finance Committee, Canadian Association of University Teachers

One function among the many legitimately assigned to a university is to develop an awareness of and an understanding of the society in which we live. This society of course has local and national as well as international aspects, all of which require attention. The university thus has an important role to play in the development of community and national identities. If we assume that university faculty play an important or even dominant role in the learning process, then we can properly expect that faculty members at Canadian universities be familiar with the Canadian situation and further be committed to the development and enrichment of the Canadian community, or engage themselves to acquire this familiarity and commitment. Canadian birth or citizenship is some evidence of such knowledge and concern, although not a necessary prerequisite to it. Other functions of the university require qualifications of expert knowledge in a discipline, concern for and ability to communicate with students, and, for senior positions, appropriate experience in university work. .

The principal criterion to be used in engaging a professor must continue to be his *competence* in the broad sense of his capacity to carry out the functions for which he was engaged. Competence thus includes not only his promise and ability as teacher and scholar, but also those qualities which affect his performance within the Canadian university community. In areas where a familiarity with things Canadian is important, as for example in Canadian history or government or literature, then competence requires that knowledge. Such knowledge is not confined to Canadian citizens, although it may require residence and study in Canada. From this viewpoint, the Chairman of a department (of history, for instance, or French, English, etc.) who is unsympathetic or indifferent to the development of Canadian studies is clearly incompetent regardless of his academic qualifications, his citizenship, or national origin.

The Canadian Association of University Teachers believes that competence, in the sense referred to above, should be the sole criterion for appointment. Consequently, C.A.U.T. is opposed to any system of quotas or formal regulations which would require that some fixed proportion of faculty or of new appointees be Canadian citizens, or which would reduce or restrict the status or rights of non-Canadian faculty members. The potential damage to individuals and to institutions of any enforceable quota regulations far outweighs any possible benefits. Further, in certain areas the lack of qualified Canadians, regardless of their desirability, makes a citizenship requirement impossible to meet. For example, until very recently anthropology and sociology were virtually ignored in Canadian universities and negligible numbers of graduate degrees were granted in these areas.

The C.A.U.T. is also opposed to invoking the authority of governments and

*Reprinted with permission of the Executive and Finance Committee, Canadian Association of University Teachers. It is the text of an Association Position Paper adopted by the Executive and Finance Committee of the C.A.U.T. at a meeting on June 27, 1969.

legislatures to enforce or encourage rules concerning appointments or methods of appointments within universities.

At the same time, the C.A.U.T. is concerned with the related problem of finding positions for the graduates of Canadian universities. At present, some appointments are made on the basis of personal contacts, which in many cases may operate on international, rather than on east-west trans-Canada lines. In keeping with our recent resolution urging publication in appropriate journals of all vacancies for teaching and administrative positions, we have urged upon various groups such as the university presidents and graduate deans (through A.U.C.C.) and the various Learned Societies that by means of advertisements in *University Affairs* and by other formal and informal employment services, including Departments of Manpower or Labour, they make known to Canadian students and faculty the openings available at Canadian universities. We are confident that Canadians, given the opportunity to apply, can compete successfully with applicants from anywhere in the world.

The C.A.U.T. further urges that academic, professional, and government agencies co-operate in the preparation, publication and annual revision of five- to ten-year projections of positions available and of graduate degrees granted in each academic discipline at Canadian universities. This will allow individual students a better opportunity to plan future careers, and universities a better opportunity to encourage Canadian talents in areas of projected needs through the development of adequate graduate programmes in such areas.

The C.A.U.T. is always prepared to investigate any allegations of anti-Canadian discrimination in appointments, and to endeavour to correct improper or unsatisfactory practices.

American Invasion of the Mass Media in Canada[*] *1971*

Benjamin D. Singer

In the fall of 1969, Senator Keith Davey, himself a career advertising salesman, launched a series of hearings into Canadian mass media that galvanized the nation's attention on the importance of the communication system to the social health of Canada. In explaining his reason for the inquiry, Senator Davey said, "It occurred to me that there had never been a national accounting for the media. Most people agreed that freedom of the press presumes responsibility, but few had really stopped to assess that responsibility. It also occurred to me that Parliament might be the ideal instrument through which the people of Canada could determine whether they have the press they need or simply the press they deserve."[1]

The terms of reference of the inquiry highlighted the issue of concentration of ownership – monopoly and multi-media domination within certain communi-

---

*Not published previously; written specifically for this volume.

ties – and included such issues as the effects of technological change on the mass media. In an attempt to evaluate the *prime functions* performed by the media (for example, information, interpretation, generation of social change, and elevation of good taste) the commission examined issues such as the following: opportunities for the presentation of opposing opinions; the social analysis of the journalist's role; and, most importantly for this paper, the extent of domination and influence of foreign media – particularly American – on Canada.

This issue has been a matter of concern for years to many Canadians, especially *literati* and professional media people. Thus, the hearings were not generated in a vacuum of concern regarding American influence.

The final report of the Committee was based upon invited briefs submitted by media owners and their representatives, along with commissioned research describing access and usage patterns, economic factors, content analysis of the media, and opinion and usage surveys of samples of the Canadian population. A great deal of the material was collected from existent records based on research already conducted by the Canadian Radio Television Commission, Dominion Bureau of Statistics and other governmental and commercial organizations. However, the sample surveys conducted for the Committee are based on questionable methodology.[2]

In the present article, the data provided by the Davey Committee and other sources will be examined to determine some of the crucial patterns of influence by American media.

The newspaper is the very cornerstone of any literate society's communication system, for its formal characteristics give it great influence on the highest educated segment of the society (for example, greater depth of coverage, that it is a *demand* medium which is used at the convenience of the reader, etc.). Canadians who read daily newspapers can be expected to be conscious of their Southern neighbour a great deal of time, for as one study of daily newspapers in Montreal, Ottawa, Toronto and Winnipeg revealed, 56 percent of all the foreign news published was about the United States.[3] Thus, it can be expected that the *print audience* is not only oriented to American events but to the opinions and values that filter through those events. The finding by the Davey Committee that 94 percent of their sample of the Canadian population surveyed preferred Canadian newspapers to only 2 percent who preferred American ones, becomes less relevant in view of the high American content.[4] There was a similar finding with regard to radio, but one must again consider the very high American domination of the content – the production of records and the United States based packaged programming selections.

The Davey Committee's magazine preference questions, on the other hand, indicated a much higher regard for the American product than was so in the case of newspapers. The aggregate findings for the entire population indicates Canadian magazines are preferred 56 percent to 37 percent for American magazines. However, this figure is biased by the fact that French speaking individuals overwhelmingly opted for Canadian (French language) publications. In three provinces, British Columbia, Nova Scotia and Newfoundland, American magazines were preferred equally or more. As income and education rise, preference increases for American magazines.[5]

In 1969, Canadians purchased 131 million American magazines, compared with 34 million Canadian magazines – a ratio of nearly four-to-one.[6] Yet, the periodical both in the United States and Canada becomes less important every day that television exists. Further, the major cultural forces invading Canada from the South come through the air and cable.

It has been estimated that three-fifths of the Canadian population are within range of American broadcasters. The perfection of cable television allows the importation of programmes from hundreds of miles away, thus providing a means of penetration to audiences which otherwise would not be exposed to American influences. In 1969, according to the Canadian Radio and Television Commission, United States television stations garnered 18 percent of the total viewing hours, part of that as a result of cable linkage (17 percent of Canadian homes have cable at the present time).[7] As cable hookups increase so will the penetration of American *stations* – but one must also be aware that recent data indicate that of the 60 percent of CBC programming which consists of films, 82 percent have been imported, primarily from the United States.[8]

Certain border areas are particularly dominated by American television products. In the Toronto-Hamilton area, Canadian audiences devoted 34 million hours to direct viewing of Buffalo stations, compared with 43 million hours for three Canadian stations, but when one adds the contribution of American programmes carried by the Canadian stations, it is clear that United States' content predominates.[9] In another border area, Vancouver, cable-equipped homes devote 40 percent of their television time budget to American stations, but to this total one must add the American programmes carried by the Canadian stations.[10]

Even those *programmes* nominally classified as Canadian contribute American content. The CBC has contracts with the American news networks to permit it to carry American news items on the CBC National TV News. A study conducted over a period of 21 days in 1970 indicated that 20 percent of the news items on that programme were American.[11]

Given that access and utilization of American television are substantial, what kinds of effects can be inferred? One measure of such effects is stated preference on the basis that consistent exposure has a canalizing effect. The Davey Committee findings indicate that Canadians say they prefer American television 54 percent to 43 percent for Canadian television, but five out of six predominantly English speaking provinces indicate preference of American television by two-to-one or more.[12] And, as income and education increase, so does preference for the American product. In addition to *preference*, belief in *quality* may be an issue. A Gallup Poll indicated in 1969 that more than three times as many Canadians believe that American television is better than Canadian (50 percent versus 15 percent).[13]

Yet, approximately half the Canadian public also believe that the Canadian culture or way of life is being influenced too much by American television.[14]

There is some evidence that this is true. In 1967, Henry Comor, a president of the Association of Canadian Television and Radio Artists wrote in an article titled "American TV, What Have You Done to Us?":

> Canadians are more aware of United States history than of Canadian history. They are more aware of the Civil War and War of 1812 and

Abraham Lincoln than of Canadian events and statesmen. . . . I once told a reporter, facetiously, that my children thought they *lived* in the United States. And when this report was published in 45 Canadian newspapers, there wasn't a single cry of protest. No one said I was distorting the facts.[15]

It is interesting to note that an empirical test of Mr. Comor's assertion has been made. This investigator found that Canadian university students knew slightly more about American current events and had an even higher relative knowledge of American political figures than Canadian. American television newsman Walter Cronkite was known to more students than his then counterpart in Canada, Earl Cameron. Furthermore, they were likely to use American terminology rather than Canadian to describe an important institution (for example, *district attorney* – right out of the evening's American television programming – rather than the *Crown attorney*).[16]

The research noted above illustrates well the problem of the preservation of the Canadian culture – its values and sense of self-identity – that Canadians have been so fearful of losing over the decades, in the shadow of their giant neighbour. Some believe that this has now become a matter of national urgency since television far exceeds print in massive power to socialize; and the fear seems well-founded that within a generation, the will to resist cultural assimilation will have eroded and with its demise, one can expect little resistance to further economic and then political assimilation to the South.

Footnotes

1. Keith Davey, *Report of the Special Senate Committee on Mass Media*, I, No. 7, Ottawa: Queen's Printer, 1970.

2. The questionnaire was sloppily constructed and ambiguous in many places, the interviews required two to six hours – far beyond the tolerance of the majority of people – if one is to get valid answers, and no information was provided on refusal rates or sampling techniques as is usually provided in social scientific surveys.

3. Jim A. Hart, "The Flow of News Between the U.S. and Canada," *Journalism Quarterly*, 40, 1963, pp. 70-74.

4. Davey, *op. cit.*, II, p. 131.

5. *Ibid.*

6. *Ibid.*, I, p. 156.

7. Canadian Radio Television Commission, *Annual Report, 1969-70*. Ottawa: Queen's Printer, 1970, p. 21.

8. Henry Comor, "American TV: What Have You Done to Us?" in *Broadcasting and the Public Interest*, J. H. Pennybacker, W. W. Braden, eds., New York: Random House, 1969, p. 84.

9. Davey, *op. cit.*, II, p. 385.

10. *Ibid.*, p. 387.

11. Benjamin D. Singer, "Violence, Protest and War in Television News: The U.S. and Canada Compared," in Benjamin D. Singer, ed., *Social Issues in Canadian Communication*. Toronto: Copp-Clark Publishing Co., 1971.

12. Davey, *op. cit.*, II, p. 131.

13. Canadian Radio and Television Commission, *op. cit.*, p. 96.

14. *Ibid.*

15. Comor, *op. cit.*, p. 83.

16. Earle Beattie, "The Influence of U.S. Media in Canada," in Benjamin D. Singer, ed., *Social Issues in Canadian Communication, op. cit.*

Canada's "National" Sport[*]

Bruce Kidd

Canada does not have a distinctive sports culture. Virtually every aspect of Canadian sport has been conditioned by American influences. Our sports heroes, with the exception of our hockey favourites, are mostly Americans – not surprisingly when our media constantly bombard us with as much American sporting news as Canadian, and when our sports commentators consider *American* to be the standard of excellence. Our best professional athletes seek their fortunes in the United States and our best amateurs seek the semi-professional status and the specialized coaching and facilities that are available through US athletic scholarships. Canadian sport impresarios – from track and field to tennis and golf – depend upon the *drawing power* of US athletes to attract spectators to their events. Canadian physical educators rely upon their American counterparts to prepare their teaching manuals, conduct their coaching clinics, and so on. Even our fitness fads are imported. Lloyd Percival has preached the benefits of jogging for more than twenty years, but it was an American Airforce major, Dr Kenneth Cooper, who fathered the present jogging boom. Canadians in search of a distinctive national culture get no help from sports.

To be sure, not every Canadian sport has been Americanized in the same fashion. In track and field and swimming, for example, the lack of adequate year-round facilities and the scarcity of good coaching has forced many Canadian athletes to go south: as a result, half the members of our 1968 Olympic team in these sports attended university in the United States. In football, on the other hand, opportunities for professional employment in the Canadian Football League have encouraged many American athletes to come north. This essay confines itself to one sport – hockey, our national game.

The Americanization of Canadian hockey is the direct outgrowth of the commercialization of hockey that occurred first in the United States and then in Canada, at the turn of the century.[1] Social conditions at the time – growing urbanization, shorter working weeks, the popularization of the press – were ideally suited to the promotion and sale of sport as a spectator attraction, and hockey was one of the most exciting games available for sale.[2] Ever since the British garrisons, which had been the focal point of most Canadian sport before Confederation, were sent home in 1872, Canadians had crossed the border to compete and exchange sporting ideas.[3] And hockey, which had always flourished in Canada, quickly caught on in the United States. By 1926 six of the ten teams[4] in what was generally recognized as the best Canadian hockey league, the National Hockey League, were located in the United States and owned by Americans.[5]

Although few US-born athletes have demonstrated outstanding skill at hockey, American entrepreneurs have been able to stage first-class hockey by importing Canadian players, coaches, and managers. Neither country has ever raised

*Reprinted from *Close the 49th Parallel, etc.: The Americanization of Canada*, edited by Ian Lumsden, by permission of University of Toronto Press. © University of Toronto Press 1970.

barriers against the free flow of hockey talent between the two countries.[6] Enjoying generally a more lucrative market – larger population, higher incomes – than their Canadian counterparts, American hockey entrepreneurs have been able to pay higher salaries and attract the best Canadian players away from the Canadian teams that employed them. Complete statistics are difficult to obtain, but it appears that since the turn of the century there has been a general increase in the number of hockey teams operating in the United States and a general decline in the number operating in Canada. It is difficult to avoid the conclusion that American capital has put Canadian hockey out of business in Canada. Today, all but five of the forty-five North American commercial hockey teams are located in the United States and all but six are owned by Americans.[7] With ownership comes control: ten of the twelve directorships of the NHL, which rules over both commercial and non-commercial hockey in the two countries, are held by American corporations.[8] The players may all be Canadian, but as NHL president Clarence Campbell said recently, "The NHL has never been a Canadian organization."[9] Not surprisingly, this non-Canadian organization has rarely acted in the best interest of the Canadian community.

It makes no sense to blame the Americans for their control of hockey, distasteful as that control may be. Given the commercialization of the game, its Americanization is inevitable. The particular characteristics of the takeover are unimportant. If the sport had not been exported almost entirely to the United States, control might have been acquired just as easily through the outright purchase of successful Canadian hockey corporations by American interests. No, there has been nothing out of the ordinary about the Americanization of hockey. What is difficult to explain, however, is its commercialization; or specifically, why Canadians have allowed – in fact encouraged – the sale of hockey to go unregulated for so long.

Commercial hockey in Canada is called *professional* hockey, but strictly speaking the two terms are not synonymous. In *professional* hockey the players are remunerated for their hockey efforts and thus can be distinguished from *amateur* players who are not so remunerated. The term *commercial* refers to a different aspect of the game altogether, the ownership and control of the game. In *commercial* hockey, team owners enjoy complete property rights in the players and the right of admission to actual contests, and they operate the hockey enterprise to make a private profit.

It has been the commercialization of the game, not its professionalization, that has harmed Canadian hockey. There is nothing dishonourable about professionalism in sport, for without a regular income, most highly skilled athletes would not be free (from alternative work) to develop their talents to the full. Artists need money for the same reason. But professional hockey need not be commercial hockey. Because of the costs of staging competitions between professionals, it may be necessary to charge admission to the hockey game. But it is not necessary to vest unconditional property rights in the admissions. Only in North America has spectator sport been both professionalized and commercialized. In other countries, commercial profits from spectator sport are closely controlled by the state, sometimes limited and sometimes forbidden altogether. It has not been the salaries that have hurt hockey – in fact, they have contributed to the high level of skill developed by its players – but rather the exploitation of the game for private profit.

The most galling consequence of this commercialization for Canadians is that nearly all the best hockey games are played in the United States! Where hockey is played at its best in Canada – in Toronto's Maple Leaf Gardens and Montreal's Forum – it is impossible to buy a ticket. As Ralph Allen loved to write, hockey is Canada's religion.[10] Weekends are centred around it, election campaigns and religious observances are altered to fit its scheduling, and during the annual Stanley Cup playoffs, the whole country stands still. Every family grows up listening to or watching "Hockey Night in Canada." Why we save all our enthusiasms for hockey is difficult to explain. Whatever the reason, hockey is the Canadian passion. Yet because spectator hockey is privately owned, most Canadians are prevented from seeing it at its best. What community would permit property rights in its national religion?

The Canadian community invests a great deal in the production, as it were, of good hockey players: it creates the social environment that encourages young players to aspire to greatness in the sport and to devote the necessary long hours of practice; it provides him with arenas in which to play and coaches to perfect his skills. The size of the investment is often considerable. Every hamlet boasts an arena, although its construction often requires years of saving and months of volunteer labour. Many a municipal budget is spent largely on minor hockey, to the deliberate neglect of alternative programmes. Because the development of good players is thus essentially a community enterprise, the choicest fruits of this enterprise – games between the most highly skilled of athletes – should be a community benefit. Yet they are not. If not exported directly for sale in the United States, the best games are sold here in Canada under monopoly conditions at outrageous prices.

Given the importance of hockey to Canadians, it seems incredible that major Canadian cities like Halifax, Quebec, Hamilton, Winnipeg, Regina, Calgary, Edmonton, and Vancouver do not have professional hockey teams of the highest rank. Yet they do not. But given commercial hockey's goal of profit maximization, the explanation is all too apparent. Bigger profits can be made in the United States. Take the case of Vancouver, for example. At long last a group of businessmen in that city have been offered (as of September 1969) first refusal on a newly created NHL franchise. If the Vancouver syndicate agrees to buy the $6 million franchise (no announcement has been made at the time of writing), it will bring a third NHL team (of fourteen teams) to Canada. At the most recent NHL expansion, that of 1966, Vancouver was refused a franchise and all six new franchises were awarded to US cities. The reason: television revenue. The expansion (to Philadelphia, Pittsburgh, St Louis, Minneapolis, Los Angeles, and Oakland) placed teams in the remaining northern US television markets and thus enabled the NHL to get a national TV contract from CBS. A Vancouver franchise would have brought little additional television revenue to the league, for NHL hockey (the games of the Montreal and Toronto teams) was already beamed at the Vancouver area. And the Vancouver market meant nothing to CBS.[11]

The commercialization of the game has affected the location of minor league teams too. Although it is difficult to trace a direct relationship between the growth of minor league hockey in American cities and the decline of similar operations in Canadian cities, I think the two developments are closely related. During the past decade senior semi-professional commercial teams in several Canadian cities have folded; and in 1969 the always strong junior clubs have been hit. This time, raiding has been direct: the semi-professional US college teams are luring Canadian boys away with "athletic scholarships."[12] Since the commercial game has socialized almost all Canadian athletes to the idea of playing in the United States, there is little reason to stay.

Commercialization has made hockey a high-priced, exclusive form of entertainment. In home games neither Montreal nor Toronto has played to less than full capacity for the last twenty years. Although the seating capacity of both arenas has been increased, the demand for tickets far exceeds the supply. Because of their private monopoly, the owners have been able to determine prices as they please and to restrict the sale of tickets to anyone they choose. In both cities, the option on season's tickets has become a property right, too. It is not unknown for people to bequeath them in their wills. In Toronto more than 90 percent of the tickets to Maple Leaf games are pre-sold to season's subscribers. Despite this tremendous demand for hockey seats, neither of the owners appears interested in distributing seats to a wider segment of the public. It may be a national game, but it is only a privileged – and well heeled – few that are able to watch professional games in person.

Commercialization of the game has even affected traditional Canadian television habits. The larger US market has given the American network priority over the Canadian networks in the telecasting of weekend games. They are now scheduled to suit CBS. When there is a conflict, the Canadian network must be happy with second choice. This is why "Hockey Night in Canada" is telecast in the afternoon during the playoffs.[13]

Commercialization, moreover, has disrupted amateur hockey. The profitability of commercial hockey depends primarily upon two factors: the availability of the best players and competition from alternative hockey attractions. Salaries and promotion costs – the main costs of spectator hockey – are determined by the existence of other potential employers, and ticket sales vary according to the ability of the team to field *star* players and according to the performance of other teams of equal calibre in the same area. If commercial teams could completely control the player market and eliminate all professional hockey competitors – in short, if they could gain monopoly control over the sport – then profits could be maximized. This is, in fact, what the NHL has done. Until the late 1940s a number of semi-professional (*amateur*) leagues, some of which were operated on a profit basis, competed with the NHL for hockey players and spectators. Although they enjoyed only a small percentage of the market, the NHL considered them a threat to its financial security. The NHL eventually won this competition – by completely outbidding its rivals for players – and Canadian senior hockey has been a wasteland ever since.[14] It is difficult to determine the extent to which the NHL's monopoly has reduced the number of hockey teams operating in Canada, but I believe this number to be considerable. In other countries, where professional sport has not been commercialized and where no profit motive exists to encourage the elimination of rival teams, large professional leagues thrive.[15] In Canada, good senior hockey is but a memory.

Through its victory over senior *amateur* hockey, the NHL gained almost complete control over the association which governs all amateur hockey in Canada and directs its development, the Canadian Amateur Hockey Association. Virtually every youngster who plays organized hockey outside his school, for example, possesses a registration card from the CAHA or one of its affiliates.

Although not all school boards are affiliated with the national organization, most of them use the CAHA rule-book and CAHA-approved referees. As the NHL controls the CAHA and closely supervises all its actions, it enjoys undisputed control over every aspect of the game.

By means of a series of legal agreements which it has persuaded the CAHA to sign, the NHL dictates the rules used in amateur hockey leagues and the conditions of amateur status. It dictates how the CAHA administers its programmes and spends its funds. And until three years ago, it controlled the hockey career of every boy over fourteen years of age, through an elaborate system of sponsorship of amateur teams. In 1967 a special committee of the National Advisory Committee for Fitness and Amateur Sport studying Canadian hockey, observed:

> If any organization is to operate independently, it must enjoy control over its own procedures. For a sports governing body, this means it must be able to determine the eligibility of its own members, the playing rules of its competitions, and it must be free to determine how to spend its own funds. The Canadian Amateur Hockey Association enjoys fully none of these essential rights. Under the 1958 agreement (the agreement then in effect), it has abdicated certain of these responsibilities to the National Hockey League. In order to be able to function independently, we firmly believe amateur hockey must be free of control by the NHL.[16]

The 1967 NHL-CAHA agreement replaced the *sponsorship* system with a universal draft of players twenty years of age, but the other forms of NHL control remained the same. In a subsequent report, the Hockey Study Committee concluded: "The CAHA failed to achieve the autonomy which the committee felt to be essential for the good of amateur hockey when it agreed to the 1967 NHL-CAHA agreement. . . . The committee is concerned because the *amateur* and the autonomous status of the CAHA is even more in question than it was under the 1958 agreement."[17]

The NHL-CAHA agreement has but a single purpose: to control the development of talent for the NHL's entertainment industry, now largely American-dominated. Few of the commercial hockey operators would dispute this conclusion. All hockey players and coaches seek to make their careers within the commercial leagues, they would argue. And the integration of amateur and commercial hockey supposedly ensures that players will receive a proper apprenticeship and thus make an easy transition to the professional, commercial leagues. But if one assumes, as the Fitness Council's study committee assumed, that amateur hockey is based upon an entirely different set of values and objectives, then he must conclude that NHL control is harmful.

At the community level, professional domination is harmful in many ways. The *win-at-all-costs, beat-'em-in-the-alley* ethic of the professionals has so pervaded minor league hockey that it has soured the game for many youngsters, teachers, and parents.[18] The scramble to gain control of young players (the Fitness Council study discovered that the registration cards of boys as young as fourteen and fifteen were being bought and exchanged on the basis of their playing abilities[19]) has disrupted many homes and the education of many young hockey players. As part of its study, the hockey committee compared the records of Ontario high school students who played hockey for teams *not affiliated* with the school with those of other students. The results bore out what has been widely believed:

> From this research, we can now report there were significant differences in certain respects between the two groups, and that sound reasons exist to indicate these differences were related to the playing of Junior OHA hockey.
>
> It is important to note that the hockey-playing and non-hockey-playing [students playing hockey for school teams are included in the "non-hockey-playing" population] students in this study were alike in their first year in secondary school. . . . After a similar start in Grade 9, a divergent pattern of school behaviour began to appear which became most pronounced around the fourth and fifth years of secondary schooling.
>
> The hockey-playing students performed progressively more poorly on Grade 11 and Grade 12 school examinations. On every one of six standardized achievement tests given in Grades 10 and 11, they also performed more poorly than their non-hockey-playing peers. In terms of completion of Grade 13, only 5.9 percent of the 511 hockey players graduated compared with 10.7 percent of the non-hockey-playing group.[20]

As long as amateur hockey is considered by the NHL as a training ground for its professional players, the disruption of education must follow.

NHL control prevents thousands of Canadians who enjoy hockey at the community level to conduct the game as they see fit. One recent illustration should suffice. In the 1967 agreement, the amateur association agreed to lower the age of junior competition to enable the NHL to turn young players into professionals a year earlier. At the CAHA meeting a year later, the regional association representing 200,000 of 265,000 registered players voted to re-establish the higher age limit. But the CAHA national executive, which bargains with the NHL, refused to make the change.[21] Early in 1969 CAHA executive secretary Gordon Juckes formally requested permission from the NHL to raise the age limit, but the NHL has refused to reconsider.[22] The reduced age limit is a serious blow to junior hockey, depriving the clubs of their most experienced players and banishing the players to the uncertainties of senior hockey. It is because they have lost a full year of junior hockey that so many young players are accepting US athletic scholarships. At a US college they are guaranteed a few extra years of good competition.[23] The new age ruling has also led to the establishment of two maverick junior leagues, one on the prairies and one in western Ontario.[24] The breakdown of junior hockey is a steep price to pay for the inability of the national association to conduct its own affairs in the face of NHL domination.

The NHL-CAHA agreements have hampered our hockey teams in international competition as well. The lengths to which the NHL may go to eliminate senior competition and protect its monopoly profits is readily demonstrated by its now successful attack on the Bauer experiment with the National Hockey Team. Prior to the 1964 Winter Olympic Games, the CAHA chose one of the top amateur teams in the country to represent Canada in international competition. Early in the 1960s, however, it became clear that a single amateur club, no matter how much it was supplemented by amateurs from other clubs, could no longer guarantee the success in international hockey that the Canadian public expected. The Russian, Czechoslovakian, German, and Swedish teams were steadily improving. Even the United States was entering teams equal to the best senior teams in Canada. At this time senior hockey in Canada was on the wane, particularly because of the opposition of the NHL.

In 1964, upon the initiative of the Reverend David Bauer, a truly national amateur team was selected and trained to represent Canada at the Olympics. An important component in the Bauer plan was that members of the National Team would be encouraged to combine university study with their hockey playing. In 1965 the team moved to Winnipeg, and two years later a second national team was formed and located in Ottawa. Although both these teams have proven far superior to any single senior team, they have been unable to regain Canada's supremacy in international hockey. In the 1969 World Tournament, Canada finished fifth. Largely as a result of these losses, a non-profit Hockey Canada Corporation has been established to finance and administer the National Team. Hockey Canada's first objective was to persuade the International Ice Hockey Federation to allow nine instantly reinstated professionals to play in international competition. The Montreal Canadiens and the Toronto Maple Leafs, both represented on Hockey Canada's Board of Directors, have promised to supply the players. Now that international hockey competition promises to be opened to professionals, the need for a specially trained national amateur team has disappeared. But all the same, it will be instructive to consider why that experiment failed.

It is popularly held that Canada could never have regained the world hockey championship with a team of amateurs, but was fated to the bottom of the world league until it could be represented by the NHL's professional players. Without question, the NHL exhibits the best players in the world, but that is not being contested. The real question is whether a team of specially prepared Canadian semi-professionals could beat the rest of the world. The NHL never gave Father Bauer a chance to prove his case.

If the National Team was to prosper, it had to include the top amateur players in the country. This the NHL never allowed it to do. In the 1967 NHL-CAHA agreement, the CAHA agreed that none of its teams (including the National Team) could "approach, negotiate or discuss employment with an unsigned drafted player before October 21 in any playing year without prior consent [of the NHL]." The NHL players' draft is simply a gentleman's agreement between member clubs not to negotiate with a player *drafted* by another club. But an *unsigned drafted player* is still an amateur player. By this clause, the National Team was prohibited from discussing hockey with the most talented young players until two months after it began its practices.[25] In another clause, the CAHA agreed not to use any of its player-development funds for the development of players for the National Team.[26] And finally to restrict the National Team, the CAHA national executive recently voted that "Canada's National Team not recruit junior-age hockey players," a ruling that eliminates 10,770 registered junior players as potential candidates for the team.[27] The Hockey Study Committee concluded, "It is rather tragic to note that professional hockey is obviously concerned about competition from one CAHA amateur team (the National Team) while it enters into agreement with the CAHA to develop to the highest possible level literally thousands of amateur teams from Senior to Bantam to serve its own purposes."[28] What is ahead for the National Team as selected and organized by Hockey Canada, is difficult to predict. Vis-à-vis the rest of the world, its performances can only improve. As professional players and unlimited body checking will now be permitted in international play, Canada should regain her world supremacy in the March 1970 tournament and should enjoy a playing edge for several years to come. The real problem will arise years later when the Europeans improve to the calibre of the Canadian-based NHL teams. Suppose Montreal, Toronto, and Vancouver all experience bad years. Can Hockey Canada get help from Chicago or Los Angeles? Not likely. At present only the Canadian-based teams contribute to the National Team, although Canadian citizens will continue to form most of the other eleven teams in the league. The NHL Players' Union has urged that all Canadian hockey players be allowed to play for Canada,[29] but the American-based teams are not expected to permit their players to participate. These US-based Canadians may even return to haunt us as members of the US National Team.

It has often been claimed that, without commercialization, Canadian hockey would never have become the national institution it now is, nor would Canadian hockey players be able to earn as much money from the game as they do today. But professional sport in other countries – British soccer, for example – has proven successful, without commercialization. Commercialization is not necessary for the success of professional sport. Yet it *is* necessarily responsible for the problems of Canadian hockey, the flight of the game to the United States, and the NHL's ruthless drive for monopoly. Once profit maximization became the goal of the NHL, it was inevitable that its leaders would transplant the game to the richer markets of the United States and seek monopoly control of the sport here in Canada. So that it could enjoy monopoly prices for its games, commercial hockey has driven good senior hockey out of business. So that it could dominate the supply of players, it has gained tight control over amateur hockey, with the result that hockey at the local level has been severely hampered and the Bauer experiment with the Canadian National Hockey Team has been sabotaged. It is perhaps difficult to believe that the same organization which brings us the Stanley Cup Playoffs each spring also works against what I have argued are the Canadian interests in hockey, but that conclusion is inescapable.

The true villains of the piece are not the owners of the NHL teams, but rather the institution of commercialized sport which they personify. Stafford Smythe and his colleagues on the NHL Board of Governors have not acted deliberately to depress Canadian hockey; they have merely tried to maximize profits for their hockey corporations. It is unfortunate that the by-products of these business decisions are so unpleasant. The profit motive simply should have no place in spectator sport. Since a sport like hockey is so much a part of the national culture and since the community contributes so much to the development of its athletes, the staging of hockey games should properly be a community enterprise.

To decommercialize Canadian hockey, each of the Canadian clubs should be compelled to become non-profit corporations. Several advantages would immediately ensue. A non-profit NHL team would plough back all its profits into community hockey. (Although the NHL now boasts about the sums of money it pays annually to the CAHA for player development, these payments appear to be small in relation to profits.[30] Such a change should also bring about a more open ticket selling policy. More significant benefits would depend, of course, upon the extent to which the teams abandon their profit maximization objectives and seek to become a community service. If professional hockey could assist schools and amateur clubs in the development of sportsmanlike hockey in Canada – and not simply publicize itself or interfere, as it does at present[31] – then the benefits would be tremendous.

To repatriate Canadian hockey, however, a more radical step is necessary: the creation of a truly national non-commercial professional hockey league with teams in at least a dozen Canadian cities. To get started, the Canadian league would immediately have to buy players away from the existing NHL, as the fledgling American Football League bought players from the established National Football League to get started several years ago. Government backing might initially be necessary, but I am confident the new league could soon stand on its own feet. The existing NHL clubs only *own* players ultimately because each of them have agreed not to seek another team's players. In fact, most players are on one-year contracts. The existing NHL will not give up its present monopoly without a tremendous struggle; but with determined leadership, the new league could be formed.

If hockey stays commercialized, the Canadian community will continue to be exploited by it, while the best brand of the sport will be marketed elsewhere. Change will be difficult to effect, however, and not only because of the opposition of the commercial sports operators and their apologists, the sports press.[32] Sport in Canada rarely generates its own change, but tends to be shaped by other forces in the society.[33] Until more Canadians become concerned about the effects of unregulated commercialism upon other aspects of Canadian society, it is unlikely they will ever be concerned about the effects of commercialism in sport.

Postscript

In the few weeks since this article went to the editor, American interests have moved one step closer to total control of the NHL. Three days before Christmas the Medical Investment Corporation of Minneapolis acquired majority ownership of the Vancouver Canucks and the NHL's fourteenth franchise. John Munro, the federal minister of health and welfare, has begun to express concern about "the apparent transfer of power in the NHL to US owners although our country is still and is likely to continue to be the main source of talent for US teams," but he is quite unwilling to challenge the NHL's power over Canadian hockey. In particular, he has condemned the National Team to dependence upon handouts from the NHL for its players. In a recent reply to suggestions that Hockey Canada hire Bobby Hull for the National Team, Munro said: "Now remember that Hockey Canada is representative; it includes the NHL. Mr. Hull has a contract with the NHL. Hockey Canada cannot encourage him to breach that contract unless it wants a war, financial and otherwise – and no co-operation from the NHL. *We know how a lack of co-operation in recent years hurt the National Team*" (italics mine).

At the moment the National Team's most serious antagonists are Canada's fellow members in the International Ice Hockey Federation who have just reversed their earlier decision to allow professional players in the 1970 World Championship. Canada has quite rightly refused to go along with this double-dealing and has withdrawn from the tournament. But we should not vent all our rage upon the opportunistic Europeans. After all, if the NHL had not already wrecked Canadian amateur and semi-professional hockey, the National Team would not be quite so dependent upon those professional players.

Footnotes

1. "Strangely enough, professional hockey as such did not begin in Canada, but in Houghton, Michigan, during the winter of 1903-04. A dentist, Dr. J. L. Gibson, introduced paid Canadian imports . . ." Nancy and Maxwell Howell, *Sports and Games in Canadian Life*, p. 206. As I shall explain shortly, in North America, *professional* hockey invariably means commercialized professional hockey.

2. The special economics of commercial sport has been described by the commissioner of the National Football League as follows: "On the playing field, member clubs of a professional sports league are clearly competitors – and every effort must be made to promote this. But in their business operations, member clubs of a league are less competitors than they are partners or participants in a joint venture . . . What sharply distinguishes member clubs of a sports league from ordinary businessmen joined together in a trade association is their predominant identity of interest. Whereas the ordinary businessman may view the business failure of a competitor with equanimity or even satisfaction, the members of the sports league cannot. This wholly alters the fundamentals of their relationship . . . Every sports league must come to terms with this recognition. In the NFL there are innumerable recognitions of this partnership principle." Peter Rozelle, "A Commissioner Comments on Anti-Trust in Sports," *Virginia Law Weekly*, June 4, 1964. Essentially the same case is presented as an economic model in J. C. H. Jones, "The Economics of the National Hockey League," *Canadian Journal of Economics*, February, 1969.

3. Nancy Howell and Maxwell L. Howell, *Sports and Games in Canadian Life*, Toronto, 1969, p. 60.

4. The six teams were the Boston Bruins, the Chicago Black Hawks, the Detroit Red Wings, the New York Americans, the New York Rangers, and the Pittsburgh Yellow Jackets.

5. Frank J. Selke, *Behind the Cheering*, Toronto, 1962, p. 102.

6. I am aware of only two such barriers in sport. In the Canadian Football League each of the nine commercial clubs has agreed to play no more than fourteen American players on its team at a single time. In the National Collegiate Athletic Association in the United States, foreign athletes over the age of twenty-three are ineligible for official competition.

7. The five teams are the Montreal Canadiens (NHL); the Montreal Voyageurs (American Hockey League), a Canadiens farm team which began operation in 1969, the Quebec Aces (AHL); the Toronto Maple Leafs (NHL); and the Vancouver Canucks (Western Hockey League).

8. The ten US NHL teams are the Boston Bruins, Chicago Black Hawks, Detroit Red Wings, Los Angeles Kings, Minnesota North Stars, New York Rangers, Oakland Seals, Philadelphia Flyers, Pittsburgh Penguins, and St. Louis Blues.

9. "Kidd Attack on Pro Sport Called Off Track," *Telegram*, Toronto, September 9, 1969. In a subsequent statement Mr. Campbell said that the N.H.L. only continues to operate from Canada to avoid harassment from congressional investigation in the United States. "US Legal Climate against NHL Moving," *Globe and Mail*, Toronto, October 14, 1969.

10. Christina McCall Newman, ed., *The Man from Oxbow: The Best of Ralph Allen*, Toronto, 1967, p. 18. See also Frank Moritsugu, "Let the Probers Look at THIS Religion," *Toronto Daily Star*, April 17, 1965.

11. Jones, "Economics of the National Hockey League," pp. 18-19. Also "By Dick Beddoes," *Globe and Mail*, January 21, 1969. Clarence Campbell has said that Canadian public opinion forced the league to guarantee one of the new franchises to Vancouver. "NHL hand forced by Voice of People," *Toronto Daily Star*, September 12, 1969. But I suspect that television revenues played a significant role in this decision too. CBS has been losing money on its contract with the NHL and W. C. McPhail, its vice-president for sports, has said that unless the rating for hockey telecasts improves, the present one-year contract will not be renewed. "NHL Given One Year to Attract TV Fans," *Toronto Daily Star*, August 5, 1969. With the immediate prospects for television revenue diminishing, the importance of a strong franchise, self-sufficient at the box office, becomes much greater. Although it cannot offer much television revenue, Vancouver is likely to sell all of its seats. When five of the six present expansion clubs are losing money, that old-fashioned box-office revenue Vancouver promises can be very appealing.

12. "Kids Turning to U.S. Colleges," *Telegram*, March 24, 1969; "Only Two Junior Hockey Clubs Escape U.S. Raiding Parties," *Globe and Mail*, September 6, 1969.

13. "U.S. TV Networks Still Dictates NHL Playoff Times," *Toronto Daily Star*, September 25, 1968.

14. *Report on Amateur Hockey in Canada by the Hockey Study Committee of the National Advisory Council on Fitness and Amateur Sport*, Ottawa, 1967, p. 10. Referred to hereafter as *First Report*. A more popular explanation for the decline of senior hockey is television, but the Hockey Study Committee indicates that the decline was well advanced by 1954, before television was widesprad in Canada.

15. For example, Australia, where in Melbourne alone thirty-six professional football clubs operate successfully.

16. *First Report*, p. 10.

17. *Report on Amateur Hockey in Canada by the Hockey Study Committee of the National Advisory Council on Fitness and Amateur Sport*, Ottawa, 1968, pp. 9-10. Referred to hereafter as *Final Report*.

18. "Fathers, Mothers, Punch Imlach, Are the Curse of Kids' Hockey," *Toronto Daily Star*, January 21, 1965. Also Newman, ed., *The Man from Oxbow*, pp. 18-20.

19. *First Report*, pp. 15-16.

20. *Ibid.*, p. 27. The comparison was made with the assistance of the Carnegie Data Bank of Information about Ontario secondary school students.

21. *Final Report*, pp. 13-14.

22. "NHL in Control, CAHA Requests Age Limit Boost for Its Juniors," *Globe and Mail*, January 29, 1969.

23. "Kids Turning to U.S. Colleges," *Telegram*, March 24, 1969.

24. "CAHA Rebel Sees Growth in Ontario," *Globe and Mail*, January 29, 1969.

25. *Final Report*, p. 6.

26. *Ibid.*

27. *Ibid.*, p. 5.

28. *Ibid.*, p. 6.

29. "Players Association Wants 25 Best in NHL to Play Russians," *Globe and Mail*, May 30, 1969.

30. The CAHA receives about $800,000 annually from the NHL and its affiliates, or about $20,000 per commercial team. For the six month's period ending February 28, 1969, Maple Leaf Gardens declared a profit of $810,090 or $1.10 per share. At the time, a single share was selling for about $28.

31. One constructive – albeit commercial – contribution some professional players are making to Canadian hockey is the establishment of summer hockey schools. If these could be co-ordinated with community recreation programmes, even more boys could enjoy this specialized form of instruction.

32. A few sports journalists have complained about the size of commercial sport's profits, however. See, for example, Melvin Durslag, "Owners Want Blood and the Law Helps," *Toronto Daily Star*, September 20, 1969. For an illuminating account of the mechanics of sports promotion, see Bruce A. MacFarlane, "The Sociology of Sports Promotion," unpublished MA thesis, McGill University, August, 1955.

33. It is questionable whether sport has been a force for change in any society. I know of only one case where sportsmen en masse have been in the vanguard of social change. In 1848, when Prussia invaded the German State of Baden to suppress Baden's newly promulgated liberal constitution, the Hanau Turnverein, a sport club, sent 300 armed gymnasts to repel the invaders. P. C. McIntosh, *Sport in Society*, London, 1963, p. 189.

5 Deviant Behaviour and The Administration of Justice

No book dealing with critical issues in Canada would be complete without a section on deviant behaviour and the problems that relate to it.

While it is clear that all deviance has one common element, someone adjudged it as such, this label subsumes an exceedingly wide range of behaviour, that is performed by all kinds of people with many different motivations in a wide variety of circumstances. The particular acts of people that are labelled deviant are subject to significant variations over time, from culture to culture, and even from group to group or individual to individual within a given society.

The criminal law itself treats a number of kinds of behaviour as deviant, but at the same time it can be said that all of the behaviours that are proscribed by the criminal law are not necessarily considered deviant by all or in some cases even a majority of people in the society as a whole. Likewise, there are some kinds of behaviour that may not fall under the jurisdiction of the criminal law, but which are generally felt to be deviant by a large proportion of people in the society, and sanctioned accordingly.

For this chapter, we have chosen articles that illustrate some, although by no means all, important issues in the area of deviant behaviour at the societal level. Each section meets the criterion of importance in a slightly different way.

Crime and delinquency refer to violations of the law by adults and juveniles. Such behaviour has been of traditional and chronic concern in our society. Explanations of crime and delinquency have been difficult to formulate as a result of the fact that these labels subsume such a wide variety of activities whose prevalence frequently seems to be differentially distributed throughout society, although the cause of that variation is not at all clear. The articles selected for this section are aimed at describing and trying to understand some of these differences.

Approximately ninety percent of all adult Canadians use alcohol, a behaviour pattern that for most persons is in conformity with the norms of the groups to which they belong. However, the consumption of alcohol leads to health and social problems for hundreds of thousands of Canadians who become alcoholics. The distinction between those who use alcohol and those who abuse it is not easily or clearly defined. We have selected articles for this section that reflect these facts and underlying problems.

A short time ago the widespread use of a variety of drugs by adolescents was not a critical issue in Canadian society. Today, it is at the center of a great debate in which social and medical, as well as moral and legal issues are involved. The articles chosen for this section document the extent and patterns of drug use among young people across Canada, and on the basis of these data suggest principles from which prevention programs might evolve.

Perhaps the most crucial issue underlying the occurrence of high levels of deviant and criminal behaviour in a society is what is to be done about it. Of particular concern in democratic societies is the manner in which such behaviour can be dealt with within the prevailing notions of justice. The articles in the last section attempt to document some of the specific kinds of problems that arise when an attempt is made to maintain social order and, at the same time, protect the rights and liberties of individuals within the society. While the whole scope of criminal justice can hardly be dealt with in a single subsection, we have attempted to include materials that relate specifically to the kinds of problems that were dealt with in the earlier sections of this chapter.

A. Crime and Delinquency

The first part of P. J. Giffen's article on "Rates of Crime and Delinquency" in Canada, presents a summary analysis of the kinds of problems that surround the gathering, use, and interpretation of available statistics in this area. The discussion provides a background against which the data he presents can be meaningfully understood and interpreted. With these problems in mind, Giffen proceeds to give a comprehensive overview of crime and delinquency throughout the country. Data are provided on crimes known to the police and also characteristics of persons who have been convicted of crime. The author notes that the populations represented at each of these stages may be substantially different from the populations of people who actually commit criminal or delinquent acts. The data show variations in crime rates over time, as well as by region, province, and rural-urban areas in Canada. Employing conviction data, Giffen examines differences among persons who have been found guilty of criminal or delinquent acts according to the background characteristics of age, sex, place of residence, education, religion, and country of birth.

In the next selection, Lynn McDonald raises the question: "Is the Crime Rate Increasing?" and then conducts a statistical test on the conventional notion that it is. On the basis of her analysis of conviction rates for various offence categories between 1950 and 1960, the author concludes that "the alarmed discussion of swiftly rising crime rates is simply not warranted." Where minor increases in rates have occurred, they tend to be for the less serious acts such as summary conviction offences and parking violations. For rates of more serious crimes in general as well as for specific crimes of violence, the data do not support the contention that the crime rate is on the increase. McDonald goes on to test the relationship between crime rates and size of police force, feeling that "the efforts made by society to apprehend and prosecute criminals" might influence the crime rate. After examining the material related to this hypothesis, she concludes that rates for violent offences are not positively correlated to the size of the police force, while for non-violent offences only breaking and entering increases as the size of the police contingent increases.

While delinquency is traditionally thought of as a *lower class* phenomenon, more and more attention is being directed toward the study of delinquent behaviour at other levels of the class structure. This re-focussing can be attributed in part to the realization that much of the difference that had long been observed in the delinquency patterns of lower as opposed to middle and upper class adolescents is far less a function of real differences in behaviour than it is of differential access to, or treatment by, the legal system. Edmond Vaz in "Juvenile Delinquency in Middle-Class Youth Culture," presents and analyzes data on the "self reported delinquency" of middle class high school boys from four different Canadian communities. Vaz emphasizes "the relationship between differential delinquency involvement and (a) the active participation of boys in legitimate teen-age activities, and (b) their peer orientation." In the process he develops a strong argument for the existence of a middle class youth culture that is highly supportive of delinquent behavior among middle class adolescents, regardless of whether or not that delinquency is ever officially recorded as such.

B. Alcohol Use and Alcoholism

Jan de Lint's "Alcohol Use in Canadian Society." discusses the distribution of alcohol use in terms of its implication for health and other problems related to drinking. One principal finding in this article is that the statistical distribution of alcohol use is not characterized by clustering of drinkers around certain levels of consumption. Rather, the distribution is smooth, and remarkably stable. This indicates that the way to reduce the number of problem drinkers at the heavy consumption levels is to reduce per capita consumption.[1] De Lint indicates that approximately 10 million Canadians use alcohol at least occasionally.

While not all persons who are characterized as heavy drinkers become alcoholics, it is certainly from the ranks of the heavy drinkers that many alcoholics are drawn. However, quantity and frequency of consumption are not the only criteria for alcoholism; drinking practices prevalent in the society, and interference with social and physical functioning are also to be considered. Wolfgang Schmidt, in his article "The Prevalence of Alcoholism in Canada," addresses himself to issues related to the definition and measurement of alcoholism. He examines the prevalence of alcoholism in different countries and in the provinces of Canada. Schmidt gives special attention to what are perhaps the most thorough epidemiological studies of alcohol use anywhere. They were conducted in Frontenac County in Eastern Ontario during the 1950's and 1960's, and they produced valuable information about what happens to problem drinkers over extended periods of time.

Footnote

1. The article presented here provides a general statement about the use of alcohol. Interested readers are referred to more specific and technical papers appearing elsewhere.
De Lint, Jan E., and Schmidt, Wolfgang, "The Distribution of Alcohol Consumption in Ontario," *Quarterly Journal of Studies on Alcohol*, 29, December, 1968, pp. 968-973.
Lederman, S., "Alcool, alcoolisme, alcoolisation: Donnés scientifiques de caractère physiologique, économique et social," Institut National d'Etudes Démographique, Travaux et Documents, Cahier No. 29, Paris: Presses Universitaires de France, 1956.

Schmidt, Wolfgang, and de Lint, Jan E., "Estimating the Prevalence of Alcoholism from Alcohol Consumption and Mortality Data," *Quarterly Journal of Studies on Alcohol*, 31, December, 1970, pp. 957-964.

Smart, Reginald G. and Schmidt, Wolfgang, "Blood Alcohol Levels in Drivers not Involved in Accidents," *Quarterly Journal of Studies on Alcohol*, 31, December, 1970, pp. 968-971.

C. Drug Use and Abuse

The use of alcohol and alcoholism are phenomena that have been with us for a long time. The late 1960's witnessed the onset of a chemical revolution among many young people in North America. The use of drugs among adolescents became something that was no longer restricted to minority group youths from the ghettos of large urban centres. Kids of all ages and from all social class backgrounds began to *turn on* using not only the drugs of their parents' generation (for example, alcohol, tranquilizers and stimulants) but they also exploited the pharmacopoeia of underground chemists and illicit drug distributors. Not long after adolescents were smoking pot, dropping acid, and doing speed and junk, parents, school officials, and law enforcement agents learned of the growing popularity of marihuana, LSD, methamphetamine, and heroin. Several surveys have been conducted from coast to coast in order to ascertain the extent of drug use among students. These are reviewed by Reginald G. Smart and Dianne Fejer in "The Extent of Illicit Drug Use in Canada: A Review of Current Epidemiology." While these surveys are of uneven quality and generalizability they nonetheless document that though the use of drugs among students is far from universal it is certainly widespread and no section of Canada is immune.

One of these community studies is also presented in this section. Whitehead's surveys of drug using practices among students in Halifax are the only such studies conducted at two points in time one year apart. "The Epidemiology of Drug Use in a Canadian City at Two Points in Time: Halifax, 1969-1970" clearly points out that the rates of use of a variety of drugs, especially hallucinogenic drugs, is increasing very rapidly. It is suggested that the popularity of experimenting with marihuana is becoming part of the general youth culture and is no longer restricted to an insulated drug culture.

There are many implications for increasing rates of drug use among students. Not the least of these is that drug use is a general phenomenon rather than a specific activity differentially focussed on certain chemicals. The article by Smart, et al., "The Prevention of Drug Abuse by Young People: An Argument Based on the Distribution of Drug Use," demonstrates that the total frequency of drug use in a number of different high school populations has the same kind of distribution that describes the consumption of alcohol. That is, most users are light users, fewer are moderate users, and even fewer are heavy users. This situation prevails in communities that have considerably different average rates of drug use and in the same community at two points in time when rates of drug use differ. Prevention of drug abuse in the next generation is dependent on reducing the per capita consumption of the general public, and per capita consumption can only be reduced when many people modify their drug using habits. Prevention programmes to date have not been based on such a principle and this may well be a reason why they have been so ineffective.

D. Selected Problems in the Administration of Justice

This section begins with the Canadian Committee on Corrections' statement of the "Basic Principles and Purposes of Criminal Justice." In this selection the Committee sets forth a series of "propositions as indicating the proper scope and function of the criminal and correctional processes." These propositions provide an interesting focus for an analysis of some of the problems that exist in the administration of justice in democratic societies such as ours. The conflicts between ideals surrounding individual rights and liberties and the practical objectives of maintaining order in a complex society are felt most acutely in countries where personal freedoms are as important as the maintenance of social order and control.

John Hogarth's "Towards the Improvement of Sentencing in Canada," provides some valuable insights into the sentencing process as it presently exists in Canada, along with recommendations on how it might be brought more in line with the objectives of crime prevention and control. One of the major problems in the present sentencing structure is that although there continues to be noticeable lack of professional training in the magistrates' courts, they are nonetheless vested with an enormous amount of discretionary power. Hogarth also points to the very high utilization of imprisonment in Canada in comparison to other countries, restrictions on the use of probation, reliance on fixed-term type sentencing, and the lack of uniformity in sentencing, as additional factors that tend to undermine the objectives of the criminal law.

Margaret Hughes discusses "The Role of Law in the Control of Alcohol and Drug Use." In doing so she raises a number of points concerning the difficulties in applying legal restrictions to the drinking and drug use of individuals. In reviewing past efforts aimed at the legal control of drug use and drinking behaviour, the author raises a number of relevant points concerning the fine line between *reasonable interference* resulting in the denial of individual liberties, and the actual effects of attempts to legislate in the area of alcohol and drug use.

"Criminal Law and Non-Medical Drug Use," which is part of the interim report of the LeDain Commission, contains a detailed discussion of the appropriateness of the criminal law in this area. The commission outlines the basic legal-philosophical arguments for and against legal intervention against individuals who use drugs, and sets forth a series of recommendations based on the committee's findings up to that time.

In the final selection, Boydell and Grindstaff attempt to document "Public Attitudes Toward Legal Sanctions for Drug and Abortion Offences." In doing so they emphasize the importance of maintaining a reasonable balance between public sentiment and legal sanctions in democratic societies. This is particularly difficult in those borderline areas of the criminal code, such as abortion and drug use, that are presently the object of widespread controversy. In addition to presenting data for the sample as a whole concerning the specific legal sanctions that respondents feel should be given for a variety of drug and abortion offences, the data are also cross-tabulated according to their background

443

characteristics. This permits the authors to describe differences in severity of sanctions applied according to the variables of age, education, income, religion, and religious attendance.

Rates of Crime and Delinquency*

P. J. Giffen

It is one of the less important paradoxes of our time that most discussions of criminal statistics begin with the expression of grave doubts about the reliability of the official figures and then present these statistics in various combinations as if they faithfully portrayed the real world. Apparently nobody is happy about the state of criminal statistics, but no serious student of criminology can get along without them. There is no easy or immediate way out of this dilemma. If generalizations are to be made about the amount of crime and the number of criminals, these facts must, with rare exceptions, be derived from the statistics published by government departments. The generalizations may become less speculative as the agencies collecting the statistics bring about more adequate returns from reporting bodies, and as empirical studies yield formulae for estimating the ratio of actual to reported crime. Meanwhile, responsible writers will continue to emphasize the limitations when they present criminal statistics.

Sources of Canadian Statistics

The Judicial Section of the Dominion Bureau of Statistics is responsible for collecting national statistics on crime and delinquency in Canada and for preparing the annual volumes of the various series of statistical publications.

Police Statistics, published annually from 1920 to 1959, brings together information derived from police departments throughout the country. Of direct interest to the student of crime are the tables of offences known to the police, by the type of offence and locality, as well as the information on the number of arrests or summonses and the number of prosecutions for each type of offence. Starting with the 1960 series, this information is organized in a separate bulletin, *Crime Statistics*, and the other information on police matters is published in two companion volumes, *Police Administration Statistics* and *Traffic Enforcement Statistics*. The changes are part of recent efforts by D.B.S. to improve all the annual statistics dealing with the administration of justice. A new system of uniform crime-reporting, developed in co-operation with a committee of the Canadian Association of Chiefs of Police, has resulted in more reliable information on crimes known to the police since 1962.

The steps taken to increase the proportion of police departments filing returns appear to have had some success. Whereas in 1956 only 276 police departments

*Article by P. J. Giffen, from *Crime and Its Treatment in Canada*, 1965, edited by W. T. McGrath, by permission of The Macmillan Company of Canada Limited.

reported, the situation was described as follows in the Introduction to *Crime Statistics, 1960*:

> Monthly reports were received from 767 departments representing 80.6 percent of potential contributors. There were 108 departments or 11.3 percent who submitted less than twelve monthly reports and 77 departments or 8.1 percent who did not report.

Reports from the Quebec Provincial Police had not been received by 1961, but, according to the Introduction to *Crime Statistics, 1961* (the latest available at the time of writing), that police force would commence reporting in 1962. Until all police departments report regularly, police statistics cannot be used to determine the amount of crime on a national basis.

The quality of the reporting also remains such as to raise doubts about the validity of the information, as the following note in the Introduction to *Crime Statistics, 1961* indicates:

> The data published in the tables of this report leave much to be desired in the way of completeness and uniformity, even though there has been some improvement in recent years.

An examination of some of the figures in the 1960 and 1961 *Crime Statistics* reveals differences between large urban centres that make sense only if interpreted as reflecting differences between police departments in the classification of offences and the adequacy of reporting. In Table 1 the numbers of crimes of four major types known to the police of Montreal, Toronto, and Vancouver are compared for the two years. The population reported to be under the jurisdiction of each police department in 1961 is indicated under the name of the city.

TABLE 1

Selected Offences "Known to the Police" of Montreal, Toronto, and Vancouver, 1960 and 1961

Offence	Montreal (1,155,178) 1960	1961	Toronto (1,595,809) 1960	1961	Vancouver (376,808) 1960	1961
Theft	13,265	21,532	33,277	31,694	14,212	13,875
Breaking and Entering	4,933	6,644	8,138	7,157	4,698	4,752
Fraud	18	6	2,536	2,836	60	50
Assault Causing Bodily Harm	99	637	1,159	1,220	242	202

Source: Dominion Bureau of Statistics, *Crime Statistics 1960* and *1961*.

It seems unlikely that Montreal actually experienced such a dramatic increase in thefts between 1960 and 1961, since the other two cities showed a declining number. An increase in the efficiency of reporting appears to be involved; this impression is strengthened by the disproportionate increase also shown in the cases of breaking and entering and of serious assaults in Montreal. The enormous discrepancy between Toronto and the other two cities in known cases of fraud points to the conclusion that similar offences may be differently classified by police departments; many offences that would be regarded as frauds in Toronto may, for example, be classified as thefts in Vancouver and Montreal. The relative rarity of "assault causing bodily harm" in Montreal may be due to the tendency of the police to classify such offences as *common assault*. Whatever the reason for the discrepancies, their existence makes the statistics of limited usefulness for research.

Statistics obtained from the courts are published annually by D.B.S. in two series, *Statistics of Criminal and Other Offences* and *Juvenile Delinquents*. Whereas the police statistics on offences can tell us nothing of the characteristics of offenders, the courts can provide data on the sex, age, marital status, residence, ethnic origin, and several other characteristics of the people who appear before them, as well as information on the disposition of cases. Moreover, the classification of offences can be based on the judicial process instead of on the judgment of the police.

In Canada, the value of court statistics is enhanced by a Criminal Code that applies throughout the country, and by an integrated system of court jurisdictions. The United States Bureau of Census attempted to collect court statistics from 1932 onward, but the published series, *Judicial Criminal Statistics*, came to an end in 1945 because of war conditions, "plus the more important fact that the series as it was being conducted was not a success and could not offer reliable measurements of what the courts did."[1] The main obstacles were the failure of many courts to report and the difficulty on interpreting the returns in the light of differences in criminal law between states.

Comparison of police statistics in Canada with the two series based on the courts shows that a higher proportion of judicial districts than police jurisdictions have reported, and that the number of judicial districts reporting has varied less over time. Although in recent years no judicial district in the country has failed to report, according to the statistics, some courts within districts have apparently been remiss. A mimeographed note provided with *Statistics of Criminal and Other Offences, 1959*, indicates this:

> The number of adults appearing before the courts charged with indictable offences in 1959 was 34,812, an apparent decrease from the 1958 figure of 38,415. This may be partially explained by the failure of several courts, including that of a large urban centre, to submit returns to the Dominion Bureau of Statistics.

Correctional institutions at various levels are a third source of information on criminal matters. Since 1937, in accordance with an agreement between D.B.S. and the Department of Justice, penitentiary statistics have been collected and tabulated by D.B.S. and published in the annual report of the Commissioner of Penitentiaries.

Prior to 1957, general information on the population of correctional institutions of all types was included in a section of *Statistics of Criminal and Other Offences*. In 1961 a separate volume entitled *Correctional Institutions Statistics, 1957-1959* appeared, containing tables on total population and population movements by province and type of institution (but nothing on the characteristics of the prisoners). Annual volumes containing similar information have appeared since. Recently, committees of the Canadian Corrections Association have collaborated with D.B.S. in planning much more extensive annual series on institutional populations. Annual series on training-schools, adult prisons, probation, parole, and after-care are expected to result from these deliberations.

Criminal Statistics as Samples

If criminal statistics are to be used as indices of amounts and types of crime or of numbers and characteristics of criminals, we must take into account that they describe only a sample of the universe of offences or offenders. The problem does not exist if we adopt a strictly legalistic position and say, in effect, that no act can be called a crime until a court of law has declared it so, and no person can be called a criminal until a court has found him guilty. Few students of the subject would be willing to observe this restrictive ordinance if it meant giving up an interest in the actual incidence of potentially punishable acts and potentially culpable perpetrators.

Unfortunately, the ratio of the known to the unknown is a mystery, and probably differs by time and place and type of offence.*Crimes known to the police* are obviously only a portion of the total crimes committed. The vested interests of the offender, the victim, the police, and the local government may combine in various ways to determine whether the offence ever becomes part of a statistical table. It seems likely that bank robberies, for example, rarely go unreported by the victim, whereas many cases of rape, incest, and blackmail are never revealed to the police. Where the *victim* is a willing participant, as he is usually in gambling, bootlegging, and prostitution, the appearance of the act as a *crime known to the police* will depend largely upon the initiative of the law-enforcement authorities; policies of enforcement in these spheres are notoriously variable.

When we proceed from the official statistical debut of the act as a *crime known to the police* to the appearance in the statistics of a conviction and the appearance of the offender as a convicted person, additional selective forces intervene. Somebody must be arrested, charged, brought to trial, and found guilty – a series of steps that involves numerous contingencies. Hence, the statistics derived from the courts are an even smaller sample than the *crimes known*. The relative size of the sample apparently varies with the type of crime. In 1960 the thefts known to the police numbered 159,299; the number of cases concluded was 62,366, or 39.1 percent. The number of prosecutions was in the ratio of 89 percent of the number of arrests and summonses. In contrast, the number of concluded cases of assault causing bodily harm was in the ratio of 77 percent of the offences known to the police, and the prosecutions were in the ratio of 93 percent of the arrests and summonses. While these exact ratios should not be taken seriously without a thorough examination of the statistics, they do indicate a considerable difference between crimes as regards the probability of their appearing in court statistics.

The drop in numbers between the reporting of offences and the registration of court convictions is probably much greater for juveniles than for adult offenders. In dealing with juveniles the police may handle the matter without laying a charge, or the court may consider advisable the withdrawing of the charge in favour of an unrecorded disposition – that is, the matter is settled informally without a finding of delinquency being entered on the record. In 1944 an attempt was made to ascertain the frequency of the latter practice.[2] Only thirty-six courts supplied information, but the figures showed that, for every three cases given a formal hearing, four were handled informally, as *occurrences*. Changing methods of dealing with delinquents may explain many of the apparent fluctuations in rates of delinquency. In 1950 the province of Quebec passed the Schools for the Protection of Youth Act, which provided an alternative procedure to that of the Juvenile Delinquents Act. If the young person is found to be *in need of protection*, he does not appear in the statistics as a delinquent. The dramatic decrease in Quebec's delinquency rate from 202 per 100,000 in 1950 to 87 per 100,000 in 1952 may be, in large part, due to the use of this alternative. We have no way of estimating how widely alternative methods of dealing with juvenile offenders are used in other provinces, but the trend appears to be in this direction. The official statistics on delinquency may increasingly underestimate the incidence of illegal acts by juveniles.

Between the conviction of offenders and their statistical appearance in the prison population, the sample declines very sharply. Of the adults convicted in Canada in 1960 for indictable offences, 35.2 percent were sentenced to jail, 5.3 percent to reformatory, 0.6 percent to training-school, and 8.3 percent to penitentiary. The prison population is a highly select group of individuals.

While a damning case can be made for the inadequacy of criminal statistics as facts about representative samples, it does not follow that they must be abandoned for research purposes. Pending the extensive study that will be necessary to determine which statistics are most reliable and what inferences are justified, certain obvious precautions can be observed. One is to take seriously only fairly large differences in rates, and to check whether these differences agree with other evidence, including the findings in comparable jurisdictions. The statistics on other more reliably reported forms of deviant behaviour of which rates are known to correlate with rates of crime may give clues as to the reliability of the criminal statistics. Another precaution when calculating rates is to offset the possible fluctuations in enforcement and reporting from year to year by using averages for a number of years.

The Calculation of Rates

The convention in studying criminal statistics has been to convert absolute figures to per capita rates. Although the practice is followed here, the tacit assumption that the ratio of crime to population is a measure of *criminality* is not valid since it implies that the opportunity (or provocation, or *temptation*) is constant. The fallacy is demonstrated in Table 2.

TABLE 2

Convictions for Impaired Driving (Summary and Indictable) in Quebec and Ontario, 1956

	Quebec	Ontario
Convictions for Impaired Driving per 100,000 pop. 16 years and over	105	152
Convictions per 100,000 Licensed Motor Vehicles	360	331

Source: P. J. Giffen, "Canadian Criminal Statistics" in *C.P.S.A. Conference on Statistics, 1960,* Papers. Toronto: University of Toronto Press, 1962, p. 80.

Since Ontario has more motor vehicles than Quebec, the use of the number of motor vehicles as the measure of opportunity gives a quite different picture of the tendency to break highway laws than does a rate based on population.

In constructing rates for embezzlement or theft by conversion, to take another example, the proclivity for this form of larceny might be measured by using the number of positions of financial trust as a base. Only for crimes against the person is population clearly the measure of opportunity.

To calculate opportunity rates for many crimes, however, we would need information that is not now made available. The nature of the information contained at present in official statistics reflects the preoccupation of criminologists with the reformation or rehabilitation of the individual criminal. The implicit assumption that this is the prime or only method of coping with criminals has led to an overwhelming concern with the characteristics of criminals and a neglect of information on the nature of crimes and the situations in which they are committed. We can, for example, find in official statistics information on the sex, age, and ethnic origin of convicted thieves but nothing on what was stolen, from whom, and under what circumstances. Most criminal statistics tell us nothing about the victims of crimes, although the importance for research of this information has often been stressed. Until such data are available, we have no alternative but to use per capita rates. They are probably the most useful compromise in dealing with totals that embody a variety of crimes, each of which could conceivably have a different measure of opportunity.

Whether the rates that can be calculated are convictions per capita or convicted persons per capita will depend upon the tabulating units used in the official statistics. Since 1949, *Statistics of Criminal and Other Offences* has used "persons convicted" as the unit for tabulating information on offenders convicted of indictable offences; this is obviously much less misleading than "convictions," which could cause an individual to appear in a table several times. For offences punishable on summary conviction, the less serious but more numerous offences, "convictions" are still used as the tabulating units. The unit for compiling juvenile delinquency data is a compromise between "persons" and "convictions" called "appearances resulting in a finding of delinquency." The juvenile who is convicted of several offences at one appearance is listed only once, according to the most serious offence, but if he appears in court later in the same year on another charge he becomes, statistically, an additional delinquent. In 1961, the 15,215 appearances resulting in a finding of delinquency involved 13,358 children, so that the use of this unit for compiling social data does not appear to be seriously misleading.

The conversion of absolute figures on crime to per capita rates also depends on the availability in other sources – this usually means census materials – of statistics on the general population that are organized in classes similar or convertible to those of the criminal statistics. Many per capita rates can be computed only for the years of the regular Census of Canada, held in the first year of each decade (1941, 1951, etc.). Rates by religion, birthplace, and years of education are of this type. The much more limited Census of Population and Agriculture, conducted in the fifth year after the regular census (as in 1956), provides a basis for rates by age, sex, and marital status for most of the significant geographical units. Rates by age and sex for the provinces can be calculated for the intercensal years on the basis of the *Estimates of Population*, published periodically by the Dominion Bureau of Statistics.

Variations in Rates of Crime and Delinquency

Differences over Time

The alarming view that crime and delinquency, as well as other forms of deviance, are continually increasing seems to be widely accepted, but the official statistics give no indication of a dramatic increase over the last couple of decades. Figure 1 shows the average annual rates of delinquency for seven five-year periods between 1926 and 1960. Apparently rates of delinquency went down during the depression, rose to a new high during World War II, declined to a low in 1951-5, and rose again in 1956-60. The decline during the depression and the rise during wartime appears to have been a universal phenomenon in industrialized societies. The common element among the numerous explanations is that family supervision was relatively strict during the depression period, when adults spent much time at home, and relatively lax during wartime, when work, service in the armed forces, and recreation drew people from the home. The fact that delinquency rates in Canada did not

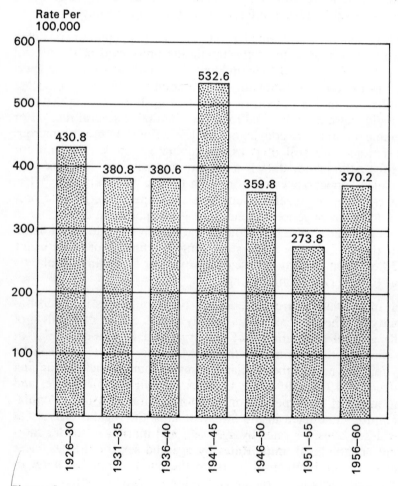

Figure 1

Rates of Juvenile Delinquency, Canada, Five-year Averages, 1926-60

Source: D.B.S. annual publication, *Juvenile Delinquents.*

increase from 1951 to 1960 as they did in the United States may be explained in part by the increasing proportion of Canadian cases that were handled without formal adjudication.

The adult rates of conviction for indictable offences for the longer period from 1901 to 1960 (see Figure 2) show an over-all trend of increase, or of better reporting, or of both. An increase over this period might legitimately be expected in view of the transformation of Canada from a predominantly rural to a predominantly urban society. The rates rose during the depression and dropped during World War II, the reverse of the juvenile pattern. In recent years they appear to have been rising again.

The belief that crimes of violence have increased dramatically is not borne out by Figure 3. The rate of "offences against the person" has remained at a low level, which means that such offences are a smaller percentage of the total than in earlier years. "Offences against property with violence" have apparently increased in recent years, but it should be noted that 90 percent of the offences thus classified are simple cases of breaking and entering, with no weapons used and without actual violence – an affluent society in which the

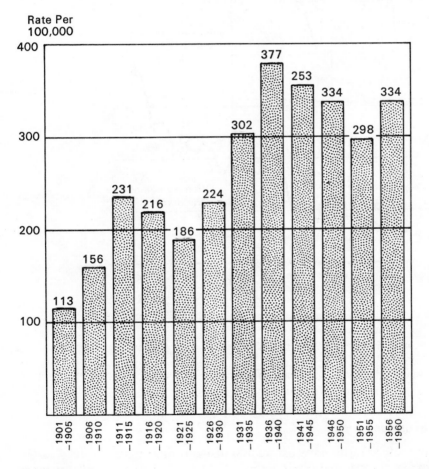

Figure 2

Rates of Conviction for Indictable Offences, Canada, Five-year Averages, 1901-60.

Source: D.B.S. annual publication, *Statistics of Criminal and Other Offences*.

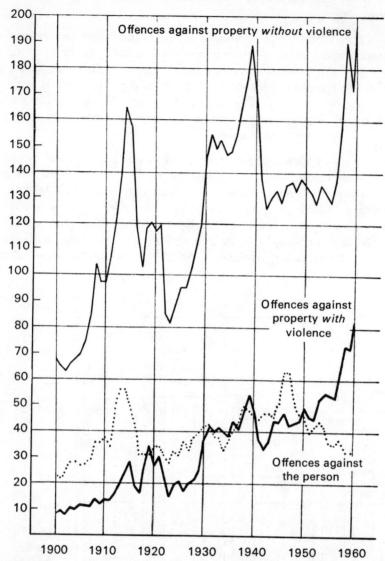

Rate Per 100,000

Offences against property *without* violence

Offences against property *with* violence

Offences against the person

Figure 3

Changes in Rates of Convictions for Three Major Classes of Indictable Offences, Canada, 1900-60.

Source: D.B.S. annual publication, *Statistics of Criminal and Other Offences.*

average householder possesses valuable and easily portable goods presents a high degree of opportunity for this type of offence.

Sex Differences

"Few, if any, other traits have as great statistical importance as does sex in differentiating criminals and non-criminals."[3] In Table 3, the sex differences in rates of persons convicted for indictable offences in the periods 1951-6 and 1957-61 are shown for Canada and the provinces. (The provinces are arranged in rank-order by total rate in 1961.) A considerable difference between the crime-rates for men and for women is found in all provinces, but the ratio of men to women varies in marked fashion between provinces. In these rates, as in so many others, the figures for Canada as a whole mask a notable disparity between regions.

TABLE 3

Persons Convicted of Indictable Offences by Sex, for Canada and Provinces: Average of Annual Convictions 1951-6 and 1957-61 per 100,000 Population 16 Years and Older of Each Sex

	1951-56*			1957-61†		
	Males	Females	Ratio	Males	Females	Ratio
Canada (excluding Yukon and N.W.T.)	537	36	15/1	558	41	14/1
Alberta	617	47	13/1	800	66	12/1
British Columbia	714	59	12/1	774	73	11/1
Manitoba	524	62	8/1	545	61	9/1
Ontario	647	43	15/1	594	46	13/1
Nova Scotia	629	31	20/1	544	31	18/1
Saskatchewan	358	21	17/1	439	27	16/1
Newfoundland	451	34	13/1	426	38	11/1
Quebec	422	25	17/1	424	22	19/1
New Brunswick	442	14	30/1	493	17	29/1
Prince Edward Island	419	16	26/1	227	4	57/1

Sources:
*P. J. Giffen, *op. cit.*, p. 82.
†Dominion Bureau of Statistics, *Statistics of Criminal and Other Offences, 1957-61*; *Census of Canada, 1961*; *Population Estimates, 1952-60.*

Since the rates for males follow, with minor exceptions, the differences between provinces in total rates, discussion of them can be left for the section on provincial differences. The female rates vary from province to province. The wide difference in sex ratios, ranging from 8/1 in Manitoba in 1951-6 to 57/1 in Prince Edward Island in 1957-61, indicates that the female rates are not simply a reflection of the general crime-rate.

No simple patterns of provincial difference in female rates are apparent from Table 3. While two of the Atlantic Provinces (Prince Edward Island and New Brunswick) have low rates for women, the other two do not. Two of the Prairie Provinces have relatively high rates, but Saskatchewan does not. Quebec is an obvious exception to the generalization that high female crime-rates go with a high degree of urbanization. The high female rates in Alberta and British Columbia fit in with their pattern of rapid population growth, but the high rate in Manitoba goes together with a relatively slow population growth from 1957-61.

Several writers have pointed out that the sex ratio in convictions for crime varies with the relative status of women; as women enjoy greater freedom, and approach equality with men, they apparently commit more crimes. Some of the provincial differences in sex ratio might be explained if they were tested against statistical indices of the status of women. Following this reasoning, we might expect the rising status of women since World War I to be reflected in an increasing proportion of female offenders, but the statistics of convictions for indictable offences show no such trend. In 1919 female convictions were 12.2 percent of total convictions. For the next 11 years, the female proportion fluctuated between 9 and 12 percent of the total. It dropped to 8.3 percent in

1931 and then fluctuated between 9 and 11 percent until World War II, when the proportion rose to 15 percent in 1942. Then the proportion of women offenders declined with minor fluctuations until a low of 5.6 percent was reached in 1957. Since then the proportion has increased somewhat, reaching 8.1 percent in 1961. These mystifying changes bear no apparent relationship to the changing status of women in our society.

Table 4 contains information about the sex of delinquents. (The provinces are again arranged in descending order of total rates in 1961.) The rates for both boys and girls vary over a much wider range than the adult rates. This may be due, in part, to the much wider discretion exercised in deciding whether or not juveniles will be brought to court. The most highly agricultural provinces (Saskatchewan and Prince Edward Island) have unusually low rates for girls. The most urbanized provinces have relatively high rates with the exception, once again, of Quebec. The differences between the extremes are sufficiently large to merit further study.

TABLE 4

Sex of Juvenile Delinquents for Canada and Provinces: Annual Average 1951-6 and 1957-61 per 100,000 Population 7-15 Years of Age

	1951-56*			1957-61†		
	Boys	Girls	Ratio	Boys	Girls	Ratio
Canada (excluding Yukon and N.W.T.)	497	62	8/1	679	92	7/1
British Columbia	969	117	8/1	1035	154	8/1
Ontario	769	97	8/1	811	133	6/1
Alberta	445	69	6/1	740	112	7/1
Manitoba	523	119	4/1	839	142	6/1
Nova Scotia	649	52	13/1	641	42	15/1
New Brunswick	447	38	12/1	604	60	10/1
Newfoundland	562	26	22/1	793	73	11/1
Quebec	205	26	8/1	413	48	9/1
Prince Edward Island	426	6	74/1	357	8	45/1
Saskatchewan	77	4	18/1	172	12	14/1

Sources:
*P. J. Giffen, op. cit., p. 83.
†Dominion Bureau of Statistics, Juvenile Delinquents, 1957-61; Census of Canada 1961; Population Estimates, 1952-60.

Broad differences between males and females in the types of serious crime for which they are likely to be convicted are shown in Table 5. Although males outnumber females in all offence categories, the ratio is much higher for some types of offences than for others. It is not surprising that males show a greater proclivity for more violent or physically daring predatory crimes, such as armed robbery and breaking and entering. The high ratio of men to women in sex offences reflects the fact that the physically aggressive sex offences, such as indecent assault and rape, which are characteristically male, are defined in our legal traditions as serious enough to be indictable, while common prostitution, which accounts for a considerable part of female crime, is not included in the table because it is punishable on summary conviction. Commercialized vice makes up a relatively high proportion of female indictable offences because it includes bawdy-house keeping and narcotics offences. In 1961, three times as many women as men were convicted for keeping a bawdy-house; although men exceeded women in narcotics convictions, the ratio was only 1.7 to 1.

TABLE 5

Numerical and Percentage Distribution of Indictable-Offence Groups* by Sex of Persons Convicted, Canada, 1961

| | Number | | Ratio | Percentage | |
	Males	Females	M to F	Males	Females
All Offences	35,516	3,163	11/1	100.0	100.0
Homicide	79	5	16/1	0.2	0.2
Assault Offences	3,693	204	18/1	10.4	6.4
Sex Offences	1,159	9	129/1	3.3	0.3
Family Offences	65	47	1.4/1	0.2	1.5
Commercialized Vice	929	376	2.5/1	2.6	11.9
Gainful Offences with Violence	7,731	132	59/1	21.8	4.2
Malicious Offences against Property	761	33	23/1	2.1	1.0
Theft	15,484	1,814	9/1	43.6	57.4
Fraudulent Offences	3,403	439	8/1	9.6	13.9
Motor-vehicle Offences	456	9	50/1	1.3	0.3
Other Offences	1,756	95	18/1	4.9	3.0

*The names of offences included in each of these groups is given in P. J. Giffen, op. cit., p. 104.
Source: Dominion Bureau of Statistics, Statistics of Criminal and Other Offences, 1961.

The differences between boys and girls in the types of offences that lead to their being convicted of juvenile delinquency, shown in Table 6, are quite marked. Although offences against property clearly predominate among the boys' convictions, girls are more likely to find themselves adjudged delinquents for a variety of misbehaviours that might be described as *running wild*. Precocity and promiscuousness in sexual relations probably account for many of the convictions listed in the statistics as "immorality", "incorrigibility", and "vagrancy", which together make up 33 percent of the female offences. If we add to them those convictions listed as "Liquor Control Act" (mostly drinking under age), "disorderly conduct", and "truancy", we have accounted for 53 percent of the total delinquencies of girls.

TABLE 6

Numerical and Percentage Distribution of Juvenile Offences by Sex, Canada, 1961

| | Number | | Ratio | Percentage | |
	Boys	Girls	B to G	Boys	Girls
All Offences	13,504	1,711	8/1	100.0	100.0
Theft	4,335	423	10/1	32.1	24.7
Breaking and Entering	3,348	65	52/1	24.8	3.7
Interferences with Property	1,204	44	27/1	8.9	2.6
Automobile Theft	781	11	71/1	5.8	0.6
Various Municipal By-laws	574	51	11/1	4.3	3.0
Highway Traffic Act Offences	352	44	8/1	2.6	2.6
Incorrigibility	346	367	0.9/1	2.6	21.4
Taking Motor Vehicle Without Consent	320	4	80/1	2.4	0.2
Disorderly Conduct	291	131	2.2/1	2.1	7.7
Having in Possession	289	12	24/1	2.1	0.7
Assault Offences	247	26	10/1	1.8	1.5
Liquor Control Act Offences	222	122	1.8/1	1.6	7.1
Truancy	124	92	1.3/1	0.9	5.4
Vagrancy	93	36	2.6/1	0.7	2.1
Immorality	83	155	0.5/1	0.6	9.1
Other Offences	895	128	7/1	6.6	7.5

Source: Dominion Bureau of Statistics, Juvenile Delinquents, 1961.

Whether the property offences of boys are really rationally planned crimes for gain, or forms of *acting out* due to status frustration (the explanation favoured by A. K. Cohen),[4] the statistics, of course, do not tell us. Certainly few of the offences labelled "automobile theft", "taking a motor vehicle without the owner's consent", or "interferences with property" are acts aimed primarily at economic gain. It is also worth noting that crimes of violence against other persons are relatively rare among juvenile offences, contrary to the impression created by the mass media.

Age Differences

All countries that keep statistics report a preponderance of young people among convicted criminals. Table 7 indicates that the rate declines with age in Canada, but that the decline is much sharper for males than for females. The increase in the rate for both sexes between the sixteen- and seventeen-year-old level and the eighteen- and nineteen-year-old level is an unexpected finding. In 1956 the older group of males had a rate that was 92 percent of the rate of the younger age-grade and the females in the older group had a rate that was 97 per cent of the rate of the younger group. Although we cannot attach much significance to such a small difference without further evidence, it does raise the possibility that the young people born in the later years of World War II are less inclined to criminal acts than those born in the earlier years. If so, the trend should show up in the criminal statistics of the next few years.

TABLE 7

Age and Sex of Persons Convicted of Indictable Offences, Canada, 1961

Age in Years	Rate per 100,000 Population in Each Age-Group		Rate as Percentage of 16-, 17-Year Rate	
	Males	Females	Males	Females
16, 17	1,844	101	100.0	100.0
18, 19	1,899	119	103.0	117.8
20–24	1,336	106	72.5	105.0
25–29	760	72	41.2	71.3
30–34	524	57	28.4	56.4
35–39	411	46	22.3	45.5
40–44	311	43	16.9	42.6
45–49	240	35	13.0	34.7
50–59	169	27	9.2	26.7
60 and Older	55	7	3.0	6.9

Number: Males — 35,516; Females — 3,163
Age not stated: Males — 1,589; Females — 158

Sources: Dominion Bureau of Statistics, *Statistics of Criminal and Other Offences, 1961*, and *Census of Canada, 1961*.

Urban-Rural Distribution

Tables 8 and 9 contain apparent exceptions to the commonplace observation that urban communities have higher rates of crime than rural areas. In 1961 the Canadian statistics for the first time showed rural rates exceeding urban rates in some provinces. It is particularly startling to find that in British Columbia the rural rate of juvenile delinquency is over twice the urban rate. However, an examination of the 1961 census reveals that any true differences in rates are obscured by changes in the criteria for classifying the population as urban or rural. The change in 1961 from the definition used in the 1956 census resulted in the exclusion from the 1961 urban population of any non-urbanized fringes within metropolitan areas and the inclusion of the urbanized fringes of smaller cities whose total population including the urbanized fringe was 10,000 or over. If the change had resulted in a large increase in the population classified as urban, some of the relative increase in rural rates might be interpreted as a result of the narrowing of the population base used in the calculations, but the actual change in population was in the opposite direction – in Canada as a whole the urban population went down by 271,537. Only in Saskatchewan and Prince Edward Island did the rural population decrease.

TABLE 8

Residence of Persons Convicted of Indictable Offences, for Canada and Provinces, 1956 and 1961. Rates per 100,000 Population 16 Years and Older

	1956*		1961†	
	Urban	Rural	Urban	Rural
Canada (excluding Yukon and N.W.T.)	283	185	361	194
Alberta	387	246	586	246
British Columbia	356	332	461	344
Manitoba	343	210	462	203
Ontario	285	204	365	186
Nova Scotia	280	205	348	223
Saskatchewan	363	126	422	129
Newfoundland	334	121	385	131
Quebec	212	142	254	162
New Brunswick	305	135	169	214
Prince Edward Island	217	56	155	19
	Number:	26,844	Number:	37,347
	Residence not stated:	567	Residence not stated:	1,332

Sources:
*P. J. Giffen, *op. cit.*, p. 90.
†Dominion Bureau of Statistics, *Statistics of Criminal and Other Offences, 1961* and *Census of Canada, 1961.*

TABLE 9

Residence of Juvenile Delinquents, for Canada and Provinces, 1956 and 1961. Rates per 100,000 Population 7–15 Years of Age

	1956*		1961†	
	Urban	Rural	Urban	Rural
Canada (excluding Yukon and N.W.T.)	443	159	546	419
British Columbia	672	526	516	1118
Ontario	535	293	707	711
Alberta	586	85	636	381
Manitoba	681	130	706	446
Nova Scotia	467	264	499	377
New Brunswick	446	113	613	241
Newfoundland	875	49	474	305
Quebec	198	40	442	172
Prince Edward Island	760	57	302	219
Saskatchewan	90	1	359	85
	Number: 9,114		Number: 16,971	
	Residence not stated: 6		Residence not stated: 3	

Sources:
*P. J. Giffen, *op. cit.*, p. 90.
†Dominion Bureau of Statistics, *Statistics of Criminal and Other Offences, 1961* and *Census of Canada, 1961.*

The confusion is increased if we take into account that each court official who reports to D.B.S. makes his own decision in each case as to whether the offender's residence is urban or rural. The criteria he uses in marginal cases may bear no similarity to the census definition of either year.

Do these changes in urban and rural rates embody changes in the pattern of offences? The rates for broad offence-groups, shown in Table 10, indicate some shifts in their relative importance. The gainful offences increased considerably in 1961, but the increase was much greater among urban than rural dwellers. The rates for assault offences decreased among urban residents and increased among rural residents, which brought the two rates close together.

TABLE 10

Types of Indictable Offences Committed by Urban and Rural Offenders, 1956 and 1961. Rates per 100,000 Population 16 Years and Older

| | Urban | | | Rural | | |
	1956*	1961†	Change	1956*	1961†	Change
Homicide	1	1	0	1	1	0
Assault Offences	37	33	−4	26	28	+2
Sex Offences	9	11	+2	6	7	+1
Family Offences	1	1	0	1	1	0
Commercialized Vice	12	14	+2	2	2	0
Gainful Offences with Violence	48	71	+23	28	46	+18
Malicious Offences against Property	5	6	+1	5	6	+1
Theft	108	166	+58	60	78	+18
Fraudulent Offences	24	37	+13	14	15	+1
Motor-vehicle Offences	25	3	−22	35	5	−30
Other	13	19	+5	8	9	+1

Number: 1956 − 26,846; 1961 − 37,001
Residence not stated: 1956 − 567; 1961 − 1,678

Sources:
*P. J. Giffen, *op. cit.,* p. 94.
†Dominion Bureau of Statistics, *Statistics of Criminal and Other Offences, 1961* and *Census of Canada, 1961.*

The radical decline in motor-vehicle offences that appears to have taken place among both populations is deceptive. The decrease is due primarily to a drop in convictions for impaired driving as an indictable offence from 2,132 in 1956 to 218 in 1961, and for driving while intoxicated from 383 to 10. The Crown may proceed by way of indictment or summary conviction on either charge, and the decrease represents a greater disinclination on the part of some Crown Attorneys to charge an accused with an indictable offence. Comparing the summary convictions for the same two years, we find that the convictions for impaired driving increased from 12,059 to 23,151, and that the convictions for driving while intoxicated increased from 1,718 to 5,906 – increases far in excess of the rate of population growth.

Educational Differences

The data provided in the criminal statistics on the educational levels of persons convicted of indictable offences yield the only usable measure of socio-economic status. Although the occupations of indictable offenders and of the fathers of juvenile delinquents are stated in the official statistics, they cannot be used to calculate rates. For 1961 this is clearly out of the question because the census used a new classification of occupations while the criminal statistics continued to use the old classification. In previous census years the categories formally corresponded, but the differences in rates between occupations calculated on this basis are so extreme that they cannot be taken seriously. In 1951, for example, the rate of indictable offenders classified as "labourers" was 1,975 per 100,000 persons in that occupation, as compared with 56 per 100,000 for persons classified as "managerial". One suspects that the information on occupations provided by court officials is based on different criteria than those used by census enumerators and coders.

TABLE 11

Educational Level of Persons Convicted of Indictable Offences, Canada, 1951 and 1961. Rate per 100,000 Population 16 Years and Over

	1951*		1961†	
	Number	Rate	Number	Rate
No Schooling	915	462	424	242
Elementary School	17,012	361	18,533	367
High School	7,590	220	14,412	252
Above High School	882	149	499	66
Educational Level Not Stated: 1951 — 2,576; 1961 — 4,811				

Sources:
*P. J. Giffen, *op. cit.*, p. 94.
†Dominion Bureau of Statistics, *Statistics of Criminal and Other Offences, 1951* and *1961*; *Census of Canada, 1951* and *1961*.

Table 11 indicates that the crime-rate declines as the level of education rises. The only obvious anomaly is that the group with no schooling has a low rate in 1961, lower than all except the "above high school" group. But the large proportion of cases "not stated" means that these rates might be differently ranked if the offenders whose education is not given were disproportionately distributed. Our suspicion of non-randomness is strengthened when we look at the differences among types of offences in the 12.4 percent of the total cases where education is not stated. Of these, 43.4 percent are motor-vehicle offenders, and 25.2 percent are commercialized-vice offenders. In contrast, only 10.7 percent are offenders convicted of theft, and 11.1 percent are offenders convicted of gainful offences with violence. In so far as people of different educational levels tend to be convicted of different types of offences, this selective reporting may give an unreliable picture of the relative criminality of the four educational levels.

The information in Table 12 indicates that the offence pattern does differ by educational level. Offenders with the most education appear to be least likely to engage in violent predatory offences and ordinary theft, but more likely to get money by fraudulent means. Violence against other persons appears to be more characteristic of offenders of lower educational attainment. The drop in the total rate for persons with above-high-school education between 1951 and 1961 is due largely to the decline in motor-vehicle offences. These offences were 18 percent of the convictions of the most educated offenders in 1956 – a much higher proportion than that found at the other three educational levels – but they declined to 2.4 percent in 1961. This apparent decline in indictable motor-vehicle offences is due largely to the decline in the offences involving alcohol and this, in turn, is explained by a change in the policies of prosecution

459

TABLE 12

Percentage Distribution of Indictable Offences by Education of Persons Convicted, Canada, 1961

	No Schooling	Elementary	High School	Above High School	Not Stated
Homicide	0.7	0.3	0.2	0.0	0.2
Assault Offences	19.8	10.4	8.5	8.8	13.0
Sex Offences	6.8	3.0	2.9	5.8	3.0
Family Offences	0.9	0.2	0.2	1.0	0.3
Commercialized Vice	1.1	2.2	3.8	3.4	6.9
Gainful Offences with Violence	15.3	22.6	18.7	9.8	18.2
Malicious Offences against Property	0.9	1.9	1.9	1.6	3.2
Theft	42.7	46.3	45.3	30.8	38.8
Fraudulent Offences	5.7	7.4	13.0	29.9	9.0
Motor-vehicle Offences	1.1	0.6	0.8	2.4	3.9
Other	4.7	5.2	4.9	6.4	4.2
Number	424	18,533	14,412	499	4,811

Sources: Dominion Bureau of Statistics, *Statistics of Criminal and Other Offences, 1961* and *Census of Canada, 1961.*

mentioned in a previous section. A few jurisdictions that earlier proceeded against drinking drivers by indictment have adopted the more common practice of charging them with summary offences.

Religious Differences

Little attention has been paid by criminologists to differences between adherents of the major religious groups in rates of crime. If large differences were proven to exist, they would be difficult to interpret since religious differences are confounded with class and ethnic differences. Also, nominal religious affiliation masks wide differences in the extent of belief in religious dogma and in participation in religious activities.

TABLE 13

Religion of Persons Convicted of Indictable Offences, 1951 and 1961. Rate per 100,000 Population, 16 Years and Older, for All Denominations with 100 or More Offenders

	1951*		1961†	
Denomination	Number	Rate	Number	Rate
Roman Catholic	13,799	356	18,979	373
United Church	4,077	203	5,087	212
Anglican	3,947	262	4,356	267
Presbyterian	1,611	267	1,309	220
Baptist	881	131	967	244
Lutheran	729	223	904	194
Greek Orthodox	453	355	425	237
Jewish	222	147	203	112
Salvation Army	139	318	218	398
Pentecostal	103	171	143	164

Other Religions: 1951 — 360; 1961 — 572
No Religion: 1951—227; 1961 — 534
Religion Not Stated: 1951 — 1,538; 1961 — 3,388
Protestant, Not Otherwise Stated: 1951 — 1,194; 1961 — 1,594

Sources:
*P. J. Giffen, *op. cit.,* p. 96.
†Dominion Bureau of Statistics, *Statistics of Criminal and Other Offences, 1961* and *Census of Canada, 1961.*

Table 13 seems to show that some fairly large differences in rates exist among religious groups in Canada, but a closer examination of the statistics leads to questions about their reliability. If the large number of offenders whose religion is not stated or whose Protestant denomination is not specified are not randomly distributed among the religious affiliations, the true picture may be quite different. Rates for the large "Protestant, not otherwise stated" category of offenders cannot be calculated because the census has no comparable classification of the general population. (Census enumerators are apparently much more successful at eliciting and recording specifics of religion than are court officials.)

However, the relatively high Roman Catholic rate cannot be accounted for by the failure to report religious preferences. The rate of conviction of all non-Catholics plus those Catholics whose religion is not stated is still lower than the conviction rate of the Roman Catholic group. In 1961 the rate for the residual group was 237, compared with 373 for those who were listed Roman Catholics.

TABLE 14

Religion of Juvenile Delinquents, 1951 and 1961. Rate per 100,000 Population 7-15 Years of Age, for all Denominations with 100 or More Delinquents in 1961

| | 1951 | | 1961 | |
Denomination	Number	Rate	Number	Rate
Roman Catholic	2,878	267	6,791	407
United Church	974	237	1,609	240
Anglican	926	343	1,402	332
Baptist	298	378	340	317
Presbyterian	299	340	328	271
Lutheran	75	121	251	255
Greek Orthodox	51	208	162	510
Salvation Army	95	721	140	684
Pentecostal	56	306	135	439

Other Religions: 1951 — 187; 1961 — 430
No Religion: 1951 — 14; 1961 — 55
Religion Not Stated: 1951 — 331; 1961 — 714
Protestant, Not Otherwise Stated: 1951 — 460; 1961 — 2,858

Sources: Dominion Bureau of Statistics, *Juvenile Delinquents, 1951* and *1961*; *Census of Canada, 1951* and *1961*.

Table 14 indicates that there are also large differences among religious groups in rates of juvenile delinquency but that, once again, the figures are to be regarded with scepticism because of the numerous cases in which religious preference is not recorded. The rank-order of religious groups in delinquency-rates is markedly different from that for adult offenders. Moreover, both the juvenile and adult rates show a considerable change in the rates of some religious groups from 1951 to 1961, although such changes are much more marked among juvenile delinquents. Either there are pronounced shifts between age-groups in the likelihood of affiliates of the various religions being convicted of offences, or the reporting by the courts is highly variable. We have no way of knowing.

Country-of-Birth Differences

The relationship between country of birth and rates of conviction in Canada, 1951-4, has been examined in a study done for the Department of Citizenship and Immigration.[5] Figure 4, based on data from this study, shows the contrast

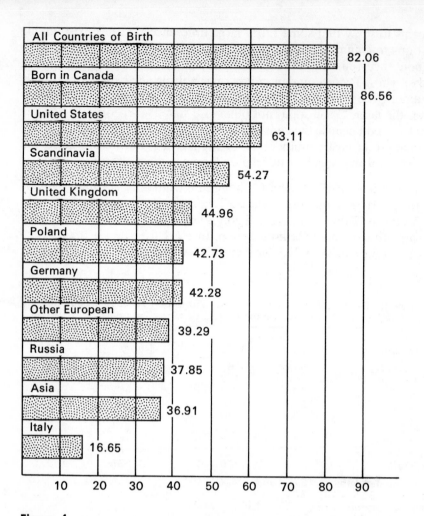

Figure 4

Average Rates of Conviction in Canada per 10,000 Males, 15-49 Years of Age, by Country of Birth, 1951-54.

between the rates of conviction of native-born males and those born in other countries. Whereas the rate of the native-born is 86.6, that of foreign-born males taken collectively is 42.8, or less than half. The rates for specific foreign-born groups range from 63.1 for the United States-born to 16.7 for the Italian-born.

The differences in rates may be due in some degree to differences in the age-distribution of males within those groups. A group made up to an unusual extent of old men would likely have a low rate, but if age were controlled statistically, the group might have a rate as high as that of the native-born. The use of forty-nine years as the upper age of the population base in the study lessens but does not eliminate the influence of age. Unfortunately, figures on convictions cross-classified by country of birth and age are not available in the official statistics.

If the discrepancy between native-born and foreign-born rates is not due to age differences, it may reflect a genuine difference in the tendency to commit crimes. A difference might be expected in view of the highly selective immigration policies of recent decades. In so far as the applicant for an immigration visa

462

TABLE 15

Birthplace of Fathers of Juvenile Delinquents, 1951 and 1961. Rate per 10,000 Males 25-64 Years of Age of Each Birthplace in the Canadian Population

Birthplace	1951* Number	1951* Rate	1961† Number	1961† Rate
Canada	4,968	3.6	11,764	3.8
England and Wales	415	9.4	211	11.7
Scotland	192	13.6	71	9.9
Northern Ireland	1	0.2	21	10.4
Other British Commonwealth	11	9.0	13	7.9
United States	116	2.6	89	11.0
Germany	21	3.1	20	3.5
Italy	74	19.6	8	0.9
Poland	73	3.2	28	3.6
Russia	84	2.7	28	3.6
Scandinavia	32	2.1	54	19.3
Other European Countries	230	5.2	59	2.8
Asiatic Countries	25	7.3	11	5.8

Father's Birthplace Not Stated: 1951 — 401; 1961 — 90

Sources:
*P. J. Giffen, *op. cit.,* p. 90.
†Dominion Bureau of Statistics, *Juvenile Delinquents, 1961* and *Census of Canada, 1961.*

must have no known criminal record, must be of good physical health and free of a diagnosed serious mental illness, and give evidence of his ability to support himself, it seems likely that many of the potential criminals are prevented from entering the country.

A part of the explanation may be that it takes time to assimilate the criminal norms, techniques, and associations of the new society; the process is at least as long and difficult as that of assimilation of the legitimate patterns, since the opportunities are weighted in favour of the latter. The relatively high conviction-rate of males born in the United States lends support to this theory, since their cultural background is closer to the dominant Canadian pattern than that of other immigrants.

The delinquency-rates of the children of foreign-born parents present a more complex picture. The second generation of a majority of the nationality groups shown in Table 15 appear, in 1961, to have higher rates than the children of Canadian-born parents. But the very considerable differences between the rates in 1951 and 1961 for some groups should caution us to attach little significance to the ranking in any one year. With so few cases involved, a change of a few children in any category except "Canadian-born parents" can make a large difference in rates. Moreover, the age distribution of males twenty-five to sixty-four years of age of each birthplace has probably changed considerably over the ten-year period, thus changing the proportion within origin-groups of men at the ages when they are most likely to be fathers of juveniles. The most surprising change in rates shown in the table is that for delinquents of Italian parentage. The number decreased by only 66 between 1951 and 1961, but this decline was sufficient to change their standing in terms of rates from by far the most delinquent group in 1951 to by far the least delinquent in 1961. The least debatable conclusion to be derived from these statistics is that children of foreign-born fathers are responsible for only a minor part of official delinquency in Canada – 20.4 percent in 1951 and 22.2 percent in 1961.

Provincial Differences

The apparent differences among Canadian provinces in rates of crime and delinquency are particularly intriguing because the relative standing of several of the provinces is not what one would expect on the basis of the degree of urbanization and growth of the province.

A test of the extent to which differences in urbanization account for provincial differences in rates is reported in Table 16. The standardized rate for each province is the rate of convictions adjusted for differences in urbanization among provinces. It is the rate that a province, given its present urban and rural rates, would have if the proportion of its population living in urban centres in 1961 were the same as that of Canada as a whole. The trustworthiness of the standardized rate is reduced by the large number of cases in which residence is not stated and by the possibility that court officials use different criteria than census officials in classifying the residences of offenders – factors discussed above in the section on urban-rural differences.

TABLE 16

Provincial Rates of Conviction Standardized for Rural-Urban Distribution of Residence. Rates per 100,000 Population 16 Years and Older, 1961 (Rank-Order of Provinces in Brackets)

	Unstandardized Rate*	Standardized Rate*	Change
Canada	313	313	
Alberta	465 (1)	489 (1)	24
British Columbia	431 (2)	428 (2)	−3
Manitoba	375 (3)	389 (3)	14
Ontario	327 (4)	315 (5)	−12
Nova Scotia	292 (5)	310 (7)	18
Saskatchewan	259 (6)	339 (4)	80
Newfoundland	263 (7)	313 (6)	50
Quebec	233 (8)	228 (8)	−5
New Brunswick	184 (9)	182 (9)	2
Prince Edward Island	64 (10)	115 (10)	50

*Using only offenders for whom residence is stated.

Sources: Dominion Bureau of Statistics, *Statistics of Criminal and Other Offences, 1961* and *Census of Canada, 1961.*

The ranking of provinces by rates of conviction is altered little by standardizing for urbanization. This seems to indicate that provincial differences in rates are not due to a significant extent to differences in the proportion of their populations living in urban centres. Only in Saskatchewan, Newfoundland, and Prince Edward Island is the rate increased very much by altering the urban-rural distribution of population. All three provinces have a considerably more rural population than Canada as a whole, but so has New Brunswick, whose rate is decreased slightly by standardizing.

The census definition of *urban* used above includes all centres of 1,000 population and over. A closer relationship between urbanization and rates of crime might be found by looking only at proportions of provincial populations in larger urban centres. In Table 17 the ranking of the provinces in conviction-rates is compared with their ranking in terms of the proportion of population in centres of 30,000 and over, and the proportion in census metropolitan areas. In addition, the provinces are ranked in terms of population increase from 1956 to 1961.

TABLE 17

Comparison of Persons Convicted of Indictable Offences. Population in Cities and Metropolitan Areas, and Rates of Growth, by Provinces
(Rank-Order of Provinces in Brackets)

	Indictable Offenders 1961*	Delinquents 1961†	Percentage of Population in Centres 30,000+, 1961	Percentage in Census Metro Areas 1961	Percentage Increase in Population 1956-1961
Canada	328	449	34.9	44.8	13.4
Alberta	476 (1)	500 (3)	44.9 (1)	46.3 (5)	18.6 (2)
British Columbia	464 (2)	684 (1)	29.0 (5)	58.0 (1)	16.5 (3)
Manitoba	391 (3)	435 (4)	36.6 (4)	51.6 (3)	8.4 (6)
Ontario	337 (4)	628 (2)	37.4 (3)	52.2 (2)	35.6 (1)
Nova Scotia	296 (5)	382 (5)	23.5 (7)	25.0 (6)	6.1 (8)
Saskatchewan	293 (6)	150 (10)	26.0 (6)	—	5.1 (10)
Newfoundland	273 (7)	374 (7)	13.9 (9)	19.4 (7)	10.3 (5)
Quebec	244 (8)	270 (8)	38.8 (2)	47.0 (4)	13.6 (4)
New Brunswick	191 (9)	379 (6)	16.6 (8)	16.0 (8)	7.8 (7)
Prince Edward Island	64 (10)	243 (9)	—	—	5.4 (9)

*Rate per 100,000 population 16 years and older.
†Rate per 100,000 population 7-15 years of age.

Sources: Dominion Bureau of Statistics, *Statistics of Criminal and Other Offences, 1961; Juvenile Delinquents, 1961; Census of Canada, 1961.*

A measure of statistical association applicable to such data is the Spearman rank-correlation. If the rank-order of the provinces in any two measures is completely similar, the correlation will be +1.0, and if they are completely reversed the correlation will be —1.0. Scores between these extremes indicate degrees of positive or negative relationship between the rank-orders.

The ranking of the provinces in rates of indictable offenders is positively associated with their ranking in the three measures, but the correlations are not high: +.58 rank correlation with population increase, +.54 with the proportion in census metropolitan areas (only the eight provinces with such areas are used), and +.53 with the proportion in cities of 30,000 and over.

The ranking of the provinces in juvenile-delinquency rates is fairly highly associated (+.76) with population increase, moderately (+.69) with the proportion of the population in census metropolitan areas (eight provinces), and hardly at all (+.29) with the proportion in centres of 30,000 persons and over.

These findings in regard to provincial differences are difficult to interpret. If we assume that all courts are equally faithful in reporting cases to the Dominion Bureau of Statistics, or at least that there are no significant differences between provinces in reporting, we are forced to conclude that the degree and type of urbanization and the rate of population increase do not have a consistent influence on crime-rates.

But when the rankings in Table 17 are examined more closely, we find that the four provinces with the highest rates of indictable offenders are all quite highly urbanized (none is less than 64 percent urban) and, with the exception of Manitoba, growing rapidly. At the other extreme, the very low conviction-rate of Prince Edward Island accompanies the least urban of provincial populations and a very slow rate of growth. The low rank-correlations between the series in Table 17 appears to be due largely to the few provinces whose conviction-rates are anomalous in terms of their urbanization and growth. Quebec is the

465

outstanding example. Although the province has a low conviction-rate, it is the second most urbanized province (using the census definition of *urban*) and it had the fourth highest rate of population increase in 1956-61. These exceptions suggest that differences in the reporting of cases may play an important role.

TABLE 18

Comparison of Rates of Indictable Offenders, Juvenile Delinquents, Divorces, Alcoholics, Illegitimate Births, and Suicides, by Provinces, 1961
(Rank-Order of Provinces in Brackets)

	Indictable Offenders	Juvenile Delinquents	*Divorces	†Illegitimate Births	‡Suicides	§Alcoholics
Canada	328	449	36.0	4.5	7.5	2,140
Alberta	476 (1)	500 (3)	78.0 (2)	6.2 (4)	8.9 (3)	1,550 (6)
British Columbia	464 (2)	684 (1)	85.8 (1)	6.9 (1)	11.8 (1)	2,380 (2)
Manitoba	391 (3)	435 (4)	33.9 (4)	6.3 (3)	7.6 (5)	1,970 (4)
Ontario	337 (4)	628 (2)	43.9 (3)	3.5 (10)	8.8 (4)	2,440 (1)
Nova Scotia	296 (5)	382 (5)	33.2 (5)	6.9 (1)	5.2 (7)	1,460 (7)
Saskatchewan	293 (6)	150 (10)	27.1 (7)	5.9 (5)	10.2 (2)	1,170 (9)
Newfoundland	273 (7)	374 (7)	1.3 (10)	4.3 (8)	3.7 (10)	915 (10)
Quebec	244 (8)	270 (8)	6.6 (9)	3.6 (9)	4.6 (9)	2,340 (3)
New Brunswick	191 (9)	279 (6)	32.4 (6)	4.4 (7)	5.0 (8)	1,230 (8)
Prince Edward Island	64 (10)	243 (9)	7.6 (8)	4.8 (6)	6.7 (6)	1,640 (5)

*Rate per 100,000 population. Dominion Bureau of Statistics, *Vital Statistics, 1961.*
†Percent of live births. *Ibid.*
‡Rate per 100,000 population. *Ibid.*
§Estimated alcoholics per 100,000 population aged 20 and over. *13th Annual Report of the Alcoholism and Drug Addiction Research Foundation of Ontario*, Toronto, 1964.

Clues to incongruities in the rank-order of provinces in conviction-rates might also be found by comparing these rates to their ranking in the rates for other *social problems* that are more reliably reported or estimated. This is done in Table 18.

The rank correlation of indictable-offender rates with divorce-rates is +.83, with suicide-rates +.64, with illegitimacy-rates +.51, and with rates of alcoholism +.35. The rank-correlation of juvenile-delinquency rates with divorce-rates is +.87, with alcoholism-rates +.58, with suicide-rates +.42, and with rates of illegitimate births +.28. In short, only the ranking in divorce-rates correlates highly with the ranking in conviction-rates of both types.

One cannot assert that the social conditions producing high rates of crime always result in correspondingly high rates of these other types of minority behaviour (despite the consistent standing of British Columbia) since other variables are known to be involved. A predominantly Roman Catholic population, for example, is likely to have a low rate of suicide and a low rate of divorce, whatever its crime-rate. Differences in the causation of the four types of divergent behaviour are indicated by the fact that they turn out to be inconsistently correlated with each other. The highest rank-correlation is +.76, for divorce-rates and suicide-rates by provinces, and the lowest is —.06, for rates of alcoholism and illegitimacy. Although this table raises interesting questions, it cannot be used as an indication of the reliability of reporting.

Another Approach to Criminal Statistics

In this chapter certain figures reported in the official court statistics have been examined on the assumption that, converted into rates, they would tell us something about differences among major social categories in amount and in types of crime. Many anomalies for which there are no apparent explanations have emerged, and these have inevitably led to questions about the reliability of the official statistics.

A more fruitful approach might be to treat the official statistics as guilty until proven innocent. With such an approach, when a difference in rates is found, the initial assumption is that the statistics are at fault, and attention is directed to discovering differences in the faithfulness of reporting or in the methods of classification that could account for it. If nothing is uncovered, an explanation is sought in differences in the administration of justice and law enforcement. Of course the research worker may eventually be driven to the conclusion that the disparity is one of those rare cases of genuine difference in rates −a residual category particularly troublesome to explain.

This suspicious approach is more likely to produce reliable official statistics than manipulation of the figures as if they reflected the real world. The responsibility for doing such studies must rest largely with the Dominion Bureau of Statistics, however, since it alone is in a position to secure and make available much of the necessary data.

Footnotes

1. R. H. Beattie, "Problems of Criminal Statistics in the United States," *Journal of Criminal Law, Criminology and Police Science*, 46, July-August, 1955, pp. 178-186.
2. Reported in Nicolas Zay, "Gaps in Available Statistics in Crime and Delinquency in Canada," *Canadian Journal of Economics and Political Science*, 29, February, 1963, pp. 75-89.
3. E. H. Sutherland and D. R. Cressey, *Principles of Criminology*. Philadelphia: Lippincott, 1955, p. 114.
4. Albert K. Cohen, *Delinquent Boys: The Culture of the Gang*. Glencoe, Illinois: Free Press, 1955.
5. Frank G. Vallee and Mildred Schwartz, "Report on Criminality among the Foreign Born in Canada," in B. R. Blishen et al., *Canadian Society* (first edition). Toronto: Macmillan, 1961, pp. 560-567.

Is the Crime Rate Increasing?
A Statistical Test[*][†]

Lynn McDonald

Sociologists have to cope with a *conventional wisdom* that offers them facts, figures and trends on the major social phenomena they study. Since hard social

*Reprinted from *The Canadian Review of Sociology and Anthropology*, 6:4 (1969), by permission of the author and publisher. This is an edited version of "Crime and Punishment in Canada: A Statistical Test of the Conventional Wisdom."
†The author wishes to thank Dr. E. H. Oksanen, Department of Economics, McMaster University, and Professor J. H. S. Ryan, Faculty of Law, Queen's University, for their criticism of the analysis, and the Dominion Bureau of Statistics for providing certain unpublished, as well as published, data.

data are still relatively scarce in Canada, the social scientist is forced either to accept the folklore or to remain sceptical, but without adequate knowledge. A particular aspect of the *conventional wisdom* that is the subject of this paper is the notion that the crime rate in Canada is increasing.

Although such a pronouncement is usually made authoritatively, the factual basis of this view has been merely assumed to be true without thorough empirical investigation. Fortunately, this is one part of the conventional wisdom that can be tested with existing statistical data.

The Data

As the data on crime statistics present numerous problems,[1] our first task is to identify these problems and to explain our methods for correcting or avoiding them.

Firstly, the categories of offences change from time to time. This has been overcome by using total offences (e.g. all indictable offences) and obtaining special runs which group specific offences together. Thus what is called *aggravated assault* in this paper covers offences in four sections of the new Criminal Code, and two in the old.

Secondly, the number of police forces reporting data changes radically over the period. To avoid this difficulty, court statistics are used for the most part and especially poor indicators, such as *offences known to the police*, are used for only one offence, parking violations, where the court statistics are considered by DBS to be less accurate.[2] Otherwise, where police-reported data are used, they are related to the populations of the areas covered by the police forces in question. This does not eliminate error, as for example x policemen covering y population are assumed to have the same effect as $2x$ policemen covering $2y$ population. Also no attention is paid to whether the population is urban or rural. The correction is obviously a crude one.

Efficiency of reporting creates the third problem. Unlike the number of reporting units, its effect can neither be estimated nor corrected. However, the changes over the period have been toward increasing efficiency, i.e., more complete reporting. Thus, it is only if an increasing rate appears that this increased efficiency poses a problem. A constant or a decreasing rate would suggest that the true crime rate is decreasing, or decreasing even more sharply, respectively, than revealed by the data.

There is no reason to suspect that the material on sentencing is affected by the number of units reporting data. For the sections on both equality and leniency of sentencing, the data consist of court records and concern the relative proportions of different sentences for that court.

Many of the statements about increased crime appearing in the popular press are based on crimes reported to the police and published in DBS's *Crime Statistics (Police)*, rather than on *Statistics of Criminal and Other Offences* which are based on court reports. The former series covers only the 1962-1966 period, a period too short for meaningful trend analysis. Comparable police-reported statistics for the years before 1962 are marked by wide variation in method of reporting as well as poor coverage in terms of quantity.

The indicator of crimes reported to the police is theoretically closer to the true number of crimes committed than charges or convictions. However, since it is so susceptible to measurement error and fluctuations in taste (what people consider important enough to report) that its one advantage does not outweigh its many faults. DBS (1967:7) does not even have confidence in its reports on murder which is a highly reported crime and one not subject to taste – all people consider it important enough to record. If the statistics on reported murders are that unreliable we must be even more suspicious of the data on other reported crimes.

Police reports on juvenile delinquency are particularly vulnerable to the peculiar policies of individual forces. The Department of Justice Committee on Juvenile Delinquency found enormous variation in these policies, and this is reflected in enormous variation in the reported statistics (Department of Justice, 1965).

It could be argued that under some circumstances a true increase in crime could be reflected in the statistics on reported crimes but not in statistics on charges or convictions. This could happen if police energies were diverted to the investigation of an increased number of reported crimes. The police would not be able to obtain as high a rate of charges or convictions because they would not be able to spend enough time on the investigations necessary to obtain sufficient evidence for legal proceedings. This argument would have some validity only if the police force per capita were to remain constant. However, the size of police forces in Canada is rising considerably faster than the population and so can be assumed to be able to handle increases in reports of crime.

People will look for trends over time and will use whatever data are available, substituting their own intuition where necessary. The purpose of this paper is to raise the quality of the data available and to make recourse to speculation less justifiable. Given DBS's proclivities for continuously *improving* the data, consequently changing it frequently, the time will never be right for the purist to do research in this field. We contend that the nature of the inadequacies of the data (where error occurs in a known direction) and the opportunity for many tests of the hypotheses, justify the use of these data, despite all their imperfections.

As there is no single generally accepted *crime rate* it is necessary to use a range of commonly used indicators to attempt to answer this question. Going from the most serious to the least these are: convictions for indictable offences; charges for indictable offences; convictions for Criminal Code summary conviction offences; children adjudged delinquent; all summary conviction convictions; traffic convictions; parking offences known to the police.

If the crime rate is indeed rising, then, it should be reflected by several of these indices, especially those relating to indictable offences. However, if the parking, traffic and total summary conviction indices do show increases, while the others do not, the hypothesis would not be refuted for these are not what is meant by *crime* by most people.

The numbers convicted or charged in these categories for each year between 1950 and 1966 were divided by the annual population, with census counts used for census years and DBS estimates for the intervening years. It might have been preferable to use a specific subset of the population, for example the population 15 and over, or the 15-35 age group, in order to better approximate the crime

TABLE 1

Summary of Crime Rate Statistics*

	Period	R^2	t	Is Rate Significantly Increasing or Decreasing?	Estimated Percentage Rate of Change per Year in Crime Indicators (percent)
Convictions for Indictable Offences[a]	1950–1966	0.02	0.40	neither	0.5
Charges for Indictable Offences[a]	1950–1966	0.00	0.40	neither	0.2
Convictions for Criminal Code Summary Conviction Offences[b]	1955–1966	0.55	3.83†	increasing	5.5
Children Adjudged Delinquent[c]	1950–1965	0.86	9.78†	increasing	0.5
All Summary Conviction Convictions[d]	1950–1966	0.92	13.78†	increasing	0.5
Traffic Convictions[e]	1950–1966	0.91	12.17†	increasing	0.6
Parking Offences Known to the Police[f]	1955–1966	0.68	4.92†	increasing	5.2

*A semi-logarithmic fit was employed to obtain an estimate of the compound annual growth rate in the crime indicator. Thus the estimating equation was of the form log $Y = a + bt$. It can be shown that the regression coefficient b is an estimate of $(1 + r)$ where r is the compound annual growth rate. The growth rate (r) is shown in percentage terms in the last column. The t statistic is the ratio of the regression coefficient (b) to its standard error.

†Statistically significant at the 5 percent level (one-tailed test).

Sources:

[a] Statistics of Criminal and Other Offences, Table 1, various years.
[b] Statistics of Criminal and Other Offences, 1958, Table 2-3; 1960, Table 17; 1961, Table 17; 1962, Table 15; 1963-1966, Table 15.
[c] D.B.S., Canada Year Book, 1957, p. 326; 1965, p. 417; 1968, p. 450.
[d] Statistics of Criminal and Other Offences, Table 17, various years.
[e] D.B.S., Canada Year Book, 1957-58, p. 321; 1960, p. 359. Statistics of Criminal and Other Offences, 1966, Table 17.
[f] Private communication from D.B.S.; Health and Welfare Division, Judicial Section.

risk population. However, as the population estimates for age groups are likely to be less accurate than for the total population, the totals were used in all but one case. The exception is for juvenile delinquents, for whom the population is the 10-19 age group.

Graphs with time as the independent variable[3] and the various crime rate indicators as the dependent are shown in Figures 1 and 2. Graphs are usually difficult to interpret by inspection alone, and, in this case, because of the number of fluctuations and the fact that different interpretations have very different social and sociological implications, there are more than the usual difficulties. To improve on subjectivity, least squares regression equations were tested, with the logarithms of the crime rate indicators as the dependent variable. The use of logarithms enables estimates of the percent annual rate of change for all the indicators to be made, which can be directly compared. These statistics (see Table 1), show that the percent annual growth in the crime rate varies from a low of 0.2 percent for an indicator of serious crime (charges for indictable offences) to a high of 5.5 percent for a less serious category, convictions for summary conviction offences in the Criminal Code. The other serious indicator, charges for indictable offences, shows a low increase, 0.2 percent, while the other less serious offences show higher increases, as 5.2 percent for parking. In other words, references to a sharply rising crime rate are based on trivial infractions only.

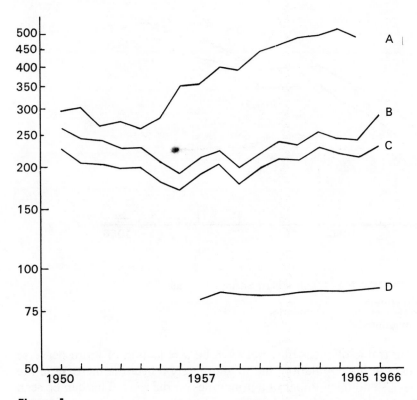

Figure 1

Crime Rates per 100,000 Population — Serious Offences
A. Children Adjudged Delinquent (Over Population, 10-19).
B. Charges for Indictable Offences.
C. Convictions for Indictable Offences.
D. Convictions for Criminal Code Summary Conviction Offences.

Values of R^2, the amount of variation in each dependent variable explained by time are also shown in Table 2.[4] These show even more clearly how poor the hypothesis of rising crime rates is for serious crime.

Time explains 0 and 2 percent only of the variation for indictable offences, respectively. It explains as much as 92 percent of all summary conviction offences (the bulk of which would be traffic) and a high 86 percent of juvenile delinquency.

The conventional wisdom could be interpreted as implying either a linear or a logarithmic relationship. (No one claims that the crime rate is mounting at an geometric rate and our graphs do not suggest this either.) A linear relationship would be a test of yearly increases in crime, at the same rate each year, with the first year of the series taken as the base. The logarithmic relationship implies that with each increase in crime the base from which the next increase is taken increases, the equivalent of interest on money being compounded each year rather than being computed from the initial deposit. Our data show that for the serious offences (Figure 1) the crime rate is not increasing in any way, and for the less serious offences (Figure 2), either the linear or the logarithmic fit very well.

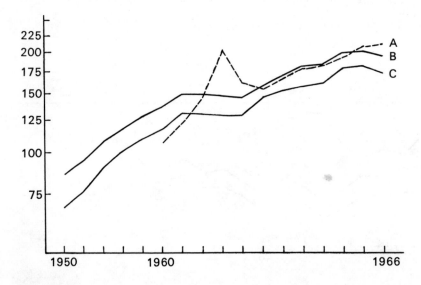

Figure 2

Crime Rates per 1,000 Population — Non-Serious Offences
A. Parking Violations.
B. All Summary Conviction Convictions.
C. Traffic Convictions.

The increase in traffic offences may not even be a reflection of more perverse driving practices in the population, but might merely reflect the increase in the number of drivers and the number of automobiles on the road. This can be seen by treating the number of traffic violations as a function of the number of motor vehicles in use and eligible for violations. In fact the number of registered motor vehicles does account for almost all (97 percent) of the variation in traffic violations, and 62 percent of the variation in parking offences. Figure 3 displays this good fit for traffic violations. It is reasonable then to suggest that people might not be becoming more law-breaking as drivers, but simply that as more people drive more cars each year the violation rate goes up.

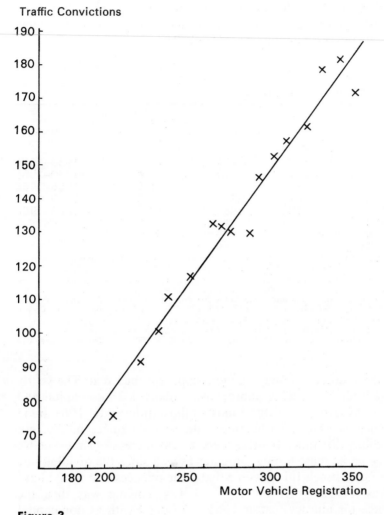

Figure 3

Traffic Violation as a Function of Motor Vehicle Registration* per 1,000 Population. $b=0.70$; $R^2= 0.97$.

*Motor vehicle registrations from DBS, *Canada Year Book*, 1957-1958, p. 837; 1965, p. 77; 1966, p. 813.

Is the Rate of Violent Crime Increasing?

Before concluding that the rate of commission of serious crimes has not been increasing we should consider some specific offences. Even though the total rate is not increasing there is a possibility of increases in the violent offences. Such variations would not affect the totals, but the total figures do not reflect the importance of the crimes involved. To consider an extreme example, if the murder rate were to triple each year for ten years the total crime rate would be unaffected, but it would be beside the point to claim that crime was not increasing.

Figures 4 and 5 show the rates of charges for the five most serious offences of violence: murder, attempted murder, manslaughter, shooting and wounding, aggravated assault.

The data show slight increases for murder and attempted murder, but slight decreases for manslaughter, aggravated assault, and shooting and wounding. The various test statistics are summarized in Table 2.

TABLE 2

Summary of Violent Crime Rate Statistics*

	Variation Explained by Time		Estimated Percentage Rate of Change per Year in Crime Indicators	Period
	R^2	t		
Murder	0.20	2.21†	0.5	1950–1966
Attempted Murder	0.36	3.15†	5.4	1950–1966
Manslaughter[a]	0.17	−1.82	−0.5	1955–1966
Shooting and Wounding[b]	0.21	−2.29	−3.0	1950–1966
Aggravated Assault[c]	0.28	−2.68	−1.6	1950–1966

*All supplied privately by D.B.S., Health and Welfare Division, Judicial Section.

†Statistically significant at the 5 percent level (one-tailed test).

[a] Manslaughter charges prior to 1955 are omitted as the offence then included criminal negligence in the operation of a motor vehicle causing death. This became a separate offence in 1955.

[b] Shooting and wounding includes causing bodily harm with intent to wound, maim or disfigure, endanger the life, prevent arrest or detention. It includes administering a noxious thing, attempt to choke, suffocate or strangle, administering drugs and traps likely to cause bodily harm (Sections 216, 217, 218, and 219 of the 1955 Criminal Code; Sections 273, 276, 277, 278 and 281 of the previous Code).

[c] Aggravated assault includes common assault, assault causing bodily harm, assault with intent, assault of a public or peace officer, assault to resist arrest, assault on bailiff, and to rescue goods seized (Sections 231 and 232 of the 1955 Criminal Code; Sections 274, 291, 295 and 296 of the previous Criminal Code).

The slight rise in the murder rate may be more apparent than real. The yearly figures show a rise after 1961, when murder was subdivided into capital and non-capital murder. As seen from Table 3 most of the murders after 1961 are in the non-capital category. The manslaughter rate only fluctuates mildly, not increasing, throughout this time. If there were a real increase in murder we would expect to see an increase in manslaughter as well since the dividing line between the two is not distinct. It is possible that some offences that would have been dealt with as manslaughter before 1961 (as hanging was then the compulsory sentence for murder), after 1961 were dealt with as non-capital murder (the sentence being life imprisonment).

TABLE 3

Annual Murder and Manslaughter Statistics

	Murder Charges per Million Population	Manslaughter Charges per Million Population	Total Murder and Manslaughter Charges per Million Population
1955	2.17	4.97	7.14
1956	1.49	10.82	12.31
1957	2.53	3.91	6.44
1958	2.05	3.57	5.62
1959	3.26	3.89	7.15
1960	1.79	3.92	5.71
1961	3.18	3.13	6.31
1962	3.55	3.55	7.10
1963	7.18	3.43	10.61
1964	3.53	3.73	7.26
1965	4.68	3.26	8.14
1966	3.90	4.45	8.35

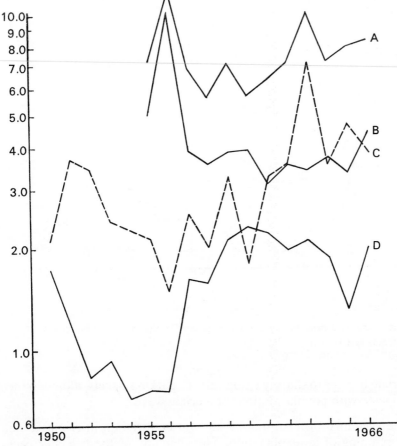

Figure 4

Rates of Violent Crime per 1,000,000 Population.
A. Murder and Manslaughter Charges.
B. Manslaughter Charges.
C. Murder Charges.
D. Attempted Murder Charges.

This possibility can be checked by fitting a trend line equation to see if the charges for manslaughter and murder taken together are increasing over the period. The estimated percent annual compound rate of change turns out to be zero, and so the hypothesis that the slight increase in the murder rate may merely reflect a change in classification is at least plausible. In any event, the increase was not great and itself was the exception among the crime rate indicators. The general conclusion that the crime rate is not increasing can still stand.

The rates for some crimes obviously are increasing. However, since the total rate is increasing at such a negligible pace, there must be other crimes for which the rate is decreasing, to offset the increases. The few increases in evidence are very slight and irregular. Slight trends in crime rates over a 15-year period cannot prove much in any event. Similar periods of increasing crime rates have, in the past, been followed by decreases and the present trends may not be any more serious than those.

The alarmed discussion of swiftly rising crime rates is simply not warranted by those few increases which are the exception rather than the rule. It would be

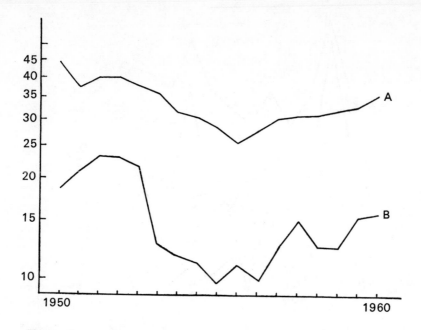

Figure 5

Crime Rates per 100,000 Population — Less Serious Offences of Violence.
A. Aggravated Assault Charges.
B. Shooting and Wounding Charges.

more appropriate to refer to sharply rising rates of parking tickets, although this would not coincide with popular notions of a crime wave.[5]

Although time accounts for a substantial amount of variation in crime, it can only be the beginning of an explanation. The changing of the calendar each January 1 is not of course what really affects the crime rate, although it is treated in the analysis as the independent variable. What is really meant is that unknown factors, which vary with time and for which time is simply a proxy, are acting to change the crime rate. These forces could be the decline of the influence of the churches, hard work and corporal punishment and increasing amounts of leisure time, the drug and comfort culture, television, and so forth, depending on one's background and prejudices.

The Relationship Between Size of Police Force and Crime Rates

However, there is another plausible influence on the crime rate — the efforts made by society to apprehend and prosecute criminals. It is one of the many paradoxes in the field of crime and corrections that increases in the strength of the police force may be followed by increases in the crime rate.

The fact that the increases for the less serious offences have been enormous, while those for indictable offences have been trivial, is indirect evidence for the hypothesis that police activity is responsible for the increase. Common sense suggests that parking offences are closely related to police activity. Traffic violations are also related to police activity although less closely. A large increase in the number of traffic policemen could deter some faulty driving, but

476

increases in the police force would probably result in an increased rate of detection of violations rather than in a decreased rate of actual violations.

The rates for summary conviction offences are especially vulnerable to police activity, for the attention paid to the less serious offences varies directly with police numbers. Presumably police forces give highest priority to the most dangerous crimes such as murder, robbery and rape, which will always be thoroughly investigated even if the force is too under-staffed to handle other reports. An increase in personnel would then be allocated disproportionately to the investigation of less serious offences.

These suggestions can be put to a number of statistical tests. Here we shall consider two hypotheses: (i) that the strength of the police force is positively related to the crime rate indicators (at least for the less serious indicators) and (ii) that the less serious the offence the greater the association will be between it and police strength.

The test consists of estimating relationships with the independent variable defined as police personnel (policemen, policewomen, and civilian employees) per capita, and with the logarithms of the specific crime rate indicators as the dependent variable.[6] [See Table 4]

TABLE 4

Summary of Police Force Strength and Crime Rate Statistics

Offence	Period	R^2	t	Proportionate Change in Crime Rate/ Proportionate Change in Police Strength
Serious Offences				
Murder Charges	1950–1966	0.04	1.26	0.6
Manslaughter Charges	1955–1966	0.00	−0.57	−0.6
Attempted Murder Charges	1950–1966	0.00	0.44	0.2
Shooting and Wounding Charges	1950–1966	0.06	−1.43	−0.5
Aggravated Assault Charges	1950–1966	0.16	−2.03	−0.3
All Indictable Convictions	1950–1966	0.00	−0.42	0.0
All indictable Charges	1950–1966	0.00	−1.01	0.0
Breaking and Entering Convictions	1950–1966	0.16	1.98*	0.4
Theft Convictions	1950–1966	0.00	1.01	0.2
Non-Criminal Offences				
Children Adjudged Delinquent	1950–1965	0.16	1.99*	0.6
All Criminal Code Summary Conviction Convictions	1956–1966	0.53	3.50*	0.8
All Summary Conviction Convictions	1950–1966	0.68	5.87*	1.0
Traffic Convictions	1950–1966	0.68	5.89*	1.2
Parking Offences Known to the Police	1955–1966	0.23	2.02*	0.7

*Statistically significant at the 5 percent level (one-tailed test). Consequently in each of these cases variation in the strength of the police force accounts for a significant proportion of the variation in the crime rate.

Source: Police data from D.B.S., *Police Statistics*, 1950-1959, Table 1; *Police Administration Statistics* 1960, Table 1; 1962, Table 20; 1963, Table 28; 1964, Table 27; 1965, Table 6; 1966, Table 6.

Note that the break in the results between the serious and less serious offences is very sharp. For virtually none of the serious offences did variation in police force strength significantly explain variation in the crime rate, while for most of the less serious offences the amount explained was substantial. Given that indictable offences include petty thefts and property damage, it is reasonable to expect an increase in police numbers to affect convictions for those crimes. Nevertheless, these categories did not show the same correlation, as the clearly trivial infractions, with the size of police force.

The data largely, but not perfectly, confirm the second of the hypotheses specified above. The rates of charges for the most serious offences of violence (murder, manslaughter, attempted murder, shooting and wounding, and aggravated assault) do not increase with the size of the police force. Of the serious non-violent crimes, breaking and entering is the only one to show a significant association.

Conclusion

The research reported in this paper is an attempt to test the fundamental belief that the crime rate is increasing. The proposition was found to lack supporting empirical evidence for the period studied, 1950-1966. This is not to say that the crime rate is decreasing. The simple conclusion to be drawn is that there have not been changes strong enough to appear in the data. The few trends found were weak and often counteracted by others in the opposite direction. Since the data allowed ample opportunity for findings of meaningful trends, it is fair to conclude that the failure to find them means that they probably do not exist.

Footnotes

1. Indeed, the DBS constantly warns the user of its statistics to exercise caution, especially for making year-by-year comparisons. Curiously, DBS ignores its own warning, especially in the *Canada Year Book* where 10-year series are common.
2. DBS Health and Welfare Division, Judicial Section, private communication.
3. This does not mean that time itself acts as an independent variable that causes changes in the crime rate, but rather that certain unknown factors that vary with time affect the crime rate.
4. Values of R^2 with the dependent variables as the crime rate indicators themselves, not the logarithms, were also tested, giving similar results.
5. The same conclusion is reached, using similar methods of analysis, in the *Report of the Canadian Committee on Corrections*, 1969.
6. Some adjustment of the police force data was required because these data are not reported consistently throughout the period. Between 1950 and 1961 the numbers of police and civilian employees reported to DBS rose sharply – primarily because each year the number of police departments reporting increase, rather than because of any real growth. However, the population of the area policed was also reported, so the final indicator of strength per 100,000 is not affected. These population figures were based on the preceding census year and had to be changed with more recent estimates.
After 1962, the population of the area policed was not reported. However, the number of departments reporting fluctuated only mildly in this period and did not increase. Consequently, the total population of Canada was used to make the ratio. This left a slight gap in the resulting ratios between the two series. The ratio in 1962 was 8 percent higher than in 1961, while for the years 1962-1966 the average was only 4 percent higher, and in the five years before the break the average ratio was identical to that in 1961. It seemed reasonable to assume that the real increase between 1961 and 1962 lay somewhere between 0 and 4 percent. Since there is no *correct* way to determine the true increase, two exploratory runs of the data were made, one fixing the increase over the 1961 base as nil, the other involving a 4 percent increase over 1961. The succeeding years were computed by adding the increases showing in the 1962-1966 series. The differences in the results using O and 4 percent turned out to be trivial. Another test was made with the 1962 ratio based upon a 2 percent increase over 1961, and the results reported in Table 4 are based on that adjustment.

References

Bauer, Raymond A., *Social Indicators*. Cambridge, Mass.: MIT Press, 1966.
Bigelow, Tupper S., *A Manual for Ontario Magistrates*. Toronto: Queen's Printer, 1962.

Canadian Committee on Corrections, *Report*. Ottawa: Queen's Printer, 1969.

Department of Justice, *Juvenile Delinquency in Canada*. Ottawa: Queen's Printer, 1965.

Decore, J. V., "Criminal Sentencing: The Role of the Canadian Courts of Appeal and the Concept of Uniformity," *Criminal Law Quarterly*, 6, 1963-1964, pp. 324-380.

Dominion Bureau of Statistics, *Murder Statistics*. Ottawa: Queen's Printer, 1967.

Friedland, M. C. and Mohr, J. W., "Canadian Criminal Statistics," *Criminal Law Quarterly*, 7, 1964, pp. 170-186.

Hogarth, John, "Towards the Improvement of Sentencing in Canada," *Canadian Journal of Corrections*, 9, 1967, pp. 122-136.

Hogarth, John, "Sentencing as a Human Process," Ph.D. thesis, Cambridge University, 1969.

Jaffary, Stuart K., "Sentencing of Adults in Canada," Toronto: University of Toronto Press, 1963.

Mewett, A. W. and Common, W. B., "The Philosophy of Sentencing and Disparity of Sentences," Report to the Canadian Bar Association, mimeo, 1969.

Ontario Magistrates Association, Report of Committee on Sentencing, mimeo, 1962.

Queen's University, "Proceedings of the Seminar on the Sentencing of Offenders," Kingston, June 4-15, 1962.

Street, T. G., "Current and Candid," *Canadian Journal of Corrections*, 5, 1963, p. 48.

Wheeler, Stanton, *Controlling Delinquents*. New York: John Wiley, 1968.

Juvenile Delinquency in the Middle-Class Youth Culture*

Edmund W. Vaz

A youth culture of middle-class adolescents is not endemic to a society. Adolescents have not always been as freely available to one another as they are today. Their community of interests, consensus of opinion, and the uniformities of action that spotlight the contemporary scene constitute a relatively new phenomenon in society, one not easily envisaged in the past. Seventy-five years ago the social structure of society, the organization of family life, educational standards, rights and obligations of the student role, and the routine activities among middle-class youth tended to handicap the emergence of a middle-class youth culture.

Few are the middle-class children today who are reared in an atmosphere of Puritan severity. No longer must children be seen and not heard, kept indoors, and off the streets. Patterns of hard work and hard saving are apt to be a thing of the past. No longer is it enough for a boy to enjoy the right to the opportunity of an education; there exists the felt right to a high school diploma, and a college degree is becoming more a matter of perseverence than of burning the midnight oil. Relaxed parental control in today's middle-class family, and the general freedom enjoyed by adolescents have been used traditionally to explain lower-class adolescent behavior. Use of the now popular term *street-corner society* is no longer warranted to describe the joint activities of lower-class boys only. The corner drug store, the drive-in, and the coffee bar are as much a precinct of the middle-class teen-ager as of his lower-class brother.

The world of middle-class boys is largely peer oriented, conspicuously non-intellectual, and is outstanding for its concern with status and the pursuit of *fun and games*. Notwithstanding the diversity and size of groups among these boys, they possess a relatively common system of values, norms, and practices, and their collective behavior patterns are distinguishable. Their tacit ratification of norms, and conformity to existing practices, foster the flow of teen-age behavior and reflect its legitimacy within the culture. This has helped strengthen the role of adolescent in the middle class, given it newly won status, and has contributed to the stability of the youth culture.

The content of the middle-class youth culture is neither delinquent nor rebellious, and seldom does it antagonize middle-class sentiments. Usually it reflects adult expectations, values, and institutions, and adult groups have encouraged development of the youth culture, advertised its prominence, and utilized its resources which has strengthened its position within the larger system. The proliferation of *extracurricular* activities has received widespread parental approval and mirrors the proclaimed educational value of the *life adjustment* and *social maturity* of the child. This congruence of attitudes between parents and educators lends structural support to the youth culture. Not only do parents encourage youth participation in social events, they also organize opportunities for regular teen-age activities. The respectability and popularity of these activities help convince parents (and adolescents) of their value, and the variety of programs testifies to widespread adult concern for adolescent participation. This tends to strengthen adolescent relationships and helps build mutual respect between adolescents and adults in the community.

Similarly, communal support of high school athletics has kept pace with the rapid growth of college and professional sports. High schools serve as preparatory training grounds for professional talent, and organized sports (e.g., Little League Baseball) has contributed widely to the general popularity of sports in the high school and community. Successful high school teams enhance community status and the reputation of families of participating athletes. Communal moral support and financial subsidization contribute to the development of athletic talent for schools, and spotlight its value for the community. The convergence of common purpose and action between community and schools reaffirms common values. Continued interest and participation by students comply with adult expectations, and promote the general reputation of schools, coaches, and of athletes in the youth culture, which helps consolidate the youth culture within the larger institutional network.

Full *membership* in the adolescent system is contingent largely upon the exercise of one's role, which requires active participation in youth culture activities and relationships. Learning the skills and nuances of a role often occurs through trial and error, but it also requires instruction from others. Middle-class youngsters are tutored early in the conduct required for future social success. Participation in age-restricted, sometimes adult-supervised social events, introduces youngsters to incipient forms of heterosexual relations and teen-age games. Older boys and the mass media are also valuable sources of instruction in the details and marginal maneuvers used in *handling* the opposite sex.

480

The significance of *socializing* for the middle-class adolescent cannot be over-emphasized. Both teachers and parents expect the child to be a *joiner*, and, to perform his role adequately, active participation in teen-age events is man-datory. Boys who pursue academic interests only are noticeably disapproved. Yet the student who excels both academically and socially is fully acceptable and mirrors the success of the educational system.

The pursuit of status is intense among middle-class adolescents, and often it is to his peers that the adolescent looks for respect. Peer-group membership and conformity to role expectations confer social approbation and tend to publicize (through frequency of interaction) collective teen-age solidarity. In a newly developing culture where norms are not fully institutionalized, where struc-tural stability and internal coherence are only partially realized, and where traditional role expectations are obscure, conformity as a moral imperative is especially helpful and desirable.

Competition

Competition pervades all parts of a boy's life in the middle-class youth culture. It influences his choice of clothes, his preference in music and girls, his necking techniques, and the manipulation of his car. Peer-group standards are often the critical criteria by which a boy forms his opinions and gauges his behavior. Throughout his daily activities competition prevails, and peers stand alert to criticize, to pass judgment, and to offer approval. Ultimately, competition with *everyman* becomes *internalized* and the *generalized other* becomes an ubiquitous audience always keeping score. The absence of others, or the fact that only strangers are present, fails to deter a boy's struggle for attention. Con-tinuously on parade, even when he is alone, the adolescent *guns* his engine, *drags* the streets, squeals the tires of his automobile (*lays a patch*), coercing attention, seeking approval.

Were competition uncontrolled in the youth culture, it might corrode friend-ships and damage group relationships. The conditions under which current teen-age activities occur tend to preserve social ties and strengthen group cohesion. Typically, adolescent activity occurs under a veneer of non-com-petitive good-fellowship and fun. This unserious quality to their joint activity fosters their belief in the impression that they create. And the rhetoric in terms of which they describe their behavior, "It's all in fun," "It's just for kicks," or "We were just having a few laughs," enables them to escape opprobrium should they be accused of more deliberate competitiveness. Increasing use of this vocabulary of motives obscures underlying competition, and tends to pre-vent them from making clear-cut distinctions among their everyday practices and games. Thus, "heavy" necking, *hooliganism, playing chicken* at 100 m.p.h., drinking bouts, and sexual escapades are often described as merely *having fun*.

Marginal Differentiation

Throughout the daily legitimate activities (dating, dances, riding about with friends, *hanging* about the drug store, playing sports, etc.) of middle-class boys, veiled competition for status stimulates their experimentation in behavior. These *operating inventions* attract others, win approval and nourish competition, and take the form of behavioral nuances, sufficiently novel to distinguish them from existing patterns and competing efforts of peers. Although all behavior is, perhaps, partly exploratory, stabs at marginal differentiation are likely to be guarded, tentative, ambiguous, and to transpire in a situation characterized by *joint exploration and elaboration* of behavior. Yet extreme conduct of any kind is apt to be strongly disapproved among *sophisticated* youths, and there exist strong motivations to conform to prevailing norms and patterns. But the boundaries of legitimacy are not impregnable, and it is during these legitimate fun-ridden activities, where boys are encouraged to join in, that unobtrusive acts lead gradually to unanticipated elaboration beyond the precincts of legitimacy. Since adolescent activities occur in a spirit of good will, creative efforts are applauded, encouraged, and behavioral novelty is seldom considered delinquent. However, innovation is tolerated only within the limits of acceptable adolescent interests. In this way behavioral differentiation does little injury to existing norms and values, and group status is not undermined. As newly developing practices gain approval, they acquire their own morality, and each move becomes circumscribed by game rules. In this setting delinquency need not emerge from anti-social motives. Delinquent acts, rooted in anti-social impulses, are apt to transgress acceptable conduct, violate middle-class norms, and be disapproved altogether. The motives for much middle-class delinquency are learned through sustained participation in everyday respectable, adolescent activities. In this manner delinquency becomes gradually routine in the middle-class youth culture.

To help substantiate some of the ideas in this paper, evidence is presented from a larger study of middle-class delinquency. Data on the self-reported delinquency of 850 middle-class boys are offered and interpreted according to their social roles in the youth culture. Evidence is presented on the relationship between differential delinquency involvement and (a) the active participation of boys in legitimate teen-age activities, and (b) their peer orientation. Data are included on the relationship between the seriousness with which boys perceive engaging in delinquent acts and their differential participation in legitimate teen-age activities. To emphasize the delinquent content of the middle-class youth culture, the relationship between differential delinquency involvement and the seriousness with which boys define engaging in delinquent acts is investigated.

Research

During the spring of 1963 questionnaires were administered to 1,639 white high school boys in grades 9 through 13 in five coeducational high schools located in four Canadian communities. Appropriate techniques were used to minimize collusion and maximize anonymity of subjects. The communities differ in size and are urban or semi-urban in character, and the high schools are located in middle-class socioeconomic areas.

Delinquency was measured by a check list of 21 items of behavior. The items are violations of the law or are offenses on the basis of which juveniles can be adjudicated as delinquent. Both serious and minor offenses are included, such as driving a car beyond the speed limit, breaking and entering, intoxication, and the use of drugs for kicks. Offenses such as gang fights, armed robbery, and rape were not included. The boys were asked how often they had committed each offense; response categories included very often, quite often, several times, once or twice, never.

To establish the socioeconomic position of subjects, three indicators were used in the following order: (a) father's occupation, (b) father's level of education, and (c) size of organization in which father works. Using father's occupation, subjects were first classified according to the Blishen Occupational Class Scale. Questionnaires initially difficult to classify, or that included only father's level of education, were reviewed and grouped according to the second indicator. Subjects whose fathers had "completed high school" or completed " some college" were classified into Group III, and those who had "finished college" or higher were sorted into Group II. A small number of remaining questionnaires, with ambiguously reported job titles only, were categorized with the help of the third indicator according to the writer's judgment. All subjects classified into Groups II ($n = 337$) and III ($n = 513$) were combined and hereafter termed "middle class."

Table 1 reveals sharp differences in the responses of younger and older boys. Important considerations in interpreting the data are the social roles of middle-class boys and the rights and obligations – varying sets of role criteria – by which boys may claim status to their roles. To the extent that a boy conforms to these criteria his peers will judge and reward him accordingly.

Some of the delinquent practices are more realistically possible and readily available for older boys as relevant criteria of status. For younger boys these practices are less meaningful to their social role. To learn the rules and tricks of smoking marijuana or of purchasing liquor takes time and effort and requires the opportunity. Youngsters are apt not to claim status in terms of these practices. Nevertheless, younger and older boys share, in part, a relatively common frame of experience. In and out of school, on and off the playing field, youngsters show deference to their teen-age elders, strengthen growing identifications, and they are eager to learn and anxious to participate. Thus, drinking games, sexual intimacy with girls, and truancy are not uncommon among these boys.

As youngsters assume gradually the role of older teen-ager new attitudes and practices are required of them. New criteria become applicable in terms of which peers judge them and, depending upon their ego-involvement in their role, they evaluate themselves. Older boys care less about the practices and criteria of status that matter to younger lads. What a youngster considers serious an older boy will define as *kid stuff*. Delinquent activities that are relatively popular among boys occupying different roles will depend on the alternative criteria available for status gain.

Table 1 shows that petty theft is the only offense committed by the majority of younger boys. Other popular delinquencies, among younger boys, include fist fighting, vandalism, gambling, stealing money, and drinking liquor. These offenses are popular also among older teen-agers, but in some cases the difference in responses is small. There is a difference of only 11 percentage points between younger and older boys who fist fight. Less than 7 percentage points separate younger and older boys who admit petty theft. About 45 percent of younger boys and 52 percent of older teen-agers report vandalic behavior.

TABLE 1

Self-Reported Delinquent Behavior of Middle-Class Boys by Age Group

Type of Offense[a]	Percent Admitting Commission of Offense Age		Percent Admitting Commission of Offense More than Once or Twice Age	
	13-14	15-19	13-15	15-19
Driven a car without a driver's license	28.6	62.3	9.1	27.9
Taken little things that did not belong to you	61.0	67.2	10.4	16.7
Skipped school without a legitimate excuse	23.6	40.8	3.9	13.6
Driven beyond the speed limit	5.8	51.2	1.3	39.7
Participated in drag-races along the highway with your friends	6.5	31.1	2.0	16.3
Engaged in a fist fight with another boy	45.8	56.0	7.1	8.7
Been feeling "high" from drinking beer, wine or liquor	11.7	39.0	2.6	17.9
Gambled for money at cards, dice, or some other game	42.2	66.0	16.9	37.4
Remained out all night without parents' permission	19.5	25.8	5.2	9.5
Taken a car without owner's knowledge	5.2	12.5	0.7	3.1
Placed on school probation or expelled from school	0.7	5.6	0.0	1.2
Destroyed or damaged public or private property of any kind	44.8	52.0	11.7	14.8
Taken little things of value (between $2 and $50) which did not belong to you	9.7	16.0	0.7	3.5
Tried to be intimate with a member of the opposite sex	18.2	37.8	7.8	17.6
Broken into or tried to break and enter a building with the intention of stealing	5.2	7.5	0.7	1.0
Sold, used or tried to use drugs of some kind	1.3	1.0	0.0	0.3
Bought or tried to buy beer, wine, or liquor from a store or adult	3.3	24.8	0.7	11.7
Taken money of any amount from someone or place which did not belong to you	30.5	32.7	7.1	6.9
Taken a glass of beer, wine, or liquor at a party or elsewhere with your friends	32.5	64.8	8.4	35.2
	n = 154	682[b]		

[a] Two items are omitted because they were used solely as reliability check measures.
[b] Fourteen cases of boys over 19 years are omitted.

Ironically, the world of younger boys is a masculine world, girls occupy little of their time. Their role in the middle class (perhaps among all social classes) is characterized by a particular image of masculinity. The values of adventure, bravado, manliness, and muscular prowess circumscribe their role, and usually they make every effort to prove that they are *all boy*. Most younger lads approve of practices that enable them to display their courage, exhibit their physical strength, and thereby *improve* their self-image. To *take a dare*, to engage in varying kinds of vandalism, fighting, and petty theft are practiced frequently among younger boys. Failure to participate in at least one of these types of games may deny a boy's claim to being *all boy* among his peers. The data indicate that typical of these boys are the more masculine offenses.

The older adolescent role requires increased participation in dominant youth culture activities. Parties, dances, sport events, cars, and girls occupy a larger part of a boy's time. *Sophistication* replaces masculinity, and a premium is put on the cultivation of social skills and a *social personality*. The rougher habits of younger lads are taboo. Yet a change in roles and the gradual transformation of a boy's self-image take time and involve uncertainty and strain. Under such conditions boys are apt to revert, occasionally, to an earlier set of responses and standards to which they are still partly committed. Thus, older boys continue temporarily their earlier delinquencies. But once they learn their new role, feel committed to its standards, and begin to judge themselves by it, earlier practices, no longer serviceable, are seldom recruited. Petty theft, vandalism, stealing money, and aggressive behavior, concomitant with the role of the youngster, become relics of an earlier role.

If the role of older teen-ager calls for sophisticated behavior, it tends also to generate a more sophisticated brand of delinquency. Yet, theirs is no criminal world, there is no community of delinquent gangs, no body of criminal values, malicious attitudes, and predatory skills. The young hoodlum, the adolescent thug, and the gang leader are types of a nether world. It is the crew-cut and the clean look, the *nice guy*, and the high school star who claim status among these boys. Drinking, drag-racing, speeding, sex practices, truancy, and gambling assume a larger part of later adolescent behavior. At age 16 a boy immediately acquires greater access to an automobile. Besides being a symbol of status the car allows the teen-ager to expand his circle of friends, makes available girls otherwise inaccessible to him, and also offers him increased opportunity to break the law. Sixty-two percent of older boys admit having driven without a permit. Over 50 percent have driven beyond the speed limit, and 31 percent admit dragging along the highway. Admittedly, the values of courage and daring underline the practice of dragging, but its value for these boys is less to demonstrate their masculinity than it is to exhibit their driving skills and to highlight the efficiency of their cars. Since the automobile is an extension of self, these practices enable a boy to increase his popularity among peers.

Drinking practices (at parties, sport events, in cars during intermission at high school dances), sex games with girls, and gambling are symbolic of adolescent sophistication, serviceable for youth culture participation, and very likely a means for acquiring popularity. Sixty-five percent of older boys admit drinking liquor at a party; 39 percent admit having felt *high*, and over 37 percent have tried to *go the limit* with a girl. And once boys begin to drink they are expected to buy their liquor.

New interests and non-academic, time-consuming activities are necessary in maintaining a boy's popularity and very likely subvert his interest in school work. Thus, truancy tends to gain popularity among older youths. Similarly, gambling very likely increases among boys who gradually obtain larger sums of money. Most of these activities are predominantly sociable forms of delinquency and, apart from the intimate stages of sexual congress, are seldom practiced in private. They strengthen peer-group relationships, consolidate normative patterns among teen-agers, and contribute to the cohesion of the middle-class youth culture.

Table 1 shows also that sociable delinquencies such as automobile offenses, drinking, gambling, and sex violations rank highest among older boys who admit committing offenses more than once or twice.

Delinquency Involvement Among Middle-Class Boys

In order to establish the differential delinquency involvement of boys, two Guttman scales were obtained. Eleven items were selected on the basis that they might measure a common dimension of middle-class delinquency and using 850 boys, aged 13-19, eight of the items scale satisfactorily. Dichotomizing each item, a reproducibility coefficient of .920 was obtained with random distribution of error. Scale items include: taken little things that did not belong to you; gambled for money at cards, dice, or other games; driven a car beyond the speed limit; skipped school without a legitimate excuse; been feeling *high* from drinking beer, wine, or liquor; bought or tried to buy beer, wine, or liquor from a store or adult; taken a glass of beer, wine, or liquor at a party or elsewhere with your friends; and tried to be intimate (go the limit) with a member of the opposite sex.

A second scale was obtained for 682 boys aged 15 to 19. Dichotomizing each item, eight items scale satisfactorily giving a reproducibility coefficient of .914. Scale items include: taken little things that did not belong to you; taken a glass of beer, wine, or liquor at a party or elsewhere with your friends; driven a car beyond the speed limit; been feeling *high* from drinking beer, wine, or liquor; driven a car without a driver's license or permit; tried to be intimate (go the limit) with a member of the opposite sex; bought or tried to buy beer, wine, or liquor; and skipped school. Each delinquency scale was trichotomized into low, medium, and high categories.

Not all boys engage actively in the social events of the middle-class youth culture, and not all delinquency is found among those who do. However, it is noteworthy that our scales highlight a non-violent component of delinquency. Items such as drinking liquor, skipping school, speeding, purchasing liquor, and sexual intimacy are noticeably sociable practices, and are conspicuously in accord with the typical, legitimate affairs of the youth culture. This kind of conduct seems to *fit* the sophisticated self-image of the older middle-class adolescent.

Two situation-type items (each with two response categories) were used to establish the peer orientation of boys. Three items were used to measure the active participation of boys in typical teen-age activities. One item deals with the time a boy spends riding about with his friends in the evenings. The second concerns the frequency of dating girls. The third item enquires about the time a boy spends around the local *hangout* in the evenings. Each item has five weighted response categories, and cases were distributed into high, medium, and low categories.

Differential Delinquency Involvement and Peer Group Orientation

Ordinarily adolescents are preoccupied with those of their own kind, friends and acquaintances who hold their values, share their opinions, and talk their language. Recurrent participation in peer activities tends to increase one's status in the eyes of peers, and opportunities (dates, parties, dances, etc.) for further social activity are the cherished rewards for conformity to prevailing norms. Under these conditions, to be a *loner* is a passport to pariahdom, but from our perspective the *loner*, the boy who is not peer-oriented, is less apt to engage in delinquency.

When each peer orientation item is tested against delinquent participation, results are significant ($p < .001$). In each case the majority of peer-oriented boys rates high in delinquency. Boys who favor parents rank lower in delinquency. To substantiate further these results, composite results of the peer orientation items were cross tabulated with delinquency involvement.

TABLE 2

Combined Items on Peer Orientation by Differential Delinquency Involvement: Middle-Class Adolescents by Age Groups

Peer Orientation	Delinquency Involvement					
	15-19 Years			All Ages		
	High	Medium	Low	High	Medium	Low
High	13.2	14.1	6.2	14.0	11.8	6.0
Medium	7.9	18.5	18.0	10.0	18.2	17.4
Low	2.9	7.8	9.4	3.7	6.5	10.7
Non-responses	0.0	0.0	0.0	0.0	0.0	0.0
	$n = 682$			$n = 850$		
	$\chi^2 = 58.03, 4df, p < .001$			$\chi^2 = 75.36, 4df, p < .001$		
	$C = .283$	$\bar{C} = .346$		$C = .287$	$\bar{C} = .352$	

Table 2 indicates that over 80 percent of high peer-oriented boys aged 15 to 19 rank high or medium in delinquency. Being parent-oriented is no guarantee against delinquency, but considerably fewer parent-oriented boys are highly delinquent. If we are correct, peer-oriented boys are more in demand in the typical carrousel of teen-age activities of which delinquency is an unanticipated result. The more a boy engages in such events the greater the likelihood of his becoming delinquent.

Differential Delinquency Involvement and Youth Culture Participation

We have described the middle-class youth culture as predominantly social in character. We have implied that the boy who has ready access to an automobile, who dates girls, attends dances, who goes to parties, and who is regularly engaged in sports is more likely to begin drinking, dragging, gambling, and to become partner to sexual practices and other sophisticated forms of delinquency. The more restricted, unsociable adolescent is less apt to become so involved.

When responses to the question, "How often do you drive about with friends in the evening" were cross tabulated with delinquency involvement, results revealed that approximately 90 percent of boys, aged 15 to 19, who drive about with friends three or more times per week, rank high or medium in delinquency. Boys who drive about once a week or less, are much less likely to rank high in delinquency. The same pattern holds for boys of all ages ($p < .001$).

The majority of boys who date girls three or more times a week are highly involved in delinquency. Most boys who seldom or never date rank low in delinquency. Again the pattern holds for both age groups ($p < .001$).

The third item asked was, "How often do you spend some time about the local 'hangout' in the evenings throughout the whole week?" When responses are matched against delinquency involvement, the results are significant ($p < .001$). With an increase in the social pursuits of boys, there is an increase in their delinquent behavior. Table 3 is important because it indicates the overall youth culture participation scores of boys and their delinquency involvement. Among boys highly active in legitimate activities about 90 percent fall into the two highest delinquent categories. Among low participants about 35 percent rank high in delinquency.

TABLE 3

Combined Scores on Active Participation in Youth Culture by Differential Delinquency Involvement: Middle-Class Adolescents by Age Groups

Youth Culture Activities	Delinquency Involvement					
	15-19 Years				All Ages	
	High	Medium	Low	High	Medium	Low
High	15.1	16.0	3.5	16.9	10.1	3.1
Medium	7.0	18.0	15.3	9.2	18.9	12.4
Low	2.0	6.9	15.7	1.9	7.9	19.4
Non-responses	0.2	0.0	0.2	0.1	0.1	0.0

$n = 682$ $\qquad\qquad$ $n = 850$

$\chi^2 = 151.26$, 4df, $p < .001$ $\qquad$ $\chi^2 = 251.67$, 4df, $p < .001$

$C = .426$ $\quad$ $\bar{C} = .522$ $\qquad\qquad$ $C = .478$ $\quad$ $\bar{C} = .586$

Active Participation in Youth Culture and Boys Perception of Delinquency Acts as Serious Conduct

The adolescent who is actively engrossed in social affairs is especially susceptible to current teen-age perspectives, attitudes, and opinions. Absorbed with his peers, listening to what they say, watching their actions, engaging in their games, prevailing teen-age attitudes gradually become part of his own behavioral and motivational baggage. Delinquency in the middle-class youth culture is an unanticipated consequence of conformity to the expected patterns of respectable teen-age behavior. Seldom is it defined illegal, and these boys rarely develop an image of themselves as delinquent. Under these circumstances certain types of delinquent practices are apt not to be taken seriously by middle-class boys. Paradoxically this relatively unserious attitude towards delinquency is learned while engaging in typically non-delinquent activities.

Twelve items were used to measure the seriousness felt by boys toward selected delinquent acts, and the distribution of scores was trichotomized into low, medium, and high categories. When responses to youth culture items are matched separately against scores on the perceived seriousness of delinquent acts, Chi-square values are significant in each instance ($p < .001$). Boys who are highly active in teen-age affairs (dating, driving about with friends, etc.) define delinquent acts less seriously than do boys who participate infrequently in such pursuits. More important is the association between overall scores on both variables (see Table 4). Again Chi-square values are significant ($p < .05$) for both age groups.

Teen-agers who are caught in the vortex of typical social activities are especially popular and enhance their social standing among peers. This is difficult to relinquish and they are apt to persist in their quest for social rewards.

TABLE 4

Separate and Combined Scores on the Relationship Between Youth Culture Activities and the Perception of Delinquent Acts as Serious: Middle-Class Adolescents by Age Group

Youth Culture Activities by Perceived Seriousness of Delinquent Acts	15-19 Years			All Ages		
	χ^2	C	$\bar{C}$	χ^2	C	$\bar{C}$
Driving about with friends in evening	77.94	S^a .319	.368	106.71	S .333	.384
Takes out a girl in evening	36.72	S .225	.275	41.11	S .214	.262
Spends time about local "hangout"	82.80	S .340	.380	104.13	S .330	.369
Youth Culture Activities: Combined Scores	83.08	S .109	.133	113.91	S .343	.420

$^a S$ = Significant at .05 level.

Through prolonged youth culture involvement they learn the prevailing attitudes and definitions and ultimately become involved in delinquency. But since this is seldom discovered and accords with routine events, neither the behavior nor the boys are apt to be considered delinquent. The seductive appeal of the middle-class youth culture and the rewards that reside therein very likely contain the seeds of delinquency.

A difficulty in appreciating delinquency among middle-class adolescents is that the majority of their everyday activities receive the blessing of parents, which tends to inhibit the development of a socially recognized image of the middle-class delinquent. This seeming immunity from the delinquent role perhaps confirms the teen-ager in his delinquent ways. Since delinquent practices emerge so unobtrusively from non-delinquent activities, middle-class teen-agers are apt less to define them as serious practices. Yet middle-class delinquency is not a happenstance affair. It is one thing for boys to break the rules, define their acts as serious and, perhaps, feel guilty. But boys who break rules and are indifferent about their violations are certainly to be viewed in a different light. The association between delinquency involvement and the seriousness with which they define delinquent acts suggests strongly a delinquent content to the middle-class youth culture. Moreover, it lends stability to the delinquent norms developing in the culture.

Table 5 reveals that the definition of engaging in delinquency as serious behavior tends to correspond with the differential involvement in delinquency.

TABLE 5

The Perception of Delinquent Acts as Serious Behavior by Differential Delinquency Involvement: Middle-Class Adolescents by Age Groups

Perceived Seriousness of Delinquency	Delinquency Involvement					
	15-19 Years			All Ages		
	High	Medium	Low	High	Medium	Low
Not Very Serious	15.4	11.7	6.3	15.8	9.9	5.4
Moderately Serious	7.2	18.0	12.2	9.5	16.9	10.4
Serious	1.8	11.0	16.1	2.8	10.1	19.1
Non-responses	0.0	0.2	0.0	0.0	0.1	0.0

$n = 682$
$\chi^2 = 102.04$, 4df, $p < .001$
$C = .360$ $\bar{C} = .441$

$n = 850$
$\chi^2 = 187.58$, 4df, $p < .001$
$C = .425$ $\bar{C} = .521$

These results subvert the idea that delinquency among middle-class boys is an occasional phenomenon.

Because behavior is illegal does not exempt it from having objective consequences for the adjustment of boys and for the middle-class youth culture. In the first place, as long as delinquency remains relatively faithful to middle-class values, it tends to reaffirm the social standing of the adolescent. Drinking games, dragging a car, *scoring* with a girl, or getting mildly drunk at a party are apt to be normative practices among these boys and are congruent with the dominant social orientation of the middle-class youth culture. Since these kinds of conduct emerge from societally endorsed activities, and once they do not get *out of hand*, they are likely perceived by parents as signs of maturity. This will prevent a boy from developing a delinquent self-conception, confirm his image of himself as an *average boy*, and legitimize his claim to the adolescent role.

In addition, conformity to legitimate teen-age norms serves to sustain existing delinquent patterns. Until middle-class delinquency openly violates middle-class values and sentiments it is not likely to arouse collective parental concern over the teen-age culture. The fact that periodic outbursts among these boys are blamed on a few *troublemakers* – whose behavior is attributed typically to personality pathology – prevents delinquency from being considered normative within the culture. Since the recreational programs of middle-class youngsters coincide with current educational programs and reflect strongly felt values of adults, this helps deflect attention from the youth culture, and its relationship to the larger social structure, as a major source of juvenile delinquency among middle-class youth.

Alcohol Use in Canadian Society[*][†]

Jan de Lint

Canadian drinking has not been given much attention in the alcohol literature. The most likely explanation for this is that the use of beverage alcohol in Canadian society, unlike its use in Jewish, French, Irish or Italian societies, is not characterized by the predominance of one particular drinking pattern or one particular alcohol problem. There are many different drinking patterns in Canada and many different problems associated with alcohol use.

An examination of the drinking patterns in a society can offer us some useful clues about the magnitude and nature of alcohol problems in that society. Particularly, the problems of intoxication and of physical damage caused by long periods of excessive drinking are closely associated with the prevalence and type of drinking patterns.

*Reprinted from *Addictions*, Vol. 15, No. 3 (Fall 1968), published by the Addiction Research Foundation of Ontario.

†This article is based on papers he delivered to the Addiction Research Foundation's seventh annual summer school at Laurentian University in Sudbury, June, 1968.

To what extent a study of drinking patterns can also provide us with meaningful information about the magnitude and nature of clinical alcoholism is less clear. It has been suggested, for instance, that drinking to relax, to unwind, or to relieve social and physical discomfort, may precede clinical alcoholism. On the other hand, many who at times drink in this manner do not become alcoholics; also, it should be noted that many factors other than alcohol use contribute to the development of clinical alcoholism.

How should drinking behaviour be studied? Some authorities in the alcohol field have gone so far as to try to develop a general theory of drinking. At present, such a theory is as impossible as a general theory of human behaviour. At best it is a frame of reference suggesting the type of factors that may be relevant in drinking behaviour. Thus it has been stated, for example, that people drink for five reasons: ritual, leisure, tension-release, to express solidarity or social differentiation, and to facilitate interaction. It has also been suggested that drinking is affected by the accessibility of alcohol and by the rules of society.

The major objection to such statements is that they are too general to have any meaning. There are too many areas of human behaviour that can be similarly defined. For instance, eating can have all these *functions* and is similarly affected by the accessibility of food and the rules of society. But no one has seriously proposed a general theory of eating.

In other words, I suggest that we should not aim at a general theory of drinking; it is not really meaningful. What we want to study instead are those patterns that can be usefully associated with the problems that face us. The questions we should ask should be practical and to the point. I would like to describe in this article the major patterns and trends in Canadian drinking, and I would also like to show their relevancy to the problems associated with alcohol use: to intoxication, to clinical alcoholism and to physical damage as a result of regular, execssive drinking.

Present Level of Consumption

An obvious point of departure in our sketch of the major aspects of alcohol use in Canada is to consider, first of all, the general level of alcohol consumption. In 1966, the latest year for which statistics are available, the average Canadian adult consumed 1.79 Imperial gallons of absolute alcohol per year – an amount equivalent to 480 twelve-ounce bottles of beer or 29 twenty-five-ounce bottles of whisky. Compared to other countries, this level of consumption is not high. The average drinker in France, Italy or Switzerland consumes at least twice as much.

Alcohol use in Canada has increased considerably during the last three decades. At present, average consumption is at least three times that of 1935. This increase is attributable in part to an increase in the proportion of adult users in the general population: at present, about 70 to 80 percent of Canadian adults use alcoholic beverages. Attitudes towards drinking have changed much in Canada since Prohibition, and very few Canadians still feel that alcohol sales should be abolished.

Changes in Drinking Patterns

The overall increase in alcohol consumption cannot only be explained with reference to a wider acceptance of drinking in Canadian society. It is also attributable to an increase in the prevalence of certain drinking behaviours. For instance, excessive alcohol drinking (for example, inveterate drinking or clinical alcoholism) usually accounts for a large share of total alcohol consumption. These drinking behaviours are much more prevalent now than in the recent past, and consequently the increased prevalence of these types of drinking behaviour *alone* has contributed more to the overall increase in alcohol consumption than has the increased proportion of users in the adult population.

The overall increase in alcohol consumption has not been brought about by similar increases in the use of beer, wine and distilled spirits. Since these three types of alcoholic beverages differ in cost, alcohol strength, taste and tradition, they are quite differently involved in the many Canadian drinking patterns. It appears that the drinking patterns involving distilled spirits and wine have increased somewhat more rapidly than the patterns involving the use of beer. Beer consumption still accounts for most of the alcohol consumption in Canada, but the trend seems to be in the direction of distilled spirits and wine. At any rate, the sales of these two beverages have increased more rapidly in recent years than the sales of beer. I will come back later to the significance of these current trends in specific alcoholic beverage consumption with reference to alcohol problems. However, before doing this, I would like to discuss other major aspects of Canadian drinking behaviour.

To know that in Canada the average yearly consumption of alcohol per adult is about 1.79 gallons of absolute alcohol has little meaning by itself. The probability of meeting someone who indeed consumes 1.79 Imperial gallons of absolute alcohol yearly – of which 58 percent is beer, 8 percent is wine, and 34 percent is distilled spirits (according to the 1966 statistics) – is obviously

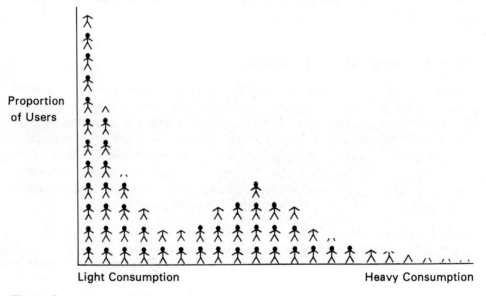

Figure 1

Distribution of Consumption if Predominant Patterns are Light Occasional Use and Regular Excessive Use

492

very small. In fact, most Canadians do not use all three kinds of alcoholic beverages, and the vast majority drink considerably less than 1.79 Imperial gallons of absolute alcohol per year.

What is of interest, however, with reference to the type of drinking behaviour present in Canadian society is how alcohol consumption is distributed over the population of adult users. One might expect some clustering of drinkers around certain levels of consumption: a lot of light, occasional drinking on the one side of the distribution curve and many excessive users on the other (Figure 1). This, however, is not the case. The distribution of alcohol use in Canada has been found to be regular and smooth: a gradually decreasing proportion of Canadian adults consume a gradually increasing quantity of alcohol (Figure 2).

It is clear that the vast majority of Canadian drinkers are very moderate consumers. In fact, as Figure 2 shows, 84.37 percent consume less than five centilitres of absolute alcohol daily. This is slightly less than three pints of beer

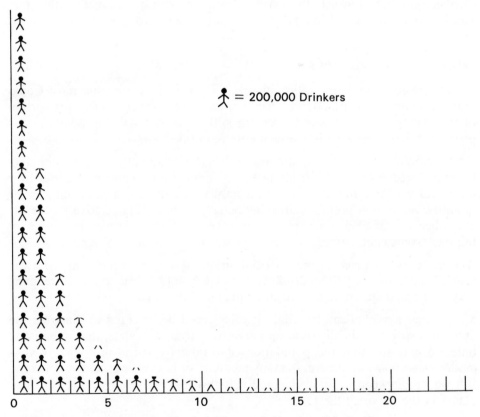

Average Daily Consumption in Centilitres of Absolute Alcohol*

84.37% (8,117,359) drink 0–5 cl. daily	9.87% (949,607) drink 5–10 cl. daily	2.96% (284,787) drink 10–15 cl. daily	1.24% (119,302) drink 15–24 cl. daily	1.56% (150,090) drink more than 20 cl. daily

*A pint of Canadian beer (5% alcohol by volume), or a 1½ ounce shot of Canadian distilled spirits (40% alcohol by volume), contains about 1.7 centilitres of absolute alcohol.

Figure 2

Distribution of Alcohol Consumption in Canada

(5 percent alcohol by volume) or three drinks containing 1½-ounce shots of distilled spirits (40 percent alcohol by volume). On the other hand, 1.56 percent consume more than twenty centilitres daily – in other words, twelve or more pints of beer, or twelve or more 1½-ounce shots of distilled spirits. Although relatively small, this group accounts for nearly 20 percent of the total alcohol sales in Canada.

Transition is Gradual

It is not difficult to appreciate the difference between the 8,117,359 drinkers on the extreme left of the distribution curve who consume between zero and five centilitres of absolute alcohol daily, and the 150,090 drinkers who consume more than twenty centilitres. The latter group is either grossly intoxicated at frequent intervals or in a continuous state of mild intoxication. What is difficult to understand is why the transition from moderate consumption to excessive consumption is so gradual. Only a relatively small proportion of drinkers gravitate towards the extreme range of consumption. On the other hand, many Canadian drinkers are dangerously close to these high levels.

Many are Beginners

Examination of the consumption distribution curve indicates that most Canadians have established moderate drinking habits. However, a large proportion of the drinkers at the lower ranges are still beginners – young adults in the process of acquiring a variety of drinking patterns.

One person may enter the population of drinkers at age 20; by age 30 he may have acquired a variety of drinking habits involving a quantity of about four ounces of whisky daily. At age 40 his habits may involve a somewhat larger quantity, but at that point his drinking behaviour may vary relatively little for a number of years. When he approaches 60 or so, his yearly consumption may fall back somewhat.

Another person's place in the distribution curve may also move up with the years, but at the age of 40 his drinking habits may not become stable. Instead, he may continue to gravitate towards the tail end of the curve.

Many other hypothetical drinking histories could be invented to illustrate the dynamic aspects of the distribution curve. It is true, of course, that at any one time we may say that the population of drinkers consists of so many very moderate, so many moderate, so many medium, or heavy, or excessive drinkers. But we should keep in mind that individual drinkers are moving to different places in the curve all the time.

Where to Draw the Line

Whatever the nature of the different drinking careers, the overall result at any one point in time is a fairly smooth distribution of consumers according to the quantities they consume. The distribution does not suggest any point, any quantity, where we seem to be dealing with different *types* of drinkers. The traits that would suggest that four-ounce drinkers are much different from five-ounce drinkers are unknown.

The tail end of the distribution curve is, of course, of particular interest to us. It contains many alcoholics in the clinical sense, but it also contains a considerable number of other drinkers. All of them consume quantities hazardous to health. It would be difficult to pinpoint exactly at what consumption levels drinking becomes hazardous. Some scientists have placed it at nine gallons of absolute alcohol yearly or about ten ounces of whisky daily. Many other factors also have to be considered, such as the age and the nutritional habits of the drinker. Whatever the case, the present distribution of consumption clearly shows that a substantial number of Canadian drinkers consume quantities hazardous to health.

Reasons for Drinking

Let us now turn to the different ways in which beverage alcohol is used in Canadian society. For what reasons do Canadians drink? Can we say, for instance, that regular social use is more prevalent than other types of use? To answer these questions we must keep in mind that the prevalence of each type of alcohol use cannot be estimated, since there is a great deal of overlap in reasons for drinking. A bottle of beer on a warm afternoon may be consumed for thirst, relaxation, taste and pleasure all at the same time. Similarly, a martini before a luncheon meeting may serve a variety of *functions*: to facilitate interaction, to make the occasion more enjoyable, to increase the appetite. But although we cannot clearly separate alcohol consumption according to different types of use, we do have some information about the relative importance of the various reasons why Canadians drink.

The use of beverage alcohol to celebrate an important event was often mentioned by Canadians who were interviewed in the course of a survey of drinking behaviour. This use is also clearly indicated by the large proportion of total distilled spirits and wines sold around the Christmas season.

Medical Use of Alcohol

With reference to the importance of medical use of beverage alcohol in Canadian society, we must draw a distinction between institutionalized medicine and traditional or home medicine. The extent to which beverage alcohol is prescribed by physicians in the course of treatment would refer to its role in institutionalized medicine. This use is relatively unimportant. However, traditional or home medical use of beverage alcohol appears very prevalent in Canadian society. Many people reportedly drink to promote sleep, to relax, to unwind, or to relieve social or physical discomforts. These are essentially medical uses of alcoholic beverages.

Another frequently reported use of beverage alcohol is as part of the daily diet. Alcoholic beverages are essentially foods, and often form part of a meal or are used to quench a thirst. From alcohol sales data we learn that beer sales are up at least 25 to 30 percent during the summer months and that large quantities of this beverage are consumed, particularly on warm days. A rather high prevalence of dietary use of beverage alcohol is also evident from the type of answer given by many Canadians when asked why they drink alcoholic beverages: they often say that they drink to quench their thirst, or to increase their appetites.

Convivial Drinking

Alcohol use in the course of entertaining guests at a party, or as a gesture of hospitality, or just to make a get-together more enjoyable, is also very frequent in Canadian society. It is of some interest that this type of use, as well as the other types that we have discussed, tends to take place more and more in the home rather than in a bar or tavern. This means that an increasing number of Canadians need to keep alcoholic beverages in the home and must learn to exercise control over their drinking. It is difficult enough at times to leave a well-stocked refrigerator alone when one feels like a late-night snack; the same would certainly apply to a well-stocked liquor cabinet or bar. The trend towards home use also implies that other members of the family are confronted with the use of beverage alcohol more directly, and at an earlier age.

I have noted that overall alcohol consumption is increasing in Canada, as is the proportionate use of the stronger alcoholic beverages – the distilled spirits and wines. These changes are the results of a wider acceptance of use and an increased prevalence of various uses of alcohol, particularly regular social use. It seems that Canada is moving in the direction of those societies where the consumption of beverage alcohol is much more a part of social life.

The Affluent Consumer

This is made easy by the prosperity currently enjoyed by many Canadians. The affluent person can afford to engage in an increasing variety of consumptive behaviours, and the different uses of beverage alcohol are among the options open to him. Income levels as well as the accessibility of alcohol in terms of cost and outlets are important factors in explaining trends in beverage alcohol use. This does not mean, however, that alcohol consumption will continue to increase as long as income goes up and as long as alcohol beverages become more accessible. Observations of drinking behaviours in other societies have shown this to be the case only where drinking is not very widely accepted and where several drinking behaviours are still not too prevalent.

It can also be predicted that the increase in alcohol consumption will be largely the result of increases in the use of distilled spirits and wines. These types of beverage alcohol are more fashionable and more intimately associated with upper-class and middle-class behaviour. They are also better adapted to satisfy the affluent Canadians' search towards more variety in their consumptive behaviours.

Thus far, I have described the major problems and trends that are characteristic of Canadian drinking and that are relevant to the problems associated with alcohol use. I would like now to examine how these specific changes in the consumption of beverage alcohol in Canadian society do indeed affect our chief alcohol problems: intoxication, alcoholism, and physical damage due to chronic excessive drinking.

First of all, I have noted a continued rise in the general level of alcohol consumption. This in itself is often considered undesirable from a public-health point of view. Many governments have traditionally taxed alcoholic beverages very heavily and have justified this taxation as a public-health measure aimed at curbing alcohol consumption and alcohol abuse.

Some statistical evidence indeed suggests an association between alcohol consumption and the prevalence of alcohol problems. Consequently it has been argued that high levels of alcohol consumption bring about a high prevalence of alcohol abuse. However, this is a rather naive interpretation of the statistical evidence. One may with equal justification argue that a high prevalence of clinical alcoholism and habitual excessive use brings about high levels of alcohol consumption. At any rate, to judge the desirability or undesirability of increased alcohol consumption in Canadian society is certainly not a simple matter.

It may be better to rephrase the question as follows: How is a wider acceptance of alcohol use and a higher prevalence of regular social drinking going to affect the incidence of alcohol problems? In addition one may ask what role alcohol taxation can play in increasing or reducing these problems.

Good Drinking Practices

With reference to intoxication, it can be argued that a higher prevalence of social drinking, particularly at home, tends to facilitate the development and dissemination of good drinking practices and therefore to reduce the incidence of intoxication and related forms of abuse.

It would seem, then, that increased alcohol taxation might not be very desirable as far as the problems of intoxication and related forms of abuse are concerned, since a further rise in the cost of beverage alcohol would tend to reduce the prevalence of social drinking.

In the case of clinical alcoholism, it is doubtful whether increased or decreased social drinking will have very much effect on the magnitude of this problem. It is conceivable, in view of the availability of a great variety of drugs other than alcohol, that the emotional states of the clinical alcoholic may eventually find forms of expression other than the frequent benders. At any rate, the cost of beverage alcohol is not likely to have much effect on this type of drinking. After all, to drink frequently to excess only requires about $1,000 a year. This is a relatively small sum of money for a person who has frequently lost all interest in other consumption items such as a car, a home, a TV set. The cost of alcohol would have to be increased very much indeed to affect this type of drinking.

Physical Damage

In the case of the third major problem associated with alcohol use – the problem of physical damage due to regular, excessive use over long periods of time – the situation is quite different. This problem will undoubtedly become more serious if the trend towards a wider acceptance of drinking, and particularly towards an increased prevalence of dietary and convivial drinking patterns, continues.

It might perhaps be argued that a program of education aimed at informing Canadian drinkers about the levels of drinking that are known to increase significantly the probability of sustaining some physical damage may help to reduce the prevalence of regular, excessive drinking. However, the continued prevalence of cigarette smoking despite its association with lung cancer shows that public education alone is not very effective. Therefore, to tax beverage alcohol relatively heavily would seem to be well justified in the case of this type of alcohol problem. It makes the hazardous habit of regular, excessive use also very expensive.

Let us now consider the situation in Canada with respect to the consumption of specific alcoholic beverages. I observed earlier that a relatively high proportion of alcohol use is in the form of beer, but that this proportion has somewhat decreased in recent years. What is the significance of this pattern in relation to problems of alcohol use?

In the alcohol literature the question of weaker versus stronger beverages has been frequently discussed. Many governments have clearly favoured the sale of weaker alcoholic beverages, usually by taxing distilled spirits considerably more heavily than beers and wines. Is this differential treatment of the specific alcoholic beverages really justified? Do distilled spirits, in fact, contribute more to alcohol problems than do beers and wines?

The evidence for this position is not very convincing. It has been shown experimentally that intoxication is much more rapid if a given quantity of alcohol is ingested in the form of distilled spirits than if the same quantity is consumed in the form of beer or wine. It has also been suggested that inebriates do not prefer the weaker beverages. Finally, it has been pointed out that in societies with high consumption of distilled spirits, such as the Scandinavian countries, the prevalence of problems associated with alcohol use is also high.

Examining the Arguments

With reference to these arguments, however, it should be noted first of all that distilled spirits in Canada and elsewhere are typically consumed diluted and at strengths not unlike that of wine. Secondly, the argument that in countries where there is much consumption of distilled spirits there are notably more alcohol problems is not meaningful. It so happens that in these countries drinking is not widely accepted and regular social use is not very prevalent. Thus, with equal justification, the incidence of their alcohol problems may be attributed to the marginal acceptance of drinking rather than to the strength of the alcoholic beverage most often used.

Finally, with reference to the statement that alcoholics tend to prefer distilled spirits, I would like to point out that excessive alcohol use in Quebec involves beer rather than the two other types of beverage alcohol, while the Skid Row drinkers in Toronto invariably consume the inexpensive Canadian wines. It is probably quite true that the typical clinical alcoholic who seeks gross intoxication prefers the stronger beverage – if he can afford it. Whether this is necessarily an argument in favour of the relatively high cost of distilled spirits, I do not know.

Differential Taxation?

With reference to other alcohol problems, let us consider what is likely to happen if distilled spirits are taxed out of reach for almost all people. This has indeed occurred in Czechoslovakia, where alcohol is consumed almost exclusively in the form of beer. Nevertheless, the alcohol problems there are apparently no less serious than in societies where other alcoholic beverages are used. Both liver cirrhosis mortality rates and the number of cases of alcoholic dementia – loss of intellectual function due to brain damage – are rapidly increasing. On the other hand, the prevalence of alcoholic psychosis has dropped markedly. It has been suggested by Czechoslovak observers that heavy beer drinkers typically think of themselves as being very healthy individuals and that alcoholic dementia and other signs of physical damage are often present in this group of people while they still consider themselves healthy.

It would appear from all the evidence available in Canada and elsewhere that differential taxation of specific alcoholic beverages is not justified. To label beer *the drink of moderation* and to associate alcoholic problems primarily with the use of distilled spirits is not supported by the facts. Desirable drinking practices are not brought about by the beverage used, but by the people who use it.

The Prevalence of Alcoholism in Canada[*][†]

Wolfgang Schmidt

A main requirement for an adequate study of the prevalence of alcoholism is a definition that effectively delimits this condition. This is a deceptively simple requirement, for attempts to define alcoholism have long been marked by uncertainty, inconsistency and conflict. I do not intend to go into an extensive critique of current definitions here, except to point out that none of the many in existence today have entirely succeeded in describing clearly what is meant by the term.

To begin with, it might be held that a definition of alcoholism should contain at least two components: the consumption of alcohol, and the damage resulting from it. We might state, then, that "alcoholism is any use of alcoholic beverages that causes any damage to the individual or society or both." But this is a very loose definition, and has little operational value. Consider two drinkers who have identical drinking patterns, each consuming one litre of wine a day. They distribute their consumption over a twenty-four-hour period in such a way that they are sober at all times. It is clear that this drinking pattern is unlikely to interfere with their normal functioning.

Definition Falls Down

Now let us assume that one of these two drinkers maintains this drinking pattern until he dies at a ripe age from a cause unrelated to alcohol ingestion, while the

[*]Reprinted from *Addictions*, Vol. 15, No. 3 (Fall 1968), published by Addiction Research Foundation of Ontario.
[†]This article is based on part of a paper he prepared for discussion at the Addiction Research Foundation's seventh annual summer school at Laurentian University in Sudbury, June, 1968.

other dies of liver cirrhosis that has been caused by his alcohol intake. According to the definition, one of these two drinkers was an alcoholic and the other was not; yet their drinking patterns were identical. The problem here is that the definition rests at least in part on consequences of drinking that are possible but uncertain. Although the consumption of one litre of wine a day increases the *risk* of incurring certain alcohol-related diseases, the concept of risk or probability cannot be part of a definition of alcoholism or, for that matter, of any disease. A definition must not only clarify a concept but also establish its objective reality. The drinking pattern I have described may be thought of as a hazardous habit, but not as alcoholism.

Define by Behaviour

To circumvent this difficulty, alcoholism should be described in terms of habitual drinking behaviour rather than in terms of the uncertain consequences of drinking. This has been attempted in the following definition: "Alcoholism is a psychogenic dependence on ethanol or a physiological addiction to it, manifested by the inability of the alcoholic to control consistently either the start of drinking or its termination once started." For the present purposes, we can drop as irrelevant the material referring to dependence and addiction. These terms would require separate definition and hence should not be part of a definition. Alcoholism, then, is any form of drinking that cannot be consistently controlled.

It is evident that this definition rests largely upon a symptom of alcoholism that is commonly referred to as "loss of control." This simply means that whenever an alcoholic starts to drink it is not certain that he will be able to stop at will. This denotes helpless dependence, which is, according to some investigators, the essence of the "disease alcoholism." The advantage of this definition is that on its basis it is very simple to make a diagnosis of alcoholism. However, its general utility is greatly limited since it does not cover the people we sometimes call "inveterate drinkers," whose drinking consists of regular intake of large amounts of alcohol without conspicuous display of drunkenness. It is quite possible for these drinkers to maintain this pattern without exhibiting loss of control.

The W.H.O. Definition

The most widely used definition, and the best so far, is that developed by the World Health Organization. It defines alcoholism as "any form of drinking which in its extent goes beyond the traditional and customary 'dietary' use, or the ordinary compliance with the social drinking customs of the whole community concerned, irrespective of the etiological factors leading to such behaviour and irrespective also of the extent to which such etiological factors are dependent upon heredity, constitution, or acquired physiological and metabolic influences."

The terms in this definition are relative and sociological. Amount of intake is irrelevant, provided that it is above some societal average or norm. But the utility of such a relativistic approach is limited also. The customary dietary use of alcohol, and the drinking customs of different communities, range from total abstinence in a teetotalling community to a very high intake in free-drinking cultures and subcultures. The chance of finding biological or psychological similarities in drinkers on the basis of this kind of classification seems small.

No Definition Satisfies

We may conclude, then, that none of the definitions available today describes objectively the drinking behaviour of all alcoholics. The most plausible explanation of this difficulty is the great variability in the manifestations of alcoholism. Each of these definitions describes the drinking of an unknown proportion of an alcoholic population, and it may well be that a single definition covering all alcoholic patterns is impossible. It is probably more useful to think of alcohol*isms* rather than of a single entity, and to define these various manifestations separately.

The problems arising from inadequate definitions are least felt in the clinical field. People who seek treatment in an alcoholism clinic can be identified as alcoholics, regardless of the type of definition one chooses to employ. In these patients, drinking has adversely affected all aspects of their lives. The amounts they have consumed must be considered excessive regardless of the measure of excessiveness one wishes to apply, and they have demonstrated over and over again that they cannot control their intake. In preparing our book *Social Class and the Treatment of Alcoholism*, Reginald Smart, Marcia Moss and I studied thousands of clinical records; we found only two in which the diagnosis of alcoholism was doubtful.

The situation is quite different if one wishes to identify alcoholics in a general population for the purpose of counting them. The task of determining how many alcoholics there are at any place in any given time requires a definition based on a set of behaviours or signs that can be recognized by relatively superficial methods of inquiry. This can be achieved by operational definitions, which are usually tailored to suit a particular epidemiological approach and do not claim to be universally applicable. In the following, I will discuss the results of such inquiries with special reference to the definitions of alcoholism that were employed.

The prevalence of alcoholism can be estimated directly or indirectly. The indirect methods rest on the assumption that the behaviour of alcoholics *en masse* will be reflected in certain statistics that are regularly reported by governments. These include hospital admissions, convictions for drunkenness and other alcohol-related offences, beverage alcohol sales data, and statistics on causes of death that are wholly or partly attributable to the consumption of alcohol. Although data like these are subject to various errors, they do convey an impression of the magnitude of alcohol problems, including alcoholism. With the help of such information, Jellinek and others have ranked a number of Western countries according to their prevalence of alcoholism. (Table 1, next page.)

Statistics Were Comparable

The countries in this table have been grouped into a number of categories reflecting the magnitude of the problem in each country. Within each category the countries are arranged alphabetically, since we believe that the data do not warrant discrimination where the differences in prevalence appear to be relatively small. The underlying conceptions of alcoholism in this tabulation rested heavily on damage resulting from excessive intake, and were thus sufficiently similar that comparison among these countries was not vitiated. It is beyond the scope of this article to attempt to explain the variation in prevalence among these countries.

Among the indirect methods of estimating the prevalence of alcoholism, the best known and most often used is the Jellinek Estimation Formula – developed by the late E. M. Jellinek, who is generally agreed to have been one of the foremost workers in the field of alcoholism. Estimates based on the Jellinek formula have been developed for many countries, including Canada.

TABLE 1

Ranking of Estimated Prevalence of Alcoholism in a Number of Western Countries (Countries are listed alphabetically within categories)

Range	Country
Extreme High	France
Upper High	Chile Portugal U.S.A.
Lower High	Australia Sweden Switzerland Union of South Africa Yugoslavia
Upper Middle	Canada Denmark Norway Peru Scotland Uruguay
Lower Middle	Belgium Czechoslovakia England Finland Ireland Italy New Zealand Wales
Upper Low	Brazil Netherlands
Lower Low	Argentina Spain

Jellinek hypothesized that the relationship between the prevalence of alcoholism and the mortality rate from cirrhosis of the liver was sufficiently constant that the former could be estimated from the latter. The proportion of alcoholic patients who develop cirrhosis of the liver has been fairly closely calculated. This being so, if one knows the number of liver cirrhosis deaths attributed to alcoholism in a given population, it is possible to work back from this figure and estimate the number of clinical alcoholics in the population. *Clinical alcoholics* in this context means persons whose medical and personal characteristics are comparable to those who have been admitted to treatment facilities for alcoholism. The validity of the formula has been criticized, but it is generally agreed that most Jellinek formula estimates that have been published to date are accurate enough for purposes of education and program development.

TABLE 2

Estimated Prevalence of Alcoholism in the Ten Canadian Provinces

	Percentage of Population Aged 20 and Over Who are Alcoholics	Number of Alcoholics
British Columbia	2.58	28,150
Ontario	2.50	100,120
Quebec	2.41	76,770
Manitoba	2.20	12,470
Alberta	1.81	14,710
Saskatchewan	1.57	8,530
New Brunswick	1.56	5,120
Nova Scotia	1.45	6,180
Prince Edward Island	1.27	750
Newfoundland	1.11	2,670

Applying the Jellinek formula to the Canadian provinces, then, we get the results shown in Table 2. The general impression gained from this table is the considerable variation in the prevalence of alcoholism among the provinces. Quebec, Ontario and British Columbia have the highest prevalence, the Maritime provinces rank lowest, and the prairie provinces are in between. The lowest rate is less than one-half of any of the three highest. These considerable differences in prevalence are a particularly interesting aspect of the epidemiology of alcoholism. There is probably no other chronic disorder of similar magnitude whose prevalence varies as widely from jurisdiction to jurisdiction and from decade to decade. It is generally said that the variation over time – and probably also over space – in the prevalence of other psychopathologies is far lower than in the case of alcoholism. This has been particularly emphasized by the incidence of the major psychoses, which some investigators say has not noticeably changed over a number of decades.

Environment is Important

The most plausible explanation for the considerable variation in the prevalence of alcoholism is that in this condition environmental factors have a singularly strong effect on prevalence. This observation is supported by the comparisons between nations, leading to the conclusion that national customs, social attitudes and economic factors greatly influence the prevalence of alcohol excess.

Although the estimation methods described so far are appropriate enough for determining the alcoholism rates of major population groups, this technique is less effective if one wishes to study the demographic characteristics of natural (as opposed to clinical) populations of alcoholics. Such information can only be obtained through field study. This leads us to the direct method of estimating the prevalence of alcoholism, which is by actual count of the known alcoholics in a given area.

The most successful prevalence surveys in practice have been those that concentrated on the complete coverage of distinct communities within the national population. This approach – examining complete groups of the population – minimizes the bias that one is likely to get when one selects only a sample. Surveys of this type are designed to count each case of alcoholism that can be discovered over a given period. The outstanding advantages of this technique are that the diagnostic standards for inclusion can be prearranged and that much more collateral evidence on personal characteristics and social background can be collected.

The Frontenac County Surveys

During the last fifteen years, two intensive field studies have been made of the alcoholic population of Frontenac County in eastern Ontario. The first was begun in 1951 and the second ten years later. The findings of these surveys have recently been summarized by Robert Gibbins. Associate Research Director (Psychological Studies) of this Foundation, who conducted the first survey and served as consultant to the second. The following is quoted from his summary:

> ... The main objectives of the studies were: (1) to provide a sound basis for estimating the prevalence of alcoholism in the province as a whole; (2) to examine the major demographic characteristics of a natural (as opposed to a clinical) population of alcoholics; and (3) to ascertain what happens to the members of such a population over an extended period of time.

> ... Essentially the same procedures were employed in both studies. ... These procedures were sufficiently rigorous to ensure that all but the most secretive alcoholics were identified. Detailed information about each case was obtained from documentary sources (e.g., police and hospital records) and from reliable and strategically located informants (e.g., physicians, public-health nurses, social workers, clergymen, employers, and selected city and county officials). For survey purposes, alcoholics were defined as individuals whose histories revealed well-established patterns of undisciplined alcohol use which had culminated in damage to their health in general and/or to their financial and social standing. Cases who satisfied the requirements of this rather loose working definition were further classified as "problem drinkers," "alcohol addicts," or "chronic alcoholics."

> Classification as a *problem drinker* required evidence of excessive drinking of a repetitive nature and, as a consequence of this, an upset in domestic equilibrium to the extent that a family member, friend or associate complained, expressed concern, or sought advice from someone in authority; or a material reduction in work efficiency and dependability to the extent that it had become a matter of concern to an employer or business associate.

> Before an individual was classified as an *alcohol addict* there must have been evidence of a seemingly irresistible desire for the effects of alcohol; loss of control of drinking; an apparent inability to break the drinking habit; and deterioration of interpersonal relations as a consequence of the loss of control and inability to stop drinking.

> Classification as a *chronic alcoholic* required evidence of a prolonged period of excessive drinking which resulted in the development of one or

more of the complicating diseases of alcoholism, e.g., liver cirrhosis, delirium tremens, Korsakoff's psychosis, and so forth.

TABLE 3

Alcoholics per 1,000 Persons Aged 20 and Over in 1951 and 1961

Year	Adult Population	Total Alcoholics	Alcoholics per 1,000 Adults
1951	43,606	698	16.01
1961	53,138	1,245	23.43
Increase in alcoholism rate			7.42
Percentage increase in alcoholism rate			46.37

Table 3 shows that a very substantial increase in the rate of alcoholism occurred in the county during the ten-year period between surveys. In 1951 there were approximately 16 alcoholics per 1,000 adults and in 1961 approximately 23 per 1,000 – an increase in rate of slightly more than 46 percent.

To provide a basis for estimating the number of alcoholics in the province as a whole, the 1961 adult population of the county was stratified according to factors which influence prevalence, such as age, sex, and rural-urban distribution. Rates of alcoholism were calculated for these strata and projections made from them to the equivalent strata in the provincial population. *The resulting estimate for the province in 1961 was approximately 90,000 alcoholics.* Of these, an estimated 75,100 were males and 14,900 females. It is worth mentioning that the survey estimate corresponds quite well with an independent estimate of 93,450 obtained by means of the Jellinek Formula. . . .

Table 4 shows the distribution of problem drinkers, alcohol addicts, and chronic alcoholics in the county in 1961.

TABLE 4

Classification of the 1961 Alcoholic Population

Category	Percent
Problem Drinker	39.5
Alcohol Addict	43.2
Chronic Alcoholic	17.3

As mentioned earlier, a major objective of the two investigations was to ascertain the fate of members of a natural alcoholic population after an extended period of time. Table 5 shows the status in 1961 of the majority of cases detected in 1951.

TABLE 5

Status in 1961 of the 1951 Alcoholics

Status in 1961	Percent
Active	36.0
Inactive	22.8
Dead	17.6
Missing	23.6

The group designated "Active" is comprised of those individuals identified as alcoholics in both surveys. The group labelled "Inactive" is made up of individuals who were identified as alcoholics in the first survey but not in the second.

The cases labelled "Missing" were individuals in the 1951 survey who were not residing in the county in 1961, and who did not appear in the provincial death records. It is presumed that the majority of this number had emigrated from the county.

TABLE 6

Causes of Death in the 1951 Alcoholic Population

Cause of Death	Percent
Diseases of the circulatory system	41.4
Accidents	14.4
Diseases of the digestive system	11.9
Respiratory diseases	11.8
Vascular lesions	9.4
Malignant neoplasms	8.9
Other	2.2

Table 6 shows the leading causes of death among those who died during the period between the surveys. It is worthy of note that the chief difference between this listing of causes of death and that obtained for the general adult population of Ontario is the higher percentage of deaths due to accidents and gastro-intestinal disease – which includes cirrhosis of the liver – among the Frontenac County alcoholics.

TABLE 7

Classification of the 1951 Alcoholic Population According to Degree of Alcoholism in 1951 and Status in 1961

Degree of Alcoholism in 1951	Status in 1961				
	Active (percent)	Inactive (percent)	Dead (percent)	Missing (percent)	Total (percent)
Problem Drinker	30.9	30.9	13.2	25.0	100.0
Alcohol Addict	45.3	14.0	16.0	24.7	100.0
Chronic Alcoholic	27.3	9.1	54.4	9.1	100.0

Table 7 shows that status at the time of the second survey varied according to presumed degree of involvement with alcohol in 1951. The data in the table indicate quite clearly that the mortality rate during the years between surveys was considerably higher for the chronic alcoholics than for either the problem drinkers or the alcohol addicts. They also suggest that persons classified as problem drinkers in 1951 were far more likely to be inactive in 1961 than those classified as alcohol addicts or chronic alcoholics.

The group of apparently inactive alcoholics (22.8 percent – Table 5) is of considerable interest, for several reasons. Since no evidence could be found of their having been admitted to any of the county's hospitals or clinics, or of their having received formal therapeutic assistance from the county's professionals (or AA) for alcoholism or its complications, it is not unreasonable to suggest that *"spontaneous recovery" from alcoholism did occur in 22.8 percent of all cases during a ten-year period.*

As shown in Table 8, the "inactive" group was composed mainly of individuals who had not progressed beyond the "problem drinker" stage.

TABLE 8

Classification of Those Listed as Inactive in 1961 According to Degree of Alcoholism in 1951

Category	Percent
Problem Drinker	74
Alcohol Addict	23
Chronic Alcoholic	3

Most of them were in occupations requiring some formal training or degree of skill, and were steadily employed in a closely supervised working environment. It is particularly noteworthy that 23 percent of the inactive cases were classified as alcohol addicts and 3 percent as chronic alcoholics in 1951. The fact that they were able to become abstinent, or at least to modify their drinking behaviour to the point of unobtrusiveness, with little or no sustained professional assistance, should dispel some of the unwarranted pessimism about the prognosis of alcoholism.

A further finding of these surveys concerns the social class distribution of the alcoholics that were identified. It is frequently said that "alcoholism is no respecter of persons." Statements of this sort are often meant to imply that, at least with respect to such broad categories as socio-economic class, the risk rates and prevalence rates are about equal. Investigations concerned with these questions, including the Frontenac County surveys, have challenged the credibility of this contention. From a comparison of the occupations of the alcoholics in the survey it became evident that the higher occupational categories had lower rates of alcoholism that the lower categories. The rates also varied according to education, with the highest rates among those having little formal education. This finding accords well with the results of many other investigations, which also indicate an inverse relationship between occupational status and the prevalence of alcoholism.

The Epidemiological Method

The data that have been presented so far indicate considerable differences in rates of alcoholism among geographic regions, between males and females, and among various subgroups of a general population. The mapping of rates in such a manner is generally referred to as the epidemiological method. Its potential value is twofold. Firstly, knowledge of prevalence may give information that is immediately useful in the organization and administration of treatment services. Secondly, and probably more importantly, all the main factors in the etiology and development of a disorder – genetic, physical or social – can be investigated by epidemiological methods. In these investigations, the first step is usually to establish that the rate differentials exist. This information is derived from the study of the distribution of the disorder in relation to time, space, or the distinguishing characteristics of the social groups affected. From these distributions, one attempts to uncover clues about factors responsible for the variation in risk rates. An example may clarify the ensuing process of investigation.

It has been consistently found that rates of alcoholism are much higher in urban than in rural areas. In order to explain this difference, one has to search for components of urbanism that may be responsible for the relationship. Such components may suggest themselves on grounds of widely held beliefs, by intuition, or by analogy to other social problems that also occur with higher frequency in urban areas. In the case of alcoholism, an investigator would select for study certain seemingly significant components of the relationship between the higher rates of alcoholism and the urban milieu. The following might be considered: the easier accessibility of alcohol due to more numerous public drinking places, the probably greater tolerance of drinking in urban life than in the rural areas, and the generally higher socio-economic level concomitant with city living. The latter may be particularly relevant, since it is known that personal income and per-capita consumption are correlated.

It should be pointed out that evidence derived by these methods is always circumstantial, in that it may be sufficient to suggest a causal relationship but can never give final proof of it. Different methods have to be applied at this stage of an investigation, but it is beyond the scope of this article to go further into these possibilities.

The Extent of Illicit Drug Use in Canada: A Review of Current Epidemiology[*]

Reginald G. Smart and Dianne Fejer

More and more interest is being expressed in illicit drug use. It is widely believed that marihuana, LSD, speed, and other mood-modifying drugs are frequently taken by some segments of the Canadian population. One salient fact is that few studies of the extent of present usage are available in published form. It is extremely difficult to obtain any estimates of drug usage which could be seen to apply to more than a narrow geographic area. However, a number of surveys of illicit drug use have been made in Canada. These surveys vary in size, method of sampling, validity of conclusions and range of drugs covered; taken together they constitute at least a beginning for an epidemiology of drug use. The major purpose of this paper is to review all available surveys of illicit drug use in Canada in an effort to contribute to an understanding of the epidemiology of drug use. Further purposes are to indicate populations or subgroups so far unexplored as to their drug use, and discuss some of the difficulties involved in making accurate drug surveys.

In preparing material for this review a number of decisions as to its scope were made. The surveys reviewed all contain data on illcit psychoactive and hallucinogenic drugs, including marihuana, LSD, solvents, other hallucinogens and amphetamines, especially *speed*. Surveys concerned only with alcohol and tobacco or with the narcotic drugs such as heroin, morphine, etc., were not included. Also, the review has been limited to studies reporting original data on samples or populations with known attributes. Of course, studies stating, without empirical support, that some specified proportion of a particular

[*]Not published previously; written specifically for this volume.

508

population uses drugs have been left out. A study reported by Radouco-Thomas et al. (1968, 1969) was concerned with drug use among students in grades 11 to 14 in Quebec. However, this study has not reported rates of use of specific drugs but only that 9.7 percent used hallucinogens such as marihuana, LSD, glue, etc. In all, some twenty-two studies with specific drug use are reviewed. Their major features are summarized in Table 1.

Marihuana

Marihuana is the drug most often studied in usage surveys. In all, 22 surveys have been concerned with marihuana usage, compared to 17 for LSD, 15 for glue, and 13 for amphetamines. It should also be noted that all of these studies are for adolescents or young adults; none are concerned with users outside of the college age (approximately age 24). Most of the surveys involving marihuana are for high school populations or for high school age adolescents (16/22).

The largest and most carefully designed studies have been carried out in Toronto (Smart and Jackson, 1969; Smart, Fejer, and White, 1970), Halifax (Whitehead, 1969; Whitehead, 1971), Montreal (Laforest, 1969), London (Stennett, Feenstra, and Aharan, 1969),[1] Niagara Counties of Southern Ontario (Smart, Fejer, and Alexander, 1970), British Columbia (Russell, 1970), and Ottawa (Halpern and Mori, 1970).[2]

The first Toronto study, conducted in 1968, found that 6.7 percent had used marihuana. When this survey was repeated 2 years later, use had increased to 18.3 percent. In Halifax the first survey in 1969 indicated 6.63 percent had used marihuana. As in Toronto, marihuana use in Halifax increased in 1970 (to 17.3 percent). The Montreal survey, conducted in 1969, found 8.54 percent of the students used marihuana and in 1968 in London, 5.75 percent. The three other recent surveys (1970) in Niagara Countries of Ontario, in British Columbia, and in Ottawa found 12.4 percent, 19.7 percent and 19.0 percent respectively using marihuana.

All of these studies were based on adequate samples representing the whole school district and chosen at random or on some acceptable sampling basis. The London survey obtained questionnaires from all students at school on the day of survey and represents a sampling only in that the absentees were not included.

It is worth pointing out that the first study made in Toronto (Smart and Jackson, 1969) involved two methods of estimating the numbers of marihuana users. In one method respondents were asked about their own marihuana use. In the other, persons taking part in group discussions (one person from each class participating) were asked to say how many persons in their class had used marihuana. The two methods gave highly similar results and this tends to create considerable confidence in the data derived from the questionnaires. The studies done in Halifax, Montreal, and Niagara Counties used the same drug questions as in the Toronto study and, hence, these studies should have the same reliability.

Several studies have involved relatively large samples but there is little information on how they were selected. For example, the study by the Canadian

Home and School and Parent-Teacher Federation (Kucharsky, 1969) appears to be national in scope. It includes 2,249 students from six provinces and found 8.11 percent use of marihuana. However, the methods by which provinces, schools, and respondents were selected is not yet available. Also, the studies of Renfrew students (Renfrew County School Board et al., 1969) and those in Edmonton (Division of Alcoholism, 1969) are based on samples selected in an unknown manner. The survey in Edmonton was done by students themselves and is the only survey to use this method. It found a high proportion of marihuana users, 19 percent, while Renfrew found only 5.85 percent.

Several studies were made with rather small, specialized samples and, hence, have data only of local importance. The Fort William study reported data for 214 high school students and the Port Arthur study for only 101 students from special summer sessions for failing students. These two studies obtained usage rates of 8.92 percent and 13.0 percent. The study by Byles in 1967 is also small and select. Byles studied a particular suburb of Toronto and collected data on marihuana use only; incidentally, only 2 percent of his interviewees used marihuana, but the survey was done in 1966. However, the report made by Byles in 1968 included samples from four sub-groups – upper middle class, lower middle class, training schools, and Yorkville. In his total sample of 508, Byles found that 23 percent had tried marihuana and about 10 percent of males and about 6 percent of females outside of training schools and Yorkville, had tried marihuana.

It is surprising that so few studies have been made of marihuana use in Canadian universities, as a number of such studies have been made in the United States (Eells, 1968; Imperi, Kleber, and Davie, 1968). Only studies by Campbell (1969) and Brady et al., (1970) are concerned with marihuana use in a total university population. In his first survey Campbell found that almost 20 percent of 619 students at Bishop's University had used marihuana. Following up a year later with a sample which included about 80 percent of students in the first survey, he found marihuana use had increased to about 27 percent. Similarly, the recent study at the University of Western Ontario by Brady et al. found 23.2 percent of the students surveyed had used marihuana. The study by Menard at Loyola College reported that 15 percent of male and 7 percent of female first year students had tried marihuana. Since they were asked the questions on registration day, their marihuana use probably occurred during their high school years and not as a result of their being university students. Webster's survey (1968) found that only 5 percent of 105 students in an introductory psychology course had smoked marihuana. To date, then, there appear to be few surveys of marihuana use in large Canadian universities or multiuniversities. Of course, this is one of the major relatively untouched areas for later epidemiological studies.

It appears, when surveys, especially the largest and most reliable ones, are grouped together for the same periods that rates of marihuana use are remarkably similar, considering the geographic, linquistic, and cultural variables separating the areas. The four surveys conducted in 1968 and early 1969 (Toronto, Halifax, Montreal, and London) gave rates of 6.7, 6.63, 8.54, and 5.75 respectively. Also some of the rates for other studies conducted in 1968, Renfrew County (5.85%) and the Canadian Home and School National Survey (8.11%), are not very different from them. Although those in Edmonton (19%) and Lakehead (9% and 13%) are substantially different.

The five most recent surveys (Toronto, Halifax, Niagara Counties, British Columbia, Ottawa) showed rates considerably higher than the earlier surveys. The rates for these areas were 18.3 percent, 17.3 percent, 12.4 percent, 19.7 percent, and 19.0 percent respectively. The two areas, Toronto and Halifax, where two surveys were conducted showed marihuana use had more than doubled in the interval between the first and second survey. If the rates for the four largest surveys conducted in 1968 and early 1969 are averaged the marihuana usage for this period becomes 6.9 percent. The average for the five most recent high school surveys (1970) is 17.54 percent.

With so few university populations surveyed an estimate of marihuana use for that population would be premature.

Lysergic Acid Diethylamide (LSD)

Seventeen surveys enquired about LSD use and the general features of all of them were discussed in the above section; no study was exclusively devoted to LSD use. The large high school surveys in Toronto, Halifax, Montreal, and London, conducted in 1968 and early 1969, found that 2.5, 2.37, 3.02, and 1.24 percent of students, respectively, had tried LSD at least once. For each city, far fewer students have taken LSD than have tried marihuana. Again, for this time period, there is considerable similarity in the rates for Toronto, Halifax, and Montreal but, in London, LSD was used by only about half as many students as elsewhere. In addition, the Lakehead studies reported rates similar to London (.47 and 1.00 percent). It seems that LSD use was much greater in very large cities than in moderately large ones in 1968 and early 1969. The best estimate of LSD use for high school students in large Canadian cities would appear to be about 2.5 percent in 1968 and 1969.

The other studies conducted about the same time as those mentioned above enquiring about LSD varied considerably in their findings. The sole "national" study reported 2.24 percent LSD use but it is not known how many of its students were in large cities. Byles' study (1968) found that about 1.5 percent of males and only .5 percent of females in the middle class samples had used LSD. Once again, the Edmonton study has rates many times higher than found elsewhere at this time; about 9 percent of the students in this study reported LSD use.

The five surveys conducted in 1970 found rates of LSD use much higher than the earlier studies. In Toronto 8.5 percent had used LSD, 8.1 percent in Halifax, 8.0 percent in the Niagara Counties, 6.6 percent in British Columbia and 10.0 percent in Ottawa. As can be seen, the rates for these areas are very similar. For Toronto and Halifax LSD use appears to have tripled when compared to the earlier surveys in these cities. Also LSD use does not appear as confined to large cities in 1970 as it was in 1968 and early 1969. In the Niagara Counties most of the students lived in moderately large cities such as St. Catharines and Welland and LSD use here was almost identical to Toronto and Halifax. If the rates for these five surveys are averaged the most recent estimate of LSD use would be 8.24 percent.

Three studies of LSD usage relate to university populations. Campbell's (1969) first study at Bishop's University found that only .65 percent had used LSD.

But this increased to 3.12 percent in the follow-up survey. At Loyola College 1.57 percent of first year students had tried LSD. With only three studies obtaining such different results, no estimate of LSD use could be made for college level students. The University of Western Ontario survey enquired about use of hallucinogens other than marihuana and found a rate of 13.1 percent, but LSD use was not specified.

In summary, the most recent surveys show that LSD is used by about half as many students as have tried marihuana. However, for both the high school and one university population resurveyed, LSD use appears to be increasing at a rapid rate. In Toronto and Halifax LSD use tripled in the 1 to 2 years between surveys while marihuana use only doubled.

Glue

Substantial numbers of young persons are believed to inhale glue containing toluene and other toxic substances. Indeed, the range of glues and other solvents used for mood-modification seems to be very wide. Some of the 15 surveys which asked questions about solvents were concerned only with glue.

All but one of the surveys reporting information about solvent use involved high school age students. The 1968 and 1969 surveys in Toronto, Halifax, Montreal, and London showed that 5.7, 3.12, 1.93, and 10.2 percent of high school students had sniffed glue. Glue use, then, varied to a factor of 5 with London the highest use area and Montreal the lowest. This was the largest variation in these cities for any of the illicit drugs. Byles' study of adolescents in a Toronto suburb found that 7 percent had sniffed glue. The Hayashi studies found that 8 percent of regular high school students but 12 percent of those in summer sessions had sniffed glue. The Canadian Home and School (1969) study found that about 6 percent had used glue, a figure close to the average of the largest studies. Byles' (1968) second study found that glue use rates were about 8.5 percent for middle class boys but only 1 percent for girls.

If the four largest surveys in 1968 and 1969 were averaged, the best estimate is that about 5.2 percent of high school students sniffed glue at least once. However, it should be noted that the rates for these four studies show little clustering about the mean.

The 1970 studies also show large variations in the rates of glue use from area to area. In Toronto (1970) questions were asked about the use of glue and other solvents separately. Glue use was lower in Toronto in 1970 than in 1968, 3.8 percent, but solvent use was higher than glue use, 6.3 percent. Glue use had doubled in Halifax between surveys to 7.2 percent. Niagara Counties showed a rate of 7.6 percent and in British Columbia 12.4 percent of the students had used glue or other solvents. The lowest rate of glue use among high school students in 1970 was found in Ottawa: only 3 percent of the students here reported glue use. Despite these large variations the rates do appear to be higher in 1970 than in the earlier studies. The average for these five surveys[3] is 7.04 percent.

The survey conducted at the University of Western Ontario by Brady et al. was the only one to include glue use for a university population. They found the usage rate much lower than for the high school populations, 2.0 percent.

Stimulants (Speed)

All but two of the 13 studies of stimulant use involve high school students. Five of these studies were concerned only with stimulant use in general, five enquired only about the use of speed – one specifying methedrine, and three enquiring about the use of stimulants and speed separately.

The studies in Toronto, 1968, Halifax, 1969, and Montreal, 1969, found that 7.3, 6.42, and 5.82 percent of high school students had ingested stimulants at least once. Obviously, the rates of use were similar, with an overall average for stimulant use of 6.5 percent for these three cities. Of course, the proportions of these users who had used speed was uncertain.

The early studies enquiring specifically about speed use also produced similar results. The London study found that 5.6 percent of the high school students had tried speed. While in Fort William and Port Arthur, the rates were 4.21 and 5.0 percent, respectively, although small samples were involved.

The 1970 studies did not show any great differences in either speed or stimulant use from earlier studies. In Toronto, 6.7 percent of the students reported using stimulants and 4.5 percent used speed. In Halifax, 6.9 percent had used stimulants; while in Niagara Counties, 9.0 percent reported stimulant use and 5.6 percent speed use. The Ottawa survey showed 5.0 percent speed use and the British Columbia survey which asked specifically about methedrine use, found 3.7 percent of the students had used it.

Campbell's (1969) second study was the only university survey to enquire about speed use. Only 3.28 percent of the students at Bishop's University had used speed. This rate was considerably lower than that in high school populations. But, of course it may not represent the rate among university students in other areas. The University of Western Ontario survey asked about stimulant use but specified nonmedical use. They found that only 4.1 percent of the students had participated in the nonmedical use of stimulants. However, this figure cannot be directly compared to stimulant use among high school students since medical and nonmedical use were not differentiated for these latter populations.

Unexplored Areas

To date, most of the studies of illicit drug use have concentrated on the high school populations, in Eastern Canadian cities. In particular only 2 out of 22 surveys have been conducted in Western Canada. Clearly more studies in Western cities, or small towns, and rural areas would expand the epidemiological data considerably.

Follow-up surveys such as these conducted in Toronto and Halifax are also important. From these surveys it has become evident that illicit drug use cannot be viewed as a static phenomenon. Surveys conducted in 1968 or 1969 no longer reflect the current drug use rates. In order to follow the trends in illicit drug use it will probably be necessary to conduct surveys at 2 year intervals in many areas of Canada.

So far, very little is known about the use of drugs by any young adults beyond high school age. A few suggestive studies have been made for marihuana and

TABLE 1

Illicit Drug Use Surveys in Canada

Population Studied	Place and Year	Sample Size	Data Collection Technique	Drug	Percent Ever Used	Authors	Remarks
Relatively random sample of students in grades 7, 9, 11, and 13 in Metropolitan Toronto	Toronto 1968	6,447	40 minutes, self-administered, anonymous, questionnaire	marihuana LSD glue stimulants	6.7[a] 2.5[a] 5.7[a] 7.3[a]	R. G. Smart D. Jackson	Large sample with good representation. Data given on grade and sex differences and on many social variables.
Relatively random sample of students in grades 7, 9, 11, and 13 in Metropolitan Toronto (Grade 6 students also surveyed but excluded here for comparative purposes)	Toronto 1970	6,890	40 minutes, self-administered, anonymous, questionnaire	marihuana LSD glue solvents stimulants speed	18.3[a] 8.5[a] 3.8[a] 6.3[a] 6.7[a] 4.5[a]	R. G. Smart D. Fejer J. White	For drug use rates essentially a repetition of 1968 Toronto survey. Also gives data on parental drug use and student alienation.
Relatively random sample (25% of all students in grades 7, 9, 11, and 12 in Metropolitan Halifax)	Halifax 1969	1,606	144 item, self-administered, anonymous, questionnaire	marihuana LSD glue stimulants	6.63[a] 2.37[a] 3.12[a] 6.42[a]	P. C. Whitehead	Study has large sample with good area representation. Data given on grade and sex differences. Covers also many social variables.
Relatively random sample of students in grades 7, 8, 9, 10, 11, and 12 in Metropolitan Halifax (for comparative purposes data for grades 8 and 10 were not included here)	Halifax 1970	1,081	self-administered, anonymous, questionnaire (modified version of 1969 questionnaire)	marihuana LSD glue stimulants	17.3[a] 8.1[a] 7.2[a] 6.9[a]	P. C. Whitehead	For drug use rates essentially a repetition of 1969 survey.
Relatively random sample (1/15 of all high school students in Fort William)	Fort William 1968	214	self-administered, take-home, anonymous, questionnaire	marihuana LSD glue speed	8.92[a] .47[a] 7.94[a] 4.21[a]	T. Hayashi	Frequency data given but poorly presented. Only about 1/3 of the users represented. Little age and sex differentation.
High school students attending summer school for failure of one or more exams in the preceding year in Port Arthur	Port Arthur 1968	101	self-administered, take-home, anonymous, questionnaire	marihuana LSD glue speed	13.00[a] 1.00[a] 12.00[a] 5.00[a]	T. Hayashi	Subjects may not be viewed as representative of high school students. No grade breakdown nor frequency data.

514

Sample	Location/Date	N	Method	Drug	%	Author	Comments
Grade 11 and 12 students at an Edmonton high school	Edmonton 1968	652	structured interview, anonymous, conducted by other students	marihuana LSD	18.10 9.05	*Concept*, a publication of the Division of Alcoholism, Edmonton	Study also presents interesting data on reasons for drug use. However, methodology may be questioned—interviews conducted by grade 10 students.
Freshmen at Loyola College on registration day (graduated from high school less than 2 years before and who lived within 30 miles of Montreal)	Loyola College 1968	700	15 to 20 minute questionnaire handed out at registration	marihuana LSD	15.00 (male) 7.00 (female) 1.57	L. C. Menard	A special population and generalizations cannot be made to high school or university students.
Area sampling, students in grades 8, 10, 12 and 14	Montreal 1968	4,504	self-administered, anonymous, questionnaire	marihuana LSD glue stimulants	8.54[a] 3.02[a] 1.93[a] 5.82[a]	Lucien Laforest	Study has large, fairly representative sample. Data on age, grade and sex differences as well as on many social variables.
All students in Introductory Psychology Class at University of Toronto	Toronto 1967	105	self-administered, anonymous, questionnaire	marihuana	5.00	D. C. Webster	Study is only of one class and cannot be considered representative for the university.
All full-time university students at Bishop's University	Bishop's University 1968	619	self-administered, anonymous, mailed, questionnaire	marihuana LSD	19.55[b] .65[c]	I. L. Campbell	Part of an intensive study of drug use including questionnaires on family and group life and alienation plus MMPI and TAT data.
All full-time university students at Bishop's University	Bishop's University 1969	609	self-administered, anonymous, mailed, questionnaire	marihuana LSD speed	27.26 3.12 3.28	I. L. Campbell	Follow-up study (complete one year later) shows increase in use. Of students studied 79.80% same ones as given first questionnaire.
Random sample of students age 12.5 to 18.5 from a suburb of Toronto	Toronto 1966-1967	155	structured interview	marihuana glue	2.00 7.00	J. A. Byles	A study of the social class variables associated with alienation of youth.

continued

Table 1 continued

Population Studied	Place and Year	Sample Size	Data Collection Technique	Drug	Percent Ever Used	Authors	Remarks
Stratified random sample of Toronto adolescents from four sub-groups in Toronto: 1) upper-middle class, North Toronto, 2) lower-middle class, South-East Toronto, 3) youth in training schools and detention, 4) Yorkville, age 12.5 to 18.5	Toronto 1968	508	structured interview	marihuana LSD glue	23.00 15.00 10.00	J. A. Byles	Total sample use is not very valuable since 1/3 of the population belongs to the two special groups, Yorkville residents and delinquents.
High school students from 6 provinces in Canada	Alberta Saskatchewan Ontario Quebec New Brunswick Nova Scotia 1969	2,249	self-administered, anonymous, questionnaire	marihuana LSD solvents	8.11 2.24 5.86		No information was available on sampling procedure. Contains data on use of other drugs, students' attitudes toward drugs and social characteristics.
High school students in Renfrew County	Renfrew County 1969	2,083	questionnaire	marihuana	5.85	Renfrew County School Board et al.	
All high school students in all 12 schools in London, Ontario	London 1968	11,454	self-administered, anonymous, questionnaire given in classroom	marihuana LSD glue speed	7.9 (male) 3.6 (female) 1.88 (male) .6 (female) 11.3 (male) 9.1 (female) 6.7 (male) 4.5 (female)	R. G. Stennett H. J. Feenstra C. H. Aharan	Extensive study, all students in London given the opportunity to participate. No detailed frequency data.
Relatively random sample of students in grades 11 and 12 of high school, college (grades 13 and 14) and university. Each education level was represented according to its proportion in the student population	Province of Quebec 1969	8,500	147 item, self-administered, mailed, questionnaire	hallucinogens (marihuana, LSD, and glue)	9.67	S. Radouco-Thomas A. Villeneuve M. Hudon C. Tanguay D. Monnier C. Gendron C. Radouco-Thomas	Data analysis preliminary. Unfortunately, no data on prevalence of use of each drug given independently is available.

Sample	Location/Year	Size	Method	Drugs	%	Authors	Comments
Relatively random sample (25% of students in grades 9, 10, 11, 12, and 13 in Welland and Lincoln Counties)	Niagara Counties 1970	5,900	45 item, self-administered, anonymous, questionnaire	marihuana LSD glue stimulants speed	12.4[a] 8.0[a] 7.6[a] 9.0[a] 5.6	R. G. Smart D. Fejer E. Alexander	Large sample with good representation. Data given on grade, sex, many social variables and also parental drug use.
Relatively random sample (10% of all students in grades 8-13 in six school districts of British Columbia)	British Columbia 1970	3,430	15 to 20 minute self-administered, anonymous, questionnaire	marihuana LSD methedrine glue and solvents	19.7 6.6 3.7 12.4	J. Russell	Large sample selected. Data given on age, sex, social variables, attitudes toward and knowledge about drugs.
All students in grades 7-13 present on day of testing in Ottawa completed one either on illicit drug, alcohol, or tobacco questionnaire.	Ottawa 1970	not specified	anonymous, self-administered, questionnaire	marihuana LSD glue speed	19.0[d] 10.0[d] 3.0[d] 5.0[d]	G. Halpein G. Mori	Large sample, provides also information on grade, sex, and drug information sources, as well as a comparison with other studies.
Sample of classes (Cross section of academic disciplines) at University of Western Ontario.	University of Western Ontario 1970	487	anonymous, self-administered, questionnaire	marihuana glue stimulants other hallucinogens	23.2 2.0 4.1 13.1	J. F. Brady D. R. Ross C. F. Grindstaff E. F. Ryan	Sample slightly over weighted with law students. Includes data on attitudes toward drug use, as well as a variety of social characteristics.

[a] "Percent Ever Used" refers only to the last 6 months.
[b] "Percent Ever Used" refers to both high school and university.
[c] Only while in university.
[d] "Percent Ever Used" refers only to last 2 months.

517

LSD. However, only the studies by Campbell and Brady et al. involve drug use during the university years. The most pressing epidemiological need is for studies of drug use in a variety of post high school populations. Typically, studies of university students come to mind, but it should be remembered that many young people enter the work force, or various nondegree institutions such as community colleges, technical institutes and the like. The extent of their drug usage appears to be a complete mystery.

A further unexplored area is the use of illicit drugs by older *squares*, that is, persons holding regular jobs and accepted social roles who are not students. It is widely stated that many such *squares* experiment with, or regularly use, drugs such as marihuana and LSD for kicks, euphoria and self-exploration. Anecdotal reports in magazines and newspapers have described this drug usage. However, no systematic observations have been made of its nature or extent and some such observations are needed on this sort of drug use.

The Difficulties Involved in Making Accurate Drug Surveys

The studies described above illustrate the difficulties of surveying drug use. Most of the studies reported have utilized anonymous questionnaires in which respondents report their drug use. Usually, the veridical nature of the responses has to be assumed although there are obvious opportunities for respondents to prevaricate. In the Toronto study, two methods of estimation were used and the results for marihuana use, at any rate, were very similar. The Quebec and Halifax studies, using the same drug use questions found very similar rates of usage for marihuana, stimulants, and LSD. If students are lying on these questionnaires, as is sometimes claimed, they are doing so in a very consistent manner. Nevertheless, few questionnaire studies do provide any check on the veracity of the responses, although this could be done by various methods such as asking the same question in different ways, administering the same questionnaire on two occasions or by checking with estimates of other peoples' behaviour. Any of these consistency checks would lend greater credence to questionnaire derived estimates of drug usage.

The second major difficulty is related to sampling. Many of the reported surveys (for example, Kucharsky, 1969) are not based on any well-constructed sample, and several others (for example, Menard, 1968) are based on samples from populations which are very special and of little general interest, for example, failing high school students or first year freshmen on the day of registration. Of course, populations are easiest to sample if their main features are known and if they exist in some aggregate form such as the class lists available for high school and university populations. It is not merely accidental that most completed surveys are for high school populations; they are more readily sampled than university students where courses and classes overlap so extensively. Attempts to survey samples of the general population for drug use data have not been made, partly because major difficulties would ensue in establishing a representative sample. However, some such survey will eventually be necessary to provide a complete epidemiological picture.

Many of the sampling deficiencies cannot be specified in detail for the studies reported here. For example, the one "national" study reported data from provinces without any indications of how they or the schools within them were selected. Similarly, the study in Edmonton gives no indication as to how the school or students were sampled. It cannot be over-emphasized that careful selection of the sample from a known population is essential before inferences can be made about drug use data.

Footnotes

1. It should be noted that the questions for the London survey and the British Columbia survey enquired about drug use at any time, whereas those in Toronto, Halifax, Montreal, and Niagara Counties enquired about use in the "past six months".
2. The Ottawa survey enquired about drug use in the "past two months".
3. For Toronto glue and other solvents were averaged giving a rate of 5.0 percent.

References

Brady, J. F., Ross, D. R., Grindstaff, C. F., and Ryan, E. F., "Non-Medical Drug Use Among Students at the University of Western Ontario," University of Western Ontario, 1970.

Byles, J. A., *Alienation and Social Control*, Interim Research Project on Unreached Youth (Phase 1), Toronto, 1967.

Byles, J. A., *Alienation, Deviance and Social Control*, Interim Research Project on Unreached Youth (Phase 2), Toronto, 1969.

Campbell, I. L., "Marihuana Use at Bishop's University (A Preliminary Statistical Report)," Bishop's University, Lennoxville, 1969.

Campbell, I. L., "Marihuana Use at Bishop's University (A Second Preliminary Statistical Report,)" Bishop's University, Lennoxville, 1969.

Division of Alcoholism, Alberta Department of Health, "Survey Reveals Frequency and Use of Alcohol, Drugs among Students," *Concept*, 2, No. 3, 1968.

Eells, K., "Marihuana and LSD: A Survey of One College Campus," *Journal of Counseling Psychology*, 15, 1968, pp. 459-467.

Halpern G. and Mori, G., "Drug Use and Drug Education," Ottawa Board of Education and the Addiction Research Foundation, Ottawa, 1970.

Hayashi, T., "The Nature and Prevalence of Drug and Alcohol Usage in the Port Arthur Board of Education Summer School, 1968," Fort William, Addiction Research Foundation, 1968.

Hayashi, T., "The Nature and Prevalence of Drug and Alcohol Usage in Fort William Schools," Fort William, Addiction Research Foundation, 1968.

Imperi, L., Kleber, H. D., and Davie, J. S., "Use of Hallucinogenic Drugs on Campus," *Journal of the American Medical Association*, 264, 1968, pp. 1021-1924.

Kucharski, H., "Progress Report: Use of Drugs and Alcohol by Young People," National Family Life Committee, The Canadian Home and School and Parent-Teacher Federation, 1968-1969.

Laforest, L., "The Incidence of Drug Use Among High School and College Students of the Montreal Island Area," Office de la Prévention et du Traitement de l'Alcoolisme et des Toxicomanies, Québec, 1969.

Menard, L. C., in paper presented at: Loyola Conference on Student Use and Abuse of Drugs, Loyola Collge, Montreal, 1968.

Radouco-Thomas, S., Villeneuve, A., Hudon, M., Monnier, M., Tanguay, C., Tessier, L., Lejeunesse, N., Gendron, C. and Radouco-Thomas, C., "Enquête sur l'usage des psychodysleptiques (hallucinogènes) dans les collèges et universités de la province de Québec, Partie I," *Laval Médical*, 39, 1968, pp. 817-833.

Radouco-Thomas, S., Villeneuve, A., Hudon, M., Tanguay, C., Monnier, D., Gendron, C. and Radouco-Thomas, C., "Enquête sur l'usage des psychodysleptiques (hallucinogènes) dans les collèges et universités de la province de Québec, Partie II," *Laval Médical*, 40, 1969, pp. 103-107.

Renfrew County School Board, Pembroke Police Department, and Pembroke R.C.M.P. Detachment, "Secondary School Drug Survey," Pembroke, 1969.

Russell, J., "Survey of Drug Use in Selected British Columbia Schools," The Narcotic Addiction Foundation of British Columbia, Vancouver, 1970.

Smart, R. G., Fejer, D. and Alexander, E., "Drug Use Among High School Students and Their Parents in Lincoln and Welland Counties," Toronto, Addiction Research Foundation, Substudy 1-7 & Jo & Al-70, 1970.

Smart, R. G., Fejer, D. and White, J., "The Extent of Drug Use in Metropolitan Toronto Schools: A Study of Changes from 1968 to 1970," Toronto, Addiction Research Foundation, 1970.

Smart, R. G. and Jackson, D., "A Preliminary Report on the Attitudes and Behaviour of Toronto Students in Relation to Drugs," Toronto, Addiction Research Foundation, 1969.

Stennett, R. G., Feenstra, H. J. and Aharan, C. H., "Tobacco, Alcohol, and Drug Use Reported by London Secondary Schools," London, Addiction Research Foundation and London Board of Education, 1969.

Webster, C. D., "Marihuana Use Among Freshmen at the University of Toronto: Preliminary Survey," Addiction Research Foundation, Substudy, 2-22-68, 1968.

Whitehead, P. C., "The Incidence of Drug Use Among Halifax Adolescents," Halifax, Dalhousie University, 1969.

Whitehead, P. C., "The Epidemiology of Drug Use in a Canadian City at Two Points in Time: Halifax, 1969-70," presented to the National Research Council, Committee on Problems of Drug Dependence, Toronto, February 17, 1971.

The Epidemiology of Drug Use in a Canadian City at Two Points in Time: Halifax, 1969-1970[*][†]

Paul C. Whitehead

Several cross-sectional studies have been conducted in order to ascertain the epidemiology of the use of drugs for various high school populations. Some of these have focussed on fairly representative samples of well-defined urban populations, for example, adolescent students in Toronto (Smart and Jackson, 1969), Montreal (Laforest, 1969), and Halifax (Whitehead, 1969, 1970). A survey conducted in Lincoln and Welland Counties of Ontario (Smart, et al., 1970) included persons living on farms, in rural nonfarm houses, small villages, and towns. Surveys in London (Stennett, et al., 1969) and Ottawa (Halpern and Mori, 1970) focussed on the total populations of high school students, while a survey in British Columbia (Russell, 1970) directed its attention to selected schools. Some other studies are based on fairly large samples of unknown or questionable representativeness. These include a "national" survey conducted by the Canadian Home and School and Parent-Teacher Federation (1969) and a study of Pembroke-Renfrew students (Renfrew County School Board, Pembroke Police Department, and Pembroke R.C.M.P. Detachment, 1969). Still other studies are of relatively small samples ($N=101$-216) from fairly select areas: Fort William (Hayashi, 1968a), Port Arthur (Hayashi, 1968b),

*Revised version prepared specifically for this volume of a paper presented to the National Research Council Committee on Problems of Drug Dependence, Toronto, February, 1971.

†Financial support of this project from the following sources is gratefully acknowledged: the Youth Agency of the Province of Nova Scotia; The Welfare Grants Division of the Department of National Health and Welfare (#552-21-3); and the Dalhousie University Faculty of Graduate Studies Research Development Fund.

North Vancouver (Rush, 1968), and Regina (King, et al., 1969). Similarities and differences among some of these surveys and the results they obtained have been noted elsewhere (Smart and Fejer, 1969; Smart, Laforest, and Whitehead, 1971; Laforest, et al., 1970; Whitehead, et al., 1970; Smart and Whitehead, 1970).

As useful as these surveys have been in providing information about epidemiological aspects of the use of drugs among adolescents at a particular point in time, they have the disadvantage of all cross sectional research. They provide no information as to the dynamics of the situation. They are solely descriptive and provide no perspectives about trends or change. To date, only two attempts have been made to survey the same population at more than one point in time in order to measure whether there are changes in the patterns or rates of drug use among adolescents. Schools in Toronto were originally surveyed in 1968 and a follow-up was conducted two years later in 1970 (Smart, Fejer, and White, 1971). The purpose of this paper is to present the results of the resurvey of the drug use practices of a population of adolescent students in Halifax, Nova Scotia. The elapsed time between the two surveys is one year. This is the only known study that uses a one year interval.

Methodology

The original survey was conducted during April of 1969 when 1606 students from grades 7, 9, 11, and 12 completed questionnaires about their attitudes and behaviour toward the use of drugs (Whitehead, 1969; 1970). The classes of students comprised a twenty-five percent random sample of the classes in grades 7, 9, 11, and 12 from the Halifax Metropolitan area.

A similar survey was conducted one year later – April, 1970 – in order to obtain measures of the stability or change of the drug use pattern among adolescent students in this community. A total of 1526 students are in the 1970 sample. However, the grades sampled were slightly different than in 1969. In 1969 grades 7, 9, 11, 12 were sampled. In 1970 we decided to include classes from grades 8 and 10 in order that we might compare the patterns exhibited by students in grades 7 and 9 in 1969 with those of the same general cohort when they reached grades 8 and 10 in 1970.

The data for the 1970 survey were collected during a four-day period in mid-April. A modified version of the questionnaire used in 1969 was employed. The principal modification was that the 1970 instrument was much more brief than the one used in 1969. In the 1969 survey approximately 5 percent of the questionnaires (mostly all from seventh graders) were excluded from the analysis because they were incomplete due to students not having had sufficient time to finish. The items excluded have in themselves no relevance to this paper. However, this modification was important because in 1970 all the students had sufficient time, during the one class period allotted, to complete the questionnaire. There was no loss of respondents due to incomplete questionnaires.

There is, as in 1969, good reason to have faith in the credibility of the data (Whitehead, 1969). The part of the instrument that provides the data for this paper has previously been shown to give reliable estimates when matched against usage estimates not based on self-report (Smart and Jackson, 1969).

In both 1969 and 1970 each class was randomly selected in advance and permission was obtained from the school principal to gather the data. With the teachers out of the room, students were promised confidentiality and anonymity both in writing and verbally by the research assistants who administered the questionnaires. The administration of the questionnaires was scheduled in such a way that in almost every case all students in each school who were to participate in the survey did so during the same class period though, of course, not in the same classroom. There was little opportunity for students to interact with one another either while completing the questionnaire or while some had completed it and others had not. Students did not know in advance that they were to participate in the survey. At no time was the original sample of randomly chosen classes compromised for practical or other considerations.[1]

All students were given the option not to participate in the survey. Only two students in the classes refused to complete the 1970 questionnaire and only three completed questionnaires were excluded from the analysis because they contained obvious lack of seriousness or caring on the part of the respondent. In 1969 only eleven students refused to participate.

The sample was chosen in terms of the following proportions: a twelve and one-half percent random sample of classes from grades 7, 8, 9, and 10 was chosen along with a 25 percent random sample of classes in grades 11 and 12. The 1969 survey was based on a 25 percent random sample of classes in grades 7, 9, 11, and 12.

Results

In most of the sections to follow we will examine the rates of *users* of various drugs. For our purposes we will, for the most part, define *use* in terms of its minimum category: that is, having used that drug one or more times during the six months prior to completing the survey qualifies one as a *user*. In a later section we will take up the topic of frequency of use.

Total Sample

The comparative rates of drug use among students in 1969 and 1970 are presented in Table 1. This table allows us to compare the rates of use in the total samples and for that part of the 1970 sample that is from the same grades (7, 9, 11, 12) as the 1969 sample. The 1970 rates favour the patterns displayed by the two higher grades since they are disproportianately represented in the column that focusses on only those students from grades 7, 9, 11, 12. This will not be a factor in later tables when we will examine comparisons within grades.

Inspection of Table 1 makes quite clear that there are significant[2] increases in the rates of use, for eight of the ten types of drugs, among these students between 1969 and 1970. This increase is statistically significant whether one compares the 1969 rates to either the total 1970 sample or only to that part of the 1970 sample comprising grades 7, 9, 11, 12. The rates of increase, for the rates of use, of the eight drugs are in some cases considerable: tobacco (18 percent), alcohol (28 percent), barbiturates (63 percent), opiates (81 percent), glue (132 percent), marihuana (162 percent), LSD (237 percent)

TABLE 1

Use of Drugs: Total Sample, 1969-1970
Number and Percentage of Students Using Drug at Least Once in Last Six Months

Type of Drug	A 1969		B 1970		C 1970 (7, 9, 11, 12 only)		Rate of Increase (C-A/A × 100)
	Number	Percent	Number	Percent	Number	Percent	Percent
Tobacco	758	47.3	846	55.4	603	55.8	18.0
Alcohol	640	40.0	727	47.6	555	51.3	28.2
Marihuana	106	6.6	223	14.6	187	17.3	162.1
Stimulants	103	6.4	94	6.2	75	6.9	7.8
Tranquilizers	96	6.0	107	7.0	81	7.5	25.0
Glue	50	3.1	108	7.1	78	7.2	132.2
Barbiturates	48	3.0	70	4.6	53	4.9	63.3
LSD	38	2.4	110	7.2	88	8.1	237.5
Other Hallucinogens	35	2.2	89	5.8	64	5.9	168.2
Opiates	26	1.6	43	2.8	31	2.9	81.2
N's 100%	1,606		1,526		1,081		

and other hallucinogens (168 percent). The rates of stimulant and tranquilizer use did not increase significantly between 1969 and 1970: 6.4 percent versus 6.9 percent and 6.0 percent versus 7.5 percent, respectively.

Comparison by Grade

In 1969 the pattern of drug use was characterized by increases in the rates of drug use from grade 7 to grade 9 and from grade 9 to grade 11 with a decrease from grade 11 to grade 12. There were two exceptions to this. The peak rate for glue sniffing occurred in grade nine and the rates of marihuana use increased from grade 7 to grade 12. In spite of these trends there were no significant differences between the rates for grade 11 and the corresponding rates for grade 12. The pattern for the 1970 survey is only slightly different with a trend toward higher rates in grade 12, but again there are no significant differences between rates in grade 11 and those in grade 12 (Table 2). Peak rates in 1970 are predominantly in grade 12 where 67.2 percent of the students have drunk alcohol and 26.4 percent have smoked marihuana. The rates of use of tranquilizers and barbiturates are both 10 percent, and 13.8 percent of the students have tried LSD at least once. A higher proportion of grade 11 students report having used other hallucinogenic drugs one or more times (8.3 percent) than twelfth graders (6.3 percent) but this difference is not statistically significant. Opiate use is reported by 3.7 percent of the tenth graders and 3.3 percent of the eleventh graders, but neither of these is significantly higher than the 1.6 percent reported by the twelfth graders. In 1969 the peak rate for glue sniffing was found in grade 9 (5.2 percent) where it occurs again in 1970 (7.8 percent). The 1970 peak rate in grade 9 (7.8 percent) is not significantly higher than the 7.4 percent rate of use among eighth graders.

There is relatively little variation in the rates of those who have at least experimented with tobacco between grade 8 and grade 12. The greatest jump is between the 54.3 percent grade 8 rate and the 58.7 percent rate shared by grades 11 and 12.

Grades eight and ten were included in the 1970 survey in order to make comparisons possible between a sample of students who were in grades 7 and 9 in

1969 and a sample from the same general cohort one year later. Grade twelve was sampled both years so we can check for changes between the sample of the grade 11 cohort in 1969 and a sample from the cohort when they got to grade 12 in 1970. The dominant pattern is that samples from the same general cohort had higher rates of drug use in 1970 than in 1969. Many of these differences are statistically significant.

One of the largest increases – both in relative and absolute size – occurred for marihuana use among the 1969 eleventh grade cohort, 10.1 percent, and the same group in 1970, 26.4 percent: a 161.0 percent increase in only one year. LSD and other hallucinogens also displayed an increase in popularity within cohorts between 1969 and 1970 to a greater extent than some other types of drugs. A notable exception to this pattern is that 5.4 percent of the ninth graders reported using stimulants in 1969 while less than 1 percent of the 1970 tenth grade sample did so.

Comparison by Drugs

There are no significant differences in the rates of use of stimulants and tranquilizers between 1969 and 1970 for grades 7, 9, 11, 12 (Table 2). Three other drugs have significantly higher rates of use in a single grade only. Significantly more seventh graders have used the following drugs at least once in 1970 than in 1969: tobacco (48.3 percent versus 33.4 percent); barbiturates (5.0 percent versus 1.4 percent); and opiates (3.4 percent versus 0.6 percent). There is significantly more use of hallucinogenic drugs other than marihuana and LSD among seventh graders (3.1 percent versus 0.2 percent) and eleventh graders (8.3 percent versus 4.2 percent). And, significantly more seventh graders (39.8 percent versus 21.1 percent) and twelfth graders (67.2 percent versus 54.9 percent) have consumed alcohol in 1970 than in 1969. Glue, LSD, and marihuana display more widespread increases. The first three have significantly higher rates of use for three of the four grades in question while the 1970 rates of marihuana use are significantly higher than the 1969 rates in all four grades.

Just as the rates of marihuana use increased from grades 7 to 12 in 1969 so do they maintain a fairly similar pattern in 1970. However, the 1970 rates are significantly higher than those in 1969. Among seventh graders the increase was from 1.4 percent to 7.3 percent, for ninth graders 6.2 percent to 12.3 percent, eleventh graders 10.1 percent to 23.4 percent, and for twelfth graders 12.4 percent to 26.4 percent. *The rates of increase range from 98 percent among ninth graders to 421 percent among seventh graders.*

Comparison by Sex

In 1969 males generally had higher rates of drug use than females but few of those differences were statistically significant. Of the forty male-female comparisons (ten drugs and four academic grades) only six were significantly different. In each grade, significantly more males than females used alcohol at least once and twelfth grade males had significantly higher rates of tobacco and marihuana smoking than twelfth grade girls. Slightly more comparisons of males and females in the 1970 survey produced significant differences (Table 3). Ninth grade males had significantly higher rates of stimulant use

TABLE 2

Use of Drugs by Grade: 1969-1970
Number and Percentage of Students Using Drug at Least Once in Last Six Months

Type of Drug	SEVEN 1969 No.	%	SEVEN 1970 No.	%	EIGHT 1970 No.	%	NINE 1969 No.	%	NINE 1970 No.	%	TEN 1970 No.	%	ELEVEN 1969 No.	%	ELEVEN 1970 No.	%	TWELVE 1969 No.	%	TWELVE 1970 No.	%
Tobacco	165	33.4	126	48.3	139	54.3	248	51.4	153	57.1	104	55.0	213	57.6	213	58.7	132	51.4	111	58.7
Alcohol	104	21.1	104	39.8	85	33.2	183	37.9	109	40.7	87	46.0	212	57.4	215	59.2	141	54.9	127	67.2
Marihuana	7	1.4	19	7.3	13	5.1	30	6.2	33	12.3	23	12.2	37	10.1	85	23.4	32	12.4	50	26.4
Stimulants	15	3.0	13	5.0	10	3.9	26	5.4	12	4.5	9	5.0	44	11.9	31	8.5	18	7.0	19	10.0
Tranquilizers	12	2.4	12	4.6	9	3.5	32	6.6	15	5.6	17	9.0	31	8.4	35	9.6	21	8.2	19	10.0
Glue	18	3.6	19	7.3	19	7.4	25	5.2	21	7.8	11	5.8	7	1.9	26	7.2	0	0.0	12	6.3
Barbiturates	7	1.4	13	5.0	9	3.5	14	2.9	14	5.2	8	4.2	19	5.1	16	4.4	8	3.1	10	5.3
LSD	2	0.0	12	4.6	12	4.7	11	2.3	12	4.5	10	5.3	15	4.0	38	10.5	10	3.9	26	13.8
Other Hallucinogens	1	0.2	8	3.1	16	6.2	12	2.5	14	5.2	9	4.8	16	4.2	30	8.3	6	2.3	12	6.3
Opiates	3	0.6	9	3.4	5	2.0	8	1.7	7	2.6	7	3.7	10	2.7	12	3.3	5	2.2	3	1.6
N's 100%	495		261		256		483		268		189		370		363		258		189	

TABLE 3

Use of Drugs by Grade and Sex: 1969-1970
Number and Percentage of Students Using Drug at Least Once in Last Six Months

Grades SEVEN, EIGHT, NINE

Type of Drug	SEVEN 1969 Males No.	%	SEVEN 1969 Females No.	%	SEVEN 1970 Males No.	%	SEVEN 1970 Females No.	%	EIGHT 1970 Males No.	%	EIGHT 1970 Females No.	%	EIGHT 1969 Males No.	%	EIGHT 1969 Females No.	%	NINE 1970 Males No.	%	NINE 1970 Females No.	%
Tobacco	94	37.0	71	29.6	73	57.0	53	39.9	76	56.3	63	52.1	140	54.5	108	48.0	84	59.7	69	52.3
Alcohol	75	29.6	29	12.1	78	60.9	26	19.5	49	36.3	36	29.7	125	48.4	58	25.8	66	49.3	43	32.6
Marihuana	2	0.8	5	2.1	13	10.2	6	4.5	7	5.2	6	5.0	20	7.8	10	4.4	25	18.7	8	6.1
Stimulants	9	3.5	6	2.5	9	7.0	4	3.0	6	4.5	4	3.3	16	6.2	10	4.4	11	8.2	1	0.8
Tranquilizers	8	3.1	4	1.7	10	7.8	2	1.5	6	4.5	3	2.5	16	6.2	16	7.1	8	6.0	7	5.3
Glue	8	3.2	10	4.1	11	8.6	8	6.0	9	6.7	10	8.3	15	5.8	10	4.4	16	12.0	5	3.8
Barbiturates	3	1.2	4	1.7	8	6.3	5	3.8	5	3.7	4	3.3	9	3.5	5	2.2	10	7.5	4	3.0
LSD	1	0.4	1	0.4	8	6.3	4	3.0	6	4.5	6	5.0	5	1.9	6	2.7	11	8.2	1	0.8
Other Hallucinogens	1	0.4	0	0.0	6	4.7	2	1.5	6	4.5	10	8.3	8	3.1	4	1.8	13	9.7	1	0.8
Opiates	2	0.8	1	0.4	7	5.5	2	1.5	4	3.0	1	0.8	5	1.9	3	1.3	7	5.2	0	0.0
N's 100%	254		241		128		133		135		121		258		225		135		133	

Grades TEN, ELEVEN, TWELVE

Type of Drug	TEN 1970 Males No.	%	TEN 1970 Females No.	%	ELEVEN 1969 Males No.	%	ELEVEN 1969 Females No.	%	ELEVEN 1970 Males No.	%	ELEVEN 1970 Females No.	%	TWELVE 1969 Males No.	%	TWELVE 1969 Females No.	%	TWELVE 1970 Males No.	%	TWELVE 1970 Females No.	%
Tobacco	38	56.7	66	54.1	120	60.3	93	54.7	136	64.2	77	51.0	67	63.8	65	42.8	57	60.0	54	57.5
Alcohol	33	49.3	54	44.3	137	68.8	75	44.1	139	65.6	76	50.3	79	75.2	62	40.8	70	73.7	57	60.6
Marihuana	9	13.4	14	11.5	26	13.1	11	16.5	58	27.4	27	17.9	20	18.9	12	7.9	33	34.7	17	18.1
Stimulants	4	6.0	5	4.1	28	14.0	16	9.4	23	10.9	8	5.3	9	8.7	9	5.9	14	14.7	5	5.3
Tranquilizers	3	4.5	14	11.5	10	5.0	21	12.4	25	11.8	10	6.0	10	9.6	11	7.2	10	10.5	9	9.6
Glue	2	3.0	9	7.4	4	2.0	3	1.8	17	8.0	9	6.0	0	0.0	0	0.0	8	8.4	4	4.3
Barbiturates	2	3.0	6	4.9	16	8.0	3	1.8	14	6.6	2	1.3	6	5.7	2	1.3	7	7.4	3	3.2
LSD	4	6.0	6	4.9	12	6.0	3	1.8	23	10.9	15	9.9	7	6.6	3	2.0	17	17.9	8	8.5
Other Hallucinogens	4	6.0	5	4.1	13	6.5	3	1.8	21	9.9	9	6.0	3	2.9	3	2.0	10	10.5	2	2.1
Opiates	1	2.5	6	4.9	7	3.5	3	1.8	10	4.7	2	1.3	2	1.9	3	2.0	2	2.1	1	1.1
N's 100%	67		122		200		170		212		151		106		152		95		94	

526

(8.2 percent versus 0.8 percent), glue sniffing (12.0 percent versus 3.8 percent), LSD tripping (8.2 percent versus 0.8 percent) and opiate use (5.2 percent versus 0.0 percent) than ninth grade females. Seventh grade males have significantly higher rates of tranquilizer use (7.8 percent versus 1.5 percent) than their female classmates and more eleventh grade males have used barbiturates than females. Rates of tobacco use are significantly higher for seventh grade males (57.0 percent versus 39.9 percent) and eleventh grade males (64.2 percent versus 51.0 percent) than their female counterparts. Ninth grade males (9.7 percent versus 0.8 percent) and twelfth grade males (10.5 percent versus 2.1 percent) have significantly higher rates of use of hallucinogenic drugs other than marihuana and LSD than comparable females. Males have significantly higher rates of marihuana use than females in grade nine (18.7 percent versus 6.1 percent), eleven (27.4 percent versus 17.9 percent), and twelve (34.7 percent versus 18.1 percent). Significantly more males than females have at least experimented with alcohol in grades seven (60.9 percent versus 19.5 percent), nine (49.3 percent versus 32.6 percent), eleven (65.6 percent versus 50.3 percent), and twelve (73.7 percent versus 60.6 percent). Of the seventeen significant differences between males and females in the six grades – sixty comparisons in all – seven occurred in grade nine, four in grade eleven, and three each in grades seven and twelve.

Drug Preferences

In the 1969 survey we found that the most popular drugs used by adolescents were tobacco and alcohol with marihuana running a distant third. The order of preference for the total sample of the other seven drugs was as follows: stimulants, tranquilizers, glue, barbiturates, LSD, other hallucinogens, and opiates. The 1970 survey indicates some change in the relative rates of use of these drugs for the total sample. However, the overall differences are not statistically significant (Table 4) in spite of the fact that most of the 1970 rates are significantly higher than the 1969 rates. Again in 1970, tobacco (55.4 percent) and alcohol (47.6 percent) have been tried by many more students than any other drug and marihuana (14.6 percent) is still a fairly distant third. However, in 1969 the rate of marihuana use (6.6 percent) was quite similar to the rates of use of some other drugs, for instance, stimulants (6.4 percent) and tranquilizers (6.0 percent). In 1970 the rate of marihuana use (14.6 percent) is twice as high as that of any other drug lower on the preference scale. For example, LSD ranks fourth at 7.2 percent, glue fifth at 7.1 percent and tranquilizers sixth at 7.0 percent. Ranks seven to ten are occupied by stimulants (6.2 percent), other hallucinogens (5.8 percent), barbiturates (4.6 percent), and opiates (2.8 percent).

The largest shift in rank order is observed for LSD. In 1969 it was rather low on the preference scale, eighth position, but in 1970 it moved up to fourth in preference. Stimulants decreased in popularity from fourth to seventh position as did barbiturates from seventh to ninth position. Tranquilizers, glue, and other hallucinogens display only minor shifts in position from 1969 to 1970. Opiates rank lowest in order of preference (tenth position) in 1970 just as they did in 1969.

The rank order correlation between the drug preferences of males and females was quite high, $R = .87$, in 1969. The same is true in 1970, $R = .82$. In comparing the rank order for males and females in 1969 with the corresponding rates in 1970 we find that the correlation coefficients are .75 and .77, respectively (Table 5). These are lower than the other rank order relationships but still statistically significant. Hence, we again find changes in patterns of drug use that are gradual and suggest trends rather than dramatic changes.

TABLE 4

Rank Order of Drug Preference: Total Samples, 1969-1970

Type of Drug	Rank 1969	Rank 1970
Tobacco	1	1
Alcohol	2	2
Marihuana	3	3
Stimulants	4	7
Tranquilizers	5	6
Glue	6	5
Barbiturates	7	9
LSD	8	4
Other Hallucinogens	9	8
Opiates	10	10

Rank order correlation (Spearman's Rho) = .81 ($p < .01$)

Frequency of Use

Thus far we have discussed the use of various drugs in terms of the minimum category of use, that is, the number of persons who report having used each substance at least once in the six months prior to completing the questionnaire. We turn now to a brief examination of the frequency of use for the various substances. Our respondents who had used drugs were asked to categorize their frequency of drug use into the four following groups: one or two times, three or four times, five or six times, and seven or more times. The maximum use category for cigarettes was "20 or more per week" and for alcohol it was "above four or more times per month." In spite of the fact that rates of drug use increased significantly between 1969 and 1970 the distribution of the frequency of drug use did not change significantly. It remained very much as it was in 1969. Almost half of those who have used tobacco have done so on a regular basis and less than ten percent of those who have used alcohol have done so

TABLE 5

Rank Order of Drug Preference for Males and Females: 1969-1970

Type of Drug	Males 1969	Males 1970	Females 1969	Females 1970
Tobacco	1	1	1	1
Alcohol	2	2	2	2
Marihuana	3	3	5	3
Stimulants	4	5	4	8
Tranquilizers	5	7	3	4.5
Glue	8	6	6	4.5
Barbiturates	7	9	7	9
LSD	9	4	8	7
Other Hallucinogens	6	8	9	6
Opiates	10	10	10	10

Males 1969 − Females 1969 $R = .87$ ($p < .01$)
Males 1970 − Females 1970 $R = .82$ ($p < .01$)
Males 1969 − 1970 $R = .75$ ($p < .01$)
Females 1969 − 1970 $R = .77$ ($p < .01$)

"above four or more times per month." Most users have tried the other drugs only infrequently and very few users have used these drugs seven or more times. For example, 13.8 percent of the twelfth graders have used LSD at least once; over seventy percent of these have used it only one or two times and about ten percent have used it seven or more times.

Discussion

Surveys designed to ascertain the extent of drug use among adolescent students were conducted at two points in time in Halifax, Nova Scotia. Both the 1969 and 1970 surveys were based on random samples of classes within grades seven to twelve. Grades eight and ten were surveyed only in 1970.

All data reported in this paper are based on self-reports of the students. Thus, the usual problems of validity and reliability associated with such measurement strategies apply in spite of the precautions we have taken. There is also the additional difficulty of whether students – especially the younger ones – really know what drugs they have in fact taken. Drugs available on the street are known to vary considerably in terms of quality and potency. Furthermore pushers are known to sometimes misrepresent the actual nature of the drugs they sell. We of course have no control over these matters. However, two points should be kept in mind concerning this situation. First, laboratory evidence indicates that a sizeable proportion of drugs actually contain what they are alleged to contain. Two-thirds of the samples alleged to contain LSD,[3] marihuana, and methaphetamine (speed) analyzed by Marshman and Gibbins (1969, page 23) actually contained the alleged chemicals. Second, the very fact that many young people are willing to try a potentially dangerous substance, regardless of what it may actually be, is important. It means that if the substance actually was what it was purported to be, for example, an opiate derivative such as heroin, they would have taken it.

General increases in the rates of reported drug use are observed for eight of the ten types of drugs from 1969 to 1970. The fact that there were increases during this one year period will likely surprise few persons. However, the magnitude of the increase may in some cases be greater than had been anticipated while in other cases the fact that there were no significant increases will warrant closer examination.

Marihuana is the only drug that was used by significantly more students from grades seven, nine, eleven, and twelve in 1970 than in 1969. Over seven percent of the seventh graders have now reported at least having tried it, and 26.4 percent of the twelfth graders do the same. Experimental use of marihuana seems to no longer be restricted to the drug culture; it is likely becoming institutionalized as part of the larger youth culture. Increasingly, it is something that must be tried as a part of growing up. In 1969, 12.4 percent of twelfth graders had at least experimented with marihuana. In 1970, 26.4 percent have done so. *If* each year the rate of marihuana use continues to increase by the same number of percentage points, then, we would expect that the rates of those at least experimenting with it for the years 1971 to 1975 would be as follows: 1971 – 40 percent, 1972 – 54 percent, 1973 – 68 percent, 1974 – 82 percent and 1975 – 96 percent. In just three years (1973) the popularity of experimenting with marihuana would surpass the current popularity of experimenting with alcohol. If the rate of increase remained the same – 113 percent from 1969-1970 – this level would be achieved by early 1972. Of course, as we have information of only two points in time we have no definitive way of determining the nature of the pattern of increase. The projections mentioned above are conveniently based on the assumption that the pattern of increases will be a linear one. However, it is far more likely that the pattern would be curvilinear, reach a peak, and level off well before experimentation with it became universal. Such a pattern would seem to be similar to that of tobacco and alcohol.

We were surprised to find that the rates of stimulant and tranquilizer use did not increase significantly in any of the grades between 1969 and 1970. Reported increases in the popularity of tripping on speed and then taking downers, frequently in the form of tranquilizers, led us to exepct the contrary. We can only speculate as to why the 1970 rates showed no marked increase in the use of stimulants. It may be that, while there was no overall increase in the percentage of persons using stimulants, the type of stimulants used shifted considerably. For example, it may be that stimulant users in 1969 used some pep pills while the 1970 users included a number of speed freaks who inject amphetamine. If such a shift took place it is also quite likely that some of the speed freaks were not at school to complete the questionnaire. They may have simply been absent due to tripping or have dropped out of school. This argument may, of course, be raised with respect to the representativeness of any of the rates presented in this paper. Nonetheless, the probability of missing school among those whose drug of choice is speed is greater than for those who favour alcohol, or marihuana.

There is a general trend for the rates of use for each drug to increase from one grade to the next grade during a given year; however, few of these increases are statistically significant. Hence, increases – and where they occur, decreases – in the rates of use from grade to grade represent a pervasive but gradual pattern. We do not have a situation where drugs are solely, for example, a high school phenomenon. In such a case there would be sizeable jumps in rates from the junior high to the high school level. What we have instead is a situation where drugs are becoming more and more popular at all levels of the educational system. There is some suggestion that rates of use for some drugs (especially marihuana and alcohol) may be increasing at a higher rate in the early (especially grade 7) rather than the later grades. Nonetheless, the weight of the evidence indicates that the pattern of diffusion is a fairly stable one.

It is important to note that there are relatively few significant differences across adjoining grades in either 1969 or 1970 but that there are many significant differences between the rates in 1969 and those in 1970. The absolute time factor – in this case one year – is more important than the more relative factor of year in school in determining rates of usage of many drugs.

Glue sniffing was significantly more popular in 1970 than in 1969 among students in grades eleven (7.2 percent versus 1.9 percent) and twelve (0.0 percent versus 6.3 percent). However, these rates are much lower than those for the higher status drugs such as alcohol, marihuana and LSD. Furthermore, the peak rate for 1970 is found in grade nine (7.8 percent), the same grade as the 1969 peak rate indicating that glue sniffing is still kids' stuff. Grades eight and seven have the next highest rates.

The rank order of drug preferences did not shift significantly between 1969 and 1970. The only dramatic change is that LSD went from eighth in order of preference to fourth. This provides further evidence for the increase in the popularity of psychedelic drugs. Marihuana maintained its same position relative to other drugs (third) but its absolute position changed significantly. In 1969 its rate of use was similar to that of other drugs (for example, stimulants), but in 1970 its rate of use is twice that of the fourth place drug. As experimentation with marihuana becomes more commonplace we would expect this difference to become even greater. It is important to note, however, that even though there are almost across-the-board increases in rates of drug use these are not parallel to the absolute increase in the use of marihuana. The increasing popularity of marihuana is not being matched by other drugs. Other Cannabis products (for example, hashish) may likely be sharing this popularity.

The frequency distribution of use among users of psychoactive drugs has not changed significantly between 1969 and 1970. Most users tend to be infrequent users and relatively few users could be described as frequent or regular users of psychoactives. This pattern was also found to characterize students in Halifax in 1969, students in Montreal in 1969, and in Toronto in 1968. Such distributions of drug use conform to the log normal curve expectancy. This curve describes a distribution where there is a relatively large number of infrequent users, relatively fewer moderate users and even fewer frequent users. It has been shown that this curve describes the distribution of drug use in Halifax, Montreal, Toronto, and Lincoln and Welland Counties in Ontario even though these communities have different rates of drug use at different points of time (Smart, Whitehead and Laforest, 1971).

Conclusions

The epidemiology of drug use among adolescent students in a single community was compared for two points in time, one year apart. An anonymous self-report questionnaire was administered to random samples of classes within specified grades of the Metropolitan Halifax school system. Except for tranquilizers and stimulants, significantly higher rates of drug use were observed for 1970 than 1969. The greatest increases were for the psychedelic drugs: marihuana, LSD, and other hallucinogens. The largest absolute increases were for rates of marihuana use. The fact that 18 percent of twelfth grade females and almost 35 percent of twelfth grade males have at least some experience with marihuana suggests that experimentation with marihuana is becoming institutionalized as part of the youth culture and is less and less restricted to a drug subculture. We must be cautious about extrapolating the pattern displayed by rates of marihuana use to what may in the future happen to the rates of other drugs now enjoying some popularity among adolescents. The fairly widespread fad involving marihuana may well be drug-specific and may never spread to heroin use, for example. However, there is reason to be concerned about the possibility that some of the other psychedelics may follow the path of marihuana. The use of LSD, for example, is reported by 13.8 percent of twelfth grade males.

In spite of the general trend toward significant increases in the rates of use it is important to note that other changes in the patterns of use beween 1969 and

1970 are slight. So are the increases as one moves from grade to grade. The distribution of drug use is not something that seems to fluctuate widely from time to time. This suggests that the idea of using at least some drugs is becoming institutionalized and that the pattern of diffusion is fairly stable. This further suggests that other factors such as access to drugs and programmes oriented toward prevention are not having uneven impacts.

Future surveys will be needed in order to ascertain more clearly the nature of trends in changing patterns of drug use. For example, we are at present unable to do any more than speculate as to what the rates of use for particular drugs will be next year. Measurements taken at three or more points in time would be a great advantage. These sorts of measures will be important if we wish to base educational, treatment, and preventative programmes on sound empirical foundations. Further, such surveys would be of assistance in helping to evaluate the efficacy of such programmes and aiding those whose job it is to suggest public policy on this matter. For example, when the Le Dain Commission wrote its interim report it had no information at its disposal concerning the patterns of drug use among high school students from the same community at two points in time (The Commission of Inquiry into the Non-Medical Use of Drugs, 1970).

Surveys of this sort are not the only kinds needed however. There is a sizeable need to examine populations that are not in high school: dropouts, college students, recent graduates, young professionals, and the general adult population are groups whose nonmedical use of drugs must be ascertained before we can truly come to grips with the scope and magnitude of the nonmedical drug use phenomenon. Nonetheless, we must begin somewhere and the great importance that our society places on young people and the functional importance of high school education dictates that this is a good place to begin conducting epidemiology studies of drug use on a continuing basis.

Footnotes

1. This is due in large measure to the immense and conscientious cooperation in both 1969 and 1970 that was accorded to us by the Board of School Commissioners, the principals of each of the schools, and the teachers of each of the classes. However, none of these is in any way responsible for the conduct, content, or shortcomings of the research project or any reports that deal with it.

2. Throughout this paper we use *significant* in the statistical sense of not being attributable to chance at the .05 level. That is, the probability is less than five out of one hundred that a difference this large is a product of chance.

3. Fifty-four percent of the samples "contained LSD in a relatively pure form" and only nine percent of the fifty-seven samples alleged to be LSD contained "no drug at all" (Marshman and Gibbins, 1969, page 24). One must also consider the possibility that the samples sent for analysis were those whose quality was most questionable.

References

Canadian Home and School and Parent-Teacher Federation, "Progress Report: Use of Drugs and Alcohol by Young People," National Family Life Committee, The Canadian Home and School and Parent-Teacher Federation, 1969.

Commission of Inquiry Into the Non-Medical Use of Drugs, "Interim Report of the Commission of Inquiry Into the Non-Medical Use of Drugs," Ottawa: Queen's Printer for Canada, 1970.

Halpern, G. and Mori, G., *The Ottawa Drug Survey: Univariate Results*. Ottawa: Research Office, Ottawa Board of Education, 1970.

Hayashi, T., "The Nature and Prevalence of Drug and Alcohol Usage in Fort William Schools," Fort William, Addiction Research Foundation, 1968a.

Hayashi, T., "The Nature and Prevalence of Drug and Alcohol Usage in the Port Arthur Board of Education Summer School, 1968," Fort William, Addiction Research Foundation, 1968b.

King, J., McDonald, D. and Salloum, H., "A Survey on the Use of Marihuana and LSD in the University of Saskatchewan, Regina Campus, and in Regina High Schools," 1969.

Laforest, Lucien, "The Incidence of Drug Use Among High School and College Students of the Montreal Island Area," Québec, Office de la Prévention et du Traitement de l'Alcoolisme et des Autres Toxicomanies, 1969.

Laforest, Lucien, Whitehead, Paul C. and Smart, Reginald G., "Tranquilizers: Drug or Medication?" Paper presented to the Canadian Foundation on Alcoholism and Drug Dependence, Halifax, 1970.

Marshman, Joan A. and Gibbons, Robert J., "The Credibility Gap in the Illicit Drug Market," *Addictions*, 16, Winter, 1969, pp. 22-25.

Renfrew County School Board, Pembroke Police Department, and Pembroke R.C.M.P. Detachment, "Secondary School Drug Survey," 1969.

Rush, G. B., "A Brief on Marihuana Use and School Leavers Presented to the Commission of Inquiry into the Non-Medical Use of Drugs," 1969.

Russell, John, "Survey of Drug Use in Selected British Columbia Schools," Vancouver, The Narcotic Addiction Foundation of British Columbia, 1970.

Smart, Reginald G. and Jackson, David, "A Preliminary Report on the Attitudes and Behavior of Toronto Students in Relation to Drugs," Toronto, Addiction Research Foundation, 1969.

Smart, Reginald G. and Fejer, Dianne, "The Extent of Illicit Drug Use in Canada: A Review of Current Epidemiology," Toronto, Addiction Research Foundation, Substudy 2-7 and 20-69, 1969.

Smart, Reginald G., Fejer, Dianne and Alexander, Eileen, "Drug Use Among High School Students and Their Parents in Lincoln and Welland Counties," Toronto, Addiction Research Foundation, Substudy 1-7, 1970.

Smart, Reginald G., Fejer, Dianne and White, Jim, "The Extent of Drug Use in Metropolitan Toronto Schools: A Study of Changes from 1968-1970," Toronto, Addiction Research Foundation, 1971.

Smart, Reginald G., Laforest, Lucien and Whitehead, Paul C., "The Epidemiology of Drug Use in Three Canadian Cities," *British Journal of Addiction*, 66, March, 1971.

Smart, Reginald G. and Whitehead, Paul C., "A Typology of High School Drug Use: Medicinal Usage, Mood-Modification, and Tripping," Toronto, Addiction Research Foundation, Substudy 4-7 Wh-70, 1970.

Smart, Reginald G., Whitehead, Paul G. and Laforest, Lucien, "The Prevention of Drug Use Among Young People: An Argument based on the Distribution of Drug Use," *Bulletin on Narcotics*, 23, June, 1971.

Stennett, R. G., Feenstra, H. J. and Aharan, C. H., "Tobacco, Alcohol, and Drug Use Reported by London Secondary Schools," London, Addiction Research Foundation and London Board of Education, 1969.

Whitehead, Paul C., "Drug Use Among Adolescent Students in Halifax," Halifax, Youth Agency, Province of Nova Scotia, 1969.

Whitehead, Paul C., "The Incidence of Drug Use Among Halifax Adolescents," *British Journal of Addiction*, 65, No. 2, 1970, pp. 159-165.

Whitehead, Paul C., Smart, Reginald G. and Laforest, Lucien, "Multiple Drug Use Among Marihuana Smokers in Eastern Canada," Paper presented to the National Research Council Committee on Problems of Drug Dependence, Washington, D.C.; "La Consommation d'Autres Drogues Chez les Fumeurs de Marihuana de l'est du Canada," *Toxicomanies*, 3, January-April, 1970, pp. 49-64.

The Prevention of Drug Abuse by Young People: An Argument Based on the Distribution of Drug Use[*]

Reginald G. Smart, Paul C. Whitehead and Lucien Laforest

Concern about adolescent drug use has reached epidemic proportions in North America even if drug use itself has not. Documentation of this concern does not need to be extensive and various reviews have been made of the extent of drug use in various populations.[1] Although there is a tendency to see all illicit drug use as harmful or dangerous, many professionals are chiefly concerned with preventing excessive use or demonstrably harmful abuse. So far, preventive programs suggested (for example, see Smith and French[2]) have been based upon education about the harmful effects of drugs or the development of counter cultures.[3] Neither of these approaches has been closely derived from scientific evidence about the nature of youthful drug use and neither has been shown to be effective as yet. Clearly, there is a need to develop preventive approaches to drug abuse in North America. The purposes of this paper are to (i) present data concerning the distribution of drug use in a variety of high school populations and (ii) indicate the implications which this distribution has for the prevention of drug abuse.

Most studies of the extent of drug use report data for numbers of users and non-users and, occasionally, data for the frequency of use. The latter is often described in terms of a few categories and the distribution of drug use can rarely be appreciated from such studies. There is a need to know the distribution of drug use among drug users taking all of their drugs together. It is of prime interest to understand the basic distribution of drug use and to know whether different drugs have similar or different distributions. It will be argued here that the value of many educational or legal controls on drug consumption will depend on the nature of the underlying distribution and on whether it varies with geographic and cultural contexts.

There are two basically different expectations about the distribution of drug use in young persons. Certain clinical reports and descriptions of heavy drug users suggest that the distribution might be bi-modal, with most persons average or *normal* in drug use and a smaller high point in the heavy or *abusing* category. On the other hand, De Lint and Schmidt[4] and Ledermann[5] have found that the consumption of alcohol in several countries describes a log normal distribution. This is a curve in which there are many infrequent users, fewer moderate users, and even fewer heavy users. The implications arising from a knowledge of the distribution of drug use are considerable. If *normal* and *abusing* drug use can be differentiated then educational and preventive programs need only focus on preventing drug abuse. However, if there is no clear distinction between users

[*]Article to appear in *Bulletin on Narcotics*, 23, No. 2, June, 1971. Printed with permission of *Bulletin on Narcotics* and authors.

534

and abusers then all forms of drug use may have to be modified in order to prevent *abuse*.

This paper reports the distribution of drug use found in five large scale studies of high school students. These studies were made in four different places over a period of three years and all involve large adequately chosen samples. The drug use questions employed were tested against a second method of estimation which gave similar results.[6] Considerable confidence can be held in the reported data on drug use.

Method

The details of the conduct of the five studies are described in the original reports.[7] Only certain broad similarities and differences will be noted here. All five studies were based on large samples of high school students, chosen at random from the total population. The sample sizes were 6,447 in Toronto – 1968, 8,568 in Toronto – 1970, 5,900 in the Niagara Counties, 4,501 in Montreal, and 1,606 in Halifax. In total, some 27,022 students were involved in these studies. The 1968 Toronto sample was chosen to include 120 students from grades 7, 9, 11 and 13 in 20 percent of the high school districts in Toronto. A similar practice was used in 1970 except that grade 6 was included. In Montreal, grades 8, 10, 12 and 14 were sampled to provide proportionate sampling of the two languages (French and English) and the two religious groups (Catholic and Protestant). The sample in Halifax was a 25 percent random sample of classes from grades 7, 9, 11 and 12. Virtually the same questions about drug use were asked in all five studies and similar tables and statistical analyses have been performed on the data. Four of the studies were done at the same time of the year (April), and the Niagara Counties study was done in February. The first Toronto study was done in 1968. The Halifax and Montreal studies in 1969 and the second Toronto study and the Niagara Counties study in 1970.

It is obvious that the three studies have some differences in methodology. The sampling of grades, and of the total populations was not identical, although each sample is representative of its own population. The grades sampled were slightly different, for in Halifax and Montreal, there is no grade 13. In addition, the studies were done during three different years. Nevertheless, it is rare to find surveys in widely spaced areas which are similar in any important characteristics.

Data from five high school drug use studies were employed in determining the fit of the log normal curve to the drug scores of users. The drugs involved were alcohol, tobacco, glue, marihuana, LSD, other hallucinogens, opiates, tranquillizers, stimulants and barbiturates. All five studies enquired about the use of these 10 drugs and for each drug there were four categories related to frequency of usage. These were 1-2 times, 3-4 times, 5-6 times, and 7 plus times in the past six months. Responses in each category were assigned to the mid-point so that the drug use frequencies were 1.5, 3.5, 5.5 and 7.5 respectively. Each drug use then had a score for each of the drugs used (1.5 to 7.5) and a total score varying from 1.5 to 75.0 comprising the sum of the scores for the 10 individual drugs. Only the total scores were used here. Persons who were not users of any drugs obtained scores of zero and were not included.

Results

The distribution of drug use scores were compared with the expected values derived from the log normal expectancy. The methods used were described by Croxton and Cowden.[8] Merely by gross inspection of Figures 1-5 it can be seen that these five studies have produced similar distributions of total drug use. Croxton and Cowden also describe a skewness test to statistically determine the goodness of fit. They suggest that if skewness measures are .20 or lower then log normality has been achieved. The skewness measures are .01, .03, .11, .18 and .20 and all within the acceptable limits. All of the distributions are of the same shape, although the means vary from 6.51 to 11.16. It should be noted that although drug use increased substantially from 1968 to 1970 in Toronto the shape of the curve did not change.

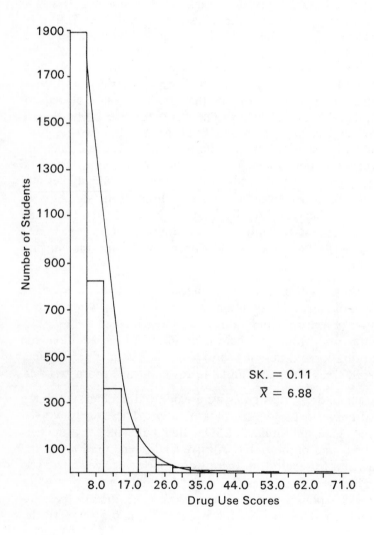

Figure 1

Logarithmic Normal Curve Fitted to Drug Use Scores of Toronto High School Drug Users, 1968.

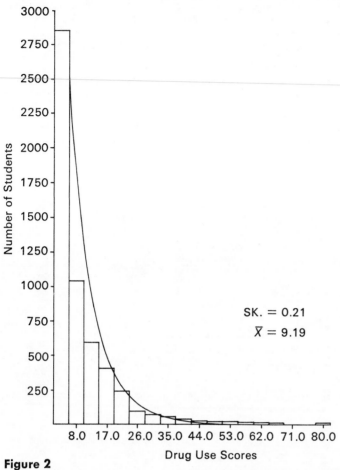

Figure 2

Logarithmic Normal Curve Fitted to Drug Use Scores of Toronto High School Drug Users, 1970.

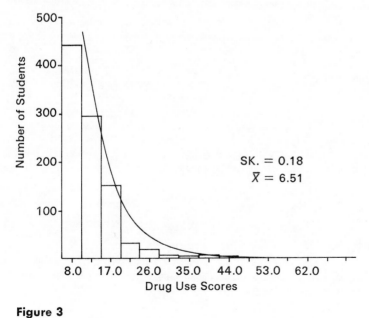

Figure 3

Logarithmic Normal Curve Fitted to Drug Use Scores of Halifax High School Drug Users, 1969.

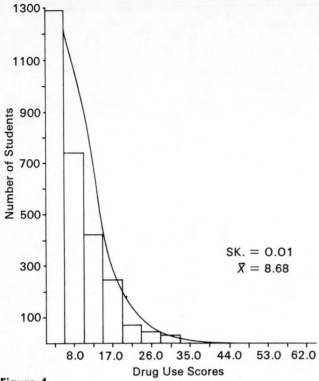

SK. = 0.01
$\bar{X}$ = 8.68

Figure 4

Logarithmic Normal Curve Fitted to Drug Use Scores of Montreal High School Drug Users, 1969.

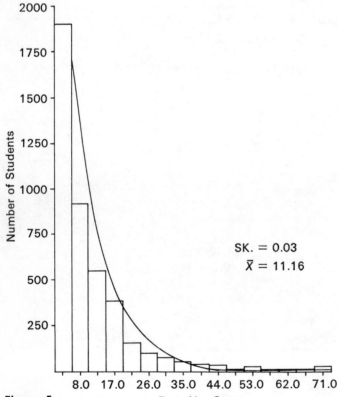

SK. = 0.03
$\bar{X}$ = 11.16

Figure 5

Logarithmic Normal Curve Fitted to Drug Use Scores of Niagara Counties High School Drug Users, 1970.

Discussion

It has been shown that five large scale studies generate drug usage data describing a log normal distribution. These studies were made in widely separated areas and they range over a three year period. The studies in Toronto in 1968 and 1970 showed that drug usage had increased substantially but the character of the distribution remained the same. These data strongly suggest that, at least for high school students, the basic shape of the drug use distribution will be similar in different places and at different times. Of course, it would be well to have similar data from different cultures and efforts are being made to obtain them. In this connection it should be remembered that the log normal character of the alcohol consumption data holds for Canada, Finland, the United States, and France.[9]

The findings of this study clearly show that the distribution of drug use is not bi-modal but smooth and continuous. This suggests that there is no clear differentiation of drug users into *normal users* and *abusers* on consumption alone. Any definition of drug abuse in terms of extent of use must be arbitrary. It will be necessary then to define points in the distribution above which some physical or psychological pathology occurs. Schmidt and De Lint[10] have shown that about 15 c.l. of absolute alcohol is the average amount consumed by alcoholics per day and 10 c.l. has been shown to be associated with various physical pathologies such as liver cirrhosis.[11] Some such damaging level of drug consumption will also have to be determined in order to give meaning to the term *drug abusers*. Studies being made of hippies and dropped out young persons show that almost all of them would fall in the top 10 percent of the distribution of drug use but these studies have not been completed.

The log normal distribution also provides some interesting predictions about the prevention of *drug abuse* however that comes to be defined. Let us suppose for a moment that the log normal distribution describes drug use in a variety of cultures and at different times. This suggests that the distribution of drug use will retain the same character after successful efforts have been made to increase or decrease consumption. This has already been shown to hold for the increase in Toronto from 1968 to 1970. What this means is that the numbers of drug abusers cannot be reduced unless per capita consumption of drugs falls. There will be no way to cut off the *heavy* or *abusing* part of the distribution. In order to reduce *drug abuse* it will be necessary to lower the whole consumption curve and lower per capita consumption. Any successful effort to reduce drug abuse will mean that most people in the population will have to use fewer drugs such as alcohol, tobacco, and psychoactives. Per capita consumption can only be reduced when many people modify their consumption habits.

Efforts at the prevention of drug abuse by young people probably depend upon convincing or forcing people in general to use fewer mood-modifiers. This process may take several generations to achieve and it may depend upon educational programs or public policies as yet untried.

Of course, the problems of drug use and abuse are not confined to young persons. A recent study of high school drug users[12] showed that users of illicit drugs often had parents who were heavy users of psychoactive drugs. Our work suggests that it will be necessary for parents and adults in general to reduce their overall drug use in order to prevent drug abuse by adolescents of the next generation. This general position predicts that changes in drug laws or public education campaigns against drug abuse will fail unless they reduce drug consumption by the public at large.

Footnotes

1. Dorothy Berg, "Extent of Illicit Drug Use: A Compilation of Studies, Surveys and Polls," unpublished report, Bureau of Narcotics and Dangerous Drugs, 1969; R. G. Smart and Dianne Fejer, "The Extent of Illicit Drug Use in Canada: A Review of Current Epidemiology," in Craig L. Boydell, Carl F. Grindstaff and Paul C. Whitehead, (editors), *Critical Issues in Canadian Society*. Toronto: Holt, Rinehart and Winston of Canada Limited, 1971. R. G. Smart, Dianne Fejer and Eileen Alexander, "Drug Use Among High School Students and Their Parents in Lincoln and Welland Counties," Toronto, Addiction Research Foundation, Substudy 1-7 & Jo & Al-70, 1970.

2. Kline Smith and French, "Drug Abuse: Escape to Nowhere, A Guide for Educators," National Educational Association, 1967.

3. J. T. Ungerleider, "Information About Project D.A.R.E." Los Angeles: Drug Abuse Research and Education Foundation, 1969.

4. J. E. De Lint and W. Schmidt, *Quart. J. Stud. Alc.*, 1968, 29, pp. 968-973.

5. S. Ledermann, "Alcool, Alcoolisme, Alcoolisation. Donnés Scientifiques de Caractere Physiologique, Economique et Social," Institut National d'Etudes Démographiques, Traveau et Documents Cahier no. 29, Paris: Presses Universitaires de France, 1956.

6. R. G. Smart and D. Jackson, "A Preliminary Report on the Attitudes and Behavior of Toronto Students in Relation to Drugs," Toronto, Addiction Research Foundation, 1969.

7. Smart, Fejer and Alexander, *op. cit.*; Smart and Jackson, *op. cit.*; P. C. Whitehead, "Drug Use Among Adolescent Students in Halifax," Youth Agency, Halifax, Nova Scotia, 1969 (Support for this study was received from the following sources: the Youth Agency of the Province of Nova Scotia, the Welfare Grants Division of the Department of National Health and Welfare, and the Dalhousie University Faculty of Graduate Studies Research Development Fund.); L. Laforest, "The Incidence of Drug Use Among High School and College Students of the Montreal Island Area," Office de la Prévention et du Traitement de L'Alcoolisme et des Autres Toxicomanies, Quebec City, 1969; R. G. Smart, D. Fejer and J. White, "The Extent of Drug Use in Metropolitan Toronto Schools: A Study of Changes from 1968 to 1970," Toronto, Addiction Research Foundation, 1970.

8. F. R. Croxton and D. J. Cowden, *Applied General Statistics*. Englewood Cliffs: Prentice-Hall, 1955.

9. De Lint and Schmidt, *op. cit.*

10. W. Schmidt and J. E. De Lint, "Estimating the Prevalence of Alcoholism from Alcohol Consumption and Mortality Data," *Quart. J. Stud. Alc.*, 31, December, 1970, pp. 957-964.

11. G. Pequignot, *Bulletin de L'Institut National d'Hygiene*. Paris: Tome, 13, 3, July-September, 1958.

12. Smart, Fejer, and Alexander, *op. cit.*

The Basic Principles and Purposes of Criminal Justice*

Canadian Committee on Corrections

The Committee accepts the following propositions as indicating the proper scope and function of the criminal and correctional processes.

1. The basic purpose of criminal justice is to protect all members of society, including the offender himself, from seriously harmful and dangerous conduct.

The Committee regards the protection of society not merely as the basic purpose but as the only justifiable purpose of the criminal process in contemporary Canada.

The inclusion of the offender as a member of society entitled to full protection is important. This principle prevents the application of correctional measures against convicted persons too harshly or for too long.

2. The basic purposes of the criminal law should be carried out with no more interference with the freedom of individuals than is necessary.

Society should receive the maximum protection from criminals that is consistent with the freedom of those to be protected, at the same time inflicting no more harm on the offender than is necessary.

To accomplish this, the number of laws must be limited to what is essential, since too many laws invite public rejection and increase the scope of state interference while reducing its effectiveness. Police and court procedures must ensure that the process of enforcement will be carried on effectively but with a minimum of interference with the individual. The suffering caused by the sanctions of the criminal law must also be limited. Unduly harsh sanctions not only create a sense of injustice and impair the treatment potential of correctional measures, but also reduce the impact of law in general. There is also the risk that an increase in the severity of sanctions contributes to an escalation of the war between crime and its control.

As Professor Fitzgerald has put it:

> The aim of crime prevention in a free society is part of the larger aim of producing a society in which the citizen can fulfill himself in the pursuit of his individual happiness, free from want, disease, and external interference. The pursuit of this aim naturally entails some measure of state interference with individual liberty. But unless a society is careful to keep a check on the measure of interference, it may end by losing more in the way of liberty than it gains in freedom from want, disease, and crime.[1]

*Canadian Committee on Corrections, "The Basic Principles and Purposes of Criminal Justice," in *Report of the Canadian Committee on Corrections*, Roger Ouimet, Chairman, 1969, pp. 11-19. Reproduced with the permission of Information Canada.

3. Recognition of the innocent must be assured by proper protection at all stages of the criminal process.

This is taken to be self-evident.

4. No conduct should be defined as criminal unless it represents a serious threat to society, and unless the act cannot be dealt with through other social or legal means.

The Committee has not been asked to direct its mind to the question whether specific acts should be designated as crimes. However, there can be no criminals and no one liable to correction under our system unless there be pre-existing legislation, designating such conduct as criminal and imposing upon the actor a liability to legal correction. It would appear to the Committee that there are some matters which are at the moment designated as crimes and yet which are in general agreement not appropriate to be dealt with by the criminal law. To apply the criminal process to such matters is to impose an intolerable burden upon the whole process of correction.

The Committee adopts the following criteria as properly indicating the scope of criminal law:

1. No act should be criminally proscribed unless its incidence, actual or potential, is *substantially damaging to society*.

2. No act should be criminally prohibited where its incidence may adequately be controlled by social forces other than the criminal process. Public opinion may be enough to curtail certain kinds of behaviour. Other kinds of behaviour may be more appropriately dealt with by non-criminal legal processes, e.g. by legislation relating to mental health or social and economic condition.

3. No law should give rise to social or personal damage greater than that it was designed to prevent.

To designate certain conduct as criminal in an attempt to control antisocial behaviour should be a last step. Criminal law traditionally, and perhaps inherently, has involved the imposition of a sanction. This sanction, whether in the form of arrest, summons, trial, conviction, punishment or publicity is, in the view of the Committee, to be employed only as an unavoidable necessity. Men and women may have their lives, public and private, destroyed; families may be broken up; the state may be put to considerable expense: all these consequences are to be taken into account when determining whether a particular kind of conduct is so obnoxious to social values that it is to be included in the catalogue of crimes. If there is any other course open to society when threatened, then that course is to be preferred. The deliberate infliction of punishment or any other state interference with human freedom is to be justified only where manifest evil would result from failure to interfere.

Briefs received from the principal Canadian churches endorse this point of view. Much anti-social behaviour is kept in check by social agencies other than the police and the courts. Fear of discovery with concomitant loss of social and economic status must operate in many cases as effectively as the fear of legal punishment. The family and the general environment must surely more effectively condition the young either for good or evil than do the isolated lessons of the criminal law. As the Wolfenden Committee reported:

> Unless a deliberate attempt is to be made by society, acting through the agency of the law, to equate the sphere of crime with that of sin, there must remain a realm of private morality and immorality which is, in brief and crude terms, not the law's business.[2]

With that proposition, the Canadian Committee on Corrections is in substantial agreement. The Committee expresses no view on the legislative recommendations of the Wolfenden Committee, most of which have now passed into law in England.

We do, however, desire to emphasize that it is the substantive criminal law including the power of the courts and their sentencing policy which primarily determines the flow of convicted persons to the correctional processes. For example, the extent of the legislative limitations on abortion will determine the extent in terms of liability to correction of those performing abortions in Canada. The existence, extent and function of the correctional services is basically determined by the creation and perpetuation of offences and sentences.

Our terms of reference do not extend to an overall examination of Canadian criminal law. It is, however, our conviction that such a comprehensive examination of the Criminal Code and related Canadian statutes and that body of *quasi-criminal* law enacted by the provinces is a matter of the greatest urgency. The designation of murder, rape, assault and theft as crimes does not require extensive justification: the consequences to the victim are obviously grave. In the case of most offences there is objective proof of damage. However, there is a grey or borderline area – if common drunkenness is to continue to be classified as an offence, the correctional process must be prepared to cope with common drunks; if wandering abroad without visible means of support is to be criminal, then the correctional processes must continue to provide for vagrants. If the offering of contraceptives for sale is to be a crime, then the correctional processes must remain charged with responsibility for dealing with such offenders. There are many who see drunkenness as a social deficiency or disease to be dealt with through social, psychological, or medical and legal agencies rather than criminal courts; vagrancy as a social misfortune to be dealt with by welfare and counselling agencies; the sale or use of contraceptives as essentially a matter of morals rather than criminal law. The criminal process is resorted to infrequently with respect to certain kinds of offence created under existing laws. This is true of some sexual offences. There seems to be some justification for a belief that unenforceable legislation is harmful since it teaches disrespect for all law. Only long term research, as yet only of the most meagre proportions in Canada or elsewhere, will provide an adequate factual and philosophical basis for a comprehensive criminal law system. While we are concerned that piece-meal reform will add further confusion, this lack of long term research should not deter us from recommending action where adequate knowledge of glaring deficiencies in the existing system is presently available.

It should here be noted that there is considerable evidence to suggest that in prohibiting certain kinds of conduct and imposing criminal sanctions upon its occurrence, one may be providing the most effective and corrupting publicity for the practice rather than the prohibition. The practices of smoking marijuana and sniffing model glue come immediately to mind as examples of the double and dangerous effect of description and disapproval. Much research is needed into the causative relationship between introduction, description, exploitation, procuration and corruption.

Crime is not a unified activity but consists of a large number of widely differing types of conduct. Crime is made up of a large number of types of conduct, distinct in why they are called crimes, in their history as crimes, in their moral, social and psychological implications, and in the extent to which they are condemned by the public.

The President's Commission on Law Enforcement and Administration of Justice put it this way:[3]

> Many Americans also think of crime as a very narrow range of behaviour. It is not. An enormous variety of acts make up the *crime problem*. Crime is not just a tough teenager snatching a lady's purse. It is a professional thief stealing cars *on order*. It is a well-heeled loan shark taking over a previously legitimate business for organized crime. It is a polite young man who suddenly and inexplicably murders his family. It is a corporation executive conspiring with competitors to keep prices high. No single formula, no single theory, no single generalization can explain the vast range of behaviour called crime.

The terms commonly employed to designate crimes do not adequately describe particular kinds of activity. *Murder* may in practice be applied to such widely diverse activities as killing in the course of armed robbery on the one hand and mercy-killing on the other; *rape* may range from over-aggressive seduction to kidnapping and sexual assault by a gang of ruffians. It may be that the educative function of the criminal process is limited by the extent to which legal terms reflect real-life situations; certainly, effectiveness of any sentencing guides to be included in criminal law presupposes a definition and classification of offences which bears a close relationship to the particular kinds of behaviour dealt with by the courts.

The Committee recommends that the Government of Canada establish in the near future a Committee or Royal Commission to examine the substantive criminal law. The Committee or Royal Commission should also direct its attention to the classification of crimes with a view to developing a system of classification that would distinguish between illegal acts on a more realistic basis.

5. *The criminal justice process can operate to protect society only by way of:*
(a) the deterrent effect, both general and particular, of criminal prohibitions and sanctions;
(b) correctional measures designed to achieve the social rehabilitation of the individual;
(c) control over the offender in varying degrees, including the segregation of the dangerous offender until such time when he can be safely released or, where safe release is impossible, for life.

The Committee believes that the rehabilitation of the individual offender offers the best long-term protection for society, since that ends the risk of a continuing criminal career. However, the offender must be protected against rehabilitative measures that go beyond the bounds of the concept of justice. Some modern correctional methods, such as probation, suspended sentences and medical treatment are part of the arsenal of sanctions but are not conceived as punishments. Their purpose is rehabilitative. Whatever their purpose, however, it cannot be assumed that such treatment methods are necessarily more humane and more effective in practice than moderate penalties. Treatment is not more humane than punishment if it imposes more pain, restricts freedom for longer periods, or produces no results regarded as desirable by the individual concerned.

It is most difficult to ascertain the extent of the deterrent effect of legal prohibition, arrest, trial, conviction and sentence, and under what condition it operates. It has been suggested that likelihood of detection, arrest and conviction is the best deterrent and that the nature of the sentence that follows conviction is of less importance. For the established member of the community, the risk of public trial is no doubt also a deterrent. However, the Committee is of the opinion that risk of punishment is a deterrent in certain areas of behaviour where the offender is motivated by rational considerations. The Committee is further of the opinion that the removal of profit from crimes that involve financial gain would also serve as a powerful deterrent if made effective in practice. Some persons commit violent crimes for reasons we do not fully understand, and these offenders do not respond to current methods of treatment. Such persons cannot be left at large to repeat their antisocial acts. They must, therefore, have their liberty restricted to ensure the protection of society.

All three techniques are subject to be limited by current ideas of fairness and justice.

6. The law enforcement, judicial and correctional processes should form an inter-related sequence.

There must be consistency in philosophy from the moment the offender has his first contact with the police to the time of his final discharge. In the past, there has been some conflict in aims among the different processes. The aim of corrections has been rehabilitative while the aims claimed for the criminal law have included retribution, deterrence, segregation, denunciation of evil and declaration of moral principles. However, in recent years it is being increasingly recognized that the law enforcement, judicial and correctional processes all share a common over-riding aim: the protection of society from criminal activity. Once this is fully recognized the necessity for the three processes to work in harmony will be accepted.

7. Discretion in the application of the criminal law should be allowed at each step in the process: arrest, prosecution, conviction, sentence and corrections.

To implement the Committee's proposition that the criminal law should be enforced with a minimum of harm to the offender, discretion should be exercised in cases involving individuals who are technically guilty of an offence but where no useful purpose would be served by the laying of a charge. Where a charge is laid, discretion should be exercised as to the manner in which the law is applied.

This means the police should have appropriate discretion whether to lay a charge and, if a charge is laid, whether to release the accused or hold him in custody. The prosecution should have appropriate discretion to determine whether a charge is to be laid or proceeded with, and whether conviction on a lesser charge would satisfy the requirements of justice. The court should have the power to dispose of a case without conviction and should have a wide range of alternatives open when a sentence must be imposed. The correctional services should have as much discretion as possible in planning and executing a treatment program.

Discretion should, of course, always be exercised with the protection of the community in mind.

8. *The criminal process, including the correctional process, must be such as to command the respect and support of the public according to prevailing concepts of fairness and justice; the process should also, as far as possible, be such as to command the respect of the offender.*

The Committee's conclusions as to the steps required to develop a system of justice that will command the respect and support of the public are set out in the appropriate sections of this report. However, it might be helpful to summarize here in brief form some of the problems that require attention in any effort to develop a unified and efficient system of justice.

Investigation of Offences

While there can be no criminals if there be no criminal prohibition, it is also true that there can be no convicted persons to be corrected unless suspected offences are investigated with a view to establishing the nature of the occurrence and the apprehension of the offender, if there be one. Substantive law is only a literary exercise unless there be police to enforce it. Like the substantive criminal law, the procedural law governing the investigative process effectively limits the flow of offenders to the correctional process. There are those who maintain that police powers should be greatly extended in Canada in order that offenders should not go uncorrected. There is another school of thought which maintains that police powers must be limited in that too great a police power will give rise to feelings of injustice which will not only gravely affect the community's respect for law in general (a respect upon which law ultimately depends) but also may seriously affect the possibility of the rehabilitation of one who has been apprehended as a result of what he considers an unjust investigation.

Procuring the Attendance of a Suspect in Court

Apart from the civil liberties aspects of the problem of ensuring that a person charged with crime appears to stand his trial, there appears to be little doubt that the treatment of a suspect between his original apprehension and the time of trial has a serious bearing on any corrective measures which are to be applied to him in the event of conviction. The Committee takes the general view that no person should be held in custody before his trial unless there are clear and compelling reasons for so doing. A person held in custody pending trial and who is subsequently acquitted may well be embittered to a dangerous extent; a person held in custody pending trial who is convicted may be faced with a sentence completely inconsistent with his earlier detention, e.g. the imposition of fine or of a period of probation.

Representation of a Suspect

Once again serious questions of civil liberties and equal justice arise. Legal representation of a suspect is however linked directly with the question of the eventual sentencing of one who is convicted of crime. "Failure to provide an adequate legal aid system thus tends to increase recidivism." (Third United Nations' Congress on the Prevention of Crime and the Treatment of Offenders.) Furthermore, in this area there appears to be a grave risk of a justified lack of respect in both the public and the offender for a system which leaves some persons disadvantaged on the ground of poverty.

The Judicial Function

In keeping with the general philosophy of the report, the Committee has directed its attention to the necessity that justice must be seen to be done. About 95 percent of all criminal cases in Canada are disposed of by magistrates courts. An enquiry was commissioned into the actual operation of magistrates courts across the country and we have directed our minds to the qualifications and training of those appointed to the Bench.

Conviction

Traditionally it has been regarded as inherent in the criminal process that one who is judged to have committed a crime is to be convicted of crime and thereby made subject to the penological or correctional process. Here again the question of the proper scope and function of the criminal law is raised. Are all of those presently convicted of crime apt subjects for the penological and correctional services? This problem of appropriateness is particularly present with regard to those charged with the commission of a criminal offence but who appear to suffer from a mental deficiency or disorder to which their anti-social conduct can be related.

Sentencing

This report assumes a criminal code which is related to social reality and a criminal process which provides the sentencing authority with the opportunity to make an appropriate disposition of a particular offender. The Committee sees the overall end of the criminal process as the protection of society and believes that this is best achieved by an attempt to rehabilitate offenders in that society is given long term protection at least expense in human values and material resources. The Committee believes that traditionally punishment has been over-stressed as a means of crime prevention yet it does not deny the necessity for punishment as a sanction and it accepts that in some cases the person may be so dangerous as to justify his segregation from the community for periods up to the whole of his life.

Correctional Services

Without adequate correctional services based on a shared general philosophy, the chronologically earlier stages of the criminal process will not ensure the protection which society properly demands from criminal damage.

Present penal and correctional institutions must be reassessed both in the light of the role that they are expected to play and the practicability of their discharging this role. Where punishment is imposed for deterrent reasons, penal facilities must be made available. If correction rather than punishment is to be the goal, then both institutional and community based correctional agencies must be created and maintained.

On these declarations of principle, the Canadian Committee on Corrections rests this report.

Footnotes

1. P. J. Fitzgerald, *Criminal Law and Punishment*. Oxford: Clarendon Press, 1962, p. 146.
2. Cmnd. 247, 1957, p. 24, para. 61.
3. President's Commission on Law Enforcement and Administration of Justice, *The Challenge of Crime in a Free Society*. Washington: United States Government Printing Office, 1967, p. v.

Towards the Improvement of Sentencing in Canada*

John Hogarth

Part I

Introduction

Most people would agree that the protection of society through prevention and control of crime should be the ultimate objective in sentencing. There is little agreement, however, as to the most effective method of achieving this objective. Some people would argue that the rehabilitation of convicted offenders is the best method of preventing crime. There are others who believe that it is the deterrent effect of criminal sanctions that offers the greatest protection. Still others maintain that detention of dangerous or anti-social offenders is the only guarantee that the offenders concerned will not commit further crime, at least during the period of custody. Finally, there are those who feel that criminal sanctions find their justification not in the prevention of crime but rather in an alleged moral right and duty vested in the courts to inflict suffering on convicted offenders as an expression of society's revulsion to their crimes. Each of these approaches has its advocates and it is not difficult to discover reported cases in which the courts have emphasized one or more of them. What is interesting and significant at the present time is the apparent trend for a majority of criminal courts to minimize their traditional role of social vengeance and to maximize their modern role of social control. The main difficulty in making this transition arises from the fact that the effective control of crime through sentencing requires an ability on the part of the courts to determine the best method of preventing further crime in individuals appearing before the courts and to

*Reprinted from the 1967 (Volume 9, No. 1), pp. 122-136, issue of the *Canadian Journal of Criminology and Corrections* published by the Canadian Criminology and Corrections Association, 55 Parkdale Avenue, Ottawa, Ontario, Canada.

make those decisions that are most likely to promote desired changes in their behaviour.

Limitations imposed by lack of knowledge and by lack of treatment facilities undoubtedly impose sharp restrictions on what the courts may achieve. But sentencing must take place within the framework of existing knowledge and resources. Within this framework the effectiveness of sentencing decisions will depend primarily on the degree to which the courts are able to make best use of available information. Both the quantity and the quality of information and the manner in which it is used will influence how decisions are made and determine their effectiveness. Efficient information-use, therefore, becomes the touch-stone of effective sentencing decisions. In part 2, I will examine some of the problems facing the courts in making better use of available knowledge and experience. But first let us review the main characteristics of sentencing in Canada.

Sentencing in Canada

There are eight features of sentencing in Canada which distinguish our system from that which exists in most other countries.

1. Enormous Discretionary Power Vested in Magistrates' Courts

The Canadian magistrate has a broader jurisdiction to try cases and a greater discretionary power in sentencing than that given to any single lower court judge in Europe, the Commonwealth or the United States. A magistrate's court, or its equivalent, is the only court that can deal with offences punishable on summary conviction. This category includes all provincial and municipal offences as well as summary offences under federal legislation, and amounts to some ninety-eight percent of all cases. The magistrate has absolute jurisdiction to try certain indictable offences, including theft, possession and false pretences where the value of the property concerned is under fifty dollars, and certain assaults. These amount to forty-four percent of all indictable cases. With the consent of the accused, a magistrate may deal with most of the remaining indictable offences, and the vast majority of accused, when given a choice, elect trial in magistrates' courts. Another fifty percent of indictable cases come into the magistrates' courts in this way, making a total intake of one hundred percent of all summary offences, and ninety-four percent of all indictable offences.

The breadth of the Canadian magistrates' jurisdiction to try cases becomes significant when coupled with enormous discretionary power. With few exceptions, the Canadian Criminal Code lays down only the maximum penalty that may be imposed. Depending on the offence, a magistrate sitting alone may: sentence to life, commit to preventive detention, impose whipping or forfeiture or fines in any amount. In short, he may impose any penalty except death. No lower court judge sitting alone in any other country is given this power.

Despite the fact that the Canadian Magistrate's Court has the broadest criminal jurisdiction in the Western World, Canadian legislators have been reluctant to provide these courts with the status or facilities commensurate with their responsibilities. In many areas, magistrates' courts are situated in old and decrepit buildings, often in a back room of a police station. Magistrates' salaries in some provinces are as low as those paid to the lowest paid professionals. In many provinces most magistrates do not have professional qualifications of any kind. A great many magistrates' courts still are not supported by probation services and only courts in a few of the larger centres have psychiatric facilities available to them.

2. *The Frequent Use of Imprisonment in Canada*

It appears that Canadian courts use imprisonment in a significantly greater proportion of cases than courts in most other countries. We imprison almost 50 percent of those convicted of indictable offences. The corresponding figure in the United Kingdom which uses a similar classification of offences, is 38 percent. During 1960, the rate of committal to penal institutions by population sixteen years of age or over, was as follows:[1]

Norway	–	44 per 100,000
U.K	–	59 " "
Sweden	–	63 " "
Denmark	–	73 " "
Finland	–	153 " "
U.S.A.	–	200 " "
Canada	–	**240** " "

The higher rate of imprisonment in Canada may be due, in part, to a higher crime rate, but probably it also reflects a lack of community resources, and, possibly, a more punitive attitude on the part of the courts.

3. *Restrictions on the Use of Probation*

Probation finds its way into our law through the back door. By a 1921 amendment to the Criminal Code the courts were given discretion to add a condition to the then existing recognizance for suspended sentence, requiring the offender to report to an officer designated by the court. To this day probation is tied to this ancient form of recognizance, and is subject to very severe restrictions on its use. As a result, probation is limited to first offenders and in certain circumstances to second offenders. There are no restrictions on the use of probation in the United Kingdom, except for murder where a mandatory life term must be imposed. Restrictions of various kinds exist in several United States of America, and in some European countries, but none appear to be as severe as those in our law. As a result, probation is used by our courts in only 18 percent of indictable cases. This contrasts with 24 percent in the United Kingdom and over 50 percent in the United States federal courts.

The law pertaining to probation needs to be re-written giving this form of disposition independent legal status and broadening the class of offenders to which it may apply.

4. *Reliance on the Definite Fixed-term Type of Sentence*

The Canadian Parliament has been reluctant to extend the use of indeterminate and indefinite types of sentences beyond special categories of offenders. An indefinite sentence is one in which the court sets the maximum and usually the minimum (for example, a sentence of five to ten years), and an administrative agency determines the exact date of release within those limits. An indeterminate sentence is one in which neither a maximum nor a minimum term is set, the court exercising no judicial control over the length of time spent in custody. We have one example in each type on our law [*sic*].

Under the Prisons and Reformatories Act,[2] courts in British Columbia and Ontario are empowered to use a "definite – indeterminate" type of sentence; the definite period of which fixes the minimum period of custody, and the indeterminate period the maximum, with the provincial parole boards in each of these provinces setting the exact date of release within these limits. The Preventive Detention provisions of the Criminal Code relating to Habitual Criminals[3] and Dangerous Sexual Offenders[4] are the only provisions in our law for indeterminate sentences in which there are no limits on the length of time spent in custody, complete discretion being given to the National Parole Board.

For the most part we have relied on fixed sentences in which the length of sentence is determined at the time of disposition, subject only to parole and remission. In most countries, there has been a movement away from this type of sentence. This movement is grounded in the belief that if sentencing should be based on the offender and not the offence, the duration of custody cannot be determined in advance, but only after observing the offender's response to treatment. The extreme form of indeterminate sentence is probably repugnant to most Canadians as it would mean that, however minor the offence, the offender might be subject to indefinite incarceration; and alternatively, however serious his crime, he might be released immediately after study and observation. The indefinite sentence, on the other hand, should have greater appeal as it seems to make a sensible division of responsibility in determining the length of custody between the courts and the correctional agencies, and it ensures that both individual and community interests are protected. This type of sentencing structure relieves the courts of having to speculate about the offender's likely response to treatment. The court in fixing the minimum and maximum terms, addresses itself to two simple questions: What is the minimum length of custody that should be imposed *regardless of response to treatment*, bearing in mind the need to provide at least short term protection to the community and the deterrent aspect? What is the maximum period of custody that should be imposed, *even if the offender does not respond to treatment*, bearing in mind that the commission of an offence does not warrant unlimited interference in the life and liberty of the subject by the State?

5. *Lack of Professional Training in Magistrates' Courts*

Judges and magistrates from other countries are surprised to learn that many Canadian magistrates do not have legal or other professional qualifications, despite the fact that they exercise enormous sentencing power. In Ontario, over seventy percent of magistrates are legally trained. In other provinces, the proportion is well below fifty percent. The present situation is partly due to an historical development in which professionally qualified candidates for the position were not always available. The reluctance of lawyers to seek appointments as magistrates is also due to the fact that the legal profession in Canada has paid little attention to criminal law problems and a criminal practice has never attracted much prestige, in or out of the profession. It is also true that legislators in many provinces have not seen fit to provide the salaries or conditions of employment that would make the position attractive. Finally, it cannot be denied that in some provinces a major criterion for selection still appears to be political loyalty to the party in power. While it would be naive to expect patronage to be removed entirely from judicial appointments, there have been encouraging developments in a number of provinces indicating that greater care can be exercised in making these appointments.

6. *No Requirements for Receiving Information Prior to Sentence*

In most advanced countries, courts are required to make a formal pre-sentence inquiry prior to sentencing young offenders, first offenders, or any offender to long terms of imprisonment. No formal restrictions are imposed on Canadian courts. Some judicial control is exercised by the appeal courts, but in practice the majority of offenders convicted of indictable offences are sentenced without an inquiry of any kind being made.

7. *Lack of Uniformity in Sentencing*

There is bound to be some variation in sentencing practice in a country as large and diversified as Canada. Provincial and regional variations in crime and in resources to meet it are likely to have an impact. Table 1[5] shows the distribution of sentences by province in indictable cases. The figures denote the use of particular forms of disposition as a percentage of the total number of offenders sentenced in the province.

TABLE 1

Range in Sentence Practice by Province, 1964

	Highest Percentage	Lowest Percentage	Average Percentage
Suspended Sentence With Probation	28.72	11.91	18.59
Suspended Sentence Without Probation	20.52	7.64	11.64
Fine	31.15	20.49	24.05
Institution	53.50	32.48	45.70

In units as large as provinces, individual differences between courts tend to cancel out giving a superficial impression of uniformity. A more accurate assessment of the situation can be made from an examination of differences in practice between judicial districts within provinces.

Table 2[6] shows the variations in sentencing practice by judicial district in Ontario during the year 1964. The figures denote the use of particular forms of disposition as a percent of the total number of offenders sentenced in the judicial district.

TABLE 2

Range of Sentence Practice by Judicial District Ontario, 1964

	Highest Percentage	Lowest Percentage	Average Percentage
Suspended Sentence With Probation	43	0	24
Suspended Sentence Without Probation	34	0 (2 districts)	7
Fine	39	2	24
Gaol	60	4	24
Reformatory	37	1	12
Penitentiary	23	0 (2 districts)	6

The enormous variations revealed indicate that despite the excellent initiative taken by the Ontario Magistrates' Association in holding judicial conferences and sentencing seminars, wide differences persist which appear to be too great to be explained solely in terms of differences in the kinds of cases appearing before different courts.

8. *Lack of Legislative Activity in the Field of Criminal Law*

Our Criminal Code is essentially the abortive English Draft Code[7] of 1878. It was drafted at a time when the courts operated on the tariff system and retribution and deterrence were the predominant themes. Since 1878, there has not been a major re-examination of the law relating to sentencing, and our law continues to reflect these themes. Certain changes were introduced in 1954, as a result of the recommendations of the Criminal Code Revision Committee,[8] but these changes did no more than make alterations in the maximum penalties provided for certain offences. The continuing shift in emphasis from meting out punishment based solely on the offence towards preventing crime through reforming, deterring or incapacitating offenders poses a host of entirely new sentencing problems, calling for a fundamental re-examination of the law related to sentencing.

Sentencing now occupies a central position in the administration of justice and treatment of offenders. Further improvement in the methods of dealing with the offenders will depend in part on improvements in the disposition process. It would, therefore, seem timely and appropriate to give serious attention to the drafting of a *Model Sentence Statute*. This statute would not only consolidate existing provisions in the law relating to sentencing and remove anomalies, but would also translate the broad policy recommendations of the Archambault,[9] Fauteux,[10] and Ouimet[11] commissions into legislation. A failure to do so at this time would only give support to those who believe that Canadians lack either the ability or the desire to do more than make pious pronouncements about penal reform. Failure to act would also lend credence to the view that commissions on the penal system are appointed as an expedient method of avoiding immediate action.

Effort directed towards drafting specific legislation will undoubtedly act as a stimulant to further thinking and it might inject a note of realism into discussions about the specific changes that are both desirable and practical. It would be wrong to make specific suggestions at this time about the machinery that should be used in drafting a model statute, except to say that the drafting committee should be composed not only of lawyers but also of people representing a broad range of professional skill and experience. The draft proposals should also be given the widest publicity so that a full debate will be possible. No doubt there will be differences of opinion as people directly concerned are likely to take positions reflecting their particular professional interests. However, it should not be beyond the wit of the drafters to come up with a statute that represents a sensible balance of professional opinion.

Part II

I stated in Part I that within the framework of existing knowledge and resources, efficient information-use becomes the touch-stone of effective sentencing decisions. In this Part, I will examine the problem further.

When a judge or magistrate makes decisions with the prevention and control of further crime as his primary objective, he is in effect addressing himself to the problem of predicting the likely effect of particular types of sentences on the offender before him, and, in some circumstances, on potential offenders. Whether done systematically and deliberately, or haphazardly and intuitively, these predictions are made by relating information concerning the offender before the court to previous experience with similar offenders. At one extreme, the court may carefully examine a large body of information derived from probation officers' reports, psychiatric reports, statements made in court, and other sources; or it may rely on only one or two pieces of information, such as the apparent age of the offender and his criminal record.

It may well be true that magistrates who rely on one or two simple criteria for estimating the likely impact of particular forms of sentence on offenders are able to make more effective sentencing decisions than magistrates who attempt to handle a large body of pre-sentence information. One of the most widely held myths in the folklore concerning sentencing is that the more information the court has the better able it is to make effective sentencing decisions. This myth reflects, in general, a lack of understanding of the complexities of the decision-making process, and in particular, a failure to appreciate the peculiar manner in which the communication of information has an impact on decisions. In any event, both the quantity and quality of information, and the manner in which it is used, is likely to influence how decisions are made and determine their effectiveness.

In this connection, the role of the probation officer and psychiatrist in assessing offenders for the courts assumes great significance. If this role is to be strengthened, the format and content of the pre-sentence report will need close examination.

Criteria for Selecting Pre-Sentence Information

To be of practical value to the courts in sentencing, information contained in pre-sentence reports should, as far as possible, satisfy four tests: namely, reliability, validity, relevance and efficiency.

Reliability

Pre-sentence information is reliable if, for example, two or more probation officers collecting the same information are likely to agree on what that information is, although they may still disagree as to the implications to be drawn from it. In this sense, criminal records drawn from the R.C.M.P. finger-print files are likely to be reliable indicators of recorded convictions, being subject only to clerical errors; while information concerning inter-familial relationships obtained through interview and observation, while perhaps just as important, is likely to be prone to various ratings depending upon the skill and experience of the probation officers concerned.

In recent years, considerable research, mainly by psychologists, has been directed towards testing the reliability of various kinds of diagnostic information that often finds its way into social histories. Research has also been directed towards discovering ways of improving the reliability of ratings made by social workers and others. Unfortunately, it appears that little of this experience has filtered through to the training of those who assess offenders for the courts. I have a hunch that if research were to be focused on the reliability of information commonly presented to the courts through the medium of pre-sentence and psychiatric reports, a number of profound and terrible truths would be revealed, but I will not press the point.

Validity

Information is valid if it accurately represents what it purports to represent. The test of validity is met by pre-sentence information if it makes genuine distinctions between offenders and non-offenders or between offenders of different types. For example, using early psychological tests, it was possible to obtain reliable measures of differences in I.Q. scores between delinquents and non-delinquents. However, I.Q. scores are not direct measures of intellectual potential, but only measures of performance in a test situation. Since they depend in part on learned verbal skills and familiarity with performing assigned tasks, these early tests consistently underestimated the intelligence of most delinquents. Improved non-verbal intelligence tests and better testing procedures are now yielding more valid results which suggest that there is little difference in real intelligence between delinquents and non-delinquents.

The selection of valid information among the mass of data that could be collected is becoming more difficult. Criminology and corrections are in the midst of a virtual *fact explosion*, and problems are posed by the need to sift the mountain of information that is available. Only a fraction of this information is immediately useful and, indeed, much of it is likely to be proven invalid. The intellectual junk yard is piled high with discarded theories and discredited concepts. At any one time, information considered diagnostically significant tends to depend more on the current mood and fashion in corrections than on scientific evaluation. As a result, the style and format of pre-sentence reports tend to become institutionalized and seem to be based more on the highly stylized folklore and jargon of corrections than reliable evidence as to the validity of its contents or manner of presentation. This only encourages a certain scepticism on the part of judges and magistrates about using modern sentencing aids. This scepticism will not be dispelled until it can be convincingly shown that by using pre-sentence and psychiatric reports more effective sentencing decisions can be made.

Relevance

Pre-sentence information is relevant if it is specifically directed to the objectives the court has in mind and the alternatives available under the law. There seems to be a tendency, particularly in the case of psychiatric reports, for the courts to be presented with elaborate diagnoses that are largely out of place in the court setting, however reliable and valid they might be in other situations. Sometimes treatment plans are put forward that are not realistic, either in terms of what the law will permit or in terms of what can be accomplished with existing resources.

Certain basic questions must be asked: What kinds of information about offenders do the courts need to have in order to make effective sentencing decisions? What specific items of information are relevant to those characteristics thought to be important? Is it possible within the framework of existing pre-sentence procedures to obtain reliable measures of these characteristics? The ultimate test of the relevance of pre-sentence information is to be found in the answer to this question. Will the courts be able to make more efficient sentencing decisions with the help of this information than without it?

Irrelevant information does not play a neutral role in sentencing decisions. If irrelevant information has played a part in a court's decision, then it must follow that the decision was less effective by reason of that fact. Even if irrelevant information is not given much weight by the court, it can impair the impact of pertinent information. The possibility of *information overload* should be constantly borne in mind.

The problem of relevance tends to diminish as clinicians become more familiar with the special features of court work, enabling them to focus their reports on those often limited purposes that can be achieved in sentencing. *Use for Purpose*, should be a guide-post in formulating assessments and making plans for the court.

Efficiency

Pre-sentence information is efficient if it makes an independent contribution to the diagnosis or prognosis in the case and does not merely duplicate the contribution of other pieces of information. It is generally known that some kinds of pre-sentence information have greater diagnostic and prognostic significance than others. For example, it is known that the nature and extent of an offender's criminal record is the greatest single predictor of success under any form of correctional treatment. The age of the offender is also highly significant, but not in the way generally assumed. Young offenders are not generally better risks than old offenders. Marital, occupational and residential stability are also significant, but a law of diminishing returns seems to operate in which the prognostic value of information tends to diminish rapidly after the above-mentioned factors are included.

There are many items of information that could be used in a report. The most efficient way of using this information is the one that uses the least number of factors without sacrificing predictive power.

The noticeable tendency for pre-sentence reports to become longer is unfortunate when all the evidence points towards the need to become more selective. This need will not be met until probation officers and others who prepare assessments for the courts are provided with better training in the skills of handling information. In the present state of knowledge it is not possible to give wholly satisfactory answers. But our knowledge is increasing, and in the course of further research it can be expected that those who assess offenders for the court will be given the tools to make a more discriminate use of information available to them.

Making the Best Use of Information

Getting information before the courts that meets the tests of: reliability, validity, relevance and efficiency is only part of the answer to the problem of improving sentencing. Equally important is the problem of ensuring that courts make the best use of information placed before them. Sentencing decisions are likely to be influenced not only by the quantity and quality of information, but also how it is assessed and used. Until a great deal more is known about the processes of information handling in sentencing, it would be dangerous to make specific suggestions. However it is possible to identify those aspects of the problem that might usefully be explored.

It is generally known that magistrates and judges tend to develop distinct sentencing styles characterized by the frequency in which pre-sentence information is asked for and the specific manner in which individual pieces of information seem to influence decisions. Research into the psychology of decision-making in other areas of human behaviour suggests that differences in the way in which decisions are made are associated with differences in how the individual perceives the facts upon which the decisions are made.[12] Social perception tends to be selective, most people only seeing part of the picture and often only what they wish to see. It has been demonstrated that differences in social perception are associated with differences in age, experience, attitudes and personality.[13] Some personality types such as the well-known "authoritarian personality"[14] have such a rigid conceptual framework that they find it impossible to make subtle distinctions in a complicated or ambiguous fact situation. All this suggests that great care must be taken in making judicial appointments. However startling it may seem to some, it would appear that personality factors should be given some consideration. It should not be beyond human ingenuity to devise ways and means of obtaining pertinent information about prospective candidates to the bench in a way that is consistent with the dignity of the judicial office.

Less radical suggestions can also be made. It is known that errors in social perception can be minimized through training experiences in which the individual is exposed to the perceptions of others, thereby sensitizing him to facts and issues previously overlooked.[15] In this connection, sentencing seminars built around hypothetical case situations are a form of sensitivity training, and should be encouraged.

Other Considerations

So far I have discussed those aspects of the sentencing problem in which science can play a predominant role. However, only part of the sentencing problem concerns scientific considerations; equally important are value considerations, and the two aspects must not be confused. The scientific aspect of sentencing involves determining the risk involved in taking one of various courses of action open to the court. In coping with this aspect of the problem, the use of all modern prognostic aids, including mathematical prediction devices and computers, is fully justified. But computers can never take risks; they can only determine what they are. Determining what risks will be taken and the actual taking of risks in the light of the evidence are, fundamentally, value judgments. This aspect should always be a matter for the personal judgment of the court, bearing in mind the need to effect a balance between concern for the individual as a person and concern for community protection. Yet one often hears expressions of concern, epitomized by fear of the computor, that science will make unwarranted inroads in the discretionary power presently enjoyed by the courts and will *de-humanize* sentencing. In my view, this concern is unnecessary, and is grounded on a mistaken conception of both the meaning of discretion and the human element in sentencing. Real discretion can only be exercised in full awareness of pertinent information. Decision-making in ignorance of pertinent information is not the exercise of discretion, it is pure speculation.

In any event, factual questions do not admit of discretion. Discretion only enters into the decision-making phase at the level of making value judgments in the light of the best information available. Information provided by science can only widen the scope of possible alternatives open to the court and thereby increase its real discretionary power.

Can it be seriously argued that sentencing in ignorance of pertinent information is somehow more human? It can be argued on the other side that effective sentencing is in the long term interests of both the offender and society. More importantly, it must be pointed out that the human aspect of sentencing has nothing to do with science, and is in no way threatened by the use of scientific sentencing aids. Indeed by making it easier for the courts to settle the scientific issues quickly and effectively, it will be possible for the courts to concentrate a greater proportion of their time and effort in coping with the far more difficult human aspect of the problem.

These considerations have a bearing on the true value of the pre-sentence report. Perhaps the greatest impact probation has had on the penal system has been in the degree to which it has humanized the sentencing process. Whether or not pre-sentence reports have always contained the most useful information is not the whole story; they have enabled judges and magistrates to see offenders as ordinary individuals, in many ways more like their fellow human-beings than the stereotype of the typical criminal. As pre-sentence reports become more scientific, this function of the report is likely to be minimized. Perhaps the solution will be found, once the techniques are developed, in a greater use of mathematical prediction. The prognostic aspect of the pre-sentence enquiry is likely to be done better by actuarial methods, and it would leave the probation officer free to concentrate his efforts on writing a straightforward description of the offender and in developing a better plan for him.

Conclusion

The introduction of prevention and control of crime as a primary objective in sentencing has made the application of criminal sanctions an exceedingly difficult task. It is unlikely that a simple solution will be found as the problem has many facets requiring action on a number of levels. Improvement in this area ultimately rests on the expansion of treatment resources and on the enlargement of knowledge through research. It is hoped that research projects now under way, when published, will make a contribution to this end. In the meantime, a number of improvements can be made of a more immediate and practical nature. In this paper a number of suggestions were made and they are briefly summarized below:

1. There is a need for a fundamental re-examination of the law related to sentencing. The drafting of a "Model Sentencing Statute" would give shape and direction to this task.

2. Attention should be given to improving the standing of magistrates' courts. This will involve the provision of adequate court and office facilities, an improvement in magistrates' salaries and, in some areas, a change in present methods of selection to the bench.

3. Provision should be made for initial and on-going training for all judges and magistrates.

4. Probation services should be extended to all criminal courts. Where services exist they should not be permitted to come under such heavy strain that their efficiency and ultimate value to the court are impaired.

5. Probation officers and others who assess offenders for the courts should be given better training in the skills of information handling so that the diagnostic and prognostic value of the pre-sentence report can be improved.

6. Provision should be made for the establishment of continuous research programs as a necessary and normal part of the sentencing process. Machinery should be established to feed the results of this research back to the courts and correctional agencies.

Footnotes

1. Nils Christie, paper read to Research Symposium at National Institute of Mental Health, Washington, D.C., 1963; Leslie T. Wilkins, *Social Deviance*. London: Tavistock, 1964, p. 83; Dominion Bureau of Statistics, *Statistics of Criminal and Other Offences*, 1960.

2. Prisons and Reformatories Act, *Revised Statutes of Canada*. Ottawa: Queen's Printer, 1952.

3. Criminal Code, *Revised Statutes of Canada*, Chapter 43, 44, Section 660. Ottawa: Queen's Printer, 1960-61.

4. Criminal Code, *op. cit.*, Section 661.

5. Canada, *Statistics of Criminal and Other Offences*. Ottawa: Queen's Printer, 1964.

6. Dominion Bureau of Statistics, in response to a special request from the Centre of Criminology, 1966.

7. Report of the Royal Commission Appointed to Consider the Law Relating to Indictable Offences. London: H.M.S.O., 1879.

8. Report of the Criminal Code Revision Committee (1949-53). Ottawa: Queen's Printer.

9. Canada, Report of the Royal Commission to Investigate the Penal System of Canada (Archambault Report). Ottawa: King's Printer, 1956.

10. Canada. Report of the Committee to Enquire into the Principles and Procedures followed in the Remission Service of the Department of Justice of Canada (Fauteux Report). Ottawa: Queen's Printer, 1956.

11. Canadian Committee on Corrections, appointed May 1965 by the then Minister of Justice, Mr. Guy Favreau. Chairman: Justice Roger Ouimet.

12. Leon Festinger, *A Theory of Cognitive Dissonance*. New York: Evanston, Row, Peterson, 1957. See also Sherif and Hovland, *Social Judgement*. Newhaven and London: Yale University Press, 1961.

13. T. M. Newcombe, *Personality and Social Change*. New York: Dryden, 1943. See also P. F. Lazafeld and others, *The Peoples' Choice*. New York: Duell, Sloan & Pearce, 1944.

14. T. W. Adorno and others, *The Authoritarian Personality*. New York: Harper, 1950.

15. Milton J. Rosenberg and others, *Attitude Organisation and Change*. New Haven and London: Yale University Press, 1960.

The Role of Law in the Control of Alcohol and Drug Use*†

Margaret F. Hughes

Law is the instrument that our society uses to create, maintain and enforce desired relationships between individuals and the state, and between individuals within the state. For our purposes in this discussion, we may divide the law into two categories: criminal and civil. In the former, the state initiates the action and is responsible for carrying it through prosecution to conviction or acquittal. In the latter, the state merely provides the courts and officers that an aggravated citizen may use to obtain relief. At the moment, it is the criminal law that is the primary means of controlling the use of alcohol and drugs.

In our society, laws are based on the principle that the personal freedom of the individual members of society must be protected. This is particularly true of our criminal law, which is based on the belief that the state should penalize or confine a subject only if he is found guilty of conduct that has interfered with some right deemed important to society as a whole. In other words, society does not interfere with the personal freedom of its individual members unless it is absolutely necessary; and the determination of the situations in which interference is deemed absolutely necessary depends on one's view of the purpose of the criminal law.

Two Schools of Thought

At the present time there are two main schools of thought on the purpose of the criminal law, and this difference of opinion has important implications for us. Perhaps the best known proponent of the first school is Lord Devlin, a highly respected English criminal judge. According to Lord Devlin,[1] a society must possess a common morality; and because society has the right to preserve itself, it has an unconditional right to enforce this common morality. He says that the chief method of enforcing this morality is the enactment and enforcement of criminal law. For example, in terms of this discussion, if addiction to alcohol is sinful conduct, society has the right to interfere with the alcoholic's personal freedom and in effect "save the alcoholic from himself."

The second view of the purpose of the criminal law is exemplified in the report to the Parliament of the United Kingdom, in 1957, of a special committee on homosexual offences and prostitution headed by Sir John Wolfenden. The committee took the view that the function of the criminal law is "to preserve public order and decency, to protect the citizen from what is offensive or injurious, and to provide sufficient safeguards against exploitation and cor-

*Reprinted from *Addictions*, Vol. 16, No. 2 (Summer 1969), published by Addiction Research Foundation of Ontario.

†This article is edited from a paper presented to the seventh annual summer school of the Addiction Research Foundation of Ontario at Laurentian University in Sudbury, June, 1968.

ruption of others, particularly those who are specially vulnerable because they are young, weak in body or mind, inexperienced, or in a state of special physical, official or economic dependence."[2]

The committee went on to say: "It is not, in our view, the function of the law to intervene in the private lives of citizens, or to seek to enforce any particular pattern of behaviour, further than is necessary to carry out the purposes we have outlined."[3]

The committee stressed that it was not condoning or encouraging private immorality, but that "there must remain a realm of private morality and immorality which is, in brief and crude terms, not the law's business."[4] In other words, in terms of this discussion, the mere fact that a person is an alcoholic would be insufficient to justify society's interference with his liberty. Before interference would be justified, the person, as a result of using alcohol, would have had to commit some act that had in some way endangered the well-being of others.

The Wolfenden Committee's view of the distinction between law and morality is not new. According to John M. Murtagh, Chief Justice of the Court of Special Sessions in New York City, St. Thomas Aquinas was saying very much the same thing in the thirteenth century. Judge Murtagh says that his own philosophy of the criminal law is based in large measure on the teachings of St. Thomas, which he describes as follows:

> Basically he [Aquinas] taught that human law, or in this connection, criminal law, must be based on the moral law, that in effect we must start with the violations of the moral law or, if you prefer, of accepted standards of social behavior. But he went on, and this is what I want to emphasize: it is not the function of human law or criminal law to take over the entire moral law; rather human law should limit itself to implementing the moral law in that narrow sphere of activities where violations thereof have a substantial impact on others. In plain English he taught that criminal law should be dealing with acts of violence against the person and property; that it was not the function of human law to make men saints – that was largely a matter for the individual himself, and for society through the home, the church, and the school, by teaching and encouraging morality. But the law should not avail itself of the organized authority of the state to force a person to become saintly whether he wills it or not. He taught that indeed we, as individuals and as an organized community, have a right and a responsibility to persuade and to educate, but not to coerce.[5]

Now I am not saying that either of these philosophies of the purpose of the criminal law is the one in which you must believe; what I am saying is that you must choose a philosophy, and the choice you make will undoubtedly affect your opinion of the role the criminal law should play in the control of alcohol and drug use. I believe that although morality and the criminal law will overlap at times, crime cannot be equated with sin. As the Wolfenden Committee suggested, the state must not interfere with the freedom of an individual unless interference is necessary to preserve public order and decency or to protect other individuals from injury, exploitation or corruption. I want to make this clear because my philosophy will be reflected in any evaluation that I make of existing or proposed laws that are intended to control the use of alcohol and drugs.

Criminal law is intended to control conduct, whether we wish to control it because it is immoral or because it threatens public order and decency. Leaving aside for a moment the philosophical purpose, let us consider two essential ingredients of any successful criminal law. In our society, to be successful, a law must be supported by the majority of the population, and those who transgress it must be punished. Except in a police state, the laws must reflect the customs and attitudes of the majority of the people who are subject to them. Those who propose or enact laws often seem to assume that all the lawmaker has to do is declare "Be it enacted that . . ." and in some miraculous way the prescribed standard of conduct will effectuate itself. This is simply not the case.

Why Prohibition Failed

The Ontario Temperance Act of 1916 illustrates this point. This Act forbade the possession, transportation and sale of intoxicating liquor except in very limited circumstances. As soon as it was enacted it was violated, in many cases quite openly, by a great number of people. Why? Because the legislators had not given adequate consideration to the attitudes of the population and to the available means of enforcement. The law was in opposition to the customs and desires of too many people. The existing law-enforcement machinery was unable to eradicate the drinking habits of such a large proportion of the population. Evidently, the legislators had declared a prohibitive standard and assumed that it would somehow effectuate itself.[6]

True, no one is seriously proposing that we attempt total prohibition today; but prohibition taught us a lesson that we must bear in mind as we examine and propose revisions to our existing legislation.

When Penalties are Effective

The support of the majority of the population is not, in itself, sufficient to ensure that a criminal law will in fact regulate conduct. There will always be persons who will consider violating a law, whether or not they support it in theory. As a result, penalties for violations of the law are provided in the hope that the threat of punishment will supply a motive for a potential violator to refrain from doing what the law forbids. The effectiveness of a threat of punishment in controlling behavior depends upon four factors:

> – the severity of the punishment;
> – the speed with which it will be exacted;
> – the degree of certainty that it will be exacted;[7] and
> – the ability of the actor to control his behavior.

This last factor is most significant. Without this ability, the deterrent effect of the threatened penalties will be negligible. For this reason, I will distinguish later on between the role of the law in controlling the social or non-addictive use of alcohol and other drugs and its role in controlling the use of these substances by addicts. The apparent inability of the addict to refrain from using alcohol or narcotics, regardless of the laws and the penalties threatened, makes this distinction essential.

Now that we have considered the function and the essential elements of a successful criminal law, let us examine our present laws. Do they reflect the attitude of the majority of the population? Are they enforceable? Do they control the use of alcohol and drugs?

Today, mixed attitudes still exist towards the use of alcohol. To some, its use is sinful and should be condemned by the law; but I think it is fair to say that to the majority it is a source of pleasure and relaxation. Its use at home and at social gatherings is acceptable, provided that some degree of moderation is observed – at least in public. However, great reproach and disdain are directed towards those who show the effects of continual, excessive use of alcohol. The opposite attitude seems to exist towards the use of drugs. To a minority, drugs are a source of pleasure and relaxation; but to the majority, drugs are extremely dangerous and should only be used for medicinal purposes and under a doctor's supervision.

Present Legal Control

What, then, are the applicable laws? Alcohol is available over the counter, without a prescription, to anyone over 21 years of age. The Criminal Code of Canada makes it an offence to create a disturbance in a public place by being drunk, and in Ontario, the Liquor Control Act makes it an offence to be drunk in a public place. The Ontario Liquor Control Act also provides for the issuing of an interdiction order, which is a judicial order prohibiting a named person from purchasing, possessing or consuming any liquor within the Province. There are drinking-driving offences, such as careless, impaired or intoxicated driving. However, as long as the individual drinks at home and does not reach the point where his use of liquor renders him incapable of managing his affairs, dangerous to himself or others, or mentally incompetent, the law leaves him alone.

Similarly, the drug addict is not fined or imprisoned merely because he is a drug addict. There is a strong tradition in English law that a person cannot be punished simply for being a certain sort of person; he can only be punished for committing an act that is proscribed or for failing to perform an act that is required by law. Thus the drug addict is punished, not for being a drug addict, but for having been found in illegal possession of a narcotic, or trafficking in or importing a narcotic, at a specified time and in a specified place.

The drug addict can run afoul of the law in other ways: a narcotics user is generally unable to obtain enough drugs to support his habit legally, and must resort to illegal purchases. The expense of illegal purchases generally requires him to engage in other criminal activity for financial support, and thus he is likely to come into contact with other criminal laws such as the laws against theft.

The question now is, do these laws really control the use of alcohol and drugs in our society? Let us begin with the use of alcohol. The deterrent function of the criminal law is most effective with people who are not alcoholics – who have not lost control of their drinking. If moderate drinkers wish to avoid a prescribed penalty, they will not engage in the prohibited act – whether that act be public drunkenness, impaired driving or any other offence. It is with non-addicted drinkers as well that social control in the form of interdiction has the greatest chance of being effective.

Reasonable Interference

Although technically the present laws, such as the prohibition against impaired driving, do constitute an interference with the freedom of those people who are able and prepared to use alcohol moderately, the interference is reasonable and, I think, is accepted by the majority of the population on the basis of the need to preserve public order and to protect others from injury. In fact, our present laws do not interfere to any greater extent with the freedom of those who are *not* willing or able to use alcohol moderately. Society will not interfere with the freedom of these people unless they violate a criminal law.

How effective are the laws in controlling the actions of those who wish to use narcotics socially? Indeed, can there be such a person as a "social narcotics user"? The difference between the use of alcohol and the use of narcotics is not merely that alcohol is legally available and that no prescription is required to obtain it, but that only a relatively small proportion of those who drink become alcoholics. In contrast, the continual use of narcotics almost inevitably results in addiction.

Are the Drug Laws Succeeding?

For our purposes let us define a social drug user as a user who is not addicted. The law is attempting to control his use of narcotics and certain other drugs by making it virtually impossible for him to obtain them legally and by providing very severe penalties if they are found in his possession, even in the privacy of his own home. However, the frequent reports about the widespread use of drugs – generally non-narcotic and apparently non-addictive – by hippies and other young people make one question the degree to which the law is succeeding in its attempts at control, even with people who are apparently not addicts.

Finally, let us consider the extent to which the law controls the use of alcohol or narcotics by addicts. I think we can sum it up by saying that the deterrent function of criminal law is relatively ineffective with this group of people; the same can be said for interdiction orders. Our laws were originally based on the belief that addiction, especially to alcohol, was the result of the addict's moral weakness and that the deterrent effect of a jail sentence would induce him to "stiffen his spine" and control his behavior. If he did not so regulate himself, his moral lapse warranted punishment.

Today, many authorities believe that an addict is incapable of refraining from consuming alcohol or narcotics. He cannot control his need for these substances and therefore he is not deterred by the prospect of penalties – regardless of their severity or the certainty of their exaction. Addiction, in this view, is a disease; and punishing an addict without providing treatment for his disease does not deter him from repeating his offence, nor does it deter other addicts from committing the same offence.

On the other hand, there is growing medical and legal support for the view that an addict *is* capable of some degree of control over his behavior and that in fact he often uses his addiction as a blanket justification for behavior that is irresponsible. On this view, the deterrent function of criminal law may well be effective with many addicts – depending upon the degree of control possessed by the particular addict involved.

The relative ineffectiveness of the criminal law as a deterrent in the case of people who have lost control of their behavior has been recognized, and our laws are in a state of transition. Our laws do not require that medical treatment be given to imprisoned alcoholics, whether they are convicted of alcohol-related or other crimes.

A Questionable Distinction

On the other hand, the federal Narcotic Control Act of 1961 contains a provision for the treatment of imprisoned drug addicts in special centres. This provision is now being implemented. However, the Act's treatment provisions apply only to those convicted of narcotic offences: possession of, or trafficking in, narcotics. In other words, if a drug addict traffics in narcotics to support his habit he may receive treatment; but another addict, caught stealing to support his habit, will not – he is merely imprisoned. The wisdom of this distinction is questionable.

We are moving towards a general acceptance of the view that addiction, to alcohol or narcotics, is not a moral lapse but rather a disease over which the addict may or may not have some degree of control. As acceptance of this concept increases, we will reach the stage where treatment will be available for all addicts who have been convicted of criminal offences and sentenced to jail or prison. This raises several interesting problems. Can we force an addict to accept treatment aimed at curing him? Assuming that we can, should we?

If an addict is convicted of an offence, should he be allowed to choose between jail or treatment, or should society make the decision for him? If the choice is up to him, and the conditions of treatment are less congenial than jail, few addicts are likely to opt for treatment. Should we be required to keep the length of mandatory treatment sentences proportionate to the sentence that the addict would have received if he had been jailed for the offence? Taking the Narcotic Control Act as an example: if the maximum sentence for possession of narcotics is seven years, should we be able to sentence the addict to ten years' compulsory treatment – or even worse, to treatment for an indeterminate sentence, perhaps until he is completely cured? This might mean a lifetime of confinement.

The Demand for Compulsory Treatment

This is not merely an academic discussion. The reluctance of addicts to admit that they have a problem and to enter into and sustain a treatment program voluntarily has led members of the helping professions to demand that the addict, for his own good, be forcibly brought into contact with treatment. Some have suggested that this should be accomplished by seizing upon an addict's infraction of some law, even if it is a minor infraction that might otherwise be overlooked, to convict him and give a lengthy sentence so that ample time for treatment would be available. In fact, it has even been suggested that we develop a civil commitment procedure whereby we could compel an addict to undergo compulsory treatment even though he has not been detected in the commission of any offence.

One's evaluation of the pros and cons of these various solutions will depend upon one's basic philosophy of the purpose of the criminal law. The ambition to help our suffering fellow man is a laudable one, and from the limited field experience I have had as a social worker I know the frustration that one can feel in trying to help people. However, I do not believe that the purpose of the law is to make men saints – to help them in spite of themselves – but rather that society must interfere with the liberty of a subject only when he has committed some act that endangers public order and decency.

Will Compulsory Treatment Work?

However, if one believes that society should interfere with an individual's liberty to help him in spite of himself, the gain to be realized from such a sacrifice of civil liberties must be evaluated. Can we successfully impose treatment upon an addict against his will? Is not personal motivation essential? I do not believe that it makes much difference to an addict who is deprived of his liberty that this deprivation is to help him and not to punish him. Compulsion generates anger, resentment, and resistance – none of which are conducive to rehabilitation. As a result, if it cannot be demonstrated that in at least the majority of cases we can in fact successfully impose treatment and cure the addict despite himself, the sacrifice of civil liberties is too great. The end will not justify the means.

Prospects for the Future

Today the proposition is firmly held that a man may be taken out of society only on the basis of what he has done and not on the basis of the sort of person he is; and I think it is fair to say that it will be difficult to reshape our legal process to allow the compulsory confinement of a sane person for treatment of a non-contagious disease when he has not been convicted of a criminal offence. This does not mean, however, that such legislation is impossible to obtain in the future. It is possible; but its passage and its acceptance by the majority of the population will require that the helping professions advocating such a fundamental change undertake an extensive public-relations program. Part of this program will undoubtedly need to be a demonstration that a much higher rate of cures is achievable with present treatment techniques than the public currently believes is possible.

Footnotes

1. The Hon. Sir Patrick Devlin, *The Enforcement of Morals*. Maccabean Lecture in Jurisprudence of the British Academy, London: Oxford University Press, 1959.
2. *Report of the Committee on Homosexual Offences and Prostitution*. London: H.M. Stationery Office, 1957, para. 13.
3. *Ibid.*, para. 14.
4. *Ibid.*, para. 62.
5. John M. Murtagh, "Alcohol and the Law," in S. P. Lucia (ed.), *Alcohol and Civilization*. New York: McGraw-Hill, 1963, pp. 234-235.
6. B. Shartel and B. J. George, Jr., *Readings in Legal Methods*. Ann Arbor: The Overbeck Co., 1962, p. 50.
7. *Ibid.*, p. 60.

Criminal Law and Non-Medical Use of Drugs: Some Comments and Recommendations of the Le Dain Commission*

Commission of Inquiry into the Non-Medical Use of Drugs

The Commission's Terms of Reference

Although the Commission's terms of reference do not refer expressly to law they clearly invite a consideration of its role in relation to the phenomenon of non-medical drug use. The nature and application of the law in this field is one of the social factors presently related to drug use, and it is also an essential factor to be considered in determining what the Federal Government may do to reduce the problems involved in such use. It would be idle to seek recommendations for governmental action if a consideration of law were to be excluded.

International Framework

Federal law in relation to non-medical drug use fulfils international obligations arising under the *Single Convention on Narcotic Drugs, 1961*. Canada is required by this Convention to make the manufacture, distribution, and possession of certain drugs for non-medical (or non-scientific) purposes a penal offence, although considerable discretion is left as to the choice of appropriate penalties. The Convention can only be amended by agreement; if a country can not secure amendment it must abide by the Convention as it is or withdraw from it altogether by denouncing it.

Constitutional Framework — The Criminal Law Basis of Canadian Legislation

Canadian legislation in this field, consisting principally of the *Narcotic Control Act* and the *Food and Drugs Act*, rests constitutionally on federal legislative jurisdiction with respect to the criminal law. The prohibitions in these statutes are as much a part of the criminal law as the Criminal Code of Canada. The offences created under both statutes are criminal offences. There is no way in which a federal legislative prohibition, violation of which is punishable by fine or imprisonment, can be considered as other than criminal law.

Canadian legislative policy is to make certain drugs available for medical or scientific use, under strict controls, but to prohibit the distribution, and in some cases the possession, of some drugs for other purposes. A violation of any of the legislative prohibitions, whether applicable to drugs for medical or non-medical

*Commission of Inquiry into the Non-Medical Use of Drugs, *Interim Report of the Commission of Inquiry into the Non-Medical Use of Drugs*, "The Extent and Patterns of Non-Medical Drug Use in Canada," Chapter III, pp. 275-327; "The Law," pp. 503-526, 1970. Reproduced with the permission of Information Canada.

purposes, is a criminal offence. The regulatory aspects of quality control, licencing, inspection, information returns, and the like, merely establish the conditions on which certain conduct is permitted. Conduct which does not comply with these conditions is prohibited as a matter of criminal law. This, at any rate, is a rationale for treating Canadian food and drug legislation as resting on criminal law power rather than on jurisdiction over trade and commerce, which, being limited to interprovincial and international trade, is too restrictive for the control of transactions taking place wholly within a province.

Within the present international and constitutional framework the legislative options – that is, the choice of general approaches to legal regulation of non-medical drug use – are not very wide. Unless it is possible, because of the national dimensions of the problem of non-medical drug use, to find a new constitutional basis for such regulation in the general power (or *Peace, Order and Good Government* clause) it would appear that federal regulation must continue to rest on the criminal law power, as directed to the prevention of harm from dangerous substances.

The Appropriateness of the Criminal Law in Relation to Non-Medical Drug Use

In the initial phase of this inquiry serious questions have been raised concerning the appropriate role, if any, of the criminal law in relation to conduct in the field of non-medical drug use. Some witnesses have asserted that the criminal law should not concern itself at all with the manufacture, distribution, possession or use of drugs for non-medical purposes, although witnesses taking this extreme position suggest that the state has a responsibility for seeing that its citizens are properly informed of the dangers of drugs produced and distributed under these conditions. Other witnesses take an intermediate position that the state has a responsibility to restrict the availability of harmful drugs and substances (and that at the federal level this necessarily involves criminal sanctions) but that the criminal law should not be applied to prevent an individual from doing alleged harm to himself. In other words, this view would concede the role of the criminal law in prohibiting the distribution of harmful drugs but would deny it any application to simple possession for use. A third view that has been put before us is that the criminal law may be properly applied against possession for use but only on a clear showing of serious potential for harm to the individual concerned. In fact, this view is indistinguishable in principle from that which holds that the effective restriction of availability (justified on the ground of potential for harm) requires the prohibition of possession for use.

These contentions, and others to be referred to below concerning the present administration of the law, require us to consider the nature of the criminal law and its general appropriateness and effectiveness in relation to the phenomenon of non-medical drug use. A radical challenge has been laid down to the philosophic basis of the law in this area.

The John Stuart Mill Thesis

Those who contend that the criminal law has no application to the conduct involved in the manufacture, distribution and possession of drugs for non-medical use rest their case, for the most part, on the notion that the prohibited conduct is an example of crime without a victim. They contend that the criminal law should be reserved for conduct which clearly causes serious harm to third persons or to society generally and that it should not be used to prevent the individual from causing harm to himself. They often invoke John Stuart Mill's celebrated essay *On Liberty* as philosophical authority for their position. In it, Mill states as his central proposition:

> The object of this Essay is to assert one very simple principle, as entitled to govern absolutely the dealings of society with the individual in the way of compulsion and control, whether the means used be physical force in the form of legal penalties, or the moral coercion of public opinion. That principle is, that the sole end for which mankind are warranted, individually or collectively, in interfering with the liberty of action of any of their number, is self-protection. That the only purpose for which power can be rightfully exercised over any member of a civilized community, against his will, is to prevent harm to others. His own good, either physical or moral, is not a sufficient warrant. He can not rightfully be compelled to do or forbear because it will be better for him to do so, because it will make him happier, because, in the opinions of others, to do so would be wise, or even right. These are good reasons for remonstrating with him, or reasoning with him, or persuading him, or entreating him, but not for compelling him, or visiting him with any evil in case he do otherwise. To justify that, the conduct from which it is desired to deter him, must be calculated to produce evil to some one else. The only part of the conduct of any one, for which he is amenable to society, is that which concerns others. In the part which merely concerns himself, his independence is, of right, absolute. Over himself, over his own body and mind, the individual is sovereign.

Mill goes on, in a passage which is not as often quoted, to make an exception to this doctrine where persons below the age of maturity are concerned:

> It is, perhaps, hardly necessary to say that this doctrine is meant to apply only to human beings in the maturity of their faculties. We are not speaking of children, or of young persons below the age which the law may fix as that of manhood or womanhood. Those who are still in a state to require being taken care of by others, must be protected against their own actions as well as against external injury.

What he would justify in the way of coercion to prevent the young from causing injury to themselves is not clear. But it is clear that his doctrine necessarily assumes the capacity for truly free and responsible choice. This is an important qualification insofar as the problems presented by non-medical drug use are concerned.

Mill argues against restrictions on the availability of allegedly dangerous substances as an interference with the liberty of the individual who may seek to use them, but once again he makes an exception in favour of protection of the young. Pertinent passages on this point include the following:

> ... On the other hand, there are questions relating to interference with trade, which are essentially questions on liberty; such as the Maine Law, already touched upon; the prohibition of the importation of opium into

China; the restriction of the sale of poisons; all cases, in short, where the object of the interference is to make it impossible or difficult to obtain a particular commodity. These interferences are objectionable, not as infringements on the liberty of the producer or seller, but on that of the buyer. . . . When there is not a certainty, but only a danger of mischief, no one but the person himself can judge of the sufficiency of the motive which may prompt him to incur the risk: in this case, therefore (unless he is a child, or delirious, or in some state of excitement or absorption incompatible with the full use of the reflecting faculty) he ought, I conceive, to be only warned of the danger; not forcibly prevented from exposing himself to it.

Mill meets head on the argument that there is no such thing as harm to oneself that does not cause some harm to third persons or society in general.

The distinction here pointed out between the part of a person's life which concerns only himself, and that which concerns others, many persons will refuse to admit. How (it may be asked) can any part of the conduct of a member of society be a matter of indifference to the other members? No person is an entirely isolated being; it is impossible for a person to do anything seriously or permanently hurtful to himself, without mischief reaching at least to his near connections, and often far beyond them. . . .

I fully admit that the mischief which a person does to himself may seriously affect, both through their sympathies and their interests, those nearly connected with him, and in a minor degree, society at large. When, by conduct of this sort, a person is led to violate a distinct and assignable obligation to any other person or persons, the case is taken out of the self-regarding class and becomes amenable to moral disapprobation in the proper sense of the term. . . . Whoever fails in the consideration generally due to the interests and feelings of others, not being compelled by some more imperative duty, or justified by allowable self-preference, is a subject of moral disapprobation for that failure, but not for the cause of it, nor for the errors, merely personal to himself, which may have remotely led to it. In like manner, when a person disables himself, by conduct purely self-regarding, from the performance of some definite duty incumbent on him to the public, he is guilty of a social offence. No person ought to be punished simply for being drunk; but a soldier or a policeman should be punished for being drunk on duty. Whenever, in short, there is a definite damage, or a definite risk of damage, either to an individual or to the public, the case is taken out of the province of liberty and placed in that of morality or law.

But with regard to the merely contingent, or, as it may be called, constructive injury which a person causes to society, by conduct which neither violates any specific duty to the public, nor occasions perceptible hurt to any assignable individual except himself; the inconvenience is one which society can afford to bear, for the sake of the greater good of human freedom. If grown persons are to be punished for not taking proper care of themselves, I would rather it were for their own sake, than under pretense of preventing them from impairing their capacity of rendering to society benefits which society does not pretend it has a right to exact. But I can not consent to argue the point as if society had no means of bringing its weaker members up to its ordinary standard of rational conduct, except waiting till they do something irrational and then punishing them, legally or morally, for it. Society has had absolute

570

power over them during all the early portion of their existence; it has had the whole period of childhood and nonage in which to try whether it could make them capable of rational conduct in life.

The Hart-Devlin Controversy

The principles affirmed by Mill have been a point of reference for divergent legal philosophies concerning the conduct which is appropriate for criminal law sanction. The issue is often referred to as one of *law and morals*. The two leading exponents of the contending points of view in modern times have been the English legal philosopher, H. L. A. Hart and the English judge, Lord Devlin. Hart has expressed various ways in which the issue has been put as follows:

> Is the fact that certain conduct is by common standards immoral, sufficient to justify making that conduct punishable by law? Is it morally permissible to enforce morality as such? Ought immorality as such to be a crime?

Hart's answer is no, as is Mill's, but he adds that "I do not propose to defend all that Mill said; for I myself think there may be grounds justifying the legal coercion of the individual other than the prevention of harm to others" (*Law, Liberty and Morality*).

Devlin's answer is yes, on the general ground that "Society is entitled by means of its laws to protect itself from dangers, whether from within or without" (*The Enforcement of Morals*).

As Hart himself points out, however, the expression of the issue as one of law and morals is not strictly appropriate to the drug crimes, in which the concern is the protection of the individual from physical and psychological harm, albeit harm to which he may voluntarily expose himself. It is not the suppression of conduct simply on the ground that it fails to conform to an established code of morality, although moral judgment on the deviant character of the conduct is no doubt involved to some extent. Hart refers to this protection of the individual against himself as *paternalism*. He says:

> But paternalism – the protection of people against themselves – is a perfectly coherent policy. Indeed, it seems very strange in mid-twentieth century to insist upon this, for the wane of laissez faire since Mill's day is one of the commonplaces of social history, and instances of paternalism now abound in our law – criminal and civil. The supply of drugs or narcotics, even to adults, except under medical prescription is punishable by the criminal law, and it would seem very dogmatic to say of the law creating this offence that *there is only one explanation*, namely, "that the law was concerned not with the protection of the would-be purchasers against themselves, but only with the punishment of the seller for his immorality." If, as seems obvious, paternalism is a possible explanation of such laws, it is also possible in the case of the rule excluding the consent of the victim as a defence to a charge of assault.

Hart finds Mill's argument against restriction of the availability of harmful substances extreme, and inapplicable now in the light of the far-reaching paternalism of the modern state. On this point he says:

Certainly a modification in Mill's principles is required, if they are to accommodate the rule of criminal law under discussion or other instances of paternalism. But the modified principles would not abandon the objection to the use of the criminal law merely to enforce positive morality. They would only have to provide that harming others is something we may still seek to prevent by use of the criminal law, even when the victims consent to or assist in the acts which are harmful to them.

The Right of the State to Restrict the Availability of Harmful Substances

Thus it is important to keep in mind, and particularly in view of the exception which Mill makes to his own doctrine in favour of protection of the young, the distinction which Hart makes between paternalism and *legal moralism*. In our opinion, the state has a responsibility to restrict the *availability* of harmful substances – and in particular to prevent the exposure of the young to them – and that such restriction is a proper object of the criminal law. We cannot agree with Mill's thesis that the extent of the state's responsibility and permissible interference is to attempt to assure that people are warned of the dangers. At least, this is our present position, particularly in the light of such recent experience as the thalidomide tragedies. Obviously the state must be selective. It can not attempt to restrict the availability of any and all substances which may have a potential for harm. In many cases it must be satisfied with assuring adequate information. We simply say that, in principle, the state can not be denied the right to use the criminal law to restrict availability where, in its opinion, the potential for harm appears to call for such a policy.

The Right of Society to Protect Itself from Certain Kinds of Harm

Without entering into the distinction between law and morality, we also subscribe to the general proposition that society has a right to use the criminal law to protect itself from harm which truly threatens its existence as a politically, socially and economically viable order for sustaining a creative and democratic process of human development and self-realization.

The Criminal Law Should Not Be Used for the Enforcement of Morality Without Regard to Potential for Harm

In this sense we subscribe to what Hart refers to as the *moderate thesis* of Lord Devlin. We do not subscribe to the *extreme thesis* that it is appropriate to use the criminal law to enforce morality, regardless of the potential for harm to the individual or society.

If we admit the right of society to use the criminal law to restrict the availability of harmful substances in order to protect individuals (particularly young people) and society from resultant harm, it does not necessarily follow that the criminal law should be applied against the user as well as the distributor of such substances. There is no principle of consistency that requires the criminal law to be used as fully as possible, or not at all, in a field in which it may have some degree of appropriateness. We do not exclude in principle the application of the criminal law against the user since it is a measure which can have an effect upon availability and the exposure of others to the opportunity for use, but the appropriateness or utility of such an application must be evaluated in the light of the relative costs and benefits.

The law enforcement authorities and the courts have tended to see the offence of simple possession as related to the effective suppression of trafficking. The officers of the RCMP have testified that law enforcement against trafficking is more difficult without a prohibition against simple possession.

The judicial approach is reflected in the reasoning of the British Columbia Court of Appeal in the *Budd* and the *Hartley and McCallum* cases, in which the Court saw the suppression of use as the most effective means of suppressing trafficking. "If the use of this drug is not stopped," the Court said, "it is going to be followed by an organized marketing system."

During the initial phase of the inquiry we have received recommendations for changes in the law respecting the offence of simple possession. Some have proposed the repeal of the present prohibition against the simple possession of marijuana. Others have suggested that the simple possession of the amphetamines without a prescription should be made a criminal offence. These proposals and the experience so far with law enforcement in the field of non-medical drug use oblige us at this time to consider the merits of the offence of simple possession.

The present state of our empirical studies of law enforcement in the field of non-medical drug use does not permit us to express a considered opinion of the operational relationship between the offence of simple possession and the offence of trafficking. We are unable to estimate the relative effect on enforcement against trafficking of the absence of an offence of simple possession. We are unable, for example, to draw comparisons, in this respect, between the enforcement against trafficking in narcotics, cannabis, and restricted drugs, and enforcement against trafficking in controlled drugs, for which there is not an offence of simple possession. We do not know if meaningful comparisons of this kind can ever be drawn, in view of the many other factors in each case which may influence the patterns of trafficking and their detection. *At the present time we are not convinced of the necessary relationship between the offence of simple possession and trafficking, or of the necessity of such an offence for effective law enforcement against trafficking. We do feel, however, that further study and consideration must be given to the contention of the law enforcement authorities on this point, and for this reason we are not prepared* at this time *to recommend the total elimination of the offence of simple possession in respect of non-medical drug use.*

At the same time we have very serious reservations concerning the offence of simple possession for use which prompt us, as an interim measure, to recommend a change in the law respecting it. Our reservations apply to the offence of simple possession generally in the field of non-medical drug use and not to any one or more of the psychotropic drugs, in particular. *In effect, while we feel the offence of simple possession should be retained on the statute book, pending further investigation and analysis, which we hope to carry out in the ensuing year, its impact on the individual should be reduced as much as possible.*

Our basic reservation at this time concerning the prohibition against simple possession for use is that its enforcement would appear to cost far too much, in individual and social terms, for any utility which it may be shown to have. *We feel that the probability of this is such that there is justification at this time to reduce the impact of the offence of simple possession as much as possible, pending further study and consideration as to whether it should be retained at all.* The present cost of its enforcement, and the individual and social harm caused by it, are in our opinion, one of the major problems involved in the non-medical use of drugs.

Insofar as cannabis, and possibly the stronger hallucinogens like LSD, are concerned, the present law against simple possession would appear to be unenforceable, except in a very selective and discriminatory kind of way. This results necessarily from the extent of use and the kinds of individual involved. It is obvious that the police can not make a serious attempt at full enforcement of the law against simple possession. *We intend during the ensuing year to attempt to determine the relative cost in actual dollars and allocation of time of the enforcement of the drug laws, but it is our initial impression from our observations so far that it is out of all proportion to the relative effectiveness of the law.* Although accurate statistics are not available to us at this time of either the extent of cannabis use or the number of cases of simple possession of cannabis cleared by the law enforcement authorities during the past year, conservative estimates of both suggest that the total number of cannabis users brought to court may be under one percent.

The law which appears to stand on the statute book as a mere convenience to be applied from time to time, on a very selective and discriminatory basis, to *make an example* of someone, is bound to create a strong sense of injustice and a corresponding disrespect for law and law enforcement. It is also bound to have an adverse effect upon the morale of law enforcement authorities.

Moreover, it is doubtful if its deterrent effect justifies the injury inflicted upon the individuals who have the misfortune to be prosecuted under it. It is, of course, impossible to determine the extent to which the law against simple possession has deterrent effect, but certainly the increase in use, as well as the statements of users, would suggest that it has relatively little. The relative risk of detection and prosecution may be presumed to have a bearing upon deterrent effect.

The harm caused by a conviction for simple possession appears to be out of all proportion to any good it is likely to achieve in relation to the phenomenon of non-medical drug use. Because of the nature of the phenomenon involved it is bound to impinge more heavily on the young than on other segments of the population. Moreover, it is bound to blight the life of some of the most promising of the country's youth. Once again there is the accumulating social cost of a profound sense of injustice, not only at being the unlucky one whom the authorities have decided to prosecute, but at having to pay such an enormous price for conduct which does not seem to concern anyone but oneself. This sense of injustice is aggravated by the disparity in sentences made possible by the large discretion presently left to the courts.

Finally, the extreme methods which appear to be necessary in the enforcement of a prohibition against simple possession – informers, entrapment, Writs of Assistance, and occasionally force to recover the prohibited substance – add considerably to the burden of justifying the necessity or even the utility of such a provision.

Despite these reservations, the Commission is not prepared to recommend the total repeal of the prohibition against simple possession without an opportunity to give further study and consideration to: (a) the possible effect of permitted use on the nature and development of trafficking; and (b) the possible effect of the lack of an offence of simple possession on the effectiveness of law enforcement against trafficking.

At the same time the commission is of the opinion that no one should be liable to imprisonment for simple possession of a psychotropic drug for non-medical purposes. Moreover, it believes that the discretion as to whether to proceed by way of indictment or summary conviction should be removed. *Accordingly, the commission recommends as an interim measure, pending its final report, that the narcotic control act and the food and drugs act be amended to make the offence of simple possession under these acts punishable upon summary conviction by a fine not exceeding a reasonable amount.[1] The commission suggests a maximum fine of $100.* Such a change would in fact reflect, and bring the law into closer conformity with recent sentencing practices, at least for first offenders, in cases of simple possession of cannabis or LSD.

Furthermore, this change would be within the scope of Article 36 of the *Single Convention on Narcotic Drugs, 1961*, which only requires "imprisonment or other penalties of deprivation of liberty" for *serious offences.*

The Commission also recommends that the power conferred by section 694(2) of the Criminal Code to impose imprisonment in default of payment of a fine should not be exerciseable in respect of offences of simple possession of psychotropic drugs. In such cases, the Crown should rely on civil proceedings to recover payment.

The Commission would further recommend that the police, prosecutors and courts exercise the discretion entrusted to them at various stages of the criminal law process so as to minimize the impact of the criminal law upon the simple possessor of psychotropic drugs, pending decision as to the whole future of possessional offences in this field.

Unless we are prepared to prohibit some or all of the controlled drugs altogether, whether under prescription or not, as some countries have done, we see serious difficulties (perhaps even greater than those which have arisen with cannabis) in attempting to enforce a criminal law prohibition against simple possession for non-medical use. In the first place, it would not be practicable to impose or attempt to enforce such a prohibition for possession of drugs obtained under prescription, even though the use might no longer be justified on generally accepted medical grounds. The same would apply to members of the same family or to friends to whom such drugs might be given for non-medical use. In other words, the extent to which these drugs can presently be obtained and used under prescription by the adult world – and indeed are used, if we are to draw the logical inferences from production figures – is such that the enforcement of a prohibition against simple possession for the non-medical use of such drugs would inevitably involve even greater discrimination and sense of injustice than that which is bringing the law with respect to cannabis into disrepute. Since such a prohibition might be expected to be directed and enforced mainly against what the police considered to be *excessive* use by young people it would be a further cause of youthful alienation and resentment of the older generation. This would only be reinforced by increasing use of amphetamines and barbiturates by adults.

Further, in view of the paranoia associated with the excessive use of amphetamines and methamphetamines (the level of use which characterizes the *speed freak*), we do not think it would be socially helpful or desirable to attempt to apply the criminal law and the enforcement methods which seem to be necessary to the simple possession of these drugs for non-medical use. We believe that such a course could lead to a substantial increase in violence and other undesirable social effects. We place much more hope and confidence in education and cultural controls as a means of reducing the use of *speed*. There is reason to believe that such controls may be beginning to operate effectively through the influence of peer group opinion and the judgment of leading opinion formers in the drug culture.

We fully share the general concern which has been expressed to us concerning the extent and effects of amphetamine and methamphetamine use, but we do not feel that we have a sufficient understanding of the phenomenon at this time to make long term recommendations with respect to it. In the first place, we do not have a reliable impression of its extent, although there are reasonable grounds for believing that it has in recent years been steadily increasing. But is it still increasing, or is it levelling off, or is it declining? We do not know. Is speed likely to be a temporary phenomenon which will burn itself out in a relatively few years, as a result of the problems which it creates and the general contempt in which it is held by large sections of the youthful drug culture? Who can say? We do not at this time have any real sense of conviction about the probable future pattern and extent of amphetamine use in Canada. Other countries, such as post-war Japan, have experienced amphetamine epidemics. Because of very extensive use, and particularly use by adults, Sweden has seen fit to proscribe their use altogether. We have not yet been able to judge how successful they have been and what the social effects of such repression are, although we understand from preliminary impressions that there is now an extensive illicit traffic in such drugs from neighbouring countries such as Germany and the Netherlands, and that the unlawful possession of amphetamines has become a middle-class status symbol with conspiratorial overtones, which history has shown to be the inevitable consequence of the prohibition of a substance which a large proportion of the population desires.

It would not appear that the excessive use of amphetamines by young people has assumed the same relative importance in Scandinavia as it has here. The emphasis is rather on excessive adult use. Are we moving in Canada into a similar pattern of excessive adult use? It has been suggested to us that this may be the case, but we do not feel confident about expressing an opinion on this possibility at the present time. We would want to give further consideration to the conditions which have produced this phenomenon in other countries during the post-war period, and to compare them with present conditions in this country. It is our impression at this time that the government would not be warranted in following the example of other countries in a total prohibition of amphetamines or barbiturates without clear evidence that such a step is warranted by the extent and levels of use. We doubt very much if such a step would ever be justified in Canada. *At the present time, we advocate closer controls on the availability of these drugs, including controls on production, importation and prescription.*

Strong representations have been made to the Commission during the initial phase of its inquiry for radical changes in the law respecting cannabis. In particular, many witnesses have urged the *legalization* of marijuana – that is, that this drug be made legally available through government licenced or operated channels of production and distribution. Several witnesses have urged that if the Commission is not prepared to recommend such legalization at the present time, it should at least recommend a *moratorium* or suspension of all marijuana prosecutions pending publication of its final report. The Commission has also frequently heard the proposal that cannabis should be removed from the *Narcotic Control Act* and placed under the *Food and Drugs Act*.

Several arguments are advanced for the legalization of marijuana. They may be summarized as follows:

(1) the use of marijuana is increasing in popularity among all age groups of the population, and particularly among the young;

(2) this increase indicates that the attempt to suppress, or even to control its use, is failing and will continue to fail – that people are not deterred by the criminal law prohibition against its use;

(3) the present legislative policy has not been justified by clear and unequivocal evidence of short term or long term harm caused by cannabis;

(4) the individual and social harm (including the destruction of young lives and growing disrespect for law) caused by the present use of the criminal law to attempt to suppress cannabis far outweighs any potential for harm which cannabis could conceivably possess, having regard to the long history of its use and the present lack of evidence;

(5) the illicit status of cannabis invites exploitation by criminal elements, and other abuses such as adulteration; it also brings cannabis users into contact with such criminal elements and with other drugs, such as heroin, which they might not otherwise be induced to consider.

For all of these reasons, it is said, cannabis should be made available under government controlled conditions of quality and availability.

It should be observed that many of the witnesses who have advocated the legalization of cannabis have also advocated an age limit under which it should not be available, similar to the prohibition against the sale of alcohol to minors. Eighteen and over has been an age limit frequently suggested. Thus, even among those who advocate the legalization of cannabis there are those who have reservations about its use among young people, and the implications of criminal law proscription of it, insofar as they are concerned, are among the chief problems involved in such use today. A *legalization* of cannabis which continued to prohibit its sale to persons under 18 years of age would be one which favoured adults rather than young people, and although it would undoubtedly have the indirect effect of making cannabis more easily available to young people, it would leave the issue of the use of cannabis by the young essentially unresolved.

We think it is significant that a number of those who advocate the legalization of cannabis are sufficiently concerned about its potential for harm to young people to advocate an age limit for its availability. This obviously deepens as one seeks to ascertain what is considered to be the appropriate age limit – is it 18, 17, 16, 15, 14, 13, 12, 11, 10, 9, 8, 7? We do not mean to suggest that such concern necessarily justifies the maintenance of the present legal status of cannabis, but merely that it throws additional perspective on the debate concerning its potential for harm.

This is, of course, the essential question with respect to cannabis at this time. It is idle to pretend that cannabis was brought under its present criminal law proscription on the basis of clear and unequivocal scientific evidence of its potential for harm. Although the precise historical reasons for the decision to suppress its use are somewhat obscure, there is no evidence that scientific judgment played a leading role. There did, however, develop an international climate of official opinion, strongly opposed to its use. This opinion was based in part on the experience of certain countries, but it was also strongly influenced by American insistence. Thus it is fair to say that Canadian policy found increasing support in the opinion of the international community. The spread of the use of cannabis, particularly among the young, and the effects of the criminal law attempt to suppress it now call for a fresh look at the justification of the law, and in particular, at the alleged personal and social harm caused by such use.

The issue now is whether Canadian policy is to turn on potential for harm, or whether it is to turn on the extent of use and the apparent incapacity of the law to prevent the spread of such use. It is a difficult judgment to make. The law has had to throw up its hands in the past, as in the case of the failure to enforce the prohibition against alcohol. It is not clear, however, that we are yet at this point with cannabis. The debate and the perception of the issues have turned on a difference of opinion as to the potential for harm. At this point, it is not possible to give assurance concerning potential for harm.

The question is: How long can society wait for the necessary information? It is very serious that the scientific information concerning cannabis lags so far behind the rapidly developing social problem caused by its illegal status. It is useless to apportion blame. We have referred above to the necessity of research and a fundamental change in the attitude of government towards research. Given a sufficiently comprehensive and aggressive program of research, when are we likely to know enough, one way or the other, to justify a decision on legalization on the basis of potential for harm? It may be that we shall not be able to learn enough in time, at least with respect to potential for long term harm, before we are obliged to take a decision on another basis – that is, on the basis of calculated risk, or the lesser of evils.

At this time, we do not feel that Canadian perceptions of this problem or our knowledge warrants a recommendation by us on the basis of calculated risk or the lesser of evils.

For the following reasons we are not prepared at this time to recommend the legalization of cannabis:

(1) First, it is our impression that there has not yet been enough informed public debate. Certainly there has been much debate, but too often it has been based on hearsay, myth and ill-informed opinion about the effects of the drug.

We hope that this report will assist in providing a basis for informed debate not only as to the effects, but as to other issues, including the extent to which science is capable of providing a basis for public policy decision on this question.

(2) There is a body of further scientific information, important for legislation, that can be gathered by short term research — for example, the effects of the drug at various dose levels on psychomotor skills, such as those used in driving.

(3) Further consideration should be given to what may be necessarily implied by legalization. Would a decision by the government to assume responsibility for the quality control and distribution of cannabis imply, or be taken to imply, approval of its use and an assurance as to the absence of significant potential for harm?

(4) A decision on the merits of legalization can not be taken without further consideration of jurisdictional and technical questions involved in the control of quality and availability.

Footnote

1. [Letter of Disagreement]

March 15, 1970.

I find myself in disagreement with my colleagues on the Commission in respect of the offence of simple possession of cannabis. In my opinion the prohibition against such possession should be removed altogether. I believe that this course is dictated at the present time by the following considerations: the extent of use and the age groups involved; the relative impossibility of enforcing the law; the social consequences of its enforcement; and the uncertainty as to the relative potential for harm of cannabis.

Marie A. Bertrand

Public Attitudes Toward Legal Sanctions for Drug and Abortion Offences*

Craig L. Boydell and Carl F. Grindstaff

Introduction

In recent years both social scientists and legal experts alike have directed a great deal of attention to questions concerning the scope, purpose, and effectiveness of the criminal law. Such questions present special dilemmas in democratic societies where conflicts often arise between the maintenance of order and the preservation of individual liberties. An earlier selection in this volume contained the Canadian Committee on Corrections' statement of "The Basic Principles and Purposes of Criminal Justice." In this statement the Committee established a set of principles that pertain to the criminal law:

> 1. No act should be criminally proscribed unless its incidence, actual or potential, is *substantially damaging to society.*

*Reprinted from the July, 1971 (Vol. 13, No. 3) issue of the *Canadian Journal of Criminology and Corrections* published by the Canadian Criminology and Corrections Association, 55 Parkdale Avenue, Ottawa, Ontario, Canada.

2. No act should be criminally prohibited where its incidence may adequately be controlled by social forces other than the criminal process. Public opinion may be enough to curtail certain kinds of behaviour. Other kinds of behaviour may be more appropriately dealt with by non-criminal legal processes, e.g. by legislation relating to mental health or social and economic condition.

3. No law should give rise to social or personal damage greater than that it was designed to prevent.[1]

The Committee goes on to state that although the criminal law has traditionally been associated with the imposition of sanctions, a sanction should only be used as a last recourse.[2] When guidelines such as these are applied to certain aspects of the criminal law as it presently exists in Canada, serious questions may be raised as to the adequacy of that law. One particular area that seems to have attracted the most attention in this regard is the present structure and implementation of the law pertaining to crimes that have no identifiable victims. Edwin Schur in *Crimes Without Victims* has given this area much of its initial impetus by providing a solid base from which further investigation has emanated. The concept of "crimes without victims" according to Schur, "refers essentially to the willing exchange, among adults, of strongly demanded but legally proscribed goods and services."[3] Schur maintains that legal intervention in such activities as drug use and abortion constitute "attempts to legislate morality for its own sake."[4]

When we attempt to apply the principles set forth by the Committee on Corrections to *crimes without victims*, we are confronted with a number of problems. First of all, while acts of drug use and selling, and abortion and the like, may have no clearly identifiable victim (that is, they do involve an exchange between consenting adults), are they nonetheless "substantially damaging to society?" How does one measure or document such damage? Further, can we determine that making such acts legal or illegal is necessarily an important factor that affects such actual or potential damage?

Second, can these victimless crimes be "adequately controlled by social forces other than the criminal process." This possibility assumes that if certain of these acts were made legal, as, for example, has already been done with homosexuality in Canada, they would still be considered deviant by the society as a whole and therefore in need of treatment and/or control. This would not necessarily be the case, as some activities derive their deviant status from the very fact that they are proscribed in the criminal law. Consider, for example, the case of drinking behaviour before and after prohibition, or the difference in the deviant status of marijuana use as opposed to alcohol use at the present time. If, however, we do assume that the cancelling of criminal sanctions for certain kinds of behaviour would not affect the general public's view of these acts as deviant, then the issue of whether or not these acts could be effectively dealt with by other than legal means would become an empirical question.

Third, in considering the issue of the law giving "rise to personal or social damage greater than it was designed to prevent," we are again left with the problem of trying to assess the amount of such damage either to the society, by virtue of an individual's deviant act, or to the individual as a result of his being sanctioned for that act. Clearly, it is with regard to these "crimes without victims" that the nature of this balance is most fragile. It is also within the context of these types of crimes that the conflict between maintaining the order that is necessary for any society to exist and at the same time preserving the rights and freedoms of individuals is felt most actutely.

Arguments both for and against changing the legal code often make reference to public sentiment in support of their positions. While such appeals are certainly in keeping with the importance assigned to public opinion in democratic societies, one rarely sees a concrete demonstration that public opinion has indeed been tapped. Some would argue that congruency between policy decisions and public opinion may be assumed to exist when those decisions originate from duly elected representatives. Another point of view would have it that the law itself should be used to initiate social change and that once laws are changed public opinion will follow suit. Developments in the civil rights movement in the United States lend partial support to this viewpoint. In essence this position assumes that the leaders of a society *know what is best* for the society as a whole, in both a structural and a moral sense. Even if we were to assume this to be true it would still seem inadvisable to act without some feeling for public sentiment on a given issue.

This is not to say that if public sentiment does not clearly support a recommended change in the criminal code that the recommendation should then be discarded. The disparity between executive policy and public attitude may lie in the fact that the public at large does not have access to the same information that led to the suggested revision in the first place. If this is the case, then it would seem to be the responsibility of those supporting the revision to disseminate such information. This may then lead to a change in public opinion. If it does not, it would seem to be a reasonably clear indication that the change being proposed is out of step with public sentiment and probably inadvisable at that time.

The data presented in this paper are part of the findings of a research project that attempted to document public attitudes concerning sanctions that should be applied to a wide variety of illegal activities, some thirty in all. The study was conducted in London, Ontario during the summer and fall of 1970. A mail questionnaire, which was pretested in a substantial pilot study,[5] was sent to a two percent sample of household heads in London.[6] Approximately fifty percent of the questionnaires were returned, 451 of which were in usable form.[7] At the outset, the respondent was given the following coded list of penalties that he might assign to the crimes described in the questionnaire:

- (0) No penalty
- (1) A fine
- (2) Probation
- (3) 30 days or less in jail
- (4) 31 days to six months in jail
- (5) Six months to two years in jail
- (6) Two years to five years in jail
- (7) Five years to fifteen years in jail
- (8) Fifteen or more years in jail
- (9) Execution

On the questionnaire the respondents were asked to indicate the most frequent penalty that they felt should be given for each particular offence. In addition, they were asked to indicate the minimum and maximum penalty that should be given for such offences.[8] Also, the respondents were asked to supply background information about themselves that could later be cross-tabulated with response patterns on the various questionnaire items. Such background information is extremely important if we are to understand in depth the nature of public opinion with regard to a particular issue. With it we can not only determine what proportion of the public holds a given opinion on an issue, but also whether or not there are variations in attitudes according to such characteristics as age, educational level, income, religion and the like. Understanding the nature of such variations would seem to be important if we are to understand the exact nature of public sentiment concerning the use of legal sanctions. Information such as this might give important insights into the types of changes that would be most in line with public attitudes at a given time as well as the probable reaction of the public to changes that are presently being proposed.

We shall now turn to a detailed analysis of the *most frequent* response category for offences relating to drugs and abortion. The respondents were asked to indicate what penalty they would assign most frequently for the following seven activities that relate to these two types of *crimes without victims.*

Drugs
1. A person uses marijuana.
2. A person uses a dangerous drug other than marijuana, for example, heroin, LSD, cocaine, etc.
3. A person sells marijuana.
4. A person sells a dangerous drug other than marijuana, for example, heroin, LSD, cocaine, etc.

Abortion
5. A female has an induced abortion without legal approval. What penalty should be assigned to the female?
6. A medical doctor performs an abortion of a female without legal approval. What penalty should be assigned to the doctor?
7. A person other than a medical doctor performs an abortion without legal approval. What penalty should be assigned to the non-doctor?

The data relating to these questions are first presented for the sample as a whole. In subsequent sections they are analyzed according to the background characteristic of age, education, income, religion, and religious attendance.[9]

Total Distribution of Response

TABLE 1

Percentage Distribution of Penalties Assigned by Total Sample

	No Penalty	A Fine	Probation	IMPRISONMENT						Execution	No Response
				30 days or less	31 days to 6 months	6 months to 2 years	2 years to 5 years	5 years to 15 years	15 years or more		
Marijuana use	27	23	22	9	8	4	1	1	—	—	5
Hard Drug Use	15	13	26	12	14	11	4	1	1	—	4
Marijuana Sale	4	9	6	8	15	22	16	7	7	1	5
Hard Drug Sale	1	4	3	5	6	20	23	18	14	2	4
Abortion (Female)	56	11	14	5	4	4	2	—	—	—	4
Abortion (Doctor)	41	21	10	3	4	7	7	1	2	—	4
Abortion (Non-doctor)	4	6	2	6	13	24	23	13	4	—	6

Note: All rows total 100 percent.

Drug Use

The first two items in Table 1 show the percentage distributions of penalties assigned for the use of marijuana and hard drugs. The majority of respondents feel that something less than a jail sentence is the most appropriate penalty for both marijuana use (72 percent) and drug use (54 percent). Twenty-seven percent indicate that there should be no penalty for using marijuana, while 15 percent feel that hard drug use should not be legally sanctioned.

Drug Sale

The sale of drugs is viewed more severely in the eyes of the public than their mere use. A person selling marijuana is given a no penalty adjudication by only four percent of the respondents. Seventy-six percent indicate that some form of jail sentence or even execution should be given. For the sale of hard drugs 88 percent of the respondents indicate a jail term or execution. The majority (57 percent) feel that the penalty should be at least two years in prison, while more than a third (34 percent) assign sentences of five years or more.

Abortion

A majority of the respondents (56 percent) feel that no penalty should be assigned to the female who has an illegal abortion, while 15 percent assign a jail sentence. The penalties assigned to doctors who perform abortions without legal approval are only slightly more severe with 24 percent indicating a jail term, in most cases less than two years. For both the female and the doctor, however, the largest single disposition is no penalty. In contrast, a non-doctor who performs an abortion is severely sanctioned. Only four percent feel that no legal sanction is called for, while over 80 percent assign a prison sentence, including 40 percent who indicate that the sentence should be in excess of two years.

Age

The respondents were divided into four age categories: Under 30 years of age (N=89); 30-39 (N=94); 40-49 (N=128); and 50 years and older (N=133).[10] Given present notions concerning the so called *generation gap* we might expect to find markedly different response patterns by age, particularly with regard to these crimes which have been the subject of recent controversy. The differences might not be as great as we would have normally expected because we have so few people in our sample under the age of 20.

Drug Use

In examining responses related to marijuana use (Table 2) we find that a minority of all age groups assign a jail sentence. The youngest age group is least likely (16 percent) and the respondents aged 40-49 most likely (31 percent) to prescribe jail terms. Forty percent of the respondents under 30 assign no penalty at all (again this is the most lenient group) while the oldest age category, 50 and over, show the smallest no penalty adjudications, 20 percent.

TABLE 2

Percentage Distribution Assigned for Drug Offences by Age

| | No Penalty | A Fine | Probation | IMPRISONMENT | | | | | | Execution | No Response |
				30 days or less	31 days to 6 months	6 months to 2 years	2 years to 5 years	5 years to 15 years	15 years or more		
Marijuana Use											
Under 30	40	25	16	6	6	3	1	—	—	—	3
30–39	31	20	22	8	10	5	2	1	—	—	1
40–49	23	19	23	13	12	4	1	1	—	—	4
Over 50	20	27	23	8	6	5	2	—	—	—	10
Hard Drug Use											
Under 30	20	13	27	11	12	9	3	2	—	—	3
30–39	14	13	29	9	12	15	5	1	1	—	1
40–49	17	11	25	13	11	12	5	2	1	1	2
Over 50	9	17	23	12	18	7	4	1	—	1	8
Marijuana Sale											
Under 30	10	14	8	6	18	17	12	5	6	—	4
30–39	5	7	5	7	13	25	15	9	11	1	2
40–49	3	5	2	5	15	28	20	9	7	1	5
Over 50	—	11	5	13	14	19	17	6	7	1	7
Hard Drug Sale											
Under 30	3	1	4	8	9	18	26	15	11	2	3
30–39	1	3	2	3	6	25	17	25	15	1	2
40–49	—	2	2	4	5	20	29	20	13	2	3
Over 50	—	7	2	5	4	20	20	17	15	3	7

Note: All rows total 100 percent.

In very general terms, the youngest age group is the most lenient in sentencing patterns, while the other age categories show no definitive trends in sentencing procedures relating to marijuana use.

The person who takes hard drugs is viewed more severely by all age groups. By and large, about half as many people in each age category give no penalty for hard drug use in comparison to marijuana use, and about twice as many in each age category assign a jail term. The youngest group is least likely to assign a prison sentence (37 percent) and most likely to give no penalty (20 percent), while the respondents aged 40-49 are the most severe in proscribing jail terms (55 percent), and the 50 and over category is least likely to assign no penalty (nine percent). Thus, the relationship between the age groups in penalty assignments is much the same for marijuana and hard drug use. That is, the youngest respondents are most lenient while the other age categories vary somewhat in their sentencing practices.

Drug Sale

The selling of drugs (whether marijuana or hard drugs) is more harshly sentenced than either the use of marijuana or hard drugs (Table 2). A person who traffics in marijuana is given a jail sentence by a majority of the respondents in all age categories. The under 30 group is least likely to give a jail sentence (64 percent) and most likely to assign no penalty (10 percent) in comparison to any other age group. In terms of the more severe penalties, two years in jail or more, the youngest group is again the most lenient with 23 percent assigning penalties of this magnitude. The most severe sentencing is given by the 40-49 age category, with the oldest group next to the youngest in terms of leniency. Again, the youngest people are the least severe, but it does not follow that the oldest group is the most severe.

The trafficking in hard drugs is seen as the most serious crime of all, at least as far as sentencing is concerned. Less than 10 percent in any age group assign less than a jail term and almost all of these give fines or probation. When it comes to assigning sanctions for the sale of hard drugs, the previous patterns observed by age tend to break down altogether; there are no significant sentencing differentials by age. The youngest group assign the fewest severe penalties (28 percent assign prison terms of five years or greater or execution), but the oldest group is least likely to assign a jail term at all (84 percent). All age groups are represented in the execution category and between 28 and 41 percent assign penalties of more than five years in prison.

Abortion

A minority of all age groups assign a jail term to the female who undergoes an illegal abortion (Table 3), and there are no significant differentials apparent by age in this sentencing. The oldest age category is least likely to assign no penalty than any of the other age groups which are quite similar in their responses, but even in this case 44 percent of the oldest group prescribe no penalty.

TABLE 3

Percentage Distribution of Penalties Assigned for Abortion Offences by Age

	No Penalty	A Fine	Probation	30 days or less	31 days to 6 months	6 months to 2 years	2 years to 5 years	5 years to 15 years	15 years or more	Execution	No Response
						IMPRISONMENT					
Abortion (female)											
Under 30	64	6	12	5	3	6	2	—	—	—	2
30–39	62	9	14	1	3	4	5	—	—	—	2
40–49	59	10	13	6	2	4	2	1	1	—	2
Over 50	44	16	14	8	5	2	1	—	—	—	10
Abortion (doctor)											
Under 30	47	20	10	2	7	3	5	2	2	1	1
30–39	45	22	14	2	4	6	3	1	2	—	1
40–49	48	15	5	2	2	10	10	2	1	—	5
Over 50	26	25	12	5	5	9	7	1	2	1	7
Abortion (non-doctor)											
Under 30	4	6	1	4	9	15	38	19	2	—	2
30–39	2	4	1	9	17	21	26	15	3	—	2
40–49	6	3	2	7	13	34	14	9	7	—	5
Over 50	2	10	2	6	14	24	17	12	2	—	11

Note: All rows total 100 percent.

A slightly different pattern emerges when the respondents are asked what penalty should be assigned to the doctor who performs an abortion without legal approval. Again, the oldest group is least likely to indicate that no penalty should be assigned, but unlike the case of the female they are also more likely to assign some form of prison sentence than either of the two younger groups. In general, however, the differential sentencing by age in relation to this crime is small.

The penalties assigned to a non-doctor who performs an illegal abortion are quite severe for all age groups, comparable to the sentencing patterns observed for hard drug trafficking. At least three-quarters of each age group assign a prison term, but, contrary to expectations, the oldest group assigns the least severe penalties. They assign a larger proportion of fines and moderate jail terms than the other groups and are least likely to assign a long prison term. When we compare the percentage in each age group choosing prison terms of two years or greater, we see that the youngest group is nearly twice as likely to choose sanctions of this severity than either of the older two age groups (59 percent to 30 and 31 percent).

Education

The respondents were divided into four educational categories according to the amount of schooling they had completed at the time of the survey. The categories consisted of: not completed high school ($N = 88$); completed high school ($N = 181$); some university ($N = 115$); completed university ($N = 52$). The percentage distribution of responses by educational category are presented in Tables 4 and 5.

Drug Use

For marijuana use there appears to be no relationship between level of education completed and severity of sanctions applied. The only noticeable difference is that the completed university category assigned less severe jail terms when such sentencing was indicated as an appropriate penalty. Between 20-30 percent of each age group assigned a jail term, usually less than six months.

For the use of hard drugs, however, there is a much more noticeable distinction between education categories. Although there is virtually no difference by education in the assignment of no penalty, there is a definite difference between the least and most educated groups in the severity of penalties assigned. The university graduate category is the least likely of all groups to assign a minor penalty of a fine or probation (29 percent) and correspondingly the most

TABLE 4

Percentage Distribution of Penalties Assigned for Drug Offences by Education

	No Penalty	A Fine	Probation	30 days or less	31 days to 6 months	6 months to 2 years	2 years to 5 years	5 years to 15 years	15 years or more	Execution	No Response
Marijuana Use											
Some or no high school	21	25	23	6	9	2	2	1	—	—	11
High school graduates	27	22	18	12	9	5	2	—	—	—	5
Some university	34	24	24	6	3	6	1	2	—	—	—
University graduates	23	19	33	12	13	—	—	—	—	—	—
Hard Drug Use											
Some or no high school	16	14	27	2	13	8	5	—	2	—	13
High school graduates	14	13	24	13	16	11	4	2	—	1	2
Some university	16	15	30	10	12	11	4	2	—	—	—
University graduates	14	8	21	27	13	13	2	2	—	—	—
Marijuana Sale											
Some or no high school	5	10	4	5	12	18	14	6	9	1	16
High school graduates	3	9	6	9	15	21	19	8	5	1	4
Some university	4	9	5	8	11	27	16	10	10	—	—
University graduates	6	6	4	8	27	23	15	4	7	—	—
Hard Drug Sale											
Some or no high school	3	8	1	8	1	17	20	14	14	3	11
High school graduates	—	3	3	4	10	24	22	18	11	2	3
Some university	—	3	3	5	3	16	29	22	18	1	—
University graduates	2	2	2	2	8	25	19	23	13	4	—

Note: All rows total 100 percent.

586

likely to assign some form of jail sentence (57 percent). The least educated is the least severe group in this regard as only 30 percent assigned a jail sentence. This is an interesting finding as it tends to go counter to the fairly widespread notion that tolerance for *deviant* forms of behaviour increases with education. Although this finding does not necessarily refute that notion in general it at least should sensitize us to the fact that the type of deviance being considered is an important factor.

Drug Sale

The sale of marijuana invokes a similar response from all educational levels treated here. No group is very likely to assign no penalty, a fine or probation. One minor difference is that the college graduate group is slightly less likely to assign a major sanction of five years to execution, although severity of sanctioning at this level does not decrease directly as education increases. The *sale* of marijuana is treated more harshly by all groups than the *use* of hard drugs.

For the sale of hard drugs the lines between educational categories can be drawn more clearly. The less than high school educated group is the least severe of all the groups in terms of the severity of sanctions applied. Twelve percent indicate that either a non-jail term or no penalty is appropriate as compared to six percent in each of the other groups. Seventy-seven percent of the least educated group assign some length of jail term or execution compared to over ninety percent in each of the other categories. When we examine the more severe sanctions (five years to execution) the two lesser educated groups are noticeably less severe than both the college graduates and those with some college experience. In general, with some qualifications in mind, the people educated to the highest level prescribe the most severe penalties for the use or sale of marijuana and hard drugs.

Abortion

TABLE 5

Percentage Distribution of Penalties Assigned for Abortion Offences by Education

	No Penalty	A Fine	Probation	30 days or less	31 days to 6 months	6 months to 2 years	2 years to 5 years	5 years to 15 years	15 years or more	Execution	No Response
Abortion (female)											
Some or no high school	45	12	15	6	2	6	1	1	—	—	11
High school graduates	57	10	12	4	4	6	3	—	—	—	3
Some university	62	10	15	5	3	1	2	—	1	—	2
University graduates	60	11	19	4	4	—	2	—	—	—	—
Abortion (doctor)											
Some or no high school	33	13	8	3	5	13	7	2	2	2	12
High school graduates	37	22	11	3	6	7	7	2	2	—	3
Some university	47	24	13	4	2	3	4	1	1	—	1
University graduates	50	19	10	—	6	6	9	—	—	—	—
Abortion (non-doctor)											
Some or no high school	8	8	2	6	7	17	20	13	3	—	16
High school graduates	3	7	2	8	15	22	22	12	4	—	5
Some university	1	2	—	6	18	29	25	16	3	—	—
University graduates	6	8	8	4	10	30	15	13	4	—	2

Note: All rows total 100 percent.

With regard to penalties assigned to a female for having an illegal abortion the least educated group is generally the most severe. They are the only group in which a majority of the respondents do not indicate no penalty as the appropriate sanction. However, fewer than 20 percent of any group give a jail term. For the medical doctor who performs an illegal abortion, the severity of sanctions applied tends to be greater for the two least educated groups. There is a fairly clear line of demarcation between the two least educated groups and the two most educated groups. This can be seen in the distribution of no penalty responses (34 and 37 percent for the least educated groups, 47 and 50 percent for the most educated group), and to a lesser extent in jail sentencing in that the use of a prison term is deemed appropriate by 34 and 27 percent respectively of the groups with the least education, as opposed to 15 and 21 percent respectively for the two university groups.

There is virtually no direction in the relationship between educational level and severity of sanctions deemed appropriate for the non-doctor who performs an illegal abortion. The distribution of responses for the some university category is strikingly more severe than the other three groups. Ninety-seven percent indicate that some form of jail sentence would be most appropriate, including 44 percent who assign a sentence of two years or more. However, this does not seem to be a part of any general pattern that might relate severity of sanctioning for this crime with educational level.

Income

The respondents were divided into five income groups according to the total annual family income. These groups, along with the number of respondents in each, are as follows: Less than $3,000 per year ($N=63$); between $3,000 and $5,999 ($N=156$); between $6,000 and $9,999 ($N=112$); between $10,000 and $14,000 ($N=49$), and over $15,000 per year ($N=66$). The percentage distributions of responses according to income classification are presented in Tables 6 and 7.

Drug Use

The use of marijuana is least severely sanctioned by the highest income group; 41 percent assign no penalty and only 14 percent assign a jail penalty, the maximum of which would not exceed six months. The lowest income group is the least likely to assign no penalty to a person who uses marijuana, but it does not follow that when penalties are chosen that their sanctions are more severe than those in other income groups. If we combine all non-jail responses (no penalty, a fine, and probation), there is a fairly stable increase in such judgments as income increases: slightly under 65 percent for the two lowest income brackets; 75 and 76 percent for the $6,000 to $10,000 and $10,000 to $15,000 brackets respectively; and 86 percent for the highest income group.

For the use of hard drugs, we again note that the highest income group is least likely and the lowest income group most likely to assign no penalty. However, in the actual imposition of sanction it does not necessarily follow that the former group is least severe and the latter group most severe; prison terms are assigned by 36 percent of the under $3,000 category and 38 percent of those making over $15,000. If we combine the non-jail responses we find virtually no pattern, in contrast to the increase noted for marijuana use above. In the

TABLE 6

Percentage Distribution of Penalties Assigned for Drug Offences by Income

| | No Penalty | A Fine | Probation | IMPRISONMENT | | | | | | Execution | No Response |
				30 days or less	31 days to 6 months	6 months to 2 years	2 years to 5 years	5 years to 15 years	15 years or more		
Marijuana Use											
Under $3,000	14	25	25	10	5	5	1	2	—	—	13
$3,000–$5,999	24	19	20	10	13	5	3	—	—	—	6
$6,000–$9,999	28	25	22	10	6	6	1	1	—	—	2
$10,000–$14,999	27	24	25	6	6	4	—	2	—	—	6
Over $15,000	41	24	21	8	6	—	—	—	—	—	—
Hard Drug Use											
Under $3,000	9	14	32	9	11	5	5	2	2	2	9
$3,000–$5,999	13	14	19	11	17	14	6	1	1	—	4
$6,000–$9,999	12	13	34	10	13	11	3	1	—	1	2
$10,000–$14,999	19	12	23	14	10	12	4	4	—	—	2
Over $15,000	24	9	26	18	9	8	1	2	—	—	3
Marijuana Sale											
Under $3,000	3	13	6	10	9	16	16	5	5	2	14
$3,000–$5,999	3	6	3	7	13	20	19	8	12	1	8
$6,000–$9,999	4	13	5	10	17	23	19	3	4	1	1
$10,000–$14,999	4	8	4	6	10	29	14	19	6	—	—
Over $15,000	8	6	11	6	21	26	9	4	8	—	1
Hard Drug Sale											
Under $3,000	—	9	5	13	5	19	17	10	8	3	11
$3,000–$5,999	—	4	1	3	5	18	24	17	20	2	6
$6,000–$9,999	—	3	4	4	6	21	27	21	12	1	1
$10,000–$14,999	—	2	2	4	2	27	27	24	10	2	—
Over $15,000	5	1	3	3	11	21	18	24	11	3	—

Note: All rows total 100 percent.

comparison of marijuana use and drug use by the various income groups, the higher income groups become relatively more severe in their sentencing. For example, in the under $3,000 group, the proportion giving jail sentences rose from 23 percent for marijuana use to 36 percent for drug use, an increase of 56 percent. If we examine the $15,000 plus category, we find that 14 percent prescribed prison sentences for marijuana use but this figure increased to 38 percent for drug use, *a rise of over 170 percent.*

Drug Sale

The sanctions assigned for the sale of marijuana and hard drugs suggest nothing in the line of a clear association between sentencing for trafficking and income level. For marijuana, the highest income group was the most likely to assign no penalty (eight percent), but there is little else in the data that would suggest a consistent pattern in the severity of sanctions applied according to income. With regard to the sale of hard drugs, the highest income group is the only one that was represented in the no penalty response category. However, it is the lowest income group that assigns the most lenient sanctions: fines, probation or moderate jail terms. The under $3,000 group has the highest percentage of those assigning a fine or probation (14 percent), the lowest percentage assigning some form of jail sentence (75 percent), and the lowest percentage of responses between five years in jail and execution (21 percent). Response patterns for the other four groups are almost identical.

Abortion

The lowest income category is the only one in which the majority of respondents do not indicate that there should be no penalty for the female who has an abortion without legal approval (44 percent). This group is also the most

589

TABLE 7

Percentage Distribution of Penalties Assigned for Abortion Offences by Income

	No Penalty	A Fine	Probation	IMPRISONMENT 30 days or less	31 days to 6 months	6 months to 2 years	2 years to 5 years	5 years to 15 years	15 years or more	Execution	No Response
Abortion (female)											
Under $3,000	44	11	16	5	6	5	3	2	—	—	8
$3,000–$5,999	54	15	9	6	2	5	2	—	1	—	6
$6,000–$9,999	59	8	17	6	2	4	1	—	—	—	3
$10,000–$14,999	62	12	12	4	8	—	2	—	—	—	—
Over $15,000	62	5	20	1	3	2	6	—	—	—	1
Abortion (doctor)											
Under $3,000	22	21	6	6	5	14	13	—	2	2	9
$3,000–$5,999	39	21	8	3	5	10	5	1	1	1	6
$6,000–$9,999	47	19	14	4	5	3	4	3	1	—	—
$10,000–$14,999	39	23	12	2	4	2	8	2	4	—	4
Over $15,000	51	21	9	—	3	8	6	2	—	—	—
Abortion (non-doctor)											
Under $3,000	3	8	2	6	19	22	14	6	2	—	18
$3,000–$5,999	2	5	2	6	13	24	22	13	5	—	8
$6,000–$9,999	4	4	2	7	14	23	26	16	3	—	1
$10,000–$14,999	4	6	2	8	12	21	27	16	4	—	—
Over $15,000	6	8	5	3	8	27	24	12	4	—	3

Note: All rows total 100 percent.

severe in the sense that it has the largest proportion assigning prison sentences for this offence (21 percent). The doctor who performs an illegal abortion is also sanctioned the most severely by the lowest income category. They account for the lowest percentage of no penalty responses (22 percent versus 51 percent for the $15,000 and over category) and the highest percentage of prison terms (42 percent). The highest income group appears to be the most lenient for this crime in that they have the highest percentage of no penalty responses and the lowest percentage of responses indicating a prison sentence, although in the latter case the differential between the three middle groups is minimal.

The data on penalties for a non-doctor who performs an abortion are very difficult to interpret for the lowest income group because of the very high percentage of non-responses (18 percent). The other four groups are very similar to one another, with the highest group being slightly more lenient than the others. Generally, the lowest income groups prescribe the most severe sanctions and the highest income groups give the least severe.

Religion

Respondents were divided into categories as follows: Protestant ($N=325$); Catholic ($N=65$); Jewish ($N=1$); other ($N=18$); and none ($N=31$). The Protestant and Catholic categories were the only ones with a large enough representation to warrant analysis. Tables 8 and 9 provide the percentage distributions for these two groups.

Drug Use

For both marijuana and drug use, Protestants are slightly more inclined to assign no penalty than are Catholics, although both view hard drug use as con-

TABLE 8

Percentage Distribution of Penalties Assigned for Drug Offences by Religion

	No Penalty	A Fine	Probation	IMPRISONMENT						Execution	No Response
				30 days or less	31 days to 6 months	6 months to 2 years	2 years to 5 years	5 years to 15 years	15 years or more		
Marijuana Use											
Protestant	26	23	22	10	9	5	1	—	—	—	4
Catholic	18	28	25	12	2	3	2	1	—	—	9
Hard Drug Use											
Protestant	14	15	23	13	15	12	3	1	—	—	4
Catholic	9	12	35	9	12	6	6	2	2	2	5
Marijuana Sale											
Protestant	3	10	5	8	14	22	18	8	7	—	5
Catholic	3	8	3	9	20	22	14	6	9	—	6
Hard Drug Sale											
Protestant	1	4	2	5	6	20	24	19	14	1	4
Catholic	2	5	5	6	5	18	18	20	15	3	3

Note: All rows total 100 percent.

siderably more deviant than marijuana use. Despite the fact that Protestants are more likely to assign no penalty for both offences, they do not correspondingly give lighter penalties when sanctions are chosen. In the case of marijuana use, 25 percent of the Protestants assign jail sentences compared to 20 percent of the Catholics. For hard drug use the figures are 44 and 39 percent for Protestants and Catholics respectively, although in this case the Catholics assign a greater percentage of the most severe sanctions.

Drug Sale

When we examine the percentage distributions for the sale of hard drugs and marijuana little if any real difference can be identified in the response patterns of Protestants and Catholics. Catholics have a slightly higher percentage of response in the non-jail sanctions (12 percent to 7 percent) and a correspondingly lower percentage indicating a jail term (85 percent as opposed to 89 percent). However, these differences are relatively small and the response patterns from penalty to penalty are virtually identical.

TABLE 9

Percentage Distribution of Penalties Assigned For Abortion Offences by Religion

	No Penalty	A Fine	Probation	IMPRISONMENT						Execution	No Response
				30 days or less	31 days to 6 months	6 months to 2 years	2 years to 5 years	5 years to 15 years	15 years or more		
Abortion (female)											
Protestant	56	12	14	5	3	3	2	—	1	—	4
Catholic	46	9	15	6	3	6	5	2	—	—	8
Abortion (doctor)											
Protestant	38	22	10	3	5	8	7	2	1	—	4
Catholic	38	15	8	6	9	5	6	2	3	2	6
Abortion (non-doctor)											
Protestant	2	6	2	6	13	27	22	12	4	—	6
Catholic	6	5	2	12	14	17	17	18	3	—	6

Note: All rows total 100 percent.

Abortion

The crime of abortion is one for which we might have anticipated considerable differences between Protestants and Catholics in view of the latter's stronger ideological opposition to abortion in general, regardless of its legal status. While we do find some differences in this regard, they are not nearly as large as might be expected. In the case of sanctioning a female who has an abortion without legal approval, Catholics are less likely to give a no penalty response, and also more likely to give a penal sanction. For the doctor who performs an illegal abortion, Catholics are again more likely to assign a penal sanction (35 percent to 26 percent). However, the same percentage of Catholics as Protestants (38 percent) indicate that no penalty should be given to the doctor. Finally, in the case of a non-doctor performing an illegal abortion, Catholics are more likely to assign no penalty, and the distributions of penalties themselves reveal very little, if any, real difference between the two religious groups.

Religious Attendance

Although religious denomination is an important sociological variable that is often associated with attitudes and behaviour of individuals, it is also well recognized that the mere identification with one religious group or another is in no way an indicator of the amount of commitment an individual has to that group, or his general state of religiosity. Since religious commitment is itself an important variable, attempts are often made to measure it and determine the extent to which it might be related to other social and psychological phenomena. Here we have taken the attendance of religious meetings as a partial index of religiosity and have organized the respondents into four categories according to the frequency with which they attend religious services: one or more times per week ($N=82$); one or more times per month but less than once per week ($N=108$); only on special occasions ($N=191$); and those who never attend religious meetings ($N=57$).

Drug Use

There are some significant differences in the percentage distributions of responses among attendance groups both for use of marijuana and hard drugs. For marijuana, those who never attend religious services are almost five times as likely to assign no penalty (58 percent) than are those who attend once a week or more (12 percent) and more than twice as likely to assign no penalty than either of the two middle attendance categories (25 and 26 percent). With regard to severity of sanctions, it is the two middle attendance groups (1-3 times per month and special occasions) which are the most inclined to assign jail sentences for the use of marijuana. While the highest attendance group is the least likely to leave marijuana use unsanctioned, they do not at the same time assign the stiffest penalties, but rather are far more inclined than the other groups to give a fine or probation.

While all groups treat hard drug use more severely, the pattern among groups is essentially the same as that for marijuana use in terms of the relative likelihood of assigning no penalty (non-attenders 35 percent, highest attenders

TABLE 10

Percentage Distribution of Penalties Assigned for Drug Offences by Religious Attendance

	No Penalty	A Fine	Probation	IMPRISONMENT 30 days or less	31 days to 6 months	6 months to 2 years	2 years to 5 years	5 years to 15 years	15 years or more	Execution	No Response
Marijuana Use											
Once/week or more	12	36	26	9	5	1	2	—	—	—	9
1-3 times/month	25	18	28	10	9	4	1	2	—	—	3
Special Occasions	26	25	17	9	12	6	1	1	—	—	3
Never	58	7	18	7	—	4	3	—	—	—	3
Hard Drug Use											
Once/week or more	5	21	32	9	13	12	2	—	—	—	6
1-3 times/month	15	11	24	17	13	7	5	1	2	1	4
Special Occasions	14	12	24	14	15	11	4	3	—	1	2
Never	35	12	26	3	11	11	2	—	—	—	—
Marijuana Sale											
Once/week or more	—	10	2	15	9	21	23	7	6	1	6
1-3 times/month	2	6	6	12	18	21	16	6	9	—	4
Special Occasions	6	7	6	5	15	23	18	8	7	1	4
Never	5	18	7	2	19	25	5	9	5	—	5
Hard Drug Sale											
Once/week or more	—	6	2	6	4	16	26	24	9	2	5
1-3 times/month	1	5	3	6	9	21	23	13	16	—	3
Special Occasions	1	2	3	4	5	22	22	20	13	4	4
Never	2	.5	—	2	9	21	24	18	17	—	2

Note: All rows total 100 percent.

5 percent and the two middle groups about 15 percent) and the greater use of jail term by the middle attendance groups (46 and 48 percent) as opposed to the highest attenders and the non-attenders (36 and 27 percent respectively).

Drug Sale

None of the attendance groups are very likely to assign no penalty for either the sale of marijuana or hard drugs. The sale of marijuana is however treated more leniently by those who never attend religious meetings than the four other groups whose sanctioning patterns are very similar. Thirty percent of the non-attenders assign either no penalty, a fine or probation as opposed to between 12 and 19 percent for the other groups.

However, when it comes to the sale of hard drugs, not only do all groups treat this as the most serious drug offence, but the differences among the groups in sanctioning behaviour disappears both in terms of the likelihood of assigning non-jail sanctions and in the severity of the jail sentences applied.

Abortion

The severity of penalties assigned to both the female and the medical doctor involved in an illegal abortion increase directly as attendance of religious meetings increases. The higher the church attendance of the group the less likely it is to assign no penalty and the more likely it is to assign a jail term. Not only is the direction of the relationship clear, but the differences between each of the attendance groups is also quite distinct.

The penalties assigned to the non-doctor who performs an abortion do not show this same direct relationship. The percentage choosing no penalty does

593

increase as attendance decreases, but for all groups the percentage is quite small (between two and five percent). When we examine the percentage of each group choosing jail terms, the relationship breaks down altogether. Eighty percent of the highest attendance group and 81 percent of those never attending religious meetings, prescribe jail terms. The percentage assigning terms of two years or greater for these same two groups is identical (42 percent).

TABLE 11

Percentage Distribution of Penalties Assigned for Abortion Offences by Religious Attendance

| | No Penalty | A Fine | Probation | IMPRISONMENT | | | | | | Execution | No Response |
				30 days or less	31 days to 6 months	6 months to 2 years	2 years to 5 years	5 years to 15 years	15 years or more		
Abortion (female)											
Once/week or more	35	15	17	9	4	6	5	—	1	—	8
1-3 times/month	46	13	17	7	4	4	3	1	—	—	—
Special Occasions	64	9	13	3	3	3	2	—	—	—	3
Never	81	9	5	—	3	2	—	—	—	—	—
Abortion (doctor)											
Once/week or more	22	23	10	5	6	7	12	4	4	1	6
1-3 times/month	33	22	13	2	5	9	5	3	2	1	5
Special Occasions	45	19	10	4	5	7	5	—	1	—	4
Never	65	14	9	—	2	3	7	—	—	—	—
Abortion (non-doctor)											
Once/week or more	2	7	—	6	14	18	21	20	1	—	11
1-3 times/month	3	5	—	10	15	34	15	8	5	—	5
Special Occasions	4	6	4	6	11	21	27	14	4	—	3
Never	5	5	5	4	16	19	26	12	4	—	4

Note: All rows total 100 percent.

Summary and Conclusions

The purpose of this study is to provide information about public attitudes toward legal sanctions relating to the crimes of illegal abortion and the use and sale of drugs. These crimes are currently under rather extensive investigation by the legal, judicial, and legislative organizations in Canada, and it is important in a democratic society that public sentiments about such matters be solicited and taken into account. In addition to general public attitudes, we tabulated the individual responses obtained in our study by various background characteristics to determine if any attitudinal variation exists between different subcategories of the society.

The general response pattern of 451 household heads in London, Ontario shows that a majority assign less than a jail sentence for both marijuana and hard drug use, although marijuana is viewed more leniently. The sale of drugs is treated much more severely, with a majority of the respondents assigning prison terms for the selling of marijuana and other drugs (over 75 percent in both instances). Penalties assigned for illegal abortion vary considerably according to which person in the situation is being sentenced. The pregnant female is rarely given a jail term (16 percent) and a majority of the respondents assign no penalty. A medical doctor who performs such an abortion is sentenced more severely, but only slightly so. Less than 25 percent of the respondents assign a prison term and over 40 percent give a no penalty judgment. A non-doctor who performs an illegal abortion is treated very harshly, with only four percent of the respondents assigning no penalty and over 80 percent prescribing prison terms.

Age is a differentiating variable in most cases. For sanctions relating to marijuana and hard drug use, the youngest age group is the most lenient in its sentencing pattern. However, the other three age groups show no consistent trends. This same relationship is evident in the sanctioning of marijuana sales. This sentencing differential breaks down when hard drug selling is the crime. All groups give equally severe penalty sanctions.

Penalty differentials by age group for illegal abortion vary by the abortion situation. The youngest group prescribes the most lenient sanctions for the female and the doctor while at the same time assigning the most severe penalties to the non-doctor who performs such an abortion. In general, the oldest group gives relatively severe sentences for the female and the medical doctor, but it is the most lenient of all the groups in sentencing the non-doctor. These seemingly *inconsistent* differential sentencing patterns by age may be a function of differential experience with the various illegal abortion situations.

No significant relationship was found between educational level and either of the marijuana offences. For both the use and sale of hard drugs, however, there is, contrary to what one might expect, a tendency for those in the two university categories to assign the most severe sanctions and the least educated group to be the most lenient. For abortion, the least educated group tends to be the most severe in assigning sanctions for both the female and the medical doctor who performs an illegal abortion. The non-doctor is treated most harshly by the some university category. Why this group should be significantly different than the others, particularly those completing university, is not at all clear.

For marijuana and hard drug use, the highest income group assigns the most lenient penalties. Although the lowest income group tends to be most severe in sanctioning these crimes, no clear pattern emerges. Marijuana and hard drug sale penalties show no consistent association with income level. Generally, the findings relating to each abortion crime show that the lowest income groups prescribe the most severe sanctions and the highest income groups give the least severe. This differential could possibly correlate with financial accessibility to illegal abortion procedures.

There are no clear penalty differences by religion for the use and sale of drugs and marijuana. The penalty sanctions are quite similar. We find some differentials relating to abortion between Protestants and Catholics, but the differentials are not as great as might be expected, given the nature of Catholic opposition to abortion in general. In fact, the proportion assigning no penalty to the doctor performing an illegal abortion is exactly the same for Protestant and Catholic (38 percent) and for the non-doctor, the Catholic sanction in some cases is less severe.

Those who never attend religious services were far less likely to assign sanctions for marijuana or hard drug use than any of the other attendance groups. The non-attenders were also less severe in their sanctioning of the sale of marijuana although the differences were not as great. For the sale of hard drugs, however, the differences in the sanctioning behaviour among religious attendance groups virtually disappeared.

The severity of sanctions increased significantly as attendance of religious services decreased both for the female and doctor involved in an illegal abortion. However, there was no comparable pattern for penalties assigned to the non-doctor who performed an abortion.

The purpose of this paper has been to document public attitudes relating to penalty sanctions for crimes currently under legal and potential consideration for change. Only when such public attitudes are known and taken into account can the democratic process work to its fullest potential. The importance of assessing public opinion in democratic societies cannot be over-stated.

Footnotes

1. *Report of the Canadian Committee on Corrections*, Roger Ouimet, Chairman, Crown Copyrights, Queen's Printer: Ottawa, 1969, p. 12.
2. *Ibid.*, p. 13.
3. Edwin M. Schur, *Crimes Without Victims: Deviant Behavior and Public Policy*. Englewood Cliffs, N.J.: Prentice-Hall Inc., 1965, p. 169.
4. *Ibid.*, p. 169.
5. Part of the pilot study along with a detailed discussion of the rationale behind its use is contained in "Public Attitudes Toward Legal Sanctions: A Pilot Study" in Gallagher and Lambert, *Social Process and Institution: The Canadian Case*. Toronto: Holt, Rinehart and Winston of Canada Limited, 1971.
6. The fact that this is a sample of household heads and not the population in general should be noted. This means that the background characteristics of our sample are weighted heavily with those old enough to be heads of households and also with males who are far more likely to be household heads than are females. In the latter case this meant that the cross-tabulation of responses by sex, generally an important sociological variable, was not plausible because of the relatively small number of women respondents. Also the women in our sample as household heads would probably not be typical of women in general.
7. Most researchers have found that a return rate between 10 and 50 percent is about all that can be expected for questionnaires of this nature, with about 35 percent being the average. We achieved a usable rate of return of about 45 percent which is reasonably high. The question still arises, however, concerning the extent to which our sample is representative of the general population of household heads from which the total sample of 1000 was drawn. This issue is given rather detailed treatment in the general presentation of the research findings for this project, "Public Attitudes Toward Legal Sanctions in London, Ontario," (presently in manuscript form).
8. Although only the *most frequent* response category is analysed in this paper, the rationale for using the other two response categories should be noted. One of the problems in gathering data of this type is that it is impossible to specify in full detail all of the variables that would normally go into a decision concerning the sanction that should be assigned for a particular offence. Such variables as the degree of injury suffered by a victim; what motivated the act; social characteristics of both the victim and offender such as age, sex, social class and race; and even the general attitudes, or demeanor of the offender; and many others are constantly brought into play when persons, either informally or in official capacities, are asked to make judgments about the behaviour of others. In adding the *minimum* and *maximum* alternatives we have attempted to take into account factors such as these. The respondent is being asked, in effect, to consider the offence, not as a single universally typed act, but as a category of an offence that may assume a wide range of variation.
9. We have included the percentage of persons in each category who did not respond to a particular item, rather than merely calculating the percentages on the basis of those who did respond. (This should give the reader a better sense of the actual meaning that might be assigned to the data.) While the actual reason for failure to respond is not specifically stated, it can be assumed that in a large percentage of cases it resulted from doubt on the part of the respondent as to the appropriate response. When the percentage of no responses gets larger it is sometimes difficult to interpret the data in a table for we do not know exactly how these responses might have been distributed throughout a given category. It is often assumed that they would be distributed in the same way that those who did respond are distributed. Another reason for including the no response figures is that distinct patterns often emerge in this category according to the background characteristics.

The reader may note for example that there is a tendency for the least educated, lowest income, and oldest age groups to have the highest percentages of persons who did not respond. If, as suggested, the major reason for not responding is uncertainty, then these patterns may indeed give us a more detailed picture about the actual nature of public opinion in these categories.

10. The numbers in parentheses ($N = $) represent the actual number (N) of respondents in each category.

DAT